Acts of Teaching

ACTS OF TEACHING
How to Teach Writing, Second Edition

A Text, A Reader, A Narrative

Joyce Armstrong Carroll, Ed.D., H.L.D.
and
Edward E. Wilson
Abydos Learning International
(formerly NJWPT)

Foreword for First Edition by Janet Emig
Foreword for Second Edition by Edmund J. Farrell

Teacher Ideas Press
An imprint of Libraries Unlimited
Westport, Connecticut • London

Heinemann
Portsmouth, New Hampshire

Library of Congress Cataloging-in-Publication Data

Carroll, Joyce Armstrong, 1937–
 Acts of teaching : how to teach writing : a text, a reader, a narrative / Joyce Armstrong Carroll and Edward E. Wilson. — 2nd ed.
  p. cm.
 Includes bibliographical references and index.
 ISBN 978–1–59158–517–6 (alk. paper)
 1. English language—Composition and exercises. 2. Report writing—Study and teaching (Secondary) 3. Report writing—Study and teaching (Elementary) I. Wilson, Edward E. II. Title.
 LB1576.C31717 2008
 808.'04207—dc22 2007027275

British Library Cataloguing in Publication Data is available.

Library of Congress Catalog Card Number: 2007027275
ISBN: 978–1–59158–517–6

First published in 2008

Libraries Unlimited/Teacher Ideas Press, 88 Post Road West, Westport, CT 06881
A Member of the Greenwood Publishing Group, Inc.
www.lu.com

Heinemann, 361 Hanover Street, Portsmouth, NH 03801
A division of Reed Elsevier, Inc.
www.heinemann.com

Printed in the United States of America

The paper used in this book complies with the
Permanent Paper Standard issued by the National
Information Standards Organization (Z39.48–1984).

10 9 8 7 6 5 4 3 2 1

CONTENTS

CONTENTS

FOREWORD TO ACTS II

The second edition of *Acts of Teaching: How to Teach Writing* is a splendid book. A well-thumbed copy should rest atop the desk of every teacher of English language arts as a nagging reminder of the infinite richness of the subject each professes. In it teachers will find no gimmickry, no facile suggestions on how to occupy students on those Monday mornings that threaten vacuity. As Janet Emig rightfully notes in her foreword to *ACTS I*, readers will discover that solid research provides foundation for the book's principles, which in turn spawn a myriad of pedagogical practices.

Those practices can be trusted, based as they are not alone upon the best of scholarly research and thought but also upon the classroom experiences, direct and derived, of the two eminently gifted teachers who have authored the volume, Joyce Armstrong Carroll and Edward Wilson. As founders of the New Jersey Writing Project in Texas, now Abydos Learning International, the authors have worked with thousands of teachers since 1979, have been in hundreds of classrooms and scores of school districts, and, in keeping with the central purpose of the National Writing Project, have trained over 500 selected teachers to be teachers of fellow teachers.

Students that they themselves are, what the authors did not know firsthand from their own years as exemplary classroom teachers they have been willing to learn from both direct observation of, and reports from, teachers in their workshops. The new edition of *Acts of Teaching* is replete with anecdotes about and detailed practices of scores of teachers whose work in the classroom is consonant with current scholarship.

The word *current* is critical, for the world, and with it both scholarship and the profession of English, are in a time of accelerating change largely brought about by electronic technology. Cognizant of the rapidity of that change, the authors, who have long required that trainers for Abydos Learning International undergo additional education every three years to be recertified as teachers of teachers, have extensively revised *Acts of Teaching* for this new edition. Moreover, recognizing that students, like the world around them, are undergoing constant change, they provide readers with the full arc of students' cognitive and linguistic development, from conception to adulthood. The consequence is that teachers of English language arts can contextualize the dynamics of both their students and their curriculum, familiarizing themselves with what should have preceded their own teaching and anticipating what should follow once youngsters depart their classrooms. Finally, the authors provide teachers of other subjects ways by which writing can help students appropriate and construct knowledge in disciplines outside of English.

If each teacher of English language arts attends to the contents of *Acts of Teaching*, his or her classroom, like every one of its antecedents and successors, will be rich with language activities. In it an observer will find students reading and writing in a variety of modes and genres, conferring with peers, proudly sharing their work orally and visually, consistently taking ownership of their learning. In it, one will not find deadly workbooks or worksheets: grammar and mechanics attendant to composing will be being taught not in isolation but in the context of writing itself. The observer will find the teacher modeling for students what is to be learned, being readily available as a resource as individuals create, and serving as a counselor following their acts of creation. Humming with engaging and worthwhile things to do, the classroom will be one students eagerly attend. Implicit in such a class will be the ultimate aim of American education—to free students to become lifelong autonomous learners and contributors to a democratic society.

Practicing teachers will find the second edition of *Acts of Teaching* to be both a needed refresher course on what they once knew but have forgotten and a stimulating seminar on what they never knew but now need to know. Novice teachers will discover it to be nothing less than a godsend.

—Edmund J. Farrell, Professor Emeritus of English Education,
The University of Texas at Austin

FOREWORD TO ACTS I

In the lost 1970s, when the New Jersey Writing Project was just a whippersnapper, I received a call one morning from a state coordinator of the English language arts. She had heard about the Project and wanted to consider offering several institutes the following summer to teachers in her state. She was however considering several other models of teacher education as well. What unique virtues did our project have?

I spoke—I thought eloquently—about writing as a process, about the highly interactive exchange between a teacher and her own writing, a teacher and her student, a teacher and her students' writing, a student with another student, and one student's writing with another student's writing. She listened thoughtfully to my highly detailed description of the Project, then asked what textbooks and other written materials I could send her to use in a comparative presentation to her board. When I said that we had none beyond a very basic brochure, there was a palpable withdrawal of interest over the miles. Then she said that her board was uncomfortable without "manipulatives" to contemplate and that she would probably recommend another heavily texted project from our region. And she did.

The incident revealed a tension those of us who espouse writing as a process have experienced over the fifteen years since the Project was formed: how to honor the tenets we believe in while yet providing the specific guidelines and help that stay true to those tenets, such as proffering, when needed and when requested, appropriate readings, activities, and advice.

Through *Acts of Teaching,* Joyce Armstrong Carroll and Edward E. Wilson provide compelling solutions to this dilemma by giving just such help, advice, and solace.

The virtues of this source book are too many to catalog, but three are especially noteworthy. First is the seamless connection between theory and practice. The classroom processes and activities they recommend are based always on the most current, valid theories of learning, writing, and thinking. They know, and appropriately apply, their Bruner, Donaldson, Murray, Vygotsky, and others.

The second is how well they know those classrooms they serve. Carroll and Wilson's advice is grounded in their almost daily observation of diverse teachers, students, and learning situations. They reveal that always discernible difference between those who spend vast amounts of time in the classroom and comprehend with sophistication what they see, like Jane Healy, Ann Dyson, and John Goodlad, and those who don't, like Tracy Kidder in *Among Schoolchildren.*

More, Carroll and Wilson can do what they say, what they recommend. Both are brilliant teachers who can cope on the spot with almost any learning challenge that greets them. Teachers consequently know that they can be trusted above the hit-and-runners who appear from academe or elsewhere and reveal immediately their own discomfort with the creative mess of daily learning and teaching.

Finally, their humanism shines through. They not only see and teach; they believe profoundly in the model of teaching writing they espouse, a model distinguished by its respect for children, for teachers, for learning, for the democratic process in and out of the classroom.

—Janet Emig, Professor Emeritus of
English Education, Rutgers University

PREFACE
A Parable

The first-graders entered the room quietly and with purpose. They rummaged in their desks, pulled out writing logs, each uniquely "loved up" with frayed, worn covers and turned-back pages, and began writing. Soon a timer bell sounded. They pushed their logs into their desks, walked to a miniature wooden house tucked in the corner of the room, and lifted its roof. The house held books. Each child chose one, found a comfortable place, and began reading. When the timer rang again, the students returned the books and took their places, cross-legged, on a wonderfully inviting carpet in the front of the room. Because we were so absorbed with *kidwatching* (to use Yetta Goodman's term), we were moderately startled when the teacher appeared, book in hand, to take her place on the wooden rocker positioned on the carpet's edge.

Sharon Chamberlain begins school with fifteen minutes of uninterrupted sustained silent writing followed by fifteen minutes of uninterrupted sustained silent reading, we entered into our field notes.

Sharon held *Sylvester and the Magic Pebble* by William Steig for all the children to see. The students, enthralled, made comments and observations about the book's cover. If they strayed from the point, she gentled them back into reexamining details. She invited predictions, descriptions, and associations.

After this book talk, Sharon wrote three words from the story on the board: *perplexed*, *puzzled*, and *bewildered*. "These will be our spelling words, boys and girls. Listen for these big words when I read." The students, delighted with the challenge, readied themselves for close listening.

Sharon read *Sylvester* with all the verve associated with a first reading, although we suspected she had read it dozens of times. The students intervened, quipped, and questioned, demonstrating their involvement. When she finished, Sharon engaged the students in the spelling and meaning of the "big" words, after which they evaluated their predictions, and discussed the story. Moving to the writing activity, Sharon produced an intriguing brown pouch from her pocket that contained colored glass pebbles. Giving one pebble to each child, she said, "This is your special pebble. It will help you write something wonderful when you return to your seat." Over and over she repeated those sentences like an incantation.

Then the children moved into more talk, this time to generate writing. Among ideas about the colors, shapes, and things they themselves could be changed into, the children decided they could make up how they got their pebbles, because, as one child offered, "If we all say 'teacher,' it will be bor-r-ring."

She's doing appropriate things to prepare these diverse students for a rich language experience, we wrote. *These students are so happy you can tell they think they are having fun. She is allowing them to learn through exposure and discovery to reading and writing. Mostly, though, she is there with kind suggestions and few corrections. She is giving these students ample time to be actively creative, inventive, and discoverers.*

So they wrote, filling long pages with writing about how they "found" their pebbles, what their pebbles looked like, and what happened because of their pebble's "specialness." Then they shared.

Sitting on the author's chair, Michael read his two and one-quarter pages. This was his opener:

Fig. P.1. Michael's Lead.

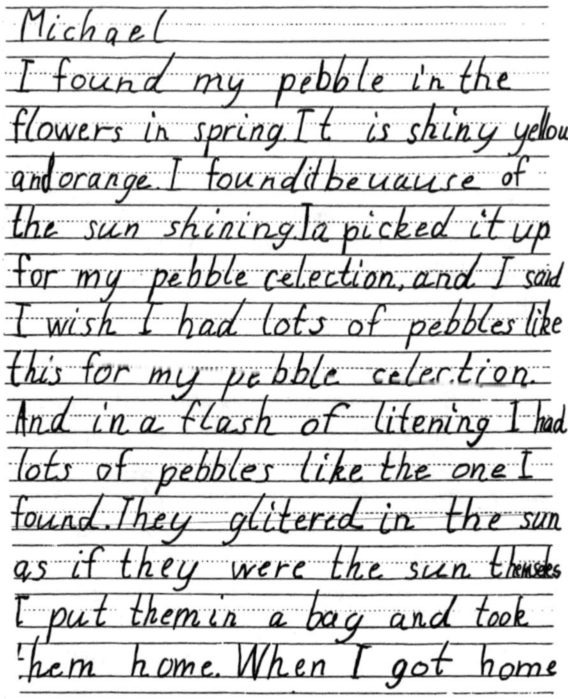
Michael
I found my pebble in the
flowers in spring It is shiny yellow
and orange. I founditbeuause of
the sun shiningIa picked it up
for my pebble celection, and I said
I wish I had lots of pebbles like
this for my pebble celection.
And in a flash of litening I had
lots of pebbles like the one I
found. They glitered in the sun
as if they were the sun themseles
I put them in a bag and took
them home. When I got home

I found my pebble in the flowers in spring. It is shiny yellow and orange. I found it because of the sun shining. I'd picked it up for my pebble celection, and I said I wish I had lots of pebbles like this for my pebble celection. And in a flash of litening I had lots of pebbles like the one I found. They glitered in the sun as if they were the sun themseles.

[I found my pebble in the flowers in spring. It is shiny yellow and orange. I found it because of the sun shining. I'd picked it up for my pebble collection. And in a flash of lightening I had lots of pebbles like the one I found. They glittered in the sun as if they were the sun themselves.]

Michael's writing proved that by January of first grade he had internalized a sense of narrative and descriptive detail, at least partly due to the print-rich environment Sharon had created. After this opener, Michael developed a clear plot line, one obviously based on the original story.

Fig. P.2. Michael's Story.

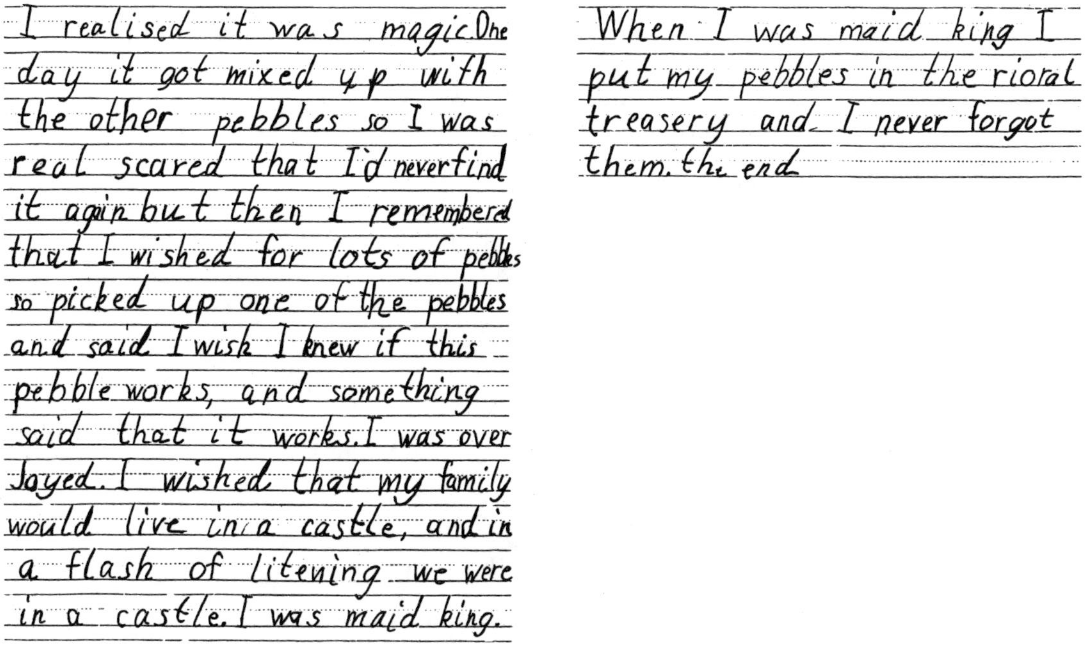

> I realised it was magic.One day it got mixed up with the other pebbles so I was real scared that I'd never find it agin but then I remembered that I wished for lots of pebbles so picked up one of the pebbles and said I wish I knew if this pebble works, and something said that it works.I was over Joyed.I wished that my family would live in a castle, and in a flash of litening we were in a castle.I was maid king.
>
> When I was maid king I put my pebbles in the rioral treasery and I never forgot them.the end

I put them in a bag and took them home. When I got home I realised it was magic. One day it got mixed up with the other pebbles so I was real scared that I'd never find it again but then I remembered that I wished for lots of pebbles and said I wish I knew if this pebble works, and something said that it works. I was over joyed. I wished that my family would live in a castle, and in a flash of litening we were in a castle. I was maid king. When I was maid king I put my pebbles in the rioral treasery and I never forgot them. the end

[I put them in a bag and took them home. When I got home I realized it was magic. One day it got mixed up with the other pebbles so I was real scared that I'd never find it again but then I remembered that I wished for lots of pebbles and said I wish I knew if this pebble works, and something said that it works. I was overjoyed. I wished that my family would live in a castle, and in a flash of lightening we were in a castle. I was made king. When I was made king I put my pebbles in the royal treasury and I never forgot them. the end]

Fig. P.3. Kyle's Lead.

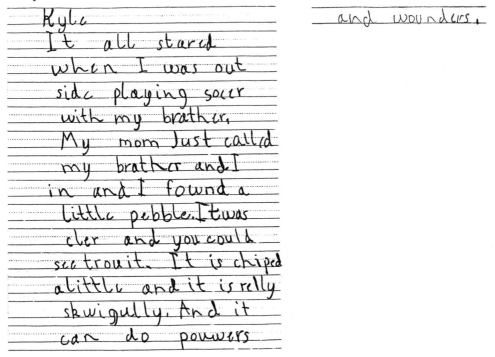

Kyle's writing also showed the benefits of much reading and writing.

> *It all stared when I was out side playing socer with my brother. My mom Just called my brother and I in and I found a little pebble. it was cler and you could see throu it. it is chiped a little and it is relly skwigully, And it can do powers and wounders.*

[It all started when I was outside playing soccer with my brother. My mom just called my brother and I in and I found a little pebble. It was clear and you could see through it. It is chipped a little and it is really squiggly. And it can do powers and wonders.]

The powers and wonders occurring in this classroom weren't coming from any pebbles. Sharon Chamberlain had created a nonthreatening environment that allowed students to connect and take risks.

The next time we visited Sharon's class, the students entered; again they wrote, read, and gathered on the carpet. This time Sharon introduced *Amelia Bedelia*, but this time she only wrote one word on the board—*idiom*.

Idiom! Idiom? We questioned in our notes. *Why, we taught some college freshmen who thought Idiom was their roommate's name!*

"This is your vocabulary word today, boys and girls. Where do we usually find the words we use for our vocabulary and spelling words?" They knew, of course, that those words come from the books they read.

"Yes that is true, but today you must listen with different ears. Today you will not hear me read the word *idiom*. Instead, if you listen with those different ears, you will know by what Amelia

Bedelia says and does what the word *idiom* means." The children couldn't wait for the story to start.

We couldn't get enough of this class and the children couldn't either. They thought everything they did was fun because everything they did held meaning and challenged their growing brains. Everything they did related to everything else they did. Because Sharon integrated reading and writing with listening, speaking, viewing, thinking, and skills, learning was cognitively appropriate and natural.

The students reveled in Sharon Chamberlain's praise and encouragement and they grew. But one day she was absent from school. When she returned, Heather Mitchell greeted her with a story she had written.

"Can you come over? You've got to see Heather's story." Sharon invited over the phone.

As soon as we arrived at Sharon's classroom, she thrust Heather's four-page story at us with no explanation. We approached Heather's writing with expectation. Her title "The Meanist Sub," and her sense of authorship, "by Heather Mitchell," immediately caught our attention. We were hooked and quickly began reading.

Fig. P.4. Heather's Writing, Pages 1 and 2.

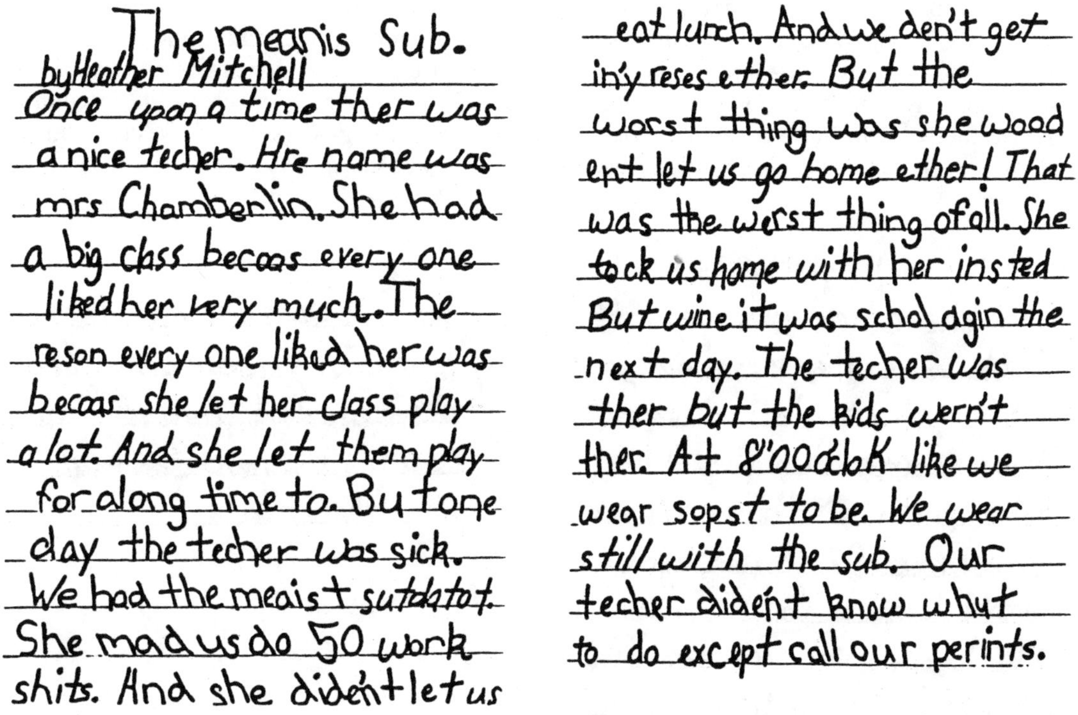
The meanis Sub.
by Heather Mitchell
Once upon a time ther was
a nice techer. Hre name was
mrs Chamberlin. She had
a big class becoas every one
liked her very much. The
reson every one liked her was
becoas she let her class play
a lot. And she let them play
for along time to. But one
day the techer was sick.
We had the meaist sutdtot.
She mad us do 50 work
shits. And she didn't let us

eat lunch. And we den't get
iny reses ether. But the
worst thing was she wood
ent let us go home ether! That
was the werst thing of all. She
tock us home with her insted
But wine it was schol agin the
next day. The techer was
ther but the kids wern't
ther. At 8'00clok like we
wear sopst to be. We wear
still with the sub. Our
techer dident know whut
to do except call our perints.

[Once upon a time there was a nice teacher. Her name was Sharon Chamberlain. She had a big class because everyone liked her very much. The reason everyone liked her was that she let her class play a lot. And she let them play for a long time too. But one day the teacher was sick. We had the meanist substitute. She made us do 50 work shits. And she didn't let us]

[eat lunch. And we didn't get any recess either. But the worse thing was she wouldn't let us go home either! That was the worst thing of all. She took us home

with her instead. But when it was school again the next day, the teacher was
there, but the kids weren't there at 8 o'clock like we were suppose to be. We were
still with the sub. Our teacher didn't know what to do except call our parents.]

When we read "50 work shits," we exclaimed, "That is exactly what they are! Out of the
mouths of babes . . . "

Indeed, Heather had written great truth. On the one hand, the mindless circling of sounds, the
endless drawing of lines, the senseless coloring of pictures that match words, the isolated skills
detached from anything real must have seemed "mean" to this six-year-old, so in the hyperbolic
language of childhood, Heather exaggerated what may have been five worksheets into fifty. On
the other hand, because of these worksheets, Heather may have experienced what Adrienne Rich
calls "psychic disequilibrium." As Rich describes it, "When someone with the authority of a
teacher, say, describes the world and you are not in it, there is a moment of psychic disequilibrium,
as if you looked into a mirror and saw nothing" (Rosaldo ix). Because genuine writing is an
extension of self on paper, and because worksheets are not genuine writing, when doing the assigned worksheets, Heather very well may have seen nothing.

As we read on, we discovered that not only did Heather have strong feelings about worksheets
as opposed to the real reading and real writing she was accustomed to, but also she was able to
develop her feelings into a story with characters, plot, a conflict, and a resolution. As Jerome
Bruner tells us in *Acts of Meaning*, "Our capacity to render experience in terms of narrative is not
just child's play, but an instrument for making meaning that dominates much of life in culture"
(97). Heather tries to make meaning about someone giving first-graders "50 work shits." In her
mind, it seems, that person is capable of even more dastardly deeds.

Fig. P.5. Heather's Writing, Pages 3 and 4.

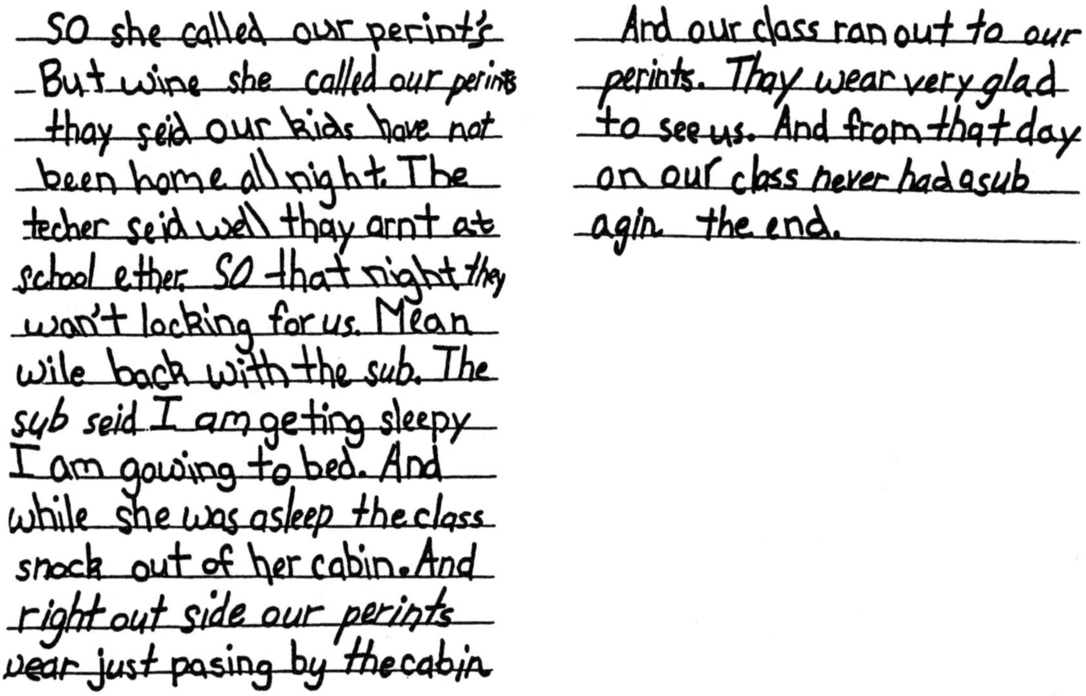

SO she called our perints
But wine she called our perins
thay seid our kids have not
been home all night. The
techer seid well thay arnt at
school ether. SO that night they
won't locking for us. Mean
wile back with the sub. The
sub seid I am geting sleepy
I am gowing to bed. And
while she was asleep the class
snock out of her cabin. And
right out side our perints
vear just pasing by the cabin

And our class ran out to our
perints. Thay wear very glad
to see us. And from that day
on our class never had a sub
agin. the end.

[So she called our parents. But when she called our parents they said, "Our kids have not been home all night." The teacher said, "Well, they aren't at school either. So that night they went looking for us. Meanwhile, back with the sub. The sub said, "I am getting sleepy. I am going to bed." And while she was asleep the class snuck out of her cabin. And right outside our parents were just passing by the cabin.]

[And our class ran out to our parents. They were very glad to see us. And from that day on our class never had a sub again. The end.]

We noted the exclamation point when the sub wouldn't let the students go home. Also, we noticed the parents did not rush right out to find the children. First-graders must surely think adults do everything at night, but it is Heather's next line that remains one of our favorites—a segue with remarkable aplomb that returns her readers to the story. "Meanwile back with the sub."

By her fourth page, Heather has delightfully, eloquently, and clearly demonstrated that she knows the elements of a story. Daily reading and writing, daily mini-teaches on various story elements, daily speaking, listening, examining, predicting in a joyfully literate classroom paid off. Clearly, the self-sponsored writing Heather accomplished during Sharon's absence exclaims loudly that she knows what writing is and is not: It is telling stories; it is not filling in worksheets.

Through Heather's writing we know that Sharon knows what the process of teaching writing is and is not. Writing engages students in grappling with words on blank pieces of paper to craft those words into meaningful experiences; it is not assigning worksheets. Teachers like Sharon know it takes hard work to transcribe thoughts so self and others comprehend them. They know they must walk alongside their students throughout the entire writing process. They know that writing is one of our most rigorous intellectual activities. And they know how to teach in a way that helps writing happen.

Heather's writing verifies the importance of this type of teaching. Teachers who teach writing in a way that promotes energy not lethargy about writing create risk-taking environments in which students are enabled to accomplish their writing. Teachers who foster students' writing about what they know enable students to gain confidence and skill to make their points as powerfully as did Heather.

Acts of Teaching II helps teachers teach writing in a way that promotes excitement about writing. It offers strategies for creating comfortable environments that encourage risk-taking in writing, and it shows teachers ways to foster student writing about what they know in order to gain confidence and skill, rather than having students write simply to respond to a vague prompt that is not tied to the students' world.

Heather makes her point. The importance of being able to do that is exactly what makes this book significant.

INTRODUCTION
Our Flattened World

The future belongs to a very different kind of person with a very different kind of mind—creators and empathizers, pattern recognizers, and meaning makers. These people—artists, inventors, designers, storytellers, caregivers, consolers, big picture thinkers—will now reap society's richest rewards and share its greatest joys.

—Daniel H. Pink □

A BIT OF BACKGROUND

When we wrote *Acts of Teaching* in 1993, there were two prevailing paradigms in education. The Product Paradigm—educators who held to the factory model for the organization and operation of schools with its attendant routines, formulae, assembly lines, standardizations, top-to-bottom management systems, and either/or philosophy—and the Process Paradigm—educators who held to an informational model as appropriate for schools with its concomitant flexibility, technologies, collaborations, global empowerments, and both/all philosophy.

We, in 1993, making a case for process, quoted futurists such as Marvin Cetron and Owen Davies, John Naisbitt, Patricia Aburdene, and others. We cited Robert Reich, Denis Doyle, and other economists and educators who warned against the factory-model school and the passive pouring of facts and attitudes into empty vessels. We praised dynamic, interactive processes, good teachers, and smart, forward-looking administrators. Mostly we cautioned against cog jobs encouraging teachers to prepare students for cognitive ones. A mere decade and a half later most of their predictions have come true.

Pointing out that the twenty-first century will demand innovative thinkers, we supported our case with the rise of lasers, robotics, telecommunications, aerospace, microscopic power, neural net computers that think like people, magnetic levitation technology, superconductivity, quantum dots, nanomachines, genetic engineering, and change.

Quoting the Hebrew proverb, "Do not confine your children to your own learning for they were born in another time," we argued for a shift to the process paradigm. We used Kuhn's definition of paradigms as "achievements that for a time provide model problems and solutions to a community of practitioners" (viii) as a useful way to describe shifts in political, economic, and academic worlds. We supported the new process/information paradigm as one with unprecedented achievement that was attracting adherents away from the product paradigm. We challenged adherents to meet new and redefined challenges. We quoted Kuhn, "To be accepted as a paradigm, a theory must seem better than its competitors, but it need not, and in fact never does, explain all the facts with which it can be confronted" (17–18).

We identified reading, writing, thinking, and collaborating as educational needs for the twenty-first century. We called for a restructuring of schools and intensive teacher training and re-training with administrative support, monitoring, and modeling.

We presented the then radical notion that writing is best taught as a process with grammar taught within the context of writing, that students taught by trained teachers who write will score better than those taught by untrained teachers who don't write, and we had the scientific research to prove it. We held to writing as thinking and thinking as the fundamental skill for the twenty-first century.

Historical Perspective

The Product/Formula Paradigm

The product/formula paradigm, sometimes called the factory or industrial model, traces its roots to the manufacturing and industrial changes that marked the transition from an agrarian and commercial society to a modern and industrial one. Caine and Caine contend "it was only natural, perhaps, that schools would also adopt the basic tenets of the industrial model as guides for effective education" (12–13). The factory model of education, moored to a nineteenth-century paradigm, has served as the standard for public education since the Industrial Revolution in the United States.

Inasmuch as U.S. public education has always been bound to economic and social influences, it is not surprising that the rise of industry influenced not only the organization and governance of schools but also the architecture. Schools resembled factories. Students sat in rows simulating assembly lines, often performing mindless, boring, repetitive exercises that would prepare them for endless hours of cog jobs—jobs that required repeating relatively simple tasks. While a few students were set on advanced tracks to prepare them for the top jobs, most students spent their days listening to lectures, taking notes, making outlines, and memorizing for tests—in short, learning to understand and follow instructions. Students followed rigid rules and orders, predetermined classifications, and a top-down system of authority. "Discipline and reliability were core virtues" (Reich 11).

Teachers eventually felt alienated in this system. They didn't control the curriculum, hand down the rules, choose the texts, establish the environment, or even determine schedules. Within this paradigm, it was not unusual for teachers to have changes made in their teaching schedules days before the advent of school, even though such changes allowed little time for preparation.

Students, too, felt alienated. Class interaction was limited since most students consistently viewed the necks of the students sitting in front of them. Little, if any, collaboration occurred. Students caught in a discussion were often accused of cheating. "No talking" was allowed. After all, talking on the job meant a slowing of productivity and had to be halted, so students had to be programmed. In the classroom, the teacher was the boss who made all the decisions and meted out assignments, rewards, and punishments. Curriculum was lock-step. That learning could be interesting or even fun appeared to be anathema. As a matter of fact, in the 1930s and 1940s, "at Ford's River Rouge plant, laughter was a disciplinary offense—while humming, whistling, and smiling were evidence of insubordination" (Pink 178–179). Likewise, schools were joyless places.

Administrators often felt alienated. At the top, they were expected to make sound decisions consistently, correctly, and without counsel. They recited the "district line," expecting little or no opposition. They were the big bosses. And they were often lonely.

Parents were perhaps the most alienated of all. They sent their children to school but had little say in any decision making. Like students, parents were expected to obey the rules and to exhort their children to do the same. They were expected to buy into the school policy without question. PTA meetings, usually superficial social gatherings, lacked academic substance. Open house events promised some interaction with the faculty, but time was limited and discussions lacked privacy.

Everyone was a cog in a wheel.

Yet the product paradigm served its purpose in a world that demanded "high-volume, standardized production in which large numbers of identical items could be produced over long runs, allowing fixed costs to be spread as widely as possible. Whether it was wheat, steel, or even insurance, the same overarching rule prevailed: Every step . . . was to be simple and predictable, so that it could be synchronized with every other step" (Reich 11).

The product paradigm produced a workforce that labored at the same task day after day, month after month, year after year with a chosen few propelled toward top positions. After a given number of years, both groups retired with gold watches.

> *Alex told me that he had worked in the local flour mill as a kid. "My job," he said, "was to wait until three bags of flour came down the conveyor belt. I took hold of them by my forearms and placed them on another conveyor belt. I was a human forklift."*
>
> *"Your forearms?" I queried. "Why didn't you use your hands?"*
>
> *"Because they go numb after a while. But I can tell you, I celebrated when only two came down. I didn't care why. I didn't investigate. If two came down that meant I could sit and rest. That was the boss's problem, not mine."*

All that has changed. Or has it? We still go into classrooms, especially secondary classrooms, where every student sits in a preordained row like little cogs.

The Process/Information Paradigm and NJWPT

Since 1979, the New Jersey Writing Project in Texas has trained thousands of teachers and hundreds of thousands of students in the process paradigm—sometimes referred to as the information paradigm of the information age. NJWPT stands as the largest writing project in the state of Texas and the most enduring project to rise up out of the Bay Area Writing Projects. The New Jersey Writing Project began in 1977–1979 as a consortium of Rutgers University, Educational Testing Service, and demographically disparate school districts across the state as an answer to the call of Jim Gray from the Bay Area Writing Project at Berkley. The project received validation and designation in 1979 as a National Diffusion Network Project when its name morphed into the New Jersey Writing Project in Texas. Since then it has trained teachers in New Jersey, Nevada, California, Texas, Oklahoma, Illinois, and Florida.

NJWPT has and continues to enjoy the reputation as the largest literacy project in Texas. Its program, both unified and coherent, merges theory and pedagogy and encourages teachers to implement its philosophy of process uniquely—according to their teaching styles and the learning styles and needs of their students.

In addition to the project's three-week basic training model, it trains teacher-trainers. These trainers model the implementation of literacy as a process in their classrooms and in the classrooms of others, becoming paradigm pioneers, helping peers shift philosophies from product to process. Presently, there are approximately 500 NJWPT/Abydos certified trainers. Certification extends for three years, after which trainers recertify, setting conditions and standards for renewal and retraining.

Dr. Janet Emig, keynoting the 1991 NJWPT Annual Trainers'/Teachers' Conference, looked out over the audience and said, "This is where true educational reform begins."

Dr. D. Max McConkey, Executive Director of the National Dissemination Study Group (NDSG) and Director of The NETWORK, Inc., praised the quality of NJWPT at its 1992 Teachers'/Trainers' Conference, calling it "the best state-wide implementation model" he had seen. In 1993, he reiterated his assessment:

> *The New Jersey Writing Project* was one of the first and finest writing programs validated and disseminated by NDN. For the last decade, a principal focus for dissemination of that project has been in Texas, where a unique, statewide effort, the *New Jersey Writing Project in Texas,* has produced truly amazing results. . . .
>
> It would be one thing if the project simply perpetuated its original good work, but I found that NJWP-TX has gone well beyond the scope of its initial program, staying entirely contemporary with current research and practice. (Letter to NJWPT Trainer, Kaye Dunn)

After a two-year research project designed to study the ability of teachers to acquire teaching skills and strategies, Joyce and Showers conclude, "Teachers are wonderful learners" (379). We concur. Teachers tire of gaggles and gimmicks. They tire of presentations by people who have lost touch with the inner workings of schools, but when information is relevant, interesting, and practical, when the theory is merged with the pedagogy, when they can see immediate ways to apply the theory in their classrooms, they see training and retraining as effective. After more than three decades of working with teachers in writing and the integration of the language arts, we concur.

In the September 13, 2006, issue of *Education Week*, Pendred Noyce, a trustee for the Noyce Foundation, questions the evaluation and impact of staff development. As we read her article, we found NJWPT meets her suggested standards—especially "the reason we do professional development is so that students will learn more" (36). Of course, students are the prime raison d'être of all teachers' work; we proved that in 1979. "Students of teachers so trained [in NJWP] showed statistically significant and educationally important increases in their writing performance" (Carroll 1984, 325).

Abydos Learning International

Enter Abydos Learning International. Subsuming the New Jersey Writing Project in Texas and its sustainability, Abydos builds on almost a half-century of the solidly sound work of Harvard's Janet Emig whose studies in the late 1960s first probed how published authors write and continued with her seminal research on how students write. With such a firm foundation, NJWPT grew grand and strong, earning through the study referenced above by Carroll, the coveted National Diffusion Network designation and coming to Texas just in time for the first high-stakes test, the Texas Assessment of Basic Skills (TABS).

That marked the beginning of the NJWPT sustainability factor. The project has proven itself effective repeatedly in Texas through TABS, TEAMS, TAAS, not to mention the SAT, the TPRI, plus all the other alphabetic tests we impose on students, and is making a positive difference on the Texas Assessment of Knowledge and Skills (TAKS) in school districts where it is properly implemented and supported. Built upon true scientific research, designed and monitored by the Educational Testing Service in Princeton in collaboration with Rutgers University, New Jersey, and tested in project and control school districts across New Jersey 1977–1979, it is a proven project (Carroll 1984, 315–333).

Continued research out of NJWPT/Abydos Learning includes a dissertation study conducted by Vivian Athens Eads through Baylor University which replicated the data of the NJWP original study (Eads 1989). Virginia Ellen Metz's doctoral dissertation, "Training Teachers to Teach Writing: Impact on Teacher Attitudes and Student Products" (1993) from Texas A & M University, used NJWPT as a basis as did Kelley R. Smith's (now Barger) dissertation "Home Literacy Experiences: The Effects of Collaborative Familial Interactions of Student Writing and Reading Ability and Performance" (2000) from Texas A & M University, Commerce. Robin D. Johnson's forthcoming dissertation from Texas A & M University, Commerce, will replicate the Emig Attitude Survey designed by the Education Testing Service and administered to the first NJWP Writing Institute with "A Study of the Effects of a Three-Week Teacher Training in Writing on Teacher Attitude, Student Attitude, and Student Achievement." Additionally, trainers recertify every three years using the latest research and strategies, which broadens us all.

Today, in step with the recent trend in rediscovering what is sound and good, schools are turning to that which has proven lasting, durable, and workable—that which is successful and wholesome. NJWPT/Abydos Learning International has worked district by district, teacher by teacher, student by student to earn this luxury of sustainability. It has avoided fads, commercialism, and scare tactics by staying true to the basics of writing and reading as processes, grammar taught within that process in systematic, hands-on, eco-friendly ways, that is using authentic strategies and authentic student writing and not mountains of worksheets that kill trees, and in foundational staff development. It has embraced research built not upon conjecture, spurious results, or falsified numbers but upon the hard and fast rules of science. While others floundered and foundered, NJWPT knows how people learn and has always built upon that knowing in sound ways.

NJWPT/Abydos Learning International is not a program. Programs are reactionary because they try to repair something gone awry or something negative. They are always temporary, always following, never leading. They impose. Abydos Learning has grown out of a project born of vision. Vision grows out of a philosophy. It leads, opens the way to success, permits growth, flow, and natural development. It proposes. Educational systems will not be saved or changed by programs but by people with vision; therefore, NJWPT/Abydos Learning has no intention of resting on its laurels; we look to the challenges with confidence armed with the data of success.

THE GLOBAL AGE

Since the original publication of *Acts of Teaching,* the notion of globalization has risen up, entering the educational arena this twenty-first century. Given that *globalization* has so many meanings, ranging from the economic to social and cultural, we hold to Coatsworth's explanation: "Globalization is what happens when the movement of people, goods, or ideas among countries and regions accelerates" (in Suarez-Orozco 2004, 38). We see globalization as an extension of the process paradigm with a series of processes that deeply affect education. As Rotberg reminds us, "A nation's priorities are typically reflected in its education system. As a result, when a country is subject to major societal shifts—political, demographic, or economic—it focuses attention on its education system and seeks to 'reform' that system so it becomes more consistent with the changing societal context" (xi).

Students in the Global Age

Whether we like it or not the truth is that in a milieu where students access each other on the Internet, on cell phones, or IM-ing an evening away, where they text message during classes, while walking, waiting in airports, or even while out on dates, students sitting in rows facing the teacher looks downright archaic. Even primary students whip out their "cells," plug in their iPods or Zunes, and tune out what they perceive as irrelevant. Similarly, albeit not quite equally, seeing students sitting in small groups for reading and sharing is beginning to seem quaint in these days of world-wide interconnectedness and mind-boggling technologies that cut across boundaries, languages, ages, and cultures. When "it has been estimated that a billion people across the world saw the second plane hit the South Tower in real time" (Giddens xii), class time must drag for this accelerated generation.

Challenges in the Global Age

Globalization presents new challenges and nudges us to redefine old challenges. The operative word *complexity* begs a comparison. Since we are teachers, comparing a lesson on the elements of a narrative to the increasing complexity of the world makes an apt metaphor.

The nursery rhyme "Little Miss Muffet," a simple template for the parts of a story, presents readers with two characters, one setting, an easy plot, conflict, and resolution. But when we juxtapose it with *Charlotte's Web*, *To Kill a Mockingbird*, or *War and Peace*, the elements increase to an excruciating complication of numerous characters, complex plots, myriad subplots, and intricate conflicts—not all resolved satisfactorily.

We know young people no longer live in a "Miss Muffet" world where things move slowly and simply. Their world continually quickens; everything speeds up; the contexts constantly change. That acceleration requires shifts in theories, teaching, training, methodology, pedagogy, curriculum, indeed, even shifts in an understanding of what learning is: If we don't shift, we shall lose all our students.

If the Muffet metaphor doesn't work, consider this: In 1993 the Pentium® successor to the 486 line of microprocessors from Intel® made its debut. It boggled our minds with its almost unbelievable capability and speed (FSB Speeds: 50 MHz to 66 MHz; CPU Speeds: 60 MHz to 300 MHZ). Today, Intel Core 2 is so fast, it makes the Pentium look heavily underpowered (FSB Speeds: 667 MT/s to 1333 GHz; CPU Speeds: 1.60 GHz to 2.93 GHz). In less than a decade Intel Core microarchitecture offers higher performance, greater energy efficiency, and more responsive multitasking while it enhances user experiences in all environments.

Echoing what we wrote in 1993, Suarez-Orozco reminds us yet again that

An intellectually curious, cognitively autonomous, socially responsible, democratically engaged, productive, and globally conscious member of the human family in the 21st century cannot be educated in the 20th century factory model of education. The regimented mastery, internalization, and mechanical regurgitation of compartmentalized facts and rules that served the Industrial Age are anachronisms. The pandemic boredom among children and youths in European and U.S. schools stems from the redundancy in much of today's schooling. (2005, 212)

But what have we done? We have met this challenge with enormous numbers of tests thrust at students—tests that invite limited teaching, formulae, and rote responses. When the world scene clamors for multiple perspectives using flexible thinking and synthesized knowledge, our educational system has reduced learning to A, B, C, D choices, fill in the blanks, and mindless worksheets.

When the world scene calls for sound thinkers, deep readers, clear writers, and tolerance of others, many educators fret over test booklets, no. 2 pencils, and scores. When fluency of thought, reading, writing, and working together mark the literate, many educators, eschewing research and credibility, want the quick fix.

In the Oscar award–winning film *Why Man Creates*, there is an animated sequence depicting two snails conversing.

One snail says, "Have you ever thought that radical ideas threaten institutions, then become institutions, and in turn reject radical ideas that threaten institutions?"
"No."
"Gee, for a minute I thought I had something." (Sohn 39)

Indeed the first snail had something—it had encapsulated a paradigm shift. It could have been referring to the ideological paradigm shift from totalitarian to democratic governments; the economic shift from high-volume, standardized production to a continuous process of reinvention; the academic paradigm shift from product to process; or the twentieth-century model of education juxtaposed with what is needed for the twenty-first century. We have only to transpose phrases *teacher workshops* with *intensive teacher training* or *teachers' lectures* with *students creatively scaffolding their learning*, or *boss* for *leader* to understand the range and the depth of this shift. First institutions—political, economic, and academic—are threatened by new ideas; then these new ideas become institutions.

Shifts in the Global Age

Shift in Perceptions

"In a rapidly globalizing world, peoples from Asia, Mexico, Latin America, and parts of Africa migrate because of better labor market opportunities abroad or political turmoil at home. Some leave because they wish to become cosmopolitan; others seek a safer space to preserve their traditions . . . liberal democracies face not only burgeoning numbers of immigrants, but also their own hidden assumptions about the scope and limits of tolerance for cultural diversity" (Shweder, Minow, and Markus 4). But some teachers still whisper to each other, "He's black," and sit the Latinos in the back of the room.

Shifts in Ideologies

Consider the ideological shifts that threatened (and continue to threaten) political institutions in Iraq, Iran, and Korea. Consider the economic shifts that threatened (and continue to threaten) organizational institutions such as the Big Three automakers, the steel producers, the three or four major food processors. Consider the educational shifts that threatened (and continue to threaten) academic institutions, such as scope and sequence of curriculum, restructuring, pre-K education, systemic reform, team teaching, violence in schools, vast numbers of students from other countries, No Child Left Behind, even the concept of public education itself, such as vouchers, alternative schools, or for-profit private schools (Walsh 1). Consider terrorism.

Most teachers, administrators, and board members do not want to be the second snail. They do not want to be the dinosaurs Janet Emig describes with "dismaying ratio of tail to brain, awaiting only total ossification" (1971, 171). Realizing that enormous change is here, they want to become what futurist Joel Barker calls "paradigm shifters" (Sparks 22). They are the innovators; they are the visionaries; they see the need for change, they agree that "schools organized on the factory model do not open doors to the future; they imprison students in their own minds" (Caine and Caine 15). Understanding the necessity of training, retraining, and continuous learning, they are eager paradigm pioneers, helping to restructure schools, and motivate students who will soon enter the new world of change. And *change* is the key word. We have a friend who is a VP for AT&T. She told us, "We have startling new technologies but we feel the public is not quite ready for them yet."

Shifts in Technologies

The term *technologies* returns us to the term *globalization.* Although introduced into the English lexicon as early as 1944, it is attributed to Theodore Levitt because of his 1983 article in the *Harvard Business Review* titled "Globalization of Markets." An umbrella term, *globalization* includes a series of economic, social, technological, cultural, and political changes that increase interdependence, integration, and interaction among people and companies in disparate locations.

Giddens in *Runaway World* explains that while it is not a "particularly attractive or elegant word," it is ubiquitous. "I haven't been to a single country recently where globalization isn't being intensively discussed. In France, the word is *mondialisation.* In Spain and Latin America, it is *globalizacion.* The Germans call it *Globalisierung*" (7). However, we are not interested in the political or economic pro/anti positions on globalization; our interest lies in how it marks quickening change and how that change impacts education.

Shifts in the Job Market

Globalization raises the question: What will students need to become successful, productive people in the twenty-first century? With data claiming that manufacturing jobs have declined from 28 percent to 11 percent and will drop to 2 percent by the year 2030, most jobs will be in some area of the service sector, people will need to be able to read, write, think, compute, and collaborate. "The knowledge and skills required for higher education and for employment are now considered equivalent" (ACT 2006; American Diploma Project 2004, in Graham and Perin 8).

Skills for the Global Age

Daniel H. Pink in his *A Whole New Mind* presents a compelling case for what he calls the "conceptual age." Flirting with profundity, he holds we will move from the left-brain directed thinking of the information age to the right-brain directed thinking needed for the conceptual age. He claims the three As—abundance, Asia, and automation—are causing us to turn to a high-concept, high-touch paradigm. While not totally dismissing left-brain thinkers because some will be needed, Pink believes most left-brained people will be outsourced or replaced by technology in this flattened world because of economic reasons. What the new paradigm will demand are people of high concept, which "involves the ability to create artistic and emotional beauty, to detect patterns and opportunities, to craft a satisfying narrative, and to combine seemingly unrelated ideas into a novel invention" (51–52). Further, he contends that this flattened world will need people of high touch, which "involves the ability to empathize, to understand the subtleties of human interaction, to find joy in one's self and to elicit it in others, and to stretch beyond the quotidian, in pursuit of purpose and meaning" (52).

Reading

That reading is a necessary twenty-first-century skill is a given. Districts who know their data initiate evidence-based reading instruction with "practices grounded in sound and rigorous research with well-prepared and skillful teachers" (Tierney and Readence 2).

Certainly specialized skills are needed, but according to the most recent UIS data, there are an estimated 781 million illiterate adults in the world, about 64 percent of whom are women (www.Uis.unesco.org).

The National Center for Education Statistics in 2005 stated, "Over half of adults scoring at the lowest literacy levels are dropouts, and almost a quarter of these persons are high school graduates" (Graham and Perin 7).

A new international study of reading literacy, International Comparisons in Fourth-Grade Reading Literacy: Findings from the Progress in International Reading Literacy Study (PIRLS) of 2001, released by the U.S. Department of Education's National Center for Education Statistics (NCES), found "significant gaps in reading literacy achievement between racial/ethnic groups, between students in high poverty schools and other public schools, and also between girls and boys" (timss.bc.edu/pirls2001i/PIRLS2001_news.html).

In 1991, a Harris poll "found that only one-third of employers think that recent high school graduates show 'the ability to read and understand written and verbal instructions' " (O'Neil 6). The Organisation for Economic Co-operation and Development found in 2000 that U.S. graduates' literacy skills are lower than those of graduates in most industrialized nations, comparable only to the skills of graduates in Chile, Poland, Portugal, and Slovenia (Graham and Perin 8).

In her groundbreaking book on immigration and ethnicity *The Transnational Villagers*, Peggy Levitt shows occupations according to racial-ethnic groups in Table I.1 (226). When juxtaposed with the education of those same groups during the same time period, it is clear that education impacts occupations in Table I.2 (224).

With these data as a sampling, it appears that high on the list of necessary skills are the basics of reading and writing. The citizens of the twenty-first century will need to read and write to simply keep up with expectations of continuing education. They will need to read quickly, predict

Table I.1. Current Occupation of Selected Racial-Ethnic Groups in the U.S., 1996–99

Racial-Ethnic Group	Occupation					
	Managerial and Professional (%)	Technical, Sales, and Administrative Support (%)	Service (%)	Farm, Forestry, Fishing (%)	Precision, Production, Craft, Repair (%)	Operators, Fabricators, and Laborers (%)
White	31.8	30.2	12.1	2.4	11.0	12.5
African American	18.8	29.5	22.4	1.0	7.9	20.4
Native American	19.9	26.8	18.9	3.2	12.4	18.8
Asian	34.1	30.2	13.9	1.3	7.8	12.7
Dominican	11.6	25.7	27.8	—	4.7	30.2
Non-Dominican Hispanic	13.7	23.9	20.7	6.2	12.9	22.6
Total	28.5	29.4	14.2	2.6	10.8	14.5

Source: U.S. Census Bureau; Current Population Survey; March 1996–99; Public Use Data.
Note: Includes all persons age 15 and older.

Table I.2. Education of Selected Racial-Ethnic Groups in the U.S., 1996–99

Racial-Ethnic Group	Educational Attainment of Adults					
	0–8th grade (%)	9–11th grade (%)	High School Graduate (%)	Some College (%)	College Graduate (%)	Post Graduate (%)
White	5.2	12.7	32.3	26.3	16.0	7.5
African American	8.4	21.4	33.3	25.2	8.4	3.3
Native American	8.2	21.2	33.5	25.6	7.9	3.6
Asian	8.4	12.5	20.5	22.9	24.1	11.6
Dominican	25.4	26.7	21.5	20.0	5.0	1.4
Non-Dominican Hispanic	25.4	23.0	25.2	18.2	6.0	2.2

Source: U.S. Census Bureau; Current Population Survey; March 1996–99; Public Use Data.
Note: Includes all persons 15 years and older.

accurately, infer thoughtfully. They will need to be able to read screens of all sizes since everything will not be hard copy and computers of all types will be more common.

Writing

Writing is thinking on paper. Writing and reading are ways into knowing, learning, and communicating, so it is no surprise to read Peggy Harris's "Writing Boosts Learning in Science, Math, and Social Studies" in the September 2006 headline of *The Council Chronicle*.

A report to Carnegie Corporation of New York, *Writing Next: Effective Strategies to Improve Writing of Adolescents in Middle and High Schools*, the first meta-analysis of experimental and quasi-experimental research on pre-collegiate writing instruction in two decades, cites the New Jersey Writing Project's initial study (58) under studies supporting writing as a process.

Conducted by Steve Graham, a professor at Vanderbilt, and Dolores Perin, a professor at Columbia, under the aegis of the Alliance for Excellent Education, *Writing Next* recommends eleven key elements of effective adolescent writing instruction:

1. Writing Strategies

2. Summarization

3. Collaborative Writing

4. Specific Product Goals

5. Word Processing

6. Sentence Combining

7. Prewriting

8. Inquiry Activities

9. Process Writing Approach

10. Study of Models

11. Writing for Content Literacy (11)

Each of these key elements are integral to NJWPT/Abydos and form the basis of this book. Teachers trained by NJWPT/Abydos in these key elements and who receive administrative support are more authentically equipped to prepare students for the literacy challenges of the twenty-first century.

Students will be expected to write apt, clear, and lively prose in the workplace. Few readers will take the time to ponder over garbled sentences or incoherent memos. Even fewer readers will have patience with inappropriate style or tone. With information bombarding the world at record rates, unwieldy writing will find no place in it.

Yet "seventy percent of students in grades 4–12 are low-achieving writers" (Peersky et al. 2003 in Graham and Perin 7). In a 2005 report, the National Commission on Writing grimly states, "Poorly written applications are likely to doom candidates' chances for employment" (4).

We once heard on National Public Radio that Hewlett-Packard with its network of over 400 offices all over the world, a network connected by computers, generates 8 million pages of discourse a day. Clearly there are those who write those pages, and just as clearly there are those who read and respond.

Thinking

Thinking with its attendant skill *inquiry* promotes the development of ideas through close examination, description, inference, analysis, comparison and contrast, creating, synthesis, and evaluation. In short, inquiry is traveling Bloom's taxonomy.

Given accelerated change coupled with anticipated permutations yet unexpected innovations, students must learn to how to think logically creatively, learning how to think about thinking. Further, students need strategies to become metacognitive learners who know what they have learned and how they have learned it. They must not just be able to think but also to think through their own thinking so that they can repeat the process. This level of thinking insinuates their learning and affords them an edge over those who have no notion of their learning processes.

Metacognitive learners will be a credit both to themselves and to their employers. Already corporations are spending millions of dollars on training. "According to Roger Semerad, senior vice president at RJR Nabisco, corporations are spending $40 to $50 billion a year on training employees" (Atkins 32). Metacognitive learners will become an invaluable asset in a world where retraining and continuous learning is the norm. As Lauren Resnick, director of the Learning Research and Development Center at the University of Pittsburgh, said, "In the old industrial model, thinking was left to the manager, and doing to the hired hands. Today, to be competitive, what seems to be required is thinking throughout the production process. Competitive high-performance work organizations seek entrants to the work force who can think their way through unfamiliar problems, who can use complex tools, and who are able to envisage the place of their own activity in the much broader activity of the workplace" (O'Neil 7).

Computing

Computer literacy rules and will continue to rule in the twenty-first century. With blogs and blogs bigger than blogs such as MySpace, chat rooms, online classes, Instant Messaging, and ICQs

("I Seek You," created in India and now owned by AOL), students are agog with cyberspace. When my computer goes on the fritz, I call a student to remedy the problem. Computer fields such as database designers, senior developers, video and computer forensics, and forensic accountants lure students into jobs. Young entrepreneurs such as Vitaly Feldman, twenty-five, and Alexander Koretsky, twenty-four, who launched MetroHorse in June 2006, provide models for what students might accomplish. MetroHorse, an online company, is forecasted to earn $500,000 in its first year, $50 million by 2008.

If these figures aren't seductive enough, consider what challenges computers offer students. Biocomputing is the hot arena. Computer scientists in this field work on ways to integrate some aspect of the computer into our bodies with biochips that will tell us what to do and what not do. Our personal biochip will interface directly with the computer. Computer wizards are hard at work on a heads-up display instrument (HUD) that is somewhat like a small TV screen placed on the inside lens of a pair of glasses. The wearer will see both the screen and the environment.

What student wouldn't be intrigued by the intricate interaction between the physical and mental realms that produce a combination of concepts known as wetware? Simply put, scientists are working on a chip that will be downloadable directly into the brain.

These are some areas in computer land that are under construction. Of course, those students unable to read, write, think, and collaborate fluently will never be able to get a ticket. They will be on the outside looking in, further and further behind in the world scope.

Collaborating

Collaboration, another essential twenty-first-century skill, snugly fits into the surging globalization/conceptual age where no one person is be expected to know everything or even to understand it equally. As a nation of mini-experts, we have learned to respect the depth of knowledge of the other.

In school, rather than expecting each student to do what every other student does, collaborative classrooms enable students to work together synergistically. With a goal of the "whole being greater than the sum of its parts," relationships, teamwork, cooperation, and partnerships replace working alone, solitary undertakings, competition, and solo ventures.

> Learning to collaborate suggests a different kind of education than one designed to prepare a relatively few talented young people to become professional experts. . . . A greater emphasis is placed on interactive communications linked to group problems, definitions, and solutions. Students learn to articulate, clarify, and then restate for one another how to determine questions and find answers. . . . Students would learn how to share their understandings, and build upon each others' insights. (Reich 23)

Change, complexity, flexibility describe our times, but there is also something to say for sustainability. "Everything old is new again," Peter Allen's famous lyric incorporated into *All That Jazz* by Bob Fosse, predicted the recent frenzied trend of making over, remaking, recycling, reclaiming. The media, indeed the world, has suddenly and intensely become conscious of sustainability as its ultimate luxury. From Earth Day celebrations, tree hugging, and Green Peace to environmentally friendly products and buildings, ecological forms, and Whole Foods, people are turning to that which has proven lasting, durable, and workable—that which is successful and wholesome.

Now we use fiber optics to make vases, recycled aluminum bark to hold candles, eco-friendly Provista plastic to weave bowls, cardboard BeeBoard to construct desks, steel tongue with a sustainable aluminum shell for chairs, scrapile for tables, and cork for chaise lounges, while old porcelain ornaments again decorate homes. Smith & Hawken offers moss-covered animals, and Kristian Vedel makes handmade birds. We can buy gardens in bags, we long for a gas-efficient hybrid car, eschew meat and leather and fur, make jewelry from black gold, pernambuco wood, and cacholong stone, resurrect old silverware, turn old cafeterias into posh restaurants, design clothes that are luxurious but durable and easy to wear. Today people care less about big floor plans and marble countertops but more about how their new place might increase dependence on fossil fuels or if their home emits toxic chemicals. Even our vacations are taking on the trappings of ecology and the organic. In short, we all seem to want a sustainable and healthy life for all life forms—and that would and should include children.

SIMULTANEOUS LITERACY

Simultaneity in literacy, a form of academic multitasking, distinguishes and will continue to distinguish the literacy of the twenty-first century. Listening, speaking, reading, writing, computing, and collaborating will form the basic requirements of literacy, along with presenting skills and oral communication, but as Alvin Toffler, well known for *The Third Wave* and *Powershift: Knowledge, Wealth, and Power at the Edge of the 21st Century*, predicts, "The illiterate of the year 2000 will not be the individual who cannot read and write, but the one who cannot learn, unlearn and relearn" (Toffler, edu-cyberpg.com).

Think of "Simultaneous Literacy" as a series of overlays placed on a projector. To achieve, students will need layers of skills, first listening, speaking, reading, writing, computing, collaborating, and presenting. But concomitantly, they will be learning, unlearning, and relearning new technologies and spiraling information as they hone aptitudes in design, story, symphony, empathy, play, and meaning (Pink 65–66). Left-brain directed thinkers will learn or relearn ways to tap their right brains to be successful in a multicultural, cross-cultural, global world. Right-brain directed thinkers will be affirmed for their abilities to see the big picture and to synthesize. Both will learn to work in areas that computers can't do less expensively or more quickly.

This multiplicity of literacy, this broadening of the term, has been coming for several decades. When we conducted advanced seminars in the late 1980s to extend the work of the institutes, we used Robert J. Sternberg's *The Triarchic Mind*. His theory suggests that success comes within a sociocultural context. People who are successful know how to capitalize on their strengths and minimize their weaknesses. "They exhibit differences in the flexibility with which they can bring various styles to bear upon a variety of problems, with some people exhibiting more flexibility than others" (295). Ahead of its time, Sternberg's theory views intelligence as a form of developing competencies, and competencies as forms of developing expertise. In other words, for Sternberg, intelligence is modifiable rather than fixed. For us, his word *competency* is another word for *literacy*.

Howard Gardner in *Frames of Mind: The Theory of Multiple Intelligences* defines intelligence as "the ability to solve problems, or to create products, that are valued within one or more cultural settings" (x). By now everyone in education has studied his original seven intelligences:

- Linguistic intelligence: a sensitivity to the meaning and order of words.

- Logical-mathematical intelligence: ability in mathematics and other complex logical systems.

- Musical intelligence: the ability to understand and create music. Musicians, composers, and dancers show a heightened musical intelligence.

- Spatial intelligence: the ability to "think in pictures," to perceive the visual world accurately, and re-create (or alter) it in the mind or on paper. Spatial intelligence is highly developed in artists, architects, designers, and sculptors.

- Bodily-kinesthetic intelligence: the ability to use one's body in a skilled way, for self-expression or toward a goal. Mimes, dancers, basketball players, and actors are among those who display bodily-kinesthetic intelligence.

- Interpersonal intelligence: an ability to perceive and understand other individuals—their moods, desires, and motivations. Political and religious leaders, skilled parents and teachers, and therapists use this intelligence.

- Intrapersonal intelligence: an understanding of one's own emotions. Some novelists and or counselors use their own experience to guide others.

Most know that in 1999 Gardner introduced an eighth intelligence, the naturalist intelligence, in his work *Intelligence Reframed: Multiple Intelligences for the 21st Century*. Referring to Charles Darwin as exemplar of this type of intelligence, Gardner says the naturalist recognizes and classifies plants, minerals, and animals, including rocks and grass and all variety of flora and fauna. The ability to recognize cultural artifacts like cars or sneakers may also depend on the naturalist intelligence. He holds that some people are inherently good at recognizing and classifying artifacts.

We suggest thinking of each of Gardner's intelligences as *a literacy*.

Then Thomas Armstrong, holding that "Every child is a genius" (1), identifies twelve qualities in *Awakening Genius in the Classroom*—curiosity, playfulness, imagination, creativity, wonder, wisdom, inventiveness, vitality, sensitivity, flexibility, humor, and joy (2–3). We hold each of these qualities characterizes a literacy.

Continuing our analogy of layered transparencies superimposed upon each other, by now a large but not unwieldy pile, we add the literacy of the different disciplines, topped with a literacy of life. We contend, therefore, that the overarching features of "Simultaneous Literacy" are flexibility and the ability to synthesize—to put together two or more things in a new and different ways, to see relationships in order to gain new insights, and to academically and socioculturally multitask. These mega-abilities will earmark the literate citizen of the twenty-first century.

FUTURE TRENDS

- A vibrant entrepreneurial era

- Reading, writing, and typing the movements of sign language

- More information but a poverty of attention

- An overabundance of informational sources

- Integrated literacy, music, and technology using a cross-curricular model

- New ways to download

- Online market places

- Mailable taste testers

- Mobile takeout meals

- Genetic engineering

- Interactive TV

- Multimedia storytelling

- Linguistic rights

- The democratizing of democracy

- Sexual equality

- Scaremongering

- OV fertility watches

- Increased gaming experiences

- Consumer-generated media

- Robot hands

- Smart phones

- Electric ears

- End of the "going to work" era

- Living a "Web lifestyle"

- Large-scale immigration

- The rise of "global cities"

- Interdisciplinary centers, programs, projects, and departments

- Transnationalism

CONCLUSION

The information age defined writing as a complex of cognitive processes; the globalization age redefines writing as a complex of cognitive processes embedded in a social context. The Asia Society, in *Math and Science Education in a Global Age: What the U.S. Can Learn from China*, warns, "While American scientific research is widely admired, there are grave concerns about the quality of math and science education in the United States" (9).

"The Russian education system is moving, sometimes fitfully and sometime with surprising speed, to address the issues" (Canning and Kerr in Rotberg 49) of the twenty-first century while "South Africa has taken on an educational transformation of immense proportions compared with what almost any other country has tried in the last few decades (Crouch in Rotberg 75). "Chile's educational reform measures generally respond well to the needs of the system, have not caused a great deal of stress on teachers, and have the potential to improve student learning once they are fully implemented" (McMeekin in Rotberg 105).

All must look at teaching with eyes on those who want the freedom to know and express. As Donald Graves says, "A democracy relies heavily on each individual's sense of voice, authority, and ability to communicate desires and information" (1978, 5). He suggests that students be regarded less as receivers and more as senders. If students can only read and listen but cannot speak or write, cannot send, they are robbed of an essential right—the freedom of expression.

Still students of product teachers who write only on the teacher's assigned topic most often neither send authentic messages through their writing nor receive peer-group or teacher responses. So students try at first to fit their meaning into formula, but the results usually read as phony scholarship or contrived trivia. Most meet deadlines, yet many continue to use poor grammar within wooden writing. Eventually they give up or content themselves with anorexic paragraphs, underdeveloped bursts of what is conventional, what is safe—paragraphs starved for substance, devoid of voice or risk or discovery. Education in the product paradigm may have once served its purpose, but it no longer works.

The movement from product to process to globalization requires change and integration. Writing as a process means giving students time to prewrite, write, postwrite, proofread, and edit their papers. It means teaching writing, not just assigning it. It means teaching the various forms for writing so students think through their meaning, their purpose, the needs of their audience, and match it with the most appropriate genre. It means encouraging students to collaborate with peers and to conference with teachers during the writing. It means permitting students to determine to some extent the timelines needed for completed papers to be submitted to teacher and subsequently to be published. At all levels, students should experience the delight of publication. It means teaching grammar and mechanics within the writing process. It means hard work, self-satisfaction, discovery, and making decisions. It means making classrooms joyfully literate places.

Writing is a process. The word *process* attaches proper significance to the way writing happens, the way writing has always happened. Everyone has a process, but each writer's process is idiosyncratic. Recognizing that process not only frees the writer but frees the teacher to facilitate not commandeer writing.

Soon, students discover that writing serves other functions, not the least being a look at self on the page in order to know self, to write one's meaning down to better understand that meaning. Teachers discover that writing taught as a process provides coherence for students in a fragmented world, and that students who write begin to think more holistically, see patterns, work through knots, think as they write, then share that thinking through collaboration with peers.

Both discover that the entire topography of the classroom changes.

APPLICATION

Using cash register tape or sentence strips, create a timeline of your writing journey.

PART

I

THE PROCESS

1

PREWRITING: MORE THAN THE BEGINNING

> If writing a book is impossible, write a chapter.
> If writing a chapter is impossible, write a page.
> If writing a page is impossible, write a paragraph.
> If writing a paragraph is impossible, write a sentence.
> If writing a sentence is impossible, write a word
> and teach yourself everything there is to know about that word
> and then write another, connected word and see
> where the connection leads.
> —Richard Rhodes □

OVERVIEW OF WRITING AS A PROCESS

Just the other day we received an e-mail from one of our trainers who is an ELA coordinator for a high-powered district. She shared her concern.

> I notice in the classroom visits I do around the district so many teachers say to their students: "Don't just sit there; start writing." "Writing isn't staring; it's pen moving on paper." "Writing isn't talking." And so on.
> It really distresses me that they expect kids to take a prompt or even look back at their own prewriting and begin immediately. Several times I could tell the whisperings of the kids had to do with writing.
> Help! I feel like teachers are reinforcing the panicky feeling we have when we're asked to write.

When we read her e-mail, we realized, even after all these years, classrooms exist where writing is taught without any real understanding of the process or its recursive nature. Despite knowledge of the terms *prewriting*, *writing*, *rewriting*, and *editing*, some teachers still misunderstand these ongoing and sometimes simultaneous acts. They bear out Tolstoy's famous reminder, "It is not the word that is difficult to comprehend, but the concept behind the word which is not understood."

What distinguishes teachers who have been trained in teaching writing as a process from those who know the terms but don't understand the concepts behind the terms is that the former writes with and stays with the students every step of the way; the latter assigns, collects, and corrects.

The Writing Process Journey: The Beginning, Middle, and End

Before we launch into several chapters on each phase of process, let's us provide quick handy definitions. Each of these will be fleshed on in the succeeding chapters.

- Prewriting/Creating: The journey begins as the teacher offers one or many ways to nudge writing, to get the juices flowing, to capture illusive ideas, to find or focus on a topic.

- Writing/Organizing: Once students have settled into an idea, they write. During writing (sometimes called drafting), they elaborate on the topic, solidify their purpose, and organize the chaos of prewriting. Sometimes an idea dies, so the student travels back to prewriting.

- Rewriting/Correcting, Revising, Reformulating: Generally the longest part of the journey, students work to get the words right, the meaning clear; they work on spelling, punctuation, grammar, sentences, paragraphs, and craft.

- Editing/Checking: Others read the draft to suggest changes, spot inconsistencies, recommend reworking, find flaws in logic or out-and-out mistakes.

- Proofreading/Polishing: During this final leg of the odyssey, students prepare the piece for the eyes and minds of others by finding and correcting any lingering errors or problems.

- Publishing/Distributing: The journey ends when the writing goes public.

PREWRITING

Much has been written about prewriting. Some call it percolating (Romano 1987, 56); some call it rehearsal, a term Donald M. Murray attributes to Donald Graves (in Carroll and Wilson *Acts* 87); some call it creating (Cowan and Cowan 2). No matter what the term, all agree that prewriting is intrinsic to the writing process. All agree on its idiosyncratic nature and complexity. Consider the diverse activities found under its heading: note taking, outlining, reading, thinking, dreaming, reverie, doodling, imagining, talking, and fooling around. Additionally, there are specific prewriting strategies, which will be defined in this chapter, such as freewriting, sentence stubs, journal writing, brainstorming, listing, invisible writing, blueprinting, drawing, looping, dialogue, reporter's formula, the pentad, classical invention, classical invention for the contemporary student, cubing, hexagonal, and webbing. Since the ultimate purpose of prewriting is to find or focus a topic, most anything that gives rise to ideas constitutes prewriting.

A Poet Describes Her Writing Process

Listening to Linda Pastan at a poetry reading, we were struck with her idea drawer, an actual drawer in a chest standing in her writing room. There she collects ideas, like leaves, which float in and out of her life. When a poem is in the making, she has learned to recognize its beginnings so she can work on it from its first awakening. She tells how some fragments in her idea drawer are not ready for poems. These fragments have not been fully wakened to her as poet. So she stores all the fragments—lines written on scraps of papers, grocery cash registers slips, a page—for use when poems are not busy waking her up.

She goes to her idea drawer and stirs some from their sleep. Sometimes one or two wake up, and she gets busy making them into poems. Sometimes she puts ideas back to sleep and coaxes others into being. Some ideas become poems that need rewriting. When she is not ready to rewrite because of other forces on her writing, she places them back in her drawer. The next time she pulls from her drawer, she might find a fragment of a poem or a poem that is ready for more rewriting. Pastan understands, practices, and shares the recursive nature of her writing process.

We imagine Pastan in a Magritte painting, raking poem fragments. We see her writing these into a giant poem. We think: Perhaps teaching writing should be like leaves moving in the breeze—implicit, with all the rich metaphors of leaves and fall and wind and raking and the resurrection of spring.

The Power of Prewriting

When we mandate prewriting instead of introducing it as a way to plumb the writer's mind for ideas or as a way to focus an idea, then any prewriting strategy becomes artificial or even detrimental to the composing process. The power of prewriting strategies lies in their benefit for students because they provide a heuristic; they form the basis for inquiry that can lead the student from the simple to the more complex, the more sophisticated. They are meant to be experienced not ordered.

George Hillocks Jr. in his article "Synthesis of Research on Teaching Writing" found,

The focus of instruction with the greatest power is what I have called inquiry. This approach should not be construed as discovery teaching in which students are presented with problems or tasks and set free to pursue them. On the contrary, the method involves using sets of data in a structured fashion to help students learn strategies for using the data in their writing. . . . The results of these studies indicate that the process of observing and writing is far more effective in increasing the quality of student writing than the traditional study of model paragraphs that illustrate the use of strategies. (77–78)

Effective use of prewriting allows for connections between what is taught and what is thought. We engage students in strategies rather than locking them into prewriting as a stage apart from anything that holds meaning for them. Certainly prewriting taught in isolation is a carryover from product paradigm teaching. When taken out of context, it may only foster "pseudo concepts" that seem to be grasped abstractly but are not (Vygotsky 1962, 66). Prewriting is more than sitting down with paper and writing on a topic with a designated number of supporting details; it is a way of learning to perceive, a way of thinking, a way of choosing potentialities from the writer's life to use as grist for writing. It is living the writing.

Richard Larson says,

One source of help in finding this plan [heuristic] may be the psychologists who have studied the phenomenon of *creativity*, as Gordon Rohman demonstrated in the report of his experiments with *prewriting* exercises a few years ago in writing classes at Michigan State University, which were based in part on theories by Rollo May and Arthur Koestler about the process of creating. These writers argue that if a student is to create, to "bring [something new] into birth" (Rollo May's words), he must learn to understand thoroughly his experiences, the data he has to work with—what May calls his *world*." (quoted by Larson, 146–147)

Prewriting strategies are the tools for finding that world.

Grandmother loves to garden. When she does, she uses four tools: a spade, a shovel, a fork, and a trowel, all well worn from years of breaking ground. The spade digs deep—getting into the depths of the earth, turning the soil so new nutrients get close to tender shoots. The shovel is for general digging. She says, "You can use it as a hoe if you just slide the blade along the top of the ground." The fork breaks up the big chunks and uncovers the worms she will use during the heat of the day when she leaves her garden to fish at the tank just below the rim of the canyon. The trowel serves for small chores, when she gets on her hands and knees to gently loosen the soil. As grandmother readies her garden, one tool is not more important than the other—they are different. So, too, with prewriting strategies.

Prewriting as a Manifestation of Thinking

If students think randomly, more than likely their prewriting will be rambling and disjointed. If students think sequentially, more than likely their prewriting will resemble a shopping list. Thus, a case may be made that prewriting evidences thought. In prewriting, this thinking is recorded, thereby rendering it a potential source for subsequent writing.

In classrooms where prewriting is taught, modeled, and practiced as an ongoing activity, as liberating, students learn its value as a collection from which to draw. They also begin to differentiate among the prewriting strategies, choosing the one most fitting their purpose. Some strategies warm up the writer, get the brain in gear. Others help generate ideas, while still others focus an idea. Prewriting heuristic techniques become enriched sources since they take the writer through a thinking process.

It is not enough to give a student topic and assign "writing." Nor is it enough to give a student an experience and say, "Write about it." Students need to have a repertoire of prewriting strategies to draw from just as Linda Pastan drew from her idea drawer. Then students develop a habit of thought and learn to choose and use the appropriate prewriting strategy as a way of interpreting the world and experiencing it as rich rootstock.

Prewriting Problems

Oversimplifying

Often texts or teachers oversimplify prewriting, suggesting it as an activity undertaken only at the beginning of the process. This oversimplification belies the difficulty of how to teach the techniques of writing while at the same time allowing for the tentativeness of the act; how to provide strategies while keeping those strategies from becoming linear stages.

Jumping from Prewriting to Publishing

Another problem occurs when the teacher jumps from prewriting to publishing, ignoring the writing and rewriting, the very times needed to maximize teaching and employ modeling. So students embrace prewriting but eschew the hard work of grammar, syntax, diction, the tough act of correcting what Emig calls those "stylistic infelicities" (1971, 43) and the even tougher act of crafting the piece. Another problem happens when texts divide the process according to hard-and-fast guidelines: prewriting on Monday, drafting on Tuesday, rewriting on Wednesday, editing on

Thursday, handing in the final copy on Friday. This approach neither allows students to develop the discipline of revisiting their prewriting, reworking a draft, nor does it encourage students to begin an entirely new portion after revising if warranted. It certainly does not promote thinking or reflecting upon what they have written or insight into their processes.

Staying Power

Ironically, one problem with prewriting is its staying power. Since teachers and students enjoy its freedom, they want to remain in prewriting. These teachers and students point proudly to bulging writing folders filled with starts, bits, lists, loops, unfinished stories, half-written how-to's, quotations, reactions, notes, and other proof that prewriting lives in their classrooms. But when closely inspecting the contents of those folders, we sometimes find little or no evidence that shows an attempt to take the prewriting further. We find superficiality or hastily written final copies, lack of elaboration, or frustration because students are not experiencing the benefits of the full process, or there is lack of closure because of a quantum leap from prewriting to publishing.

Thinking Prewriting Is a Finished Piece

Some student writers maintain an interesting attitude but potential problem about prewriting. Like Moses, they treat their prewriting as tantamount to tablets of stone brought down from the mountain. They perceive no need to change their writing in any way, nor do they have the motivation to change it. They often quip, "But I wrote it, didn't I?" For them, seeing their teacher writing, resisting the seduction of not changing anything, accepting the challenge to reenter the piece to discover the writing's potential, becomes a powerful model and makes their reentry into their writing easier, or at least more realistic.

Internalized Prewriting

Then there is the phenomenon of prewriting "by grace." Some writers—even some student writers—sit down and write a draft without seeming to have to prewrite at all. Perhaps here the prewriting has already taken place internally or "tacitly," to borrow Michael Polanyi's term (20). Students come to the task already armed with an idea or a focus, already finished with prewriting either done in the head or completed through some substrata of the psyche. This phenomenon may happen to any student, at any time, without warning. It may also be the modus operandi of specific writers. In any case, it is upsetting to untrained teachers who insist on evidence of prewriting, who do not themselves write, who may hold rigidly to lock-step instruction, or who may view this as the "down from the mountain" syndrome.

The difficulty with this internalized prewriting lies in the fact that, unlike jogging or chin-ups, thinking cannot be seen. Without any type of physical manifestation, other than a poised pencil or furrowed brow, or until a time when classrooms will be equipped with a technology that permits lights positioned above students' desks or tables to glow with the same intensity as the students' minds, teachers are left to interpret the veracity of this unseen prewriting. Because some students prewrite mentally, teachers who write know how to look for observable signs of mental prewriting. They note students who stare out the window before they write, those who talk before writing, or those who doodle their prewriting. They become keenly aware of activities, which to the untrained eye may look like off-task behavior, that are really evidences of prewriting.

The actor Kevin Kline spoke to a group of business people about the boss who fired the employee for leaning back with his feet on the desk. The boss could not accept the fact that the employee was thinking. Kline's humor revealed a subtle truth: sometimes thinkers lean back and put up their feet. In classrooms where thinking occurs, in classrooms where thinking is encouraged and nurtured, teachers find ways to allow students to lean back and put up their feet. Some teachers establish thinking corners with beanbags and pillows, or they create isolated areas corded off with refrigerator boxes.

Tracy McDonald encourages her second graders to set cardboard light-bulbs on their desks when they are thinking so classmates do not bother them. This concept is not exclusive to the elementary school. Linda Maxwell provides pillows and carpet squares in the back of the room for her twelfth-grade students to use when they need time to think. Trivializing what cannot be seen is to give mere lip service to cognition.

Facilitating Prewriting

We recommend facilitating prewriting three ways. The first way is to introduce all the prewriting techniques—freewriting, wet ink, trigger words, free association, invisible writing, writing roulette, sentence stubs, journal writing, brainstorming, listing, blueprinting, drawing, looping, dialogue, reporter's formula, the pentad, classical invention, classical invention for the contemporary student, cubing, hexagonal, and webbing—teaching one after the other in rapid fire, until all have been experienced. This way, students develop a repertoire of strategies. From that point on, they have choices, choosing among the prewriting strategies, trying them out with different genres, or picking one they decide will work best.

The second approach is to introduce an appropriate prewriting technique guaranteed to produce the type of writing desired. For example, when students write a newspaper article, we teach reporter's formula (who? what? where? why? which? how?) as the natural prewriting strategy to generate such an article. When students work on narratives, we suggest dialogue or writing roulette as prewriting techniques most likely to help students focus on characters or plot development.

We model a different prewriting strategy during a mini-teach as part of an integrated lesson on writing. This third way of facilitating prewriting strategies takes into account the activities underway. For example, when working with students studying the Holocaust, we take several children's books or excerpts from young adult novels to generate prompts for prewriting (see Chapter 13); we may arrange discussion groups or class discussion followed by several minutes of freewriting; while the pentad might jog still another prewriting. By generating several prewritings related to one topic, students collect many starts from which to make a commitment to a longer, sustained, more substantive paper.

PREWRITING STRATEGIES

Since prewriting is recursive, folding back upon itself if more thinking is needed, we suggest students engage in several prewriting strategies or use the same strategy several times. That way, if one doesn't work, another may. Building a repertoire and encouraging choice promotes a comfort zone that invites fluency and specificity. Prewriting strategies also serve varied purposes. While the prewriting strategies listed below may be used for purposes other than those designated—for example, freewriting may be a warm-up or a way to find or focus an idea thereby blurring purposes—this list reflects the most natural heuristic of starting with simple warm-ups and ending with strategies that result in text analysis.

Prewriting Warm-Ups

Freewriting, wet ink, trigger words, free association, and invisible writing are prewriting strategies used to stimulate the brain, to get the kinks out, to rev up the motor for further writing. They may be used repeatedly as anticipatory sets or as sponge activities, the latter being for those minutes of downtime that sometimes occur after a lesson but before the bell.

Freewriting

Explanation. The mother of all prewriting is freewriting because it is just that: writing freely about whatever comes to mind without regard during the flow for punctuation, spelling, mechanics, grammar, or usage. Freewriting is the mind's dictation. The point is to freely receive the mind's offerings and record them, to simply get down as quickly as possible the thoughts flowing through the brain. Because the brain works faster than the hand, many writers even abbreviate when they freewrite in an effort to write as closely as possible what the mind says. Therefore, when the mind takes a turn, the writer takes the same turn. Often in these twists and curves lies the surprising view, the intuitive leap, the hidden memory. Think of freewriting as a dialogue between the brain and the hand.

Implementation. When implementing freewriting, we find ten- or fifteen-minute challenges work best at first. The idea is to get the juices flowing. During that time, students write freely. The point is to get down whatever comes into their minds. We remind them of what William Faulkner advises, "Get it down. Take chances. It may be bad, but it's the only way you will get something good." In time we gradually increase the time challenge. Since freewriting is the truest, purest, and most common prewriting technique, students learn to go with its flow.

Remarks. After implementing freewriting, all other prewriting techniques become variations, adaptations, or extensions of that strategy, either in their call for freely getting ideas down or in their permission not to become concerned at this point in the process with punctuation, spelling, or mechanics.

Wet-Ink Writing

Explanation. As a close cousin to freewriting, wet-ink writing invites nonstop writing in minuscule bursts of time. Wet-ink writing derives its name from the days when writers dipped their quill pens into ink and wrote until the pen went dry before dipping it in again. So this strategy invites students to write so quickly there is literally no time for the ink to dry. Since the hand wearies quickly when not lifted from the paper, this prewriting strategy should not extend over one to two minutes. Its purpose is to allow the subconscious to sneak in an idea.

Implementation. To implement wet-ink writing in the classroom, we initiate a start and stop signal. We remind students not worry about mechanics since the purpose of this warm-up is to increase fluency. If they cannot think of anything to write, we tell them to write, "I can't think of anything," or "Nothing comes to mind," until something does—and it usually does because the brain refuses to be bored.

Remarks. Wet-ink writing allows students to measure the fluency of their writing against themselves. That is, the more they engage in these minuscule bursts of writing, the easier it becomes to get words on paper.

Trigger Words

Explanation. Trigger words combine freewriting and free association. The idea is to jog the memory with a carefully chosen word. Since the brain is capable of almost infinite connections, trigger words sometimes serve as both a warm-up and a strategy for finding an idea.

Implementation. To implement trigger words, we call out a word and everyone writes words, phrases, sentences, or anything that comes to mind. A variation of this, especially for a warm-up, is to invite different students on different days to call out a word for this purpose. Afterwards students share what they have written.

Remarks. Trigger words also may be used as a mini-teach. For example, if the word *bats* acts as the trigger, someone always writes *Batmobile* or *Batman*, a clear allusion to the Batman movies or comics, so we use that response to teach the purpose of allusions in writing or literature. Because the trigger word *bumblebee* usually results in someone writing the word *buzz*, we use *buzz* for a micro-mini-teach on onomatopoeia.

Trigger words may reinforce a skill taught earlier. For example, we invite appropriate adjectives when we give trigger nouns such as *flower*.

Free Association

Explanation. Free association belongs in the warm-up category because it gets students thinking. We use "Good Water" by Diane Wakoski as our model. Her first four lines read:

> the cup holds
> a ball,
> the ball becomes
> a skull . . . (in Carroll and Wilson 1997, 20)

This prewriting strategy breaks the usual thinking patterns; it literally frees students to tap the resources of their brains. Free association shows students the myriad ways their minds work as they process information and make connections. As Ornstein and Thompson say metaphorically in *The Amazing Brain*, "There are perhaps about one hundred billion neurons, or nerve cells, in the brain, and in a single human brain the number of possible interconnections between these cells is greater than the number of atoms in the universe" (21).

Implementation. To encourage this associative thinking, we read Wakoski's poem and talk about her connections. For example, what about a ball is like a skull? What else could the cup hold? Then we invite students to come up with their own first line and follow Wakoski's pattern. We tested this with students on many grade levels. They all embraced the challenge, most finishing the entire poem, making it loop back to the first line. Many worked on it and published it in their anthologies. Through writing this, some found topics they used in other genres. Here are some examples.

Buddy in third grade wrote:

> the cup holds
> the water
> the water
> turns into
> rainbows

Jocelyn, a fifth-grader, wrote:

the Reese's® taste
like pudding,
the pudding becomes
a rock,
the rock breaks
into pebbles,
the pebbles become
soil,
the soil becomes
water,
the water forms
a puddle.
the puddle looks
like pudding.

An eighth-grade boy started his poem:

the test is
for students
students resent
the test

A high school student contributed

the house thrush nests
in the ligustrum
the ligustrum scents
the night

Students make connections by associating the previous noun with something, by thinking part to whole or vice versa, by linking the words grammatically, sequentially, or by some other logical connection. Many students gravitate to metaphors and similes. We invite students to share their associations and talk about how they arrived at them.

For a twist on inviting students to write text innovations using the patterns of noted writers, see Claudia Brancato's *Borrowings*.

Remarks. Free association provides a rich and unusual way to expand vocabulary, reinforce spelling, or challenge work on parts of speech. Students find synonyms or antonyms for a free association as one way to expand vocabulary.

Another implication for this strategy is its possible use for collaboration. In one variation, groups work their way from one word to another on long strips of cash register tape or large pieces of butcher paper.

In still another variation, individual students or groups design their own versions of free association by giving the first lines and specific directions. They check to make sure their challenge will work, and then they present it to another person or group.

Finally, free association is an appropriate way to begin class. It warms up the brain, sets a tone in the classroom, and readies the students for work. It also may be used to conclude class by using words from the day's lesson.

Invisible Writing

Explanation. This idea comes from *A Community of Writers* by Peter Elbow and Pat Belanoff (11). Theoretically, invisible writing makes students write more, increases their concentration on "the emerging meaning inside your head," invites deeper focus of the mind, and helps them realize how often they lose track of what they are writing when they stop to reread, rethink, or listen to the critic inside. Peter Stillman calls this strategy "Invisible Ink" (173).

Implementation. We distribute two paper clips, two sheets of plain photocopy paper, and a sheet of carbon paper to each student. Students place the carbon between the two sheets of paper and affix it with a paper clip on the bottom and top. With that in place, each student receives a wooden skewer (or "dead" ballpoint pens may be used). Coupling invisible writing with trigger words, we give a word, for example, *destiny* as a prompt. Some teachers permit students to choose their own word or topic. Students then write with pausing until they come to the end of the page. Afterward they read what they have written and talk about it. (This may also be accomplished on the computer with the screen turned off.)

Remarks. We find that students either love this strategy or hate it. Those that love it speak to its intrigue, how they found what they wrote almost like finding a treasure. They thought not being able to see what they wrote kept them totally focused. Those that hate it are equally adamant. They dislike "giving up control"; they see no purpose to it and they were bothered by the way their paper "looked." Interestingly, students in both groups found some nuggets worth developing.

Prewriting for Narratives

Often warm-ups produce nuggets worthy of further elaboration or those that beg for a story. Sometimes when we ask students to write a story, they reply, "I don't know what to write." One way to break through the "I don't know" barrier is through collaborative narratives.

Writing Roulette

Explanation. Writing roulette, a prewriting strategy undertaken by a group, yields a collaborative narrative. These group-generated stories may be shared and enjoyed aloud—usually to grand chuckles or outright laughter. They may be honed and polished by individuals or the group. The products of writing roulette may provide the grist for future mini-teaches on the elements of a narrative, transitions, focus, voice, style, tone, legibility, punctuation, and spelling. Fun, they work on every grade level.

Implementation. Each student takes out a sheet of paper and writes his or her name in the top right-hand corner. We direct students to begin a story, telling them their beginning will be passed on to another student. Sometimes we conduct a bit of brainstorming first. Students write quickly until we call, "Time." At that signal, each passes his or her paper to the right. The student receiving the paper reads what has been written and continues the story line. And so it goes until we say, "This time when you receive the story, bring it to a close." Then volunteers share their stories.

Remarks. Students find writing roulette enjoyable and nonthreatening. Teachers like the way it fosters fluency and provides a way into the narrative. The word *roulette* connotes chance, which makes this strategy interesting because each student anticipates what is coming. With a tangible story in a prewritten form in hand at the conclusion of this strategy, students have something with which to work. There may be flat characters, hints of other elements, and little or no elaboration, yet the spontaneity yields funny, weird, sometimes poignant, but usually creative stories. Writing roulette could end there, but the true power of this prewriting strategy lies in what it enables teachers to do as follow-ups.

We brainstorm all the skills we needed to produce this group story: everything from handwriting to reading, from following a plot line to injecting trouble. After the brainstorming, class discussion centers on the implications of writing roulette. What ultimately emerges is a realization that writing and reading improves by writing and reading, and that knowledge and correct use of grammar, punctuation, and usage aids readers' understanding of what has been written.

Writing roulette also supports reentry for revision. A mini-teach on transitions using *signposting*, John Trimble's word, solidifies transitions in context. Trimble talks about transitional words and phrases that signal "the kind of thought that is coming next" (51). Students easily remember the parallel between the image of signposts that help travelers find their way along roads, and signposts that help readers find their way through the writing. Transitional words and phrases, repetitions, and rhetorical devices become important because they are applicable immediately to the group story. Signposting gives students—who have been exposed to large doses of jump cuts on television and in film and who often eschew transitions expecting the reader to follow their thoughts—a concrete device when writing that will help the reader. Additionally, working collaboratively on a story underscores the need for transitions because students readily see after this strategy that not everyone follows the connections throughout the story in the same way.

Prewriting to Find a Topic

One of the most obvious reasons for prewriting is to find a topic. Sentence stubs, journal writing, brainstorming, listing, blueprinting, and drawing enable students to call upon their own knowledge and experiences and those of others to find a topic. When these strategies are used in the classroom, students rarely complain, "I don't have anything to write about."

Sentence Stubs

Explanation. Sentence stubs are open-ended pieces of sentences meant for the students to finish and meant to spark enough interest so that more writing follows. The idea is that when the students finish that sentence stub, they continue writing out of it in an effort to find or follow a topic.

Implementation. We teach sentence stubs two ways. We write a sentence stub on the board or overhead and invite students to finish the sentence and continue with whatever thought it generates. We write too. Here is a sampling of our sentence stubs:

Today I thought . . .

Once when I was little . . .

I like . . .

My wish list would include . . .

I wish I knew . . .

Everyone has a defining moment. Mine was . . .

The second way we work with sentence stubs is by using Bonni Goldberg's *Room to Write*. Her invitations to write are sometimes funny, sometime eye-popping, sometimes wise, but always inspiring. We read a "stub" of something she has such as "Today pick an abstract concept like truth, beauty, evil, or love . . . " (56), we stop, and everyone begins to write. We find this resource usually sparks some good prewriting.

Remarks. Sentence stubs are to be used sparingly, and then only as a nudge. Short, simple, positive, and universal, they appeal to all students regardless of background or grade level. For instance, "My favorite vacation . . . " is not a good sentence stub because all students may not have had a vacation but "If I could take a trip . . . " works because everyone can relate to that possibility. Another caution: sentence stubs should not be negative or invite negativity. We realize some powerful writing is born of adversity, but that is the student's choice and should not be the result of a teacher-generated sentence stubs. Do not use stubs such as "My most embarrassing moment was . . . " or "I hate . . . " or "The most despicable person I ever knew was . . . "

Journal Writing

Explanation. Keeping a journal, perhaps the most ancient of all prewriting techniques, goes back to antiquity. There are records King Sargon of Agade (2334–2279 B.C.) who wrote detailed personal accounts on cuneiform tablets as did his daughter Enheduanna (Barnstone and Barnstone 1). The literati always kept journals: the classic *Walden* by Henry David Thoreau, for example, but neophyte writers keep journals, too. Case in point: the other day at dinner with friends, someone mentioned the term *hrair limit*. Immediately Javier took a small book from inside his coat pocket and made some notes. We know we will see that term erupt sometime in some way in something Javier writes.

> *Mother kept her journal in dad's unused bookkeeping ledgers. Her writing extends from page edge to page edge; it ignores all lines and margins. When she was in her eighties, she bequeathed to us a legacy of over fifty of these large rectangular books filled with memories, thoughts, collected maxims, facts, speculations, poetry, stories her mother told her, and those of her mother's mother.*

Among the first to legitimize journals as prewriting was Dorothy Lambert. Her "Keeping a Journal" (1965), was followed by Joyce Armstrong Carroll's "Journal-Making" (1972), Anne Ruggels Gere's extension of journals as a way to learn in *Roots in the Sawdust* (1985), and Toby Fulwiler who gathered much of the existing information on journals in his *The Journal Book* (1987). Since then, journals have become a staple in most classrooms.

Journals gain power through accumulation and connection. When people keep journals there is a commitment to writing, usually at a certain time each day, so it becomes habitual. Over a period of time this writing takes on a life, begins to speak. Returning to earlier entries, because of time and space, journal keepers regard them with a fresh eye. Shards nudge their way into honed pieces, longer writing. Bits of one entry may blur into parts of another; some, however, are never touched again. These may have served another purpose, perhaps "getting something out of the system," or as Natalie Goldberg puts it, "I want the students to be 'writing down the bones,' the essential, awake speech of their minds" (4). Whatever their function, journals remain a testimony to the mysterious workings of the mind.

Some people confuse journals kept at school with diaries kept at home. Diaries lock in the most intimate feelings, the most intimate reflections—the goings and comings of family members, problems, that kind of thing. Journals open up reflection on interesting topics, questions, not intimacies. In this world of immediacy, where quick answers, brief news reports, and instant replay are the norm, keeping a journal provides a place for students to attain depth of thought, substance, continuity, and elaboration of an idea.

Writing in journals is primarily a reflexive act—from self for self. Therefore, writing in journals is often abbreviated, fragmented, sometimes surreal. In a sense, journals are like dreams. Susanne Langer could have been describing journals when she wrote, "The most noteworthy formal characteristic of dream is that the dreamer is always at the center of it. Places shift, persons act and speak, or change or fade—facts emerge, situations grow, objects come into view with strange importance, ordinary things infinitely valuable or horrible, and they may be superseded by others that are related to them essentially by feeling, not by natural proximity. But the dreamer is always 'there'" (in MacCann 201).

This is an apt comparison with the journal writer, who is always at the center of the entry. Consider Will Durant's description of Leonardo da Vinci's journal, "He wrote five thousand pages, but never completed one book. . . . They are written from right to left. . . . His grammar is poor, his spelling is individualistic . . . he is 'a medley of brilliant fragments'" (217). Da Vinci's jumbled drawings of bones, plants, buildings, geometrical forms, airplanes, horse's heads, and organs of human beings juxtapose with written explorations, treatises, descriptions, vivid accounts of battles, and eloquent aggregations on science and art. But always da Vinci is center.

Implementation. Implementing journals must be accompanied by many specifics. All must be clear on the journal's purpose, the time relegated to journal keeping, its privacy, and how the journal is to be used. The class may brainstorm, discuss, and eventually create a list of dos and don'ts that all class members—teacher and students—are expected to uphold.

On the one hand, allow plenty of time for the habit of journal keeping to root. At first, students may write superficially, but in time and with proper instruction and modeling, students find their authentic voice and their own rhythm. On the other hand, if the enthusiasm for journal keeping wanes and writing deteriorates into a mundane list of daily routines, forgo the journal for a time. Give it a rest.

Above all, journals should not be employed simply as a classroom management tool. All too often a teacher implements the journal to give students something to do during roll call and other housekeeping tasks. Students soon realize this is not so much a strategy as it is a time consumer, so their entries become the trivial, bed-to-bed, bland, boring: "I got up. I brushed my teeth. I went to school on the bus." If the teacher wants to underscore the value of journal keeping as valuable and important, the teacher should keep a journal, write in it during journal time, and occasionally share excerpts.

Remarks. So common have journals become and so widely are they used in academe that misunderstandings and misconceptions have run rampant. Some teachers who initiate the journal as a way for students to chronicle what they have read or those who use journals as dialectical notebooks in other disciplines may regard journals in English language arts as a way to peek into the personal. They are misinformed. The journal as prewriting is a place to write and no one, especially not the teacher, has the right to enter that domain unless invited. Students choose sections to share. If journals are used to respond to reading or if they are used in other disciplines, discussion of what is an appropriate entry helps students understand the journal's purpose.

Renaming school-kept journals refreshes the concept and realigns it to its classroom purpose. A more specific name often focuses the objective. Some students name their own journals: "Joan's Prewritings," "My Math Journal," "What's Happening?" "Prewriting Perks," "Jesse's Journal," "Notes by Nanci," or "The Log Lady." Others prefer more generic names such as logs, learning logs, reading logs, literature logs, content journals, dialogue journals, dialectical notebooks, and notebooks.

We recommend teachers introduce a "Writer's Notebook." This notebook, if handled properly, inculcates the habit of jotting. Random images, quotations, a peculiar facial expression, a snippet of dialogue, a line from literature, a thought, as well as longer, more sustained writing find their way onto the pages.

> *When my father slowly slipped away with cancer, I kept a writer's notebook. In it I wrote many things—memories of Daddy, his idiosyncrasies, his funny jokes, his incredible linguistic punning—but I also wrote his chemo protocols, his meds, our visits to the doctors, his time in the hospital; I chronicled his slow passing, and even little things like a fly vainly fussing against a window, things that usually go unnoticed except when death stands waiting.*
>
> *Years later when I could bring myself to read that notebook, it was tantamount to looking through an antique stereopticon. I experienced cognitive stereoscopy. It was as if I had inserted the double-image card with one view of Daddy on one side and another view of Daddy on the other side. As I looked through the glass, the two views merged into one three-dimensional memory. Keeping a writer's notebook gave me that gift.*

Brainstorming

Explanation. Brainstorming is a collaborative prewriting strategy. In a sense, the class becomes a macrocosm of the microcosm of the brain because this strategy works the way the brain works, students make connections the way neurons make connections in the brain. The purpose of brainstorming, as with all prewriting, is to unfetter the brain and get the ideas down. Decisions on those ideas will come later.

Implementation. When implementing brainstorming, students call out what they associate with the prompt. Teacher or designated scribe writes all offerings on a chart or board. Brainstorming allows students to "storm their brains" aloud and listen to the storming of others. We find that during brainstorming, students freely advance ideas without worrying whether their ideas sound silly or unrelated. Also, students piggyback on the ideas of others, listen to all offerings, and find inspiration and insight for their own responses. After a brainstorming session, students may discuss ways to move on the ideas generated by the group.

Remarks. Because brainstorming generates a group list, even the most reticent students get caught up in it. And since it is totally noncritical, wonderful ideas often present themselves. As Einstein explained, "As one grows older, one sees the impossibility of imposing one's will on the chaos with brute force. But if you're patient, there may come that moment, when while eating an apple, the solution presents itself politely and says, 'Here I am!'" (Sohn 35).

Listing

Explanation. Listing is perhaps the most familiar of the prewriting activities. People make shopping lists; they generate "things to do," "pros and cons," "dos and don'ts" lists; almost everyone has written a wish list or two. Listing calls upon both the left and right sides of the brain because lists may be logical with one thing following the other in sequential order, or they may be serendipitous with one item causing an unexpected turn, a surprising thought, or an intriguing possibility.

Implementation. The trick when implementing listing is for students not to generate one list, but several. Students take the general topic then quickly write all the associations that come to mind. Then they use their associations to prompt additional lists. For example, friends may be the general topic. This prompt may spark associations of *food, parties, school, football games,* and so forth. Each of these, in turn, may become a prompt. After several minutes on each prompt, students study their compilations in search of connections, or items that seem to go together. Then they focus on the connection as they begin to freewrite.

We often invite students to list the alphabet vertically down a page. When finished, we encourage them to write connections they have with each letter. Afterwards, they write about that connection. For example, for the letter A, we would write *Acts of Teaching.* After that, we might write how the book came to be, how the second edition came to be, or we might write the many stories we have about the book. That single letter may spark many ideas.

Remarks. Often with listing, the idea does not lie in something actually listed but rather in the exploration of the connections among the words, phrases, or sentences on the lists. The idea may hide between the lines, so the writer uses inference skills to ferret it out. It is as if the idea resides in the spaces of the lists, not in the words themselves. Think of listing as an individual brainstorming session.

The Quicklist

Explanation. Paula Brock developed a variation of listing for her high school students. She wanted an idea to jump-start her student writers. She wanted something theoretically sound yet pedagogically easy. She named her variation "Quicklist" because it generates writing quickly and is easy to implement.

Implementation. When we use Brock's idea, we ask students to take out notebook paper, fold it down the red margin, and then fold the outside edge in to meet the red margin. This creates three columns. Students label the skinny first column "names," the middle column "descriptions," and the right-hand column "anecdotes." They quickly write names of family, friends, pets, places, even vehicles in the first column. In the second column, they write meaningful adjectives. In the last column, students jot notes that jog their memories about events, situations, or stories associated with what they have listed in column one.

Remarks. Brock calls her Quicklist idea "an irresistible invitation to actually participate in writing" (16), protection against all the "I can't think of anything to write about" excuses. She and we find it a genesis for ideas hidden in name, descriptions, and anecdotes. By providing students with this concrete avenue into thinking, they are bolstered in their confidence and find a "security blanket against the great unknowns" (16).

Blueprinting

Explanation. Blueprinting rises out of an idea in Peter Stillman's book *Families Writing* (13–16). As a prompt for finding something to write about, Stillman suggests drawing a floor plan of a house or apartment remembered.

Implementation. For a bit of novelty, when we teach blueprinting, we show students how to construct a house of paper. Students fold a sheet of 8.5″ × 14″ lightweight blue paper in half, short end to short end, and crease. They fold it in half again short end to short end but only pinch the top to mark the mid-point. Using the mid-point, they fold the left side over to the pinched mark and crease. They fold the right side over to the pinched mark and crease. This creates a paper gate, often called a gatefold.

On the left-hand "gate," they take the top left inside corner, fold back so that its point lies parallel to the left vertical side to make a small triangle—a "nacho fold" in kid-talk—and crease. They repeat for the right side. This creates a paper shirt.

To make the "dormers," they open the left "gate," place a finger inside the small triangle, and push it out to form a larger triangle that they press flat. This forms the left side of the "house." They repeat for the right side. This creates a paper house.

Students are now ready to prewrite. They open their houses and draw a floor plan of a house, apartment, or room that is important to them. They label each room or items in a room: kitchen, my bedroom, TV room, basement, Dad's workroom, Sis's room, bed, bureau, closet, and so forth.

On another part of their paper houses, they use their labels as column heads, listing beneath words, phrases, sentences, names, or activities under the appropriate columns as the memory jumps from one to the other. For example, "living room" may yield: listening to the radio, doll's wedding party, visitors, big sofa, and stories. When they feel they have exhausted their memories, they reread what they have written. Looking for connections, they circle these and draw those connections with a network of lines. "Radio" may connect to iPod or stories may connect to one particular story. On a fresh sheet of paper they freewrite about these connections.

Remarks. Blueprinting, closely tied to drawing and doodling, allows students to re-create places that hold memories worth writing about. The visualization of some remembered place catches the writer off guard sometimes, and in that instant can be clarity of perception that illuminates an idea.

Drawing/Doodling

Explanation. Drawing enables students to create visual metaphors that often represent extraordinary ways to look at ordinary things, events, people. Sometimes topics are lodged in a basically nonverbal mode and need to make their first escape through nonverbal means.

Implementation. After students read a story, discuss an issue, or receive some other prompt, they draw what they think or feel. It is important to distinguish this drawing from art. As a prewriting strategy it is a way to release visual images from the mind not an attempt to create art. (See Carroll's "Drawing into Meaning: A Powerful Writing Tool," Appendix H.)

Remarks. Traditionally, teachers think of drawing as an activity for primary students, but with the growing corpus of information gleaned from brain study and cognitive developmental research, more teachers on all levels consider it a powerful prewriting tool. In her book *Authors of Pictures, Draughtsmen of Words*, Ruth Hubbard recounts a story about e.e. cummings, who drew and painted daily. When asked once by an interviewer if the drawing got in the way of the writing, cummings replied, "Quite on the contrary: they love each other dearly" (5–6).

Prewriting to Focus a Topic

Many times as students journey through the grades, they receive assigned topics, especially on tests. Then they are expected to focus that topic or to use the common phrase, "narrow the topic." Looping, dialogue, and reporter's formula help students do this. With each of these strategies, students begin with a general or broad topic and strategically progress to the specific, thereby practicing a deductive line of argument or thought.

Looping

Explanation. The beauty of looping, a term coined by Peter Elbow (1981, 59), lies in the fact that students experience a prewriting strategy that not only helps them focus but also enables them to find their "centers of gravity" (1973, 20). These centers pull the students. Nuggets—unrefined ideas, or gems—polished notions, often nestle within the prewriting where they hold some attraction, some writing potential. As one student aptly renamed them, they are "centers of 'grab-bity.'"

Implementation. We introduce the concept of looping by reading a children's book that loops such as any of the several variations of *If You Give a Mouse a Cookie* by Laura Joffe Numeroff and Felicia Bond. After they understand the concept, we brainstorm possible topics and alight on one by consensus. Students write it on their papers. Then students freewrite five to ten minutes on that topic. Next they read what they have written, remaining alert to what tugs them— what grabs them. When they circle that "center of 'grab-bity,'" they complete the first loop. At this point in the looping experience, students share their "centers of gravity." This helps them see that given the same general topic and the opportunity to explore that topic, each person gravitates to a different center, a different focus.

For the second loop students use their individual centers of gravity from the first loop as their prompts. Now each writer loops off in his or her own specific direction. Again they write five to ten minutes. Again they read what they have written. Again they circle their centers of gravity, thereby completing the second loop.

After the third loop is achieved by repeating the strategy, students discuss what they have written. Some immediately see a pattern—from general to specific—and feel comfortable about a deductive approach to their paper. Others may see that they need to loop further. Still others may see too much repetition. Whatever, the students have something to pursue.

Remarks. Before sharing, we share a quote from Clarissa Pinkola Estes's *Women Who Run with the Wolves.* "Looping is when an animal dives under the ground to escape and pops up behind the predator's back. [It] is a way of diving down and coming up behind the issue and seeing it from a different perspective. Without the ability to see, truly see, what is learned about ego-self and the numinous Self slips away" (59). We talk about this quote and how it pertains to what we have experienced during prewriting looping. Then students share. Students who notice a repeated idea realize that idea is worth their concentration. Students who realize they strayed from the topic have also learned a valuable lesson and may loop again to refocus.

When assigned an essay on a broad subject such as the Civil War, looping helps students narrow it to something manageable, something that speaks to them. Looping teaches them one way to build an organized, focused piece of writing.

Dialogue

Explanation. Dialogue works well as a prewriting activity because it is natural. Since people dialogue daily on various topics, we can capture this naturalness as potential for writing. Students take the assigned topic and create a hypothetical conversation between two people or among more people about that topic. (See Priscilla Zimmerman's "Writing for Art Appreciation" [31–45] in Anne Ruggles Gere's *Roots in the Sawdust.*) This strategy stretches students because they must look at the topic from multiple perspectives. During this stretching, students are often surprised, intrigued, or find themselves wanting or needing more information.

Implementation. We ask students to take the topic and, using it as a prompt, quickly generate a list of persons, events, dates, ideas, words, and phrases it generates. (This part of the strategy resembles trigger words.) Then we invite students to circle two or three items on the list that suggest potential for writing. Students freewrite on each of these for several minutes. Using the information generated during the freewriting, they prewrite a dialogue. Providing the first line as a model helps students get started. For example, Mary told Tom, "I'm getting married." To avoid dialogue turning into monologue, limit the number of lines allocated to each speaker. Ultimately students rework the dialogue into a draft.

Remarks. This strategy permits ancillary teaching of the various conventions for formatting, indenting, and punctuating dialogue. Dialogue invites students to hear at least two sides of the topic, gets them to use their imaginations and sense of humor, and provides a way to analyze a topic.

Reporter's Formula

Explanation. Reporter's formula is a prewriting technique based upon the standard journalistic approach to gathering information—who? what? where? why? when? how? By using the reporter's basic questions, students may plumb the depths, uncover the hidden, startle the unexpected onto the blank page.

Implementation. We follow Linda Rief's model for this technique, adapting it slightly from *Seeking Diversity*. This strategy may be accomplished in one class period as a get-acquainted activity to establish comfort zones.

1. Distribute three $5'' \times 8''$ index cards to each student as they enter the room.

2. Invite students to choose a partner, preferably someone they don't know, know the least, or someone they want to know better. Allot three minutes.

3. After students are settled, instruct them to fold two cards in half and number each section respectively 1, 2, 3, 4. They number the unfolded card 5. Allot one minute.

4. In section 1, remind students of who? what? where? why? when? how? Then let them generate four to five questions they want to ask their partner. Allot five minutes.

5. Students ask their partners the questions they have generated and record answers in section 2. Allot four minutes for each person for a total of eight minutes.

6. Students read the answers. They circle the one answer they like best, want to know more about, or the one that surprised them. In section 3 they generate four to six more questions that focus on the circled answer. Allot five minutes.

7. In section 4, students record their partners' answers. This time they try to capture the exact words and body language of their partners. Allot four minutes for each person for a total of eight minutes.

8. Students use card numbered 5, both sides if needed, to write a draft based on the gathered information. Encourage students to hook the reader immediately with a zippy opener, use direct quotes, and find an angle. Allot ten minutes.

9. Students read their drafts to their partners who confirm or correct the facts and point out what they like. Allot two minutes for each person for a total of four minutes.

10. Students revise, title, and put their name on the card. Allot three minutes.

11. Invite volunteers to share aloud. Allot five minutes. Students then give this gift of words to their partner.

12. Debrief. Allot two minutes.

Remarks. This strategy also works as an introduction to research. (See Chapter 12.) Students learn that research involves gathering data, analyzing that data, identifying a focus, refocusing, gathering more data, synthesizing, and presenting the information concisely and precisely. Some teachers stop before number eight to conduct a mini-teach on leads to integrate appropriate openers with this prewriting strategy.

Rhetorical Prewriting Strategies

Rhetoric, *eiro* in Greek, means, "I say." When students practice rhetorical prewriting invention such as the pentad, classical invention, classical invention for the contemporary student, and cubing, they develop strategies that enable them to come closer to what they want or need to say.

The Pentad

Explanation. The pentad, an elegantly simple strategy, invites writers to examine an event, a happening, or a piece of literature as if it were a drama with actors, acts, scenes, purposes, and agencies pivoting on human motives and motifs. Adapted from Kenneth Burke's five key terms of dramatism, fully explained in "The Five Key Terms of Dramatism" (155–162) as well as in his *A Grammar of Motives*, the pentad turns the elements of drama into generating principles or questions. By concentrating on one of these five terms, the most dramatic, students are freed from writing everything, but emerge with a depth of focus and a blend of one or two of the other elements.

For example, students prewriting about Robert Frost's "Out, Out!" (See Carroll and Wilson [eds.] *Poetry After Lunch* 70) begin with this generic set of questions:

Actors: Who did the action?

Acts: What was done?

Scenes: When or where was it done?

Agencies: How was it done?

Purposes: Why was it done?

Considering the answers, the students write from what they find as the dramatic crux of the piece, not excluding anything but rather focusing on how everything else is connected to the drama. Several students choose to focus on the actors: the boy, the sister, the doctor, the saw; some concentrate on the act: the sister calling, the cutting of the hand, the giving of ether; others opt for the scene: the hills of Vermont or the yard; a couple choose the agency: distraction, working too many hours, too young; a few choose the purpose: the reason for the boy's death. Although each student writes to his or her chosen focus, all find their focus encompassing the other elements, albeit tangentially.

Implementation. When implementing the pentad, we talk about the topic, read, and discuss the literature students are about to explore through prewriting. Then we invite students to draw a five-pointed star as their prewriting graphic. At each point on the star they write one of the elements of drama—actor(s), act(s), scene(s), agency(ies), and purpose(s). In the center of the star they write their topic or the title of the literature. Students make a commitment to one point on the star and freewrite to that focus.

After freewriting, we spend time modeling how to connect the elements. We draw a triangle to join the focus element to one or two other points emphasized most, the parts most dramatized. That triangle becomes the central idea for their paper. For example, Mario focused on the saw. He personified it. He placed it in the yard and he attributed it to the boy's ultimate death. While he stayed focused on the actor/saw, he also touched upon scene and agency.

Remarks. Using the pentad minimizes rambling because students focus on one element. They dramatize or emphasize that focus but not to the exclusion of other significant elements. Students realize the pentad helps them come closer to uncovering the human motives in any given "drama."

Classical Invention

Explanation. Classical invention, an adaptation of the principles found in Aristotle's *Art of Rhetoric*, the oldest extant textbook on the subject, is all about discovery. Aristotle believed in the practical value of rhetoric and that rhetoric facilitates discovery. Therefore, he set forth principles he believed helped reveal qualities in precepts such as truth, wisdom, and a sense of the aesthetic. Aristotle held that if speakers defined their topic, compared and contrasted it, explained its relationship to other like topics, investigated its circumstances, and provided testimony about the topic, their speeches would be thorough and well organized. Aristotle's principles are still applied to speeches and to writing.

Implementation. We implement classical invention as a heuristic; we move students hierarchically from the simple to the more difficult. Working together first as a class to model, we choose an interesting topic. We guide students through the generic questions (applicable to a wide range of topics from *Macbeth* to perfume) based on Aristotle's principles. If answers give rise to other questions, we encourage students to follow that line of thought. We keep in mind that classical invention is not a rigid set of rules.

- Definition: Define the topic. What connotations may be applied to this topic? Can this topic be divided into parts?

At this beginning point, students use dictionaries and thesauri for basic definitions, denotations, and connotations, and any divisions of the topic. For example, one group we worked with chose the topic "drugs." They used various dictionaries to define drugs. They offered their definitions of drugs. They divided drugs into prescription and street drugs. Thesauri helped them see the verb and adjectival forms of the word.

- Comparison: How is this topic similar to other like topics? To what degree? How is it different? To what degree?

On this level, students thought of some drugs as similar to and different from other drugs. They compared medicines to narcotics. When they got into degrees of difference, they started with aspirin and compared it to opium. They did the same thing with other drugs.

- Relationship: What causes or caused this topic? What are its effects? What came before it? What are its opposites?

When writers work with relationship they are looking for cause and effect or antecedent and consequence. Students researched the source of antidepressants and then traced its effects. They considered the consequences of cocaine abuse and attempted to ascertain its antecedent. They tried to find opposites such as tranquilizers versus stimulants.

- Circumstance: What makes this topic possible? What would make it impossible? What are some past facts about this topic? What are some future predictions about it?

Circumstance in Aristotelian terms emphasizes the qualities and conditions that make something possible or impossible. We urged students to examine history to help their predictions. With the topic drugs, students talked about how high technology and research monies make possible the variety and effectiveness of prescription drugs, but they talked about how drop-outs, gangs, or lack of adequate policing make street drugs possible. They made predictions.

- Testimony: Find statistics about the topic. Are there any sayings, rules, laws, precedents, or maxims about this topic? What do creditable sources say about it? Have there been any testimonials about it?

Testimonials have always been part of what makes people buy into a product, an idea, or a project. Investigating what people say about a topic provides prewriting information that writers work into drafts as supporting evidence. For example, reading what the editors of *The Michigan Daily*, in their supplement *Student Life*, said in an editorial titled "Pot: The Newest 'U' Tradition" (Reaske and Willson 109–111) is considerably different from reading *Worst Pills Best Pills*, which was based on data from the National Disease and Therapeutic Index, and a medical advisory board of eighteen medical doctors (Wolfe 1988). Discovering degrees of credibility is perhaps the most important research and life skill for students.

Remarks. When students follow Aristotle's principles in their prewriting, they make discoveries. Indeed, it is difficult not to. They may have to scramble into the libraries or on the Internet for some answers, but the research is organic, rising out of the questions. There is direction and organization, and when students have finished the heuristic, they have much preliminary information to use. Perhaps, like the people of Athens—who delighted in the power of language to move minds and influence actions, who considered it somewhat magical—students may also begin to consider the results of classical invention as somewhat magical.

Classical Invention for the Contemporary Student

Explanation. Richard L. Larson tailored the principles of Aristotle to fit the needs of today's students. Larson's "Plan for Teaching Rhetorical Invention" constitutes a useful heuristic for writing about single items, events, or processes, abstract concepts, collections of items, or completed events, propositions, or questions. This rhetorical approach, both simple and practical, provides a systematic way to approach any topic. Perhaps more importantly, teachers may use these heuristics to model additional questions even better suited to the needs of their curriculum and students.

Implementation. Taking heavy cardboard, we divvy up Larson's fifteen questions applicable to "Writing about Single Items (in present existence)" (152) and mount them on the cardboard. We arrange these around the room as sophisticated centers and divide the students into groups. Each group decides upon a single item to research. Students have chosen such disparate items as a soda can, a pencil, a shoe, a keychain, perfume, and eyeglasses. We begin with "What are its precise physical characteristics (shape, dimensions, composition, etc.)?" Starting so concretely clearly outlines for students a way to analyze any item. From that point questions range from "How do the parts of it work together?" to "Who uses it? For what?" Students working in groups shift from center to center answering the questions and referring to some of the appropriate reference books we leave at each center. After answering all the questions as part of prewriting, students collect enough information to write their papers. If they think they need more, we encourage further research.

When guiding students into writing about events, abstract concepts, collections of items, groups of completed events, including processes, propositions, or questions, we use the appropriate heuristic of questions as probes based on Larson (152–154). With these rhetorical strategies, students have an organizing principle to guide them in ferreting out pertinent information on any given topic.

Remarks. Larson explains,

As for invention—until very recently we have done little to help the student. When we awakened to the simple notion that we needed to help the student gain ideas, we resorted too often to what I call the "smelly-looky-feely" gimmicks that were based on the notion that if students could be brought alive to the sensual world around them, they would have things to say. Which was right, as far at it went. But rhetorical invention has a profounder meaning than awakening students to their senses and having them produce haiku about autumn leaves, sandpaper, and limburger cheese. We live not only in a sensual world but in a world of ideas and concepts, and it is to this world that rhetorical invention addresses itself. (144–145)

Cubing

Explanation. Cubing, a prewriting strategy defined by Gregory and Elizabeth Cowan in *Writing,* helps students study a subject from a variety of perspectives (21). During this strategy, students quickly shift perspectives on a topic, usually a thing, by describing it; associating it with some experience, person, or event; applying it in some way; analyzing it by breaking it into parts; comparing to and/or contrasting with something; arguing for or against it—taking a stand. By writing something for each of these categories, students progress through Bloom's taxonomy and use higher levels of thinking.

Implementation. We introduce cubing by distributing a commercially wrapped cube-shaped caramel candy. Together as a class we progresses through these six cubing levels using the caramel as the thing we are cubing and sharing our responses aloud.

1. How would you describe the caramel you are holding to someone who is not in the room?

2. Does the caramel remind you of something you have experienced? Does it make you think of someone, something, or some event in your life?

3. What kinds of things can you do with or to the caramel?

4. Think of the caramel in parts. How would you separate the caramel into those parts?

5. What other confection is similar to the caramel? How it is like that confection? What other confection is unlike the caramel? Explain the difference.

6. Do you like caramels or not? Why or why not?

After this oral model, each student chooses something to cube in writing. After writing the six perspectives, each student makes choices about whether or not to incorporate all of the sides or several of the sides into their papers, focus on one perspective, blur two or three sides together, or omit a side that emerges as weak or unrelated.

Remarks. Teachers sometimes make a large cube with the different perspectives written on each side to make cubing concrete. This technique is especially helpful for visual learners, young students, or those needing structure.

Prewriting about Literature

Aristotle cautions, "It is not sufficient to know what one ought to say, but one must also know how to say it." So often when writing about literature (or other subjects), students know what to say but are at a loss about how to say it. The prewriting strategies of hexagonal writing and webbing reconcile the *what* with the *how*.

Hexagonal Writing

Explanation. Hexagonal writing is a heuristic for writing about literature. Based on the ABCs: Aristotle's principles, Bloom's taxonomy, and Cowan's cubing, Carroll's hexagonal writing enables students to produce six perspectives on a piece of literature, which then may be shaped into a unified response or paper. In addition, it provides an inventive way to teach literature, one that engages the student through its systematic movement into higher levels and more challenging thought. Hexagonal writing results in an authentic, layered response because it moves students from simple plot summaries toward elaborated text analysis. By providing a heuristic for responding to a literary piece, as the chart below shows, students move from the plot summary, Bloom's knowledge level, through evaluation, called the judgment level in his cognitive taxonomy.

A Cognitive/Prewriting Taxonomy

Bloom's Taxonomy	Cowan's Cubing	Carroll's Hexagonal
1. Knowledge/Memory	Describe it	Literal level/plot summary
2. Comprehension	Associate it	Personal Allusions
3. Application	Apply it	Theme (social/universal)
4. Analysis	Analyze it	Analyze/literary devices
5. Synthesis	Compare/Contrast it	Literary Allusions
6. Judgment	Argue for or Against it	Evaluation

Implementation. To help students see the connections between cubing and hexagonal writing, we have students create a cube.

1. We distribute three different colored 15″ × 3″ strips of construction paper to each student.

2. Students measure off five 3″ squares on each strip, making a clear line to distinguish each square.

3. They leave the first square blank on the first strip.

4. Students write D/P (Describe/Plot) in the second square.

5. Leaving the third square blank, they write A/PA (Associate/Personal Allusions) in the fourth square.

6. Leave the last square on the strip blank.

7. On the second strip, they write A/T (Apply/Theme) in the second square and A/A (Analyze/Analyze) in the fourth square.

8. On the third strip, they write C/LA (Compare/Literary Allusions) in the second square and A/E (Argue/Evaluate) in the fourth square.

9. When the strips are complete, we challenge students to fold these three strips on the lines and fashion them into a cube. All the letters must show, no tape, glue, or staples may be used, and the cube must be capable of being tossed in the air without coming apart. (Students who finish first may help others make their cubes.) Now each student has a concrete representation for the hexagonal process he or she will apply when responding to literature.

10. At this point, we teach or reteach plot, personal allusions, theme, ways to analyze a piece of literature, literary allusions, and how to evaluate. We model each side using some short piece of literature, so students are clear about the terms and our expectations. We spend particular time on theme and then how theme impacts the other parts of the hexagonal. In other words, if the theme of a piece is "loneliness," then the elements in the selection need to support that theme. When thinking of connections to other literary selections, students think in terms of that theme: loneliness. This helps students realize the parts all integrate with the whole. If the theme is truly the theme—the central core of the piece, then the rest of the piece stands as its supporting evidence.

As we walk students through the heuristic, they turn their cubes to the appropriate letters. In time, they work this heuristic individually. Eventually it becomes internalized when students respond to literature by giving more than a rehash of the plot.

Remarks. Hexagonal writing works equally well at any level—for the advanced high school student prewriting for a paper on *Hamlet* and for the kindergartener who may be orally engaged in discussing *Beauty and the Beast*. The following chart (Table 1.1) parallels how a teacher might develop the hexagonal heuristic for high school or for kindergarten. The structure is the same for both levels, only the vocabulary changes.

Table 1.1. Hexagonal Heuristics for Two Levels

Hamlet	Beauty and the Beast
1. Retell the plot of *Hamlet*	1. Tell the story of *Beauty and the Beast* in your own words
2. Does *Hamlet* remind you of anything or anyone in your life?	2. Does this story make you think of something or someone?
3. Brainstorm possible themes.	3. What is the author trying to tell you?
4. Choose a scene from *Hamlet*. Discuss the figurative language in that scene.	4. What parts of *Beauty and the Beast* are believable? What parts are unbelievable?
5. Based on the theme, how is *Hamlet* like or unlike other literary selections you have studied?	5. How is this story like other stories you have heard?
6. Answer these three questions in sentences: a. Did you like *Hamlet* or not? b. What make you think/feel that way? c. What specifically in the play made you think/feel that way? Quote this and explain.	6. Answer these three questions: a. Did you like the story *Beauty and the Beast*? b. Why do you like or not like it? c. Can you remember something in the story you especially liked or did not like?

Cindy Joor presented hexagonal writing to her first-grade class in conjunction with her lesson on shapes in math. Each student received six different-colored triangles that they glued onto a large sheet to form a hexagonal. "They thought that was cool," she told us.

Then she read Ed Young's *Seven Blind Mice* and the students immediately noticed that their colored triangles matched six of the mice. She took them through the process described above, and sent us the results. We have chosen Sam Patterson's writing as proof that this technique may be taught to young children. (See Fig. 1.1, Sam Patterson's Hexagonal Writing, page 28.)

Intermediate teachers use hexagonal as a six-week focus. The first week they teach plot; the second week they work on text-to-self, text-to-text, text-to-world connections; the third week they introduce theme and so forth.

By using hexagonal writing, middle and high school teachers have at their disposal a ready way to discuss literature. For example, when approaching an anthologized short story unit, we recommend beginning with one story to invite either written or oral plot summaries as a way into the story.

For the next story, students summarize and then share personal allusions. We typically use the third story to build on the two previous stories before students discuss theme. When approaching the fourth story, we review the preceding three, plus an analysis of one or several of the story's literary devices.

For story five, students access the skills from the preceding four levels but concentrate on comparisons and contrasts with other literary works, films, song lyrics, current events, historical events, or whatever the teacher thinks appropriate. The important thing to remember at this level is that thought and making connections are most important.

Finally, students evaluate the sixth story after they have taken that story through all its other levels. This heuristic serves two purposes: students experience using all levels of cognition on one piece of literature, and they learn the importance of not making a snap judgment by jumping from a simple reading of the story or plot summary to a judgment of that story.

Generally there are several remaining stories remaining in the unit. We invite students to choose one for their individual application of hexagonal writing, one they will eventually polish

Fig. 1.1. Sam Patterson's Hexagonal Writing.

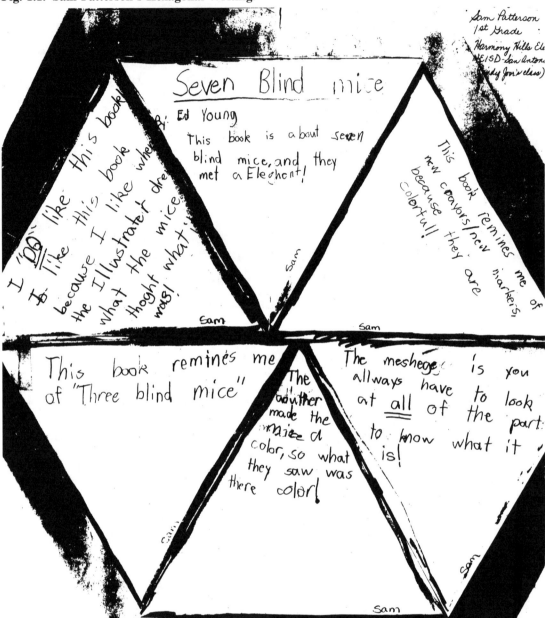

as a final paper. We use this same approach with younger students with trade books or selections from their language arts or reader texts.

Webbing

Explanation. Webbing, sometimes called *semantic webbing* (Freedman and Reynolds 677), *semantic mapping* (Pearson and Johnson 324), or *clustering* (Rico 10), exists as one of the most popular of the prewriting techniques. It enjoys this popularity for three reasons: its versatility, its controlled easiness, and its instant tapping of right and left modes of thinking and learning. Webbing generates ideas for all modes of writing and helps students organize ideas related to or integrated with a core idea or topic.

Implementation. Students of any age draw the diagram—a central circle with extending lines—because it looks so much like a sun and its rays, an image that makes sense in an archetypical way to students. The central thought, topic, story, or literature title is written in the "sun" with tangential thoughts radiating out from its center. Some versions of this technique encourage writing along the line; others terminate the line with a word that is then circled; still others use arrows to indicate the direction of the thought. Whatever the version, enacting this prewriting technique enables writers to access what Rico calls their "design mind" (28). Working with webbing usually results in a plethora of ideas that may be turned into writing.

Remarks. Webbing makes visible an invisible, nonlinear process of mixed and matched thought, associations, experiences, moods, dreams, imaginings, and feelings. Writers first spill out onto the page without anxiety. When they reenter the web in search of patterns, they call upon the "design mind" and then the "sign mind" (Rico 17). Rico calls it "writing the natural way"; Euclid calls it bringing order out of chaos.

Inverse Clustering

Explanation. A variation, especially for literature, on webbing or clustering is Gabriele Lusser Rico's "inverse clustering."

Implementation. She reads a piece of literature, a poem or excerpt from fiction or nonfiction or something from another discipline—once. Students listen. As she reads it the second time, they pull out words or phrases and jot them around a blank circle—hence the inversion of webbing or clustering. When she finishes the second reading, they name the circle and use it and the words and phrases they pulled to literally re-create their own writing. She gives them three minutes to improvise.

Remarks. To read more on this technique and see many student samples, check Rico's book, in second edition, *Creating Re-creations: Inspiration from the Source.*

CONCLUSION

Some teachers try to categorize prewriting by making it into a stage, one taken on Monday then followed by a different stage each day resulting in a finished product on Friday. In a true writing classroom, writing does not happen that way—on command on designated days. Although time certainly may be set aside for prewriting, the process simply does not occur in clear, lockstep stages. There are times when an idea hits with such force time is wasted hunting for another idea. When that happens, less time is needed generating the idea and more time is needed for extending and elaborating it. There are other times when several days are required to discover an idea or a focus. Still other times what at first seemed to be a good idea or a workable focus emerges as faux and needs to be totally scrapped because nothing will come of it. Then there are times when the writer returns to prewriting after several drafts or even during revising or proofreading the final copy. Thus, just as the process of writing is recursive, so is each of the processes within that process. The skilled teacher allows for these ebbs and flows, for individual rhythms, for the turning inward and turning outward nature of writing.

Because of the recursive nature of the writing process, prewriting weaves in and out of it. Prewriting allows the writer to move in and out of experiences. The moving in, where the writer turns inward to reflect substantially on the topic, and the moving out, where the writer takes the experience from a distance to see it an a more objective light, allows for continual re-creations in the writing—re-creations of experiences, of moments, of hopes, of dreams. Like digging in the garden soil before the sowing, during the growing, and while harvesting, prewriting happens throughout the process.

Prewriting also allows for the dormancy of writing—not just a single piece, but myriad pieces, much like Linda Pastan's "leaves." Ideas in one piece of writing may lie dormant for years and then upon rereading or reworking, a sleeping idea may awaken and present itself. It may even find its way into other pieces, totally different pieces, the writer pursues.

While certainly not new, the film *Why Man Creates* by Saul Bass remains germane to the writing process, especially to prewriting. Produced in the sixties, it chronicles the creative processes and parallels the writing process (Carroll, "Visualizing" 1982). In it Bass defines creativity as "looking at one thing and seeing another." To sum up prewriting, it could be said that prewriting is looking at one thing and seeing another.

APPLICATION

Divide into groups. Each group chooses one or more of the prewriting strategies to try. Afterwards in a large group session, discuss findings, observations, and implications.

2

WRITING AND ORGANIZING

> I see every book as a problem that you have to solve. That is what dictates the form you use. It's not that you say "I want to write a space fiction book." You start from the other end, and what you have to say dictates the form of it.
>
> —Doris Lessing ☐

GETTING IT ALL TOGETHER

In prewriting students find meaning; in writing they find form. To do it the other way around is artificial. If students are given a "form," writing becomes formulaic. When students have freedom in prewriting but are moved into writing with mandates of form, they become disenfranchised, give up ownership, and lose motivation. As a result students jump through hoops with little or no investment. They ask the form questions, "How long does this have to be?" "How many paragraphs do you want?" Those who own their writing, however, often argue in defense of their decisions on form and are reluctant to change simply for a grade. Their questions are based on meaning, "Do you understand what I mean here?" "How can I say this better?" "I think this would better as a story, than an essay. Don't you?"

Organization, a slippery word in writing, sliding in and around other words such as *focus* or *coherence*, *unity*, even *clarity*—all abstract terms to the neophyte student writer. In this chapter, we discuss the levels of organization in a way that brings the wonders down for easier implementation of the concept.

LEVELS OF ORGANIZATION

We daily hear teachers administer good advice, "Now make sure your papers are organized." "Stay focused." "Stay on topic." "Don't stray from your topic." "Remember the rubric." Good advice but too ephemeral. Students need sound, concrete ways to develop a sense of organization and then a sound, concrete way to check it. (See Carroll's *Guide to Writing with Depth.*) We propose a hierarchical structure for students to work within so they comprehend and achieve organization in their writing.

Purpose

The foundational level of organization builds upon author's purpose. If students know why they are writing what they are writing, the initial fight to turn their random, unfocused ramblings of prewriting into comprehendible pieces of writing becomes an inviting challenge not an over-whelming task.

Armed with their prewriting, students first determine the *why* of their writing. Knowing if they want to persuade, inform, argue, express, or develop an idea, tell a story, or entertain influences their decisions on genre, organizational patterns, and ultimately how they will craft their pieces. So determination number one is the answer to the question: Why am I writing this?

If students are writing to a teacher-generated assignment, then some discussion must ensue about purpose. This is exactly why it is so important for teachers to model. Modeling solidifies the purpose by showing the assignment as opposed to just telling it.

Understanding Audience

Let's be honest here. Students most often write to the teacher or to some disembodied "they" who score their writing on tests. To gain a handle on the structure and usage of language, students need to develop a sense of audience. To assist students with *voice* and *organization*, we recommend that teachers couple their assignments with a theoretical audience.

High school: For high school teachers, we suggest examples such as, "Look at your prewriting. Find a nugget you can develop to convince a fifth-grade student not to meddle in drugs." Then as models, we search through our prewriting, find that nugget, and talk/write a portion of a model to show teachers how to show students how specific that writing can be.

"Reread your prewriting on *Grapes of Wrath*. Find something that connects to your life, to a time when you had to make a sacrifice. Write that to share with your family at some family gathering or holiday get-together." Again we model for teachers the model for students.

Middle school: For middle school teachers, we suggest examples such as, "Let's take what we did on hexagonal writing for "A Day's Wait" by Ernest Hemingway and make some decisions. Pretend this prewriting will be developed into an essay for an Ernest Hemingway contest. Your paper will be read by Hemingway experts, and the winner will get a free all-paid vacation to the theme park of your choice." What parts of the hexagonal will you save? Will you discard any? Let's think of our hook. How will we hook an expert?

Elementary school: For elementary teachers the assignment and audience might sound like this. "We watched the live-action movie of *Charlotte's Web*, we read the book, and we did those centers for prewriting [classical invention] so we could define each, compare and contrast them, show what caused them to happen, what made the movie and the book possible, and what people have said about the movie and about the book. Now we are ready to write so we can share what we know. We are going to write an article for *Cricket Magazine*. We know kids our age read that magazine, but we can be sure all of them don't know all the things we found out in our inquiry. We want our articles to be filled with fascinating facts that will make kids think." Again, we begin by modeling the process so teachers can jump-start their students.

Structure and Usage of Language

Too often students study structure and usage separately. What good is structure if it is not used? And how can students learn to use English effectively without understanding structure? We believe—and research bears this out—that teaching structure and usage within the context of writing helps students realize that they are flip sides of the same coin.

By providing students with the textual event (the unit of discourse), the method of transmission (writing), and the audience (the societal/educational level, time frame, and region of the audience), students can make informed choices about the lexicon (vocabulary) and grammar (syntax) of their writing. For example, those high school students writing for fifth-graders should choose a different level of vocabulary and syntax than those middle-schoolers writing for a Hemingway expert. This level of organization is crucial to the effectiveness of a piece.

Appropriate Genre

Genre, a word that comes from the French, is a category of literary composition. In literary criticism, it refers to a type of literature or literary form. In writing, genre refers to the forms writers use as structure. As a convenient but arbitrary model, genre offers form for the human imagination and serves students with models for writing.

Moving prewriting into genre helps students organize meaning since readers expect certain elements in certain genre. Little children know stories contain characters involved in problems that get solved before the story ends. Essays inform, persuade, argue, or classify; and, unless the poem is of epic proportions, readers expect verse to be short, sometimes to rhyme, and to appear on the page in a certain way. Therefore, the genre students choose emphasizes, dramatizes, or makes the meaning clearer for their audience/reader. Form does not freeze; rather it shapes the shapelessness of prewriting. (A list of genres may be found in Appendix A.)

Focus and Coherence

Focus is the lens of writing and coherence is its Velcro. Without focus, writing wanders haphazardly on the page, ideas run pell mell; readers feel as if they are looking through an unfocused camera lens with everything fuzzy and blurry. Focused writing sustains its purpose, ideas are connected; readers feel they are viewing the piece through a tightly focused camera lens with everything lucid and clear. Focus also speaks to rhetorical stance and point of view so that both remain consistent throughout the piece.

Without coherence, sentences and paragraphs are disjointed, disconnected, jumbled masses of words, phrases, and clauses. Just as something inserted between two pieces of Velcro keeps it from cohering, so, too, an unrelated thought inserted between sentences or paragraphs muddles the writing. Coherent writing glues sentences to sentences and paragraphs to paragraphs in ways that make sense. (See Chapter 4 in Carroll's *Guide to Writing with Depth.*)

This level of organization assists students in choosing organizational strategies that best present their ideas clearly and effectively.

Craft

The last level of this heuristic is the most difficult. When writers craft their work, they organize it in an altogether different way than they do when considering their purpose, audience, genre, focus, or coherence. Crafting is not simply ranging the vocabulary to fit the audience but judging the effectiveness the rhetorical emphasis of figurative language, repetition, and other elements that create mood, tone, and style. Judith Newman in *The Craft of Children's Writing,* second edition, suggests even young writers employ four concepts—intention, organization, experimentation, and orchestration (5), each of which influences how the writer will craft the piece. She says, "Because writing requires attention to so many different kinds of information at the same time, writers cannot always use everything they know when they write. They must be free to decide what aspects of the writing process will engage their attention for the moment" (84). Writers want to be understood, but they also want to be unique.

TEACHING GENRE AS STRUCTURE

In Betty Edwards's *Drawing on the Artist Within* there is an exercise that invites participants to draw lines that represent feelings (not pictures or symbols such as hearts or crosses—just lines, no words). These lines become analogs for human emotions: anger, joy, depression, loneliness, love, and so forth. Her results indicate that while there is great variety, since no one's lines are exactly alike, there is a structural similarity, an almost visual vocabulary for like feelings. This similarity seems to point to a shared intuition, one that contributes to a collective understanding (66–95). In other words, given the same word, for example *bliss*, people draw similar lines to express that feeling, and others looking at those lines "get" the same feeling.

We tried this with teachers and students, as they listened to poems and short stories with the same results. They scratched stubby lines to approximate simple ideas; made twisted lines to parallel convoluted or complicated thought; ran jagged lines, often all over the page, to indicate something unpleasant; and used symmetrical lines or flowing lines to convey the beautiful or the lyrical. When we debriefed the activity, both groups remarked that they found it interesting that line, so simple a form, could be used to express meaning which others understand. What they discovered or uncovered as most interesting, though, is that the meaning came first.

We used this as a case in point: if a simple line can convey meaning, we asked them to consider form within the complexity of writing. They agreed that writers use intrinsic forms that readers understand. Prewriting runs rampant with fragments, ramblings, turns, pauses, tentativeness, in short, with idiosyncratic messiness that makes for "sloppy copies," but when writers turn prewriting into a form fit for an audience, they make decisions about their purpose and how best to shape their meaning. Knowing the structure of different genres provides the basis, either consciously or subconsciously, for those decisions.

We follow that activity by exposing students to choice of genre. Elementary students who have had their field of vision narrowed to the narrative are just as limited as secondary students who have had their field of vision narrowed to the essay. Instead, we open them up to different genres and the right to choose among them. Their meaning dictates their form.

INQUIRY AND CHOICE OF GENRE

Students who get their meaning down first and then work it into an appropriate form use critical thinking skills. Making intelligent decisions about form involves having a repertoire of options and a series of questions, being exposed to print-rich environments with a multiplicity of genres that act as literary models. Further, rich discussion about those literary models invites speculation and commentary on the efficacy of form, structure, and craft—not merely that three witches open *Macbeth*, but how does that opener work? Not that Eric Carle designed holes for the pages of *The Very Hungry Caterpillar*, but how do those holes contribute to Carle's meaning? Then students connect these models to their writing. They keep records of their reading and writing as they taste often of different genres. If a student gets stuck in nonfiction, for instance, the teacher might nudge some poetry or fiction.

> *There is an anecdote about Dorothy Parker, celebrated journalist known for her acerbic wit. During the Q & A after one of her speeches, a teacher asked if she had any rules for student writers.*
> *"Oh yes," said Ms. Parker, "I have six."*
> *Everyone quickly retrieved paper and poised pens in anticipation.*
> *"Read, read, read, and write, write, write," she said dramatically.*

STRATEGIES FOR TEACHING GENRE

Strategies for teaching genre vary in scope, depth, and approach. We caution teachers to adapt and adopt them for their grade levels. "You are the boss of your classroom," we say. We don't want teachers on any grade level to omit examples of modes, genres, or shaping techniques as too sophisticated. We do want teachers of all grade levels to help students realize—through reading, writing, guidance, modeling, and encouragement—a respect for each writer's craft while simultaneously gaining enough confidence to experiment with various genres in their own work.

We fully intended to culminate a first-grade demonstration lesson on insects by inviting the students to write a story about spiders. But they were eager and bright, so we decided to take a risk despite the twenty teachers observing us.

"Boys and girls, we were going to ask you to write a story, but you are so smart, we'd like to try something different. Would you like that?" They assured us they would, and their excitement matched the challenge.

Together we created quires, eight-page books for their writing. We put those aside and assembled "spiders" using Oreo cookies and licorice. Then we said, "Now you know how to make spiders. Use your book to tell other first-graders how to make them." We modeled.

They trundled off to write informational books, telling their readers how to make spiders. Jennifer wrote:

Fig. 2.1. Arachnids.

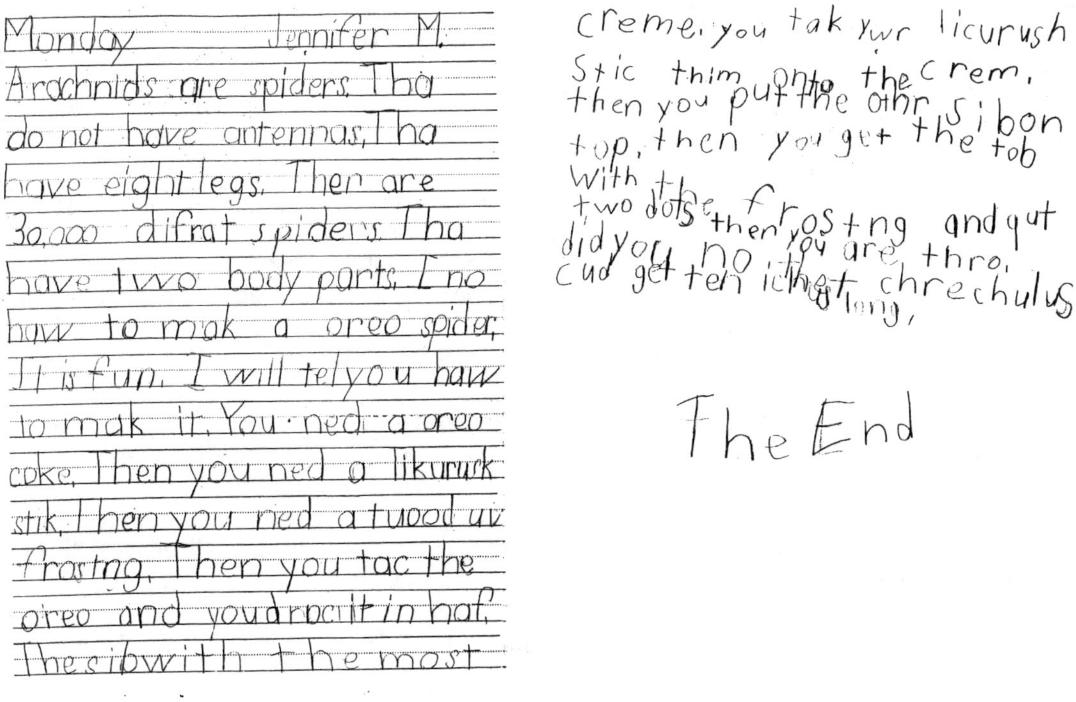

Monday　　　　　　　　　　　　　　　　　　　　Jennifer M.

Arachnids are spiders. Tha do not have antennas. Tha have eight legs. Ther are 30,000 difrat spiders. Tha have two body parts. I no haw to mak a oreo spider. It is fun. I will tl you haw to mak it. You ned a oreo coke. Then you ned a likurusk stik. Then you ned a tuood uv frostng. Then you tac the oreo and you droc it in

haf. The sib with the most creme. You tak ywr licuruswh stic thim onto the crem. Then you put the othr sib on top. then you get the tob with the frostng and gut two dots. Then you are thro. did you no thet chrechulus cud get ten ichus long.
  The End

[Arachnids are spiders. They do not have antennas. They have eight legs. There are 30,000 different spiders. They have two body parts. I know how to make a Oreo spider. It is fun. I will tell you how to make it. You need an Oreo cookie. Then you need a licorice stick. Then you need a tube of frosting. Then you take the Oreo and you break it in half. The side with the most cream. You take your licorice. Stick them onto the cream. Then you put the other side on top. Then you get the tube with the frosting and put two dots [for eyes]. Then you are through. Did you know that tarantulas could get ten inches long? The End.]

It became clear to us that these first-graders understood the difference between narrative and informative writing as they juggled for their place in line. We overheard one girl say to a classmate, "Anybody can write a story, but we are really smart, aren't we?"

If we hadn't issued the challenge, we know these first-graders would have written wonderful stories, but by raising their awareness to another genre, we opened them up to what they already knew.

AWARENESS OF GENRE

When raising awareness of genre, we suggest beginning with the ones students know. Then move them into areas that are new. The following is a list of awareness activities for students:

- Together create an anchor chart of favorite genres and specific titles within those genres.

- Discuss the modes of writing such as narrative, descriptive. Record lists on anchor charts to display around the room. As additional modes are discovered, add to the list.

- In small groups, students brainstorm the genres they use when writing.

- Consistently use reading and literature as sources for various genres—short stories, novels, editorials, political columns, advertising copy, poems, song lyrics, essays, and so forth. Discuss these.

We also encourage teachers to broaden students by practicing some or all of the following awareness activities:

- Introduce, define, and explain general terms such as *shaping*, *form*, *mode*, and *genre*.

- Review reflexive and extensive writing.

- Model writing in different genres.

- Encourage students to experiment with various genre.

- Reward risk-takers.

The influence of the teacher in expanding the awareness of the student is invaluable.

Robert Cormier, the author of *The Chocolate Wars, I Am the Cheese,* and other fine works of young adult literature, said at an ALAN Workshop at NCTE, "I am a writer today, because a teacher in seventh grade called me a writer. From that moment on, I was never anything else."

LITERARY EXPLORATION

In partnership with the genre awareness campaign of the writing teacher is the continual extension of students' exploration of literature, as reading, information, entertainment, and as writing. Most writing teachers also teach reading or literature; as lovers of words, they daily experience reading/writing connections. Students who compartmentalize reading and writing have difficulty synthesizing the two.

Some teachers combat this problem of synthesis by adopting a literature-based approach to the study of language. Such a strategy uses a major literary work as the focal point of all learning. If *Hamlet* were the center of study, students choose journal topics, make analogies, write multi-genre papers as ways into their learning, and engage in other integrated study. Grammar mini-teaches and lexical word banks augment ongoing readings and discussions of the play.

Other teachers work through a thematic strand of literature and employ a wide variety of genres within that strand. For example, their students take the themes in the focal novel and dramatize them. They write mini-plays or poems as a part of their study. These mini-plays and poems reflect the themes they are studying. Students develop "play sheets"—a page with blank speaker balloons down the page. By using these, students do not become bogged down in the formal logistics of writing a script. Therefore, form does not overwhelm meaning. Sometimes they construct a biography of their favorite character or collaborate on sequels.

Still other teachers acquaint students with wide-ranging genre selections through short daily readings that help them develop an appreciation of the variations of forms and the styles of different authors, and the B-flat personal narrative essay becomes the pungent, powerful narrative poem.

Literary exploration incorporates the study of skills, genre, literature, spelling, reading, listening, speaking, and viewing with writing. If students truly explore, they truly make discoveries. Rather than force-feeding literacy, we help teachers create environments where students freely range over possibilities. In this way their students make important connections between their writing and its form.

HEURISTIC STRATEGIES

Heuristic strategies, discussed in Chapter 1 in relation to prewriting, are also productive, systematic ways to move students from prewriting into writing. The questions of classical invention applied to a topic, for example, may be reapplied to the prewriting those original questions generated. Although independent thinkers often ask themselves questions as guides to give their thoughts form, students, who may or may not have achieved this level of independence or who may not have been trained in inquiry techniques, sometimes require a heuristic model to help them. We offer four heuristics to help organization: dialogue with self, the shaping conference, status of the class, and a taxonomy of questions.

Dialogue with Self

Increasing students' confidence in their abilities to make decisions lies at the heart of dialogue with self. We begin by inviting students to write a dialogue with themselves about their prewriting.

This yields insights, if not immediately, then after students have reread and thought about their writing. Much like the prewriting activity of dialogue, we give students a first line. They continue the dialogue by assuming at least two different perspectives. This strategy leads students closer to form.

Me 1:   I'm reading my prewriting to see if there is some form hiding in the words.

Me 2:   It was easier when the teacher just told us what to write.

Me 1:   But she didn't, so get on with it.

Me 2:   OK. All my stuff seems to be about friends. It's like I'm on a friend kick.

Me 1:   Is all the prewriting saying the same thing?

Me 2:   All pretty much, except the one about Francey.

Me 2:   What's different about that piece?

Me 1:   Well, I was really angry she had to move away. I wrote a lot of stuff about kids' rights. I mean her parents decided to move so she had to move and leave all her friends.

Me 2:   Sounds like you'd like to convince her parents of something.

Me 1:   Yeah. I'd like to persuade them to move back.

Of course, all students' dialogue with self does not point so clearly to form as the above example. If it does not, we follow up with a shaping conference. After all, the prewriting is there, some students need additional nudges to see the organization lurking within it. Most of the time, though, dialogue with self provides the needed focus, time, and direction to be beneficial.

The Shaping Conference

Because the shaping conference promotes discussion, even debate, it helps students clarify meaning, purpose, audience—even interest. After students read their prewriting, peers talk honestly about how it came across; we remind them that they are looking for form. Does the prewriting foreshadow a passionate plea for change that begs to be a letter? Does it promise a solid argument that needs the form of essay? Is it an intensely emotional reaction that demands the condensed form of a poem? Does it want to become a story?

Sometimes in shaping conferences, especially with extremely disparate prewriting, group members brainstorm a variety of forms to which the prewriting lends itself, as well as the pros and cons of each form. Ultimately, though, the student writer makes the decision.

Status of the Class as a Heuristic

Atwell's status of the class (89), which she credits to Donald Graves, allows students to hear the options and ideas discussed by others. This dialogic often spurs the reluctant writer. The different responses proffered by others become the heuristic, the series of stepping stones, for students to consider.

The need for a class status arises out of "abandonment" of teacher selected assignments and "whole-class deadlines." With classes of students working at their own pace independently, this strategy provides a way for teachers to graph what students have done, are doing, intend to do. We recommend beginning status of the class as a heuristic immediately after students have done some prewriting. It works like this:

- Create a chart with all the students' names written down the left-hand side followed by a series of boxes for the days of the week.

- Each day we ask students to brief us on their writing.

- As we work through the class list, we ask probing and heuristical questions to lead student in productive directions, to clarify misunderstandings or misconceptions, and encourage. For example:

  "Janeen, what are you going to do today."

  "I think I am going to start a new draft."

  "What are you writing about?"

  "The time my bike got run over in the driveway."

  "What organization form will it take?"

  "I don't know yet."

  "What about a play?"

  "No, I don't think so."

  "Have you considered a memoir?"

  "No, but maybe that is what I want."

  "What will you have to do to determine what form you want?"

  "Consider which works best."

And we move to the next student. Although this may seem to take time, the status of the class as a heuristic does not have to be experienced by every student every day. In classes where reading and writing happen simultaneously, not only can the teacher use status of the class as a heuristic, but also for classroom management.

A Taxonomy of Questions

If the previous strategies fail to help students find form, we suggest a direct approach. Students work through the following questions as a large group, in pairs, with the teacher, or alone.

- Why are you writing this piece?

- Who is your audience?

- What is their age, their educational level? Where do they live?

- How do you want your audience to feel?

- What do you want them to think?

- What do you want your audience to do after they read your piece?

- What form does this writing sound like it wants to become (e.g., poem, play, story)?

- How might your writing look on the page?

- Can you change the form but keep your message? Will your purpose be as clear?

In using these strategies with students for many years and after conducting many debriefings, we have found that students come to finding form from a different points in the discovery process. Some use preliminary notes, only the very beginnings of prewriting to choose form. Others make the decision after a trial run of a draft. Still others keep reworking the prewriting until the form presents itself.

The importance of discovering form is the freedom of marrying meaning and purpose to meet the appropriate structure, the freedom to move from idea to poetry to travelogue to protest letter; it allows students the freedom to find the best venue to say what they have to say. The more experience students have in selecting an organizational structure, the more critical they become. Through awareness and literary exploration students become facile in fitting the appropriate structure to their meaning. Organization gives form and informs writing.

FICTION

"Fiction is an imaginary but usually plausible and ultimately truthful prose narrative which dramatizes changes in human relationships. The author draws his materials from experience and observation of life, but he selects and shapes them to his purposes, which include entertainment and the illumination of human experience" (Altenbernd and Lewis 14).

However brief or lengthy a piece, whether it be an anecdote, vignette, short story, novella, or novel, it contains dramatic action that is concrete and specific, shows a purpose, manifests a relationship to life, and contains creative aspects. The length of the piece usually determines the level of complexity.

We always tell students if they can recite "Little Miss Muffet" they know the essential elements of fiction. To put that to a test, I invite them to fold a paper in fourths. We draw a smiling Little Miss in the center of the first block, a frowning Little Miss center with a small spider in the right-hand corner of the second block, a shocked Little Miss side-by-side a large spider in the third block, and a large spider in the center with a small Little Miss disappearing off the last block.

We then identify the protagonist and antagonist, setting, action (plot), problem (trouble), and solution. We label the beginning, middle, and end. We talk about who told the story.

After this micro-mini-teach, students find it easy to see how longer pieces, more complex pieces have multiple characters, characters in conflict with themselves, subplots, several problems and solutions. They understand that *story* may be simple or complicated. After they internalize this, they understand how authors break from these elements or change them to fit their meaning.

Students like to write, read, and listen to fiction. Kindergartners revel in their early scribbles and drawings talking them into stories; second-graders exhaust readers or listeners with books that run chapter after chapter, detail after detail in the sheer delight of the writing. Little ones eagerly gather around the teacher to hear a story read or told, but so do middle and high school students.

Implementing the Writing of Fiction

Writing fiction strikes students as easy for several reasons: familiarity with the genre, they like the genre, and they are able to tap their own experiences for the basic "stuff" of a story; it is the fundamental way people organize their reality. As Jerome Bruner explains in *Acts of Meaning*, "stories make 'reality' a mitigated reality. Children . . . are predisposed naturally and by circumstance to start their narrative careers in that spirit. And we equip them with models and procedural tool kits for perfecting those skills. Without those skills we could never endure the conflicts and contradictions that social life generates" (97). Because of the gamut of techniques and permutations fiction takes, students benefit from understanding the general characteristics of all fiction.

General Characteristics of Fiction

- Anecdotal/narrative/plot items—the story drives the plot.

- Cause and effect pattern of events—the audience experiences the "action-reaction cycle" (Sedlacek 50).

- Significant conflict—emotional or physical risk.

- Character development—the audience gains insights into motivations, personalities, and feelings; three-dimensional versus one-dimensional characters.

- Dialogue—authentic to the characters.

- Awareness of audience—tone and style that convey a genuine sense of readership.

- Emotional significance—for the characters and audience.

- Change—the character changes emotional, physically, mentally.

- Literal, social, and universal implications—the stories work on one or all levels.

- Discovery by audience—insights discovered.

- Setting—emotional, physical, imaginary.

- Description—of character(s), mood, tone.

- Point of view—first-, second-, third-person, or omniscient.

- Voice—author's personality and unique understanding of characters and setting.

Problems Writing Fiction

Two major problems occur when students write fiction. The first problem—not dealing with possibility and plausibility—leads students to think anything goes. Fiction may be possible or impossible, but it must be plausible. Aristotle says, "One should, on the one hand, choose events that are impossible but plausible in preference to ones that are possible but implausible; but on the other hand one's plots should not be made up of irrational incidents" (25, I.27).

Gods in myths, for example, reflect the human condition, but if the story becomes irrational, we scoff. We absorb the plausibility of a mermaid disobeying her father and falling in love with a human in *The Littlest Mermaid* because experience has taught us that love is strong enough to cause someone to change. Although we may reject the existence of mermaids, we accommodate them, and accept, perhaps as analogy, perhaps as symbolic, the tension between lovers who are different and whose deep love overpowers disbelieving parents and personified evils.

When students write fiction, they are writing from their own experiences in fictional ways. For example, if a student writes a bucolic piece about a family gathering where no problem arose, to fictionalize the event, students should consider not *what happened* but *what could have happened*.

They go against Aristotle when they eschew the impossible but plausible in order to choose the possible but implausible, piling one irrational incident upon another. In short, students often strive for the unconvincing possibility rather than the likely impossibility.

We clarify this for students by showing an Alfred Hitchcock film. We discuss how this master storyteller helps the audience identify with the characters no matter how impossible the situation because the story is always plausible. Hitchcock said, "Making a film means, first of all, to tell a story. That story can be an improbable one, but it should never be banal. It must be dramatic and human. What is drama, after all, but life with the dull bits cut out?" (Truffaut 103). Hitchcock provides a good place to start understanding possibilities and plausibility.

The second problem—not fully developing characters—leads students to create flat, one-dimensional, coloring-book characters who lie lifelessly on the page. Round characters who rise up actively from the pages are the ones with whom we identify; they make us laugh; we root for them and boo them; we love, hate, worry about them; and we weep with, for, and because of them. Students who strive for dramatically elaborated three-dimensional characters develop someone with whom the reader identifies. Characters are the central focus in fiction. Even if they are animals—we forget Winn-Dixie is a dog, Charlotte is a spider, or Olivia is a pig—because the author depicts through them the changing human condition.

To help students develop characters, we invite them to prewrite for a few minutes. We ask them to list all the people they have come in contact with during the previous twenty-four-hour period. Then they circle several they found more interesting even if they do not know names. For example, once while waiting for a table in a restaurant, we met the most fascinating woman who lived in the Village in New York City. She was an artist who regaled us with stories until we parted company, going to different tables. In Paris we sat on a bench with an old man who was Jean Cocteau's friend. In neither case did we catch the names, but we could snuggle them both into a story as full-blown characters.

To flesh out the character, students create a dialogue with them, asking and answering questions until the character comes alive, takes on a life, makes choices, and acts in characteristic ways. Or, if the character does or says something uncharacteristic—something surprising—students respond as they would to a real person.

If dialogue doesn't work to round out the character, students may jot some notes by the character and think of people they know with those characteristics. Also, students may round out the character through memory joggers (Carroll 2002, 32–33) or "Rounding the Character" (Carroll 2007, 100).

Types of Fiction

Short Story, Novella/Novel

Specific fictional genres exhibit their own special attributes—the most significant are breadth and depth. The short story by definition is finite, with "tight plotting, close character development, and concise, effective expression" (Sedlacek 49). Because the short story has had a magical and wonderful evolution, examining contemporary short stories is imperative when teaching this genre. Although modern short stories continue the beginning, middle, and end structure, not necessarily all contemporary short stories do. Writers such as Baxter, Max, and Oates take liberties with something so pat, arguing that the predictability fails to match contemporary life.

The old standard of "once students master this form, then they can break the rules" needs rethinking. Does mastery of aging, traditional characteristics ensure that students will be able to write for today's audiences or even understand today's literature? Certainly Dickensonian descriptions engaged people who received serials weekly in popular magazines such as the *Godey's Lady's Book*. They had time to consider the significance of warts on noses and the way streetlights reflected in gutter water, but today's readers want immediacy. Today's writers withhold beginnings, leave off endings; sometimes their stories are only middles.

We, echoing IRA and NCTE, recommend balancing the classics with the contemporary. We urge teachers to stay abreast of contemporary fiction—the short story did not languish after Edgar Allen Poe—it changed. Unfortunately, many textbooks omit contemporary fiction because of copyright costs. With the present emphasis on multi-ethnic literature, we encourage teachers and students to search and share a variety of short story authors.

Although it is impossible to know all the best contemporary writers, intolerance of ethnically diverse authors has led to a lack of recognition of these writers. As long as we select solely from those writers we all know and love—Wordsworth, Shelley, Keats, Poe, Emerson, Dickinson—how will students ever find Linda Hogan, Lisa See, Toan Ngyen, Rita Dove, Walter Dean Myers, Arundhati Roy, and others? Students need to know the Pulitzer Prize winners to understand the richness of differences and learn to accept these differences. They need to examine their prewriting for places where they can illuminate their cultures through story.

Sudden or Flash Fiction

Sudden or flash fiction, sometimes called mini-sagas, one of the newest of the evolving forms of the short story, is abrupt, brisk, a quick read. With short exposition, development is pared to necessity. Characters are complicated in the way fragments of a broken mirror are complicated. The author does not reveal everything, inferring motive and story elements. The uninformed reader usually and initially classifies this form as unelaborated; but, as in Oriental flower design, many readers adore the "less as better" form, considering it another way to write a story. *In media res*—"in the middle of things"—takes on another level of meaning in sudden fiction. Transitions, like those in film and on television, are replaced with jump cuts.

Joyce Carol Oates maintains, "Very short fictions are nearly always experimental, exquisitely calibrated, reminiscent of Frost's definition of a poem—a structure of words that consumes itself as it unfolds, like ice melting on a stove. The form is sometimes mythical, sometimes merely anecdotal, but it ends with its final sentence, often with its final word. We who love prose fiction love these miniature tales both to read and to write because they are so finite; so highly compressed and highly charged" (Shapard and Thomas 246).

Author Barry Targan offers this advice for writing sudden or flash fiction:

In writing, the short-short story rather than the more common short story comes closer to the classic *étude*, and for this reason is better suited to some of the initial needs of the creative writing student. Particularly, the main advantage is this: the writer can get a great deal of specific practice with various elements while staying within a true fiction form. He can pose specific technical problems of characterization, tone, mood, or whatever, and solve the problems in the terms of real stories. Using the short-short story, he avoids the artificiality of the set piece of assignment while at the same time protects himself from an uncertain commitment of energy and time entailed in the short story, for a short story is open-ended in the way a short-short story is not. That is the beauty of it. The short-short story can no more get out of hand, go beyond its natural aim, than could Leonard have drawn more on one sheet than size and design would allow. (Shapard and Thomas 247)

Sometimes students begin with short-short stories and gather impetus as they write.

Fables

Students approach the traditional fable with its stated moral, stereotypical animal characters with optimism and success. Because we enjoy these oldest genres of literature—fables, myths, legends, and tall tales—they lend themselves equally to writing and reading. If a student's prewriting promises an anecdote with a clear lesson or strong advice, we encourage the student to continue working in this genre. We share

- examples of traditional fables (Aesop)

- contemporary fables (Sumiko Yagawa [Katherine Paterson (trans.)], *The Crane Wife* or Brian Jacques, *Redwall* or *Mossflower*).

We invite students to tap prior knowledge by

- selecting animals with personalities similar to that of people in the prewriting

- writing out a moral

- experimenting with the form of fable.

As students progress in their development, Thurber's fables offer fine examples of the modern form of this genre. Students soon discover that although deceptively simple, the fable is not simple to write. When students decide to tell their story as a fable, they are well on their way to understanding the critical decisions writers make while employing their craft. They learn that deciding on genre is much like deciding on what to wear. The closet may be full, but the choice reflects what they want to project. We advise students to consider the form of fable if they want to disguise an experience. Who can argue with a violent rooster, a wayward chicken, a wolf who preys on the young, or a greedy pig?

Myths

The myth and related forms, the legend and tall tale, have distinct characteristics yet all have the traits of adventure and exaggeration. The nature myth explains natural phenomena, the hero myth extols admirable virtues, and the epic examines religion, history, and culture. Few have used the myth to illuminate the workings of the mind more powerfully and poignantly than Joseph Campbell. He says in *Creative Mythology*, "In what I am calling *creative* mythology . . . the individual has had an experience of his own—of order, horror, beauty, or even mere exhilaration—which he seeks to communicate through signs; and if his realization has been of a certain depth and import, his communication will have the value and force of living myth—for those, that is to say, who receive and respond to it of themselves, with recognition, uncorked" (3).

Other forms of myth lead students to fairy tales, science fiction, and the Gothic (horror) thriller. The fairy tale—concerned with things that cannot really happen, about people and creatures who do not exist—holds logic within its unreality. Whereas although containing some of same elements of the fairy tale, science fiction finds its roots in scientific theories and discoveries; it combines the known and the unknown. The Gothic develops a gloomy or terrifying atmosphere with uncanny, macabre, supernatural, or melodramatically violent events. The modern Gothic explores psychological states. As long as students have dreams and are not required to have a license to practice their imagination, these genres offer myriad opportunities. Teachers and parents should not dismiss these genres as frivolous, outdated, or detrimental to young writers.

One way of moving students from prewriting to myth is by helping them see the subjectivity of their experiences. Most students have been involved in an adventure or a frightening brush with danger. If students place these experiences in an exaggerated setting or add a colorful character, they are on their way to transforming experience into myth. Exaggeration allows the story to take on larger dimensions. Dealing with outside forces over which the writer has no control through the concept of the *deus ex machina* (a "god" who solves all problems is lowered onto the stage by some mechanism) gives the writer the opportunity to end myth with a renewed sense of confidence and control.

Legends

Legends also spring from reality. Myths, with heroic people not supernatural beings as protagonists, borrow the episodic structure of the epic, add romantic elements, and include the possibilities of diversity. The stories surrounding John F. Kennedy, Bobby Kennedy, Martin Luther King Jr., and César Chavez rise up as modern legends. Marilyn Monroe is half legend, half myth. Students love to discuss legends surrounding celebrities—Anna Nicole Smith, for instance. The sixth-grade girl who writes the cliché, "My dad is a knight in shining armor," has begun a medieval legend. The fifteen-year-old boy who pines in his writing about the beautiful, unattainable girl has the makings of a medieval romance. When prewriting hints at unsolvable situations, then dragon slayers cannot be far behind. Wise sisters with troubled siblings invite "heroes" armed and ready for personal battle.

The legend is so closely related to the folktale, that studying the difference is tantamount to splitting hairs. One of the foremost contemporary folklorists Jan Harold Brunvand, author of *The Vanishing Hitchhiker* and *The Choking Doberman,* records the differences this way as he writes about his urban legend collection:

> It contained the results of some twenty years' study of many highly captivating and plausible, but mainly fictional, oral narratives that are widely told as true stories. We folklorists call them urban legends, although modern legends might be more accurate term.
>
> The book sets forth the history, variations, and possible meanings of some popular belief tales found in contemporary storytelling, such as those about hitchhikers who vanish from moving cars, alligators lurking in New York City sewers, rats that get batter-fried along with the chicken in fast-food outlets, convertibles filled with cement by jealous husbands, housewives caught in the nude while doing laundry, hairdos infested with spiders, pets accidentally cooked in microwave ovens, and so on....
>
> Calling urban legends folklore requires an explanation. The usual definition of verbal folklore is material that gets orally transmitted in different versions in the traditions

of various social groups. Proverbs, riddles, rhymes, jokes, anecdotes, and ballads are among the folk forms that circulate in oral and usually anonymous variants, comprising the folklore of the people among whom they are known. Urban legends, despite their contemporary sound, display the same characteristics as older verbal folklore. They pass from person to person by word of mouth, they are retained in group traditions, and they are inevitably found in different versions through time and space. If an urban legend at first seems too recent to have achieved the status of folklore, further study often reveals its plot and themes to be decades or even centuries old. And even a new story partly disseminated by the mass media soon becomes folklore if it passes into oral tradition and develops variations. (ix–x)

Urban tales are a part of the fabric of being storytellers. Encouraging students to become researchers of the oral tradition, something that may have begun in their prewriting, allows them to become writers and recorders of modern legends.

Tall Tales

Tall tales emphasize humor, a strong sense of national identity, an outlandish exaggeration, and unblemished imaginative heroes. "The characteristic of the tall tale that distinguishes it from other humorous stories is its blatant exaggeration. Our older tall tales—with their swaggering heroes who do the impossible with nonchalance. . . . They are such flagrant lies that the lyingest yarn of all is the best one, provided it is told with a straight face and every similitude of truth" (Arbuthnot and Sutherland 245).

Imagination summons the tall tale. The everyday excuses we dream up on the spot to save ourselves embarrassment or reprimand are ways into the tale. The lamer our excuse, the greater is the opportunity to invent a wonderful tale. Tardy excuses take on whole new dimensions as tall tales. Exaggeration becomes a byword for the writer. The teller of the tall tale must show profound reasonableness and logic and accuracy while having everything take place in the middle of hilarious lunacy.

Sometimes something snuggled in prewriting holds the promise of point through exaggeration. Amazingly students rereading their prewriting find these gems.

Three Quick Ways to Shape Fiction

Story Maps. The story map is a visual plotted out by students to better understand contemporary fiction. The map of *Maniac Magee* is a good example of mapping a story (see Fig. 2.2). By creating this visual, the student deals with the novel's flashbacks in a linear fashion. Writers like Robin McKinley, in her novels *The Blue Sword* and *The Hero and the Crown*, play with time. Readers are sometimes surprised to find that the second novel of the series is a prequel to the first. Student-made story maps assist students in reconciling the variations in modern literature by helping them give shape to the story. When students write these stories, making story maps help them to form their stories during the act of writing.

Dialogue. Dialogue allows the writer to catch up the reader on background. "The Sniper" has been on the rooftop for many hours when Liam O'Flaherty's story opens. Without dialogue, the reader would have no idea why the sniper is on the roof. This device is hardly new to fiction. Zeus and Athena discuss how Odysseus got himself in the mess he is in long before the reader meets the hero.

Fig. 2.2. *Maniac Magee* **Map.**

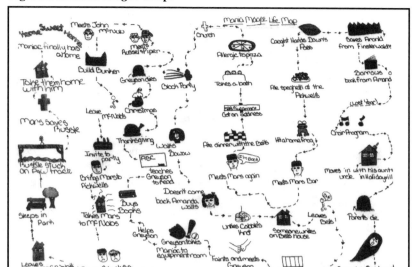

By giving the reader an intimacy with the character, dialogue also permits the reader to hear the authentic voice. We know so much about the grandfather in *Knots on a Counting Rope* because his dialogue stays true from beginning—"I have told you many times, Boy. You know the story by heart . . . listen carefully. This may be the last telling. . . . I promise you nothing, Boy. I love you. That is better than a promise" (2)—to the end—"Now Boy . . . now that the story has been told again, I will tie another knot in the counting rope. When the rope is filled with knots, you will know the story by heart and can tell it to yourself. . . . I will not always be with you, Boy. . . . You will never be alone, Boy. My love, like the strength of blue horses, will always surround you" (Martin and Archambault 32).

Perhaps most importantly, dialogue reveals the character. We speak what we are. In William Golding's *Lord of the Flies*, Piggy confronts Jack with the truth, asking, "What are we: Human? Or animals? Or savages?"

The reply answers the questions and defines the character Jack, "You shut up, you fat slug!" (82).

Naming Characters. Maxine Hong Kingston, answering our question about how students should go about naming their characters, wrote in a personal letter to us, "I've noticed that most minority students write about stereotype Caucasian lovers. When you remind them to give their characters surnames, particularly of their own cultural background, many students will make a breakthrough that will amaze you" (1). We help students use real names as they write, explaining they can fictionalize them in the final draft. This keeps students focused and authentic.

Fiction has moved away from Dick, Jane, and Spot. Characters like Abuela in the children's book *Abuela* by Arthur Dorros, or Elena Serafina Capalbo Chiradelli of Renée Manfredi's *Pushcart Prize, XVI* short story "Bocci" are infinitely more interesting. The more real the characters, the better the understanding and response from the reader.

Whether the student reveals everything about the character depends upon style and genre. But students must know the character, get under the skin, delve into the heart. This is exactly why students write best what they know—they can fictionalize their friends, family, enemies—but when they enter the realm of the phantasmagorical, they lose their touch with reality and people their writing with phony cookie-cutter characters. We sometimes invite students to write histories for their main characters. When students do this, they often uncover their characters' hidden motivations.

The short story and its related forms are natural for storytellers. Student writers often find their voices when writing in this genre. As they master the showing and not telling, they truly capture the narrative.

DRAMA

Drama, a literary form first designed for theater, now includes film, television, video, and YouTube. Students who thrive on the joys and tragedies of life, the wild swings of humor and pathos, find drama an exciting and challenging medium to explore. Although relatively few students have seen professional stage productions, film and television are natural extensions of their lives. The visual learner adapts to the drama/script easily. These students often "see" what they write. They want the reader to "see" their story. Script writing helps these students move into this genre.

The play has been a staple of English language arts teachers for years. Teachers have played records of dramas such as Dickens's *A Christmas Carol* or Shakespeare's *Hamlet*; they have divvied up the parts of Shaw's *Pygmalion* or Wilder's *Our Town*, but the computer invention YouTube of Steve Chen, Chad Hurley, and Jawed Karim has changed our definition of drama forever. It has "created a new way for millions of people to entertain, educate, shock, rock and grok one another on a scale we've never seen before" (www.time.com/time/2006/techguide/bestinventions). Called "a portal into another dimension," these videos indeed open drama to another dimension, one related more closely to students. Currently, the site shows more than 12 million videos per day—a number that is "doubling on a month to month basis," Chen said.

Drama is meant to be seen. Writers as well as actors, directors, and camera crews all share in production. Too often students experience plays as scripts. Hence with video and YouTube, students more directly experience drama. After all, "the play's the thing"—or should be.

The magazine *Scholastic Scope*, often used in English language arts classrooms, consistently provides one of the best sources for contemporary stories presented in play form. Students of all levels and abilities enjoy reading these plays and find affirmation in this genre. They provide excellent models for a student-written drama that may be lurking in their prewriting.

Drama for the Very Young

Working with drama, film, and video does not have to be confined to secondary students. Elementary and early childhood students understand the natural workings of drama. Three-, four-, and five-year-old students reenact classic tales. When working with little ones, we read a fairy tale and discuss how we could make it different. The children write their own versions, illustrating and dictating as is developmentally correct. They roleplay their stories, and often someone videotapes the production. The students then write, making shape books, flap books, or quires. The drawing and writing become symbolic representations of their dialectics (logical discovery of truth). Together we watch their productions and talk about them. Writing and visual literacy merge and emerge in ways that often surprises all of us.

For example, their symbolic reenactment becomes a manifestation of psychodrama. They not only demonstrate their understanding of a story such as *The Little Red Hen*, but also they reveal their understanding of parent/child social structures while integrating the literature into their lives. They act out attitudes and social behaviors. Observing these students is akin to watching what

Suzanne K. Langer calls the "symbolic transformation of experience" (44). They make metaphors; they make meaning. And using drama allows the meaning to happen in concrete, reinforcing ways. The students' multiple viewings of their stories and the stories of their schoolmates constantly gird up their emergent literacy.

The Collaborative Nature of Drama

Students cannot be totally independent and self-sufficient while working with drama. Not only does drama insist on collaboration but also it exercises imaginative muscles. Playing out riddles helps students understand life. Out-of-reach adventure becomes attainable because film can take place anywhere, anytime. The most ordinary problems and events take on new meaning. For example, in Charlie Chaplin's *The Gold Rush*, the famous "Dance of the Rolls" sequence has Charlie daydreaming that the girl he loves from afar has come to his lonely cabin as his Christmas guest. Proudly he jabs forks into two bread rolls and goes into a dance. Cunningly photographed, it appears that Chaplin's huge head and the tiny roll "feet" are one body, and with a wonderful range of facial and pantomimic gestures, Charlie does his "dance"—an episode that has to be seen rather than described to be fully appreciated for its grace and imagination in depicting a lonely man wishing for a dance.

Film and video allow viewers to review and re-experience moments and ideas. To use D. W. Griffith's words, "Above all else I want to help you to see." Drama creates new environments with each production whereas film and video enable multiple viewings.

One-act plays, documentaries, cartoons, musicals, serials, and news programs offer unique opportunities for students to see their prewriting come alive, to work together, and to "see" writing for a different audience.

POETRY

Students working with poetry are like a well. Water comes flowing forth or the well is clogged and dry. Another difficulty arises with what students do with the poem after they write one. We help students recognize poetry within their own writing by continually sharing contemporary and traditional poetry. Discussing what they like about the poems they hear encourages students to think about why a particular poem works and how students can shape their feelings and ideas into poems of their own. It helps them listen to the well inside them.

When considering poetry, there is no need to consider the genres as exclusive of each other. Writers continually push established genres to the limits; they continue to develop new genres. Contemporary poems often tell a story, lyric poems deal with emotions, and both sometimes contain dialogue. For neophyte poets, these two subgenres are good departing spots. As writers mature, reading extensively and studying all types of poetry become their life work, but for novices the narrative and the lyric mark comfortable starting places.

The Narrative Poem

Generally, the narrative poem is told chronologically with poet the persona of the poem. In some cases, the poet assumes another persona. Sometimes the poet tells about the persona of the poem. Narratives like "Sarah Cynthia Sylvia Stout Would Not Take the Garbage Out" by Shel Silverstein and Ericka Mumford's "The White Rose: Sophie Scholl 1921–1943" in Paul Janeczko's *The Music of What Happens* are excellent examples of the poet telling about someone else. Sarah

Cynthia Sylvia Stout reminds children of themselves or someone they know, whereas Mumford writes a historical account of Sophie Scholl, a Nazi resistance fighter in Germany. Using these as models, we encourage students to reread their prewriting to see if there is a poem about themselves or someone else hiding there.

The Lyrical Poem

Songs hook students into the lyric poem. The ancient lyric was a poem accompanied by the lyre—hence its name. Today we refer to the words of a song as the lyrics. Oral in its tradition, intended to be read aloud rather than sung, musical elements still impact the lyric poem—patterns, rhymes, the sound of words. Generally more emotive, the sound of the words join with the feelings of the poem.

Barbara Drake says a lyric usually is:

- personal or individualistic;

- emotional; concerned with feelings;

- musical, not necessarily metrical, but sound elements—such as rhythm and rhyme—are an integral part of its sense (consequently, paraphrasing and translating are difficult);

- organized by association rather than by chronology;

- compressed, so that figurative speech, allusion, and so forth suggest rather than state explicitly (153).

While students are not likely to be writing song lyrics as papers in most classes, sometimes a lyrical line or two extracted from a prewriting solidifies a point in a piece. Sometimes essays and stories are lyrical, such as William Stafford's poem "The Animal That Drank Up Sound," also available as a children's picture book. The poem, part myth, part fable, tells a mysterious and compelling story rich with imagery and words that create a mood that blends with sound. Is it lyric or narrative?

Barbara Drake advises,

The point is not to discourage anyone from writing a modern narrative poem either long or short, dealing with the past or present. One should, however, be cautious of this tendency toward the artificial, inflated rhetoric of a period piece. Faced with the dominance of the lyric, it might be a challenge to experiment with narrative in poetry, and doubtless instructive to think of how your present poetry might be changed by developing its narrative or dramatic qualities. Other questions also arise: should your poetry imitate life? should lyric poetry become more musical, more abstract, more associative? is poetry an effective medium for social criticism or the exploration of aesthetics or psychology? Set yourself a problem of one of these areas and experiment with the idea of genre. (174)

Free Verse and Line Breaks

In the twentieth century poetry began to break away from the structure of rhythm and the predictability of rhyme. Ezra Pound and his followers called it free verse. The purpose was to "compose in the sequence of the musical phrase, not in sequence of a metronome" (Nims 306). Students like this open form because it comes closer to their world, and allows them to arrange words to emphasize meaning; teachers like it because it leads to lessons on craft. Without a rhyme or meter dictating form, free verse relies of other ways to engage the reader. Part intuition, part visual, part aural, students writing in this form place the words in their natural positions.

Line breaks lend emphasis to the last word on the line and the first word of the next line. The meaning within the line dictates the break.

When working with students who want to write poetry, remember what Stephen Berg and Robert Mezey say, "The best poems of the last twenty years don't rhyme (usually) and don't move on feet of more or less equal duration (usually). That nondescription moves toward the only technical principle they all have in common" (ix).

Good Versus Bad Poetry

Teaching poetry is difficult. Helping students distinguish between good and bad poetry is even more difficult. Reading models is the best approach. Poet X. J. Kennedy discusses good vs. bad poetry in his book *Literature: An Introduction to Fiction, Poetry, and Drama.* He uses two poems on the same subject—death of defenseless animals. One example is William Stafford's "Traveling Through the Dark," and the other is Rod McKuen's "Animal Rights." When juxtaposing the two poems, students easily discern the difference. Stafford's poem rings rich with imagery and metaphoric language. McKuen's poem manipulates the audience's emotions with trite phrases and cute images. Stafford does not tell. He takes the reader through the experience of finding a dead deer while traveling along a treacherous road. The poem never says the driver feels bad, but the reader knows it to be true. Great poets do not tell.

Providing models such as these help students develop their poetic sense. It is not unlike developing a taste in clothes or food. The intellectual palate must be readied.

Techniques to Shape Poetry

Prewriting that sings with imagery, figurative language, and impacts the audience with an immediacy of power and emotion cries out for poetic form, not formula. Students discover their own patterns by freely experimenting, trying as many forms as they find interesting, then changing the rules as meaning dictates. Free verse sometimes finds rhyme; lyric poems can turn narrative. Students discover when writing poetry that meaning is the its only limit.

Students who panic, "But I can't write a poem," should begin in the comfort zone of the traditional prose trial draft. After drafting, sharing in groups, receiving help in noting striking phrases, images, or figures of speech, they are on their way to a poem.

Poet Richard Hugo suggests:

- Make your first line interesting and immediate. Start in the middle of things. When the poem starts, things should have already happened.

- When rewriting, write the entire poem again.

- Don't erase. (It's gone then.) Cross out or circle. (You may want to reconsider.)

- If you want to change something—first try leaving the same words but play with the syntax.

- Use strong verbs. Don't overuse "to be" forms.

- Consider the aptness of each word.

- Use "love" only as a transitive verb (for at least 15 years).

- End more than half your lines and more than two-thirds of your sentences on words of one syllable.

- Don't use the same subject in two consecutive sentences.

- Maximum sentence length: 17 words.

- Minimum sentence length: 1 word.

- No semicolons.

- Make sure each sentence is at least four words longer or shorter than the one before it.

- Don't use more syllables or more words than you absolutely need.

- Use any word that you "own." Don't be afraid to possess words. If you love them enough to own them, you will be secure with them. If you don't love them enough to own them, you will have to be very clever to write a good poem.

- Beware of certain words that seem necessitated by grammar to make things clear but dilute the drama of your poem (e.g., meanwhile, while, as during, and, a, an, the, this, that).

- If you ask a question, don't answer it, or answer a question not asked, or defer. (If you can answer the question, to ask it is to waste time—and words.)

There will be a new list tomorrow (Workshop given in 1982).

The Sound of Poetry

When reading their drafts aloud, students begin noting the natural groupings of words. The sounds that words make when placed next to each other. These words can extend into lines of a poem. They can be rearranged, changed, or omitted to sound better in the mouth and to the ear. Removing all the article/determiners from prose helps students discover the poetic nature of words. After they have done this, they return them, consider them, and work to make the line specific, not vague. When students in poetry or prose, circle abstract words and replace them with a concrete image, they are on their way to better writing.

Listening is a big part of the process. The sound and rhythm of words come into play. If the sound is off, students usually discover they have too many words. In the film *Amadeus*, the court musician erroneously remarks of Mozart's work, "There are too many notes," but when writing poetry students can indeed have too many words. The line and poem become weighted down. On the other hand, students need to exercise prudence against the tendency to cut arbitrarily because they often cut information needed to make the poem work. Poetry, more than any other genre, raises students' awareness to the importance of craft.

Imagery

Marking descriptive words and phrases that "show instead of tell" leads students into writing strong imagery in both poetry and prose. Writers deal in sight, sound, touch, smell, rather than telling about those objects, ideas, or feelings. Imagery brings life to the poem.

Imagery supplies breadth to a poem while metaphor keeps it breathing. Poet Alfred Noyes did not write the simile, "the road was like a ribbon of moonlight." Instead he used a metaphor, "the road was a ribbon of moonlight." The metaphor strengthens the line. Moves it along. The writer and reader see the twists and turns of the moonlight on the road.

When students first attempt poetry they should remember:

- Keep the poem concrete. Write what you know.

- Assume the persona of the poem. Become the main character.

- Do not tell everything. Give a snapshot of what the reader needs to see. What is obvious, what is wordy, what is extra needs to be cut from the poem.

- Take the reader through the experience. Let the reader vicariously participate in the poem.

- Remember to add conflict or tension.

Abstraction in Poetry

In poetry, ambiguity not abstraction rules. Ambiguity invites intellectualizing; it allows the reader to have different interpretations. Abstractions spiral into infinity—no one knows what the poem is trying to say. Concrete images give body to the idea.

More than any other poetic technique, ambiguity and concrete imagery fit the characteristics of the global/conceptual paradigm. Ambiguity invites the magnificent interconnections of the mind. Concrete imagery turns ideas into images.

Tracy, one of our students, wrote draft after draft of poems like:

Butterfly
Fly, smooth, pretty
heart, love, fly
cocoon, love, pretty
butterfly, me, fly.

When she grouped, her peers asked what the poem was about. She confided, "I feel like the only way I can escape my family situation of fourteen brothers and sisters, and unemployed parents is by becoming a butterfly." Her group gave her good advice. "Why don't you just write that? We didn't know what was going on. It's too abstract."

Tracey revised. The result:

Cocoon me
Mother's pregnant again.
For every year since I was two
She has had a child.
At sixteen, I want to be cocooned,

wrapped tight,
So one day I may come out
Wings bright.
I will butterfly
Away from the tight beds
of two kids on my right,
two on my left.
I will find the sky
and space to fly.

Tracy mastered a major concept in poetry. She replaced the abstractions with what caused the abstractions. Then everyone understood the poem.

NONFICTION

Nonfiction is such a complicated genre that most experts puzzle over its definition. William Knott devotes an entire chapter in his book *The Craft of Fiction* attempting to distinguish fiction from nonfiction, and M. H. Abrams in *A Glossary of Literary Terms* ignores it completely. Facts do not distinguish nonfiction from fiction. Neither does topic; both include writings about science, technology, popular culture, women's issues, urban issues, economics, politics, travels, psychoanalysis, television, nature, baseball, or anthropology. With that dilemma in mind, we embrace the following definition: Nonfiction is the writing of actual happenings, true events, and real people.

Students examining their prewriting find that is exactly what has occupied them—writing real "stuff" about their world. Shaping that reality is their next step. As Zinsser reminds us, "Nonfiction is the place where much of the best writing of the day is being done. Yet many writers and teachers of writing continue to feel vaguely guilty if they prefer it to fiction—nonfiction is the slightly disreputable younger brother in the royal house of literature. No such guilt is necessary. While the keepers of the temple weren't looking, nonfiction crept in and occupied the throne" (57).

We have heard of the burgeoning genre "creative nonfiction," which further blurs the distinction between fiction and nonfiction, but at this point in students' writing we believe it is best not introduced as it will muddy the waters of their understanding.

LETTERS

The letter is the expression of one person to another. In contemporary life, letter writing seems a lost art. Few individuals spend time or energy writing letters when cell phones, e-mail, and text messaging are accessible. But we have trouble recalling phone calls from yesterday, we erase e-mail, and text messaging disappears, whereas letters last far beyond lifetimes. Letters can be the writer's personal connection to an impersonal world.

As always, audience and purpose are major determiners. Informal letter writing to friends and family equals long talks over the kitchen table. We recollect past experiences and exchange news. We probe problems and emotions that we may not or cannot express face to face. We apologize; we work through disagreements because the brain has had time to overrule the tongue. Letters make life more interesting.

Letter writing activities engage students in ways that cannot be duplicated. When studying past events, students write grandparents asking them to recall certain events as they remember them. History may be explored through such letters.

Letters that address public issues are no less engaging. These letters inform, persuade, argue, protest, or support. Students have strong opinions, and letter writing provides a unique—and totally appropriate—venue for expressing these opinions.

For many students the letter as genre offers a new experience. Because we emphasize writing for an audience, letters promise not only an audience but also one that will actually read and respond. Letter writing becomes a powerful inducement to produce authentic writing.

A Note about Letters as Fiction: The Epistolary Tradition

Samuel Richardson wrote the first English novel *Pamela; or Virtue Rewarded* (1740), in epistolary form, which means an exchange of letters conveys the narrative. Probably no one used the epistolary more imaginatively than Bram Stoker in *Dracula*. The novel, a story of change, is told through letters, recordings, and news articles.

Although we have placed letters in nonfiction, they should not be discounted as a form for fiction. Nor should any form be restricted. Christopher Nolan writes his autobiography as if it were the biography of Joseph Meehan in *Under the Eye of the Clock*. Nolan is frequently compared to James Joyce, William Butler Yeats, and Dylan Thomas; John Carey says about him, "Plain statements and straightforward reportage now intermix with the bravura passages, allowing Nolan new kinds of tonal contrast, a new capacity for extended narrative, and a new realism" (Nolan x).

AUTOBIOGRAPHY

Because autobiography focuses on the writer, it is the ultimate reflexive writing. James Olney says autobiography allows the memory to bring "back some things, neglecting other things . . . seems to argue that selfhood is not continuous; for it brings up one self here and another self, and they are not the same as one another" (25–26).

Students who write reflexively, who find their own lives to be the primary focus of their writing, need a chance to examine their "one self and another self," look at where they have been, and project where they hope to go. This genre belongs in a prominent place in the repertoire of young authors.

Each year teachers and students hear funny, sad, frightening, and happy stories about each other's lives. Some of these stories are especially arresting, so they have an impact.

A stunning example comes from a sophomore class who wrote about turning points in their lives. The class had been writing since the beginning of school, more than six weeks. Everyone was getting to know each other, so they were comfortable sharing.

Lucy read, "It was the second week of August and everyone had been having a wonderful time. The party was at the park and all the family was there. My dad and my uncle were getting ready to leave. My brother, Raul, decided to leave with them, too. When he walked to the car, the shot rang out." As Lucy continued, the class became silent and still; everyone sat riveted as her love and her pain took over the room.

The death of Lucy's brother because of a passing gang encounter became a defining event in her life. Her unyielding intolerance of the gang mystic and her persistent questioning of why that happened never faded during the year, therefore gangs and gang members were not popular in first period. Autobiography did that.

Autobiographical Selections

Teachers can direct students to autobiographical selections at the appropriate level, for example, secondary choices include *A Christmas Memory* by Truman Capote, *West with the Night* by

Beryl Markham, *AKE* by Wole Soyinka, and *Hunger of Memory* by Richard Rodriguez. Autobiographical writing by Maya Angelou, Dylan Thomas, Anne Frank, and Helen Keller also interest students. Intermediate students like *Homesick: My Own Story* by Jean Fritz, and *ME ME ME ME ME Not a Novel* by M. E. Kerr.

Libraries Unlimited has a smashing series called "The Author and YOU" that provides windows into the lives of popular children's authors. For example, *Alma Flor Ada and YOU* opens with "To Poetry"/"A La Poesia" and is replete with wonderful stories about her experiences, her writing, her Latina identity, and her many books. Further, she offers ideas for teachers and librarians on writing, inquiry, using books and newspapers, retellings, dramatizing, creating characters, and so forth. In short it is a repository of information and ideas. This is an autobiography that goes beyond the formulaic, "I was born on . . . "

Another in this series worth sharing and emulating is *Jane Kurtz and YOU*. Most fascinating in this autobiography is how each chapter focuses on writing and the writing process, how authors come up with interesting ideas, hunt for those precious details that bring the writing alive, craft their diction, and find their voice. Because Kurtz spent most of her childhood in East Africa, and because we fancied the *Tarzan* movies, we especially loved the sections where she answers such questions as "Were you hot all the time in Africa?" "Did you speak Amharic or English?" "What did you eat?" "Who did you play with?"

Other autobiographies and biographies in this series include: *Gerald McDermott and YOU*, *Jim Aylesworth and YOU*, *Toni Buzzeo and YOU*, *Mary Casanova and YOU*, *Bob Barner and YOU*, and *Jacqueline Briggs Martin and YOU*. Alma Flor Ada has a forthcoming *Alma Flor Ada and YOU*, volume 2, which covers more of her huge corpus of writing.

Suggestions for Writing Autobiography

- Create a personal timeline—include whatever comes to mind—small events may prove significant.

- Create a story map of your life—draw the pictures and symbols to enrich the meaning.

- Search through old letters and notes, look for memorabilia—find the things that jog memories.

- Interview family members and friends about past events—consider the other point of view.

- Select the event that is significant and reveals the most—let the metonymy of that event reflect life.

- Consider starting points of memoir—sometimes it is best to start at the end, or after an event has occurred.

As students work through autobiographical writing, they arrive at intersections that allow them to continue on or change direction by rearranging, or altering facts. The real test at the intersections is keeping the writing true but not necessarily accurate. Accuracy can be dull, drawn out, and boring, whereas the truth liberates and holds interest. For example, if a student tells about a broken leg caused by not heeding Mother's repeated advice, then that student may reconstruct the events so Mother gives a final warning rather than leaving the warning wedged in between other episodes. What is important is not the accuracy of *when* the warning was given, but that the warning *was* given. Writers of nonfiction make these decisions of truth and accuracy in order to empower the truth. Students begin to realize that revising the accuracy while maintaining the truth heightens the dramatic effect and enables work on craft.

BIOGRAPHY

Students who are curious about their own lives are curious about the lives of others. Those who attend favorite rock star concerts, quote a special relative, follow a politician, or know all the statistics about an athlete are ready to research and write biography.

Often students study heroes as a major thematic strand in literature or social studies. To connect students and biography, we recommend they begin their study close to home by brainstorming people they consider heroic. To collect information about their hero, they interview people and develop surveys to uncover the opinions of family and friends. We want them to learn about assessing data, so they tally the surveys, examine the results, and compile questions to further reveal details hinted at but not made clear. Finally, if they determine they need more information, they return to their sources.

But students also need models, so they study classic and contemporary models of heroes. The students read, search, and discover, collecting information that can serve as comparisons to their heroes. With more information than they can use, students realize all that data makes it easier to write a biography plus they have learned the power and value of the apt quotation and documentation. Suggestions for writing biography:

- Read biographies as writers and analyze how they are written.

- Limit biographies to a certain period or certain event.

- Place periods and events within a broader historical context.

- Interview people who know the subject.

- Read the writings or view the accomplishments of the subject.

- Interview the subject and use his/her own words.

- Strive for true picture of the subject.

Although most student-authored biographies tend to be shorter character portraits not lengthy works, writing biography gives students experience in authentic research and encourages inquiry. Frequently, when students begin to evaluate others' lives, they learn about their own.

THE MEMOIR

Memoir, related to biography, is eyewitness accounts of writers' participation in events and with characters around them. Its strong sense of objectivity coupled with a place to analyze and interpret, makes memoir an interesting genre for students.

An excellent genre to couple with social studies, memoir places the writer within an historical context. Richard Beach says, "[Memoir] recounts experiences which portray another person whom the writer knew in the past" (1). He delineates further:

Memoir differs from portrait (writing about someone in the present) in that students usually have more direct access to the subject of a portrait: they can interview the subject of a portrait, while they must depend more on their memories in writing about someone in the past. As with phase autobiography, memoir writing is most successful when it focuses on specific events or incidents representing characteristic behaviors. (5)

When examining prewriting for organizational purposes, students need to keep all these distinctions in mind. Does their prewriting call for autobiography, biography, memoir, or portrait?

THE INTERVIEW

Students need to practice conducting interviews before they ever actually conduct one. Heuristics such as reporter's formula and classical invention offer departure points to develop questions for the interview. Key aspects of interviewing include:

- Ask open-ended questions.

- Think before responding to the interviewee.

- Encourage the interviewee to talk.

- Be honest when asking questions. This isn't an exposé.

- Admit ignorance—if the interviewee refers to something unknown to the interviewer, show curiosity.

- Do not be afraid to cut parts out of the interview.

- Do not try to record every word in an interview. Only record those statements that will make good quotes.

THE ESSAY

Dennis, a sophomore in a large suburban school district, was writing about George Bernard Shaw. Dennis discovered he had something in common with Shaw—a caustic sense of humor. Upon the suggestion of his teacher, he had read some of Shaw's classic works and his biography. Then he wrote about Shaw, "Shaw was also known as a Saist." When the teacher read the paper he asked Dennis, "What do you mean by 'saist'?" Dennis replied, "You know, Shaw wrote *s a's*."

S A's or Saist—students know the word *essay*. They may not be able to spell it, nor consider themselves essayists, but the essay has been the standard for school writing for the last one hundred years. Often the reason for assigning the essay is, "You'll have to write essays in college." Yet colleges vary so much—from institution to institution and department to department—that preparing students for college by teaching them only the essay is like bailing out a sinking boat with a colander.

With the enormous stress placed on test scores of late, no further rationale is needed for teaching the essay. Students simply have to be able to persuade, inform, classify, define, describe, and document using this form. Each essay has it own idiosyncratic characteristics and guidelines. While in their purest state there is nothing wrong with any of these essays, the problem occurs when teachers "teach" the essay. When weekly assignments "Write the persuasive essay in five well-constructed paragraphs to turn in Friday" are given, form dictates meaning. Far better for teachers and students to explore contemporary essays and find real reasons to write real essays for real audiences.

A more deductive approach to writing essays might be saner and more profitable for students. When teachers help students find what they have to say, they allow students to make decisions about how best to say it. When that happens real writing, authentic writing occurs. The characteristics of essays are shown below.

Table 2.1. Characteristics of an Essay

Type of Essay	Purpose of Essay	Major Characteristics Essay
persuasive	to persuade	• uses facts and opinions • uses emotional arguments
how-to	to give steps or procedures	• linear steps from beginning to end • sequence is important
narrative	to tell a story	• personal in nature • has a beginning, middle, and end • uses flashbacks
definition	to define an issue or problem	• has a clear bias • has facts to support definition • offers no solution
problem/solution	to consider a problem and offer a solution	• clearly states the problem • considers causes of the problems • offers at least one solution to the problem
comparison/contrast	to compare similarities and consider differences	• follows a comparison 1. first describes similarities in terms of elements of A compared to elements of B and then describes differences in terms of elements in B contrasted to elements in A. OR 2. first describes all similarities in terms of A and B, then describes all differences in terms of A and B. OR 3. taking a topical approach, describes similarities and differences of A and B in relation to each topic.
informative	to inform	• clearly gives the information
descriptive	to describe object or thing	• use spatial, time, or order sequences
documented	to accomplish any purpose	• uses quotation, facts, statistics from documented sources to support ideas

Isolated, essay forms can be boring and trite. Writers with a voice, style, and purpose never confine themselves to strict forms. Instead an essay might persuade while at the same time describe. Another essay might inform and define using a personal narrative. Contemporary essays exist everywhere in fine publications. Essayists such as Joan Didion are not bound to a form; instead they use their style, wit, and voice to say what they need to say. Unfortunately, many students are not given the freedom to use their style, wit, and voice—which they do have—to express themselves. This is a shame, yet no consumer advocacy group exists to protect the essay and students from the abuses of this genre.

Organizing the Essay

Kenneth A. Bruffee in *A Short Course in Writing* details four common patterns for the essay. He provides "a new model for learning the principles of discursive writing" (1). His patterns allow students freedom to choose subject matter and advance opinions, but set specific guidelines for presenting that information. These patterns present form but not formula; they give students workable, expandable structures within which to write.

Bruffee's organizational patterns and the shaping of those patterns have always been an important lesson in the three-week NJWPT/Abydos Writing Institute, but never more important than now given state-mandated writing tests, the new SAT essay, and the essay questions on each of the English AP® exams. In order to write for these on-demand assessments, students must internalize options for quickly but precisely organizing and presenting well-crafted responses. Bruffee's patterns offer opportunities and scaffolds for successful persuasive and argumentative writing.

When these forms are taught as a natural outgrowth of what students have to say, rather than as formulae, then students develop a deeper understanding of the power of organization. The forms are given here to explore *with* students not to prescribe *to* students. The anecdote at the conclusion of this section illustrates one way this exploration can happen.

Fig. 2.3. Bruffee's Organizational Patterns.

TWO REASONS

Introduction
Proposition

First reason developed
Explanation or defense

Second reason developed

NESTORIAN ORDER

Introduction
Proposition

Second best reason developed
Minor reasons

Major reason developed

STRAWMAN AND ONE REASON

Introduction
Proposition

Main opposing argument
Refute the opposition

Major positive reason
developed

CONCESSION

Introduction
Proposition

Important opposing
argument

Concession
Positive argument developed

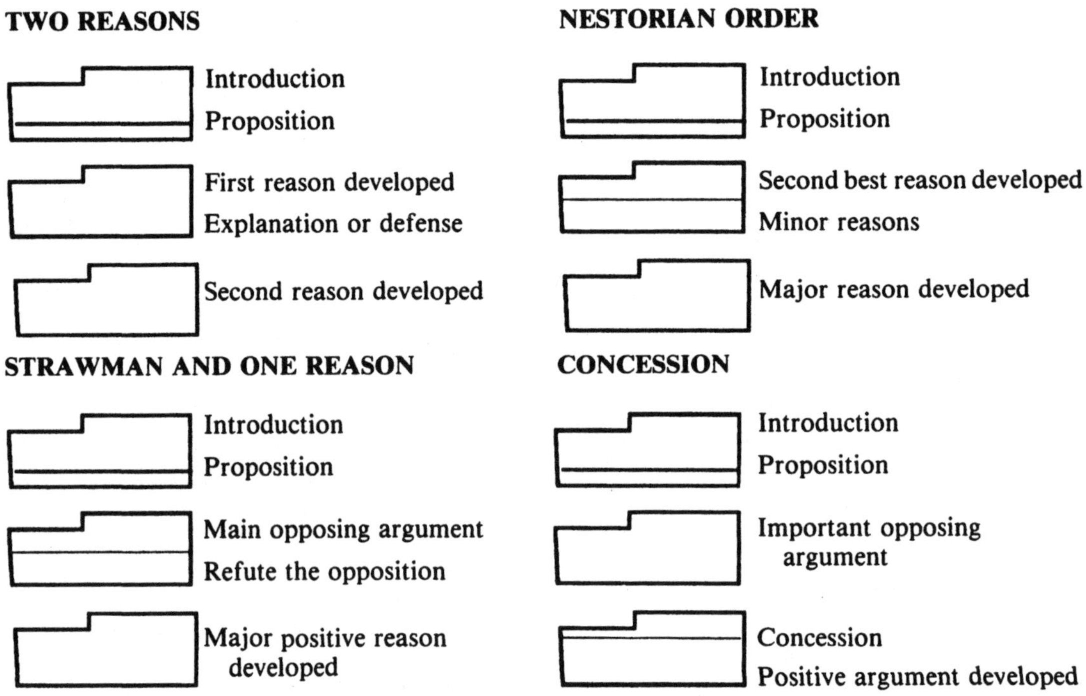

Two Reasons

Two reasons (or three or five or fifteen) is the easiest pattern because it gives students a straightforward way to organize their ideas, points, arguments, or steps. Students write one reason, idea, point, argument right after the other sequentially and support each with evidence. This pattern is favored by testing agencies and traditionalists.

Nestorian Order

Ministers favor this organizational pattern because of their purpose. They want to start with a punch and end with a bang. They want to leave their congregations with a ringing idea or a poignant concept for the week.

In testing situations, Nestorian order is a winning pattern. Students begin with their second best idea, one they usually know well and can support. They follow this with other ideas, points, arguments, or steps, which they usually know less well or in lesser depth, but they conclude with their best point, argument, or step. By saving their best for last, graders are left with a strong impression instead of ramblings or dwindling rhetoric.

Strawman and One Reason

In examining the strawman pattern, students find they can raise an opposing point, argument, or idea and then systematically invalidate it. After deflating the opponent, students go on to present their points, arguments, or ideas. Lawyers use strawman because their goal is to knock down the opposing argument, thereby discrediting the opposing view and winning the case.

Concession

When considering concession, the rhetoric of politicians, students learn to use this pattern when there is opposing data to their argument that cannot be refuted. In using this pattern, students concede the existence of an opposing viewpoint, argument, or idea but then proceed to elaborate on their data. In scholarship or research, to ignore the opposing information reduces the credibility of the writer. Students learn writers must at least acknowledge the opposing viewpoint—even if they cannot counter it—to make their views viable.

WHAT WORKS AND WHAT DOESN'T: SHAPING THE ESSAY

Jodi came to our office and pronounced, "You can't teach below level, disadvantaged students how to organize—they could never use Bruffee's patterns."

Accepting the gauntlet she had thrown down, we replied, "Yes you can."

We asked Jodi what her outcomes were for her unit of study. She wanted her students to use Bruffee's organizational patterns. She said they were going to write an essay on *Of Mice and Men* by Steinbeck and she wanted to see the patterns used. We set up an action research arrangement. We would watch Jodi one period, and she would watch us the next. This is a reflection of what happened:

Monday—Jodi

Jodi gave the writing assignment topic: "The Moral Dilemma in *Of Mice and Men*." She asked for a thesis statement but received blank stares. She asked questions about what they could write about. Two students offered topics that she vetoed. Going to the board, she wrote: "George did the correct thing by taking Lenny's life." She informed them this was their thesis statement. After distributing a handout of Bruffee's four organizational patterns, she explained each pattern and then assigned prewriting due the following day.

Monday—We

As the students came into class, we provided large sheets of butcher paper and divided the class into two groups. Explaining the rules of brainstorming, we asked them to brainstorm all the things they could think of that related to the book. Hesitantly, they started. With markers they made lists on the butcher paper. We discussed both lists after they displayed them on the wall.

Together we prioritized the items in order of interest and starred those that held the highest interest. These we wrote as statements on paper strips that we also displayed.

Tuesday—Jodi

Students, instructed to write their rough drafts from their prewriting, spent the entire period writing drafts. Few had any prewriting. Some slept, some talked.

Tuesday—We

We gave each student a swatch of butcher paper and asked if they had a personal favorite from Monday's list of starred statements. Most did. Those that did not offered to pick one. They wrote their favorite statements on the butcher paper. We asked students to find an opposing viewpoint on the master list that contradicted their statements. Some students found opposing ideas faster than others. Because some were having trouble, we completed this orally. Finally, every student, with the help of the class, wrote down an opposing statement. The students had previously done webbing, so we invited them to complete a web on their butcher paper. After they completed their web, they starred what they liked best, and then wrote more about each.

Wednesday—Jodi

Students were instructed to revise their papers by using a revision "check sheet" that covered spelling, subject-verb agreement, and fragments. They spent the period working on their papers. Most recopied Tuesday's draft more neatly.

Wednesday—We

Students were given six 5″ × 8″ index cards—two yellow, two blue, and two green. They were asked to label the yellow cards Pro, the blue cards Con, the green cards Props. After we modeled Bruffee's guidelines for propositions, they wrote propositions on the green cards.

We shared their statements. Then, as we modeled, they placed the Pro and Con cards on opposing sides of their desktops. Next, we instructed them to use their ideas from the butcher paper as support for their statements. This was difficult. They asked many questions, but we continued to model and encourage them to try different supports by sharing them with their peers. The class became the place for trial-and-error discussion of what constitutes supporting arguments. By the end of the period everyone had at least two supports for each statement. (At this point we began to interchange the terms *statement*, *thesis statement*, and *proposition*.)

Thursday—Jodi

Jodi instructed the students to write their final drafts. She told them they were due Friday.

Thursday—We

We showed students how to consult *Of Mice and Men* to find supporting textual evidence for the ideas on the cards. At this point, we had to distribute more cards because the students wrote several supports on one card. We discussed the value of having one support per card. The students decided one support per card was easier. We felt if we had given better directions, the students would not have had to use up valuable instructional time redoing what they had done. When we shared this observation, the students agreed but they added they liked figuring out a better way of doing it. We decided students make the best teachers.

After the students wrote one argument and one supporting quote per card, we modeled how to expound, explain, or elaborate the idea and quote and how to integrate the text. We made a list of ways we deepened our writing during modeling: repetition, facts from the book, personal anecdotes, examples, instances and more details, and comparison/contrast. Students spent the remainder of the period following our model.

Friday—Jodi

Students handed in their papers and worked on a vocabulary handout. When we examined the papers, all of them were organized using the "Two Reasons" pattern. None of the papers incorporated quotes from the books to support any idea.

Friday—We

Using the cards as manipulatives, each student arranged and rearranged his or her cards according to Bruffee's organizational patterns that we wrote on the board and modeled. Students experienced realizations: some configurations required fewer cards; others required all the cards. We then asked students to identify which pattern best fit what they had to say and make a commitment to that organizational pattern. They arranged and rearranged their cards. When they decided on a pattern, we rubber banded the cards together and labeled it by its pattern. We concluded class with a mini-teach on transitions.

Monday—Jodi

Jodi's class began a new unit of study.

Monday—We

To review Friday's mini-teach, we examined essays to identify where transitions were needed. Students wrote transitions to connect the cards, suggesting the transitions be written on white cards. This took the rest of the period.

Tuesday—We

We modeled writing drafts and gave students rules for conferencing. Only a few students took advantage of the conference. They spend the period transferring their prewriting from the cards to notebook paper.

Wednesday—We

We introduced the concept of audience, but the students decided audience wouldn't change the way they wrote this paper. After a mini-teach on ratiocination of "to be" verbs, students ratiocinated their papers. More students conferenced. They had almost finished and felt pleased with their papers.

Thursday—We

After conducting a mini-teach on leads and sharing examples of the typical, action, dialogue, and reaction lead. Students wrote a lead for their papers. We followed this with the grouping technique "Say Back." By the conclusion of class, every student had a lead that worked.

Friday—We

We asked students what they needed to complete their papers. Most felt they were close to completion. We explained the concept of clocking; they decided they could be ready Monday to clock.

Monday—We

We went through the clocking technique. Students were given time to make the corrections based upon the clocking sheets. We debriefed about their chosen organization patterns. No one chose the easiest "Two Reasons."

Because Jodi worried about objectivity on the assessment, an impartial party read the papers. A teacher from another high school in the district evaluated the papers. This teacher did not know which papers came from which class.

The data showed that students who used "Two Reasons" were assessed one to two grades lower than the students who used the "Nestorian Order," "Strawman and One Reason," or "Concession" as organizational patterns.

The implications are clear. First, meaning dictates form. Students who made the decisions on how to organize their papers based on the best structure for what they had to say scored better than those who chose the "easy" pattern. Second, teachers must model not tell students how to organize. Third, students will use more sophisticated organizational patterns if they see them modeled in concrete ways and if they are taken through the experience. Students cannot abstract organization. Possibly the most important lesson, though, proved teaching is not telling, it is not assigning—it is experiencing.

SHAPING THE HEXAGONAL

While Bruffee's organization patterns work wonderfully well, we also recommend shaping hexagonal writing, especially for literary analysis. After the six sides of the hexagon have been flushed out with prewriting, we encourage students to manipulate those sides, deciding which one would make the best lead, where theme would work best, how they would conclude. Since the prewriting has been done on half-sheets of paper, manipulation is easy and challenging.

After they have made their decisions, we draw six blocks vertically on the board or on chart paper in four or five columns, and then ask individual students to tell us how they organized their prewriting. The sample shown in Table 2.2 shows the kinds of responses we usually get.

Table 2.2. Responses to Shaping the Hexagonal

Student A	Stubent B	Student C	Student D
Personal allusions	Plot	Theme	Plot
Theme	Theme	Literary devices	Personal allusions
Plot	Literary allusions	Literary allusions	Theme
Literary devices	Literary devices	Evaluation	Evaluation
Literary allusions	Evaluation	Plot	Literary devices
Evaluation	Personal allusions		Literary allusions

Immediately students see that not everyone shapes their prewriting exactly the same way. We spend time asking students to justify their organization. Why did you combine plot and personal allusions? Why did you drop personal allusions? How can you evaluate before you explore literary devices and allusions? And so forth. The lesson always ends with the dictum: Meaning dictates form.

CONCLUSION

When students move from their messy prewriting into structured writing modes, genre offers them choices. When writing teachers encourage the freedom of choice, the freedom of genre, then meaning takes on a force that moves the writing. Genre is not a mold into which plaster is poured, it is clay that needs kneading, shaping, and firing. It is the clay that may be a dish, a bowl, or a sculpture. Genre frees students from the mundane and inane, from neurotic formulae that shackle thought. Independence as a learner, as a person, cannot totally be achieved if teachers not meaning dictate form.

Tess Gallagher writes in her introduction to Raymond Carver's *A New Path to the Waterfall*:

Ray had so collapsed the distance between his language and thought that the resulting transparency of method allowed distinctions between genres to dissolve without violence or a feeling of trespass. . . . Ray used his poetry to flush the tiger from hiding. Further, he did not look on his writing life as the offering of products to a readership, and he was purposefully disobedient when pressures were put on him to write stories because that's where his reputation was centered and that's where the largest reward in terms of publication and audience lay. He didn't care. When he received the Mildred and Harold Strauss Living Award, given only to prose writers, he immediately sat down and wrote two books of poetry. He was not "building a career"; he was living a vocation and this meant that his writing, whether poetry or prose, was tied to inner mandates that insisted more and more on an increasingly unmediated apprehension of his subjects, and poetry was the form that best allowed this.

Students, too, have inner mandates, and they need to practice finding the form that best allows the expression of these mandates. Teachers of writing can use form as a way to allow for expression.

APPLICATION

We like to say, "The line you choose determines the genre you choose." Go through your prewriting looking for a line that strikes you, a line that sings, a line that promises potential. Underline it. Then decide what genre that line beckons. Share with your group. Draw conclusions.

3

WRITING AS A SOCIAL ACT

What the child can do in cooperation today he can do alone tomorrow.
—Lev Semonovich Vygotsky □

THE WRITING GROUP, CONFERENCE, AND DEBRIEFING

We have noticed a trend toward interaction—on TV, we are urged to call in votes for our favorite dancers, teams, politicians, and survivors. Starbucks panders to those who want go to a coffeehouse with people. Barnes and Noble encourages folks to visit while checking the books and magazines. Churches, once quiet, sober places of worship, have turned into amphitheatres of histrionics with shouting, arms waving, and witnessing. Even Las Vegas has interactive slot machines.

Students, with iPods and Zunes plugged into their ears, with music blaring from their car speakers, with their distracted or bored demeanors who have been baby-sat by "electronic miracles" over six hours a day throughout their young lives, who live with one parent who works, who join gangs for companionship, who are latchkey kids, who in high school number 7,000 drop-outs every school day (in Graham and Perin 7; Pinkus 2006) suggest that many students need significant opportunities for interaction and a sense of belonging. With these challenges facing educators, it seems that collaboration, in this case, collaboration within the writing process, offers one way for students to experience collective goal setting and meaningful cooperation.

While the present demands collaboration, projections into the future also call for collaborative skills. As Robert B. Reich projects, "It is not enough to produce a cadre of young people with specialized skills. If our enterprises are to be the scenes of collective entrepreneurship—as they must be—experts must have the ability to broadly share their skills and transform them into organizational achievement; and others must be prepared to learn from them" (24). Reich focuses this report on what education can and should do to contribute to the emerging economy. Clearly he makes the point that the more students learn about collaborating, the better their preparation for entry into the new global economy.

Since writing paradoxically absorbs both solitary and collaborative time—time spent writing alone juxtaposed with time spent receiving responses from others—students who write should also learn and practice collaborative strategies. Once, after students had completed a group technique, Marsha, a freckle-faced redhead, quipped, "You know, we can't do this solitary work alone." Writing is solitary work, but at some point in this solitary sojourn we want and need the input of others.

The strategies presented in this chapter extend students' learning and eventually become intrinsic to their writing processes. Therefore, the ease with which these strategies are implemented during writing instruction often determines the degree of their immediate success. Repeating these strategies often and at appropriate times promotes the integration of these strategies into each student's writing processes and into their lives. Three major ways to teach and practice collaboration in the writing classroom are (1) the writing group; (2) the writing conference; (3) the writing debriefing.

Writing Groups

Trust and Immediacy

Trust is the foundation of the writing group. So important is trust to the writing process that without it writing groups take on an inauthentic, even phony feeling—a sense of simply going through the motions. Therefore, we caution teachers when they set up groups to convey to students a true grasp of the power of people interacting. Facilitating so that learning occurs builds trust because the students see the power. Through continual and successful grouping, students learn to trust and return that trust in others, themselves, and writing.

Writing is immediate because the words on the paper call for response. In the classroom, this call provides students with firsthand practice in giving and receiving feedback, following the procedures of the group technique, attending and listening, tolerating ambiguity, responding genuinely, learning how to question, increasing sensitivity to others, and decreasing game-playing and manipulation. Further, students learn to focus on their writing and the writing of others in purposeful ways.

Satellite Skills

Writing groups not only enhance writing and reading skills (especially reading aloud, with expression), but they also help students develop satellite skills such as flexibility, decision making, higher-level thinking, interaction, tolerance, discovery, listening, and leadership. Students working in groups foster these skills in simultaneously overlapping ways. Writing in different modes and for different purposes, for instance, calls not only for flexibility in writing but also in sharing that writing with others. Sometimes the writing calls for pairing with just one other student; other times the writing requires feedback from a larger group. Also, deciding upon the group's purpose prompts students to consider appropriate responses. For example, deciding if an idea is worth writing about necessitates a different response than deciding upon the vitality of a lead.

Group cohesiveness happens when there is positive feedback and an absence of ridicule, both developed through an understanding of the sensibilities of others and reinforced through modeled verbal and nonverbal interaction. When teachers model by sharing their own writing to invite responses, students learn what comments help, encourage, or extend writing. Conversely, they learn what might thwart further writing or sharing. This develops tolerance and a facility with responsive language as students work to build-up not put-down the writing of peers.

Creating an environment where discovery can occur means constantly furnishing a secure place where students may comfortably work together to analyze writing, risk new styles, find fitting genres, experiment with workable structures, and practice solving linguistic and metalinguistic problems. Ultimately, students make the final decisions about their writing, but they learn the nuance of response by listening to others. This leads to more informed choices, ensures ownership, and calls upon high-level thinking skills. Through group work, students learn to receive input from others while taking the responsibility for their own decisions. Often this interaction leads to a deeper understanding coupled with better decisions not only about the writing but also about the decision-making process itself.

Writing groups also help students develop or refine leadership skills because the group becomes a learning community. If writing groups are well integrated into the English language arts classroom, students find them a place to belong and a place where their contributions are valued. Because writing is a complex of processes, sharing with others and hearing the writing of others heightens students' awareness about writing. They begin to realize they may excel in one area of writing, imagery for example, but have problems with creating apt metaphors. They also discover their weakness may be another's strength. As they begin working with these strengths and weaknesses, they often learn self-respect and respect for others. Therein lies one of the energies of the writing group.

Finally, writing groups are fun. Sharing a funny anecdote, hearing a gripping story, musing over a powerfully written poem can be fun in two senses of the word: (1) the fun of delight—delight in language, in discovery, in the learning process itself; (2) the fun of fruition—fruition in closure, in completion, in making the writing whole through others. Fun in writing groups should not be confused with rollicking laughter, boisterous behavior, or acting up. Rather, fun in writing groups more closely matches what William Glasser defines as five basic human needs: survival, love, power, freedom, and fun. These needs are built into our genetic structures (43). Writing groups furnish the fun of involvement and investment that gives rise to true emotion in the classroom. Caine and Caine cite several studies that support the interconnectedness of emotion and learning, concluding "that the enthusiastic involvement of students is essential to most learning" (57). Through writing groups, students engage in a process that will prepare them in positive, substantive ways for a future that will demand responsibility and collaboration, decision making, meeting challenges, posing and solving problems, serious study, and a sense of humor.

When implemented correctly and consistently, writing groups become the foundation for writing communities and writer's workshop.

Writing Group Strategies

The group strategies suggested here have been developed and used by writing teachers affiliated with the New Jersey Writing Project in Texas (NJWPT) for over three decades. We have adapted pointing, telling, summarizing, and showing from Peter Elbow's work (1973, 85–92). Highlighting is a visual group strategy adapted from June Gould (115). Large group share is a variation of Lucy Calkins's share meetings, and process share comes from her *Lessons from a Child* (111). Analytic talk first appeared in the November 1981 *English Journal* (Carroll 101). Double Dyads is an adaptation of "Peer Revision," an unpublished group strategy developed by a NJWPT/Abydos trainer.

The notion of reading twice, which is incorporated into most of the group strategies, is based on the observation that listeners first experience a piece then they analyze it. Reading twice is not wasted instructional time, rather it is time spent developing finer listening skills and deepening sensitive responses.

Pointing

Explanation. Pointing invites group members to suggest what they find effective in a piece of writing. Best used early in the writing process when students are fragile, it is the most nonthreatening of all the strategies.

Implementation.

1. Divide students into groups of four or five.

2. Writers read the whole piece, pause, and then read again.

3. Listeners listen. Upon second reading, listeners jot down words, phrases, images, anything that successfully penetrates their skulls.

4. After each reading, listeners point out what they liked.

5. Nothing negative is allowed. Writers may not begin, "This is terrible, but . . . " Listeners may not even mumble, "That's the worst thing I've ever heard . . . " All are charged to seek what works.

Remarks. Through pointing, students become acquainted with each other and with the technique of grouping. They learn how groups function, develop spoken and unspoken norms of behavior, receive positive responses from peers, uncover the best in the writing, and discover that the group is a nonthreatening place.

Telling

Explanation. Telling enables listeners to become aware of every possible reaction they may have to the writing. It sets up an environment that works much like a full battery of physical tests so students don't overlook something important. Telling is the MRI of techniques.

Implementation.

1. Divide students into groups of five or six.

2. Writers read the whole piece, pause, and then read again.

3. Listeners listen. Upon second reading, listeners pretend they are hooked up to a variety of instruments that record everything that occurs to them: blood pressure, pulse, EKG, EEG, CAT scans, bone scans. They monitor their proprioceptions—those reactions that occur in the subcutaneous tissues of the body such as goose bumps, hair standing on end, blushes, sweaty palms, chills, or sudden tearing.

4. After each reading, listeners tell what their "instruments" have recorded.

5. Nothing negative is allowed since honest physical reactions are simply "recorded."

Remarks. Like pointing, all responses during telling are positive. Telling fits the needs of those inexperienced in grouping or those fragile about their writing. Knowing the reactions of others (or even that there were reactions) to a piece of writing can be helpful to the writer. Telling meshes thinking and feeling.

Showing

Explanation. Showing provides a way for listeners to share perceptions that are tacit, that is, locked in the mind. Tacit knowing is sometimes unlocked through the use of metaphor. Responding to another's writing through metaphor often unblocks reluctant responders since students see this strategy as inviting a response that cannot be "wrong."

Implementation.

1. Divide students into groups of four.

2. Writers read. Pause. Read again.

3. Listeners listen. Upon second reading, listeners jot down metaphors that match the writing: voices, weather, motion or locomotion, clothing, topography, colors, shapes, animals, fruits, vegetables, musical instruments, or songs. Some listeners doodle or draw their metaphors as they listen.

4. After the reading, listeners share their metaphors or drawings and talk about their responses.

Remarks. According to Michael Polanyi, tacit knowing is an inarticulate intelligence by which we know things in a purely personal manner (64). Attempting to put that knowing into precise words or accurate descriptions is sometimes impossible. By the use of metaphor (or simile), listeners come closer to what they know and are able to share, albeit indirectly.

Student A: Your writing reminds me of an eggplant.

Student B: I hate eggplant. Does that mean you hate my writing?

Student A: No, I thought it smooth and, well, there was something regal about it—you know deep purple reminds me of royalty.

Student B: Yeah. Now I get it.

Mary: When you read I saw an old faded pair of jeans.

Jesse: Cliché, huh?

Mary: No, I meant it had a comfortable feel about it.

Summarizing

Explanation. Summarizing invites listeners to synthesize what they have heard in four ways. It prevents parroting because its purpose is to let the writer know what stood out, what stuck in the listener's consciousness.

Implementation.

1. Divide students into groups of five.

2. Writers read the whole piece, pause, and then read again.

3. Listeners listen. Upon second reading, listeners:

   a. focus on what they think is the main idea;

   b. write that main idea a single sentence;

   c. choose one word to express the main idea;

   d. think of a synonym to express the main idea.

4. Listeners share their summaries.

Remarks. Because it provides immediate application, this strategy is appropriate to couple with mini-teaches on main idea, paraphrasing, summing up, synopsizing, or research.

Plus and Minus

Explanation. Plus and minus is a tabulated version of thumbs up, thumbs down. Best used on rough drafts, it gives students an indication of first reactions to specifics in the writing.

Implementation.

1. Divide students into groups of ten. Assign each a number from one to ten.

2. Distribute one chart to each group member (see Table 3.1).

3. A writer reads his or her paper through once.

4. In turn, each student reads each of the criteria in the first column.

Table 3.1. Plus and Minus Chart

Criteria	Groups Members									
	1	2	3	4	5	6	7	8	9	10
Title catches the reader's attention										
First two sentences hook the reader										
Purpose is clear										
Uses phrases that work										
Appeals to reader's interest										
Vocabulary is appropriate to audience										
Reels the reader in										
Believable characters										
Not confusing										
Ending works										
Grammar OK										
Language is fresh										
Overall evaluation										

5. Group members signal thumbs up or thumbs down for each criteria.

6. The writer places a (+) if a group member gives a thumbs up or a (–) if a group member gives a thumbs down. The signs go in the column that corresponds to each student's number.

7. After the group has finished their charts, they study them to consider appropriate revisions.

Remarks. Because Plus and Minus is almost in a game format, students find it agreeable. Students like the idea of receiving so much feedback, especially because they tabulate it themselves and then use the tabulations to make decisions about their writing.

Highlighting

Explanation. Highlighting provides verbal and visual feedback. Much like pointing, it enables the writer to understanding what listeners find outstanding and effective.

Implementation.

1. Divide students into groups of four or five. Remind students to bring a highlighter or colored marker to group.

2. Writers read the whole piece, pause, and then read again.

3. Listeners listen. Upon second reading, listeners jot images they like.

4. After the reading, listeners repeat back these images.

5. Writers highlight these images on their papers.

Remarks. June Gould contends that "meaning resides in images, and highlighting reinforces image making." Because modeling helps students make important connections, often after hearing each other's images, students seem to include more imagery in subsequent writing. Also, highlighting may be adapted to other elements in the writing such as dialogue, metaphor, characterization, repetition, and diction.

Large-Group Share

Explanation. Large-group share is a time, usually early in the process, when the entire class meets. Its purpose is to provide a forum for students to test their ideas, to see if others think their ideas worth the commitment of continued writing (i.e., taking the piece through the process).

Implementation.

1. Gather students together in a tight group.

2. Invite those who wish to share their idea, their purpose, their audience, and where or how they intend to publish.

3. Class members respond informally.

Remarks. Large-group share is particularly effective at the onset of extensive writing when audience is a paramount consideration. Following is an excerpt from a large group share with twelfth-graders.

Student A: I'm looking at *The Black Collegian*. I'm trying to get an interview with our mayor. I want to talk to him about his career. Since he is African American, I think this magazine might be interested in his views if I can get them down well enough. *Writer's Market* says they take stuff on careers.

Student B: Do they take freelancers?

Student A: You bet and they pay!

Student C: Did you know there's another magazine interested in that topic?

Student B: No. Which one?

Student C: *Career Focus.*

Student D: I think I'm going for the athlete. *Texas Coach* is always looking for articles and I want to do something about how important trainers are to a football team.

Student E: I'm writing an editorial for the local paper.

Student D: On what?

Process Share

Explanation. Process share helps students focus on how their papers came to be and what they still need. Recognizing their writing processes and hearing others describe theirs help students relax, go with their processes, and not fight them. This cuts down on frustration.

Implementation.

1. Divide students into groups of seven.

2. Writers talk about where they are in the process or share what they have written thus far. Together students informally probe their processes using the following questions as a guide:

    a. What problems have you encountered?

    b. How did you go about solving them?

    c. Have you made any changes? What were they? What prompted them?

    d. What are you planning to do next?

    e. What help do you need from this group?

3. After this, the class meets to debrief what was learned.

Remarks. This strategy is most beneficial at the beginning of a paper that entails research. It helps students understand that writing research is also a process, and it asks for the responses of others.

Say Back

Explanation. Say back is one of the most constructive strategies because it begins with positive comments and concludes with helpful suggestions. This strategy works best about midway through the process, when students think they have included everything in their writing or know they have some muddles but are unsure about how to clarify them.

Implementation.

1. Divide students into groups of four or five.

2. Writers read. Pause. Read again.

3. Listeners listen. Upon second reading, they jot down two things:

    a. what they liked;

    b. what they want to know more about.

4. Listeners *say* these *back* to the writer.

Remarks. The beauty of this strategy is its adaptability. Workable with any grade level, say back fosters extending the writing and elaborating upon it in a positive way.

Analytic Talk

Explanation. Analytic talk enables students to share their writing in order to elicit specific responses on specific areas of concern. This strategy works best when the writing has been through several drafts and is ready for final polishing. After peer feedback, students hone the parts of their writing that still cause problems.

Implementation.

1. Divide students into groups of five.

2. Writers read, pause, and then read again.

3. Listeners listen. Upon second reading, they take notes—a word or phrase—to help them remember anything they may wish to comment upon.

4. After the reading, the group comments, suggests, advises, and discusses by following specific questions:

    a. Was the lead effective?

    b. Was the beginning/introduction clear and interesting?

c. Would I continue reading if I read the opener in a magazine?

d. Was there a lazy or phony question such as, "Have you ever been in love?"

e. After hearing the beginning, am I sure what the writing is about?

f. Did I ever get lost during the reading? If so, where?

g. Did I ever get confused during the reading? If so, where?

h. Does the piece have voice?

i. Do the sentences link together? Do the paragraphs?

j. Was I left hanging at the end? If so, was it intentional and effective, or was it caused by lack of information?

Remarks. These questions may be modified, but generally they work well since they focus on parts of the paper such as leads, theses, coherence, conclusions, without using terms students find threatening. Analytic talk provides "congenial motivation," to borrow William Stafford's term.

Olympic Scoring

Explanation. Olympic scoring approximates the evaluation system used at the Olympic games. Students work with one element of writing (in this case, character development) by grouping on that element with two different partners. Each writer then compares the values received in each of the ten areas and makes decisions for further work on the paper.

Implementation.

1. Writers reread their papers and fill out a score sheet (Table 3.2) for themselves.

2. Divide class into groups of two.

3. Partners exchange drafts one and two.

4. Distribute one copy of the score sheet to each student.

5. Partners complete the score sheet for each other. They assign points 1–10 (1 is lowest; 10 is highest) to each area just as a judge would assign points to an Olympic participant.

6. Students repeat steps 3–5 with a new partner.

7. They study all three score sheets and revise accordingly.

Remarks. This strategy may be adapted to any or all elements within a particular genre. It works best when used in conjunction with mini-teaches. For example, if the mini-teaches have centered on writing about characters, developing characters, rounding out flat characters, and so forth, then Olympic scoring on character provides the logical check on the application of those lessons. Equally effective, Olympic scoring may be constructed for conventions, grammar, or most anything taught in relation to writing.

Another level of collaboration can be achieved with this strategy through mini-teaches on the

Table 3.2. Olympic Scoring Sheet

Writer's Name _____ Partner's Name _____

Draft One	Score	Draft Two	Score
1. Characters' appeal		1. Characters' appeal	
2. Quality of characters' names		2. Quality of characters' names	
3. Authenticity of characters		3. Authenticity of characters	
4. Characters sound real		4. Characters sound real	
5. Characters look real		5. Characters look real	
6. Characters are consistent		6. Characters are consistent	
7. Characters are not stereotypical		7. Characters are not stereotypical	
8. Quality of dialogue		8. Quality of dialogue	
9. Story has beginning, middle, end		9. Story has beginning, middle, end	
10. Overall quality		10. Overall quality	
Total		Total	

appropriate elements within the genre and then encouraging groups of students to develop Olympic scoring sheets for those elements. Students may use Table 3.2 as a model.

Double Dyads

Explanation. The strategy double dyads is related to proofreading. Used immediately before the final copy is to be handed in, it allows peers to become editors. Further, this strategy facilitates input from two persons within a given structure, so it is effective with students not yet accustomed to grouping or with somewhat unruly students.

Implementation.

1. Divide students into groups of two.

2. Distribute two "Preparing for Publication Sheets" (Table 3.3) to each student.

3. Partners exchange papers.

Table 3.3. Preparing for Publication

Writer _____

Reviewer _____

Read the essay and rate the writing honestly in the following categories.	Super–outstanding	Really good	Just OK	Not so hot—could be better	Really needs help
How well does the introduction catch your attention?					
How well does the writer give you a clear objective of where the paper is heading and what the writer wants to say?					
Does the paper flow?					
Does the writer prove what he or she intended to prove?					
Does the writer document borrowed materials correctly?					
Does the writer wrap up the paper nicely with a sense of finality?					
Does the writer do a good job of convincing you of what he or she believes?					

What is the strongest part of the paper?

What is the weakest part of the paper?

Discuss the paper with your partner.

4. Each student silently and carefully reads the paper and marks the sheet accordingly.

5. After marking the sheet, partners discuss the papers.

6. Students repeat the process with a new partner.

7. Students evaluate their papers after taking feedback into consideration.

Remarks. Double dyads work best with the documented essay although the Preparing for Publication Sheet may be adapted to other genre.

CLASSROOM MANAGEMENT STRATEGIES FOR WRITING GROUPS

Conducting Writing Groups

When initiating writing groups, it is important for teachers to think of themselves as facilitators who structure the classroom so that each group feels successful. Keeping three things in mind helps groups work smoothly and with purpose: (1) remain nondefensive; (2) act from a knowledge base, and (3) incrementally implement writing groups.

Remain Nondefensive

We recommend that teachers assume a nondefensive stance during writing groups, equip themselves with reasonable expectations and explicit goals, and set up writing groups by introducing specific strategies. We tell teachers that they are observers of how the groups function using those strategies. Closely noting what occurs in each group enables teachers to modify, adapt, continue, or disregard a strategy—always with future writing groups in mind. We caution teachers to expect some floundering as groups find their rhythm and warn them not to take group behaviors personally. Although teachers may sit near a raucous group, nudge an idle group, and interact with a lively group, they must remain nondefensive and refuse to take on any group. Later, during the debriefing, students may consider and reconsider the actions of the group. Debriefing often turns what may have been an unproductive session into a productive one.

"What happened in your groups today?"

"No much."

"Let's talk about that."

Act from a Knowledge Base

Teachers know that if they write with students, they teach from a knowledge base. When they perceive needs based on their own experiences as writers, they are better at eye contact, close listening, respectful comments, and insightful questions; they set a standard and expectations by modeling their own writing. Because they write, they are able to anticipate concerns, so they design mini-teaches based on those concerns as well as those they observe while students write, what they hear in conferences and during debriefing, and what emerges during writing groups.

Incrementally Implement Writing Groups

We constantly advise teachers who want to initiate collaboration but who are still inexperienced with group strategies to implement group work in increments. We recommend beginning with a nonthreatening strategy such as pointing, and with small, easy-to-structure groups, such as partners (dyads). As teachers become more facile with groups, and students become more facile in groups, both move more successfully into the complicated strategies and larger or more flexible groups.

Sometimes past experiences with groups (or lack thereof) militate against trying them, especially in middle and high school. Some teachers who have not received training on implementing group strategies are understandably reluctant to risk losing control because of the dynamics in class. If they do take the risk, the results sometimes may be less than satisfying. This may lead teachers to conclude, "Groups do not work," and they never try again. This is a disservice to students who require practice in collaboration.

According to *Writing Next,* the report to the Carnegie Corporation of New York, studies on the effectiveness of collaborative writing "show that collaborative arrangements in which students help each other with one or more aspects of their writing have a strong positive impact on quality" (16).

Students who have not collaborated since the primary grades often regard groups as "baby stuff" or a time to fool around. These students are misinformed, which is all the more reason why teachers must deeply believe in the value of collaboration and learn its techniques. The best defense is to introduce writing groups slowly and in increments. But to group because it's mandated, because others do, or because it is trendy will most certainly lead to problems.

Introducing Writing Groups

Explanation. A clear sense of purpose and an organized system for initiating groups sets the tone. When teachers project security about groups, students feel secure. To achieve this mutual understanding and security, a mini-teach works best.

Implementation. Before initiating writing groups, we conduct a mini-teach on this activity. It answers questions, anticipates problems, and provides a forum for learning.

1. Sit on a low chair in an open area in the classroom.

2. Invite the students to gather around, either on chairs drawn up close or on the carpet.

3. Together talk about group experiences they remember. Discuss why they think they worked in groups, their feelings about groups, the purposes of groups, and so forth.

4. Introduce the group technique to be used, model it with several students, and ask the remaining students to act as observers. Discuss the technique.

5. Divide the students into groups, reiterate where they may group in the room (or outside if that is permissible), and designate the amount of time they have. Caution them to keep time constraints in mind so all group members have time to share.

Remarks. When we begin writing groups this way, we discover invaluable information that helps our direction with writing groups. For example, if the class has consistently grouped in various classes and seems comfortable with the strategy, little else is necessary except to validate that and move into groups. If the class has not grouped for several years, has only grouped in one class, or if the students generally convey negativity or even hostility about groups, it is important to talk through those feelings, do more preparation with the class, and move more slowly into writing groups.

Strategies for Dividing Students into Writing Groups

Number Groups

The easiest and most efficient way to divide a class into groups is to count off. Divide the desired number for each group into the number in the class and count off to that number. For example, if we want groups of four and there are twenty-eight students in the class, we divide four into twenty-eight. The class counts off to seven. All the "ones" form a group, all the "twos," and so forth. This strategy may be used repeatedly. To vary the participants in a group, simply begin the count with a different student each time.

Birthday Groups

A fun way to form groups is by birthdays. Ask all those students who have birthdays in January to raise their hands. They become a group. Follow the same procedure for February, March, and so on. If there are too many in one month, split the group. If there are too few, combine two or even three months. An ancillary effect of this strategy is that students discover others in the class who share their birthday month. This discovery aids bonding among students.

Color Groups

Students pick colors from a box. They find matching colors and group with others who picked the same color. This strategy allows chance to intervene and often produces wonderful interactions.

Genre Groups

Often it is productive to group by genre. For example, all those working on narratives form one group; all those writing letters form another group; all those working on persuasive essays form a third group, and so on. Generally, students working in the same genre share similar problems. Through collaboration, students often find solutions to these problems.

Organic Groups

As students become comfortable with grouping, as trust and respect grow, as they become aware of each other's strengths, we encourage groups to form organically. Students choose others with whom they would like to group. This strategy sends a direct message of trust and mutual respect to students. It also provides one more way for students to make decisions and take responsibility.

Small Groups

Certain categories of writing, specific purposes, or audiences call for small, tight groups. The dyad intensifies the group experience. This may be extended to the double dyad, which allows each one of the two members of the original dyad to regroup, each with a new partner. The double dyads permit each person to receive feedback from two other people but in a structured way.

Triads work well if there is a need to connect ability levels. One student weak in some area, such as coherence or conclusions, teamed with two students strong in these areas multiplies the effectiveness of feedback. Also, the student weak in coherence or conclusions may write dynamic leads or powerful imagery, areas where the other two may show weaknesses.

WRITING CONFERENCES

Writing conferences have come a long way in the past couple of decades as teachers and students have honed the technique. Still, we like Carl Anderson's idea of thinking of them as conversations (6). Woven throughout the writing process, these conversations provide time for students to discuss their writings, so conferring demands active listening on the part of both conferees. Additionally, as Judith Sanders suggests, some 93 percent of what we communicate is nonverbal, so conferring taps the nonverbal and verbal language taking place. Both teachers and students learn that tone, expression, and gestures emerge as significant subtexts of meaning and can be as important as the words spoken.

We recommend, when arranging the room for the conference, clearly stipulating the areas where talk is and is not permitted—no talk in the writing area—small, "one-inch voice" talk in the conference area. Cluster of chairs in the conference area facilitate peer conferences. Two chairs set at an angle close together for teacher and student conversation. Another chair, the "bullpen," nearby allows a nice flow for the conference.

A masking tape demarcation line effectively and visually separates these quiet and whisper areas. One side is quiet; the other side quietly buzzes with active learning.

"The point of a writing conference isn't to get kids to revise. . . . The nature of talk in my writing workshop depends on what a writer needs or what I need as a teacher of writers" (Atwell 88).

Characteristics of Conferences

- Conferences have a purpose.

- Conferences have a structure.

- During conferences, teacher and student pursue a line of thinking.

- Teachers and students have conversational roles in conferences.

- Teachers show students they care about them. (Anderson, 7)

Introducing Writing Conferences

Explanation. Because face-to-face meetings with the teacher deter some students from choosing to confer, we recommend a mini-teach on student-teacher conferences.

Implementation.

1. Gather the students around in a comfortable area of the room.

2. Talk about talk, why we do it, what purpose it serves.

3. Discuss the importance of both student and teacher understanding productive conference

talk. Explain that for a conference to be productive, students should analyze their writing and generate several questions about that writing beforehand. These questions then kick off the conference.

4. Invite students to brainstorm appropriate questions to ask when they come to conference.

5. Model several writing conferences, such as the individual conference, the conference on wheels, the group conference (see explanations of each below). Have students role play.

Remarks. Once students experience a successful writing conference, they usually like the individual attention it provides. They usually appreciate the fact that the teacher is with them during this part of the process, ready to help, advise, and encourage. They also realize this one-on-one conversation helps their writing.

Questions to Bring to Conference

After several sessions with tenth-graders, we divided them into small groups, asked them to look at their writing, and generate questions they might ask in a writing conference. They generated the following list:

*   Is it OK to combine all my prewriting into one piece?

*   How can I stop repeating myself?

*   How will I know which piece will be worth publishing?

*   I don't use any dialogue; what do I do?

*   How do I decide what genre is best?

*   How can I get closure?

*   How did you feel when I read it to you?

*   Help me out of this dead end.

*   Is my piece too trite or too personal for others?

*   How do I know when I'm dragging it out? What's the difference between empty rhetoric, fillers, elaboration, and depth?

*   Am I clear about audience?

*   How do I delete?

*   What about a certain grammar, punctuation, or usage rule?

*   Is it too long? Too short?

*   Did I indent in the right places?

- Did I use enough imagery?

- Is this word spelled correctly?

- My characters won't come alive. Help!

- I need help on my title.

- How do I get this part to hang together?

- Show me how to rewrite this paragraph.

- I think I switched tenses. Did I?

We write these on an anchor chart. We talk about them and display them. Although this list is by no means exhaustive, it serves as a model, stays in the room, and keeps the student who comes to conference from asking, "Is this good?" Also, many of these questions provide fodder for future mini-teaches.

Strategies for Writing Conferences

Individual Writing Conferences

Explanation. Individual conferences take place between one student and the teacher. They usually occur at specific times after prewriting.

Implementation.

1. The teacher sits in a predetermined area alongside an empty but inviting chair.

2. This conference takes place in the "talk area" but a bit removed from the peer conference chairs.

3. Students sign up on a nearby board or chart if they wish a conference.

4. As students complete the conference, they erase or cross out their names and tap the next person on the list. This procedure eliminates students queuing up and keeps talk to a minimum. If the "bullpen" is used, place another chair close to the chair of the conferee. The student next in line for a conference sits in that chair and is able to listen in on the conference. Sometimes, when the second student listens, his or her questions are answered so an individual conference is not required. While this arrangement often helps the time factor, it does limit the privacy of the conferee.

5. After the conversation, students return to their places and work on their writing.

Remarks. While individual conferences allow for intensity and individualization, they are time-consuming. In some cases, students demand so much of the teacher's time, the teacher must dismiss the conferee. In other cases, no matter how nonthreatening the environment, some students remain reluctant to approach the teacher.

Marjorie Woodruff individually confers with her pre-kinder class. After Marjorie read a story about a party, she explained they would have a class Valentine's Day party, but they needed to send out invitations. After much modeling on writing invitations, Marjorie distributed paper, donned a plastic visor, drew a large square in the corner of the chalkboard, wrote in five numbers, and moved toward an area where two kinder chairs were placed side by side. As she did, students went to the board and made marks beside the numbers.

Suddenly one of the four-year-olds tugged at her skirt. "I want a conference," he lisped.

Marjorie stopped, turned to the square on the board, and studied the marks. "I don't see your name on the board, Juan," she said.

Juan also studied the marks. Finally he replied, "It's not there."

"You know the rules, Juan. You must write your name on the board and wait your turn."

With that Marjorie walked to the awaiting chairs and became engrossed in the writing of the first child on the list.

Juan proceeded to the board where he made a series of squiggles next to the number 5.

Not only did Marjorie reinforce a function of writing and her belief that students could and would write, but she demonstrated excellent classroom management.

The Writing Conference on Wheels

Explanation. The most efficient writing conference is the one where the teacher moves to the student. Since the teacher starts the conference, the teacher ends it.

Implementation.

1. The teacher sits in a chair on wheels and simply rolls from student to student.

2. If a student needs immediate help, some agreed-on signal may be used, such as raising hands or putting the writing folder to the left of the desk or table.

3. Students not conferencing may remain comfortably where they are.

Remarks. The rhythm of movement keeps the conference from bogging down. There is an element of surprise. The teacher may meet with more students and may divvy the time according to student needs. If a student is obviously deeply engaged in writing, the teacher may skip that student and return another time.

Small Group Conferences

Explanation. One way to facilitate the writing conference is for the teacher to meet with small groups of students with similar questions or concerns.

Implementation.

1. Begin by asking students how many want to conference.

2. Ask students to identify what they want to discuss during the conference.

3. Invite several to conference who have similar problems or questions.

4. Those students, in turn, read their bothersome sections so that teacher and peers may interact and respond.

5. If the question or concern has been answered to the satisfaction of the student who raised the concern or to the satisfaction of other participating students, they may choose to stay or return to their writing.

Remarks. Small group conferences work much like writing groups except the teacher acts as group leader and major responder. The teacher invites students to raise the questions, then teacher and group respond.

Large Group Conferences

Explanation. During large group conferences, students meet as a class or in groups of ten or more.

Implementation.

1. One student volunteers to share while the other students informally respond.

2. All work together to make the paper better. They offer suggestions, constructive criticism, and ask questions.

Remarks. Large group conferences also work well in classes that are experienced in collaborative learning and have achieved levels of trust with peers.

Fishbowl Conferences

Explanation. Fishbowl conferences are used to "teach students about conferences" (Anderson 2000, 90).

Implementation.

1. One student enters the "fishbowl" (conferences with the teacher in front of the class).

2. Teacher and student confer.

3. Students observe.

4. When the conference is over, they discuss what they noticed.

Remarks. This is an effective method to insinuate the purpose of conferences, practice conference talk, roles, and responsibilities before, during, and after conferences, and a way to coach students.

WRITING DEBRIEFINGS

Definition and Differences

Writing debriefings, called "skull practice," are designated interactive talk times. A few minutes, three to ten, set aside at the close of a lesson or a class period provides invaluable opportunities for students to share thoughts about what they learned, how they learned, and what they think about that learning. Debriefings balance the *what* with the *how* of learning. They are metacognitive—thinking about thinking.

Debriefings differ uniquely from class discussions, during which students state or restate specific information to a logical line of questions. Rather, debriefings permit students to sort out their helter-skelter thoughts, to reflect, to make connections, and to share those connections aloud in a public forum. Students' thinking moves not necessarily inductively or deductively, but abductively. Abductive reasoning is what C. S. Peirce calls thinking that crosses a range of possibilities (Fulwiler 16). It is crablike. Thought-provoking statements or questions raised during debriefings foster abductive reasoning because they enable students to develop analogies, draw inferences, hypothesize, test assumptions, define presuppositions, pose questions, take risks—in short, think out loud.

Oral quizzes are not debriefings. During an oral quiz, the teacher generates a set of questions (usually requiring simple recall answers) to test knowledge. The mode works somewhat like a two-lane roadway: the teacher asks the questions; students answer. An oral quiz on the act I, scenes i and ii of *Macbeth* goes like this: How many witches are in the opening scene? What does *graymalkin* mean? Who is Duncan? What is Malcolm's relationship to Duncan? And so on. While this may serve the teacher's objective on occasion, this activity often degenerates into a flat, one-dimensional exchange with the teacher filling in long gaps of uncomfortable silences and the students making little or no commitment.

Likewise, a true discussion must also be distinguished from a debriefing. In discussion, the teacher sets a purpose but allows for more spontaneity, most often with occasional open-ended questions such as, "Why did Shakespeare open *Macbeth* with three witches?" Clearly, there is a desire to stimulate thinking and invite extensions, but the teacher still leads students to the correct response. Between the question and the answer there may be other conversation or conjecture, but more often than not, after the opening question or two, flags go up as students realize they are being led to the exact answer. Not that class discussions are unproductive or meaningless, not that in some classes a question or concern might spark the group, but much of the time everyone knows the teacher's agenda, so there is a falling off of engagement and answers become perfunctory.

The Purpose of Debriefings

Teachers do not set the purpose for a debriefing because the debriefing is meant to allow students to discover nuances in their own learning, so teachers becomes facilitators.

Examples of Debriefings

Explanation. To enhance diversity, to allow a multiplicity of voices to resonate, the facilitator begins with a global statement or "iffy" question then follows the lead of those being debriefed.

Implementation I. When we conducted a debriefing on *Macbeth*, we asked, "How do think it would change the play if Shakespeare had not included the three witches?"

Students immediately knew that there was no absolutely correct answer; they knew they were being invited to think, to probe, to listen to the answers of others, to entertain possibilities. As the students responded, we listened carefully (students began interacting with each other), making further statements, or asking additional questions that arose authentically from students' responses.

"We would not have gotten that Halloween opener."

"They set everything up."

"I wasn't expecting witches in a play by Shakespeare."

"I was. Didn't they believe in witches then?"

"Weird."

"So what is it about the weird that captures people's interest?" The students began comparing the witches with the bizarre in contemporary novels, television, videos, and films. After a time, we said, "Talk to us, then, about what playwrights need to know when they write." They did.

Implementation II. Another example of debriefing, this time after writing groups, we began, "How are things happening as you write?"

"I'm getting excited because my writing is coming together."

"It was easier today than yesterday. I think it was my attitude, my mood."

"I found myself rehearsing—thinking about it."

"Yeah, I dreamed about it. It's like it's physical or subconscious thinking."

"What have you learned about your writing?" we probed.

"I can't always rewrite."

"I need quiet."

"I often want to overhaul it, take a new direction. It's frustrating sometimes."

"I started a new piece and wrote four pages nonstop, but the other day I couldn't write a thing. It's like you can't force the process."

"There was so much. I was overwhelmed. I had to put it away. It brought up too many memories I can't deal with right now."

"How about the rest of you, are emotions surfacing as you write?" We picked up on that thread, and the debriefing continued.

Remarks. Debriefing resembles Faulkner's method of developing a character, "Once he stands up on his feet and begins to move, all I do is to trot along behind him with a paper and pencil trying to keep up long enough to put down what he says and does, that he is taking charge of it. I have very little to do except be the policeman in the back of the head which insists on unity and coherence and emphasis in telling it. But the characters themselves, they do what they do, not me" (Fant and Ashley 111). Likewise, the teacher begins the debriefing and then trots along behind the students' responses.

Debriefing Guidelines

1. Create an introductory global statement or thought-provoking ("iffy") question.

2. Allow plenty of wait time. Metacognition requires an unpressured, relaxed atmosphere.

3. Listen carefully to responses.

4. Do not cross arms or legs. Body language should invite openness.

5. When students begin interacting, move away from them. That movement encourages them to continue interacting with each other.

6. If someone monopolizes, move to that person, make direct eye contact, then when the student pauses, turn to look at another person.

7. Watch for indicators that someone wants to speak, such as pursed lips, blinking eyes, leaning forward.

8. Build commentary or further questions on responses. Do not lead the debriefing to what you want them to say.

9. Do not come to the debriefing with a set of questions or an agenda.

10. Trust the students' responses to lead you to farther and deeper.

APPLICATION

1. Describe how you would divide a class of twenty-seven ninth-graders for the analytic talk strategy. Give your rationale.

2. Your students have just completed a writing group. There are several minutes remaining before the bell. Write a global "iffy" statement or thought-provoking question to begin a debriefing. Share.

4

GRAMMAR AND CORRECTING

> The fundamental purpose of language is to make sense—to communicate intelligibly. But if we are to do this, we need to share a single system of communication. The rules controlling the way a communication system works are known as its grammar, and both sender and recipient need to use the same grammar if they are to understand each other. If there is no grammar, there can be no effective communication. It is as simple as that.
>
> —David Crystal □

PUNCTUATION, CAPITALIZATION, AGREEMENT, SPELLING

Even after all these years, we remain astonished when we hear people say, "If you teach process, you don't teach grammar." Nothing could be further from the truth. They must mean process teachers don't teach grammar in isolation; they must mean we don't give students reams of mindless worksheets that take up time but do nothing to teach grammar concepts. Because the raw truth is this: Teachers who understand how students learn teach grammar within the writing process. They create environments where students write daily, without threat, and with purpose. These environments result in writing students care about, and because they own it, they are more open to ways to make that writing better. They are ready to learn the grammar necessary to clarify their meaning. They are ready to correct, revise, and reformulate their writing. When students do this, two important things happen: (1) they learn grammar in a context; (2) they—not teachers—mark up and write on their papers. They approach grammar not for the sake of grammar, but to internalize it so it becomes a lifelong skill they may securely call upon when speaking and writing.

Grammar—the rules governing parts of speech, mechanics, punctuation, syntax, function, and structure of a language—is metalinguistic. It is language about language; it is both abstract and difficult. Think about the word *noun*. No one can see, taste, touch, smell, or hear *noun* because *noun* is a designation, an abstract term that names persons, places, things, qualities, and actions. But *noun* is *not* the persons, places, things, qualities, or actions it names.

Even when students learn the seemingly simple *noun*, they must understand how a particular noun works in a particular context. Consider the sentence: *The white house has been painted*. Few would miss *house* as a common noun. However, if capital letters were added: *The White House has been painted*, the new context makes *House* part of a proper noun. With a slight syntactic change, *The White's house their dog with the local vet when they travel*, the word *house* is no longer a noun but a verb.

To truly teach grammar, not assign it or and check workbook exercises, teachers need an understanding of five basics:

1. How language works contextually and structurally;

2. How the brain processes information;

3. How grammar calls upon higher thinking skills, not rote memory;

4. Why teachers should themselves write and understand grammar;

5. That grammar taught concretely first is then understood abstractly.

Teaching grammar demands hands-on strategies that make the abstract concrete so students may correct their own writing not for correction's sake but for meaning's sake.

When students realize thinking provides the basis for analyzing writing and that there are concrete visual ways to tackle making it better, they are primed to start down the path of correcting, revising, and reformulating their writing.

Engaging in grammar analysis, students call upon their ability to abstract, a function that is carried out in the left prefrontal lobe of the brain. Interestingly, that part of the brain develops last—long thought after puberty (Sanders 1985), but now we know that neural circuitry "isn't completely installed in most people until their early 20's" (Brownlee 46). Based on this latest brain research, expecting students to understand grammar abstractly before they work with it often and concretely creates frustration. An outcome of this frustration in teachers is a giving up and giving in to worksheets. In students it translates into low self-esteem; "I can't learn this stuff no matter how hard I try." When grammar is taught abstractly with little application, students, who predictably find it difficult, decide, "I hate grammar." Either way students adopt an attitude debilitating to writing and language development. Teachers who expect students to correct their writing based on rules and abstract terminology lack knowledge about the way learners learn, and the way writers write.

Frank Smith reminds us, "We all know there is a difference between being able to produce language grammatically and being able to talk about its grammar. Most of us can speak or write conventionally without being able to specify the rules. Even the ability to write grammatically does not guarantee that we will understand what a grammarian is talking about" (190).

For students to truly understand grammar and use it correctly in their writing, they must learn it when and where it matters—within the writing process, within a meaningful context, and at developmentally appropriate times. Teachers help students most when they help students get their meaning down, and then help them reenter their writing to correct, revise, and reformulate it.

A BRIEF HISTORY OF GRAMMAR

The Greeks and Romans

To the Greeks and Romans, grammar encompassed the theory of good speech, the study of classical poets, and the methodical study of the elements of language. In the Hellenistic schools, "grammar and composition were reserved for the secondary school at the earliest" (Marrou 218), while in Roman schools "children went on to the grammaticus when they got to the age of eleven or twelve" (Marrou 359). A fitting age, it seems, in light of contemporary brain and cognitive research, since at least one aspect of Latin grammar meant the abstract analysis of letters, syllables, words, parts of speech, and meticulous distinctions and classifications. For instance, nouns at that time were still not separate from adjectives. They were studied according to the six accidents of quality, degree of comparison, gender, number, figure, and case. As knowledge of pedagogy deepened, grammar slowly evolved into actual practice on systemic structure, mechanics, and syntax of the language (Marrou 371–372).

The Middle Ages

By the Middle Ages correctness of language became an end in itself. Little note was taken of common usage or differences. This stress on correctness caused a shift away from the discovery of principles to the transmission of rules. Thus, grammar shifted from strategy to formula.

The Renaissance

Between the years 1500 and 1700 fewer than five million people in the world spoke English. But as England gained supremacy in the world, she standardized her native tongue in order to legitimize it. During the Renaissance, scholars such as Richard Mulcaster and others wrote rules to codify the vernacular. Most often these English scholars used Latin rules as their models. Applying the rules of one language to another explains why even today there are dictums such as "never split an infinitive." In Latin, the infinitive cannot be split since it is one word, but in English the infinitive is formed with two words: *to* plus the verb. Obviously two words may be "split" as in the classic *Star Trek* phrase "to boldly go."

This desire to standardize and legitimize language led to what John R. Trimble calls "literary prudishness" (84) caused by "a puristic concern for the language which gradually rigidified into morbid scrupulosity, through ignorance reinforced by others' ignorance, through a hunger for the security of dogma and absolutes; and some, it would seem, merely through the appeals of snobbery and elitism" (84).

Yet as a dynamic, living language, English is not absolute; it changes with times and purpose. Historically, words wax and wane. For example, rarely does anyone refer to a secretary as an *amanuensis.* Expressions, once fresh, have become cliché or misleading. Using "like two peas in a pod" with this global generation fails. Students more likely conjure a space pod or an iPod, rather than a pea pod. And technology alters conventions in more practical ways. The colon after the salutation in a business letter, although not formally dropped in standard English usage, is often omitted by the computer. Because paper is no longer at a premium, white space often replaces the conventional marks once used to distinguish space, change, or emphasis. In short, English invites natural growth and constant refining to achieve precise communication.

It seems prudent to heed the advice of I. A. Richards, "My suggestion is that it is not enough to learn a language (or several languages), as a man may inherit a business, but that we must learn, too, how it works" (1929, 317). People learn a language and its grammar by using it, grappling with it, writing it, reading it, listening to it, speaking it, being surrounded by multiple levels of it, and by having fun with it. Not only do people learn language best in such rich contexts, but also they come to a deeper appreciation of its power. Conversely, people rarely learn grammar through isolated fragments, mindless worksheets, boring workbooks, meaningless exercises, or mind-dulling drills.

Grammar Today

If teachers wish to avoid mindless isolated grammar drills, they need a new approach to teaching grammar. Realizing how linguistic and social context affects meaning, grammar should be taught within the writing process in three ways: by correcting, through revision, and in reformulating. Correcting focuses on what Janet Emig calls mechanical errors and stylistic infelicities. Revising centers on the sentence as a unit of discourse and will be taken in Chapter 5. Reformulating invites work with larger chunks of the writing—paragraphs, covered in Chapter 6.

Correcting

When students reenter their writing to correct it, they concentrate on punctuation, capitalization, agreement problems, and spelling. Correcting means ridding writing of those niggling distractions, the little things that get in a reader's way of understanding. For example, neglecting to capitalize a proper name may momentarily bewilder a reader. Disregarding commas or putting them anywhere confuses the reader. Adopting the bizarre habit of writing *sp* over a word instead of looking it up signals sloppiness and carelessness. While these mistakes creep in during prewriting or early drafting when students worry about ideas and flow not mechanical precision, they should be corrected before their writing goes public.

To correct is *not* to make deep changes in a paper, but to reenter the paper on behalf of the reader. That is exactly why writers do not concern themselves with correcting too early in the process. Premature attention to minutia often short-circuits the process by interfering with fluency. Writers write. They get their thoughts down. They go with the flow. Then they go back, reenter, and make the writing better.

There are three things to remember when teaching students to correct their writing: (1) begin concretely; (2) move from the concrete to the abstract; (3) create a nonthreatening environment.

Three students met with grammar questions for a small group conference with us. The first two raised simple questions easily answered. That left Donna. "Is the tense right here?" she asked pointing to a sentence that read, "My grandmother had died."

"We don't know," we answered.

"You don't know," she repeated as if she heard incorrectly.

"We don't know."

"You don't know," she stated incredulously.

"We don't know." At this point we wondered how long this would go on.

Donna, now standing arms akimbo, blurted, "Why not?"

We went to the board and wrote had died. *We circled* had, *"This is a signal word. It tells the reader that the action of the accompanying verb took place further back in time than the past action in the narrative. Since we don't know when your grandmother died in relation to the rest of the story, we can't help you out on the tense."*

"Is that why I memorized has, have, had?" *she muttered as she took her seat.*

We met with another group. When the bell rang, Donna came bounding up all smiles, "It's had. *Thanks. I wanted to be right because I'm going to read this to my family at Thanksgiving."*

PUNCTUATION

Punctuation indicates what groups of words belong together and the relationship of those groups. Punctuation also shows what the voice does in speech. Although usually thought of as simple marks, punctuation really is an abstract code. In and of itself, punctuation carries no meaning; rather it enhances meaning. For example, the following line says nothing. !!!,,, . . . ?/?//' . . . {} \\\\' ;;;: (. . .). So when most students look at a comma, for instance, they see a detached mark, something abstract. They often puzzle over it, knowing it belongs in writing, but are rarely certain where to use it or for what purpose. Comments such as, "I don't know where this comma goes" reflect their puzzlement. Teachers may help make these abstract marks more concrete by encouraging students to look at the marks with new eyes—not as difficult marks but as tools that aid meaning, and to use their grammar texts as references not as books of codified rules to be memorized.

"It was at the Alexandria Museum that punctuation and grammar were invented by Aristophanes. Before this, one word ran into the next with no spaces between them. There were no question marks, periods, or exclamation points either. Reading was hard!" (Lasky 24). Since punctuation conveys emphases, pauses, stops, tones, changes in patterns and speakers, omissions, and possessions, using these marks correctly eases reading and clarifies meaning. Working with punctuation in writing, not on worksheets, helps students learn how to use correct punctuation in a context. Frank Smith says, "Far more than spelling, punctuation requires the practice of writing and the confirmation of feedback" (188). Jeff Anderson echoes Smith, "We will save ourselves a lot of frustration if we shift our notion of teaching punctuation and grammar to one of teaching principles instead of rules" (4).

Problems with Punctuation

Students have three basic problems with punctuation: (1) punctuation rules are not absolute, so students become horribly confused and frustrated; (2) punctuation is complex, so memorizing rules in isolation doesn't help; (3) punctuation depends upon the writer's style and intended meaning. Take this simple group of words: *Tom Smith called Sarah Lou is here.* There is no one absolute way to punctuation these words—punctuating them depends entirely upon the writer's meaning. The complexity of punctuation becomes apparent when examining how three different students punctuated these words.

One used quotation marks and commas to indicate that Sarah Lou announces Tom Smith's arrival: "Tom Smith," called Sarah Lou, "is here."

Another used the same marks but in a different way. Sarah tells both Tom and Smith that Lou arrived: "Tom, Smith," called Sarah, "Lou is here."

The third student used colons and two terminals to convey a dramatic purpose: "Tom: Smith called. Sarah: Lou is here."

In truth, *Tom Smith called Sarah Lou is here* may be punctuated over seventy different ways. By using punctuation marks from the exotic virgule, the less popular bracket, the often misunderstood ellipsis, the flamboyant dash, to mundane parentheses, hyphens, apostrophes, commas, quotation marks, colons, semicolons, and the necessary terminals: periods, exclamation and question marks—varieties of meaning emerge. When students try punctuating the words—without changing the order—they come closer to understand how punctuation alters meaning.

Making Punctuation Concrete

The Comma, the Parentheses, and the Dash

Explanation. One way we make punctuation concrete so that students understand the concept, is to use the same group of words *Tom Smith called Sarah Lou is here* and concentrate on how the comma, the parentheses, and the dash change the meaning. We teach this concretely by way of comparisons.

Implementation.

- Commas. We compare the comma to a small, thin sliver—a disc that may be slid into a sentence to cause a pause: *Tom Smith, called Sarah Lou, is here.* Here the comma simply sets off a nonrestrictive phrase *called Sarah Lou* as basically nonessential information. The main clause *Tom Smith is here* conveys the important information.

- Parentheses. Role playing the parentheses as curved hands placed by the mouth, we point out that parentheses captures whispers or asides: *Tom Smith (called Sarah Lou) is here.* Here the parentheses enclose supplemental material that invites an inference.

- The dash. For the dash, made by striking two hyphens on keyboard, we use a flashing neon light as an apt comparison. We open and close our hands palms out, saying, "Wa Wa": *Tom Smith—called Sarah Lou—is here.* We ask students to picture a flashing neon sign in an out-of-the-way spot, and then picture one in Las Vegas. The former sign stands out; it is noticeable. The latter goes unnoticed because it blurs into so many other flashing signs. Because the dash emphasizes parenthetical information, thinking of it as a visual neon sign reminds students to use it sparingly.

Remarks. Consider the difference between teaching punctuation by comparison, by modeling, with a bit of humor, or by discussing it as opposed to reading definitions out of a text or distributing worksheets. The first ways challenge the brain because the students "work" the concepts; the other ways deaden the brain.

Quotation Marks

Explanation. Quotation marks set off direct speech and information cited from other sources. While students rarely have difficulty using quotation marks when excerpting information, they do have trouble using them in dialogue. The difficulty arises when they try to distinguish between direct and indirect statements. We read the two sentences:

My dad told me to go to the store.

My dad told me, "Go to the store."

as we project them on the overhead. "Both say the same thing," students say, so because they have trouble distinguishing between them, they mispunctuate them.

In this case, Dad wouldn't say, "To go to the store." Those would not be his direct words. Students catch that subtlety when they visualize the words emanating from lips rather than thinking of the marks as one more rule to learn. Eventually that concrete connection becomes internalized.

For students to understand the subtle difference between these two sentences, they must grasp the difference between saying something directly and saying something indirectly; they must realize the necessity of signaling the reader that dialogue is occurring; they must know the punctuation tools to accurately send that signal.

Implementation.

1. We focus the lesson by asking students to find direct dialogue in a story they are studying—by looking for quotation marks. They turn that dialogue into drama when we ask them to "play the parts."

2. Then in small groups we ask them to rework the story by omitting the quotation marks and indirectly saying everything in them. Together we discuss the differences.

3. To apply this concept in writing, we project a piece of writing, usually ours, on the overhead as a model. Together we look for places where indirect words may be replaced with the direct words. Then we discuss what punctuation tools we need to make our revision clear for the reader.

4. To imprint quotation marks for students, we engage them in this bit of dialogue, adapted from Kelley R. Smith [Barger] (28–29):

    "What moves when we talk?"

    "Our mouth."

    "What part of our mouth?"

    "Our lips."

    "So when we speak, others can see our lips moving as well as hear us talking. But when someone reads your writing, they cannot see nor hear the characters speak. If not punctuated correctly, a reader could think you are telling *about* what a character says. So some genius contrived a perfect way to signal direct speech—as two little lips. The two marks in quotation marks represent two lips. If you think of quotation marks as lips, you will remember to use them when one of your characters starts and stops speaking. By punctuating direct dialogue correctly, your reader will see and hear the words of the character."

5. Students reenter their writing and correct it for quotation marks. Then we move on to the attendant punctuation marks used with quotation marks: the comma to introduce the quotation and terminal marks that go inside the "little lips."

Remarks. Since quotation marks resemble lips and serve a like function, this concrete analogy acts as a reminder for students to use quotation marks while at the same time clarifying the intent of the writer for the reader. Even on the high school and college level, thinking of little lips can save students from what reads as "verbal diarrhea" when they forget to close their quotation marks.

More on Commas

Explanation. Commas mark slight separations, short pauses, and relationships between and among grammatical units. Corder and Ruszkiewicz contend, "About two-thirds of all punctuation marks used are commas" (199). But the comma, one of the weakest punctuation marks, yet one indispensable for determining meaning, bedevils students.

Confounded by what to do with this mark, students usually deal with comma decisions in one of two ways. Some simply use the "salt and pepper" method. Because they know commas belong in writing, they sprinkle them in so the paper "looks good." Other students close their eyes, put their papers in the hands of fate, and insert a comma wherever their pointing index finger falls. It is as if they consider learning the number of comma rules (more than ten, most with one or more exceptions) some cosmic overload so overwhelming they resort to sheer serendipity.

Making the Comma Concrete

Making the comma concrete helps students' comprehension. While not foolproof or totally inclusive, implementing this approach moves students into some degree of security accompanied with some depth of control.

1. Define three or four most-used reasons for the comma.

2. Provide a visual to make each reason concrete.

3. Give the model sentence as an example.

4. Invite students to reenter their writing to find an example for each reason on the chart. Write several of these on the board or a chart and discuss.

5. Students then reenter their papers to reevaluate their use of commas by comparing each of their sentences to the visual models and example sentences. When they come upon an exception, they consult their grammar books. Hence, both the teaching of the comma and the subsequent correcting take place in a real context.

Making the Comma Relevant

Making the comma relevant is another way to help students see their importance in writing.

1. Share an example such as the story of the million-dollar comma.

   The United States government lost a fortune because of a comma. A tariff passed in 1872 contained a list of duty-free items that read, "Fruit plants, tropical and semitropical." A clerk accidentally altered the line, "Fruit, plants tropical and semitropical." Those importing contended that the passage with its misplaced comma, exempted all tropical and semitropical plants from duty fees. They won.

2. The Newbery Award winner *The Higher Power of Lucky* by Susan Patron presents another example in context. Lucky's friend Lincoln takes umbrage with a traffic sign in the neighborhood that reads:

   SLOW

   CHILDREN

   AT

   PLAY

He complains that people reading the sign will think, " 'Slow children. Kids around here aren't too smart.' Or else they'll think, 'Gosh, these Hard Pan kids don't move too fast. Must be 'cause of the heat'" (23). So Lincoln remedies the sign by putting "two neat perfect-size dots, one like a period and the other a little above it (23)" next to the word *slow.*

Table 4.1. Sample Comma Chart

1. Insert a comma between two independent clauses (sentences) that are joined with a coordinating conjunction.

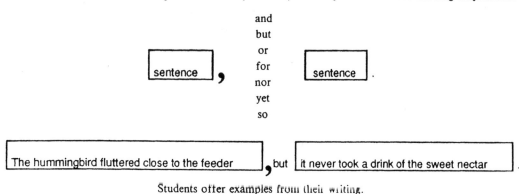

Students offer examples from their writing.

2. Use a comma after a long introduction at the start of a sentence.

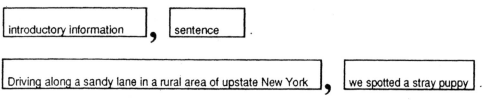

Students offer examples from their writing.

3. Use two commas to set off "grammatically unnecessary" information from the rest of the sentence.

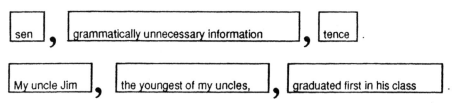

Students offer examples from their writing.

4. Use a comma after each item in a series.

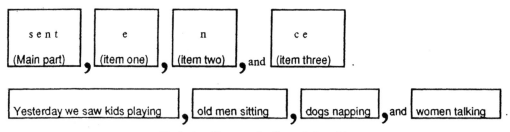

Students offer samples from their writing.

From *Acts of Teaching*, 2nd Edition, by Joyce Armstrong Carroll and Edward E. Wilson. Westport, CT: Teacher Ideas Press/Portsmouth, NH: Heinemann. Copyright © 2008.

Consider all the possible mini-teaches this excerpt presents:

a. **Adjectives/Adverbs.** The word *slow,* usually an adjective, is not used as an adjective on the traffic sign but is meant to be read as the adverb in the sense of the imperative "go slowly" or as the verb in the phrase "slow down."

b. **Imperative Sentences/Inferences.** The imperative—*you*—understood with the verb *drive* or *slow* inferred.

c. **Run-On Sentences.** *Slow children are playing.*

d. **Punctuation/Colon/Comma/Period.** Slow: Children at play. Slow, children at play.

3. Students find other examples of commas or other punctuation marks that cause confusion, such as in Lynne Truss's *Eats, Shoots & Leaves,* or they create ways commas might cause problems. They choose examples from sports, law, concert groups, money, business, school rules, or any aspect of everyday life. Share and discuss.

Cognitively moving from the concrete to the abstract is as difficult for students as moving from the abstract to the concrete is for teachers. Once a concept has become abstract, thinking of ways to make it concrete for students becomes a challenge for teachers, but a challenge worth the effort. Herbert Ginsburg and Sylvia Opper, scholars of the work of Jean Piaget, suggest one of the prime implications from Piaget for educators is that "children learn best from concrete activities" (221). Further, they state that "when the teacher tries to bypass this process by imparting knowledge in a verbal manner, the result is often superficial learning" (Ginsburg and Opper 221).

Students need plenty of models and plenty of practice to see that "all these tiny scratches give us breadth and heft and depth. A world that has only periods is a world without inflections. It is a world without shade. It has a music without sharps and flats. It is a martial music. It has a jackboot rhythm. Words cannot bend and curve. . . . Punctuation, then, is a matter of care. Care for words, yes, but also, and more important, for what the words imply" (Iyer 80).

Hands-On Cartoon Punctuation

Cartoons are wonderful to teach the skill of writing dialogue. We first saw a version of this lesson in Terry Sample's third-grade classroom and found it so effective, we have adapted it to work for all levels.

Teaching Dialogue through Cartoons

Explanation. Cartoons are a novel and effective strategy to teach the skill of writing dialogue. They have all the necessary ingredients to remind students of what they generally forget when they attempt to write dialogue. Students tend to write dialogue without characters' descriptions, such as facial expressions or body language, or the actions of the characters, such as screaming, running, moving away from, accosting, and so forth.

Implementation.

• For the model lesson, pick a cartoon with only two characters speaking. After students learn the concept, challenge students to use cartoons with more characters. We find *Baby Blues* and *One Big Happy* excellent choices. They are kid-friendly and present topics from which students can pull to fill in the missing information. Students usually read these, so they know all the characters' names from prior editions.

- Use four different-colored sentence strips. On one colored sentence strip write the dialogue of the first speaker in the first frame. On another colored strip write the dialogue of the second speaker.

- Tape these strips on a wall. Run them together.

- Through questions, lead students to discover that even though the sentence strips are different colors, the reader has no idea who is speaking.

- This inductive questioning enables a lesson on tags. Reserve the third colored sentence strip for tags, "he said/she said" or the specific name, for example, "Joe said/Ruthie said."

- Lead students to the realization of the importance of using specific names.

- At this point, we have seen some teachers engage students in lessons burying the word *said*. We prefer teachers point out that professional writers use *said* all the time. To constantly use a synonym distracts from the meaning. Even more unfortunate are the well-meaning teachers who forbid the repetition of *said,* and who insist that students substitute not only a synonym but also an adverb, for example, " 'Look,' she excitedly expressed." Instead, we recommend showing students what real writers do. They make sure the dialogue and the exposition around the dialogue conveys the excitement. While professionals may occasionally use a synonym, the dialogue doesn't read contrived. This makes for much better writing.

- We recommend several pages—124–127—from Stephen King's *On Writing*. King says, "The best form of dialogue attribution is *said,* as in *he said, she said, Bill said, Monica said*" (127).

- When we do this lesson, we keep lots of tape and many pairs of scissors handy because we show students how to manipulate the text.

- Remove the first frame. Ask the students, "Just read the dialogue. Do you have a clear idea what is happening in the frame?" The answer is always no.

- Use the fourth colored sentence strip to revise. Students become actively engaged as they suggest adding sentences describing the setting, explaining the action, and supplying the visual details in the cartoon.

Model Lesson. This is an approximate transcription of the lesson on the first frame only. Of course, there were more teacher probings and more student offerings, but the following captures the spirit of the lesson.

Teacher: We are going to do a lesson on punctuation today, but we're going to do it in a different way. How many of you like cartoons?

Students: (All hands go up.)

Fig. 4.1. Baby Blues Comic Strip.

Teacher: Let's all read this one *Baby Blues.* (Read and talk about it.) I wrote the dialogue on these two different colored sentence strips. Let's put them on the board and look at them. What should we do with this first sentence strip of dialogue? (Mommy, what do you think I should wear to school today?)

Students: Put it in quotation marks.

Teacher: Good. And the second sentence strip of dialogue? (Well, let's see . . .)

Students: Put that in quotation marks, too.

Teacher: Now let's read what we have here. If you didn't have the cartoon in front of you would that be totally clear?

Students: Well, we don't know who is speaking. It could all be Zoe speaking.

Teacher: What shall we do?

Students: Let's put the names like Zoe asked and Mommy said.

Teacher: Good idea. Let's add that.

(At this point, the students are pleased with themselves and eager to move on.)

Teacher: Is there another way we can show that two different people are speaking?

Students: (Lots of thinking—finally someone suggests a different line and someone else remembers that in books the author shows a different speaker by making a new paragraph. Eventually, they get to the notion of indention.)

Teacher: I was just wondering if someone didn't have that cartoon, if they would get the full picture—like where this dialogue happened, or even how the characters felt. Should we add some background information?

Students: Well, it's her bedroom.

Teacher: Whose?

Students: Zoe's.

Teacher: How do you know that? Did you infer?

Students: It's got little hearts and pink stripes. That doesn't look like a grown-up's bedroom.

Teacher: I think that is a good inference.

Students: And the closet shows small clothes.

Teacher: Do you think if we added some of those details it would help the reader?

Students: Yes, and we should put that Mommy is looking in the closet—with her finger to her chin.

Teacher: What does that mean?

Students: She's thinking.

Teacher: Is there any other clue that she is thinking?

Students: Those little dots.

Teacher: Those are called ellipses. When an author uses ellipses that means some words are left out, so those left out words could be something Mommy is thinking but not saying. Good.

And so on . . .

Teacher: Now I am going to assign the remaining frames to you to work on in groups. I will give each group a big sheet of butcher paper upon which to write out your frame just the way we did it together in my model.

After the groups have finished, display each group's work in the same order as the frames appear in the cartoon. Read through each and encourage commentary from other groups. The students' written exposition should provide readers with a mental picture of what the cartoonist captured.

Remarks. This is powerful learning. Hands-on cartoon punctuation allows teachers not only to teach punctuation, but also to include myriad other mini-teaches.

One of the best moments during this lesson is when students realize indenting each time the speaker changes makes everything clearer and easier to understand. Students bring in their favorite cartoons for subsequent lessons. In this way, teachers cover every skill connected to dialogue, craft, accuracy, specificity, and plain good writing. With good pedagogy grounded in sound theory, teachers trust the learning of the learners.

CAPITALIZATION

Writing, an agreed-upon system of symbols to convey thoughts and feelings, was for centuries considered a gift from the gods. As far as scholars can determine, "the process began in ancient Mesopotamia . . . around the 3rd millennium B.C." (Jean 12). But capital letters did not evolve until sometime around the fifth century B.C. when the Greek alphabet used uppercase straight letters for inscriptions in stone or metal, more rounded lowercase letters for writing on papyrus, wax tablets, hide, or later parchment (Gaur 119–121). Because the rounded lowercase letters were easier to form, they were chosen for books and documents. The more difficult uppercase letters were reserved for beginning new thoughts, headings, and formal work—to signify something important. Rules did not control that choice, efficiency did.

Problems with Capitalization

Most rhetoricians agree change is the only constant. Tradition held the first word in each line of poetry be capitalized. If contemporary poets followed that convention, their poetry would strike the eye as archaic. *The Little, Brown Handbook* offers classic advice on capitals, "Writers generally agree on when to use capitals, but the conventions are constantly changing. Consult a dictionary if you have any doubt whether a particular word should be capitalized" (Fowler 320).

The major rationale for the use of capitals is specificity. They mark beginnings of new thoughts, titles, headings; indicate *I* and *O* when they stand alone; and designate proper nouns and adjectives. Therein lies the rub—what students consider specific, for example, "their" baseball game, is not.

Classifying general (common) and specific (proper) is difficult for younger students. Often exacerbated by the "dumbing down" of textbooks, sophisticated precise words are replaced with unsophisticated ones; terms are oversimplified, often to the detriment of meaning; examples and illustrations are silly and unchallenging. In this context, textbook publishers use common nouns as proper ones. They merely capitalize the species, for example, *cat* as *Cat*. Students, who are visual learners or those who are unclear about the use of capital letters, find this confusing. On the one hand, they are told cat is a common name that may be applied to any animal in that genus: tigers, lions, and panthers. On the other hand, they read a story where the main character, a feline, is specifically addressed as Cat by the other animals in the story.

Recently while working with administrators from a large urban school district, we shared Heather Mitchell's "The Meanest Sub." We used her writing to talk about the abuse of worksheets, among other things. The following day, one of the principals brought us a first-grade workbook page on time sequence. There were three sentences on the page in random order. The students were to number them according to the time sequence in the story.

One sentence read: Spider moves to where Dog lives. Another read: Sara does not see Spider.

Clearly *Dog* and *Spider* are used as the proper names of two characters. Little wonder when we share this workbook page with teachers, especially those in middle and high school, several always exclaim, "I'm beginning to understand why my kids are confused about what to capitalize!"

And someone always asks, "Why did the author make the animal's class its name? Now kids have something to unlearn and that's harder."

We can offer no response.

Making Capital Letters Concrete

To someone learning a written symbolic code, as with a young child learning to write English, signals within that code appear complicated. After all, children delight in simply making marks. To a three-, four-, or five-year-old, a letter is a letter is a letter (to paraphrase Gertrude Stein), so to make one or several on a blank page is a feat, one worthy of celebration.

Actually grasping the concept *letter*, then *words* is a cognitive feat. When that endeavor is coupled with *uppercase* and *lowercase* distinctions along with rules that govern their use, the concept moves from complicated to confusing. To reduce the confusion and heighten the learning, we recommend teaching capitalization as concretely as possible. Following are five ways to accomplish that.

Naming

Explanation. One of the best ways to make capitals concrete is through the process of naming. Since students understand that they have a name, logically begin there.

Implementation.

1. Divide students into Group I and II. Distribute name tags. Each student in Group I writes in lowercase letters the word that describes their category: *boy/girl*. Each student in Group II writes in uppercase letters his or her specific proper name: *Roberto*, *Maryanne*.

2. Call on students according to their name tags. Talk about the problems that arise from being too general. Who should answer from a group of girls if *girl* is called, for instance? (This is a good time to discuss how people feel when addressed *boy* or *girl*.)

3. Lead students to understand why specific designations are needed and why capital letters are used to show these designations. Follow this line of thinking by extending naming to buildings, books, days of the week, months of the year, and other general and specific persons, things, or events within their experience.

4. Conclude by challenging students to create general and specific lists of things, people, and events in and around the school and the community.

5. Share and discuss. Once again the teaching must take place within a context.

Remarks. Because this strategy builds on ownership and identity, it is effective.

Capital Searches

Explanation. Working with books is another concrete way to teach capital letters.

Implementation.

1. Divide students into groups. Assign a time limit for book exploration.

2. Each group generates a list of words from the books that start with capital letters, excepting the first word in sentences.

3. Post these lists.

4. Follow with a class analysis of the words. This analysis forms the basis for generalizations about capital letters.

5. Together write these generalizations. Then compare those of the class with those in textbooks and handbooks. Discuss.

Remarks. Marrying reading and writing enhances both. Students see how capital letters are used by authors in books and how they should be used in their own writing. This is also a great strategy for generalization.

"Capitalizing" on Hyperbole

Explanation. Making abstract concepts concrete through hyperbole is fun.

Implementation.

1. Divide students into dyads, groups of two.

2. Each pair generates a story packed with titles and proper names, *which they write in lowercase letters*. Their stories should make sense, may be funny, but must contain all the elements of a narrative.

3. After writing, the dyads combine to form groups of four.

4. They exchange stories and correctly capitalize titles and proper names in each other's stories.

5. Conclude with a discussion about the function of capital letters.

Remarks. Exaggeration helps students learn because it is novel and outlandish. Because students also perceive telling stories as fun, combining hyperbole with narrative nails the concept.

Derivation Digs

Explanation. Encouraging middle- and high-school students to collect derivatives often makes the abstract concrete.

Implementation.

1. Students research words such as *sandwich* or *wisteria*. The former describes the eating habits of an earl from the geographical region of Sandwich, England; the latter describes beautiful bunches of lavender flowers named after Caspar Wistar, an American anatomist. For a list of other words, see "Words Borrowed from Names" in *The Reading Teacher's Book of Lists* by Fry, Kress, and Fountoukidis.

2. Students form groups. Each group creates a list of words with interesting derivations from proper names or places.

3. Groups share lists and discuss how common words such as *cereal* evolve from proper names such as *Ceres*, the Roman goddess of agriculture.

Remarks. This strategy fosters inquiry, develops vocabulary, and helps students understand the function of capitalization.

Sentence Checks

Explanation. It is a fact: Visuals help us remember. Advertisers know this, and it is especially true for young children.

Implementation.

1. Give each student a red crayon and a green crayon.

2. Students use their green crayons to signal capital letters at the beginning of sentences in their own writing. They use their red crayons to signal terminal marks.

3. Students circle the first letter of the first word in each sentence in green.

4. They read until they reach a terminal mark. They circle that mark in red.

5. They circle the first letter in the first word that follows that mark. They continue this procedure throughout their writing. If they only have one terminal mark in the entire piece of writing, they need to ratiocinate for sentences.

Remarks. Capital letters are relatively recent arrivals in the history of written language. Young children use them much the way they were used historically—to point out something or someone important or to draw attention to something. Consider the four-year-old who writes MOMMY or the second-grade student who titles his book THE SPOKEY HOUS and writes Chapter 1 in capital letters—GOBLEN. Once again, students gain control over the convention of the capital letter when they write and read often and when they are surrounded by a print-rich environment. Teachers use that rich language to teach the convention. Then students use what they learn about the convention to correct their own writing.

AGREEMENT

Agreement of subject and verb means that singular nouns and pronouns take singular verbs and plural nouns and pronouns take plural verbs. When that happens, subjects *agree,* or fit with, the verbs. Agreement of pronoun and antecedent means that the pronoun is the same form as its antecedent—that is, it matches it in gender, number, and case.

Discussing agreement between subjects and verbs and pronouns and antecedents is a perfect example of metalinguistic abstraction—language about language. Abstract terms such as *agreement, subjects, verbs, pronouns,* and *antecedents* become confused with terms such as *number, person,* and *gender.* Even the word *take* assumes some heightened meaning. While grammarians revel in this terminology; students writhe in it. Therefore, we emphasize once again that teachers who teach agreement within the context of the students' writing find that students' comprehension deepens and they are able to correct their writing accordingly.

Problems of Agreement Between Subject and Verb

There are three major difficulties with teaching subject/verb agreement:

1. The inability to distinguish between nouns and verbs. Even if students understand that distinction, a second problem surfaces.

2. The singular verb looks plural. If students have learned that adding an *s* makes a noun plural—*flower/flowers, boy/boys*—they have difficulty understanding why adding *s* to a verb makes it singular—*make/makes, speak/speaks.*

3. When students have difficulty in identifying the subjects of sentences, they are confused when a word or phrase intervenes between the subject and the verb. Because students have not internalized the abstract concept of *subject*, they make the verb agree with the closest noun or pronoun. If a prepositional phrase that sounds plural comes between a single subject and its verb, students choose the plural verb. Consider the sentence: *The book about animals and birds provides many interesting facts.*

Students who identify the words *animals* and *birds* as nouns and automatically as subjects write: "The book about animals and birds provide many interesting facts."

Instead of correctly identifying the noun *book* as the singular subject, they opt for the word *birds*. Thus they get the verb incorrect. The problem is not agreement; the problem lies in comprehending the subject of a sentence.

Making Subject/Verb Agreement Concrete

The Hands-On Triptych

Explanation. The triptych comes from ancient hinged three-leaved tablets and three-paneled tapestries. Because people had no means for hanging one enormous picture, they would divide it into three sections so that each section could be hung individually. By mounting them close together on a wall, the picture could be viewed as a whole.

Implementation.

1. Students create several triptychs. They write a singular or plural subject—noun or noun phrase or pronoun—in the first section, a verb or verb phrase that agrees with their subject in the second section, and a prepositional phrase in the third section. They make sure the neck and tail fit the designated space so when one student's triptych is bound with others, there is a consistency of graphic and sentence parts.

2. They make certain their words or phrases fit in the correct section and that words do not cross the vertical line separating each section.

3. Staple several triptychs together across the top of the triptych. Cover with bright tape.

4. Use a paper cutter to cut along the lines.

5. Working in small groups, students flip the sections to read different sentences.

6. They identify ones that do not agree.

7. Share on an anchor chart conclusions drawn from this strategy.

Fig. 4.2. Subject/Verb Agreement Triptych Outline.

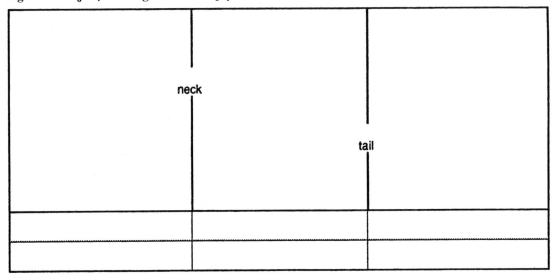

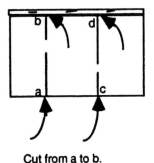

Staple and tape at top. Leave
1/2" strip at top uncut.

Cut from a to b.
Cut from c to d.

Remarks. Using the triptych not only provides a concrete way to apply subject/verb agreement, but it also reinforces the application in three ways: through writing, through silent and oral reading, through aural learning. While drawing lines from subject to predicate or vice versa, a common practice in many grammar handbooks, may help students see connections, the triptych provides a way to practice while making the concept concrete.

Problems of Agreement Between Pronouns and Antecedents

The major difficulty with teaching pronoun/antecedent agreement is the meaning of the meta-linguistic term *antecedent*. This concept could be simplified by explaining that when pronouns take the place of a noun they should match the noun they are replacing—*Jack/he, tree/it, videos/ they.* We recommend forgoing the abstract terms *antecedent, gender, number,* and *case* until the concept has been learned concretely.

Making Pronoun/Antecedent Agreement Concrete

The Match Game

Explanation. Help students think of pronoun/antecedent agreement by providing practice in matching pronouns.

Implementation.

1. Divide students into two teams. Each team generates a list of nouns. For example:

Team 1	Team 2
Nouns	Nouns
Mary	crowd
family	members
boss	academy
Mr. Smith	campus
committee	group

2. Teams exchange lists. For each noun, each team writes a pronoun that correctly replaces it. For example:

Team 1	Team 2	Team 2	Team 1
Nouns	Pronouns	Nouns	Pronouns
Mary	she	crowd	it
families	they	members	they
boss	he/she	academy	it
Mr. Smith	he	campus	it
committee	it	group	it

3. Share results. Discuss.

Remarks. Consult a good handbook for any other agreement problems, such as those based on exceptions. Expecting students to hold all the rules of grammar, usage, and spelling along with exceptions in their heads is tantamount to expecting them to learn all the synonyms in a thesaurus or all the definitions in a dictionary. Grammar handbooks should be regarded as references and students should be taught to use them for this purpose.

SPELLING

We wrote *ghoti* on the board. "What does this spell?" We asked a group of administrators who had expressed deep concern over parental complaints about the teaching of spelling in their schools.

Several volunteered, "ghetto," "ghostly," "gouty," "goatee."

"No, no, no, no. It spells fish."

They were dumbfounded, so we explained: *gh* as in enough; *o* as in women; *ti* as in ambition. *Fish.*

We continued, "There are thirteen spellings for *sh*: *shoe, sugar, issue, mansion, mission, nation, suspicion, ocean, conscious, chaperone, schist, fuchsia,* and *pshaw*. Now let's talk about spelling."

These administrators represent many who express genuine concern over what they regard as a deterioration of skills such as spelling, but who suffer from the ten myths J. Richard Gentry enumerates and then debunks in his book *Spel . . . Is a Four Letter Word*:

1. Spelling is serious business. Everyone must learn to spell.

2. People who can't spell are ignorant.

3. Spelling is supposed to be difficult.

4. Spelling errors should not be tolerated.

5. Good teachers reduce marks for poor spelling.

6. Good spellers memorize a lot of information.

7. Good spellers master a lot of rules.

8. To become good spellers, kids have to do hundreds of spelling book exercises and drills.

9. The most important thing about spelling is making 100% on spelling tests.

10. Spelling is right or wrong. Good teachers always correct spelling. (8)

Problems with Spelling

Inconsistencies, Inadequacies, and Usage

The English spelling system, both complex and inconsistent, reflects the influence of other languages: *sleigh* from the Dutch, *bayou* from the French, *stampede* from the Spanish. As if that doesn't bollix up spelling and pronunciation, factor in an alphabet about fourteen letters short of all the letters it needs for the sounds it uses. That is why letters are doubled to create necessary sounds—*au, th,* and so forth. Then there is the troublesome habit in English of varying spelling according to the sound's position as in *judge* not *juj* because English words do not end in the letter *j*. Another problem surfaces with arbitrary usage unconnected to rules, for example *basically*, pronounced *basicly*.

Homonymic Problems

Homonyms, homophones, homographs, heteronyms, and near misses also cause spelling problems. Homonyms have come to include homophones (same sound—*add* in math; *ad* short for advertisement) and homographs (same spelling—*angle* in math; *angle* to fish but different meanings). Heteronyms are homographs that are spelled the same and have different meanings but are pronounced differently (*bass*, a low male voice; *bass*, a fish). Near misses are words that sound similar or have confusing characteristics but have different meanings (*picture*, a drawing; *pitcher*, a container). These anomalies confuse adult spellers. We have a day-by-day calendar that presents one of these demons every day, for example, *apart/a part*—paradoxically, the one-word form implies separation while the two-word form implies union. Imagine how they confuse the young speller, especially the beginning speller. Consider young writers coming to words such as: *reign, rain; air, heir*, and some 385 others.

Silent Letters

Then silent letters give students grief—the *u* in *guide*, the *e* in *save*, the *p* in *pneumonia* to name just a few (Wilde 14–16). While all this makes for interesting reading, it proves discouraging for students in the throes of gaining control over the act of writing itself: to make meaning, to reason through the complexity of clarifying that meaning, to observe the conventions of language and of writing, and finally to deal with standardized spelling.

Literate Spellers

While no one expects everyone to know how to spell every word, literate people are expected to have a repertoire of words they are able to spell correctly. First-graders have their first-grade spelling, fourth-graders their fourth-grade spelling, and so forth.

Recently to focus a lesson for teachers on developmental writing and constructed spelling, we administered a spelling "test." We dictated *kinesis, pneumatic, mnemonic, inveigle, ukulele, maieutic*, and *hemorrhage*. Clearly these are not words teachers use daily, so everyone misspelled at least one of the words.

After the "test" we shared how we go about spelling a word we do not know. We applied our answers to what we know about how students go about spelling a word. We agreed that without spell check and ready access to dictionaries—both computer and book—without someone to ask—we resort to trial and error, how the word looks when written, how it feels as we write it, or we try to sound it out. The last method wreaked havoc with the words on the "test."

Interestingly, as far back as 1837, Sir Isaac Pitman worked for spelling reform. He believed all language should be written phonetically, just like his shorthand system. In 1940, the British Simplified Spelling Society lobbied for simplified spelling. George Bernard Shaw bequeathed much of his fortune to the cause of more rational spelling. Yet aside from minor changes, such as *colour* to *color* and *theatre* to *theater*, "new generations of school children are still grappling with a spelling system that dates back to William Caxton" (McCrum, Cran, and MacNeil 47).

Letters to Parents and Caregivers

Because concern about spelling is a reality and because a person's intelligence and ability are often measured by the way someone spells, it is imperative to be realistic about spelling and the teaching of spelling. Dismissing it or obsessing over it are dangerous extremes. Teachers who understand the dynamics of spelling within the larger writing process use sensible strategies to foster spelling skills.

At the outset of the school year, send home a letter that details how you will teach spelling. This greatly reduces repeated individual conferences on the topic, or misunderstandings about why spelling is being integrated with other language arts and other subjects.

Primary School Spellers

Primary teachers explain how children learn to spell, provide several examples of development from scribbles through transitional spelling, updates, and assure parents and caregivers spelling will be taken through rich writing and reading activities. They assure them if their five-year-old spells *was* as *woze* or *wus*, that is not indication poor spelling that will remain with the child throughout his or her lifetime.

These teachers avoid the term *invented spelling*. While used and understood in academe, it carries the connotation of "anything goes" and creates unnecessary concern for others. Using terms such as *kinder spelling*, or *first-grade spelling* when referring to words students use but do not yet own, words that are still in the developmental stage, words such as *wr* for *were* go far in helping those outside academe to understand.

Intermediate School Spellers

Intermediate teachers focus their letters to parents and caregivers on how they teach spelling within the writing and reading processes through word lists, word banks, and other strategies. They explain how students learn to designate their personal spelling "demons" by keeping word lists. They clarify how they explore spelling patterns and rules that work, and how they teach spelling as part of proofreading and editing skills. In these letters, teachers give examples of the more consistent spelling rules, such as doubling the final consonant before adding *-ed* or *-ing* if a word ends in a single vowel and single consonant.

Middle and High School Spellers

Middle school and high school teachers inform parents and caregivers that spelling is still an important skill. Because students are older and more independent, and because teachers at this level want to promote skills that students will be able to apply all their lives, teachers emphasize the value of proofreading: the ability to spot misspellings, strategies for figuring out how to spell words, and using such devices as spell check, hand-held computer spellers, and dictionaries, including those that list words phonetically, such as *Webster's New World Misspeller's Dictionary* (Guralnik), *The Bad Speller's Dictionary* (Krevisky and Linfield), or *Webster's Bad Speller's Dictionary* (Wileman and Wileman).

After working three weeks with a class of inner-city sixth-grade students on narratives, we were ready to write our stories into our books. We were using only the highest quality paper. We had invited the librarian in to show us the proper way to format the library cards and affix pockets to the last page. We wanted our books to be as fine as those we had read during our study. The time was perfect for a mini-teach on proofreading for spelling. The students knew they would have real audiences for their books, and they wanted them to be good. Never were dictionaries consulted more often; never were dictionaries read more closely.

Making Spelling Concrete

Four Spelling Rules

Explanation. As long ago as 1932, Leonard B. Wheat found that only four spelling rules are consistent enough to teach: doubling consonants, changing *y* to *i*, dropping the final *e* before suffixes, and writing *i* before *e* except after *c*.

Implementation.

1.   Students memorize these four rules.

2.   Divide students into four groups. Each group takes a different rule and finds examples of that rule in their writing and in their literature.

3.   Students reenter their writing to check and correct the spelling of words by applying these four rules.

4.   Share. Discuss.

Remarks. The beauty of this strategy is it makes learning the four rules doable. The side effect is students make immediate application in their writing and in their reading. Collaboration also enhances the strategy.

Develop Mnemonic Devices

Explanation. After students learn mnemonic devices to remember common spelling demons, they design some for their personal spelling demons.

Implementation.

1.   Teach two examples of mnemonic devices:

   * remember *dessert* has two letters *s*, like the dessert strawberry shortcake;

   * remember *there* is a place because it has *here* in it; *their* is a person because it has *heir* in it; *they're* is a contraction because it has an apostrophe.

2.   Students choose several words from their individual spelling lists. They create a mnemonic device for those words.

3.   Share.

Remarks. Teachers often vary this idea by adding a visual dimension. Some students remember a word if they draw it.

Model Dictionary Use

Explanation. Teachers who write with their students also use a dictionary with them. They model its importance and that it is both acceptable and intelligent to consult a dictionary when unsure of a spelling.

Implementation.

1. Write with the students.

2. When proofreading or when stuck on the spelling or the exact meaning of a word, model dictionary use.

Remarks. Students don't see adults consulting the dictionary often enough. With spell check, students see it less. When they see their teacher using the dictionary, mulling over the nuance of the meaning of a word, and checking it, they are more likely to use the dictionary.

Integrate Phonics

Explanation. Because some English words retain a predictable relationship between sound and letter, teachers teach the strategy of sounding out words as one strategy of word attack.

Implementation.

1. Choose a word that contains a predictable relationship between its letters and sound as a model. The word *bag* is a good example.

2. For words that are exceptions or do not have a letter/sound correspondence such as *phone*, teach students other appropriate strategies.

3. Students should realize that all words in English cannot be phonetically spelled, so they need to learn a repertoire of spelling strategies.

Remarks. Learning words in a context, being able to sound them out, but being able to tap another spelling strategy if necessary is the sign of a literate learner.

Spelling Patterns

Sandra Wilde lists sixteen spelling patterns in her book *You Kan Red This!* The patterns are arbitrary, historical, homophones, letter-name, letter-string, meaning related, orthographic, permutations, phonetic, preconsonantal nasals, predictable, real words, silent letters, suffixes, syllabic, and variants. She discusses some patterns in detail, with many pages of explanation and many examples; others she treats briefly. Teachers who know all the patterns are better able to use them productively with their students because we know not all students learn in the same way.

Develop Positive Attitude

Explanation. Overemphasis of spelling too soon in the writing process often short-circuits the writing because students become overly concerned with correctness to the detriment of creativity and fluency.

Implementation.

1. Allow students to make mistakes, abbreviate, and use constructed or phonetic spellings in their sloppy copies, when the ideas are flowing.

2. Then, in the manner of the published authors, as students move into final drafts, teach spelling strategies and proofreading skills so students may correct their misspelling.

3. Finally, students edit their final copy.

Remarks. Not only is this process realistic, but it also helps writers put in perspective what is important at what point in their writing. Correcting misspellings becomes a matter of timing.

Be Systematic

Explanation. When writing is meaningful, authors want it to be correct. This harries the teacher who tries to spell every word for every child who asks, "Teacher, is this right?" Developing systematic strategies for attacking unknown words helps foster independence and a heightened spelling consciousness.

Implementation. A good plan is this progression:

1. Try to sound out the word.

2. Experiment with other spelling strategies.

3. Consult the dictionary.

4. Conference with a peer.

5. Conference with the teacher.

Remarks. For lessons and more in-depth information on spelling, see Carroll's *Authentic Strategies*, 117–148.

Write and Read Often

Most people extend their vocabulary and learn their spelling by reading. Words, embedded and connected in a meaningful context, make remembering them easier. Second-grade students often astound adults with the correct names and the spellings for the various dinosaurs. They do that because they want to be precise. They know the exact names for different dinosaurs help designate the differences among these enormous animals. First-grade students correctly spell with ease the names of the Teenage Mutant Ninja Turtles—Michelangelo, Leonardo, and the others—when they write them into their stories. These are the same students who, when given the word *percolate* from a commercial spelling list, stumble and never get it. The former words are important and relevant; the latter word is archaic.

If all this seems overwhelming, think about Elizabeth McPherson's conclusion to her article "Spelling, Revisited,"

> And cheer yourself up with an ironic reversal. Not too long ago, it was fashionable to say that persnickety school ma'ams were passionately devoted to spelling and ordinary people didn't care much about it. Now the public, or some of it, is wailing about illiteracy, while good language arts teachers are using a better definition of literacy: the ability to read with pleasure and understanding, and the ability to write something real. Spelling enters into those abilities, but it isn't the most important part.

APPLICATION

1. Choose a punctuation mark. Study its uses. Design a lesson for a chosen grade level in which you concretely teach the mark so that students apply it to their writing through the process of correcting.

2. Develop or research a spelling strategy. Create a way for students to apply this strategy within their own writing.

5

GRAMMAR THROUGH REVISION

"Go ahead, I'm listening. Ratiocinate."
"What?"
"Ratiocinate. Reason. Think."
"Someone has said that only Americans could put up signs ordering the
reader to think . . . All right, I will."
—*The Murders of Richard III* by Elizabeth Peters □

TEACHING SENTENCE SENSE

Deeper and more complex than correcting, revision deals with changes on the sentence level. When correcting, students concentrate on distractions affecting their readers; when revising, students concentrate on distractions affecting their meaning. Revising demands that students reenter their writing to analyze if they have clearly expressed what they intended. Their answers determine the depth of their subsequent revision. When students revise, they quite literally make sense.

Because the act of revision is so demanding, students should have had plenty of opportunity to write, become fluent, and feel confident about putting words on paper. This confidence is essential. Feeling secure about writing provides the foundation for "re-visioning" or "seeing again." Without that security, students, who realize writing is an extension of themselves, shun anything that makes them look inadequate. If the proper groundwork has not been laid, or if writing has demeaned them in any way, they resort to mere recopying and miss the satisfaction of revising writing that matters.

Since everyone agrees that sentences are the basic constructed units of writing, revision calls upon students to spot problems of clarity within their sentences and coherence among their sentences. Once students learn sentences are made complete by grammatical form and meaning (She likes ice cream), or by context (Not he!), they have at their disposal the means to revise their writing in standard and unique ways.

In what seems to be a paradoxical statement, Frank Smith says, "It is often assumed that children need to understand metalinguistic terms like *noun, verb, sentence* (and *read* and *write*) in order to learn to read and write when in fact the opposite applies. One can learn to read and write without knowing the meaning of such terms; in fact, one cannot completely understand the terms without having first learned to read and write" (14–15).

Students may revise their sentences without labeling every word with a metalinguistic term (*subject, predicate, noun, verb*). Yet through the act of revising, they develop a deeper knowledge of those terms because this developing sense is accompanied by an understanding not only about the grammar of sentences but also about the power and meaning sentences unleash when wrought by an informed writer. This power, in turn, enables students to revise successfully.

Past Approaches to Revision

Grammar in Isolation

Hopefully the days of teaching grammar in isolation during a six-week grading period coupled with an assigned paper written in isolation and due at the conclusion of the six weeks have gone the way of high-button shoes and manual typewriters. We all remember those red marks hovering over, around, or alongside punctuation, spelling, agreement, capitalization, sentence fragments, run-on sentences, and awkward phrasings. Marked because they were easiest to grade, although time-consuming, or perhaps because teachers had little training in the act of teaching of writing, they failed to help students' writing. So obsessed did some teachers become with conformity to rules, they often bypassed what students were attempting to say. So obsessed did students become with conforming to rules, they often bypassed any attempt at artistic expression, craft, style, voice, or ever experimenting with true communication either to self or others.

Revise for a Higher Grade. In bygone days, some teachers permitted students to "revise" their papers for a higher grade. That meant rewriting it according to the marks made by the teacher, not by rethinking the meaning. Many students opted not to revise, but those who attempted to do it gave what Howard Gardner calls "rote, ritualistic, or conventional performances. Such performances occur when students simply respond, in the desired symbol system, by spewing back the particular facts, concepts, or problem sets they have been taught" (1991, 9). Gardner explains that while this approach did not preclude comprehension, it did not guarantee it either.

Loss of Coherence. Revision became worse with students began to think longer, more syntactically mature sentences were "wrong" because most often in the weaving of meaning they created a run-on, erred with a comma splice, misplaced a modifier, dangled a participle, or produced an agreement slip. Students began to doubt themselves and resorted to safe, anorexic, bland, short, choppy sentences that often invited redundancy or reflected sloppy thought. Mandated "never to begin a sentence with *and* or *but*," students lost their coherence. Papers read like disjointed jigsaw puzzles. This eventually led to negative feelings about writing.

Messages were also sent about coordination, subordination, and parallelism. Coordination became a decision about whether or not to put a comma before the coordinating conjunction—not about whether or not the intended relationship, clued by a coordination conjunction, was evenly balanced. Subordination translated into merely memorizing subordinating conjunctions, not a deep understanding of subordination as a means of indicating the relative importance of persons, events, things, or ideas.

Parallelisms presented other difficulties. Students avoided them because they called for sophisticated punctuation. Not willing to risk a *C* grade because of a comma error, students lost opportunities to play with the rhythm and repetition of language; they lost ways to make writing smoother; they lost a device to prevent unnecessary shifts in person, number, tense, and mood; and they lost the gratification to express themselves.

Most of all they lost a sense of craft.

Drill and Kill

Consider the frustration of students and teacher when after weeks of drill on subjects and predicates, after weeks of doing exercises straight from grammar books, they still saw papers teeming with mistakes. Often, if students were allowed to write after weeks of stilted grammar exercises, they become confused when confronted with real syntax. More complicated structures such as compound subjects and predicates, inverted word order, or subjects followed by *as well as* such as, *The president as well as the secretary calls the class together*, did not match the blanks they filled in on those endless experiences. Without application, all those wooden worksheets simply convinced students grammar was beyond them; they could never master it. "I'm no good at grammar," they whined, while teachers wailed, "They still don't know a sentence! How will they ever learn to revise?"

New Approaches to Revision

For many teachers and students all that has changed. There are four solid reasons why we teach revision differently today.

Grammar to Improve Writing. Contemporary composition and rhetoric scholars distinguish between grammar as an academic subject and grammar as a tool for writing improvement. (See Patrick Hartwell's article, "Grammar, Grammars, and the Teaching of Grammar," in Appendix B.) The former is a detailed and rigorous discipline. The latter, serving a different purpose, focuses what is relevant to writing (Noguchi 17). Grammar, as a tool for writing, is endemic to revising—it is sentence sense.

Grammar in Isolation Doesn't Work. Research studies such as those by Richard Braddock, Richard Lloyd-Jones, and Lowell Schoer and George Hillocks criticize isolated grammar instruction in schools.

> The study of traditional school grammar (i.e., the definition of parts of speech, the parsing of sentences, etc.) has no effect on raising the quality of student writing. Every other focus of instruction examined in this review is stronger. Taught in certain ways, grammar and mechanics instruction has a deleterious effect on student writing. In some studies, a heavy emphasis on mechanics and usage (e.g., marking every error) resulted in significant losses in overall quality. School boards, administrators, and teachers who impose the systematic study of traditional school grammar on their students over lengthy periods of time in the name of teaching writing do them a gross disservice which should not be tolerated by anyone concerned with the effective teaching of good writing. (Braddock 248–249)

Grammar Should Be Developmentally Appropriate. Cognitive developmental research suggests that teaching what is developmentally appropriate better advances students' learning. Just as there are natural stages in physical development, just as there are natural stages in the development of speech, so, too, there are natural stages in the acquisition of language skills.

Compare children stumbling while learning to walk, mispronouncing or misusing words while learning to talk, to students making mistakes while learning to write. The toddler who falls is not berated for falling but encouraged to get up and try again. The child who misspeaks is not humiliated but hears the word spoken correctly and tries to imitate.

We now know when students make mistakes, their errors don't need to be red-inked and punished with a low grade, but discussed and the skills retaught. We know highlighting the good points, modeling how to revise errors, and encouraging students to try again helps students grow into their written expression. "Students who have not yet reached a level of formal operational thought or a level of ego development where they can step outside themselves should not be forced into grammar exercises that can have no meaning for them" (Sanborn 77). By teaching grammar that students need to write effectively, by helping them match their language to audience, purpose, and genre, students learn ways language can enhance their writing and develop a better understanding about how language works.

Brain-Based Teaching of Grammar. Back in our day, we didn't have tomography machines to study the human mind, but we do today. Brain research has illuminated the incredibly complicated process of learning grammar. Antonio R. Damasio and Hanna Damasio, medical doctors who have been studying the neural basis of language for decades, believe the brain goes through three interacting sets of structures to process language. One is a large collection of neural systems that represent anything a person does, feels, or thinks. Another is a smaller number of neural systems that assemble word-forms and generate sentences. The third mediates between those two. Further, they point out that psycholinguists Willem J. M. Levelt and Merrill F. Garret also believe in the idea of mediation (89–90). We include this gross oversimplification to illustrate that teaching grammar is both physical and psycholinguistic.

Also we know the brain holds as many neurons as there are stars in the Milky Way, with the potential of making 1 million-billion connections (Nash 81); juxtaposing that with the notion of equating memorization of rules with learning grammar strikes us as primitive thinking. By contrast, teaching grammar within the writing process through revising parallels the brain's natural processes of making meaningful connections and mediating among actions, feelings, thoughts, and the capturing of it all through the highly sophisticated and complex symbolizing system we call writing.

The Importance of Grammar

Contrary to those who believe otherwise, grammar, especially grammar through revision, remains important. As Constance Weaver says in *Grammar for Teachers*, "Students do need to develop a good intuitive sense of grammar, but they can do this best through indirect rather than direct instruction. Instead of formally teaching them grammar, we need to give them plenty of structured and unstructured opportunities to deal with language directly" (5). The question is not *if* grammar should be taught, but *when* and *how* grammar should be taught. We know teaching grammar is a matter of timing (Carroll 1987, 51). "Ideally, this grammar [as a tool for writing] will be integrated with writing instruction and presented as quickly as possible so that students can use it during the revision or proofreading states of writing" (Noguchi 18).

Informed teachers in the twenty-first century understand that for students to truly understand grammar, they must learn it and apply it within the writing process. These teachers do not teach grammar in isolation, rather they incorporate it after students have generated writing and want to revise it for an audience. While academically gifted students may become effective writers no matter how they are taught grammar, integrating grammar into writing as a process turns almost everyone into a writer.

RATIOCINATION AS REVISION

Definition of Ratiocination

Ratiocination is a *systematic* revision strategy. (See Appendix C.) Students, through a process of coding and decoding clues, manipulate sentences, consider syntax and diction, activate verbs, vary sentence beginnings, avoid weak repetition, refresh clichés, develop and clarify their thinking, and revise the writing.

When teachers teach ratiocination, they:

- share visual codes as clues for students to use to reenter their writing;

- provide a schema for decoding the clues;

- model, using the students' sentences and their own writing as examples;

- teach grammar within the writing process.

When students use ratiocination, they:

- learn a concrete way to reenter their writing;

- see alternative ways to convey their meaning;

- acquire models to reference as they revise;

- use higher-level thinking skills;

- mark up their own writing;

- internalize grammar.

Rationale for Ratiocination

Using ratiocination as a revision strategy fits what Howard Gardner calls "performances of disciplinary (or genuine) understanding. Such performances occur when students are able to take information and skills they have learned in school or other settings and apply them flexibly and appropriately in a new and at least somewhat unanticipated situation" (1991, 9).

With ratiocination, students take "the information and skills" of grammar, and they, not the teachers, do the work. Students' authentic writings continually present "other settings." When they mark their own papers by coding the clues, thinking through the decoding of those clues to make their meaning clearer and their papers better, they are applying that information "in a new and at least somewhat unanticipated situation."

Ratiocination does what Wayne Booth suggests in "Rhetoric, Mere Rhetoric, and Reality": "instead [of spending a month or so preparing to pass competency exams and saving the rest of our time for genuine education] that we go about it the other way 'round, that if we think hard enough about our own notions of the basics, and then teach with full devotion according to those notions, we will find the competencies following quite naturally" (15).

Further, ratiocination as revision provides specific strategies for teaching grammar within the writing process, thereby reinforcing findings that appeared as early as 1936. At that time the Curriculum Commission of the National Council of Teachers of English (NCTE) recommended, "all teaching of grammar separate from the manipulation of sentences be discontinued . . . since every scientific attempt to prove that knowledge of grammar is useful has failed" (Monroe 392). In other words, if students do not apply the grammar they learn, there is a question about the degree of their learning.

Ratiocination Lesson

Sentence Variety and Parts of Speech

Explanation. Using ratiocination supports instruction within a context, one of the problems noted over forty years ago by Braddock, Lloyd-Jones, and Schoer. "The teaching of formal grammar has a negligible or, because it usually displaces some instruction and practice in composition, even a harmful effect on improvement in writing" (38). Students, who begin almost every sentence with *and* or *and then* in an attempt to keep their thoughts together, are not well served by the dictum, "Never begin a sentence with *and*." Taking something away from students without replacing it with something better results in frustration, or in this case, incoherence. Better to teach and model other ways to begin sentences, and use that context to teach or reteach parts of speech and sentence variety.

Implementation.

1. Students fold a sheet of paper in quarters lengthwise. Starting in the first column and at the beginning of their papers, they list the first word of each sentence.

2. Several students share the first ten or so words from their lists. As they do, write them as a list on the board or overhead.

3. Explain the purpose of these lists. They provide students with visual ways to reenter their writing to add sentence variety.

4. Circle one word from each list: a repeated article; the anticipatory subject *it*; *and*, *and then*, or *then*, or a repetitious noun or pronoun.

5. Invite the students whose work you are using as examples to accept the challenge to change that circled word, rearrange the sentence, or combine sentences.

6. All other students challenge themselves by choosing a word on their lists to circle. Quickly check to see that every student has a circled word.

7. On the overhead projector, display the following chart (Table 5.1) or one adapted for the grade level. The parts of speech are in a context and should be analyzed within that context.

8. Review the functions of the parts of speech; discuss the effectiveness of using different openers.

9. Read excerpts from good literature to show how by varying sentence beginnings writers create a certain rhythm and make their writing enjoyable to read.

10. Together revise a sentence from the teacher's writing as a model.

11. Students independently revise the sentences beginning with the words they circled.

Table 5.1. Variations of Sentence Beginnings

NOUN	Mary is an intelligent girl and pretty, too.
PRONOUN	He participated in the race.
ARTICLE	The champion received the gold trophy.
GERUND	Traveling can be inspirational, educational, and fun.
INFINITIVE	To succeed in life is her ambition.
ADVERB	Slowly and carefully, he walked through the forest.
PARTICIPLE	Having expressed his view, he left for class.
ADVERB CLAUSE	While Juan fished, Jesse worked.
EXPLETIVE	There are only six days until summer vacation.
PREPOSITIONAL PHRASE	Over the bridge the cars passed rapidly.
NOUN CLAUSE	That Mother will recover from her fall, is our wish.
ADJECTIVE	Yellow and white daisies covered the windowsill.

12. Students who have a list on the board share their "before" and "after" sentences. Discuss.

"Ben, you circled *And*. Read your before and after sentences."

"Before: And we went for a hamburger after the game. After: We went for a hamburger after the game."

"Great. Tell us what you did to make that change?"

"Dropped the *And*."

"How did you come up with that, Ben?"

"I just looked around the *and*, and discovered I didn't need it."

"What a good idea. Sometimes doing something so simple helps our writing—just taking a look around the problem. Now the sentence begins with what part of speech?"

"Pronoun."

"So, when you work on your sentences, you might want to follow Ben's idea. Look around that first word. Now let's talk about Susan's sentence."

13. Ask several students who do not have lists on the board but who challenged themselves to share their "before" and "after" sentences.

14. Students refer to these peer models and the chart as they continue revising their writing.

15. While students revise, walk around and monitor. Some students require individual help.

Remarks. When students ratiocinate their own writing, teachers eliminate mindless repetitive exercises that seem purposeless to students. Consequently, ratiocination answers Bullock's assertion in *A Language for Life*:

What has been shown is that the teaching of traditional analytic grammar does not appear to improve performance in writing. This is not to suggest that there is no place for any kind of exercises at any time and in any form. . . . What is questionable is the practice of setting exercises for the whole class, irrespective of need, and assuming that this will improve every pupil's ability to handle English. . . . Most [exercises] give the child no useful insight into language and many actually mislead him. (171)

Working with authentic sentences from students' writing intensifies the interest of the class and says loudly that the teacher wants to offer help before the paper is graded. Grappling with a student's sentence on the board together as a class creates bonds and supports the purpose for learning—to communicate more effectively, reflexively, or extensively.

When students underline sentences in alternating colors to avoid monotony and add zip to their writing, they get close to what is basic to powerful writing. When they vary sentence order to eliminate the monotony of constant subject-verb-complement order in declarative sentences, they understand the rhetoric of emphasis. When students label sentences "stringy" and realize they have lost the reader along the string, they demonstrate the importance of knowing audience. When students rework a knotted, convoluted sentence that confuses rather than convinces, they demonstrate purpose. When students watch wordiness, they indicate a grasp of directness and accuracy of expression.

When students identify and then circle "to be" verbs to eliminate the passive or to replace them with more precise verbs, they choose appropriate diction, they think about the basics of grammar, and they revise. They constantly ask themselves, "Is this the best possible way to say this?" (For a thorough explanation of ratiocination and for more lessons, see "Ratiocination and Revision, or Clues in the Written Draft" in Appendix C.)

In short, when students ratiocinate, they do what skilled writers do all the time. They revise. They craft.

Philosopher and educator Alfred North Whitehead appeals to "practical teachers" (5) to beware of "'inert ideas'—ideas that are merely received into the mind without being utilized, or tested, or thrown into fresh combinations" (1). Ratiocination as a revision tool enables students to grapple with what they are trying to say. Conversely, worksheets, workbooks, and grammar books epitomize "inert ideas" because they fail to offer students the chance to use, test, or try grammar concepts in their writing. They remain on the page mindless and boring; students see little connection between those exercises and their own writing.

Fig. 5.1. Blondie Cartoon.

Blondie © King Features Syndicate.

SENTENCE SENSE

Three noticeable problems disturb sentence sense: fragments, comma splices, and run-on sentences. Sometimes these occur because of a lack of sentence sense, but most often they occur because of poor proofreading skills or sloppy editing.

Fragments

A fragment is an incomplete sentence punctuated as a sentence. A fragment is a piece of something, a splinter. If a splinter gets under the skin, it irritates. It does not belong there. So, too, with a splinter or fragment in writing; it gets under the reader's skin and irritates, usually because it does not make sense or because the reader has to work harder to understand the writer's meaning. There are four reasons why fragments happen.

Lack of Understanding. The student does not understand the concept of a sentence. Teachers often make this assumption when they read fragments in a student's writing, but that assumption invites reconsideration. Unless the writing contains nothing but fragments, most likely the student has sentence sense but is either taking a rhetorical risk or needs help with punctuation.

Inability to Punctuate. The student has a subordinate idea but does not know how to punctuate it. Introductory modifiers and concluding modifiers most often cause this difficulty. For example:

Although he was the most qualified for the job. He didn't get hired.

The line at the voting booth was a mile long. Which caused some people to leave.

Teaching the student how to link ideas and punctuate those links helps this problem. Sometimes asking the student to rephrase ideas makes a difference.

Rhetorical Emphasis. The student wants to rhetorically emphasize a word, clause, or phrase. Using fragments for effective emphasis is acceptable. John Barth, began his essay "Writing: Can It Be Taught?" with, "Can it be learned? Sure" (1). Later in the essay, he writes, "Not necessarily by a hotshot writer, either, though not impossibly by one" (37). Of course this line makes sense in context, but it also works as a fragment. Because of its unusual syntax the reader pauses, thinks a minute. Our point is, authors use fragments for rhetorical effect. Therefore, we caution teachers to find out what the budding writer means before deciding a fragment requires drill on subjects and predicates or before possibly smothering attempts at style or craft.

The Results of Worksheets. The student inundated with worksheets that invite the "because clause" response develops a pattern of "because" fragments. *Why do you like chocolate? Because it's sweet.* Three solutions help this problem:

- Do not use worksheets that invite brief answers that become internalized as correct and show up later as irritating splinters.

- Create a literate, print-rich environment where students engage in reading and writing and have opportunity to talk about the way writers write.

- Work with sentence combining.

Comma Splices

Comma splices, sometimes called comma faults, occur when a comma joins two main clauses (grammatical sentences). They pervade students' writing. For example, it is not unusual to see sentences such as: *I love my two dogs, they love me.* The best way to take care of comma splices is by teaching the "Sample Comma Chart" from the previous chapter.

Run-On Sentences

Run-on sentences, or fused sentences, are two sentences run together with no punctuation. For example: *I love my two dogs they love me.* This problem is more often caused by sloppiness or a disregard for the writing than by the inability to see two simple sentences in the construction. "The Sample Comma Charts" also helps this problem.

> *Baffled by students who persisted in comma faults and run-on sentences, we decided on an offbeat solution since traditional approaches obviously hadn't worked. Here sat students after years of school popping commas between main clauses. Surely they could recognize a main clause as a simple sentence. So we devised a plan.*
>
> *We located a heavy wooden chair, the kind teachers used years ago, stashed away in a storeroom and lugged it to class before the students arrived. A thick rope and a pocketed thumbtack completed the preparations.*
>
> *"We've got a problem," we confided to the class. "We want to use this chair to introduce theater of the absurd to the seniors, but we need to suspend it from ceiling." They thought that idea "cool." "But it's awfully heavy."*
>
> *"We thought we'd use this rope. Where do you think we should hang it?" As we had hoped, they suggested we use the beam because the material on the ceiling didn't look sturdy enough.*
>
> *So we tied the rope to the back of the chair, lifted it slightly in the direction of the beam. Then we took out the thumbtack. At first, perhaps to be polite, they just looked at the tack and at us. Then they burst into laughter, "You can't use that!" They chorused.*
>
> *"Why not?"*
>
> *"Because it's not strong enough. It won't hold."*
>
> *We walked to the board and wrote, "I ran up the stairs, I entered my office."*
>
> *"You do it all the time," we said. "You join two strong sentences with a weak punctuation mark."*
>
> *That object lesson hit home. Did it totally obliterate comma splices and run-on sentences? Not entirely, but they definitely diminished. Sometimes a nonstandard play wins the game!*

SENTENCE COMBINING

Background

Sentence combining—pioneered by Kellogg W. Hunt and John Mellon, extended by Frank O'Hare, and popularized by William Strong and William L. Stull—effectively helps students strengthen their writing skills and practice the stylistic choices available to them. Students create more syntactically mature sentences through oral and written practice. The words in the sentences read better, the syntax flows more smoothly—not in short, choppy bits.

Typically after sentence combining practice, sentences contain "(1) the increasing modification of nouns by large clusters of adjectives, relative clauses, and reduced relative clauses; (2) the increasing use of nominalizations other than nouns and pronouns for subjects and objects (clauses and infinitival and gerundive construction, all increasingly unique); and (3) the embedding of sentences to an increasing depth" (Moffett 162–163).

While most texts refer to the sentences to be combined as "kernel sentences," and the process as "transformations," we have used more familiar terms here to avoid any confusion with transformational grammar.

Combined sentences have within them embedded or conjoined ideas. These sentences are generally longer, more complex, more syntactically versatile, and constructed with more maturity. By its very nature, sentence combining invites elaboration through the expansion and combination of simple sentences. After practicing sentence combining, students rewrite simple sentences, manipulating them into syntactically mature alternatives.

Before: I went to the football game. I saw the cheerleaders. They were dressed in blue and white. I saw the coaches. They looked worried. This was a tough game. Mojo had a reputation. They always won.

After: At the football game I saw the cheerleaders dressed in the school's colors—blue and white. The coaches, looking worried, knew this would be a tough game against Mojo because of their reputation. They always won.

Steve Graham and Dolores Perin in *Writing Next: Effective Strategies to Improve Writing of Adolescents in Middle and High Schools—A Report to Carnegie Corporation of New York* (2007) place sentence combining on their list of "Effective Elements to Improve Writing Achievement in Grades 4 to 12" (11). While they maintain that all eleven elements are interlinked, they state, "Teaching adolescents how to write increasingly complex sentences in this way [through sentence combining] enhances the quality of their writing" (18).

Ratiocination, Sentence Combining, and Balance

Earlier, we mentioned sentence combining as a way to increase sentence variety. When ratiocinating, students often combine several sentences to reinforce their meaning, or to make it clearer. Unfortunately, the down side of sentence combining happens when isolated, repeated exercises on combining sentences occur as worksheets. If students do not grapple with sentences in their writing, if they don't they fool around their own syntax, sentence combining becomes boring and meaningless.

Mrs. B., toting an overhead projector down the hall, passed two students who stood by their lockers. "Did you see Mrs. B.?" one asked. "She's got the overhead."

"That means another day of sentence combining," the other groaned.

Anything can be overdone. The point is, while sentence-combining exercises may provide practice in gaining fluency in syntax, as with every other skill, students should immediately make application in their own writing.

Balance is all. When writing, juxtaposing long, syntactically mature sentences with short ones indicates a knowledge of craft and proves that length is not the aim, meaning is. Some sentences need levels of embeds to match the complexity of the thought. Consider Merlin's plea to Stilicho in Mary Stewart's *The Last Enchantment*, "It was grim business, and it took a long time, not least because, when he would have left me to go for help, I begged him, in terms of which I am now ashamed, not to leave me" (444). Other sentences need fewer words to say more. They stand as syntactical exclamation points. Consider the impact of the shortest sentence in the New Testament: "Jesus wept."

Making Sentence Combining Concrete

Collaborative Combining

Approach sentence combining with large or small groups, in pairs, or individually, either orally or in writing, to help students realize there are many ways to combine sentences; one way is not inherently better than another. Students see that combinations are based on style, what works best, or what or sounds best in a given context. At first, avoid focusing too much on terminology (i.e., identifying parts of speech or sentence patterns). Make the experience interesting and fun. As students become more skilled at combining, introduce grammatical terms.

Modeling Sentence Combining. Write several short sentences on the board or overhead and, with the class, combine them in several different ways. (Strong and Stull offer many exercises and are good sources for sentences.) This sets a positive tone, invites everyone to participate, and models how sentence combining is done.

Using Students' Writing. Invite students to read aloud several short sentences from their writing. Write these on the board or overhead. Working together with the class, combine them. This immediate application lets students know the purpose of sentence combining.

Class Clusters. Prepare a transparency of several clusters of sentences. Mask off those not under consideration. Invite students to orally combine each cluster. Talk about the number of different ways a group of sentences may be combined. As students become comfortable with this activity, challenge them. "Who can begin this cluster with a noun? Would anybody risk beginning it with a participle or gerund (or, for the younger students, with an -*ing* word)? I can think of still another way to say this. Can anyone else?" This strategy is particularly good for the aural learner. Previously unfamiliar sentence patterns begin to "sound right." Writing several suggestions on an anchor chart also helps the visual learner.

Group Clusters. Divide students into groups. Each group works with a series of clusters related to a single topic. For example, Strong's topics range from hamburgers to health care. A scribe in each group writes out the suggested combinations, which the group later shares with the class or hands in to the teacher. Students in each group star the combination they thinks is best or most effective and present rationales for their decision. These collaborative sessions enhance learning, are less threatening than whole-class work, and are enjoyable.

This strategy works equally well with pairs of students or individual students.

Combine for Depth

Gateway to Other Topics. Use sentence combining as a way into grammar, spelling, and organization. We use parts of speech as the students suggest combinations. If we are stressing spelling, we insist on accuracy in spelling. We always discuss the logic of coordinations, subordinations, transitions, and levels of supporting information.

Literature. Use sentence combining with literature. Both Strong and Stull offer literary clusters. As students become facile with sentence combining, they enjoy the challenge of comparing their combinations to the original.

Rhetoric. After combining sentences use the outcomes to discuss how sentence combining affected the rhetoric and craft of the composition.

Ten Basic Assumptions about Sentence Combining

William Strong, author of several sentence combining books, presents comprehensive documentation on the theory and research of sentence combining. We have truncated his ten basic assumptions. Sentence combining:

- is not real writing. It is a skill-building adjunct to a language/composition program.

- is not a model of the composing process. Most sentence combining pertains to revision and editing, not prewriting or drafting.

- exercises may be cued, which target transformations, or open, which teach stylistic decision making.

- is one approach to improve syntactic fluency.

- instruction assumes that mistakes are natural and provide feedback that enables learning.

- instruction should move from oral rehearsal to written transcription.

- can be used to teach virtually any language/composition concept inductively.

- requires that teachers model editing and decision-making skills with students.

- is mainly a synthetic process, not an analytic one.

- works best when done two or three times a week for short periods and when transfer is made to real writing. (22)

PROFESSIONAL AND STUDENT WRITERS REVISE

Most writers agree that revising is a significant aspect of the writing process. In *Writers at Work,* the first in the series of the *Paris Review* interviews, Frank O'Connor answers the question, "Do you rewrite?" with, "Endlessly, endlessly, endlessly. And keep on rewriting" (Cowley 168). This series, which captures not only the words of respected authors but also excerpts of their works in progress, includes pages of the author's actual writing proving his endless revision processes.

Second-grade writers are no different. They, too, have a sense of endless revision. Latoya, who loves to write about sharks, told us she worked on her two-page shark story for "one whole week. I wrote it about twenty thousand times," she said proudly. We read one of those drafts and found that she had color-coded every *then*—five *thens* glowed.

Then *we went back to the beach and picked up seashells.* Then *I went into the beach water.* Then *these black fish started swimming.* Then *I stepped up and the fish swam away.* Then *I screamed and ran back to shore.*

Curious how Latoya revised this section, we located her published final draft—her book—displayed on the wall. We skimmed through it until we found that same section. It read:

We went back to the beach and picked up seashells. Then I went into the beach water and these black fish started swimming around my leg. I stepped up and the fish swam away, then I screamed and ran back to shore.

After ratiocinating her paper, Latoya focused on the *thens*. She obviously considered some alternatives and made some decisions. She dropped the first *then*, kept the second, and eliminated the third by combining two sentences. As she combined them, she remembered that important detail *around my leg*. She dropped the next *then*, and used the last *then* to mean *consequently*. We told Latoya she was truly a writer.

Latoya's revision process reminded us of James Thurber's. When an interviewer asked him, "Is the act of writing easy for you?" he replied, "For me it's mostly a question of rewriting. . . . A story I've been working on—'The Train on Track Six,' it's called—was rewritten fifteen complete times. There must have been close to 240,000 words in all the manuscripts put together, and I must have spent 2000 hours working at it. Yet the finished version can't be more than 20,000 words" (Cowley 88).

When queried, "Do you do much rewriting?" Thornton Wilder chose to quote a poet, "I forget which of the great sonneteers said: 'One line in the fourteen comes from the ceiling; the others have to be adjusted around it.' Well, likewise there are passages in every novel whose first writing is pretty much the last. But it's the joint and cement, between those spontaneous passages, that take a great deal of rewriting" (Cowley 105). William Faulkner admits that he wrote his great American novel, *The Sound and the Fury,* five separate times (Cowley 130).

Mary Sarton admits, "The revision process is fascinating to me. Some of my poems have gone through 60 or more drafts by the time I'm satisfied. I think it's very important for poets to have others read their work, get all the criticism they can as well as be extremely self-critical" (Strickland 157). As for revising a novel, Sarton says, "Some of this shaping is done when one has roughed out the whole thing and can revise for the dynamics of each scene in relation to the dynamics of the whole. I find myself cutting ruthlessly to keep the rising curve clean" (Strickland, 157). In poetry or the novel, Sarton knows the process of revising is organic to the balance of the final outcome.

When students get hooked on ratiocination, they share Sarton's fascination; they realize revision's power. This is especially true of middle school or junior high school students. With so much in their lives beyond their control—their growth, their awkwardness, even their privileges—they revel in revision that is presented as a form of power.

Paul Gonzales discovered his power when he wrote about a Hispanic boy named Bamboo. At first Paul's character cries as he faces danger from a gang. "On that Tuesday was the saddest day of Bamboo's life." In later drafts, however, Paul flexes his muscles, feels the power of writing, and takes control of Bamboo's fate. He concludes on an entirely different note, "On that Tuesday, Bamboo showed all the other boys his secret all right. He had been studying karate. After that they didn't bother him any more."

Paul's teacher told us how hard Paul worked on his story. "I think once he thought about how he was like Bamboo, how the big boys often picked on him, he got caught up in it."

In a personal glimpse, Anaïs Nin describes Henry Miller's process as talking through revision.

She tells how she "read the pages as he unwound them from the typewriter," then how they "talked endlessly about his work, always in the same manner, Henry flowing, gushing, spilling, spreading, scattering, and I weaving together tenaciously" (Blythe 258).

Pulitzer Prize–winning journalist for the *Boston Herald*, contributing editor of *Time*, and professor of English at the University of New Hampshire Donald M. Murray claims, "All good writing is rewriting. . . . Rearrange the sentence order so that you have strong sentences at the end of each paragraph and of the theme. . . . Rewriting helps you say what you mean. As you rewrite, and *only* as you rewrite, do you begin to become a writer" (230).

Sylvia Van, a twelfth-grade student, agrees. She rearranged sentences in "A Filial Obligation" at least three times, finally settling on this:

> *Mankind has never treated Mother Nature well. From the beginning of time we have cut down forests and helped ourselves to generous portions of Mother Nature's supply of wildlife. We have burned fields and woods, polluted streams and lakes, and we still show no signs of correcting our bratty behavior.*

It's the word *bratty* that works, and when Sylvia landed that word in that phrase, she knew the truth of Donald Murray's words, "good writing is rewriting."

CONCLUSION

Just as professional writers realize the importance of revising, so do student writers. Students who have teachers who write; students who see the revisions of professional writers in books such as *Writers at Work*; students who have the opportunity to hear professional writers; students who have commitment to writing, who are engaged in the process, who feel ownership over their writing—know writing is the most rigorous intellectual activity in which a person can engage. Writing is taking an idea, something ephemeral, and embodying it on the page so that others understand it. Students who write authentically recognize rewriting as intricately woven into the process; they welcome revision as a time to hone their work; they embrace ratiocination as a tool for this process. They think about their meaning; they consider their structure. They make decisions. They revise.

APPLICATION

Choose one of your drafts. Using "Ratiocination and Revision, or Clues in the Written Draft" (Appendix C) as your reference, color code the "to be" verbs in your paper. Count the number and challenge yourself to rid your paper of half of them using the decoding alternatives in the article. Get with a partner and compare your revisions with the originals. Draw conclusions.

6

GRAMMAR THROUGH REFORMULATION

There are no absolute rules about paragraphing and no general models of ideal paragraphs. . . . The effectiveness of any paragraph depends on how well it serves its readers, not how closely it adheres to abstract models and concepts.
—Corder and Ruszkiewicz □

THE PARAGRAPH

Reformulation suggests revising large hunks of discourse, which we call paragraphs. Paragraphing is to writing, what makeup is to actors. Both illuminate mood, tone, style—many things. Both can be topical or functional. Both help comprehension. Writers have been known to approach paragraphing intuitively or by some mathematical unit stored in some recess of their left brain. Unfortunately, if taught as a strict unit, the paragraph becomes formulaic, predictable, and boring.

We know one school district that created a school culture around what they called the "box paragraph." Comical and nonsensical in image and pedagogy, it is the ultimate in formula: Teachers assign a topic. They distribute sentence checklists that contain a predetermined, specific purpose and specified items for each sentence. For example, "Sentence three must contain a metaphor or a simile." Amazingly, students honestly try to write according to this artificial form. More amazingly, the teachers never tried to write the "box paragraph" themselves.

The work of researchers the caliber of Braddock and Irmscher make hash of such artificiality. The box paragraph exists for the uninformed. When we trained these teachers, when they analyzed their own writing processes, they agonized over the difference between what they learned and what they had taught. Because of this experience, they realized that paragraphing needs proper placement in the writing process and needs to be taught realistically.

Teachers who continue to teach *the paragraph* as if it is some pre-existing form unrelated to meaning do not understand paragraphs. Even the untrained eye can distinguish a piece of ceramic created on the wheel from one made with a mold. The former is unique, the latter, an imitation. One is created; the other is simulated—like a formula. The former flows from the hands of the potter to express feelings, intent, mood, meaning; the latter is an artificially made cast. When students become writers, they are like the potter, not the pourer. They prefer originality and eschew imitation. Imitation may be the highest form of flattery, but it can never bring with it the joy of discovery and creativity of a hand-made creation. Once they understand paragraphs, they understand the maxim, "flawed brilliance is preferred to dulled perfection."

The deepest of the correcting, revising, reformulating triad, reformulating invites students to work with large blocks of their writing. Since paragraphs represent distinct divisions of a composition, working with them requires different strategies and a different depth of purpose than does correcting "stylistic infelicities" or revising through sentence manipulation. When students reformulate, they are working a linguistic jigsaw puzzle because they:

- consider each paragraph in relation to other paragraphs, to the entire piece, and to their meaning.

- rewrite a paragraph.

- combine paragraphs.

- break apart paragraphs that are too lengthy.

- add support to a paragraph.

- write transitional paragraphs.

- move existing paragraphs around.

- put paragraphs aside for further consideration.

- remove paragraphs that do not fit.

- rearrange paragraphs for clarity.

- scrap the whole thing to begin again.

Still the practice of teaching a paragraph through patterns or formulae remains far too prevalent. The assignment, "Write a paragraph," sends an incorrect message to students, suggesting a paragraph is the ultimate goal. When following this message, students develop the confounding habit of following the formula and ignoring their meaning. They resort to counting sentences, similes, or other determiners instead of wrestling with what they are trying to say.

Nevertheless, paragraphs, not willy nilly groups of sentences, are coherent chains of thought. Unified, each paragraph works together with the next paragraph for a purpose. When taught properly and in context, students learn to embrace the real world of writing, not the hollow world of formula.

A BRIEF HISTORY OF THE PARAGRAPH

Stories abound explaining the beginnings of the paragraph, its history, and how indenting occurred. Some stories have reached the level of legend—most attributed to editorial intervention and scribal idiosyncrasies—but it all began, some say, with the illuminated manuscripts of monks. Because illumination served a cosmetic purpose and made reading easier, it became the natural guide for future indenting.

Illumination and Indention

The Book of Kells

Oscar Ogg, in his book *The 26 Letters*, recounts the story of a monk named Finnian who illuminated the *Book of Kells*, a book of the Gospels in Latin from the seventh century. Supposedly,

Saint Patrick brought semiuncials, small, decorative, readable letters dependent upon the quill, to Ireland. Irish scribes eventually became famous for their mastery of semiuncials and the beauty of manuscripts. Two such scribes, the monks Columba and Finnian, engaged in friendly competition to produce the most beautifully lettered books.

As the story goes, Columba vowed to secretly copy an original Psalter worked on by Finnian to make it finer than the original. Nightly he labored, copying the original by candlelight. One night, in what Columba consider to be a miracle, a beam of light shone through the ceiling onto a portion of the page, illuminating several letters and seeming to bless them. Because of the light, Columba was able to decorate the letters with more precision. In time this highly decorated and illuminated text became most sought after (Ogg 156–160).

Natural Inspiration

Another story describes a monk bored with copying seemingly endless words across page after page of manuscript. One day, the legend goes, he looked out the window of his cell and his gaze lingered on the sight of birds, trees, vines, plants, and the sun glowing over the landscape. Overcome with the beauty, he painted the scene in and around the first letter on each page of the manuscript. His work became renowned and demanded by the nobility, so others copied his work. Eventually illuminations graced more and more "majuscules," or capital letters in manuscripts.

Perceptual Inspiration

A third story holds that a monk who worked as a scribe came upon the idea of illuminating his manuscript as he knelt in the monastery chapel before the votive candles. Then it was fashionable to arrange the candles in figures that imitated nature—a bird, a flower, the circle of the sun—in letter shapes that suggested some sacred name, or in the shape of holy words. This monk simply transferred that concept of illumination to the letters in the manuscripts he was transcribing. Eventually these decorations became so intricate and complex that they mirrored not only nature or religion but also all aspects of medieval Europe.

Wherever the truth lies among these stories, illumination added an aesthetic quality to a manuscript page and formed the basis for contemporary graphetic variety or texture, what we consider the visual quality of typeset text. Illumination freed and rested the eye of writer and reader from the relentless letters that marched from page end to page end. It is little wonder these manuscripts were prized.

In time, Charlemagne charged the English scholar Alcuin to revise and rewrite all church literature. In training his scribes, Alcuin modified writing, systematized punctuation, and divided writing into sentences and paragraphs (Ogg 166–174).

Movable Type and Paragraphs

The advent of movable metal type perhaps most accurately illustrates how illumination served as the foundation of indention and the beginning of paragraphs. The metal letters used in printing could not capture the beauty of the illuminated letters found in the hand-transcribed books. Yet with the popularity of illuminated books, printers wanted to continue this decorative touch.

In order to integrate illumination with print, printers devised a mark used even today. They placed a pilcrow, a backward P with an extra parallel vertical line, beside the original illumination to signal the typesetters. Those spaces, which varied in size determined by the size of the pilcrow, were left free of letters so illuminators could reenter to handcraft, design, and color in those spaces. In truth, the word *paragraph* (*para* = beside; *graph* = mark) means *mark beside*.

With the law of supply and demand and more versatility with type, an ornate metal type uppercase letter replaced manual lettering and art. In time, these letters became less and less ornate. Finally, when printers used standard type capital letters, they moved them in from the margin, a contemporary testimonial to medieval illumination. Thus indention indicated the beginning of a paragraph (Ogg 204–208).

Historically, it seems paragraphs developed intuitively, illuminating then indenting, with typographic design to signal a need for a break or to help readers follow the written thought. It was Alexander Bain, a Scottish logician, not a teacher of rhetoric, in 1866 who indurated the paragraph as "simply a sentence writ large." (See Stern Appendix I.) Bain extrapolated rules from classic rhetorical and applied them to nineteenth-century writing. Teachers still teach and students still suffer through his century-old theory—always begin a paragraph with a topic sentence.

Research on Paragraphs

Both William Irmscher and Arthur A. Stern cite the research of Richard Braddock. Braddock found that publications such as *The Atlantic*, *Harper's*, *The Reporter*, *The New Yorker*, and *The Saturday Review* use paragraphs beginning with topic sentences only about 13 percent of the time. Irmscher's replication of Braddock's study concludes, "percentages vary greatly among individual writers; an overall average, however, is more likely to be closer to 40 percent or 50 percent than 13 percent" (98). Yet both found that, "Part of the problem is determining exactly what a topic sentence is" (98). So we are left with Stern's contention, "Today's paragraph is not a logical unit and we should stop telling our students it is" (111).

If scholars have difficulty determining absolutely what constitutes a paragraph and a topic sentence, and if writers use topical paragraphs only approximately 50 percent of the time, teachers who use their own writing and realistic models for teaching paragraphing come closer to helping students do what professional writers do—use the paragraph to meaningfully shape their own prose. If students are encouraged to find form in their meaning, if students learn to give that meaning shape, even if they often fall short, they are on the road to becoming self-sufficient writers.

We hear the ubiquitous question, "But how do I teach the paragraph if I don't use a formula?" Obviously teaching and grading by formula is easier, but as research suggests, it is not totally honest. Formula paragraphs and five paragraph themes exist nowhere but in archaic classrooms. Further, teaching formula paragraphs does not develop strong, independent writers. Eventually, students will pay the piper.

Form Versus Formula

It is important not to confuse formula with strategy. Formula presents a set form. It gives a recipe: There must be X number of sentences in each paragraph. The first sentence must be the topic sentence. It does thus and so. The second sentence does thus and so. The third sentence must contain a comparison. The fourth sentence . . . *ad nauseam*.

A strategy presents a plan or a blueprint within which students can write. A formula is rigid, either/or; a strategy is flexible, both/all, encouraging permutations, adaptations, and craft. Better to teach strategies within the context of real writing. Better to use models from literature and writing to analyze paragraphs. Better to help students examine their writing in relation to intended meaning. When teachers teach paragraphing that way, they foster authenticity, security, and independence.

PARAGRAPH TYPES

There are three types of paragraphs: topical, functional, and paragraph blocs (spelled *blocs* not *blocks*). Students are traditionally taught only the topical paragraph, one with a stated topic sentence, usually written at the onset of the paragraph. Students learn this topic sentence states the main idea of the paragraph and the remainder of the paragraph develops that idea. While this is sometimes true, there is also the functional paragraph, which usually serves some rhetorical purpose such as transition or emphasis. The third type, the paragraph bloc, a term coined by William Irmscher, defines "a segment of discourse longer than the paragraph that operates as a single unit" (101).

We need to teach these other paragraph types or we withhold valuable tools from students. Consider the intellectual turmoil a student experiences when being introduced to indenting direct dialogue after being drilled in topical paragraphs. Teaching all three paragraphs types provides students with a repertoire of tools for reformulating, for shaping their meaning in the most powerful way.

The Topical Paragraph

Definition

The topical paragraph is composed of sentences that contain a key sentence—most often called a topic sentence, thesis statement, or proposition—to which the other sentences are related. Clearly, *topic sentence* is most common term used and most easily understood. Topic sentences may appear anywhere in the paragraph. If a student wants to write out of the topic sentence, it will open the paragraph. If a student wants to write toward the topic sentence, it will be at the conclusion of the paragraph. Sometimes writers want to write around the topic sentence. In that case, it will be somewhere in the middle. Occasionally a writer may want a frame. Then the topic sentence may begin and a restatement of it will end a paragraph. The point is there is no absolute rule on placement.

Teaching the topical paragraph honestly—as one strategy students may use effectively and appropriately in their writing—furnishes them with a practical way to formulate and later reformulate their writing. The topical paragraph enables students to test their ideas, their logic, their sequencing, and their specifics.

Problems

To assign a paragraph, mandate its topic sentence must appear first followed by X number of supporting sentences, and expect students to replicate that form in their papers, no matter what their meaning, is to teach paragraphing formulaically. Teachers who teach this way either do not write, or they slavishly hold to some outdated or simplistic grammar book, one that belies the complex nature of this generative process.

A nontraditional college student visited our office one afternoon. She was exasperated. "What's wrong?" we asked.

"I have to do this paper for another class. The professor wants every paragraph to begin with a topic sentence with five to seven sentences in each paragraph, and he wants five paragraphs. Why do they do that? I read lots of paragraphs that aren't like that."

Sharing her frustration, we responded with another question, "What if you only need four paragraphs?"

"I guess I'll just split one in two."

That attitude neither advances students' writing nor does it foster respect for academic credibility. The woman knew better. She knew she was "doing the formula" for the grade, but she was also aware that the assignment was unrealistic for college and the world.

Another problem teaching the topical paragraph formulaically lies with teachers who do not write. They teach as if thesis statements float in the air, available for the plucking or as if students sit like a mythical Zeus with thesis statements rising full-blown out of their heads. "First your thesis," echoes down halls from classrooms on every level. This dictum leads students to erroneously dismiss prewriting with all its attendant behaviors (doodling, thinking, daydreaming, reading, drawing) as a legitimate way to discover or uncover main ideas. They strive to get anything down, hoping it will work. Normally writing does not work that way (although some rare writing comes by grace).

As students write they uncover meaning and in the meaning there is form. Again, to foist meaning into a predetermined form is to negate the entire process of thinking into writing or using writing as a mode of thinking. "Composing is not as simple as outlining and fleshing out the subtopics with prose or simply adding up parts to make a whole" (Irmscher 99). Rather, it answers E. M. Forster's question, "How do I know what I think until I see what I say?"

Teaching the Topical Paragraph

If 40–50 percent of written paragraphs are topical, we advise teachers to teach topical paragraphs as one way for students to organize information. But writing precedes shaping; it uncovers ideas. Therefore, when teachers employ strategies to cultivate the habit of writing into meaning, they teach students to write first, then shape that meaning. In the words of Paul Rodgers, compose first, and then interpret.

Students.

- Prewrite using freewriting or looping.

- Get down their thoughts.

- Follow associations.

- Make connections between ideas.

- Reread what they have written in an effort to uncover something that tugs at them, something that wants to become their topic or thesis.

- Hone this "tug" into a sentence, which becomes their key sentence or thesis statement.

- Weave that key sentence into the beginning, middle, or end of their paragraphs. More sophisticated writers grapple with the notion of implying their topic. The concept here is to write first, reformulate second.

Teachers.

- Model ways to develop paragraphs and support topics you own; show examples in literature.

- Display a chart such as the one below (Table 6.1) that illustrates the ways to achieve depth. "In truth, all literary devices may be used to elaborate. Although stringing adjectives along the way to a noun might constitute sentence expansion, that is horizontal not vertical elaboration, not depth of thought. Honing literary devices goes a long way to develop writers" (Carroll 2002, 26–27).

- Provide definitions, examples, and models for students because most are unclear about how to use facts, statistics, examples, illustrations, or instances. Students confuse details with description and are not facile in integrating anecdotes into their writing or how to use explanations, comparisons, and contrasts as textual evidence in papers.

- When teachers model ways to develop and support a topic, use their writing on an overhead, and lead students through the act of developing depth, students experience concrete examples they can emulate. The directive "Develop!" or "Support your topic sentence!" without models on how to do that serves only to baffle or frustrate neophyte writers.

- Allow plenty of time for reformulation.

Add Depth in the Topical Paragraph

When students add depth to their writing, when they layer their ideas, they ensure comprehension and enrich the topic for the reader. Layering makes writing strong. With layered ideas, the substance of a piece emerges part by part until its essence is revealed. When writing is not layered, it is weak. Without layers of meaning, writing is often superficial, shallow, or a series of generalities—a mere sketch of what could be. This sketchiness leads to misunderstanding.

Using the acronym SEE helps students understand layering. The S stands for *statement*, the sentence that states the topic. The first E represents an *extension* of that statement or a restatement; it links the statement to its elaboration. The last E stands for *elaboration*, an additional working out of the statement either by degree or by quality of development.

The metaphor of a lamp helps students visualize layering. The plug stands for the *statement*. The cord represents the *extension*. The lamp represents *elaboration*. When the plug is in the socket and the cord is attached to the lamp, the lamp can be turned on and there will be light. When a statement has been written, extended, and elaborated, readers are able to "see" the meaning.

Topical paragraphs lend themselves to layering since all the sentences in this type of paragraph are there to support the topic. One way to reinforce this notion of layering with students is to analyze a sample paragraph. The sample in Fig. 6.1 is the concluding paragraph of the epilogue in *The Story of English* by Robert McCrum, William Cran, and Robert MacNeil; we have added an analysis.

Table 6.1. Strategies to Achieve Depth, Elaboration, or Support of a Topic

Types of Depth, Elaboration, or Support	Definition, Example, and Explanation	The Model
Facts	**Definition** A fact is something that may be objectively verified, something real or actual. **Example** *You are students in Academy High School.* **Explanation** A student attending a particular school is a fact that can be verified through school records. Finding facts, writing them down along with how those facts may be verified helps students internalize the concept.	• Freewrite on a relevant topic such as school spirit. • Students freewrite on that topic. • Find or develop a topic sentence in that freewriting, such as: *We show school spirit at football games.* • Brainstorm facts that elaborate or support that topic sentence. *We show school spirit at football games.* *After every touchdown, the student body does the wave. We stand when the band plays the alma mater. We jump and cheer for our team when the players run onto the field. We wear school colors and spirit ribbons to the homecoming game. We buy spirit ribbons. We hold pep rallies before games. Classes are dismissed ten minutes early on Fridays so students can attend football games.*
Statistics	**Definition** A statistic is a fact, exact or estimated, usually stated in numbers. **Example** *There are 2,105 students in Academy High School.* **Explanation** This is a statistic because it is an exact number. Students record statistics about their classroom or the school. They may figure the number of students absent for a day, a week, or a month and organize the figures as statistical information. Based on the data gathered about the class, students may estimate absenteeism in the school, in the district. Doing this generally makes students feel comfortable with statistics.	• Take one of the brainstormed facts above and back it up with numbers. For example, students count the number of students who wear spirit ribbons and school colors for the homecoming game. • Demonstrate on the overhead how this number could be woven into the discource: *We wear spirit ribbons and school colors to the homecoming game. Last year the pep squad sold 1,610 spirit ribbons to students. That means over three-fourths of the school showed their support of the team by buying a spirit ribbon for homecoming.*

(continued)

From *Acts of Teaching*, 2nd Edition, by Joyce Armstrong Carroll and Edward E. Wilson. Westport, CT: Teacher Ideas Press/Portsmouth, NH: Heinemann. Copyright © 2008.

Table 6.1. *Continued*

Types of Depth, Elaboration, or Support	Definition, Example, and Explanation	The Model
Examples, Illustrations or Instances	**Definition** An example, illustration, or instance is a specific thing, person, or event that illuminates a general thing, person, or event. **Example** *Take John Doe, for example. He not only buys a spirit ribbon for homecoming, but he buys season tickets so he may attend every game. He sits in the bleachers near the pep squad and shouts the loudest of all. Last year he was hoarse from all the cheering.* *"I can't be on the field because of my bad leg, but I can be out there in spirit," he says. "I can be part of the cheering squad."* **Explanation** When one student describes his or her school spirit, it serves to clarify the concept of the "school spirit" for others.	• Working with your own writing on the overhead, demonstrate how to pick out a statement that is general and give a specific example. • At first introduce this type with the phrases: for example, to illustrate my point, or for instance. This sets up the habit. As students become more facile with this strategy, they will add the example, illustration, or instance without the phrase. • Use the example to show how one student with school spirit might serve as an example for other students in the school.
Details	**Definition** Details are specifics that clarify the whole; they are parts of a whole. Think of details as the close-up shot in a film. **Example** *John's school spirit epitomizes sacrifice. His "bad leg," deformed since birth, is considerably shorter than his other leg. Settling on the bench with the team would be easier for him, especially since the team has invited him, but he insists upon sitting near the pep squad. He comes to games an hour early so no one will see him dragging his leg and carrying his cushion up one tier after another tier after another tier—to the top level of the stands.* *John wears his spirit ribbon, all sparkly with green and silver glitter, on his bomber jacket. As he yells from the stands, standing at an awkward angle, arms raised, all see his green cushion with the school mascot and the cheer "Go, Cougars, go!" emblazoned on it. They notice the school motto printed across the brim of his cap. They never notice his leg.*	• Distribute index cards. • Each student punches one small hole in the card, then looks through it. The hole magnifies the details, the small things. Students write or talk about what they see. • Return to the topic of spirit ribbons to show students how giving the particulars increases the reader's sense of school spirit.

(continued)

From *Acts of Teaching*, 2nd Edition, by Joyce Armstrong Carroll and Edward E. Wilson. Westport, CT: Teacher Ideas Press/Portsmouth, NH: Heinemann. Copyright © 2008.

Table 6.1. *Continued*

Types of Depth, Elaboration, or Support	Definition, Example, and Explanation	The Model
	Explanation Because students confuse details with examples, it is important to show that the difference by juxtaposing details in relation to an example. Details are smaller bits expanded from or out of the examples. When providing details, students choose the significant particulars to show the relationship among these particulars to the whole.	
Anecdotes	**Definition** An anecdote is a brief narrative. **Example** *One Friday night John arrived at the game earlier than usual. Some kids came over from the opponents' side and began harassing him.* *"Look at the big guy sitting with his big spirit ribbon—too nerdy to get out on the field? Say, Nerd, afraid of getting roughed up? Afraid of getting your clothes dirty, Nerd?"* *Still out of breath from the climb and with some effort, John stood up. When he did, his harassers saw his deformed leg and his titled stance.* *"No. But I show my loyalty the best way I can. Go back and show your team your loyalty. What you're doing now isn't school spirit; it's just dumb!"* **Explanation** Perhaps the most ancient of all the ways to support information, anecdote adds depth to any genre. Its pervasiveness and the ease with which is incorporated into writing sometimes makes it suspect. "You mean I can tell a story to make a point?" is not an uncommon question. Yet brief vignettes, parables, and snippets of experiences often best undergird a point. People identify with people and their experiences; thus anecdotes pull readers in and cause them to nod their heads in agreement.	• Tell a story that makes a point. Ask students to think of an experience that makes a point. • Informally share these anecdotes aloud. • While not always needed or even effective, writing a story often makes the point most powerfully. Anecdotes provide students with another option for development, depth, and support.

(continued)

Table 6.1. *Continued*

Types of Depth, Elaboration, or Support	Definition, Example, and Explanation	The Model
Descriptions	**Definition** In writing, description provides the big picture, the background. Think of description as the long shot in a film. **Example** *The green and silver section of the stand undulated; it seethed with activity. From afar the green formed an enormous C for Cougar. The silver section outlined the letter. When the home team made a touchdown, each person jumped up causing the green to bulge out as if it would burst while the silver outline glistened its glee.* **Explanation** Not to be confused with details, descriptions paint pictures through visual and aural imagery. As the image intensified so the meaning is revealed.	• Choose something in the classroom to describe. Call upon volunteers to guess what it is. Continue doing with the students doing the describing as an oral activity. • Ask students to pretend they are looking at the football stands through a zoom-lens camera. They are to zoom in on one area of the stands and provide a word picture to match what they see.
Explanations	**Definition** Explanation is a statement or definition with elaboration and depth. **Example** *School spirit is the excitement and support students show at school events such as football games. While games actually take place on Friday nights, weeks and months are spent in preparation. Cheerleaders practice; the pep squad rehearses; the band marches up and down the field in daily drills making ready for their Friday night half-time show. The team works out. School clubs make and sell spirit ribbons for students to buy to wear. The entire school buzzes in anticipation. All hope for a win.* **Explanation** Explanation layers meaning: first making something comprehensible, then giving reasons, putting it in a context, analyzing it, exploring it, and finally adding any special insights or implications.	• Work with student on common statements such as "Yesterday I was absent." Then encourage them to add reasons, give a context, and so forth. They depth-charge or prove-it (Carroll, 2002). • Help students understand that explanations invite depth in writing. • Model that depth by inviting students to layer the topic sentence.

(continued)

Table 6.1. *Continued*

Types of Depth, Elaboration, or Support	Definition, Example, and Explanation	The Model
Comparisons and Contrasts	**Definition** Comparisons show likenesses; contrasts show differences. **Example** *The students in the stands look like a hive of bees. Most hover in the center, but streams of them in green and silver fly up and down the bleachers. An occasional green bee buzzes onto the field, or a silver one flits to where the cheerleaders cluster. When the team runs onto the field, it is as if the hive had been jostled by some giant's hand. All the students seem to take wing, flailing their arms in sweeping gestures.* *In contrast, the visiting team stands like zombies. They must know death is near.* **Explanation** To support or add depth to an idea through comparison or contrast is to show how that idea matches something else or how it is different from something else.	• Take any object in the room and compare and contrast it to any other object in the room. • Tell how each is alike or different. • Encourage students to choose objects and practice the strategy. • Introduce or review similes and metaphors as one way to compare, but also remind students to extend metaphors or use allegories. • Encourage students, when comparing and contrasting, to add the reasons for the comparison or contrast.

Functional Paragraphs

Definition

Functional paragraphs serve a rhetorical purpose. Students use them to arouse or sustain interest, present a special effect, emphasize a point, show a shift from one speaker to another, or provide a transition. They may be one word, one sentence, or a series of sentences. Without functional paragraphs readers may become confused, lose interest, miss a segue, or fail to catch who is speaking in dialogue.

Explanation. We find it effective to teach functional paragraphs through examples from classic and contemporary literature. This section offers a sampling of functional paragraphs used for the purposes listed above. These, or others that are appropriate for a given grade level, help students not only learn functional paragraphs but also learn how to distinguish them from topical paragraphs.

Implementation.

1. Divide students into small groups.

2. Distribute a functional paragraph to each group. They read it and identify its function.

Fig. 6.1. Excerpt From The Epilogue of *The Story of English*.

Excerpt from the epilogue of *The Story of English*	Analysis
Language has always been—as the phrase goes—the mirror to society. English today is no exception. In its world state, it reflects very accurately the crises and contradictions of which it is a part. In Britain, its first home, it has become standardized and centralized in the South, apparently cautious of change. The English of the United States (heard on television, films and radio through the world) has become the voice of the First World in finance, trade and technology. Within the United States, the huge socio-economic significance of the South and West—oil, beef, and the high-tech aerospace and computer industries—has given the voice and accents of the South-West a new and preponderant influence. In the British Commonwealth, the independent traditions of Australia, Canada and New Zealand have breathed a new life into the English that was exported from Britain two hundred years ago. In the Caribbean, it is the focus of an emergent nationalism. In Africa, it is a continent-wide form of communication. In South Africa, it is the medium of Black consciousness. In India and South-East Asia, it is associated with Third World aspirations, and, reflecting the confidence of these Asian countries, it is taking on its own distinctive Asian forms. In the words of Emerson, with whom we began [the introduction to the book], "Language is a city, to the building of which every human being brought a stone."	• First sentence is topical; it clearly states the main idea. • The second sentence limits the main idea to English. • Third sentence extends the main idea to the complexity of the world. • *Britain* signals the first support by identifying the source of English. • *United States* signals the second support by placing English into a technological, social, and economic context. • *Australia, Canada, and New Zealand* offer support through the new life they have given the language. • The *Caribbean* supports emerging English. • *Africa* uses English for communication while in *South Africa* it is a medium of Black consciousness. • *India and South-East Asia* represent areas of hope and confidence. • Countries and continents form layers of support for the topic sentence. • The paragraph links information in a systematic way and concludes with a restatement of the topic with a quotation.

3. They find another example of this type of functional paragraph. Share and discuss.

4. Students look for functional paragraphs in their own writing. Share and discuss.

5. Students reenter their writing to reformulate, by adding functional paragraphs.

Remarks. This lesson helps students recognize the difference between topical and functional paragraphs. Even the abstract terms become more concrete as students actually "work the paragraphs."

Five Examples of Functional Paragraphs

Arouse or Sustain Interest. Stephen W. Hawking, considered one of the great minds of physics during the twentieth century, author of *A Brief History of Time*, echoes questions asked since the beginning of time. His concluding paragraph clearly is designed to arouse interest and sustain that interest.

"We find ourselves in a bewildering world. We want to make sense of what we see around us and to ask: What is the nature of the universe? What is our place in it and where did it and we come from? Why is it the way it is?" (171).

Special Effect. George Bernard Shaw achieves a sardonic effect in his concluding paragraph in a letter written to Hesketh Pearson when World War II was a mere two weeks old. His one-sentence ending achieves a special effect.

"What a comfort to know that if we kill 20 million or so of one another, we'll none of us be missed!" (Weintraub 688).

Emphasis. Loren C. Eiseley, respected naturalist and conservationist, inserts a five-word, one-sentence paragraph between two long paragraphs in his essay "The Brown Wasps." This paragraph serves the essay as a syntactical exclamation point. Its emphasis resides in its brevity, its timing, and its isolation as a paragraph.

"I saw the river stop" (Decker 151).

Dialogue. When Gottfried von Strassburg, the genius of medieval romance, set up the exchange between King Mark and his chief huntsman in *Tristan and Isolt*, he relied on indentation to carry on the conversation with proper pacing and without distraction.

"Sir King," said the huntsman, "I will tell thee a marvel; I have but now found a fair adventure!"

"Say, what adventure?"

"I have found a Love Grotto!"

"Where and how didst thou find it?"

"Sire, here, in this wilderness."

"What? Here, in this wild woodland?"

"Yea, even here."

"Is there any living soul within?" (Loomis 214–215)

Transition. While the first paragraph in the prologue of James Clavell's *Shogun* sets the scene, and the third paragraph provides the depth, the second one-sentence transitional paragraph, slipped in between introduces the main character and a minor one.

"His name was John Blackthorne and he was alone on deck but for the bowsprit lookout—Salamon the mute—who huddled in the lee, searching the sea ahead" (9).

Like Shaw, Hawking, Clavell, and the rest, students, even young students, understand the need for functional paragraphs. Second-graders proved that when they wrote letters at the end of the year. Although somewhat tentative about exactly how to paragraph, they used several types of functional paragraphs.

Lance began his writing with a childlike strategy clearly meant to arouse interest, "How are you? I am fine."

David indented to emphasize, "I loved you coming to vezit us."

Shannon began her letter with all the details of their Author's Tea. She concluded with "rite now were learning about the ocean." In between the two, she wrote a one-sentence paragraph that served to emphasize her meaning, "I still remember the lesson you gave us."

And Cindy's "We went to see the Grate Berer Refe in the Omni" qualifies as a special effect in a long letter all about what they did in school that year.

These students' work with reading and writing shows all year, shows in their sense of what readers need. Taught by teachers who use writing (not exercises) as models, these second-graders grasp the idea of a paragraph and what it can do for them.

Paragraph Blocs

Definition

The paragraph bloc explains those segments in writing where a topic sentence calls for several paragraphs of elongation. When the topic sentence promises a number of causes or many implications, paragraph blocs are most prevalent. Each of the subsequent paragraphs embrace the topic not only by enumerating the causes or implications but also elaborating on each. "Thus, the paragraphing a writer chooses may be only one way—that writer's way—of partitioning the material" (Irmscher 101).

Examples of Paragraph Blocs

One of the most extreme examples of a paragraph bloc comes from Stephen Jay Gould's book *Bully for Brontosaurus.* Midway through the chapter titled, "Glow, Big Glowworm," he describes the total life cycle (egg to egg) of a glowworm offering carnivory as the focus or main idea of larval existence. Gould follows this topical paragraph with five paragraphs that operate as a single unit. He extends this unit with an elaborate four-paragraph footnote, one that covers three-fourths of the page in much smaller print (261–263).

But the paragraph bloc has been used in all types of writing. Herman Melville, in his short story "The Apple-Tree Table," sets the protagonist in search of strange sounds he hears. There follows eighteen paragraphs, most of them one line, that deal with the sound and the search. When his wife speaks, she breaks the paragraph bloc.

Uses for Paragraph Blocs

Paragraph blocs abound in books and articles that deal with theory and research in specialized fields primarily because they allow the writer to stretch topics introduced in one paragraph through several. They are most useful when

- delineating functions or dysfunctions

- identifying levels

- presenting characteristics

- itemizing concepts

- listing propositions

- enumerating components

- establishing rules

- outlining frameworks

- labeling resources

- pinpointing processes

- extending views

- determining dimensions

- making assumptions

- ascertaining implications

- advancing views

- citing causes

- addressing concerns

- constituting recommendations

- generating heuristics, planning strategies

- constructing taxonomies

- preparing purposes, distinguishing modes

- recognizing conditions, gathering indicators

- naming cycles

- formulating designs

- drafting prescriptions

- giving directions.

Paragraph blocs are prevalent; students should know them and teachers should model them.

Teaching Paragraph Blocs

- Invite students to reread their writing in an effort to identify paragraph blocs.

- If and when they do locate one, they circle the bloc with a marker and share why their meaning works best as a bloc.

- The rhetoric of their explanations is as important as the identification of the blocs. Often students discover that the bloc does not serve them best. Then they may reformulate what they have written.

Paragraph Patterns: TRI and PS/QA

To help students understand the flexibility of paragraphing, introduce the two paragraph patterns identified by Alton Becker—*TRI* is the first pattern; *PS/QA* is the second (Becker 136–140).

The acronym *TRI* stands for the *Topic*, *Restatement*, and *Illustration* pattern. When using this pattern, the writer states a topic, expands that topic, and uses examples to support that topic.

The acronym *PS/QA* stands for *Problem/Solution and Question/Answer*. Writers craft these many sentences or shape them into paragraph blocs.

TRI and PS/QA are used to analyze paragraphs not to formulate them.

Teaching Paragraph Patterns

- After teaching the *TRI* pattern, students brainstorm permutations, for example: *TIR, TII, ITR,* and *TRIT.*

- Following the brainstorming, they use these patterns to analyze their writing.

- Students find examples of each pattern in textbooks and novels. They share.

- After students have generated some prewriting and have made a commitment to take one piece through the process; after they have worked with correcting and revising that writing, they are ready to reformulate using paragraph patterns.

- Students reenter their writing.

- They mark the acronyms in the margins next to their paragraph patterns.

- Students label functional paragraphs by function.

- They mark paragraph blocs with a { } brace.

- After analyzing and identifying their patterns, they decide if they need any additions, deletions, or rearrangements.

- They reformulate accordingly.

Paragraph patterns provide structure and security for students' reformulations. They may discover they have *T* and *R* but no *I*. Or they may have a string of *I*s that relate to nothing since a topic is nowhere to be found. They may have raised a question, restated it but failed to answer it. This approach to paragraphing invites choices, higher-level thinking, decision making, problem solving, and reinforces ownership.

FROM START TO FINISH

Introductions, Beginnings, Leads

Introductions attract and hold the reader's attention and literally lead the reader into the rest of the writing. With uncomplicated pieces of writing, the introduction is usually one paragraph; with more complex pieces, it may form a bloc of two, three, or even more paragraphs. We usually call the opening section of an essay the introduction.

When we talk about fiction, especially stories, we use the word *beginning*. In both cases, the writer needs a great lead, sometimes called the hook.

Poet Richard Hugo told his audience during a poetry reading, that something should have already happened when the poem begins. Elizabeth and Gregory Cowan say, "You must hook the reader immediately. You probably have about two sentences, or 20 seconds, to do that" (173). June Gould advises, "Your lead not only has to hook the reader instantaneously but also has to be so powerful that it sets up a chain reaction until everything—even your ending—is a logical outgrowth of its promise and intention" (141).

Robert James Waller gives us an excellent example of a lead within a lead in his *Bridges of Madison County:*

> There are songs that come free from the blue-eyed grass, from the dust of a thousand country roads. This is one of them. In late afternoon, in the autumn of 1989, I'm at my desk, looking at a blinking cursor on the computer screen before me, and the telephone rings. (vii)

If we weren't hooked by Waller's sense of songs or images of blue-eyed grass and dusty country roads, that ring of the telephone surely snagged us.

Teaching Leads

- We model by using literature. We read several leads from literature of all types and then discuss the effectiveness (or not) of the lead.

- After distributing children's books, short stories, essays, or novels to the class, students read the leads to raise their consciousness of effective hooks.

- Then students read their own leads, evaluate them, try to create an electric lead, follow the spark into the introduction or beginning, and end with a flash. (See pp. 28–31 and Appendix A in Carroll's *Depth* for more on leads.)

Writers, both classic and contemporary, children and adult, fiction and nonfiction, know the importance of the effective hook. Following are some leads students may model.

Types of Leads and Examples

The Future Tense Lead (Something is in the throes of change)
"In the coming century, engineers will control the climate by flicking a switch and turning a dial. Deserts will be transformed into gardens, the polar ice caps will be melted, and the entire earth will enjoy perpetual spring."
—*The Century That Was* (James Cross Giblin, editor)

Dialogue (Someone is speaking)
"This is reading workshop, and I am Cris Tovani. You are in Room 11, and it's now fourth hour."
—*I Read It, But I Don't Get It* (Cris Tovani)

First Person Lead (Writer as participant)
"Tattered and taped, with the name 'Amy' penciled onto the dustcover in a wobbly three-year-old's hand, my copy of *The Velveteen Rabbit* sits on a shelf in my office near great works in psychology and art. Many of my colleagues—other psychotherapists and professors—would be surprised to hear that this children's book occupies such a place of honor. It does so because it has been vital to my work with hundreds of people. In fact, few sources have meant more to me than this little book."
—*The Velveteen Principles* (Toni Raiten-D'Antonio)

Setting (Place)

"To the red country and part of the gray country of Oklahoma, the last rains came gently, and they did not cut the scarred earth."
—*The Grapes of Wrath* (John Steinbeck)

Action (Something is happening) with a Bit of Dialogue

"Eva unwrapped a cinnamon Danish, opened her notebook, and stared helplessly at the wide, white pages. 'Write about what you know,' her teacher, Mrs. DeMarco, had told her."
—*Nothing Ever Happens on 90th Street* (Roni Schotter)

Reaction (Something has already happened)

"Jean: Miss Julie's mad again to-night: absolutely mad!"
— *Miss Julie* (August Strindberg)

Setting (State of mind of the character)

"Whenever my mother talks to me, she begins the conversation as if we were already in the middle of an argument."
—*The Kitchen God's Wife* (Amy Tan)

Dialogue (Someone is speaking)

"Three weeks after Granny Blakeslee died, Grandpa came to our house for his early morning snort of whiskey, as usual, and said to me, 'Will Tweedy? Go find yore mama, then run up to yore Aunt Loma's and tell her I said git on down here. I got something to say. And I ain't a-go'n say it but once't.'"
—*Cold Sassy Tree* (Olive Ann Burns)

Setting and a Physical Glimpse of Character

"I sit on the bed at a crooked angle, one foot on the floor, my hip against the tent of Mom's legs, my elbows on the hospital table. My skirt is too short and keeps riding up my thighs."
—*A Yellow Raft in Blue Water* (Michael Dorris)

Dual Narrative Lead (Two trains of thought)

"Down in the basement of my house, there is a room where I store my archives: every script I've ever worked on, photos taken of me and photos I've taken, diaries, journals, appointment books, calendars, and notebooks from all the way back to my beginnings.
"But this is only the outer room."
—*Lessons in Becoming Myself* (Ellen Burstyn)

Dialogue and Setting

"We are planning a party, a very special party, the women and I. My name is Miriam, and this is where I live. Hut 18, bed 22.
—*Let the Celebrations Begin!* (Margaret Wild and Julie Vivas)

"'Hold on, boy!' A harsh voice called to him from the dim light on Brattle Street.
"He held himself in and managed to sound calm when he asked, 'What do you want of me?'"
—*Anthony Burns: The Defeat and Triumph of a Fugitive Slave* (Virginia Hamilton)

Reaction
"And they lived happily ever after."
—*Dicey's Song* (Cynthia Voigt)

Name-Prominent Lead
"Qi Shu Fang (pronounced Chee Shoo Fong) saunters into her dressing room in the Kaye Playhouse in midtown Manhattan with an unhurried grace. Dressed casually in a black and gold sweater and warm-up pants, she cradles a huge electric teapot under one arm and carries a tin of jasmine tea in her other hand."
—*Extraordinary Ordinary People* (Alan Govenar)

Model Writing Leads

- Teachers choose one of their drafts, one with an ordinary lead. Prepare an overhead transparency of that lead. Share it with the students.

- Discuss the lead. Point out how ordinary it is, how it would not intrigue readers, how it is only one step away from, "It was a dark and stormy night." Following is a ho-hum lead we used with sixth-grade students.

  > *One day I was walking along the path in the woods on my way to Duck's Nest. I wasn't thinking much about anything until I got to the creek that serves as the mid-way point between home and my favorite swimming hole.*

- We talked about how starting with "One day, One summer day, One foggy day . . . " was ordinary and boring.

- Together we rewrote that lead several ways:

Action:	Bo, Jackie, and Musser raced over to my house shouting about going swimming.
Reaction:	Mory told me yesterday the kids were going swimming. I can't wait.
Dialogue:	"How did Duck's Nest get its name?" little Musser asked as we walked to our favorite swimming hole.
Setting:	On the other side of the woods that crept out from our back yard sat a big fat duck of water.
Character	**(a physical glimpse):** With my long baloney curls bouncing and my skinny legs racing, I couldn't wait to jump in the warm water of "Duckzies."
Quotation:	Ernest Hemingway wrote, "The only thing that could spoil a day was people" and that's exactly what spoiled mine the day I walked the woods to Duck's Nest.
Description:	The trees and bushes, looking like they had been smudged with giant emerald crayons, formed an aisle along the warm, loamy path to Duck's Nest.

Coherence

The word *coherence*, formed from the prefix *co-, together*, and the root *haerere, to cling*, means exactly that—to cling together. When sentences are coherent, one clings to the other in some sensible way; when paragraphs are coherent, one clings to the other in some related way. Coherence ensures that the writing is logical, unified, orderly, and consistent.

Internal Coherence

Internal coherence is the glue that coheres one sentence to another in a given paragraph. Students write coherently when they

- repeat a word or use a synonym,

- sustain thought,

- insert a clause that harkens back to the previous sentence,

- manipulate parallel structure,

- chain pronouns,

- establish chronology, or

- write a coordinating or subordinating conjunction to indicate the relationship between one sentence and the next.

In a well-constructed paragraph, each sentence coheres or clings to the one before it in some way.

Young or inexperienced writers often choose *and* or *and then* as a way to cohere sentences. They might write something like:

> *I went to the store. And I bought some candy. And I bought some chips. And I bought some soda pop. And I paid the lady. And then I came home.*

When we ask teachers if that paragraph is coherent, they admit it is. And while the glue is unsophisticated, each sentence does cohere to the previous one. Sometimes teachers, striving for sentence variety, proclaim, "Never begin a sentence with *and*." (For a full explanation of why *and* and *but* are perfectly proper ways to begin a sentence, see John R. Trimble's *Writing with Style*, chapter 9.)

Therein lies the problem: When teachers so mandate without teaching other alternatives for establishing coherence, students often lose the one glue they owned. Without that glue, connections and paragraphs take on a surreal quality. Akin to affixing paper together, white paste works. Children use it freely and with fascination, slapping it liberally all over the papers to make them stick together. Yet if someone took their jar of paste away without replacing it with alternatives such as rubber cement, glue, staples, tape, or a way to fold the paper, their one way to cohere would be lost and the papers would fall apart. The lesson: Strategies, no matter how unsophisticated or repetitive, should never be taken away from students until we teach alternative, better, and more sophisticated strategies.

A teacher brought us writing from her seven-year-old son. She told us that after he wrote his name, Dustin, at the top of the page, he continued

Once i saw a canoe and
there was pepl in it and they
were going down stream.

At that point he looked up at her and said, "And they got to some Indian tents." Then he mumbled, "Can't use it. Can't."
"Can't use what, Dustin?" his mother asked.
"*And*. Can't use it there."
Again he bent over his work:

They went in the tent and got
somtheing to eat.

As written, the piece is incoherent because the cohesive sentence remains lodged in Dustin's head. Interestingly, because he carefully followed the rules and had no replacement for *and*, he merely left a space for it.

Fig. 6.2. Dustin's Writing.

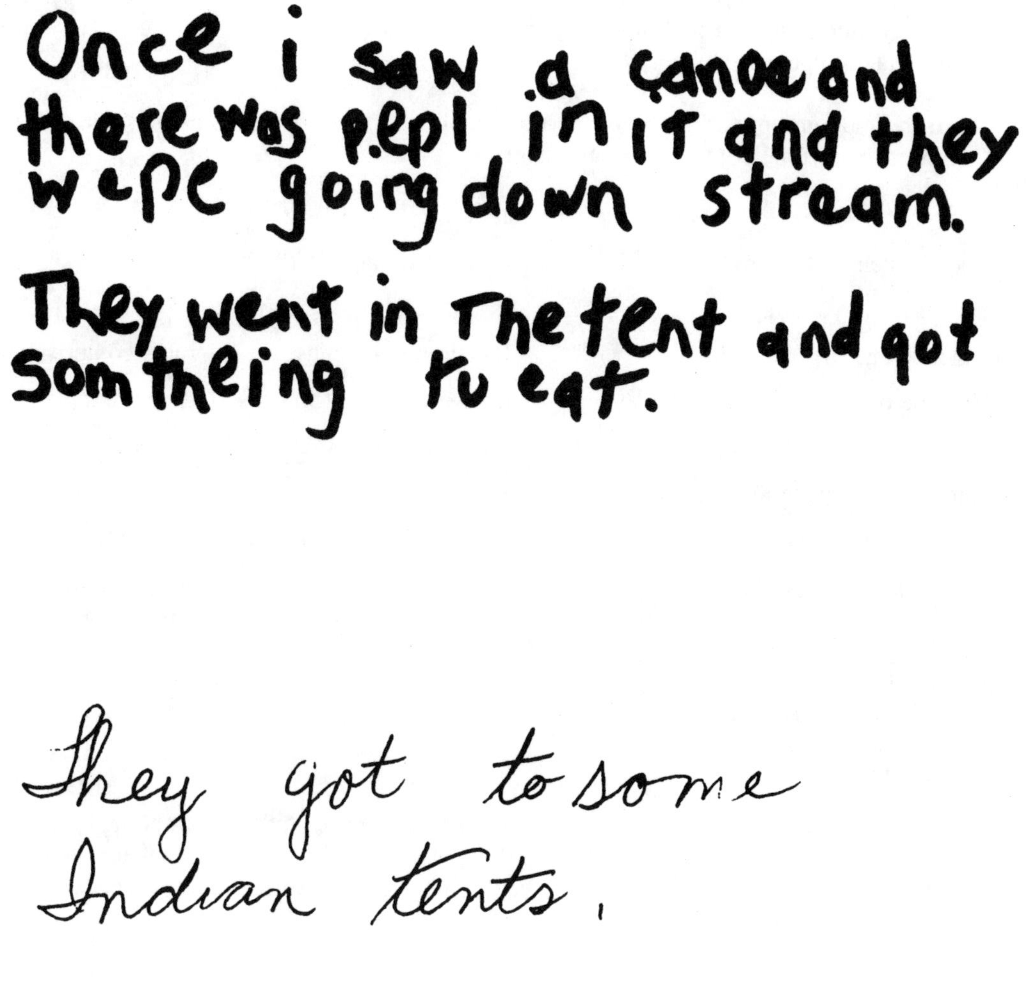

Once i saw a canoe and
there was pepl in it and they
were going down stream.

They went in The tent and got
somtheing tu eat.

They got to some
Indian tents.

External Coherence

External coherence is the glue that coheres one paragraph to another in a given piece of writing. It takes the reader's mind by the hand to turn a corner and uses transitions to best connect paragraphs together. We caution teachers to help students move from *first, next, then, finally* transitions to phrases and clauses that carry the reader's mind to the next point, step, action, argument, or item. In a well-constructed piece of writing, each paragraph coheres to the one before it in some way.

Teaching Internal and External Coherence

- Divide students into small groups; distribute various genres to each group and sheets of colorful paper 8.5″ × 14″.

- Students fold the paper in half vertically and label it *Coherence.*

- On one side they write: *Proof sentences cohere*; on the other side they write: *Proof paragraphs cohere.*

- The groups choose a page from each genre and study how the authors crafted the sentences so they clung together and how they crafted the paragraphs to do the same. They record these and prepare to share.

One fifth-grade group working with the nonfiction book *Penguins* was astonished with their results. Here is an excerpt from their group effort:

Coherence

Proof Sentences Cohere	Proof Paragraphs Cohere
In the second paragraph:	In the second paragraph:
Sentence one: penguins/birds	Paragraph one ends: . . . penguins comprise
Sentence two: all birds	their own order (Sphenisciformes) and
Sentence three: birds possess	family (Spheniscidae).
Sentence four: penguins/birds/penguins	Paragraph two begins: The origin of the
The author repeated words *birds*	word "penguin" has long been debated.
and *penguins*	The author connected the order and family of penguins to where their name came from.

Group realizations: Writers make sure their sentences and paragraphs connect.

Conclusions

William Zinsser cautions, "Knowing when to end an article is far more important than most writers realize. In fact, you should give as much thought to choosing your last sentence as you did to your first" (77). That advice applies equally well to other genres. Studying beginning and ending sentences verifies Zinsser's point.

Teaching Conclusions

To teach conclusions, we follow the same procedure as we do with leads. The bonus here is matching introductions and conclusions. When students do that, they see how the entire piece not only reinforces coherence and unity but also opens discussion of craft. Following are the conclusions to the previously cited leads. (For examples of fifteen categories of conclusions, see Carroll's *Conclusions: The Unicorns of Composition*.)

The Summary (Restates uniquely)
"Perhaps the next one hundred years will be called the 'environment century.' If so, we can thank the pioneers of the past. Some were famous, many were little known. They were males and females, kids and adults. They were all heroes for the whole earth."
—*The Century That Was* (James Cross Giblin, editor)

The Call to Action (Sets forth an expectation)
"Debates about literacy instruction rage on. The battles for greater student literacy must be fought in classrooms and can be only won by teachers, administrators, and parents who understand the complexities of reading."
—*I Read It, But I Don't Get It* (Cris Tovani)

Contemplative (Gives readers more to think about)
"What meaning will you discover as you create a legacy? Be *Real* in your own, unique way, and you will find out."
—*The Velveteen Principles* (Toni Raiten-D'Antonio)

The Surprise (Catches the reader off guard)
"She looked up and across the barn, and her lips came together and smiled mysteriously."
—*The Grapes of Wrath* (John Steinbeck)

Dialogue (Carries some truth)
"Eva smiled mysteriously. 'Thanks,' she said proudly. 'But just wait. It'll be even better . . . after I rewrite it.'"
—*Nothing Ever Happens on 90th Street* (Roni Schotter)

The Clincher (Skewers the piece with something succinct)
"Jean: . . . It's horrible! But there's no other possible end to it!—Go!"
—*Miss Julie* (August Strindberg)

The Theme (Makes clear the message)
"But see how fast the smoke rises—oh, even faster when we laugh, lifting our hopes, higher and higher."
—*The Kitchen God's Wife* (Amy Tan)

The Image (Offers the last act)
"I still have a piece of that root, put away in a box with my journal, my can of tobacco tags, the newspaper write-up when I got run over by the train, a photograph of me and Miss Love and Grandpa in the Pierce, my Ag College diploma from the University—and the buckeye that Lightfoot gave me."
—*Cold Sassy Tree* (Olive Ann Burns)

Contemplative

"As a man with cut hair, he did not identify the rhythm of three strands, the whispers of coming and going, of twisting and typing and blending, of catching and of letting go, of braiding."
—*A Yellow Raft in Blue Water* (Michael Dorris)

Contemplative and Call to Action

"I know that becoming conscious is a never-ending process. My prayer is that by the actual end of this life, I will exit wearing my own true face and be completely unmasked. Authenticity has been my aspiration. Whatever is in the shadow, own it, pull it into the light, and let it shine."
—*Lesson in Becoming Myself* (Ellen Burstyn)

The Call Back

"The women and I wink at one another and pass old Jacoba another helping of chicken soup—and so the celebrations begin!"
—*Let the Celebrations Begin!* (Margaret Wild and Julie Vivas)

The Compositional Risk (Enhances the piece)

"So Gram began the story."
—*Dicey's Song* (Cynthia Voigt)

Theme

"He hated human slavery. But through it all, he never lost his faith in people and his belief in God. He cherished freedom to the last."
—*Anthony Burns: The Defeat and Triumph of a Fugitive Slave* (Virginia Hamilton)

Dialogue

"I hope that, having been given this recognition in America, I'm able to go back to China and show them how much I have achieved here. I maintain close connection with my friends and the artistic community in China, and they are waiting for me to go home and to put on a big show."
—*Extraordinary Ordinary People* (Alan Grovenar)

None lets the reader down. Each holds a sense of finality or what Zinsser calls "the unexpected last detail" (80). The point is that the old maxim "Tell what you're going to tell; tell it; tell what you told" is no longer a viable option for conclusions. This redundant form no longer fits today's fast-paced, instant-replay, nanosecond, globalized world.

Students conduct their own investigation of leads and endings in other genres. While studying essays, students select leads and endings for discussion. David Quammen's "Strawberries Under Ice," chosen for *The Best American Essays* 1989, offers an intriguing frame.

Setting Lead: "Antarctica is a gently domed continent squashed flat, like a dent in the roof of a Chevy, by the weight of its ice."

Closing Clincher: "I believe, with Leontiev, in salvation by ice" (Wolff 212–224).

Or, if working with biography, autobiography, or memoir, students compare Eudora Welty's opening and closing lines in her memoir *One Writer's Beginnings* to Annie Dillard's *The Writing Life*.

Welty's Setting Lead: "In our house on North Congress Street in Jackson, Mississippi, where I was born, the oldest of three children, in 1900, we grew up to the striking of clocks."

Welty's Contemplative Conclusion: "As you have seen, I am a writer who came of a sheltered life. A sheltered life can be a daring life as well. For all serious daring starts from within."

Dillard's Action Lead: "When you write, you lay out a line of words."
Dillard's Quotation Conclusion: "Teilhard de Chardin wrote, 'To see this is to be made free.'"

CONCLUSION

When students study the writing of others as an avenue to their own, two powerful realizations occur. They begin reading as writers and writing as readers. They see that good leads work in all genres, and that conclusions are not synonymous with abandonment. Most importantly they see that by looking closely at parts of writing all writing aspires to be "clear, vigorous, honest, alive sensuous, appropriate, unsentimental, rhymic, without pretension, fresh, metaphorical, evocative in sound, economical, authoritative, surprising, memorable and light" (Macrorie 1970, 22).

APPLICATION

Choose a piece of your writing. Reenter it to analyze its paragraph structure. In or near the margin label each paragraph according to *TRI, PS/QA*. Use the brace { } to identify paragraph blocs.

After this analysis, meet in small groups. Discuss how your analyses impact the teaching of paragraphs.

Try writing different leads and conclusions for one of your writings.

7

POSTWRITING AND PUBLISHING

Proofreading is a special kind of reading: a slow and
methodical search for misspellings, typographical mistakes,
and omitted words or word endings.
—Diana Hacker ☐

EDITING, PROOFREADING, POLISHING

Good teachers help students internalize their writing processes. While some yearn for a neat
process, an unhampered movement through prewriting, writing, rewriting, and post writing, the
truth remains—process is complicated, recursive, and idiosyncratic. Process consists of the student's inner involvement with the nature of the stimuli—self, others, what they have read, environment, artifacts—as well as with all that is implicit in putting words on paper—getting an idea or
an angle on an idea, thinking, rethinking, determining meaning, organizing it, checking coherence,
caring enough about the topic to convey authentic voice and depth.

As if that were not enough, the final product, the culmination of the process, demands student's outer involvement with what has been written—catching those little things that speak to the
passion of the piece.

Teachers who embrace writing as a process place editing and proofreading in their proper
perspectives—at the end—and then teachers help students accordingly. When students internalize
their own processes, when evaluation, effort, indeed, the process take on as much emphasis as
grading, then writing balances itself and does not overwhelm students. Because writing becomes
integral to all students do, because they consider themselves writers, because they want their product to reflect the intensity of what they know, and because they want a product that is apt, clear,
lively, and accurate, students care as much about the final product as they do process. They learn
the balance.

Teachers, whether habitually or intentionally, frequently remain on the periphery of students'
writing noting only "externals," according to Witkin (168). In discussing the process of creative
expression, he suggests this traditional concern with only the product rests on the "incomprehensi-
bility of process to the praxis of teachers" (169). He insists involvement, so essential to the setting,
making, holding, and resolving of expressive acts, demands that teachers "enter the creative process
at the outset" (169). He reasons teachers must have a schema for conceptualizing the structuring
of the process.

This conceptualizing is no easy task, for teacher or student. The teacher must move away
from being the assigner of writing to a facilitator of processes, a guide through the stages, a
listener, a conferrer, a discoverer, a teacher, a grammarian, a helper to the writer and the writing.
We have attempted to elaborate upon these different roles, but each teacher must work that information into his or her own schema. When the teacher has a schema and communicates it, students
find their schema so the writing enriches both.

Britton and the members of the University of London Writing Research Unit agree:

Teachers have many reasons for being interested in writing processes. Their involvement with all the learning processes of their pupils requires that they understand how something came to be written, not just what is written. They can bring to their reading of a pupil's work all their knowledge of his life and his context, realizing, perhaps intuitively, that what they already know about a child and his thinking when they read his work enables them to understand and appreciate something that may be incomprehensible to another. In this respect, many teachers are far in advance of anything educational research has been able to offer them. (21)

Editing

Editing happens when another person, the editor, takes the work and makes or suggests changes. Because the editor becomes involved with the deepest structures and meaning of the piece, students in writing process classrooms learn its value. In effect, someone else works on the piece.

Editing is difficult because some teachers narrow its definition. They confuse editing with proofreading, which is the search for surface errors, not as something substantial. Bakhtin would say they only have "the ability to see the identity of a thing as a lonely isolate." They are not looking at proofreading "as a contrasting variable of all other categories" (Clark and Holquist 7). In other words, many fail to see that while proofreading addresses the stratum of a piece, editing addresses the substratum; it happens on all the layers of the writing.

So, philosophy notwithstanding, what exactly is editing? In the world of writing, there are three categories of editing: copy edits where the copy editor looks at the grammar and syntax of the text; hard edits, which deals with redundancies, gaps in logic, places where more explanation is needed, moving around paragraphs, and reworking or eliminating parts of the text; and technical edits, centering on facts and flaws such as proper attribution, incorrect data, a mistake such as inadvertently dropping the word *not*, which changes the very meaning of the piece, and incorrect information.

In the world of the classroom, editing provides another opportunity for students to deal with clarity, coherence, and meaning. Here, too, there are three types of editing: teacher and student; teacher; student and student—all take place before clocking and the collaborative effort of the Carroll/Wilson Analytic Scale for Classroom Use. (See Chapter 8.) Pedagogically speaking, the best editing is done along with the student.

Teacher and Student Editing

Students hand in their drafts—perhaps first, perhaps last. They write some questions or concerns they may have about the paper. The teacher reads the papers quickly and holistically, jotting any suggestions about organization, focus, coherence, clarity, or meaning to discuss with each student. A conference follows this edit where the teachers use their notes as talking points for one or two suggestions peppered with some positive comments. Students then work on refining their papers by incorporating some or all of the teacher's recommendations.

Teacher Editing

Teachers collects the papers, give them a fast read, make notes on Post-its®, adheres these notes to the papers, and returns them. Students then decide if they want to conference with the teacher or if the notes are sufficient nudges for further work.

Student and Student Editing

When papers are near completion, two students hunker over their papers, reading them and eliciting responses from each other. Or students exchange papers, read through them and mark with Post-its® places where the author has problems. This is not unlike the grouping technique "Analytic Talk" found in Chapter 3.

Proofreading

Proofreading, one of the most difficult writing tasks, requires that students look at their writing with different eyes. While some clearly and subjectively examine at their work, others find proofreading as if looking "through a glass darkly." Learning to read as writers, to read as readers, to write like readers is not novel in many classrooms, but learning to reenter their own text as a proofreader demands another protocol of students.

Because proofreading requires distance from the writing, some teachers let students' writing "cool down" before facilitating proofreading. It is easy for students, indeed all writers who reenter their writing too soon—while it is "hot"—to read through glaring errors. Students read what they meant and miss the errors. Then someone else reads the piece and points out the errors, so students need much proofreading practice. Simply, proofreading is correcting surface errors and is best done when performed by a number of readers.

Proofreader's Marks

Memorizing an extensive list of proofreader's marks wastes time and expends energy. While textbooks often include proofreader's marks as an answer for teacher's concerns about how to teach proofreading, teachers sometimes foist them upon students without fully understanding them.

Historically, proofreader's marks were devised to show typographers where to place capitals, commas, where to indent, where to insert a word, or where to omit a letter, and so on. Because editors could read, they used a visual code for the less literate typographers. In time these marks became standard in print shops and publishing houses. Current editors use these marks when editing the copy, although with the Internet many prefer to respond directly and electronically on the manuscripts. Few students need to edit their work as if preparing manuscripts for a typographer. (If they do become editors, they can learn these marks.) The time students spend memorizing these would be better spent actually engaged in proofreading.

Teachers play a vital role in *teaching* proofreading. Those who have experienced proofreading their own writing better understand proofreading as a skill strategy not an announced activity: "It is now time to proofread."

Clocking for Proofreading

Clocking on every paper taken through the process ensures repeated practice of proofreading. Students learn proofreading skills through the clocking strategy, which finds its roots in the brief article "Peer Proofreading" by Irene Payan (124).

Explanation. During clocking, students sit facing each other in concentric circles. This arrangement approximates the face of a clock, hence its name. The students seated in the inner circle facing out remain stationery; the students seated in the outer circle facing in move one place to the right at the teacher's signal after they check each item. In this way students practice proofreading by proofreading each other's work over and over again.

Implementation. To prepare for clocking, students assemble all the prewriting, writing, and post writing they have done for the assignment.

- Students arrange their writing in ascending order—prewriting on the bottom, final copy on the top.

- They label a blank sheet of paper, "The Proofreading Page" and number from one to the number the teacher designates. (Each number represents a different item to be checked.)

- Across the top of the proofreading page, each student writes: "This paper belongs to _____ ," and completes the blank with his or her name.

- Placing the proofreading page on top of the final copy, they take a seat in one of the circles.

Clocking works as another kind of collaboration. For each item, each student takes on an editor's responsibility. For example, if the teacher designates number three as a check for *their*, *there*, *they're*, that student proofreader is totally responsible for checking the paper for these words. If the proofreader does a sloppy job, his or her name appears next to number three for both the teacher and the peer to see.

- Students exchange papers with the persons opposite them.

- Upon receiving their partner's papers, each student writes his or her name next to the number of the item to be checked. This indicates the proofreader for that item.

- Depending on what has been taught, the grade level, and the skill of students in proofreading, the teacher chooses the item to be checked. For example, in middle school the teacher may invite students to check *its* (the pronoun) and *it's* (the contraction); in primary school, students look at the beginning of sentences for capital letters, and they look at the ends of sentences for terminal marks; in high school, dangling participles may be the teacher's choice for an item. In the lower grades, students check for fewer items. As the grades increase, so does the number of items students are expected to check.

- Students rapidly skim the paper. When they find the designated item, they check its correctness *in the context of the sentence*. If there are no errors, they indicate that in some way next to the item number (a smiley face, a positive comment). If they find what they consider to be an error, *they do not correct it*, rather they indicate page and line next to the item number for the writer to consider.

- This continues until all items have been checked.

- At the conclusion of clocking, students retrieve their papers and their proofreading sheets.

- Time is then allocated for students to study their proofreading sheets, make corrections, do any necessary revising, or maybe even some reformulation. For example, they may look up words for spelling, check grammar books, discuss a correction with a peer, or ask the opinion of the teacher.

- If the student decides a proofreader has found a valid error, the student has the opportunity to correct it. If the student disagrees with a proofreader's comment, the student leaves it as is.

- When students have had sufficient time to look over their proofreading sheets and have made corrections, they *must* sign off directly on the proofreading sheet.

- Students hand in their final proofread copies at the designated time.

Remarks. Not only does clocking teach students worthwhile habits of proofreading and editing, but also it sharpens their awareness of details, and places the responsibility upon them for an acceptable final copy. Because proofreaders identify themselves, clocking takes on the pressure of peer scrutiny.

The clocking technique enables the teacher to present instruction in a context when the learning is meaningful and important. Many teachers use clocking to present each item to be checked as a micro-mini-teach. For example, when asking students to check *their, there, they're*, the teacher quickly writes the three words on the board, covers the letter *t* in *their* and *there* and shows students the first is a person, the second a place, thereby giving the students a handy mnemonic device. Then just as quickly, the teacher points out the apostrophe in *they're* and shows the students it means *they are*. If students are allowed time to correct and edit after the proofreading, a tactic they see as improving their grade, they will soon value peers who help them elevate their papers and grades. This, in turn, lightens the teacher's paper load because students catch many peevish errors.

We have on occasion observed teachers preparing proofreading sheets ahead for the students. While this might allow for smoother transitions and a more rapid movement through the experience, we believe students should prepare their own proofreading sheets. First, since writing is a mode of learning, when students write the skill to be "clocked" on their paper, they have think time. Second, student-prepared material has the "feel" of discovery that engages students more directly. Third, when students add the items one at a time, they focus more intently on it rather than trying to do everything at once—or nothing at all.

Computerized Proofreading

Most students are familiar with software that makes writing in all its stages easier. We still remember writing articles for *English Journal, English in Texas*, and other journals where one error sent us back to retype not one but often many pages. We remember the footnoted research paper where discovering one line too many at page's end meant retyping and realigning several pages. Some of us would delete a sentence, clause, phrase, or even a word "to make it come out right." What was that all about in becoming a better writer?

However, while handy computer grammar and spell checkers have become ubiquitous, they do not replace thinking through meaning. Though they catch some spelling errors, they miss homonymic ones, foreign words, arcane spellings, typographical errors, or dialects. While grammar checkers signal fragments, passive voice, or subject/verb agreement problems, they overlook the nuances of faulty parallelisms, mixed constructions, and misplaced modifiers.

We recommend teaching checkers as tools, but we also recommend impressing upon students that nothing replaces the careful attention writers give to writing they care about, writing they have invested time and energy into producing.

SEXIST LANGUAGE

Generally, there is no place in writing for sexist language. Sexist language reflects attitudes that are better left unstated. The problem is that English has no singular neuter pronoun that refers to persons. "It" insults humanity; "he" ignores half the human race. Most writers try to rephrase in the plural to avoid this dilemma. Sometimes, however, rephrasing does not solve the sexist language reference and the singular pronoun must be used. When this occurs it is preferable to use "he or she" or "he/she." Occasionally, the use of "s/he" is found.

Some authors cite names that clearly indicate a gender and use the pronoun accordingly, although persons with names like Joyce Kilmer become problematic with this approach. Literature is full of examples of women writers who have used male names for subtle and not so subtle reasons of sexism. George Eliot, Acton, Ellis, and Clive Bell (the Brontës) to name a few. At a time when, as Tillie Olsen points out, one out of twelve published writers are men; at a time when intolerance to race, color, and creed is aberrant and undignified; at a time when cultural diversity is celebrated, there is little to gain by adhering to outdated language conventions such as those embodied in sexist language.

Authors who refer to all principals as "he," all teachers as "she," and all students as "he," need to change. Language changes. Just as the "thou" and "thee" of the Puritan era have been replaced, so should sexist language be replaced. (Of course nonsexist language can be taken to extremes as we all have seen in editorials and jokes that use words such as *humanhole* covers for *manhole* covers.) While humor and the ability to laugh at ourselves are admirable human traits, sexist language bias is not a laughing matter when it becomes embedded in the psyche of students.

Sexist attitudes, like cultural bias, are changing in schools and the effective teacher and writer will want to stay informed on these changes by using a current grammar handbook or guidebook. For an excellent guide consider, *The Handbook of Nonsexist Writing: For Writers, Editors and Speakers*, by Casey Miller and Kate Swift. They state,

> The reason the practice of assigning masculine gender to neutral terms is so enshrined in English is that every language reflects the prejudices of the society in which it evolved, and English evolved through most of its history in a male-centered, patriarchal society. We shouldn't be surprised, therefore, that its vocabulary and grammar reflect attitudes that exclude or demean women. But we are surprised, for until recently few people thought much about what English—or any other language for that matter—was saying on a subliminal level. Now that we have begun to look, some startling things have becomes obvious. What standard English usage says about males, for example, is that they are the species. What it says about females is that they are a subspecies. From these two assertions flow a thousand other enhancing and degrading messages, all encoded in the language we in the English-speaking countries begin to learn almost as soon as we are born. (4)

Writers recognize the changes in language and the need for nonsexist writing. Margaret Donaldson writes in the preface of her book, *Children's Minds*:

> While the word "child" does not convey any information as to sex, there is no similarly neutral personal pronoun in English. I have followed here, though not without some heart-searching, the tradition of using the masculine form *he* when a neutral sense is intended. It is particularly desirable when one is speaking of education not to suggest

that boys are somehow more important. The arguments in this book apply equally to boys and to girls. (x)

Donaldson is keenly aware of the bias reflected in language. As educators in the twenty-first century, as language continues to change, we need to change with our language.

As teachers write for other audiences and as students write for publication, both strive to achieve precision in language. "To go on using in its former sense a word whose meaning has changed is counterproductive. The point is not that we should recognize semantic change, but that in order to be precise, in order to be understood, we must" (Miller and Swift 8). Nonsexist language is just that, more precise.

PUBLISHING

In "Publishing: The Writer's Touchdown," Carroll quotes a drama teacher, "Writing needs some pizzazz, some zip, some zing. My speech and drama students get to show off what they have accomplished. That doesn't happen enough in writing" (1983, 93).

True. Teachers need to provide opportunities for students to print, go public, disseminate, issue, air, or circulate—in a word, *publish* their work. But who should publish, and why? What should be published, how, when, and where?

Peter Elbow states, "Writing's greatest reward, for most of us anyway, is the sense of reaching an audience. . . . Without having to muster all the courage it takes to stop strangers on the street, you can nevertheless find friends or make acquaintances who will *want* to read your words. In effect, publish" (1981, 212). Students fall under Elbow's category of "most of us" and are the *who* of publishing. The pizzazz, zip, and zing fulfill publication's *why*. Students choose *what* to publish, and the school's calendar determines the *when*, be it the choicest writing of a marking period, a semester, or an entire academic year or something students just want to share in a read-around.

Ways to Publish

The *how* of publishing varies from the stories of preschoolers drawn randomly on the back of wallpaper samples, to the work of middle schoolers neatly photocopied in plastic binders, to essays high schoolers generate on their computers. The most realistic *how* is preparing a manuscript to be sent out for publication. The *where* of publishing may be a bulletin board, the hallway, the library, *Merlyn's Pen*, *Stone Soup*, or entering a writing contest. There is no the limit to *where* of publishing.

Presently online publishing with its networks, notebooks, journals, chats, blogs, with its global audience and its testimony to the free press give students access to intoxicating publishing venues.

Writing should go public since publishing permits an audience. Publishing matters because it is the writer's solo flight, winning basket, birdie; it is the writer's curtain call, recital, aria; it is the writer's exhibit, premier, trophy; it is the writer's touchdown. And students get their applause. It comes in the form of responses, notes, reading from the "Author's Chair," seeing the manuscript in print, book fairs, read-arounds, and publishing events.

Students should write with an audience in mind. If their writing is personal, such as notes jotted in a diary, their process stops there. There is no need to worry about a fragment or incoherence. There is no need to flesh out an image or make sure the spelling is correct. If, however, writers intend their writing to be shared with others, the process of revising, editing, proofreading, and ultimately publishing takes on an importance tantamount to a school's drama production, a sporting event, a band concert, or an edition of the school's newspaper. Going public means making sure that the writing is acceptable in every way for the reader, double-checking distractions and choosing the best format.

Just as professional writers reject some of their writing early in the process, choosing for publication is worth what Faulkner calls "the agony and the sweat" of taking the piece through the entire process from prewriting through publishing, so, too, not every piece of student's writing goes through the entire process. Only after the choosing to commit to one piece does a student work it through the process schema to publishing.

Variations of Self-Publishing

Those teachers who implement self-publication need patience. Self-publication in the classroom is noisy, messy, chaotic, but exciting. The school culture that identifies quality learning with silent seatwork will be unnerved by students engaged in self-publishing. Because students are active in a process that demands collaboration, communication, synthesis, and exploration, self-publication does not suggest that the teacher has no control, or should abandon control; self-publishing calls upon good classroom management by the teacher.

Students cannot always determine prior to writing what type of publishing their work will require. The genre, the meaning, and the purpose of the writing influence the publishing and the student's decisions on where and how to publish.

Publication takes place in many different ways. For some students, writing their final copy on colorful paper with colored ink or in a hand-made book is product enough. Others live for that byline in the school newspaper. Many embrace the class anthology as their reward. Secure places in cyberspace lure many students into publishing, but a few will always submit to the school's literary magazine. We have seen some students create pieces of extraordinary power that were sent out into the world.

Author's Chair

Explanation. The author's chair, often called the "share chair," gives students opportunities to read their writing and elicit responses from an audience. Only student authors sharing their writing sit in this special "Author's Chair." Decorating it, allowing students to autograph it, or painting it in the school's colors supports the specialness of writing and sharing. High director's chairs, used in middle school and high school, sophisticate the idea.

On most days, at least two or three students eagerly want to share their writing. They wait expectantly for share time and are respectful of each other.

Implementation.

- Students meet on a rug or carpet squares with their writing.

- The teacher invites a student to share. He or she sits in the author's chair and reads. If there is a separate illustration to share the author invites a friend to assist.

- Students sit respectfully listening and applauding the writing.

- When finished reading, the author asks, "What did you like about my writing?" and calls on no more than three students.

- The author asks, "What do you want to know more about?" and calls on no more than three students.

- Students are taught how to give specific feedback.

- After the author's turn, she or he selects the next author to share.

Remarks. Initially students are hesitant or shy, but after time and positive experiences, they all want to share. Teachers find they often have more sharers than time.

The Read-Around

Explanation. The read-around, that special cumulative experience for student writers, happens on selected days through the school year, usually after writing has been completed.

Implementation.

- Students come to the read-around with their final copy ready to share what they have written in its entirety. No student may read another student's paper. It's all about ownership.

- Chairs are arranged in a large circle, or students may sit in a large circle on the floor.

- One student begins the reading. When that student finishes, the next student reads, and so on—moving around the circle until everyone has read. The students listen and respond nonverbally with nods, smiles, or applause.

Remarks. Initially some teachers find it difficult to coax students to share their writing aloud, but as they grow in their writing, work in small groups, and perceive the classroom as nonthreatening, students slowly want to share during the read-around. For these slow starters, we recommend encouraging them to read a portion of their writing, even a sentence or two. Sometimes, it's the sound of their own voice resonating in the classroom that is a deterrent—hearing it in small doses helps. No one wants to be left out.

Book-Making

Explanation. Before making books in the classroom, teachers should practice making their own books. Once teachers have mastered the knack of folding, they better anticipate where students need assistance and when they need to be left alone. No two classes, or for that matter no two students, duplicate the way they make books. Prior experience readies the teacher.

Implementation. While there are several books available about making books, we have included the direction for those we find easiest and most popular: accordion books (Fig. 7.1), eight-page books (more precisely called *quires*) (Fig. 7.2), pop-up books (Fig. 7.3), and slotted books (Fig. 7.4).

Fig. 7.1. Accordion Book.

1. Fold an 8½-by-11-inch sheet of paper in half, short end to short end.

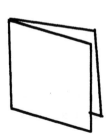

2. Fold back flaps to center fold.

There will be a cover and seven pages of text and artwork. Works well with circle stories or pattern books.

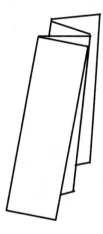

When making books follow these some general guidelines.

1. Have materials available in a publishing center or corner of the room.

2. Instruct students about these materials and label each.

3. Have prepared directions and models for making various types of books. Laminate these for extended use.

4. Teach responsibility in care and maintenance of the publishing center.

5. Find a place for display of the books.

Remarks. When teachers do not want a center, yet want students to enjoy the pleasure and pride of making their own books, teachers model one type or another at the conclusion of a paper until the students have a repertoire from which to choose.

Fig. 7.2. Quire/8-Page Book.

1. Fold an 8½-by-11-inch sheet of paper in half, short end to short end, and crease.

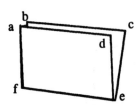

2. Fold again, short end to short end.

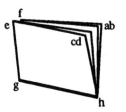

3. Fold again, short end to short end.

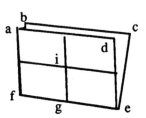

4. Open up the page to reveal the 8 sections.

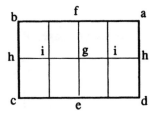

5. Make the original fold again, short end to short end. Cut from center point (g) to the mid point (i) along the crease.

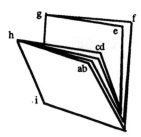

6. Open back up and fold long side to long side. Push left and right ends to center.

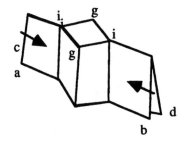

7. Fold flat along all creases to form the eight-page book.

There will be six pages for writing and artwork, and a front and back cover.

Fig. 7.3. Pop-Up Book.

1. Fold page in half and cut through the double page in two places. Do not cut more than half way down.

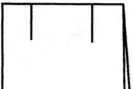

2. Fold down top panel. Crease.

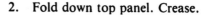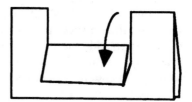

3. Make a tent shape and push the cut flap in between the outer pages.

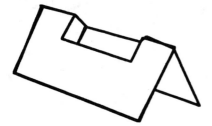

4. Turn the tent shape over as shown. Students can write on the top and bottom pages and illustrate the pop-up.

Fig. 7.4. Slotted Book.

1. Fold a sheet of paper in half, short end to short end. Cut a long sliver off the fold, leaving 1 inch on each end.

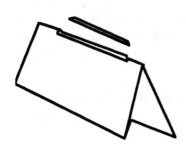

2. Fold another sheet, short end to short end. Cut a 1-inch notch out of each end of these. Do this, one sheet at a time, to as many sheets as needed.

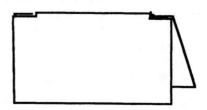

3. Take the sheet from step 1 (the sheet with the long sliver cut out). Open it and lay it flat on the table.

4. Take the sheets from step 2. Open them flat, one on top of the other, to make a stack *next to* the sheet from step 1.

(continued)

Fig. 7.4. Slotted Book *Continued.*

5. Slide the stack of sheets from step 2 through the sliver in the sheet from step 1. Stop when the notches are lined up with the sliver. You can slide the stack of sheets through the sliver all at once, or you can slide in one sheet at a time. To make it easier to slide the sheets through the sliver, you can lightly fold the stack long end to long end, then open the sheets up when they are in place.

6. Tidy up the pages so all the edges are even. Fold at the creases to make the book.

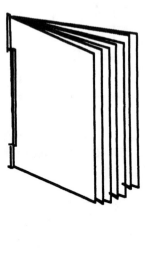

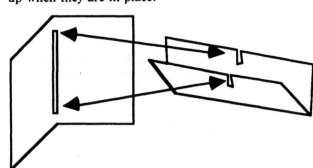

The Publishing Center

Self-publishing requires a caché of supplies. To cut a considerable expense to the teacher or the school, students, left to their own devices, with a minimum of supplies but the freedom to explore, find, make, or improvise supplies they need.

General Supplies

The printing press allowed everyone to become a reader. The computer allows everyone to be a publisher. So necessary items for publishing in the twenty-first century are computers with access to programs such as HyperStudio®, PowerPoint®, Inspiration®, Page Maker®, Quark XPress®, and others.

X-Acto® Knives—very sharp, not recommended for use without adult supervision.

Cutting mats—good cutting mats, available from art suppliers, are expensive but indestructible.

Metal rulers—these keep their shape and cannot be cut into.

Adhesives—Elmer's® is still the best and safest; glue sticks are also great.

Needles—large darning needles available from fabric stores work well.

Cover board—everything from cardboard and poster board to oak tag.

Paper—8 ½″ × 11″ or 11″ × 17″ paper of any quality and any color works.

Chicken rings—plastic rings available at craft stores for binding purposes.

String—dental floss works best for saddle stitching.

Tape—3M® plastic tape cannot be beaten for quality and durability.

Scissors—all types, including those that have fancy cutting edges.

Markers—all colors, sizes, and points—washable and permanent.

Pencils and pens.

Glue gun—at least one available with teacher supervision.

Making Self-Published Books Available

The natural place to display the students' books is the classroom. But displays need not be limited. Several librarians we know initiate student-generated rotating book displays. They place check-out cards in every book with individual call numbers. Students who wish to read someone's book simply check it out. Some librarians conduct "Reader's Choice Awards" where students who have read all the student books in a particular grade vote for their favorite. Librarians place the school emblem embossed on a gold seal on the cover of the winners' books or some such "Newbery" designation.

Librarians also use students' books as a vehicle to teach categorization skills. This aids students in using library collections. What better way to learn how books get categorized than with your own book?

Professional and Commercial Publication

Another way students get published is by preparing their manuscripts for contests, or publication in commercial magazines, journals, and books. Writing for publication is the ultimate extensive writing. Teachers often do not see themselves as writers. But if they do not write and publish, how will they share the richness of discovery? And how will they model publication for their students? Teachers are also experts in areas other than academe. For example, we know teachers who have been published on topics as diverse as genealogy, herbs, antiques, yearbooks, horses, Strawberry Shortcake collectibles, raising goats, and teaching Sunday school. English language arts teachers know more than just the practice and theory of teaching English. So do students. Students need to write for a wider audience.

But wait. Before getting all wound up in the glamour world of publishing, heed what William Stafford says about writing for publication: "By following after money, publication, and recognition, you might risk what happened to the John Cheever character who in like manner 'damaged, you might say, the ear's innermost chamber where we hear the heavy noise of the dragon's tail moving over the dead leaves'" (5). His advice is to follow the writer's compass, by "allowing in your own life the freedom to pay attention to your feelings while finding your way through language" (4). Good advice for teachers and students who write. The writer must first have something to say.

Then comes the challenge: Finding a place to get the "stuff" published. Stephen King advises writers to study the markets. "Only a dimwit would send a story about giant vampire bats surrounding a high school to *McCall's*. Only a dimwit would send a tender story about a mother and daughter making up their differences on Christmas Eve to *Playboy* . . . but people do it all the time" (19). We had a teacher who wanted to send an article on necrophilia to *English Journal*! Nothing strikes an editor as inane as the inappropriate manuscript.

Reading what writers advise about publishing may confuse the writer who wishes to publish. Some say, "Write first for yourself; then find a place to send it." Others advise, "Write what sells." Others such as Madeleine L'Engle suggest, "Whom does the writer write for? It is only a partial truth to say that I write for myself, out of my own need, asking, whether I realize it or not, the questions I am asking in my own life. A truer answer is that I write for the book" (27).

Writing for publication can be the most rewarding experience for the writer. Gloria Foster published her first article about the gray child, the child that fades into oblivion, the one no one remembers, in *Learning*. Gloria was elated when she received the notice of publication. When the magazine came out, and the cover featured a child painted gray standing unnoticed in a crowded classroom, Gloria carried the magazine around with her for days. Finally, her daughter said, "Mother get over it." Gloria finally did get over the initial elation, but she has never gotten over seeing her name in print for the first time.

Barbara Wurthmann shared a similar experience with her article "First Grade Reflections," when it was published. Barbara's confidence as a writer and a teacher increased because of its publication. When the piece was read at the school board meeting and she received recognition as a teacher who writes, Barbara understood the power of words in a new way.

The experiences of teachers mirror that of students.

Danielle and Erin decided to work together on an exposé of prejudicial attitudes and practices of department store sales clerks as part of their high school research project. They had observed on one of their shopping excursions that some people had difficulty getting waited on by some clerks, so they set up an experiment. Danielle dressed up and went to a famous shopping mall. She entered each store and Erin timed the responses of the sales clerks. They recorded their experiences and took notes. Danielle had no trouble getting assistance.

Before going back to the mall the following Saturday, Danielle and Erin stopped at the Salvation Army and purchased clothing for Erin from the discarded apparel. Erin did not comb her hair, wore no make-up, and generally appeared sloppy and unkempt. They proceeded back to the mall. This time Erin entered the shops, and Danielle timed the responses. Of the 126 stores Erin entered, she was asked to leave twenty-five. The average response time that it took the sales clerks to ask Erin if she needed assistance was seven minutes compared to Danielle's forty-eight seconds.

Erin noted rude clerks who spoke to her in a pejorative tone. Erin, who was slated to be the valedictorian, became angry. At one exclusive woman's name-brand leather goods store, she stood at the counter for twenty minutes, growing restless after waiting she asked clerks for assistance. They ignored her. Finally, the store security guard approached her to ask if he could help her.

Proud of their research, they eagerly wrote up their findings. The resulting fifteen-page account of two girls shopping—one who appeared privileged in every way, the other who lacked a privileged appearance—was powerful.

Not satisfied with writing the paper for the teacher, they wanted a wider audience. They prepared their paper as a manuscript and sent it to the management of the mall. Three days later they had a call from the assistant manager. A week later they met with the assistant and the manager. Two weeks later they presented their research at the store managers' monthly luncheon. Letters of apology and copies of store clerk policies clearly noting that discrimination because of status, race, or creed would not be tolerated sent the message that Danielle and Erin had found an audience.

Writers cannot get published if they do not send out their manuscripts. Obvious enough, but, unfortunately, some students put a great deal into their writing only to give up at this point. Publishing is not the time to become faint-hearted. Nor is it the time to play what Peter Elbow calls the "doubting game." The adage applies: "If you think you can, you can; if you think you can't, you can't." Teachers who send out for publication get published. Teachers who have classrooms where publication is encouraged, nurtured, and taught have students who get published. Some of the publications are stunning, and prestigious; some are local and ordinary—all are rewarding.

Basic Vocabulary of Publishing Manuscripts

Advance. Money the publisher pays prior to publication. The advance is against the royalty, that is, the total amount to be paid for the piece of writing.

Byline. Name of author appears with the published piece. The word *byline* is not used for books.

Chapbook. Small booklet of stories and poems, usually paperback.

Contributor's copies. Copies of the magazine or books (collected volumes) in which the author's work appears sent to the author of the issue. For academic publications, this is generally what the writer receives since publication is considered a professional honor—at the college level, it is considered a duty.

Copyright. The protection that an author has to keep someone from stealing the work. It is not necessary to register the work with the Copyright Office. The moment the author writes the work it is automatically protected. Registering is usually done after publication or infringement. Publishers generally purchase all rights or some rights when they purchase a manuscript.

Cover letter. A brief letter that accompanies the manuscript. The cover letter contains only the title of manuscript and assurance that it is not being submitted simultaneously to another publisher.

Kill fee. Fee paid for manuscript that was accepted but not used. For example, several Cold War spy novels were "killed" after the Berlin Wall came down.

Payment on acceptance. As soon as the editor accepts the manuscript for publication, payment is made.

Payment on publication. Payment is not made until the manuscript is printed—several months to a year or more after acceptance.

Query. A letter to the editor to arouse interest or to see if there is interest in what the writer is writing. A query letter contains a brief summary of the work, written in the style and tone used in the piece, length of the article, and the author's credentials.

Release. A guarantee that the manuscript is original and unpublished.

Self-publishing. The author retains all proceeds from sales because the author pays for all the production, manufacturing, and marketing of the piece. Also called vanity publishing.

Simultaneous submissions. Sending a manuscript to two or more editors at the same time and considered unethical. Most publishers do not accept simultaneous submissions. If the writer does simultaneously submit a manuscript, the writer should inform the editor in the cover letter.

Unsolicited manuscript. Any manuscript the editor did not request. Some magazines and many book publishers such as *Reader's Digest* and *The New Yorker* do not accept unsolicited manuscripts.

Preparing the Manuscript

It is important for students to understand the guidelines for preparing their manuscripts. To send a manuscript out without observing the conventions announces to the editor either the author is a beginner or the author doesn't care. Neither make an impression upon editors who receive thousands of manuscripts.

All manuscripts should be typed double-spaced. The writing of young children is the exception. Magazines that publish emergent writers often want to see the original work; in that case, a typed transcription should accompany the manuscript. No writer is too young to find an audience; for example, the magazine *Stone Soup* publishes the writing and artwork of young children.

The mailing envelope should contain the cover letter; the manuscript, including its title page; a self-addressed and stamped envelope (SASE) for the return of the manuscript. The cover letter must be a standard business letter with all of the conventions observed:

1. *Heading*: first three lines of letter

    a. writer's street address and apartment number (if any)

    b. writer's city, state, and ZIP code

2. *Date*

3. *Inside Address*: addressee

    a. name of editor

    b. title (editor, editor in chief, features editor, etc.)

    c. magazine name (underlined/italics)

    d. street address or P.O. box number

    e. city, state, and ZIP code

4. *Salutation*: formal and followed by a colon

    a. use Mr., Ms., or Dr. and the person's full name

5. *Body*: begins two lines below the salutation

    a. paragraph as any writing

    b. check for accuracy and correctness; sloppy manuscripts suggest sloppy writing

6. *Closing*: formal and followed by a comma

    a. *Yours truly* and *Sincerely yours* are the most formal

    b. writer's signature

    c. writer's name typed

The manuscript should always have a title page. It should contain:

a. title of manuscript

b. author's name

c. home address

d. home phone number

e. work address

f. work phone number

g. e-mail address

Pagination of the manuscript starts with the first page of writing, not the title page. The page number should appear in the upper right corner on each page followed by a one- or two-word short form of the article's title or the author's last name. When manuscripts are peer-reviewed or juried (readers of the magazine read the piece and advise the editor on publishing), the author's name should only appear on the title page. In that case, the identifier is the short form of the article's title: "The American Scholar/1." When manuscripts are not peer-reviewed or juried, the author's name should appear on each page as well as on the title page: "Dickens/1."

Students should affix the title page and the manuscript pages together with paper clips. Editors find staples make it too hard to turn the pages without folding up the manuscript. When placing the paper clip onto the manuscript, most writers like to first place a small slip of paper where the clip will go to keep from marring the pages or leaving rust marks.

If more than one copy of the manuscript is requested, most editors accept photocopied submissions. They even allow for a few hand-corrected typos, but onionskin paper is anathema.

The SASE

The SASE, or self-addressed, stamped envelope, is necessary for the proper ebb and flow of publishing. Since not every manuscript finds publication, teaching students to observe the conventions and enclose a return envelope with the submitted manuscript—even if the piece is on the computer and the student does not want the manuscript back—is a matter of courtesy. When preparing the SASE, a student writes his or her name and address on both envelopes—as the addressee on one envelope and as the addressed on the other envelope.

Acceptances and rejections may appear illogical or unjust to neophyte writers. For example, an editor for a professional journal rejected a fine piece on Shakespeare because he had just published an article on the Bard. Normally, he would have published the second submission but its approach to Shakespeare was too similar to the one he had just published. In this case, the published piece was inferior to the rejected one but that happens in the publishing world. Also, editors are known to accept articles because they "fit" a particular issue in tone, topic, or length—reasons that strike writers as illogical or serendipitous. But students should not become discouraged by the rejections; they must learn not take them personally.

Most editors prefer to receive manuscripts in large (9 × 12) envelopes because when manuscripts are folded and placed inside legal sized envelopes, they tend to retain the folds and become difficult to manage. Impress upon students the notion that writers strive to make everything easy for the editor. Also when preparing the envelope, writers generally do not paste the return postage directly on the envelope. Instead, they put the postage loosely in a piece of folded paper, just large enough to cover all the stamps. Then clip the postage in the slip to the return envelope. If the editor accepts the manuscript, the SASE will not be needed. This keeps postage from being wasted. While it is not necessary, again, it is a courtesy.

Now, with technology literally at everyone's fingertips, more and more editors are accepting query letters by e-mail and even proposals in that manner.

Places to Publish

For teachers. Start with an accessible professional library. Most teachers belong to the professional organization in their disciplines, so those are also good places to begin. For English language arts teachers this includes the International Reading Association (IRA), the National Council of Teachers of English (NCTE), or local affiliates of these organizations. The national organizations publish many journals for various audiences. IRA has *The Reading Teacher* for pedagogical articles, *Reading Research Quarterly* for research, a tabloid called *Reading Today*, and others.

NCTE has among others, *Language Arts* for pedagogical and research on the elementary level, and *Voices in the Middle* and *English Journal* for the pedagogical on the middle and high school levels. Their publications of *College English*, *College Composition and Communication*, *English Education*, and *Research in the Teaching of English* are for research. Most affiliates have local publications.

For teachers who write and want to explore nonacademic audiences, *Writer's Market*, published annually in hard copy and online, is the best resource for information about most magazines. Its directory lists basic publishing information on markets, fees, manuscript requirements, and so forth. Once a magazine has been found, the public library and local bookstore provide access to most publications. Reading the magazines before sending out a manuscript is a must in order to match what has been written to the most suited audience.

For students. The same advice for teachers applies for students. An excellent source for student writers is *Children's Writer and Illustrator's Market*. This directory focuses exclusively on children's and young adult publications. Published by Writer's Digest books, it does for young authors what *Writer's Market* does for adults.

CONCLUSION

John Ciardi, the poet, writes, "At a recent writer's conference I sat in on a last-day session billed as 'Getting Published.' Getting published was, clearly, everyone's enthusiasm. The hope of getting published will certainly do as one reason for writing. It need not be the only, nor even the best, reason for writing. Yet that hope is always there" (376). Ciardi is right. Hope is always there, yet he goes on to say,

Emily Dickinson found reasons for writing that were at least remote from publication. Yet even she had it in mind. She seems to have known that what she wrote was ahead of its time, but she also seemed to know that its time would come . . . she spent her last ten years writing her letters to the future. . . . The letters, to be sure, were addressed to specific friends; yet they were equally addressed through her friends to her future readers. . . . Emily spent ten years writing her poems (1,776 of them), and then ten more years stating the terms for their reception. (376)

To lead students to think everything they write is worthy of publication is unfair. We encourage teachers to allow publishing to take on broader meanings. Students need to see, feel, hear, and think about these broader meanings. To move publishing from just print, or final copy, to the self-satisfaction of the completeness of expression is the best "publishing." How does the teacher do this? By finding the satisfaction in his or her own writing, each in his or her own way: by sending out and receiving rejections; by submitting and receiving a acceptances and rejections and by sharing them with the students; by sitting in that Author's Chair and watching the faces of the students; by having hope.

APPLICATION

Choose one piece of writing you have taken from prewriting to publication. Research a journal to which you might submit your piece. Write a cover letter and prepare the self-addressed stamped envelope and mailing envelope.

8

ASSESSMENT

As a test of writing ability, no test is as convincing to teachers of English, to teachers in other departments, to prospective employers, and to the public as actual samples of each student's writing.

—Paul B. Diederich □

MEASURING GROWTH IN WRITING

We made our way down College Avenue en route to the Rutgers Library. The leaves so brilliant in their oranges, reds, umbers hung as mere pentimenti of their earlier greens. But we hardly noticed; we were on a mission. We were seeking a slim volume by Paul B. Diederich called *Measuring Growth in English*. Published in 1974 by the National Council of Teachers of English, Diederich's landmark study answered the accountability problem of assessment as writing as a process gained favor with academicians and teachers across the country. Here was a reliable way to assess large numbers of papers. Here were criteria for all English teachers. We were eager to secure the book and read what this eminent specialist in measurement, who held three degrees in Latin and Greek classics from Harvard and Columbia, had to say about grading students' papers. We were especially interested because Diederich spent twenty-five years with the Educational Testing Service (ETS) and at that time in 1977 NJWP had just entered into holistic scoring training at ETS. The project ventured into new and exciting assessment territory since the National Assessment of Educational Progress (NAEP) and ETS had just developed holistic scoring in the 1970s, and we wanted to know all about it before we arrived in Princeton.

As we read and studied, Diederich gave us more than we could imagine. In his monograph, he makes the case that English teachers have an obligation to determine how well each student writes; he makes the case for standards of accuracy in grading, measurement, record keeping, and reporting. He discusses how traditional grading procedures cause hard feelings among students, teachers, and parents, and holds that grades "ought to be reduced to the smallest possible number necessary to find out how students are getting along toward the four or five main objectives of the program" (2). He talks about reliability, and sets out the basis for first-impression scoring—the foundation for what we now call holistic scoring. He rests his defense on

> Most of the teachers had required a paper every two weeks from their students, and if they were conscientious about it, it took about forty hours a week to grade, correct, and comment on them. Now that they had a reliable measure of writing ability, the grades were superfluous, and a careful study convinced us that the corrections were more damaging than helpful. Hence they refused to grade the homework papers; they cut out most of the corrections; and they concentrated on brief marginal comments, emphasizing what the student had done well. At the end, however, they might add one suggestion for the improvement of the next paper, but rarely more than one. (4)

After discussing the effect of bias in grading and the effects of excessive correction, Diederich lays out directions for computing the reliability of essay grades and objective tests (32–41). Additionally, he deals with the factors that influence judgments of writing ability. When he gave fifty-four readers 300 papers to evaluate without a set criteria, he discovered the papers were rated differently by each reader and on different criteria—ranging from *ideas expressed* to *punctuation and spelling* to *organization and analysis* to *wording and phrasing* to *style*. There was a 43 percent variance in grades with 57 percent unexplained (10). One reader did not complete the assignment.

Diederich's Eight Qualities

Diederich culled these "eight qualities" from the factors the readers stressed.

- Ideas, their richness, soundness, clarity, development, relevance to topic, and author's purpose came from sixteen readers representing six occupational fields.

- Organization and analysis came from nine readers, some business executives.

- Wording and phrasing, the choice and arrangement of words, including the deletion of unnecessary words, what Diederich calls "the vocabulary factor," came from nine readers with no occupational bias.

- Flavor included style, individuality, originality, interest, and sincerity—personal qualities revealed by the writing came from seven readers, four of whom were either writers or editors. Diederich did not want to use the word *style* because another group of readers thought of style as it pertained to the use of language. To distinguish, Diederich chose the word *flavor*.

- Usage, punctuation, spelling came from thirteen readers; seven were college English teachers.

- Handwriting; interestingly in these days of computers, Diederich did not include "handwriting" in his original eight qualities because he used typed copies. When he discovered a concurrent study of eleven-year-olds conducted by the Italian psychologist Remondino using a method slightly different than his but where the papers were handwritten and which included the factor of "graphics," Diederich added "handwriting, neatness" when teachers rated handwritten papers (7–9).

The Importance of Diederich's Work

The reason this slim book was and continues to be so important to us and to writing assessment for the global generation is because Diederich at once disproved many myths about grading while providing a research-based and practical procedure for evaluating students' writing. His qualities have become the prototype for national and state rubrics for writing. His study furnished the genesis for general-impression holistic scoring and primary trait scoring, known as focused holistic scoring; it sowed the seeds for Vicki Spandel's six-traits writing assessment, but most importantly for us, it gave us research upon which to fashion a sound construct for *classroom* use—the Carroll/Wilson Analytic Scale for Classroom Use, which we have tested, perfected, and validated for over twenty years through classroom research on all grade levels.

Developing the Carroll/Wilson Analytic Scale for Classroom Use

Although the Diederich Scale became the foundation for the Carroll/Wilson Analytic Scale for Classroom Use, we found Diederich's Scale static. On his scale, once the items were determined and tested for reliability and validity, they remained the same and were used to assess large numbers of papers. We needed something dynamic, a scale that could be used effectively and efficiently in the changing climate of curricula that required multiple papers, multiple genres, multiple skills, multiple purposes, multiple audiences, multiple grade levels, *and* one that accommodated the developing capabilities of growing writers. Our scale had to be versatile yet sound; it had to be flexible and alterable yet consistent and stable; it had to be *reliable*. Further, it had to be efficacious and well grounded; it had to produce the desired results; it had to measure what it promised to measure; it had to be *valid*.

So we challenged ourselves to devise such a scale. It seemed logical that while there are universal attributes of good writing such as organization, focus, coherence, and so forth, we needed to identify features stressed in the *teaching* of a paper. We asked ourselves, how could teachers assess all their teaching about getting the paper started with a bang? What measure could be used when students get rid of their preponderance of "to be" verbs that bog down active writing and deter good diction? What means would evaluate the depth of writing but still address the niggling problems students have with commas? Remembering what Diederich cautioned about marking too many errors, we began to create scales for particular papers; we began working with teachers on these scales, and we urged teachers to try to create similar scales with their students.

As we continued our research, so did our trainers. Soon we made the scale part of the NJWPT/ Abydos Institute. In time, the Carroll/Wilson Analytic Scale for Classroom Use became a staple. Teachers loved them because once they became comfortable creating them collaboratively, the scales eased the burden of the paper load. Students loved them because they felt part of the assessment process, finally knowing what would be graded. Parents loved them because they saw accountability in action.

In 1993, the analytic scale was a mere paragraph in the first edition of *Acts*, with a nod to Diederich and a few sample scales in the appendix. Today, the scale is the major way teachers trained in our institutes evaluate papers.

The Carroll/Wilson Analytic Scale for Classroom Use

Explanation. In a writing process classroom, teachers introduce and model prewriting, help students organize their papers in authentic ways, teach and model ratiocination as revision and grammar, confer on drafts, and facilitate putting it all together in final, publishable form. It would be against the philosophy of writing as a process, if when it came to assessment, teachers abandoned students to grade their papers in some solitary subjective way. As Diederich says, "The average English paper corrected by the average English teacher looks as though it had been trampled on with cleated boots and has about the same effect on the student" (in Judine 38). We know from research stretching back to the 1950s and 1960s the futility of hemorrhaging on papers.

So it seems clear: As teachers we must assess students' writing, but after we have mentored them through the process, we must not forsake them at the end. But how would that work? We were not totally convinced students should assess their own papers either. The solution came to us through Diederich's work. We drew powerful pedagogical significance from his research. We adapted his qualities as items and his method for scoring as the foundation upon which to construct a system where teachers *and* students work *together* to create a scale (called a rubric in contemporary parlance) for each paper taken through the process based on what the teacher taught and what the students were expected to learn. We call this the Carroll/Wilson Analytic Scale for Classroom Use.

Implementation. The procedure of arriving at a student's grade is analytic because discrete parts of the composition are listed as a scale. Teacher and student identify items for the scale and work together to prioritize these items so they can be weighted and then rated. We recommend all teachers who teach writing as a process adopt this method for the final scoring of papers that have gone through the process. Here is how it works.

- Several days before the paper is due but before clocking, the teacher asks students to brainstorm what they were taught during the writing of the paper. The teacher or a scribe writes the students' offerings on large sheets of butcher paper to be kept for future reference.

- After reading over the list together, the teacher invites the students to continue their input by prioritizing the list, which the teacher facilitates. Typically the first time students do this, they want spelling or punctuation first on the list. The teacher nudges, "Do you think those items are more important than your ideas?" Eventually, and through deep thinking about what makes effective writing, students come up with a well-prioritized list, one that closely approximates Diederich's. If students are adamant, however, about spelling or punctuation first, teachers weight the papers accordingly; students never opt for spelling or punctuation first again.

- The teacher uses the prioritized list to work up the scale by weighting the items on the basis of 100 percent.

One of the most well-known scales, known as the Diederich Scale, was developed from an analysis of judgments of the writing of college freshmen.

	Low	Middle	High			
General Merit						
Ideas	2	4	6	8	10	
Organization	2	4	6	8	10	
Wording	1	2	3	4	5	
Flavor	1	2	3	4	5	_____
Mechanics						
Usage	1	2	3	4	5	
Punctuation	1	2	3	4	5	
Spelling	1	2	3	4	5	
Handwriting	1	2	3	4	5	_____
					Sum	_____

The spaces on the right are for subtotals with "sum" for the total rating. "If a student gets the lowest possible rating on everything, his total will be 10; if all his ratings are in column 2, his total will be 20; and similar totals for the other three columns are 30, 40, and 50. These coincide with the standard scores of 10, 20, 30, 40, and 50 corresponding to letter grades of E, D, C, B, and A" (54).

Of course, in adapting the scale, we used 100 as the base; we also moved from a 5-point scale to a 4-point scale because we found when using the 5-point scale, most teachers opted for 3, the middle number. With the 4-point scale, teachers are forced to choose between high and low. The 4-point scale also mirrors many scales used on high-stakes tests.

After studying Diederich's scale, teachers and students are able to devise their own scales so students have a say in what is scored and how it is prioritized. There are no big surprises in the grading, and students know beforehand what is expected in the paper. Here are two samples:

Sample: The Carroll/Wilson Analytic Scale
for Classroom Use—A Reflexive Paper

	1-Poor	2-Weak	3-Good	4-Excellent
General Merit	1	2	3	4
Content	5	6	8	10
Introduction	5	6	8	10
Logical order	5	6	8	10
Vocabulary	5	6	8	10
Voice	5	6	8	10
Focus	5	6	8	10
			Subtotal	_____
Mechanics				
"To be" verbs	5	6	8	10
Commas	5	6	8	10
Sentence variety	5	6	8	10
Spelling	5	6	8	10
			Subtotal	_____
			Total Rating	_____

Comments: _____

_____

For the general merit on this paper, Student X received 54 points. The teacher circled 10 for content; 10 for introduction; 8 for organization; 8 for vocabulary; 10 for voice; 8 for focus. For mechanics, this student received 36 points—10 for "to be" verbs; 8 for commas; 10 for sentence variety; and 8 for spelling. Student X's total rating was 90.

Comments read: A snapper of an intro. You make your grandfather come alive. Watch your focus, though. Here and there you strayed.

Since the analytic scale always reflects the lessons taught for a paper, this paper reflects the generous amount of time the teacher spent on leads and introductions, organization, and focus. When she introduced reflexive writing, they did much prewriting, sharing content and discussing voice in small groups and in debriefings. She modeled "to be" verbs, commas, and sentence variety.

Sample: The Carroll/Wilson Analytic Scale
for Classroom Use—An Extensive Paper

	1-Poor	2-Weak	3-Good	4-Excellent
General Merit	1	2	3	4
Content	5	6	8	10
Purpose	5	6	8	10
Structure	5	6	8	10
Coherence	5	6	8	10
Documentation	5	6	8	10
Introduction/thesis	5	6	8	10
			Subtotal	_____
Mechanics				
Sentence lengths	5	6	8	10
Commas	5	6	8	10
Quotation marks	5	6	8	10
Noun/verb agreement	5	6	8	10
			Subtotal	_____
			Total Rating	_____

Comments: _____

For the general merit on this paper, Student Z received 46 points. The teacher circled 8 for content; 8 for purpose; 8 for structure; 8 for coherence; 6 for documentation; 8 for introduction/thesis. For mechanics, this student received 34 points—10 for sentence length; 8 for commas; 8 for quotation marks; 8 for noun/verb agreement. Student X's total rating was 80.

Comments read: Overall good paper—much improved over last one. Next time concentrate on that internal documentation.

When teaching this paper, the teacher concentrated on author's purpose and the content that would inform that purpose. He spent several classes teaching coherence, showing examples, and modeling it. He also connected thesis in writing to theme in literature and showed examples of powerful essay introductions. From there he moved to organization, using Bruffee. The thrust of his work centered on internal documentation. He spent four class periods on mechanics—one on sentence lengths, one on commas, one on quotation marks, and one on agreement—all within the context of the students' paper.

- The teacher mathematically computes the items and values on the basis of 100 percent, copies the scales, and distributes it to students *before* clocking. Some teachers also make copies to be sent home to parents.

- Teachers often use the items on the scale as items for clocking.

- Students take their scales, their clocking feedback, and their papers for a final opportunity to correct, revise, and reformulate them.

- After clocking and after the students have had time to correct, revise, or reformulate for the last time, the papers are collected. Teachers, keeping the items in mind, read through the paper once quickly. Upon the second read, they circle the appropriate number for each item as described on the previous sample reflexive and extensive scales.

Remarks. The Carroll/Wilson Analytic Scale for Classroom Use enables teachers to assess quickly and effectively *exactly* what they have taught. Students, especially after the first experience with this scale, know *exactly* what will be graded. The academic beauty of this system is that students attend more closely to lessons on writing during the process because they know they will be held accountable.

> *While teaching the narrative to a group of inner-city sixth-graders for three weeks as a model for the teachers attending one of our three-week writing institutes, the day came for working together on the scale. These once-upon-a-time reluctant learners were, as kids say, "all over" this scale idea. Almost as rapid fire, they rattled off "to be" verbs, our ideas, commas, leads, protagonist, and so on. We couldn't write fast enough, the teachers observing were amazed, and then one student offered, "Choice."*
> *"What do you mean?"*
> *"You gave us choices."*
> *"How can we put that on the scale?"*
> *To which the young man replied, "I don't care if it's on the scale. I just wanted you to know that was good."*
> *We considered that our report card.*

The scale coupled with the "Comments" makes for a thorough assessment. Note: We have never had complaints using the Carroll/Wilson Analytic Scale for Classroom Use. It is both quantitative and qualitative.

> *Once we had an "almost" complaint. A mother came to question a grade on her son's composition. The teacher whipped out the scale, showed it to the mother, and explained its function. The mother asked, "This is what you taught?"*
> *"Yes it is."*
> *"All the kids agreed this is what you taught?"*
> *"Yes," said the teacher, adding, "and I made it clear this is what they should have learned."*
> *The mother turned to her son, "Is this true?" The boy nodded.*
> *The mother said to the teacher, "My business is concluded here. Please accept my apology. I will take this matter up with my son."*

As teachers change their teaching, they need to change their evaluating. Collaborating on assessment is one way to make that change. Shifting paradigms in everything but evaluation sets up disharmony and acrimony. Instead, as teachers shift to processes and global intentions, not only in writing, but also in reading, thinking, listening, speaking, viewing, and in other disciplines, they need to shift how they judge and ultimately place a grade on students' work. Evaluation as an extension of pedagogy should match its underlying philosophy. If a teacher is learner centered, then evaluation should be learner centered. There is no place in the new paradigm for "I gotcha." Of course, making such a shift is just as demanding as making the shift in teaching.

But it can be done. It must be done. Grading practices from the old paradigm have established a host of myths that teachers, students, and parents grapple with daily. Consider these myths.

Myths about Assessment

Seven different assessment myths are ingrained in the fabric of our schools. Harder to change than teaching practices, grading considerations are difficult for teachers. Other ways of evaluating student knowledge, performance, and potential, when years of state assessments, textbooks, district mandates, and habit have propelled testing and grading, leaves teachers lamenting, "But we've always done it this way!"

Myth One: Tests Tell What Students Know

Tests, even the best, only show a portion of what a student knows. "No test or single index can measure all or even most of the diverse intellectual skills that underlie intelligence, such as reasoning, insight, and practical know-how" (Sternberg 34). Considering the breakthroughs in cognition, brain theory, and multiple intelligences, not to mention the Internet with its preponderance of rapidly growing and changing information, it seems myopic to think that a test, or even several tests, could produce a totally accurate picture of anyone's knowledge.

There are problems with tests. Most tests successfully teach students how to fill in blanks, match items in a series, or bubble on a computerized grading sheet. These are norm-referenced tests, that is, the student taking the test is graded against a standard (norm) usually derived by calculating an average from a pilot group. Some administrators, perhaps in imitation of commercially produced norm-referenced tests, or in an effort to develop so-called standards, or out of some misplaced notion that standardized testing will produce standardized teaching, require blanket tests given every six weeks on a designated day by every member of a department or grade level. These administrators commit "assumi-cide" by thinking if all teachers teach then test alike, then all students will learn alike. These tests, designed as if teachers pour information into students and as if learning is exteriorized, ask students to regurgitate answers. Pejoratively called, "jug and mug" or "sit and get," this attitude ignores recent research that finds learning an active, distinctive, and incredibly complicated process.

Some tests are ancient relics, left by a retired teacher who taught Shakespeare, *Beowulf*, or Chaucer. Some are testimonials to a group of dedicated teachers who worked hours pounding out items, quotes, and true or false statements to check students' comprehension of discrete bits of information—as if identifying Polyphemus as a member of the race of Cyclopes is more important than understanding Homer's lesson, or as if drawing a line from the letter *B* to a ball tells more about the student's knowledge of letters than if that student writes a story and uses the letter correctly. Proponents often use words like *standards*, *basics*, *scope and sequence*, *aligned curriculum*, and *core information* to support tests.

How often are teachers surprised when a productive, spirited student does poorly on a test?

How often when scores are returned from outside agencies are teachers shocked when their most intelligent student receives the lowest score?

Tests and what students know do not always coincide. Perhaps this could be remedied by combining norm-referenced tests and performance-based tests, tests that are ongoing and multi-dimensional. Consider the policy of the Canadian Council of Teachers of English, "The teacher's judgment must be the main determiner of the performance of his/her students, and he/she will employ a variety of measures and observations to inform that judgment. Tests or examinations extrinsic to the classroom should play only a subordinate role in any determination of student achievement" (27).

In truth, tests tell more about what the test maker knows, what the test maker got from the material, or what the test maker wants the students to know than they tell about what the students have learned. One curiously telling addition to test-making might be to engage students in the process as with the teacher/student analytic scale.

Myth Two: Grammar Is Not Graded by Those Who Teach Writing as a Process

This myth arises from two groups. The first, composed of those who never grasped grammar, avoid grammar instruction altogether. They do not even teach it in isolation. They use writing as a process as an excuse to cover their insufficient knowledge.

The second group objects because writing as a process minimizes worksheets and exercises in grammar books. These are the ones who teach the sixteen-week grammar/usage unit in isolation. These are the ones who bemoan the status of written expression, and the fact that today's students cannot write. Yet they continue to teach as they have always taught—failing to see or refusing to see any correlation between students' writing and their teaching methods. Because they like their sixteen weeks of grammar—easy to teach, easy to grade (there is only one possible answer in the key)—they attack writing as a process on the grammar/grading front, for they know this attack will garner the most attention. The logic of this group goes something like this: If grammar is not *the* instruction, there must not be *any* instruction. They arm themselves with this rationale so they can return to worksheets and textbook exercises while claiming teachers who teach writing as a process do not teach nor grade grammar.

Nothing can be further from the truth. Of course grammar is taught and graded within the writing process. But grammar is not the *only* thing graded. For too many years the only items marked on a paper where grammar mistakes. This history of marking up papers leads to the third myth.

Myth Three: Grading Means Marking Up a Paper

Teachers who hold to this myth liberally use the abbreviations *awk, frag, sp, ww* with numerical equivalents for every mistake. Sometimes the resulting grade can even be a negative one. They play the game "take-away," subtracting points, self-esteem, security of expression, and love of writing.

Diederich, in his essay "In Praise of Praise," speculates "that all this outpouring of red ink not only does no good but positive harm. Its most common effect is to make the majority of students hate and fear writing. So far as they can see, they have never done anything on paper that anybody thought was good. No matter how hard they try, every paper they hand in gets slapped down for something or other" (in Judine 38).

Consider the message a marked-up paper sends. If writing is self-exposure, as Murray contends, if writing shows the mind at work, if writing is ownership, if writing grows out of a learning community, if writing illuminates the thoughts, dreams, and ideas of a writer, then what right does any other person have to mark the self, mind, thoughts, and dreams of that writer? Teachers rarely deface a student's artwork; why would they spoil a student's writing? Art and writing are just different symbolizing systems. Instead of a watercolor, still life, or a bucolic pastel scene to express the artist's thoughts, the writer uses words. Are these words less valuable than the brush strokes? Because writers claim their words, the teacher does not have the right, duty, or mission to mark directly on the paper.

Alternatives to marking a student's paper include the conference and self-adhesive notes. The one-, two-, or three-minute conference with a student is worth all the red marginalia. Besides, students better internalize help rendered in a conference because that help is specific and clearer than cryptic marks. Also, the student has the opportunity after this one-on-one exchange to make changes while the changes still count for something.

Self-adhesive, well-placed notes effectively point out nudges, flaws, or suggestions to students without marring their papers. Skilled teachers devise ways for students to retain these notes to prevent similar mistakes on ensuing papers.

Myth Four: It Takes Longer to Grade Writing

If teachers believe and practice myth three, then it does take a long time to grade each and every error. Called "atomistic" because not even the tiniest slip-up or the most minute mistake escapes the watchful eye and red pen of the teacher, research by the National Council of Teachers of English shows that teachers who grade atomistically spend from five to twenty minutes correcting a paper. Their drudgery translates into directives such as, "Rewrite the paper." "Correct the mistakes and hand it in again, and I will raise your grade," which does little to improve writing for most students.

Time does not have to be the ogre of grading writing. When teachers incorporate all the strategies and pedagogies associated with writing as a process, students' papers go through many drafts, peer grouping, teacher conferences, and clocking. During that process students correct most, if not all, of the stylistic infelicities. This means the teacher has more time to consider the quality of content, the organization, and the rhetoric of the writing. The teacher interacts with the paper's meaning. Instead of marking the paper, the teacher engages in a dialectic with the writer through the writing. The teacher responds to what is being said; the teacher and student work at appropriating each other's meaning.

Peter Elbow states, "It's not a question of whether we like evaluation . . . Besides, we couldn't learn without feedback. . . . There are two purposes (of evaluation). The first is to provide the audience with an accurate evaluation of the student's performance . . . The second function of evaluation is to help the student to the condition where he can evaluate his own performance accurately: teacher grades should wither away in importance if not in fact" (1986, 167).

Myth Five: Evaluation Must Take Place in the Form of a Test

Adherents to this myth reduce everything to a test. Effort and processes become lost. Writing suffers. Teacher observations, student self-evaluations, peer evaluations, and parent evaluations are unwarranted in this system—the test rules.

This myth dismisses John Dewey's idea of reflection. Why reflect on what the student has done, how the student has done the task, or why the student embarked on the learning when a multiple-choice test can be graded in fifteen minutes?

These believers also subscribe to myth one, thus compounding and intensifying myths. A single test can never be an accurate judge of what a student knows. Nor is evaluation only possible through a test. Myth five becomes further compounded when conjoined with myth six.

Myth Six: Standardized Tests Accurately Measure Students' Learning

Some state departments and legislative bodies believe that one test can prove whether or not a student has learned what is being taught. They believe that the only way to evaluate the return on tax dollars is by administering tests, which, of course, cost tax dollars. They hire testing companies and psychometricians to create tests, score them, and report the results. Testing companies, nonexistent a hundred years ago, make millions because people believe this myth.

Researcher S. Alan Cohen of the University of San Francisco levels strong criticism on standardized tests in his provocative monograph *Tests: Marked for Life?* He repeatedly questions the reliability and validity of commercially published norm-referenced standardized tests (NRSTs), what we think they test, and how test users misinterpret their results: a *validity* problem. Or the scores are inaccurate, but test users act as if they're not: a *reliability* problem (13). He believes criterion-referenced tests (CRTs), where scores are referenced to what was actually taught, are more effective and humane.

Working from the perspective of reading assessment, researchers Hoopfer and Hunsberger list many criticisms resulting from studies of standardized tests. Concerns include lack of objectivity, test bias, over-dependence on reading, over-dependence on statistical power, lack of breadth and depth of content covered, penalties for deep thinkers, penalties for careless bookkeeping, ambiguity of text and questions, reification of test scores, control of the curriculum by test constructors, lack of diagnostic value and information gain, decontextualization of the test situation, imposition of adult reality on child perception, limits to the certainty of assessment, incomplete use of rules during the testing, and assumption that informational links are the same for all students (103–119).

Mike Dilena and Jane Leaker share their thoughts about standardized tests, "These tests are often a test of test-taking skills (i.e., the ability to perform quite tricky tasks) as much as a test of authentic reading and writing" (36). We wonder at tests' validity and reliability when the only ones who validate them are the testing companies.

Howard Gardner adds his views, "The test is the ultimate scholastic invention, a decontextualized measure to be employed in a setting that is itself decontextualized. Students learn about scientific principles or distant lands while sitting at their desks reading a book or listening to a lecture; then, at the end of the week, the month, the year, or their school careers, the same students enter a room and, without benefit of tests or notes, answer questions about the material that they are supposed to have mastered" (1991, 132–133). Gardner maintains "that formal testing has moved much too far in the direction of assessing knowledge of questionable importance in ways that show little transportability. The understanding that schools ought to inculcate is virtually invisible on such instruments; quite different forms of assessment need to be implemented if we are to document student understandings" (1991, 134).

Myth Seven: Students Cannot Accurately Self-Assess

Because most students find tests a source of anxiety, as well as nonlearning events, they feel unempowered by tests and build negative views of themselves as test takers. This negativity erodes effective classroom practices. If students participate in assessment, however, they feel less disenfranchised. Madeline Hunter suggests, "Students judge their achievement by comparison with their own past record or with comparable students who have the same learning task and probability of success" (5). Diederich says, "I believe that a student knows when he had handed in something above his usual standard and that he waits hungrily for brief comment in the margin to show him that the teacher is aware of it, too. To my mind, these are the only comments that ever do any student any good" (in Judine 39). And while more research is needed in self-assessment, the niggling question remains: Who has more right to a voice in their evaluation than the students themselves?

If students become involved in self-assessments, classrooms become learning communities where everyone effectively impacts the performance of that community. In such classrooms, the infrastructure will have been laid for a genuine partnership to develop between the learner and the teacher.

Elbow says,

> There are two sources of increased trustworthiness in student evaluations. First, the student knows more than the teacher does about what and how she learned—even if she knows less about what was taught. Second, even though the student's account *might* be skewed—by her failure to understand the subject matter, or by her self-interest, or (what is in fact more frequent) by her underestimation of self—if you read that account *in combination* with the teacher's account, you can usually draw a remarkably trustworthy conclusion about what the student actually learned and how skilled she is. Because there are two perceivers and because they are using natural language rather than numbers, there is remarkably rich internal evidence that usually permits the reader to see through any contradictions and skewings to what was really going on. (1986, 226)

WAYS TO EVALUATE WRITING

There is little if any real consensus by the practitioners of the English language arts regarding terms such as *grading*, *testing*, *measuring*, *scoring*, and *assessing*. Lumped in most minds as evaluating, work and study on different ways to evaluate writing helps teachers differentiate among them by definition and purpose. Books as comprehensive as *Evaluating Writing* by Charles Cooper and Lee Odell, *Teaching and Assessing Writing* by Edward M. White, and as specific as *Portfolio Portraits* edited by Donald H. Graves and Bonnie S. Sunstein hone the theory of assessment for practical application in the classroom. Still, evaluation consistently emerges as a problem.

Grading

Teachers typically grade students' work numerically. Sometimes districts require a certain number of grades in a subject per marking period. These grades are determined subjectively, because the teacher usually establishes the criteria and judges the work accordingly. Grades pose a dilemma for both teachers and students. Jim Corder, professor at Texas Christian University, says of this dilemma:

> I have not learned what to do about grades. The chairperson, the dean, the registrar all think that there should be grades assigned at the end of the semester. So do the students. I do not. Especially in writing classes, I think that about all I should indicate at term's end is "Hey, neat work, I've enjoyed reading it," or "Thoughtful work, there, keep at it," or "You're okay, and you'll see more to do as you go along," or "Why don't you practice some particular writing chores with me for a while longer?" . . . Often early in the semester, I do not put grades on students' papers, but that makes them uneasy. It makes me

uneasy if I do assign grades. I don't know what I'll do. While I'm still trying to learn, I would not be surprised if the grades in my composition classes are generally pretty high. I don't think I am going to worry about that too much. (97)

The dilemma for students remains "stunning," as Howard Gardner describes it. In the sense of paralyzing findings, Gardner explains his term, "Researchers at Johns Hopkins, M.I.T., and other well-regarded universities have documented that students who receive honor grades in college-level physics courses are frequently unable to solve basic problems and questions encountered in a form slightly different from that on which they have been formally instructed" (1991, 3).

The truth, teachers need to change the way they assign grades. Teachers need to resist the obsessive-compulsive behavior of grading everything. Policies that dictate a certain number of daily grades and a certain number of major grades every six weeks, edicts by a dictatorial management product approach style, have little to do with learning and a lot to do with control. Some principals justify their proclamations, "If I don't mandate grades, some teachers won't have a single grade all six weeks." Instead of taking care of those isolated cases, administrators use the military approach—everyone must adhere to the controlling mandate.

There is no place in good schools for this type of grading policy.

Giving ten assignments each for a grade does not assure the assignments (1) are anything more than busy work; (2) connect to any real learning; (3) reveal what the learner is learning. When teachers assign poorly, grade poorly, or when they grade only worksheets, then they need staff development, not mandates or more blackline masters. Students do not need more assigners; they need more and better teachers.

Skilled teachers, who understand and practice a philosophy of education based upon current research and best practices, always record plenty of grades. Their classrooms, filled with rich and eager, excited students, reflect quality work. In them we find grades for oral and silent reading, prewriting, ratiocination, clocking, group work, the conference, participation, notes from debriefings, the status of the class, a grade on learning logs or writing folders, and perhaps an ongoing project to consider. For skilled teachers, students' writing is replete with opportunities to grade.

The other crucial aspect of grading is fear of failure. Most students fail because they refuse to do the work, not because they cannot do the work. When this occurs teachers must ask themselves the hard question, why? Who is the failure? The student who never grasped the concept or who doesn't care or the teacher who doesn't model, isn't explicit or motivational enough? Teachers who have high failure rates are failures themselves. They fail either at the types of assessment they devise, or in their ability to teach. There is no place in school for failure. When students do not achieve, it is a red flag. Teachers need not expend energy blaming students, parents, SES, or background and get busy restructuring assignments, reteaching, modeling more, and monitoring the students as they practice. School is a place for success and learning. In the writing classroom, where there is always more correct in a student's writing than incorrect; *failure, error,* and *wrong* are words that writing teachers need to replace with *reexamine, revise, edit,* and *next time.*

So what do grades really mean? William Glasser maintains, "high grades are a reward for quality work and are very satisfying to students' need for power. In a quality school, however, permanent low grades would be eliminated. A low grade would be treated as a temporary difficulty, a problem to be solved by the student and the teacher working together with the hope that the student would come to the conclusion that is worth expending more effort" (107). Hunter believes in the nongraded school, teachers would "expect all students to earn an 'A' or 'B,' but the time to do so will vary" (4). Diederich suggests, "Find in each paper at least one thing, and preferably two or three things, that the student has done well, or better than before. Then, if you must, find one thing, and preferably not more than one thing, that he should try to improve in his next paper. Whenever possible make this a suggestion, not a prescription" (in Judine 39).

Testing

Enormous amounts of academic time are spent testing, both in preparation for and in the taking of tests. Test sales are at a peak; estimates suggest that students do over 2,000 test items per year; 91 percent of teachers give basal tests over three times per year; 22 percent give them over nine times per year; 64 percent give their own test over three times per year; 37 percent give their own tests over nine times per year (Tierney, Carter, and Desai 22–23).

In the name of accountability, testing is touted as a measure of learning. But in the writing classroom, the test interrupts and interferes. There is something illogical about a separate test for writing. Writing is the test. Think of the absurdity of a multiple-choice test on introductions, organizational patterns, or even the elements of a narrative. If students write introductions that hook the reader, use logical organizational patterns, and include all the elements in their stories, those stories *are* the test. Even more absurd is a multiple-choice test on writing skills and conventions. Skills and conventions do not exist in some rarefied dimension; they exist as part of the larger context of communicating in the world. If students have poor skills, that dearth of expression shows in their speaking and writing.

> *Second-graders proudly read their dinosaur stories. Each child settled into the author's chair and waited for respect. Beth used a double negative, so the teacher jotted something on her clipboard. Then she noted Wayne doing it, too. When Una used the double negative twice, the teacher leaned over to me and whispered, "I have my mini-lesson for tomorrow." That teacher did not require a test to illuminate what his students needed, that need became apparent in the "test" of the author's chair. I sometimes wonder, when teachers grade worksheets, if they make note of who makes what mistakes or do they simply plow onward, armed with nothing but pseudo-concepts, through the basal, the curriculum, and their stack of blackline masters?*

Measuring

Measuring refers to a unit or system that indicates the dimensions of learning. When measuring, evaluators use descriptors such as *focus, contrast, classification, change, physical context*, and *time sequence.*

Linguistic Cues

Lee Odell, echoing Diederich, suggests that by systematically examining linguistic cues in students' writing, intellectual processes are illuminated. Odell maintains that by looking at students' initial efforts and final papers, an analysis of their intellectual processes can be described and therefore measured (106–132).

Computer Analysis

Another example of measuring is through computer analysis. By allowing the computer to count word frequencies, word choices, spelling, and other descriptors, teachers measure aspects of students' growth.

T-Units

A third example of measuring students' growth is through T-units, a term coined by Kellogg W. Hunt.

The T-unit, sometimes called idea density, measures students' syntactic maturity by gauging their ability to write sentences with sophisticated levels of thought through the use of a multiplicity of clauses and phrases without losing focus or coherence. Hunt defines T-units "as a single main clause (independent clause) plus whatever clauses and nonclauses are attached or embedded within that one main clause" (92). Because the *T* stands for *terminable*, a T-unit is the shortest grammatically complete unit that is not a fragment. Simply stated, "a T-unit is a single main clause and whatever goes with it" (93). When marking passages for T-units, scorers use a double virgule—//—much the way a line of poetry is marked. Hunt offers this example, which has been marked for T-units:

> I like the movie we saw about Moby Dick the white whale // the captain said If you can kill the white whale Moby Dick I will give this gold to the one that can do it // and it is worth sixteen dollars // they tried and tried // but while they were trying they killed a whale and used the oil for the lamps // they almost caught the white whale //. (92)

To compute the writer's average T-unit score, the number of T-units (6) is divided into the number of words (68). The result is a score of 11.3.

Hunt says, "The reason for defining a T-unit, as distinguished from a sentence, is simply that the T-unit turns out, empirically, to be a useful concept in describing some of the changes that occur in the syntax of the sentences produced by schoolchildren as they grow older. When we know what a T-unit is, we can understand certain measure of maturity that we could not understand without it" (93).

To standardized the measurement of T-units, students are given a prewriting sample, composed of short, choppy sentences to rewrite. At a later date, students are given the same sample to rewrite. Both times the instructions are the same:

> Read the passage all the way through. You will notice that the sentences are short and choppy. Study the passage and then rewrite it in a better way. You may combine sentences, change the order of words, and omit words that are repeated too many times. But try not to leave out any of the information.

After the students rewrite the passage, each student counts the number of words in his or her rewrite and records that number at the top of the paper. Students then exchange papers to check that number. The teacher marks the T-units with the double virgule and computes each student's average score. Once the posttest is complete, the teacher examines the numbers to get a measure of syntactic growth. Remember, while there are published tables on syntactic rates, T-units provide a measure of student with self *not* in comparison with others in the class or on that grade level. For example, if a fifth-grade student has a 6.1 mean T-unit in September and a 7.2 mean T-unit in May, then the measure is clear—that student shows syntactic growth. If a tenth-grade student measures 11.5 in September and 11.5 in January, there is reason to analyze the lack of improvement.

Scoring

Scoring generally refers to large-scale evaluations. Scores enable evaluators to sort or rank written work quickly. Scoring may be done schoolwide, districtwide, statewide, or even nationally as with the writing section on the College Board Examinations. Scoring is customarily done numerically. The most common scoring procedures for large-scale writing samples are holistic scoring, developed by the Educational Testing Service and primary trait scoring, developed by the National Assessment of Educational Progress.

Holistic Scoring

Holistic scoring is the most reliable way to score, sort, and rank large numbers of students' writing; it is a way to score large numbers of writing samples in a relative short period of time and it used by most states for their high-stakes writing samples.

Unlike atomistic scoring where every detail or particular feature is noted, holistic scoring allows the scorer to quickly read and rate each paper. The key to success in holistic scoring is training. Holistic scoring is difficult work and demands that those who lead the scoring sessions as well as those who do the actual scoring be well trained. There are two ways to score a paper holistically, general impression holistic scoring and primary trait, also called focused holistic scoring.

General Impression Holistic Scoring

In general impression scoring, a represented number of papers from the entire batch of papers to be scored are randomly selected, read, and rated. These supply readers with anchor papers. Well-trained readers/scorers undertake this part of the process. These anchor papers are then used to train other readers/scorers. Through a procedure of reading and discussing these anchor papers, trainees are calibrated, or socialized, to ensure a consistency of response. Occasionally a reader/scorer emerges who does not calibrate well, whose scores are always discrepant, that is, not in agreement with others who score the same papers. When this happens, that scorer is asked to act as a runner to help distribute and redistribute papers but not score them.

With general impression holistic scoring, new anchor papers are determined from each batch of papers to be scored. For example, a batch of papers from ninth-graders in 2004 have anchor papers chosen from that batch, whereas the papers from ninth-graders in 2006 have new anchor papers chosen from the 2006 batch. This means the papers are rated according to other papers in their batch. Therefore a high paper in 2004 may not be a high paper in 2006. Once the group has been trained, they rate all the papers in that batch.

Anchor papers determine what constitutes a general impression of "high/high," "high/low," "low/high," or "low/low." If a 4-point scale is used, the scorer makes two decisions. The first decision determines if the paper is high or low. If the paper rates a "high," the scorer asks, "Is this a high/high paper, or a high/low paper?" If the paper is high/high, it receives a 4. If the paper is high/low, it receives a 3.

If the first decision rates the paper "low," the scorer asks, "Is this a low/high paper or a low/low paper?" The low/high paper receives a 2; the low/low paper receives a 1. A 4-point scale prevents scorers from taking the easy way out—the middle score.

General impression is the older of the holistic methods and is not without its critics. To answer these critics, the National Assessment of Educational Progress and committees at ETS working on the Advanced Placement Program began the development of primary trait scoring or focused holistic scoring.

Primary Trait Scoring or Focused Holistic Scoring

In this version of holistic scoring, a more precise and exact guide is established. There are six guidelines considered standard: (1) Controlled Essay Reading—all papers are scored at one time; (2) Scoring Criteria Guide—a rubric of descriptors established by those controlling the readings; (3) Anchor Papers—sample papers to illustrate the scoring criteria are selected and used to calibrate the scores; (4) Scoring Checks—scores are checked during the reading and scoring to keep the scores on target to the rubric; (5) Multiple Scoring—scorers from different tables rank the papers twice. With the exception of very few scoring guides, a one-point difference between the two readings is allowed. More than that is considered discrepant; (6) Scorer profiles—records of rankings are maintained on individual readers to maintain consistency and accuracy to the criteria. Readers who have discrepant scores are eliminated from the readings (White 23–27).

The major difference between general impression and primary trait is the rubric. In the former, the criteria rise out of consensus based on close reading and discussion of the anchor papers. In the latter, certain criteria are developed before the papers are read. These items narrow the focus of the scorer who then ranks the papers accordingly.

Edward M. White urges teachers to share the scoring guides with students and even have students participate in the development of the scoring guides (122). In instances where holistic scoring is being used in large-scale assessment, real growth and understanding never occurs if the scoring guides are kept secret. Teachers and students are left with a certain amount of wonder about why a score is received and have no way of resolving questions of performance.

White goes on to consider the limitations of holistic scoring.

> The first and most important limitation is that it gives no meaningful diagnostic information beyond the comparative ranking it represents. . . . The second implication of the limited value of the holistic score emerges from its connection to its particular test group: It cannot represent an absolute value in itself. This means that every time a holistic scoring is completed, those responsible for reporting scores need to make a fresh decision about where cutting levels should be. (28)

In the classroom, teachers and students adapt holistic scoring by devising their own rubrics based on what was taught. Some teachers encourage students to practice scoring their own papers. Teachers may use holistic scoring on drafts to provide an indication of where the paper is at that time in the process. Or holistic scoring or primary trait scoring may be used on the final copy. When the scale is created in conjunction with students or created by the teacher but clearly communicated to students, scoring papers can be done quickly and with a certain amount of reliability. Because most teachers do not have another person to rate the paper, many teachers team with another teacher or invite students to be the second scorer. Since holistic scoring is done on anonymous papers, this usually is not a problem. When instituting this type of grading, teachers wisely communicate the guidelines and procedures to parents. Since most parents are unfamiliar with holistic scoring and expect atomistic grading, knowledgeable teachers reflect the research, purpose, and procedure for them.

Assessing

Assessment encompasses several of the more recent approaches to evaluation from self-assessment to portfolios, from inventories to scales. Two major divisions of assessment are self-assessment and teacher assessment.

Self-Assessment

When students engage in self-assessment teachers do not necessarily have less to grade. Some propose self-assessment to lessen the teacher's time grading. This is wrong-headed thinking. While less grading certainly might happen, it is not the reason to implement self-assessment in the class-room.

Instead, the nobler reason is to empower students. Self-assessment gives students ways of knowing about and evaluating their performance, processes, and achievement. What does it say about learning when the only way students receive affirmation is from one other person? Nowhere was this injustice more apparent to than when we conducted a debriefing with students. When we asked, "What did you learn today about your writing?" they appeared dumbstruck. When we followed up with, "How did you learn?" they became mute. When we prodded, "How could we have been more effective?" they were thunderstruck. Of course, as the debriefing continued, the students became quite adept at assessing exactly what occurred. As with any skill, self-assessment takes practice and patience. If schools want independent thinkers, if schools want students to take the responsibility for their own learning, then schools have to allow for learners to take some responsibility for the assessment of that learning. No longer will students run to the teacher for confirmation; instead, the student will run to the teacher for celebration.

This radical premise is foreign to many teachers and most students. The process of turning the student into an assessor does not happen magically or by proclamation. Teachers who say, "All self-assessments are doomed," need to talk often and authentically with students; they need to read and respond to students' writings; they need to provide models and ways for self-assessment to occur. In short, as facilitators they are the most important variable in the assessment process. Ultimately, the teacher becomes that "other voice"—other than the student's own—that students learn to consider and trust as they write and refine their writing.

Nor should self-assessment be the only type of evaluation. When the right kinds of things happen with self-assessment, students learn to evaluate the assessment itself with no one assess-ment *the* crucial one. Each evaluation has its place and purpose—together all present a total, more integrated picture to the student. As students become more secure in their self-assessments, then other evaluations become tools to gauge their conclusions.

Elbow identifies three problems with self-assessment:

1. What constitutes good student performance?

2. How does the teacher communicate the ways and means of evaluation?

3. How do teachers produce in students the ability to evaluate their own work? (1986, 176)

Students—not only teachers—should be involved in determining the answers to these questions.

When students self-assess their own writing, they provide the teacher with many opportunities for mini-teaches on the criteria of good writing, for example: Is the vocabulary suited to the audience? What keeps the reader from becoming confused? How do authors keep readers reading? Emig succinctly describes good writing as apt, clear, and lively. Irmscher's offers: "intellectual and imaginative . . . transforms the material and language in some unusual way" (156–157). Lloyd-Jones says that good writing "should be—primarily related to aims (i.e., does the piece of writing fulfill its purpose?)" (33). Student research and teacher lessons on the nature of good writing move students away from their most common and only definition of good writing—it is error free.

It seems reasonable to conclude the more teachers read and write, the more able they will be at coaxing good writing from their students, and the better they will become at identifying the characteristics of good writing. What brings student X's writing alive may sound insipid in student Y's. As students and teachers and the times change, notions about "good" are bound to change. But the bottom line is that teachers must read. Gardner points out, "it has been reported that the average schoolteacher reads a book a year" (1991, 188). To be master facilitator and evaluator of writing, the teacher must rise above *average*.

In the best classrooms, teacher and students together discover what is good, what is quality. Glasser offers his definition of quality as "whatever we put into our quality world" (102). We have applied that definition to writing: Writers achieve quality by whatever they put into their quality papers. And, according to Glasser,

> There is no doubt that they (students) know both what quality is and that to achieve it takes a great deal of hard work. When I ask them whether they have done much quality work is school, at first many say that they have. But when I ask them how many times they have actually worked hard enough to do the best work they possibly could, almost none, including the very good students, say that they have ever done as much as they are capable of doing. I think it is safe to say that very few students expend the effort to do quality work at school. . . . But for students to do quality work, it is crucial that they see that it is for their benefit, not the benefit of their teachers, school systems, or parents. (94, 96)

Types of Self-Assessment

Inventories. Students create and complete inventories to record the processes and progresses in their writing. Inventories come in many forms; the best are always student produced with teacher guidance. The poorest are usually the commercialized, mass produced, decontextualized inventories so generic students and teachers alike wonder if they were created to assess writing or the weather.

Student-produced inventories usually include some or all of these items:

- chronicles of what their writing categorized by mode, assignment, and genre;

- lists of strengths, what students do best;

- records of specifically what needs improvement;

- logs that date starts and completions;

- feelings about what they have written;

- analysis of what they have written;

- comments;

- future plans.

Movies. Movies, based on an idea from Elbow (1991, 227–231), are records kept by writers on the moment-by-moment readings of their minds. Students record what they think while engaged in the writing process. They step outside of self and record the what, when, how, and why of the writing. The results are significant because they reveal to students what they do or do not do in the writing. For the teacher, movies show an inside picture of the student's thinking. Sometimes what is not recorded is just as significant as what is. This strategy is similar to Cris Tovani's reading strategy "show me your thinking."

Observation Profiles. This type of self-evaluation requires students to note observable behaviors. This evaluation centers around the *actions* of the writer. A combination of a self-dialectical notebook and self-analysis, students record what they observe:

- themselves doing *as* they write;

- *about* the way they write;

- *from* others when they share their writing;

- about the writing itself.

Performance Profiles. Students who keep performance profiles generally find them to be descriptive not only of the process but also of the product. The performance profile uses the items shown in Table 8.1. Comments on each item are kept as short narrative notes, for example, "I

Table 8.1. Matrix for Performance Profile

	Duration	Effort	Quality	Effectiveness
Prewriting				
Writing				
Rewriting				
Publishing				

spent twenty minutes rewriting today." Before undertaking this form of self-assessment, teachers model responses that include examples from their writing and thinking.

Duration. When students consider duration, time becomes a factor. For students to realize they spent more time on prewriting and less on rewriting might indicate that they had trouble getting started, or they felt excitement for the topic, or they resisted revision. To understand and interpret duration, the items of effort, quality, and effectiveness become variables.

Effort. When considering effort, students focus on what was done and what effort they put out to accomplish what was done.

Quality. The quality factor requires students to use the internal criteria of what they think is good and the external criteria decided upon by the teacher and class.

Effectiveness. In evaluating effectiveness, students interpret how others respond to their writing.

Keeping Records. Another type of performance profile invites students to record narrative responses to the following items:

- This is what I wrote.

- This is who I grouped with and what I learned in the group.

- This is what I learned from the conference.

- This is the process I used and when I did things.

- This is the organization I used in this writing.

- This is the grade I would give my writing.

- This is the rating I would give myself while doing this writing.

- This is why I wrote this piece.

- This is what I learned from writing this piece.

- This is what I want you to know about this writing.

- Based on this writing, this is what I still want to know about writing.

As always, the best profiles always ask the follow-up question, "Why?" Performance profiles beg for follow-up conferences or provide substantial "meat" for group discussion.

Teacher-Assessment of Writing

Limited Marking Procedure

Many writing teachers limit the number of items they mark on a paper. Often they mark three to five items and then leave the rest of the paper untouched. These teachers tell students they will mark three items and then respond to the content of the paper. This method is more efficient and more psychologically sound than copious marks or a double grade—one for mechanics and one for content. Separating mechanics from the content is akin to separating the dancer from the dance. A 22/96 is ridiculous. If the mechanics are that poor, how can the writer communicate effectively? Besides, with the double grade students receive a mixed message.

Teachers who limit their marks generally make them on self-adhesive removable notes. That way the students read and remove them, leaving the paper unscarred and intact.

Portfolios

Few ideas have sparked a sense of fairness in assessment as have portfolios. They are one of the best methods to evaluate student writing—in any discipline. In a portfolio, examples writing are stored. Unlike the writing folder, which serves as a storage file for *all* writing in a given marking period, portfolios are receptacles of what students, teachers, peers, and parents deem the best writing—not unlike Jason Sapp's writing in Chapter 11. Myriad journal articles and books explain various ways to establish and evaluate portfolios. While the portfolio has much to offer, unfortunately for many, the portfolio will be nothing more than a writing folder.

Portfolios should be like the student—individual and unique. No two portfolios should look the same. As no two students nor any two classrooms are the same, it is unrealistic to expect all the portfolios to look the same, contain the same things, or reflect the same writings. Graves gives one of the most realistic views of portfolios.

As educators we are mere infants in the use of portfolios. Artists have used them . . . as a means of representing the range and depth of their best and most current work. Only in the last five years have educators latched on to the portfolio as an alternative to evaluating the literate work of students. . . .

But as young as this notion is, there are already signs that using portfolios in education is becoming a rigid process. . . . States and school systems have moved from reading about portfolios to mandating them as evaluation instruments for large school populations. Some small pilot studies were conducted to get some minor bugs removed, but sustained, long-term learning about the possibilities of portfolios as a learning/evaluation medium may be lost to us in the rush to mandate their use.

Portfolios are simply too good an idea to be limited to an evaluation instrument. Early data that show their use as a medium for instruction is more than promising. (1992, 1)

Portfolios require teachers to rethink the way they teach and evaluate. Most certainly, portfolios will cause schools to reconsider how they use their time. As we quoted Hunter earlier, the emphasis will move from time to learning. There are two possible formats that can be adopted to facilitate the implementation of portfolios: the daily model and the weekly model as shown in Table 8.2. Of course, again because of technology, many schools have electronic portfolios with shelves and shelves of VHS tapes and DVDs stored with student work.

Table 8.2. The Daily Model

Group 1	Group 2	Group 3
Reading workshop	Writing workshop	Portfolio assessment
Portfolio assessment	Reading workshop	Writing workshop
Writing workshop	Portfolio assessment	Reading workshop

The Daily Model. The daily model begins with a mini-teach. Each group applies the mini-lesson to their work. Time is not the most important feature in this model—learning is. Depending upon the teacher's need for intervention and the students' requirements for direct instruction, the teacher can work with one group or one strand. For example, if the students need a conference, the teacher confers with the groups during writing workshop. The reading group continues reading and responding, and the portfolio group works on their portfolios. Because assignment and discovery will be more important than competing to finish first, groups determine the amount of time required for each segment.

The Weekly Model. Similar to the daily model, the weekly model (Table 8.3) allows for greater depth and intensity.

Even as the glow fades on portfolios, we remember Robert Rothman's major problems with portfolio assessment. He writes,

A report analyzing Vermont's pioneering assessment system has found severe problems with it and raised serious questions about alternate forms of assessment . . . But the report by the RAND Corporation . . . found that the "rater reliability" in scoring the portfolios was very low. . . . In examining possible reasons for the low levels of reliability, the RAND report suggests that the complex scoring scales may have contributed to the problem . . . On a related point, the report also suggests that the training of the raters may have been inadequate. (1–20)

Table 8.3. The Weekly Model

Monday	Tuesday	Wednesday	Thursday	Friday
Whole-group instruction	Group 1: Reading workshop	Group 1: Writing workshop	Group 1: Portfolio assessment	Testing Review Makeup
Establish goals	Group 2: Writing workshop	Group 2: Portfolio assessment	Group 2: Reading workshop	
	Group 3: Portfolio assessment	Group 3: Reading workshop	Group 3: Writing workshop	

In 1993, we advised: "As teachers begin to use portfolios they will need training in them just as they need training in teaching writing. Giving teachers folders for portfolios and proclaiming, 'This year our school will do portfolios' is to flirt with failure" (467). Unfortunately for the most part, portfolios failed.

We also wrote,

Because the purpose of portfolios is to give a more accurate picture of students, educators will need to be slow and deliberate in their training and implementation of them. Joni Lucas writes in ASCD Curriculum Update, "With so many challenges inherent in scoring, analyzing, and evaluating portfolios on a large scale, portfolios might best be used as a diagnostic instrument and strong instructional tool helping classroom teachers to tap into the richness of student writing and learning and to reflect more clearly actual changes in instruction" (7). (467)

Apparently the challenges were too great.

Sadly, what remains a staple and the guiding event in teaching and designing curriculum in most schools across the nation is the state-mandated test.

CONCLUSION

As brain theory moves into an exact science, teachers will assess writing differently even though grading will continue to be difficult and demanding. But as teachers and students practice and understand writing as a process they will align judgment with practice.

While there is still much to know about writing and learning, teachers need to do more evaluation and assessment and less grading and testing. The nature of evaluation and assessment is based on student work and what students do or do not do. Evaluation allows teacher and student to work together rather than as polar entities. Assessment invites teacher, students, parents, and schools to look at the progress and products of students from a more global view. Authentic assessment should be used to align curriculum; it should be used to evaluate teaching and learning.

Jim Corder suggests several things when evaluating,

I have learned to consider the possibility that any essay turned in to me may be as good as it can be at that moment. Once again, I don't mean to suggest that I am pleading or recommending that all be forgiven in student writing. Hardly anyone, except my cousin Duane, gets up in the morning and decides, "I'm going to be evil today." Hardly anyone, not even some freshmen, gets up in the morning and decides, "I'm going to turn in a half-assed essay today." Most probably all believe that when they have turned in an essay, it's an okay essay. We probably ought to remember that. We probably ought to remember that any judgment we make of their writing may be rape of their judgment. All of us want justification, not denial; validation, not repudiation. If we are editors, not police officers, perhaps we can help them find their own authentication. (95–96)

Diederich sums it up best, "If a student concentrates on one error at a time, progress is possible; if he tries to overcome all of his weaknesses at once, he will only be overwhelmed. I do not know where the scientific truth lies, but I have more faith in the value of a few appreciative comments than in any amount or kind of correction" (in Judine 40). We concur having seen repeatedly the desultory effects of too much red pen on students' writing.

APPLICATION

Choose a paper you have written. Exchange it with a partner. Evaluate it atomistically, that is, mark every mistake no matter how trivial. Then evaluate the same paper according to a way discussed in this chapter. Write your findings and share them with your partner or your group.

THE THEORY AND PEDAGOGY

9

BRAIN POWER

Learning, and its synaptic result, memory, play major roles in gluing a coherent personality together as one goes through life. Our genes may bias the way we act, but the systems responsible for much of what we do and how we do it are shaped by learning.

—Joseph Le Doux □

DISENTANGLING THE GREAT RAVELED KNOT

We have several shelves of books on the brain, as many shelves with journals that deal with brain/mind/consciousness research, and an equal number of files labeled "brain" with articles, snippets, excerpts, even jokes from newspapers and magazines. Yet all that hard copy pales with the flick of the keyboard. In the beginning of 2007, if someone googled the word *brain* on the Internet, 10 out of 168,000,000 items would surface in 0.04 seconds, making writing this chapter a daunting task indeed.

When we wrote the first edition of *Acts*, we stated, "the present explosion of research on the brain—in estimates it is calculated that brain research doubles every five weeks—theories relating to consciousness, knowing, thinking, and language, as well as theories relating to paleoanthropology, differences between Eastern and Western brains, gender and the brain, the brain's anatomy, the developing brain, the aging brain, and brain disorders are literally erupting" (377). We cited James Watson, co-discoverer of the double helix DNA, who calls the brain "the most complex thing we have yet discovered in our universe." He offers it as "the last and greatest biological frontier" (iii).

We were right on target.

In 1993, brain experts from the United States, Japan, Canada, Britain, France, Germany, Sweden, Russia, and Australia convened in San Antonio, Texas, as part of the Human BrainMap Project to pursue study and to share research about this inner frontier. Spearheaded by University of Texas Health Science Center professor Peter T. Fox, BrainMap was an international effort to create a global computer database of the latest scientific developments about the brain. Fox predicted that a standardized system of recording data "will make the quality of research much higher" and could lead to improved treatments for people with neurological problems and brain injuries (McAuliffe B-1). We wrote in *Acts* in 1993, "Therefore, even as this chapter is being written, new and exciting information is emerging that will date what is here and forecast what is yet to come. This information will, of course, impact education" (377).

BrainMap continues to promote efficient compilation, analysis, and dissemination of the rapidly growing body of information about the functional organization of the human brain that can be provided by medical imaging techniques such as PET and MRI. Today on the Internet the Human BrainMap Project lists 58,100 items on the Internet in 0.11 seconds. By the time you read this, the number will be higher.

We were right on target.

In 1993, we talked about hemisphericity and the ingenious experiments Ronald Myers and Roger Sperry conducted, which included commissurotomies, noting that they earned Sperry the Nobel Prize in Physiology of Medicine in 1981. Recently, we watched *3lbs* on television and were taken through the experience of a commissurotomy on a pregnant woman. In a decade and a half, Nobel Prize–winning medicine has become fair game for weekly TV dramas.

We were right on target.

The Brain, Teaching, and Learning

That the brain impacts how learners learn and how teachers teach is best understood by remembering that neurobiology, the science of the brain, and cognitive psychology, the science of mind, have gradually blended together since the animal studies conducted on the brain during the 1950s and the subsequent work with grand mal epileptic patients during the 1960s by Roger Sperry, his collaborators, and students at the California Institute of Technology. Further, technologies such as EEG, the electroencephalogram (an early brain-monitoring device), CAT, computer-assisted tomography, PET, positron emission tomography, BEAM, brain electrical activity mapping, SPM, significance probability mapping, SQUID, a superconducting quantum interference device, MRI, magnetic resonance imaging, fMRI, functional magnetic resonance imaging, SPECT, single-photon emission computerized tomography, and NMR, a nuclear magnetic resonance diagnostic tool, enable specialized brain cartographers to directly read the brain. They are able to determine through scans what parts of the brain are energized during a given activity. (See the January 29, 2007, issue of *Time,* pages 60–61 for a famous set of brain scans.) These specialists do not see evidence of the old notion that "before you say a word, the brain must change a visual code into a sound code." They do, however, see dime-size clusters light up for nonwords that obey conventional English rules, like those found in "Jabberwocky," but do not light up for words that can have no legitimate English usage—*nlpfz.* They identify grape-size areas that process proper but not common nouns. They watch pictures of what they call "women's mental acrobatics" compared to men's compartmentalizations when both men and women are given certain words (Begley et al. 69–70).

Evoked Potential Machines

When WNET/New York distributed the PBS series *The Brain,* and when the extension of that series came out in book form as *The Brain* by Richard M. Restak in 1984, we lingered over the several pages devoted to "Jesse Salb's Evoked Potential Machine." How exciting to theorize watching brain activity on a TV monitor. We conjectured how revelatory it would be to have the electrical activity of a student's brain monitored during a writing experience. Teachers could watch moving images in color of anatomical maps of brains on TV monitors. The colors, representing the levels of engagement of different parts of the brain, would render much information about writing, the student, engagement, topics, teaching, environment, and so forth.

Fortunately, telemedicine and computer companies snapped up the technology of evoked potential machines, but unfortunately education did not. We never saw them in classrooms.

Companies also sank money into brain technology research such as sensory and cognitive components of brain resonance responses—sensory virtual goggles that give the wearer the sensation of being there. These mind machines work on the relationship between prestimulus-alpha amplitude and visual evoked amplitude. Some prototypes are the Procyon Mind Machine, the Proteus Mind Machine, the Sirius Mind Machine, and the ThoughtStream Biofeedback System—but education put its money into testing.

Brain Control Research

Consider the latest research on using brain waves applied to controlling video games. A team of neurosurgeons, neurologists, and engineers at Washington University in St. Louis has conducted experiments with an epileptic teenage boy. Their subject is the first teenager to play a two-dimensional video game, "Space Invaders," using only the electrocorticographic (ECoG) signals from his brain.

Researchers at the MIT Lab Europe demonstrated "Mind Balance," a video game where players control the characters with their brains by using wireless headsets to direct electroencephalography (EEG) cerebral data nodes positioned over the occipital lobes.

When we read about "Space Invaders" and "Mind Balance," we immediately connected that information to an article we remembered in the *New York Times*—"How Brain Waves Can Fly a Plane" by Malcolm W. Browne. This article, which appeared in the March 7, 1995, issue, suggested that new techniques in electroencephalography would help the disabled communicate by directly controlling the electromagnetic signals emitted from their brains and would allow airplane pilots to control their planes merely by thought. The article describes an Air Force program at Wright-Patterson Air Force Base in Dayton, Ohio, that demonstrated brain-actuated control. What was science fiction in the 1950s, was research in the 1960s, 1970s, 1980s, and 1990s and has become reality in the twenty-first century.

Computational Neuroscience

Consider the work of Read Montague, director of Baylor College of Medicine's Human Neuroimaging Lab, who says, "We're now moving into an age where we can start to eavesdrop on human brains in the midst of making decisions." Called computational neuroscience, this burgeoning field researches how the brain takes in energy to turn it into "freakishly efficient computation" (Berger Section B 2).

Tapping brain technology, Brain Saving Technologies (BST), founded and led by physicians intent on improving treatment and outcomes of stroke, use neuro-critical care consultation services to rapidly and effectively connect physicians with experts.

The Nicolet Viking III™ machine, which performs brainstem auditory evoked potential testing on neonates to check for auditory abnormalities while Watt, Fraser, Soni, Sett, and Clay conduct monitoring of transcranial magnetic motor evoked potentials (TcMMEP) to warn surgeons of motor tract damage, has already been replaced with Viking Quest™ or Viking Select™.

Various computer engineers are working on memory-aid systems that will completely document one's life, including every photograph, record, conversation, and other information. CNN ran this story, describing a device, much like a BlackBerry®, which recorded and then sent these audio files to a computer that translated them into text to be saved and documented.

DNA

And that DNA? Researchers recently celebrated the completion of a new digital atlas of the mouse brain, which they believe will lead them to better understand the human brain. Funded by Paul Allen, this 3-D digital map, called the Allen Brain Atlas, scanned slices of mouse brain to help identify how individual genes are "turned on" in different parts of the brain. They have already found a gene that controls appetite, but are interested in using this digital information to understand Parkinson's, Alzheimer's, autism, and addiction. Moving from mouse brains to human brains, the Allen Institute for Brain Science plans to scan human brain tissue to better understand neurological health and disease.

David Snowdon, an epidemiologist, William Markesbery, a neurologist, and Susan Kemper, a psycholinguist, working with the brains of the School Sisters of Notre Dame—"the Nun Study"—offers not only information on the effects of aging, Alzheimer's, and Parkinson's but also on memory retrieval and idea density. By evaluating the early-life autobiographies written by seventy-four sisters for idea density—that is "the number of propositions (individual ideas) expressed per ten words" (Snowdon 109)—Snowdon predicted with about 80 percent accuracy which sisters would develop Alzheimer's later in life (114).

Implications for teachers range from learning the neuroscientific data that support literacy early in life to understanding how genes, neurological health, and disease impact skills, comprehension, and learning. Once education accesses and uses what others are already accessing and using, educational institutions will change radically. But education is slow to adapt and change. If and when this happens, the changes will be immediate and have the potential of changing the very nature of learning.

WETWARE AND THE BRAIN

At the risk of reaching our *hrair* point (*hrair* is a number too large to count; it comes from the fictional language Lapine used in Richard Adams's *Watership Down*) where, from a psychological perspective, we are overwhelmed by concepts or change, we dare to mention wetware. Quite simply: What is on the chip will be immediately known. This is not science fiction; this epitomizes the globalization paradigm.

Wetware describes the integration of the concepts of the physical construct we call our central nervous system (CNS) and the mental construct we call our mind. Wetware intends to use a two-part abstraction modeled on the computer's hardware and software.

Here is how it will work: The first abstraction will concentrate on the bioelectric and biochemical properties of the CNS, especially the brain. The neurons will be the hardware and the impulses traveling the neurons will be analogized as software. The amalgamated interaction of the software and hardware will manifest through continuously changing physical connections and chemical and electrical influences. This interaction is so new there is no word or term for it yet.

The second abstraction operates on a higher conceptual level. It is logical: If the human mind is analogized as software then the first abstraction (described above) becomes the hardware. This calls into play the mind/brain/self-awareness conundrum, which is still debated.

It seems reasonable to conclude that when teachers understand these theories, the brain's components and processes, and the information gained through these contemporary technological probes, they will experience a depth of knowledge about how learners learn never before experienced in the history of education. As they apply this new information, their teaching will truly become brain compatible. As Leslie Hart says, "Hope, I think, lies in a brain-based theory serving as a guide . . . to create pilot schools, institutions that for the first time in . . . history will not reflect folklore, ritual, and cut-and-try, but will be rationalized, coherent environments designed for the society we are in, not one that has disappeared" (215–216).

Learning and the Brain

We must, therefore, concern ourselves with constantly learning. If not, we fall victim to what David Kearns, former CEO of the Xerox® Corporation defines as *uneducated*—which differs from the commonly held definition—"not knowing how to keep on learning." He cautions, "Research tells that we now have 100% new information every five years. If that trend continues, students who are in grades one through three will graduate during a time where, in some technological fields, there will be new information every 38 days. That could mean that the information they learned this month may be outdated two months from now!" (Education CyberPlayGround).

ADD/ADHD

Add to this Richard Restak who contends that "as a result of our 'make it quick' culture, attention deficit is becoming the paradigmatic disorder of our times" (2003, 47). He claims "ADD/ADHD isn't so much a disorder as it is a cognitive style" (2003, 48). Further he contends it is necessary for success in a workplace that demands employees rapidly process, shift, and comprehend information.

Dyslexia

Couple that with Daniel Pink's theory that dyslexics more readily see the big picture and will be the game-changers and thinkers of the twenty-first century. He cites Charles Schwab and Richard Branson, who were successful in the brokerage and retail music and airline industries *because* not *in spite of* their problems analyzing particulars, so they "became adept at recognizing patterns" (137–138).

Sally Shaywitz, a dyslexic specialist says, "Dyslexics think differently. They are intuitive and excel at problem-solving, seeing the big picture, and simplifying. . . . They are poor rote reciters, but inspired visionaries" (366).

All this to say that anything we write today, right this minute, may be dated tomorrow—literally—yet, according to Joseph Le Doux, the Henry and Lucy Moses Professor of Science at New York University's Center for Neural Science, we are working with an old brain in a new world. Let us examine that brain.

THE DEVELOPMENT OF THE BRAIN

The growth and development of the brain differs from the growth and development of other organs in the human body. Carla Shatz, professor of neurobiology at the University of California, explains, "The neural connections elaborate themselves from an immature pattern of wiring that only grossly approximates the adult pattern. Although humans are born with almost all the neurons they will ever have, the mass of the brain at birth is only about one fourth that of the adult brain. The brain becomes bigger because neurons grow in size, and the number of axons and dendrites as well as the extent of their connections increases" (61). So, while the neuron potential is present in the brain at birth, as these neurons grow, they become more complexly interconnected.

The Brain *In Utero*

Growth spurts occur *in utero*. At times nerve cells rapidly proliferate. On average the brain grows about 250,000 nerve cells per minute during a pregnancy, but in some twelve- to fourteen-week-old embryos, nerve cells proliferate at the rate of about 15 million per hour (Ackerman 86–87).

The Brain Eighteen to Twenty-Four Months

After birth, somewhere between eighteen and twenty-four months, the brain adds no new neurons. For the most part the cells in the brain have migrated to distinct regions and have aggregated together, that is arranged themselves with other like cells in what neuroscientists call "cytoarchitectonic" or "architecture of the cells" (Ackerman 95). Then cell bodies elongate, extend axons, form dendrites, and ready themselves for the work of creating synapses or connections with one another. There is also a pruning process that selectively eliminates some of the cells until a stabilized number of some 100 trillion or so remain (Ackerman 88).

The Brain During Childhood and Adolescence

During childhood and adolescence, the fatty insulating substance called myelin continues to coat the neural axons from lower to higher systems. This process does not end until way beyond puberty. Jane Healy contends that,

> before brain regions are myelinated, they do not operate efficiently. For this reason, trying to "make" children master academic skills for which they do not have the requisite maturation may result in mixed-up patterns of learning—reading, math, spelling, handwriting, etc.—may be accomplished by any of several systems. Naturally, we want children to plug each piece of learning into the best system for that particular job. If the right one isn't yet available or working smoothly, however, forcing may create a functional organization in which less adaptive, "lower" systems are trained to do the work. (67)

Because synapses occur between axon and dendrite, between axon and cell body, or, in the case of electrical synapses, between cell bodies directly, eventually synapses enable everything to connect to everything else. This makes the human brain a remarkable integrator of stimuli and information. Gerald Edelman calls it "the most complicated material object in the known universe" (17).

THE MAJOR STRUCTURES AND FUNCTIONS OF THE BRAIN

There is an adage held by the psychologists, neurophysiologists, chemists, molecular biologists, cyberneticists, mathematicians, quantum physicists, educators, and others studying the brain: "The organ by we which know, we know the least about." Examining the average human brain does give pause. Weighing only about three to four pounds, approximately the size of a small cantaloupe, it houses trillions cells, about 100 billion of them neurons, and it controls all activities from the mundane to the mystical, from the necessary to the aesthetic, from the reflexive to extensive, from the instinctive to the thoughtful. It is no wonder that "after thousands of scientists have studied it for centuries, the only word to describe it remains *amazing*" (Ornstein and Thompson 21).

The Brainstem

The brainstem, the oldest part of the brain, sits like the stalk of a mushroom at the top of the spinal cord. Tripartite, it consists of the medulla, pons, and midbrain. It acts as a warning system because it controls basic bodily functions associated with survival.

The Cerebellum

Cerebellum means "little brain" because it resembles, in miniature, the cerebrum. Like a wrinkled mass of tissue paper located at the lower back of the brain and long theorized as being in control of posture and movement and once hypothesized as the site of learning, the cerebellum is being re-evaluated. Considered by today's researchers as helpful in motor *and* nonmotor regions, it has been compared to a dual computer capable of contributing to motor and mental dexterity. Some researchers also now regard the *plasticity* of the brain as an important function of the cerebellum because it contributes to the automation of mental and motor activities.

The Amygdala

Shaped like an almond, this set of subcortical nuclei is located just beneath the surface of the front medial part of the temporal lobe where it causes the bulge on the surface called the *uncus*. The amygdala determines the significance of outside stimulus and triggers emotional responses, like freezing or fleeing, as well changes in the inner workings of the body's organs and glands.

The Hippocampus

The word *hippocampus* comes from the Greek *hipos* = horse, *kampi* = curve because early anatomists thought its curved shape resembled a seahorse. Le Doux tells us that the hippocampus was viewed a part of the rhinencephalon, referring to smell or olfaction. Then it was thought of as a major player in emotions, the seat of the Freudian id. "But, by the end of the 1950s, studies of H.M. and other patients had led to the conclusion that the hippocampus was crucially involved in one of the most important cognitive functions of the brain—memory" (2002, 100). The connections between the hippocampus and the neocortex put together stimuli to form global memories. "Without this capacity, memories would be fragmented" (2002, 104–105).

The Thalamus

Thalamus means "inner room" in Latin. This large mass of gray matter is located deep inside and between the two cerebral hemispheres. It relays to the cerebral cortex information received from diverse brain regions.

The Hypothalamus

Because *hypo* means "under," the hypothalamus means "under inner room" because it is located just below the thalamus. No bigger than a small bean, it is an important central monitor for many functions. Like a thermostat, it controls body temperature, but it also regulates hunger, thirst, sleep, hormones, digestion, sexuality, circulation, and emotions.

The Cerebrum

Supported on the brainstem, surmounting the rest of the brain, and forming the brain's bulk is the cerebrum, sometimes called the cerebral cortex or neocortex. It is the largest portion of the brain and is composed of gray matter that is less than three-eighths of an inch thick. It has a crumpled corrugated surface that forms the downfolds called *sulci* or fissures, and the upfolds called *gyri* or convolutions. If spread out flat, the cerebrum roughly covers an area of a small desktop. The cerebrum is divided into two symmetrical cerebral hemispheres joined by its corpus callosum. These two cerebral hemispheres are further subdivided into four lobes: frontal, parietal, temporal, occipital. The frontal lobe decides and plans. The parietal lobe receives sensory information. The temporal lobe hears, perceives, and remembers. The occipital lobe sees. The cerebrum is the part of the brain that makes us uniquely human; it is the brain that thinks.

Fig. 9.1. The Brain.

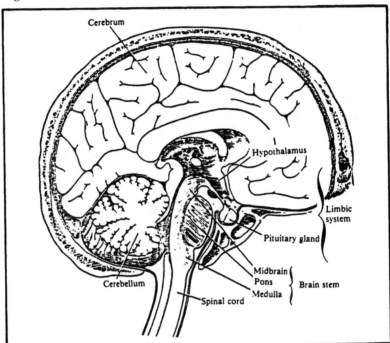

The Corpus Callosum

The two hemispheres of the brain are connected by a pencil-length, pencil-shaped bundle of approximately 300 million nerve fibers. This major neural system connects the two hemispheres and allows cross-talk and collaboration between them.

Neurons

The brain's nerve cells or neurons are not only numerous but also diverse. Santiago Ramon y Cajal, called the father of modern brain science, described them as "the mysterious butterflies of the soul, the beating of whose wings may some day—who knows?—clarify the secret of mental life" (Fischbach 49). While neurons seem to group according to kind and seem to conduct information in similar ways, they differ in shape, structure, and function. This causes researchers to speculate about the possibility of each neuron being unique. To study each of the approximately 100 billion neurons and their possible interconnections boggles the mind, especially when considering that researchers at Cambridge University spent three years analyzing the mere twenty-three neurons of a simple worm.

In her book *Endangered Minds*, Jane M. Healy suggests a convenient analogy to better understand the composition of a neuron—the human hand (51–52). By holding up the hand with fingers extended, there is immediately visible an approximation of a neuron. The palm is like the cell body or soma with its fatty part the nucleus. The extended fingers represent the dendrites, which comes from the Greek word *dendron* meaning "tree." Dendrites, in fact, resemble trees with twigs. Many dendrites have little protrusions called "spines," which is often where axons from other neurons end to form synapses. The arm to the elbow stands for the axon, from the Greek *axis* or *axle*, which is encased and insulated in a myelin sheath. The elbow represents the synapse, derived from the Greek word *clasp*, *connect*, or *join*—the site of communication between neurons. It is important to remember that the synapse does not actually touch another neuron as was once thought. Actually there is a nano space or cleft across which signals are sent.

Fig. 9.2. Dendrites.

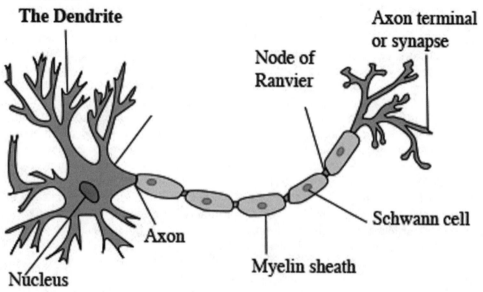

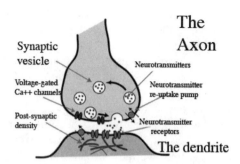

Typically neurons communicate like this: A neuron inputs information through its dendrites. The information is then processed in the cell body before being outputted as electrical impulses called "action potentials" down the axon. The axon widens near a synapse into a number of tiny buttons, which contain mitochondria, and into a number of synaptic vesicles, which contain chemical neurotransmitters ready to be released into the synaptic space. Chemical signals induce the release of the neurotransmitter molecules that diffuse across an infinitesimally small synaptic space and bind to the receptors in the new dendrite that has been activated. This is commonly called a synaptic connection and learning, knowing, and remembering are generally attributed to it.

To add to the brain's complexity, there is also a synapse that transmits signals through direct electrical coupling. "An electrical synapse is about 3 nanometers (nm), or billionths of a meter, wide, as compared with the 25-nm gap of a chemical synapse" (Ackerman 30). In short, there are chemical and electrical synapses.

Mirror Neurons

When we read Richard Restak's *The New Brain: How the Modern Age Is Rewiring Your Mind* in 2003, several things struck us. One fascinating piece of research that stretched back thirty years on movement recognition led to studies of how and why babies imitate, which laid the groundwork for the neuroscientific discovery of "mirror neurons" in monkeys. This struck us—as our marginalia prove—because we connected these mirror neurons to modeling in the classroom.

What is so exciting about this research is that it provides scientific underpinnings to pedagogically sound practices. Apparently what neuroscientists found was these mirror neurons "discharge both when the monkey performs certain movements and when the animal merely observes another monkey performing the movement" (35). Hence there may be some truth to the old adage, "monkey see; monkey do." Folk wisdom aside, Restak adds "strong evidence suggests a similar mirroring process in humans" (35). We seem to activate certain nerve cells during an activity and while observing another during that activity, "an indication that during the period of observation the brain areas responsible for planning the movements were already primed for imitation" (36).

Robert Sylwester in his 2007 book *The Adolescent Brain* mentions mirror neurons, "they create a mental template within our brain of the related neural activity that's occurring within the brain of the person we're observing" (17). Sounds like a neurological basis for modeling to us.

Finally, J. Madeleine Nash in "The Gift of Mimicry" for *Time's* "Mind & Body Special Issue," builds her article around mirror neurons. Concentrating on the implications of mirror neurons on empathy, language, and social behavior, she, perhaps overstating the case, says, "mirror neurons will do for psychology what DNA did for biology: they will provide a unifying framework and help explain a host of mental abilities" (110). Hyperbole notwithstanding, we hold that mirror neurons give us a unifying framework to support modeling. We have always maintained the power of modeling—now it seems as students watch the teacher (or others) performing an action such as writing, mirror neurons kick in, predisposing students to that activity on a subconscious level. They watch the activity, encode it, engage in it, and finally comprehend it—reinforcing our mantra, "Telling isn't teaching."

Connected to this powerful simulation equipment we call our brain, mirror neurons also hold implications for attitude, intention, and association—what Restak calls "emotional contagion" (2003, 37). Citing the findings of researchers (Blakemore and Decety, Hogg, Stosny), Restak advises we surround ourselves with people possessing qualities we wish to emulate and limit associations "with people given to pessimism and expressions of futility" (2003, 37). Therefore, if we want a pleasant classroom with happy students, if we want our students to feel positive about the act of writing, we must project that demeanor.

The Neuroglial Cells

The name "glial" comes from the Greek for glue, *glia*. Glial cells do not actually glue neurons together, rather they render a cellular support system. The brain's neuroglial or glial cells probably outnumber nerve cells ten to one. These cells do not have axons or dendrites but rather are packed between, around, and over the neurons. Not only do glials form the styrofoam "peanuts" or bubble wrap for the brain, they also nourish it and consume its waste. The only part of the neuron that glial cells do not cover is the synaptic space. Le Doux explains, "new neurons and glial cells are born in the ventricular region. From there, neurons have to find their way to their destination in order to form brain regions. Radial glial cells seem to aid in this migratory process. They give rise to fibers that extend toward the brain's surface. . . . By climbing the glial trail, neurons find their homes" (2002, 69). Pasko Rakic of Yale calls this process "the building of scaffolds" (2002, 69).

THEORIES OF THE BRAIN AND IMPLICATIONS FOR TEACHING

Common knowledge of the brain tells us that every vertebrate brain can be divided into three broad territories or zones: the hindbrain, the midbrain, and the forebrain. Joseph Le Doux tells us "the hindbrain controls very basic functions, those necessary for staying alive; the midbrain is involved in maintaining wakefulness and coarse, isolated behavioral reactions; and the forebrain coordinates complex behavioral and mental process" (2002, 35). Yet, in an effort to more fully understand the human brain, researchers in the field of neuropsychology have analyzed and continue to analyze it, comparing it, in turn, to a walnut, a hierarchical government, a machine, a computer, and constructing anatomical and metaphoric models of it. The most popular models range from Wilder Penfield's cartoon-like drawing of the motor *homunculus* (little man) to Ned Herrmann's "Whole Brain Model."

The Motor Homunculus

This model, which grew out of the experiments of Canadian neurosurgeon Wilder Penfield in the 1940s, represents the way a person would look if the proportions of the body corresponded to the brain area that controlled that part of the body. Interestingly, more brain-space aligns with the

Fig. 9.3. The Homunculus.

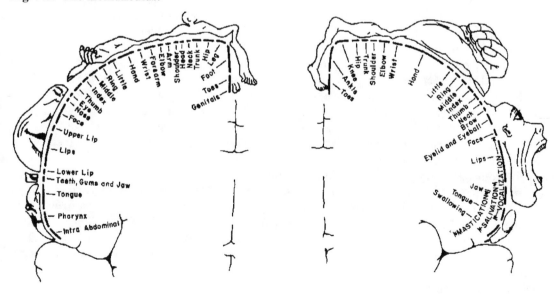

mouth and hands than for all the rest of the body. What this model contributed to the field was support for idea that the brain is organized by function. (See Fig. 9.3.)

Triune Brain Theory

Developed by Paul MacLean to explain "three formations that constitute a hierarchy of three brains in one, or what may be called for short a triune brain" (MacLean 309): the R-complex, the limbic system, and the cerebrum (neocortex).

The triune brain offers interesting implications for teaching. Considering the brain from this tripartite theory, it "is significant for educators because it provides us with a different and useful way of looking at behavior, is compatible with relevant psychological and sociological theories, and provides some coherent direction for what it will take to generate change" (Caine and Caine 52). It is important to note that just as the two hemispheres interact horizontally, the three parts of the brain interact vertically.

The R-complex

The R-complex, the brainstem, part of the midbrain area, and a primitive cortex, is the seat of instinctual behavior. By analogy, it holds as much information as a pocket dictionary and takes care of physical needs, survival, and sexuality. This part of the brain engages in rudimentary signaling, imitation, routine displays, formation of social groups, mating, ritualistic and deceptive behavior, characteristics that are primarily automatic and most resistant to change. The R-complex reacts to threat. When people downshift to the R-complex level because of a threatening experience, they freeze, flee, or fight.

Many people experience writing anxiety or panic; the thought or even the suggestion of writing poses a threat that causes downshifting. In classrooms where students downshift because of some real or imaged threat associated with writing, they display the "freeze" syndrome. They stoically sit in their places, almost catatonic, as if they cannot take out paper or move a pencil. If they do write, they write little or what is safe.

Students who display "flight" when told they will write or share what they have written, either cut the class or school altogether. If those are not viable options, they flee by putting their heads down on the desk or sit glassy-eyed with bobbing heads as they fall into a reverie that transports them, at least mentally, elsewhere. These students never have paper or pencil, lose what they have written, or only parrot back, copy, or produce minimally.

Finally there are the fighters. They deal with the threat of writing through hostile, recalcitrant behaviors. They direct these behaviors toward the teacher, toward peers, or even toward themselves. They argue about why they have to write, about their grades; they hassle about their seat; they complain about classmates, the principal, the school, rules, and regulations—all pugilistic reasons to escape writing. They perceive writing as unrelated to their world, so they use it to question, or to clench their metaphoric fists. These students write for a time, but then, in the ultimate demonstration of downshifting, wad up their papers and toss them in the trash.

If we heighten our sensitivity to the possibility that some students may have had negative writing experiences that trigger this automatic, reactionary behavior, we can circumvent this downshifting. Modifying classroom practices that convey threat while positively building upon the instinctual R-complex helps redirect these negative behaviors. For example, by modeling, we productively call upon the instinct to imitate; by incorporating a routine, we enlarge upon the innate desire for ritual; by instituting group work and cooperative projects, we capitalize on the flocking instinct. Consistently monitoring our teaching behaviors protects students from threatening writing situations. The main objective at this point is to move students into their cerebrums.

If we teach in departmentalized elementary schools, middle schools, or high schools, we need to reckon with the halo effect of threat. When students leave a threatening classroom, the brain does not immediately upshift as they enter a nonthreatening one. Nor does the brain or the maturity level of students distinguish the difference. If students regard school as threatening territory, then is it any wonder hundreds of thousands of students daily find the inside of their room, the vacant lot of their neighborhoods, gangs, drugs, or isolation preferable?

> *Recently we conducted an awareness session for a group of administrators. During break, one of the teachers commented, "I can't believe my principal came. She is terrified of writing. She even confided that she hoped you didn't make them write."*
>
> *The morning moved along with sharing and interaction. The principal remained enthusiastic, positive, and expressed pride in her teachers' efforts and their students' writing. As the morning ended, we said, "Now this afternoon we'll take you through a micro-mini experience with writing as it is taught as a process."*
>
> *The principal did not return. We conjectured that perceived threat of writing, perhaps coupled with the threat of sharing that writing, outweighed the risk of returning.*

The Reticular Activating System (RAS)

Neurologist Judy Willis reminds us of a critical element in the brainstem, the reticular activating system or the RAS. "The RAS receives input from the nerves that converge into the spinal cord from sensory receptors in the arms, legs, trunk, head, and neck. The spinal cord sends these sensory messages up through the RAS to gain entry to the brain. The RAS sets the state of arousal of the rest of the brain and affects the ability of the higher brain sensory recognition centers to receive and respond to incoming data" (18–19).

Think of it this way: The RAS is the monitoring system for incoming data. It is critical for survival. Our ancestors attending to their surroundings, to incoming sensations, images, dangers, and opportunities were not very much different than today's students attending to a classroom environment. The brain is designed to attend, and the RAS is its signal.

The reticular activating system also has many benefits crucial to learning. For example, a teacher points out the call back lead and models it. The RAS stores that information or a connection to that learning. Then when the student reads another book and comes upon a call back lead, the RAS automatically kicks in, students recognize it, and can name it. This is precisely why when we learn something new we see examples of it everywhere. Of course, the RAS has other implications besides those in learning, but we can never forget that the purpose of the brain is to learn new information.

The implication for teachers is astonishing and profound because the RAS underscores the fact that students are impacted by everything in their environment. Give them a steady diet of worksheets, which deaden all stimuli and challenge, put them in a daily threatening situation, and that RAS works overtime to alert the brain to danger, and works to avoid that danger at all costs in order to survive.

The Limbic System

The second formation is the limbic system, which includes the limbic lobe, hippocampus, amygdaloid nucleus, hypothalamus, and the anterior nucleus of the thalamus. By analogy, it holds as much information as a set of encyclopedia.

In the 1993 edition of this book, we included the limbic system as part of the structure of the brain, as did legions of neuroscience students; and, because MacLean constructed it as an all-encompassing source of the emotional aspects of behavior relating to survival, we referred to it as the visceral or emotional brain.

Since that time, while the cerebellum has gained stature, the limbic system *as a specific place* is all but defunct. Considered by Le Doux and others (1996, 2002) as imprecise and carrying unwarranted functional implications and overgeneralizations, we are abandoning it as a system applied too broadly to emotions or even as an anatomical description.

"We are at the point where the limbic theory has become an off-the-shelf explanation of how the brain works, one grounded in tradition rather than facts," says Le Doux, and as the authors of this second edition, we choose not to perpetuate something that isn't grounded in research.

But we still entertain the possibility, as does Le Doux, that MacLean was correct in holding that emotions involve relatively primitive circuits that are conserved *throughout* the mammalian development of the brain and that cognitive processes might involve other circuits and sometimes function independently of emotions. We embrace the notion that "emotion is a kind of cognition" (Le Doux 1996, 68), so we reject that emotions are housed *in one specific section* of the brain.

Based on this new view of emotions, we are also interested in the work of John and Beatrice Lacey who discovered "the heart was not just a pump but also an organ of great intelligence, with its own nervous system, decision-making powers, and connections to the brain." And we are following the work of J. Andrew Armour, author of *Neurocardiology*, who holds to the concept of a functioning "heart brain" or "little brain" that allows it to act independently of the cranial brain (in Guarneri 156).

Also, Larry Dossey's research is interesting. A psychoneuroimmunologist, he suggests that there are links between parts of the brain concerned with thought and emotion and the neurological immune systems, so we are following what is revealed in quantum mechanics, cellular memory, and nonlocal mind as a consciousness spread throughout time and space, unconfined to brain or body.

Suggesting that emotions do not reside in one place in the brain does not militate against their power when writing. There are two dominant implications for teachers of writing related to emotions. The first is the need for enthusiastic teaching; the second is ways to apply proper pressure.

Nothing replaces enthusiasm and authentic involvement in the writing process. If we write, honestly and zealously with our students, if they and we share that writing, students are more likely to become involved. If we harbor any real or imagined fears or concerns that give rise to feelings of inadequacy when it comes to writing, we should seek some training so we approach the teaching of writing with security and ardor. Students will not be fooled. Our enthusiasm carries over into feelings of genuine delight about the writing of others. In this way writing becomes a celebration in the classroom. Evidences of that celebration fill the room: writing folders, an author's chair, and books, and various displays of writing.

The Cerebrum (Neocortex)

Surmounting the rest of the brain and providing the surface of the cerebrum is the third formation—the neocortex, which quite literally means "new bark or rind." By analogy, it holds as much information as the entire New York Public Library. "The neocortex culminates in the human brain in which there develops a megapolis of nerve cells devoted to the production of symbolic language and the associated functions of reading, writing, and arithmetic. Mother of invention, and father of abstract thought, the new cortex promotes the preservation and procreation of ideas" (MacLean 332). The cerebrum is the seat of thinking.

Because the cerebrum thinks, it responds to risk. When we discuss "high order thinking skills," we assume the thinker is operating from the cerebrum or cerebral cortex where the higher brain functions occur. The cerebrum simultaneously weighs chances, considers compromises, hazards guesses, deliberates, reflects, speculates, and hypothesizes. Higher order functions manifest those of the unsophisticated child—"I bet I can throw this further than you can" to those of the sophisticated scientist—"I am hypothesizing a cure for cancer." Both take knowledge and project that knowledge into new areas or onto different situations.

While sounding perhaps too philosophical or scientific and not pedagogical enough, it is nonetheless imperative to point out that the information known about the cerebral cortex and its functions carries far-reaching implications for us. Not the least of which is that writing must occur within meaningful situations. Knowing or learning does not occur independent of other knowing and learning. Teaching students one way to write a paragraph, for example, the "box" paragraph, and relying on other teachers to teach other ways of writing paragraphs belies the brain's power to understand complexities. Speaking in "brain language," the question isn't should other types of paragraphs be taught but how best to teach them.

Because the neocortex works best within a context, writing

- about social studies offers opportunity to learn skills and mechanics;

- a remembered holiday provides a vehicle for lessons on research, organization;

- a lab report begs for organization and observation of detail;

- responses to literature are perfect times to discuss style, genre, and the observed and observable conventions;

- in logs helps synthesis and evaluation;

- letters holds teachable moments for word choice, sense of audience, and intention.

Writing takes place in the global arena of learning—it, like the neurons in the brain, may shoot off in certain directions, focus on subjectively interesting areas, make silent synaptic connections that remain tacit only to explode later in some mysterious way into a different piece of writing. Each mind is unique; each body is unique; each writer is unique. Perhaps more than anyone else in the educational system, we who teach writing best validate that uniqueness.

The Hemisphericity Theory

Hemisphericity describes "the idea that the two hemispheres are specialized for different modes of thought" (Springer and Deutsch 287). A cursory glance at even an elementary drawing of the brain reveals two hemispheres that foster conjecture about the function and relationship of these two "sides." Early Greek physicians, among the first to dissect the body, were among the first to develop theories about the brain. Hippocrates (460–377 B.C.) considered reason as well as sensations and motor activities existent in and dependent upon the brain. A. M. Lassek's book *The Human Brain from Primitive to Modern* contains a brief summary of major brain theories and experiments dating from an ancient Egyptian medical test (2000 B.C.) to the early twentieth-century neurologist Henry Head.

Twenty some centuries after Hippocrates, in the 1940s, W. P. Van Wagenen cut the corpus callosum of a patient with incurable epilepsy. A decade after that Ronald Myers and Roger Sperry severed a cat's corpus callosum, the connecting nerve tissue between the two hemispheres, and the optic chiasm, the crossover optic nerves. Ten years later, tests performed on commissurotomies, split-brain patients, led Sperry to conclude that, "Everything we have seen so far indicates that surgery has left each of these people with two separate minds, that is, with two separate spheres of consciousness" (Ornstein 117).

Extensive and ingenious experiments conducted by Sperry and others confirmed the contralaterality concept. Since the entire central nervous system in humans is bisymmetric—one side the mirror image of the other—each hemisphere of the brain controls the opposite side of the body. The left hemisphere controls the right side of the body and vice versa. This crossover or contralateral effect applies to body movement and touch and in more complicated ways to vision and hearing. Thus, when stimuli is presented to only one hemisphere of the brain, it is said to be lateralized. By conducting tests on split-brain patients, researchers identified how each hemisphere processes information. "The left hemisphere is specialized for language functions, but these specializations are a consequence of the left hemisphere's superior analytic skills, of which language is one manifestation. Similarly, the right hemisphere's superior visuo-spatial performance is derived from its synthetic, holistic manner of dealing with information" (Springer and Deutsch 54–55). Generally, the left hemisphere functions linearly, analytically, and logically. It is considered both verbal and dominant. The right hemisphere functions simultaneously, synthetically, and creatively. It is considered both spatial and intuitive.

Educational systems in Western cultures tend to emphasize and value faculties associated with the left hemisphere, which are logical and linear approaches to teaching and learning. Pervasive in all cultures, however, are discriminations about left-handedness, for example, *Webster's New World Thesaurus* lists the following synonyms for left-handed—*clumsy*, *careless*, *gauche*, and suggests further synonyms under *awkward*. The French word for left is *gauche*, which means "inept"; the Italian word for left is *mancino*, which also means "deceitful." The Spanish *no ser zurdo* idiomatically translates "to be very clever," but it literally means, "not to be left-handed." Betty Edwards in *Drawing on the Right Side of the Brain* takes a section on "The Bias of Language and Customs," but she reminds the reader "that those terms were all made up, when languages began, by some persons' left hemispheres—the left brain calling the right bad names!" (33–34).

Michael Corballis, of the University of Auckland, presents a different interpretation for this right-hand, left-brain bias. He suggests that right-handedness is unique to humans. "Perhaps this is why virtually all cultures hold the right [hand] to be sacred and the left profane, as though right handedness, like human beings themselves, is a gift of the Gods" (2).

Considering the two hemispheres perceive reality uniquely suggests that we prefer one cognitive style of teaching, learning, or administrating to another. For example, Eloise Scott Soler, in her doctoral study, found that a total of 197 Texas male school superintendents and 22 female superintendents who took the Herrmann Brain Dominance Instrument (HBDI) showed 69.1 percent of them to be left-brained, an interesting finding since educational institutions are traditionally sequential and lock-step. The superintendents in the Soler study exhibited certain behaviors that preclude change; their responses were decidedly not holistic. She recommends retraining for these people (iv–v).

Some would have a much better chance of not embarrassing themselves if they saved the hemisphericity theory, the Soler and other serious studies as a last resort, rather than jumping to them as a first conclusion. Some, oversimplifying hemisphericity, see it as an easy way to generalize their preferences and behaviors and the behaviors of others. They respond to the spate of commercially produced left brain/right brain psychographic tests, questionnaires, and surveys usually found in magazines to "test" their hemisphere preference. They use the results to justify behavior, "I can't do that. I'm right-brained." These people who misunderstand hemispericity suffer from "dichotomania, a term coined to refer to the avalanche of popular literature fostered by the speculative notions" (Springer and Deutsch 287). They take the incredibly intricate and complex nature of the brain's interconnections—so numerous, if we use Gerald Edelman's example, it would take some 32 million years to count them (17)—and interpret them via a few questions and answers in a popular magazine.

While dichotomic divisions historically have been a convenient way to organize intellectual faculties (see Table 9.1), we must keep in mind two things: (1) The original evidence about right

Table 9.1. Cross-Disciplinary Dichotomies

Suggested by	Dichotomies	
Plato	Form	Ideas
Aristotle	Body	Soul
Abelard	Particular objects	Universal concepts
Aquinas	Reason	Faith
Pomponazzi	Objective truth	Religious truth
Francis Bacon	Mind	Instincts/emotions
Descartes	Matter	Spirit
Hume	Experience of ideas	Experience of impressions
Kant	Reason	Judgment
Cassirer	Theoretical	Mythical
Langer	Discursive	Presentational
Polanyi	Explicit	Tacit
Revesz/Sapir	Imitative	Ontogenetic
Hippocrates	Reason	Sensation
Tiger	Science	Fancy
Jaynes	Language of men	Language of gods
Ornstein	Left hemisphere	Right hemisphere
Dickman	Action mode	Receptive mode
Gazzaniga	Verbal	Visuospatial
Bogen	Propositional	Appositional
I Ching	Ch'ien	K'un
Lee	Lineal code	Nonlineal code
Domhoff	Left is bad	Right is good
de Saussure	Speaking	Language synchrony diachrony
Bloomfield	Mechanistic	Mentalistic
Ogden & Richards	Symbolic	Emotive
Chomsky	Performance	Competence
Piaget	Organization	Adaptation
Bruner	Analytic	Intuitive
Vygotsky	Speech	Thought
Dewey	Other ways of thinking	Reflective thinking
Rosenblatt	Afferent	Aesthetic
Britton	Transactional	Poetic
Emig	Extensive	Reflexive

(Carroll, 1979, 75)

and left brain ways of knowing and processing information was based on studies of brain-damaged or split-brain patients, not on studies with neurologically normal people; (2) the normal brain is incredibly adaptable and is capable of almost instantaneous information transmission between the hemispheres. This militates against gross generalizations about lateralization.

While neuroscientists agree there is hemispheric specialization, they also hold that is not always so neatly separated, that experience and goals affect which brain carries out which activity. Perhaps the distinction neurologist Richard M. Restak makes based on the research of John Mazziotta and other scientists at UCLA will dispel the too-easy designation of left-brain/right-brain learners (teachers/administrators) and will serve as support for brain-balanced education. "The PET scans confirmed that the hemisphere activation differed, suggesting something quite remarkable— that hemisphere specialization is dependent on the strategy employed by the listener" (1984, 250). Restak concludes, "People may not only be of a 'different mind' on issues, but they may also use different parts of their brains to do the same thing" (1984, 250). With that information, Restak suggests that, "Division of the hemispheres into symbolic-conceptual (left hemisphere) vs. nonsymbolic directly perceived (right hemisphere) avoids many oversimplifications" (1984, 250–251).

As Carl Sagan reminds us,

> There is no way to tell whether the patterns extracted by the right hemisphere are real or imagined without subjecting them to left-hemisphere scrutiny. On the other hand, mere critical thinking, without creative and intuitive insights, without the search for new patterns, is sterile and doomed. To solve complex problems in changing circumstances requires the activity of both cerebral hemispheres: the path to the future lies through the corpus callosum. (190–191)

Think of functions of the brain as parallel computers capable of processing many steps simultaneously.

Hemisphericity is a theory with roots in localized brain function discoveries that date back to early researchers. J. Dryander illustrated diverse parts of the brain in his book *Anatomie* (1537). The Dutch woodcut shown in Fig. 9.4 shows that these early neuroscientists knew the brain was composed of parts, such as the frontal *sinciput, anterior* and the rear *occipital, posterior.* Further, it displays the brain's lobes, features still studied in neuroanatomy. The letters A through G illustrate six layers of the cerebral cortex. According to Ackerman, "In this century, observations down to the level of single cells make it possible to sort out the distinct functions of each of these layers" (x).

Paul Broca discovered of the area of articulated speech in the nineteenth century. The research with split-brain patients in the 1940s, 1950s, and 1960s contributed to the theory. Yet the data remain inconclusive, but not without implications for teaching. Three are major.

The overarching implication of hemisphericity theory is that the brain's two hemispheres interact through uniquely complicated and integrated processes. While researchers agree that the brain contains regions identifiable by function, they have found that each hemisphere is not so autonomous as originally suspected and should not be so rigidly defined. Yet original left and right brain research in learning styles, reading styles, and administration styles broaden views on how better to reach all learners.

Writing teachers who stay abreast of brain research realize both sides of the brain communicate and are involved in most activities. We design holistic, brain-balanced instruction. We focus students by purpose and audience, but allow great latitude in topic, style, genre, and mode. If the purpose is narrative, students have choices to write a story, a fable, a historical tale, a narrative poem, and so forth. We understand when some students opt for green paper with lines while others want yellow paper without lines. We know why some prefer to write with markers, some with

Fig. 9.4. Dyrander's Diverse Brain Parts.

pen, others with pencil. Our knowledge of the brain explains why some students prefer sitting by a window, some like to work alone, while still others do their best work sprawled out on the floor. They may write better in a group. We constantly ask ourselves, "What is the best way for this student to achieve? How does this student process information best?" We know all brains do not work the same way.

For us brain research informs our teaching. We give students plenty of practice sketching out their ideas through prewriting. We model how to take the best of these "sketches" through the process into a final product. The old view that they have to learn "the right way" before they can break the rules simply does not work for every learner. Sometimes it is the learner that is broken.

The third implication for teachers of writing builds upon Caine and Caine's assertion that "all knowledge is 'embedded' in other knowledge" (36). We model how parts and wholes interconnect, which offers a different vision of how teaching should occur. The old notion that fostered teaching bits that grew into bigger bits, such as sounds before letters, letters before words, words before sentences, sentences before paragraphs, paragraphs before larger pieces of discourse simply does not hold true in light of brain research.

As Margaret Donaldson says,

The old idea was that the associations were built up in quite mechanical automatic ways. They were bonds between isolated elements. The person in whom these bonds developed was passive. . . . The associations came first. Insofar as there was 'meaning' it was an outcome of the (conditioning) process by which the associations were established.

The newer account differs from this in the most fundamental way. The primary thing is now held to be the grasp of meaning—the ability to "make sense" of things. . . . It is the child's ability to interpret situations which makes it possible, through active processes of hypothesis-testing and inference, to arrive at a knowledge. (32–33)

We ask teachers to provide students with many opportunities to write with a sense of wholeness, a sense of meaning. We invite students to write poems, plays, stories, essays about social studies, in mathematics, for science—whole pieces of discourse—not lines of letters out of context, lists of unrelated words, isolated sentences, or a paragraph. We want students to feel comfortable in both the reflexive and extensive modes. We encourage students to be both creative and logical, sharing intuitions and defending propositions. When students write within a context enriched by the writings of others—books, stories, plays, poems—in places where writing really exists and where sounds, words, sentences, paragraphs hold meaning, students discover interesting and relevant contextual meaning. In this context, students see how vocabulary, style, and voice become one with craft, literary merit, and the grappling of ideas and thoughts on paper.

All this takes time, so we advise school districts to integrate curricula, schedule larger blocks of time for sustained teaching, thematic teaching, team teaching, and grouping across grade levels. Brain research also supports collaborative learning and teaching writing as a process. The point is not so much that Tanisha is left-brained or Raul is right-brained, but that all learners are whole-brain with capacities we need to tap.

The Whole Brain Model

Influenced by Paul MacLean's triune brain and Roger Sperry's left/right brain, Ned Herrmann constructed a model with paired structures that included two halves of the cerebral system and two halves of the limbic system.

Fig. 9.5. The Whole Brain Model.

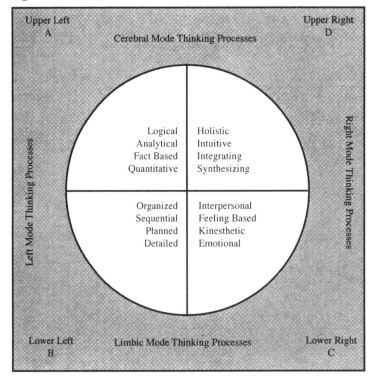

Herrmann uses this model to explain four distinct thinking modes:

A: The upper cerebral left—analytical, mathematical, technical, and problem solving;

B: The lower limbic left—controlled, conservative, planned, organized, and administrative;

C: The lower limbic right—interpersonal, emotional, musical, spiritual, and the "talker";

D: The upper cerebral right—imaginative, synthesizing, artistic, holistic, and conceptual.

Herrmann's theory holds to dominance. Believing that wherever there are two of anything in the body, one is naturally more dominant, for example, handedness. The implications in the classroom of this theory overlap with hemisphericity—an awareness of but not excuses for divergent learning styles.

MALE AND FEMALE BRAINS: THE IMPLICATIONS FOR TEACHING

There is no denying it—the brains of men and women are different anatomically and chemically. Hormones bathe the fetus with a flood of testosterone to wire the male brain and a flood of estrogen to wire the female brain. Then, during puberty, hormones cause the brain to switch on the network they laid out.

Generally speaking, because there are enormous differences among people, men's brains are larger than women's but women have larger corpora callosa with broader anterior commissures than do men. This accounts for more conversations between the two hemispheres of women, which explains bilateral thinking. Women tend to make connections quickly, jumping lickety-split and easily across that bridge of nerve fibers from one idea to another. Men, lateral thinkers, tend to stay focused on one topic until its completion. On the one hand, women think men have an alphabet tucked in their brains when they tick off, "A—yada, yada; B—yada, yada, C—yada, yada." By the letter *D*, most women "get it," which drives men crazy. On the other hand, men think women are illogical and random when they actively recruit both sides of their brains—so they dismiss woman's thinking as *creative* or *intuitive*. The point is this: One brain isn't smarter or better than the other; the brains of men and women are simply patterned differently.

Citing a series of studies that grew out of problem-solving tests, Doreen Kimura, a professor psychology at the University of Western Ontario in London, identifies some of these patterns. Women tended to outperform men in

- perceptual speed—matching items and finding displaced items;

- ideational and verbal fluency—generating certain lists by color or initial letter;

- precise manual tasks as in fine motor coordination;

- mathematical calculations.

Men tended to outperform women in

- certain spatial tasks—mentally rotating or manipulating objects;

- target-directed motor skills—throwing darts at a dartboard;

- disembedding—finding a simple shape in a more complex one;

- mathematical reasoning. (120–121)

Interestingly, men's brains are physically larger than women's, but both have the same number of brain cells. They are just packed more densely in the woman's skull.

In *The Female Brain*, Yale-trained Louann Brizendine, founder of the Women's and Teen Girls' Mood and Hormone Clinic at UCSF, says, "The brain is nothing if not a talented learning machine" (6).

Brizendine sets up a hypothetical look at the developing brain via time-lapse photography. *In utero* all brains are female until about eight weeks old. The circuitry is laid down like a blueprint. "A huge testosterone surge beginning in the eighth week will turn this unisex brain male by killing off some cells in the communication centers and growing more cells in the sex and aggression centers. If the testosterone surge doesn't happen, the female brain continues to grow unperturbed. The fetal girl's brain cells sprout more connections in the communication centers and areas that process emotion" (14). This enlarged communication center of women explains why "men use about seven thousand words per day. Women use about twenty thousand" (14). Brizendine also goes on to explain how this surge defines the innate biological destiny and perceptivity of men on women. We think knowing this about communication and emotion holds important implications in the classroom.

As physical anthropologist Marie Christine de Lacoste of the Yale School of Medicine dissected human brains, she noticed the corpus callosum was more extensive in women's brains than in men's brains. She said, "All I've shown is that there is a difference in the number of connections between hemispheres" (Johmann 26). Her findings, and those of Marian Diamond and others, led to speculation about lateralization—are women's brains more diffuse or less specialized laterally than men's brains? The theory maintained the more connecting fibers between the two hemispheres, the more communication between the hemispheres. Indeed De Lacoste found structural differences in fetuses as young as six to seven months suggesting that lateralization begins *in utero* and continues to puberty. Cautioning against sexist misunderstandings, De Lacoste explains, "We don't have two brains evolving separately, just one brain that reflects the differences in sex hormones and reproductive functions. . . . We're talking about differences in the way men and women screen information" (Johmann 113). A decade later "Allen and Gorski found the same sex related size difference in the splenium" (Kimura 123), the rear portion of the corpus callosum.

Kimura quickly points out that sex differences in cognitive functions have yet to be conclusively related to callosal size, but agrees researchers have long held the male brain is more asymmetric than the female brain. The assumption is "that men's and women's brains are organized along different lines from very early in life. During development, sex hormones direct such differentiation" (125). She adds hormones may affect cognitive patterns throughout life.

Girls develop their left hemispheres first whereas boys develop their right hemispheres first, raising the question of nature or nurture, wiring or environment. Between the ages of six and nine, girls are verbal while boys are mechanically and spatially curious. Sometime around the age of nine or ten the process reverses so by the end of puberty the processes have leveled. Teachers who recognize that gender may affect the students' writing processes individualize and allow for that diversification. For example, girls may talk more about their topics before they even put pen to paper; boys may doodle or even draw out their topic. One way is not preferable—simply different.

MEMORY

Brain research provides us with new ways to look at memory. Traditionally, we gave the highest marks to students who remembered the material best; we extolled people with quick memories. But today we are more likely to be impressed if someone checks a recorder/talking key ring.

Undoubtedly we live in an age of YouTube, Google, Wikipedia, flickr™, amazon.com, Netflix, and iTunes, with fingertip access to all manner of information. We also own technological devices such as Palm®, recorder/talking key rings, and smart phones to help our memory. Yet we know the better we understand memory, the better we understand learning. With the rapidly exploding, expanding, and changing nature of the globalization age, the emphasis has shifted from memorization as an exercise of the mind to the question of how does memory work?

Genetic Memory and Memory Codes

Robert Ornstein and Richard F. Thompson offer genetic memory and memory codes. The former are literally millions of bits of information coded in the DNA of the cell; the latter is the cellular encoding of memory in the brain. Ornstein and Thompson maintain that genetic memory and memory codes are unique for each individual. "Memories are stored among the neurons of the brain in some kind of relatively permanent form as physical traces, which we call memory traces. If only we knew the code, we could read the entire lifetime of experiences and knowledge from these traces in the brain. This is perhaps the greatest challenge in neuroscience—to understand how the brain stores memories" (133).

Categories of Memory

In the not-too-distant past, researchers divided memory several different ways. One commonly studied set of categories, recounted by Russell, include:

- episodic, memories of past episodes and events;

- factual, memory for facts;

- semantic, memory for meaning;

- sensory, memories that comes through the senses, for example, people's faces, music, aromas;

- skills, memory of basic functions such as how to throw a ball or get dressed;

- instinctive, genetic remembering, such as how to breathe, sleep, or digest food;

- collective, the access to archetypal symbols; past-life, memories of events from before birth. (82–83)

Other Categories of Memory

Declarative and Procedural Memory. Some researchers divide memory into declarative and procedural. Declarative memory holds names of things, people, occurrences, and facts, whereas procedural memory enables people to learn and remember how to do things (Klivington 171).

Short-Term and Long-Term Memory. What we hold in our immediate awareness for five to twenty seconds constitutes our short-term memory. When we remember new information over twenty-four hours or even permanently, we hold it in our long-term memory. Researchers contend that short-term memory and long-term memory reside in different parts of the brain. Also, because of observations of patients with head injuries such as concussions, data indicate a critical period is needed to switch from short- to long-term memory.

Implicit and Explicit Memory. Daniel L. Schacter, Professor of Psychology at Harvard, defines implicit memory as "past experiences that unconsciously influence our perceptions, thought, and actions." He defines explicit memory as deliberately recalled information or recognized words or materials (9). It is the one tapped most often in school.

Taxon and Locale Memory. Caine and Caine cite and synthesize the research of John O'Keefe and Lynn Nadel, when they advance taxon memory and locale memory as memory systems that help us better understand natural memory versus memorization. They see taxon memory as an information-processing model that takes signals from the sensory register and moves them into short-term memory, and, if rehearsed enough, stores them in long-term memory.

Eric Jensen calls this "Key Steps in Memory Storage Processes." Paraphrased: We received a stimulus that goes to the short-term memory. To retain this information, we must actively process it "through discussion, art, mapping, thinking, or debates" (105). Only then can it be placed in the long-term memory.

Caine and Caine list five descriptors of taxon memory. It

- takes practice and rehearsal;

- responds to rewards and punishments;

- resists change;

- remains relatively isolated but sometimes interacts with other memories;

- can recall without understanding.

In short, taxon memory is memorization.

IMPLICATIONS FOR TEACHING

In the writing classroom, taxon memories hold to prescriptive rules and conventions that students practice and rehearse. If these rules and conventions become habits, they are difficult to change. Students learn that certain topics receive better grades just as they learn that certain usage receives better grades. If mechanics are learned in isolation and only occasionally used in context—generally a context close to the way they were practiced, learners have difficulty applying them in a new context. This explains why students can study "grammar" for twelve years and still appear not to know it.

Locale Memory

Locale memory constantly creates and tests spatial, mental, or thematic maps that provide information about locations, life relationships, and ideologies. These maps are critical for establishing a sophisticated transfer of knowledge, for example, seeing the patterns or stories in our lives, and they describe interconnections through association. Locale memory has seven characteristics:

- an unlimited spatial memory system that is survival oriented;

- dynamic, contextual, and relational because it records ongoing life events and actions;

- instantaneous interconnections;

- constantly updates open-ended, flexible maps with comparisons made between past and present;

- expectations, novelty, and curiosity stimulate its interconnections;

- heightened sensory acuity;

- maps may happened instantly or take a long time to form. (Caine and Caine 37–43)

Locale memory remembers contextual learning. For example, our space, comfort, sensory perceptions all work together to develop relationships about how our writing occurs. When we develop a sense of how writing, mechanics, organization, meaning, and so forth work together to form an extension of what is known, we use locale memory. Self-discovery and exploration culled from significant experience are key for locale memories.

Although taxon memory is limited, it is needed by the locale memory. When writing, the locale memory places the topic within a context—the whole—and then calls upon the taxon memory to supply the parts—grammar, mechanics, punctuation, and so forth. This explains why students who practice skills directly within the complexity of the writing process learn them in deeper and more lasting ways. In other words, writing as a process is the thematic map that needs and utilizes the taxon memory.

Working Memory

Patricia S. Goldman-Rakic, Professor of Neuroscience at the Yale University School of Medicine, defines working memory as "the combination of moment-to-moment awareness and instant retrieval of archived information" (111). Marcel Just and Patricia Carpenter of Carnegie Mellon University refer to it as "the blackboard of the mind" (Goldman-Rakic 111). What this memory enables humans to do, explains Goldman-Rakic, is plan, predict, and sequence thoughts and ideas. Most evidence indicates that these operations occur in the prefrontal lobes of the cerebral cortex. Thus, working memory complements associative or long-term memory by activating, storing, and manipulating symbolic information short-term. An example: constructing one sentence about childhood in a story. To do this requires accessing the information about some childhood incident from the long-term memory and storing it in the working memory. While doing that, the working memory also retrieves other stored symbolic information such as the parts of speech, conventions of a sentence, lexical, and syntactical information. The working memory then manipulates all that information into a meaningful sentence. Additionally, the working memory places that sentence in the larger context of a story.

Memory as a System Property

Nobel Laureate Gerald Edelman offers "the principle of memory" (199). Highly complex, the brevity of its presentation in this chapter belies that complexity, yet no chapter on the brain would be complete without it.

Edelman, defining memory as "the ability to repeat a performance" (102), maintains that memory is a system property. He means that different memories happen in different systems of the body. For example, the memory in the DNA is different than neural memory. Identifying hereditary memory, which resides in the DNA, immune responses in the lymphocyte, reflex (neural) learning, true learning following recategorization in complex brains, and the various forms of consciousness, he contends that memory is an essential property of biologically adaptive systems, and as such involves an apparently open-ended set of connections between subjects (203–205). Further, Edelman believes these systems create a dynamic, continually changing memory, one that results in both categorization and recategorization. He states that, given its dynamic nature, "it is no surprise that different individuals have such different memories and that they use them in such different fashions" (104).

Because memory takes on the properties of whatever system or function it serves, and because each system is unique to each individual, Edelman believes memory underlies the mind and meaning. "By its nature, memory is procedural and involves continual motor activity and repeated rehearsal in different contexts. Because of the new associations arising in these contexts, because of changing inputs and stimuli, and because different combinations of neuronal groups can give rise to a similar output, a given categorical response in memory may be achieved in several ways" (102). What Edelman's theory means to us is that we make meaning through and because of our existence and that our minds create what is real for us through our culture and language. It means that categorization and recategorization should take place within contexts. It means there is not one way to learn something. In the 1990s Edelman predicted, "If the future course of science is determined at all by its present reach, we may expect a remarkable synthesis in the next century" (208). Prophetic indeed.

Memory and Understanding

The complexity of the memory militates against taking valuable instructional time on rote memorization. Memory and understanding are not synonymous. Even information stored, however briefly, in the short-term memory should be tapped for relevant tasks. When we place skills in their rightful place, as parts of a greater whole, they take new importance for the learner. Other memories and associations reinforce the skills and then they make sense. But to ask students to memorize the rules of punctuation for isolated drills makes no sense, especially when students are relatively unsophisticated to the conventions of writing or the reasons for these conventions. However, when a student tries to understand a peer's paper without punctuation, but cannot, that student begins to integrate the reason for punctuation in writing. Fragmented learning does not "take" the way integrated learning does. Meaningful connections, not only with prior knowledge, but also with emotion, place them in the long-term memory. Emotion energizes those memories.

Because movement from the short-term into the long-term memory takes time, it is good to reteach concepts at intervals during the day, week, month, or even over several months. The notion of the semester review was a good one, not because it highlighted what would be on the test, but because such a review refreshes the memory.

Novelty and curiosity enhance memory. This gives rise to the implication of having an angle. Just as journalists strive for angles on stories in order to interest readers, teachers who get an angle on a lesson better interest their students. This interest contributes to high retention of the material. The notion of a focus or an anticipatory set for a lesson is one way to achieve this, but the focus must integrate and hold meaning for the students.

When teachers teach from a script—be it a basal or an ancient lesson plan—students respond in kind. There is no spontaneity, no sparkle, no verve, and no passion. Everyone is "doing time." In that situation, students remember little. In classes where the teacher goes over and over the material *ad nauseam*, there is little motivation. That takes review to the extreme. The teacher who introduces the myth of Icarus with Jane Yolen's *Wings* or the teacher who wears an African kente to introduce the narrative knows the power of novelty, challenge, spontaneity, and teaching in a context.

People remember best when they organize and relate new material in subjective ways. In a student-centered environment, the learner manipulates the information. As Wittrock says,

> The brain does not usually learn in the sense of accepting or recording information from teachers. The brain is not a passive consumer of information. Instead, it actively constructs its own interpretations of information and draws inference from it. The brain ignores some information and selectively attends to other information. One implication is that instruction should begin with careful observation of learners, their constructive processes and individual differences. . . . Instead of age, sex, and intelligence, the strategies of learners, such as analytic and holistic strategies, promise to lead more directly to theoretically interesting instructional procedures. (101)

NEURAL PLASTICITY

For us, one of the most significant research findings about the brain is its plasticity. The word *plasticity* refers to the brain's ability to be shaped or changed through external stimuli. Now considered classic research on rats, performed by psychologist Mark Rosenzweig from the University of California and neuroanatomist William Greenough from the University of Illinois and chronicled in Marian Diamond's *Enriching Heredity*, revealed anatomical differences between rats kept in impoverished, overcrowded, and deprived environments and those kept in enriched environments characterized by larger cages, more playmates, many and varied toys that were changed often and which aroused curiosity and invited exploration.

Rosenzweig's experiments showed changes in brain chemistry and increases in brain mass for rats exposed to enriched environments. Greenough's rats, challenged by new tasks and more stimuli, actually developed new dendritic branches, which, of course, help synaptic connections. "We now have evidence to illustrate the details of the anatomical changes that do occur with modification in the environment. This evidence addresses many of the questions that concerned the early sociologists and educators, including the effects of the environment on the young as well as the elderly, sex differences, and the effects of nutritional deprivation, isolation, or crowding. It is now clear that the brain is far from immutable" (Diamond 2). What makes these data so significant is that these changes appeared in both young and mature animals.

Implications for Teaching

While we certainly don't equate rats with human beings, researchers agree that the basic plasticity principle is "constant across such species as mice, gerbils, ground squirrels, dogs, cats, and primates (e.g., monkeys, Japanese macaques)" (Healy 72). If animals benefit from enriched environments, think how much more dismaying it is to hear, "These kids can't do it. They come from a poor environment." These naysayers have warped the research; they have blurred its import. The lesson for us is neither to lament environments over which we have no control nor abdicate our responsibility because students have poor backgrounds. Rather the point, indeed the challenge, is to provide enriched environments for all children. These data indicate even those students past puberty will benefit because the primary function of the brain is to make meaning. According to Healy and corroborated by recent research on teen brains, "the process of myelination in human brains is not completed at least until most of us are in our twenties and may continue even longer" (67). Called "a work in progress" Brownlee, in her 1999 cover story for *U.S. News & World Report,* says, "the brain inside a teenager's skull is in some ways closer to a child's brain than to an adult's." As Healy states, "Any activity which engages a student's interest and imagination, which sparks the desire to seek out an answer, or ponder a question, or create a response, can be good potential brain food" (73).

Donald Hebb, one of the leading scientists in the study of the brain mechanisms of learning, contends "Every human being is creative all the time, thinking of new ways to make bread, new ways to serve breakfast, new ways to plant the garden. Creativity is not something that occurs only in the brain of outstanding individuals. It is a normal aspect of human brain function" (Restak 1984, 228–229). Learners should be encouraged to explore, to extend, to dig deep, to solve problems, to become question posers, to create.

Clearly, students should never sit idly waiting for the next worksheet; rather we should actively engage them in learning all the time. Because enrichment quite literally feeds the brain, learners must exercise their normal brain functions all the time. Simply put, the brain needs food and exercise.

Also, there are tremendous differences in the rate of brain development of children. Like Robert Kraus's protagonist Leo in *Leo the Late Bloomer*, some children blossom later than others. That is one of the mysteries of the brain. "There can be as much as a five-year difference in the early years. One consequence is that assessing children by reference to chronological age is often worse than useless. Each brain appears to have its own pace, which render the 'failing' of a child in the first year of school entirely inappropriate" (Caine and Caine 30).

While plasticity aids learning by constantly transforming the neural networks based on experience and stimuli, it also involves the neural circuits that underlie certain forms of classical conditioning. This aspect of plasticity explains why students given a steady diet of worksheets, want them, like them, and resist assignments that demand thinking or that challenge them. Plasticity explains why giving little children "story paper" leads to thinking of a paragraph as a piece of discourse in middle school and anorexic papers in high school. Plasticity is what enables us to drive to school each day without really thinking—we say we're on "automatic pilot." Plasticity is a good thing, but it can lead to poor habits yet it is also instrumental in setting up relevant circuits that lead to mastery.

Potentiality

The potentialities in any one human brain are so great and so unique and so little realized, we have a challenge before us. Edelman says, "Consider that a large match head's worth of your brain contains about a billion connections. Notice that I only mentioned counting connections. If we consider how connections might be variously combined, the number would be hyperastronomical—on the order of ten followed by millions of zeros. (There are about ten followed by eight zeros' worth of positively charged particles in the whole known universe!)" (17). That is quite a challenge.

In discussing the cerebrum, Edelman also raises questions about such things as "silent synapses" (those synapses that show no detectable firing system), the uniqueness of brain maps (how individual maps vary according to the available input they receive), the ability to categorize or recognize any number of novel objects after initially confronting only one or several similar objects. He builds upon Henry James's theory that the mind is a process as well as upon modern scientific theory that considers matter as processes. He contends that mind is a special kind of process that depends upon special arrangements of matter (6–28). He is speaking of the biology of the mind, the same biology we work with daily in our classrooms.

Often those of us who work with gifted and talented learners, AP, or advanced students define giftedness in terms of the brain. Barbara Clark, Professor in the Division of Special Education at California State University, Los Angeles, where she is coordinator for graduate programs in the area of Gifted Education, says, "A high level of intelligence is viewed as advanced and accelerated brain function" (20). We now understand that not only may the number of neurons be increased, but also the quality of those neurons may be increased. "People with extraordinary abilities, it's turning out, have learned to use their brains differently from the average person" (Restak 2003, 14). For example, Clark contends enriched environments influence glial cells because they accelerate synaptic activity. Increasing the speed of synaptic activity affects the process of learning. She maintains that changes in teaching methods and learning procedures enhance dendritic branching and neural interconnections—that there can be an actual change at the cellular level in children. "In this way gifted children become biologically different from average learners, not at birth, but as a result of using and developing the wondrous, complex structure with which they were born. At birth nearly everyone is programmed to be phenomenal" (25).

That everyone is programmed to be phenomenal is the basic thesis and philosophy of this book. Teaching writing with verve, knowledge, and as a process advances that philosophy. Giving children mindless worksheets and repetitive boring drills does nothing to champion the phenomenal in students; it deadens it. Brain researcher after brain researcher maintains to make the most of the brain is to give the brain rich experiences in an interesting and meaningful context.

"A child is born with a natural insatiable curiosity to explore and find out more about the world. . . . Yet too often in trying to help children we hinder them. We don't give them [children] problems to solve so much as answers to remember, and if this intense curiosity is not exploited, it may be wasted forever" (Russell 10).

If children literally accelerate on the cellular level through enriched environments, personal attention, interaction, diversity of experiences—if study after study in the United States, England, and Europe confirm this, then doesn't every child in every classroom deserve an education to help develop every brain to its full capacity? Knowing these data, how can we justify teaching children any other way?

STRESS

We need some degree of emotional galvanizing for memory formation and retention, but if the emotion arousal is too strong or too stressful, our memory can be impaired. In other words, stress adversely affects explicit memory by altering the functioning of the hippocampus (Sapolsky 1996; McEwen and Sapolsky 1995; Sapolsky 1998). "Thus, during highly stressful conditions, the concentration of steroid hormone (cortisol) released from the adrenal cortex rises in the bloodstream" (Le Doux 2002, 223).

When we place this information in the classroom, say a testing situation, we realize the source of our tense muscles and increased blood pressure. When we think of any stressful situation—the death of a loved one, the pressure of travel, a family problem—we realize it was immune depressant cortisol causing that headache, that cold, or that sinus infection. Eric Jensen captures the frightening side of this research:

- chronically high cortisol levels lead to the death of brain cells in the hippocampus (and remember the hippocampus deals with memory);

- chronic stress impairs a student's ability to sort out what's important and what's not;

- thinking and memory are affected under stress;

- the brain's short-term memory and ability to form long-term memories are inhibited;

- students are more susceptible to illness;

- more test stress means more sickness, which means poor health and missed classes, which contribute to lower test scores;

- stressed neurons had fewer and shorter dendrites (fewer possible connections);

- constricts breathing and changes how a student focuses;

- eyes become more attentive to peripheral areas, making it nearly impossible to track print;

- serotonin released during stress has been linked to violent and aggressive behaviors. (1998, 53–54)

With facts such as those in hand, pressure to write should elicit challenge not fear or threat. With plenty of modeling, sharing, and taking writing through the process, eustress (*eu* comes from the Greek meaning "good") not distress (*dis* comes from the Latin meaning "bad") helps students approach writing as an adventure, an opportunity to extend oneself, not as a demanded, prescribed undertaking that must be completed for someone else—or else. Teasing out meaning from the mind onto a page is difficult enough even under the most inspiring circumstances; therefore, assigning writing under duress does little to foster a love of writing, writing fluency, craft, improvement, or growth. Rather, because of downshifting, creating a stressful writing environment may simply cause writing debilitation.

The distribution of learning not only within the long-range process itself, but also during daily lessons is another perspective of stress and writing. Short interludes of writing sandwiched between the bigger burst process enables some writing to occur daily in a natural, nonthreatening, and brain/body compatible way. Micro-mini and mini-teaches focus students while guided group practice then individual application ensures challenge not coercion. Ample warm-up time helps relax the brain and renders it more receptive. Daily writing can be short, fun, and varied. All writing does not need to be perfect nor does all writing need to go through the entire process.

THE NEW BRAIN: SOME OBSERVATIONS

Almost two decades after the PBS series and book *The Brain,* Richard Restak wrote *The New Brain: How the Modern Age Is Rewiring Your Mind.* Its subtitle helps us get closer to understanding what Le Doux meant when he said we are in a new world working with an old brain.

Take risk as an example. Our old brain was wired so that our amygdala responded to dangers instinctively and instantaneously, seconds before our thinking brain kicked in with a rational response. That served us well when hunting mastodons or avoiding poisonous snakes—quick reactions saved lives. But in today's world, buffalo aren't charging at us as we leave for work. More likely we will see terrorism in action on TV as we cancel plane tickets or hear the news of an *E. coli* outbreak as we throw away the spinach in the fridge. That twenty-first century amygdala jumps into action, so we have child abuse, road rage, and shootings in schools.

Jane Healy suggests in *Endangered Minds* that children's brains may be changing (15). We know experience shapes the brain, so we asked ourselves what neuro-shenanigans were happening inside the brain of the five-year-old we watched in a restaurant. With his hand-held PlayStation®, he sat totally absorbed the entire hour his parents ate. He even tipped over a glass of water without looking up. Common sense tells us his brain is developing differently than that of a child playing mud pies in the back yard.

Let's look at attention deficit disorder as another example. Is it really the paradigmatic disorder of our era or is ADD/ADHD a cognitive style as Richard Restak suggests? "In order to be successful in today's workplace you have to incorporate some elements of ADD/ADHD" (2003, 48). Even as we accelerate our multitasking, which is not as efficient as we think it is, we seem to have less and less time. Our sense of place collapses because of technology—our world is indeed flat. And we agree with Restak, all this is not a criticism of technology but a realization that technology is antic, causing a revolution in our brain's functioning (2003, 54). And it's like kids "get that."

Consider this: Neuroscientists have discovered "mirror neurons" in the brains of monkeys that fire when they see another monkey performing a movement. Evidence suggests humans have certain nerve cells activated when doing an activity and when *observing someone else doing that activity*. While these data support modeling, they also support what Restak calls *emotional contagion*—that is we "catch" emotions from the people around us. When we're around angry people, we get angry. When we're around pessimists, we become depressed and so on. Or memeticists will tell us we have caught an idea—like an idea-virus—or a meme (pronounced *meem*). These patterns of information take on a form that others repeat. Typical memes are slogans, ideas, catchphrases, melodies, icons, inventions, and fashions. Ever hear a song in the morning—"The Wheels on the Bus" and hum it or hear it in your head all day? That's a meme.

CONCLUSION

The data available on the brain are staggering. Most of what has been presented in this chapter is either basic brain information or views that form a consensus among brain researchers. Having said that, it is equally important to note that considerable disagreement remains in many areas, for example, the connection between mind and brain, the brain and the process of aging, exceptional children and the brain, and even controversies about consciousness. These uncertainties, rather than negatives in this area, inspire continued study into this most complex and most mysterious organ in the universe.

Implications for teaching are varied and many. Perhaps, though, none have stated them as elegantly as has Merlin C. Wittrock, Professor of Educational Psychology at the University of California.

In sum, the teacher, more than the subject matter, is given new importance and original challenging functions to perform with students. The basic implication for teaching is that teachers need to understand and to facilitate the constructive processes of the learner.

The learner is also given a new, more important active role and responsibility in learning from instruction and teaching. To learn, one should attend to the information and concepts, and construct, elaborate, and extend cognitive representations of them. The teacher can facilitate these processes, but the learner is the only one who can perform them. (101–102)

Every scientist and researcher we have studied uses superlatives in describing the brain—"the most astonishing," "the last frontier," "the greatest," "the most magnificent," yet they use provisional diction when discussing its functions. For example, the following sentence: *The brain is amazing, but the physical and chemical differences between brains may be unique.* Just when researchers think they have a handle on understanding the brain, technology leads them to new information that them leads to new questions. Because we also find the brains of other creatures intriguing, for decades, the brains of monkeys and cats have been used for study. Researchers intimate that since whales and dolphins have larger brains with more folds and perhaps more specializations, they may have superior intelligences. Peter Russell recounts experiments from John Lilly's *The Mind of the Dolphin* that demonstrate that dolphins speak in stereo and hold two or three conversations at once. In one experiment, dolphins put their noses out of the water to make humanlike sounds as if they were trying to communicate with the experimenters. This was before the experimenters had any idea about the language of dolphins. Then dolphins were found teaching other dolphins to count to ten in English more effectively than the experimenters could teach them. They also live in love and harmony—not competitively. "When John Lilly, one of the pioneers in dolphin research, realized that he was probably dealing with very advanced beings, he closed down his laboratories, feeling that his research could not be ethically justified" (21).

All aspects of brain research represent a frontier. We still have so much more to learn. Truly "the organ by which we know, we know the least about."

APPLICATION

Since brain research doubles at least every five weeks, it is important to stay abreast of recent findings. Working in small teams, groups, with a partner, or individually, research recent publications or the Internet for information on the brain. Analyze the information in tandem with the information in this chapter. Does it support, validate, extend, reject, refute, corroborate, or elaborate on what is here? Be specific and be prepared to share.

10

LEARNING HOW TO LEARN

True learning involves figuring out how to use what you already know in order to go beyond what you already think.

—Jerome Bruner □

COGNITIVE DEVELOPMENTAL THEORY

We cannot overemphasize the importance of cognitive developmental theory. For we, as teachers of writing, believe that by closely observing students we can understand their cognitive structures. Since cognitive developmentalists generally chart learning through actively developing mental structures or stages that build upon each other, then it follows that if we watch what students do before, during, and after they write, in addition to studying their writing, we better comprehend the composing processes and capabilities of students.

Cognition, defined here as the process of knowing inextricably tied to learning, is most often realized through the observable actions and language students use to construct meaning as they interact with the world. Writing is such an observable action. Writing captures language and renders it perceptible. Therefore, writing, as Emig reminds us, is both a mode and manifestation of cognition. It is a way to learn and a way to learn how to learn. Further, it places that learning in the amber of permanency.

Jean Piaget, Lev Semenovich Vygotsky, Benjamin S. Bloom, and Jerome S. Bruner are four major cognitive developmentalists who have worked on the diverse processes of cognition and language and the interactive or hierarchical structure of those processes. Their theories are particularly relevant to the teaching of writing since studying them causes us to recast traditional methods. Teachers trained in the product paradigm often base instruction on the assumption that students of the same age learn the same way, through lecture, worksheets, textbooks that keep all students on the same page, or other instruction that fix lessons regardless of the needs of the learner. These teachers control all learning and perceive students' talk or too much activity as disruptive behaviors.

Interestingly and perhaps unknowingly, these educators base their teaching on the one hand on the work of psychologists such as Karl Stumpf who compared children to botanical developments or Wolfgang Kohler who compared the responses of chimpanzees to the responses of children. The Buhlers extended this emphasis on the chimpanzee-like features of children. On the other hand, some educators follow researchers such as Shapiro and Gerke who suggest children pile up imitations in a mechanical repetitive process.

In contrast, teachers who understand process look to the cognitive developmentalists to support an active environment, one that exposes students to print-rich, language-rich experiences, where they interact in meaningful ways with that environment. The cognitive developmental research supports manipulation, not just for younger children, but also for anyone, at any age, coming to a new concept. While they contend that novelty piques interest in learning, they also hold that connecting new concepts to the familiar is an important way to guarantee learning. They individualize their teaching.

As Wink and Putney put it,

> Often we have found, when working with educators, that the mystery of the various "isms, ologies, and ists" is so profound that some will discredit them as too esoteric to be meaningful, falling back on what is perceived and a more pragmatic approach, "just tell me how to do it." However, in the long run *methods* will not sustain teaching in the always-changing social cultural context. However *theory* will provide a discourse to understand, articulate, and adapt practice to meet the needs of students, even as the world changes. (8)

When we study and apply cognitive developmental research to the teaching of writing, we ground ourselves in a theoretical foundation that functions in concert with the developing abilities of students. Ultimately, teaching to these abilities fosters intelligent strategies and confidence in self and in writing.

Jean Piaget

Jean Piaget, Swiss biologist, philosopher, psychologist, and genetic epistemologist, has so influenced cognitive developmental theory that Howard Gardner credits him as "the single dominant thinker in his field" (1991, 28). It seems little wonder that someone who, by the age of eleven, had categorized all the mollusks in the natural history museum of Neuchatel, would go on to taxonomize thought. His early work with Lev and Pie in 1923, first recorded responses to a trilogy of questions: How does the child think? How does the child speak? What are the characteristics of the child's judgment and the child's reasoning? (1969, 11) Since those initial questions, Piaget has written copiously on the nature, structure, and functions of intelligence.

Piaget's Invariant Operations of Intellectual Development

Piaget contends that there are two invariant operations of mental development—organization and adaptation. These operations provide ways for getting something from the world into the mind so it can be used later. *Organization* allows an organism to integrate structures into coherent systems—it systematizes. *Adaptation* permits an organism to adjust to its environment—it fits. Adaptation occurs because of the complementary processes of assimilation and accommodation. *Assimilation* incorporates new experiences into the cognitive structure or framework. *Accommodation* modifies and enriches those new experiences. When assimilation and accommodation balance, there is equilibrium. When they are not balanced there is disequilibrium, manifested in discomfort or inner conflict.

Factors Affecting Intellectual Development

Positing four factors that influence cognitive development during any stage, Piaget believes these factors repeat in a spiral to construct knowledge:

- *maturation* refers to physical structures;

- *experience* indicates contact with objects;

- *social transmission* describes interactions with others;

- *equilibration* coordinates the other three, none of which is sufficient by itself for mental growth.

Piaget's Stages of Intellectual Development and Implications for Teaching Writing

Piaget's concept stages or periods of intellectual development: sensorimotor, preoperational, concrete operational, and formal operational are classic divisions in cognitive theory. Full explanations of each of these stages may be found in Piaget's work (representative works are referenced at the end of this book), and in any number of secondary sources. By briefly reviewing the stages in terms of their connections to thought and language, we draw implications to teaching writing.

The Sensorimotor Stage (0–2). *Sensorimotor* is a term used to describe motor activities or movements caused by sensory stimuli. During this stage, children explore their world. As they handle, manipulate, and watch, they repeat actions and patterns, recognize, imitate and even invent simple solutions. Rudimental symbolic play begins.

This period lays the foundation for thinking and eventually for writing. Two brief examples: A child observes that kicking makes things move. This observation later evolves into a sense of cause and effect. A child follows a moving object from right to left. This ability to follow something, at first with the eyes, eventually leads to the ability to sequence.

With information on the brain, especially babies' brains, increasing our knowledge, this stage takes on a new significance for teaching writing. The brain's plasticity and the powerful effect that enriched environments play in developing the density of its dendritic branches and ultimately on the neural transmissions themselves, suggest that what happens during this early developmental stage causes lasting differences for individual learners.

Consider the delight young children express upon hearing pattern books read aloud again and again. Couple that image with the delight they show when making their marks on empty pages. The ability to hear and enjoy patterns finds its roots in the sensorimotor stage. Also, the ability to make marks grows out of imitation. Even so simple a deed as giving very young children clay to manipulate establishes a message—things can be moved, changed, transformed. These concepts endure, reemerging through the acts of moving words, sentences, paragraphs, or when taking compositional risks.

Television provides us with a telling example of this. An advertisement shows a baby on the floor next to a box of facial tissues. One by one the baby takes a tissue from the box. Surprised when there are no more tissues, the baby turns the box upside down. Obviously, in plucking the tissues from the box, the baby is imitating, but in turning the box upside down, the baby shows the foundation for future problem solving, hypothesizing, experimenting, and inquiry.

Even rudimentary symbolic play such as carrying a doll or hugging a pet shows us the young child's way of acting out the world through concrete role-playing representations. Thumping the table or clapping naturally imitates a rattle or a gesture. Playing peek-a-boo initiates the ability to mentally create an image of someone or something—the powerful genesis of abstract thought.

In time, these sensorimotor beginnings become part of more elaborated symbolic play: "I'll be the mommy and you be the daddy." By school age these elemental plays surface as stories with characters, voice, tone, action, trouble, and a sense of language's rhythm. They show up first in the telling about scribbles; they grow into drawings; finally they become written stories, poems, plays.

And this stage resurfaces throughout life. We often see middle school students scribbling, high school students drawing all over dust jackets, or adults doodling.

> *May was closing in. With only a few more classes remaining before the pomp and circumstance of college graduation, seniors suffered from "senioritis." They had their lives planned. Most had job offers, although some were still looking. Many were accepted to graduate schools. A few intended to travel or visit relatives. Several were about to marry. Christi was in that group, and she could think of nothing else. Class after class she needed to be nudged away from repeatedly writing her about-to-be-new name on page after page of yellow-lined paper. She never tired of writing or reading it.*

Even at the sensorimotor level, Piaget contends children actively adapt and organize experiences. As the child grows, these actions, repeated and expanded, become sophisticated.

The Preoperational Stage (2–7). Children learn that something is like something else in certain ways during this stage of representational, prelogical thought. Because they are not miniature adults, children perceive their world through developing cognitive structures, which in turn give rise to colorful, fresh language. They process external realities in concrete ways and express themselves that way. One three-year-old told her mother, "I am the pattern and Becky [the babysitter] is the material." They think what transductively, a child-like reasoning that "moves from particular to particular" (Piaget 1969, 233).

They easily use similes, "That dog is like a car with legs." They easily create metaphors. Vardaman, in Faulkner's *As I Lay Dying*, says simply, "My mother is a fish" (79). He metaphorically connects the dead fish his sister Dewey Dell fixes for supper to his mother's dying. This transductive thinking eventually blossoms into deduction, thinking that moves logically from the general to the particular, and induction, thinking that moves logically from the particular to the general. This logical thought, however, does not begin to make its appearance until about the age of eleven or twelve (1976, 181), so we call this delightful thinking of children prelogical, and we don't discourage it.

During the latter part of this stage, more formal operations begin. To Piaget, these mental actions have their roots in the physical actions of the sensorimotor stage. Because external actions are still becoming internalized, children in this stage base their classifications on the attributes they see.

> *Two little boys were at the pool. As they splashed in the water, one of the boys spotted teen-age girls. "Look," he said pointing to the girl in the one-piece bathing suit, "she's adopted."*
> *"How do you know?" asked his friend.*
> *"She doesn't have a belly button."*

Although children make awesome leaps in cognition during this stage, Piaget identifies cognitive limits: irreversibility (sometimes called the concept of reversibility), centration, and egocentrism.

- *Irreversibility* is the young child's inability to think of an object the way it was before it changed. Children are also unable to reverse (undo) a physical action. Teachers who interrupt primary students as they read their writing, experience firsthand Piaget's theory of irreversibility. When students recommence the reading, they always begin again at the beginning. If they add something to their writing, they don't read just what they added, rather they start all over again. Children in this stage find it difficult, perhaps impossible to conceptualize that they have already shared part of the story. Since they cannot go back over their action, they begin again—irreversibility in action. It also works that way with writing. Once young writers begin a story, they write until the story is told. The concept of revision holds no meaning for them. Revision, unless it is concrete and immediate, is not a cognitively appropriate activity based on Piaget's theory of irreversibility.

- *Centration* refers to the inability of children to think simultaneously about changes that take place in two dimensions or in subgroups. In other words, they understand one set of changes but not a second set of changes. Piaget gives us an example: the classification of flowers. Children easily classified flowers into two groups—primulas and other flowers. But when children subdivided the primulas into yellow and others, they had difficulty understanding that yellow primulas were a smaller part of *all* primulas and that primulas were an even smaller part of *all* flowers (Ginsburg and Opper 125–126).

  Piaget's theory of centration gives comfort to teachers who become exasperated when students forget capital letters or terminal punctuation marks. Students involved simultaneously with writing, capitalizing, and punctuating are trying to hold more than one thing in their minds at the same time. We tell little ones, "Do one thing at a time." When they struggle to write, they are not able to think of other things. At this preoperational stage, we advise teachers to let them get the meaning down. If students, on occasion, remember other things, we tell teachers to consider that a sign of cognitive growth. Later, when students can mentally juggle more variables, they will consistently remember other things—as we do when we write. Interestingly, prewriting at any level frees the mind of this hierarchical juggling and the simultaneity of meaning and mechanics, which is why we find our prewriting filled with "errors."

- *Egocentrism* is the child's inability to see another's point of view. Most everyone knows Piaget's theory of egocentric thought. Observing young children makes egocentrism plain enough. For example, students sharing in the Author's Chair listen to peer comments such as, "I like the way you described the dinosaur," but it is unlikely those comments make any impact until students move beyond the egocentric stage. That is not to say this practice should be discontinued; it promotes listening skills, collaboration, and helps their growth toward sociocentric behavior, but it is important to realize that at this stage, children hear feedback egocentrically—they are the center of their own universe and the world spins around them.

Perhaps the most telling example of egocentrism in young children comes from Lucy Calkins. "The youngsters [two first-graders] pulled chairs close together, then each girl took hold of her story and, in unison, they read their stories to each other. Neither child listened and neither child was listened to, but both girls seemed pleased with their conference" (1986, 61).

Children are stuck in their own perception, which affects their thinking. To put this stage in perspective, think of a kindergartner, first-, or second-grade child. While some may disagree with specific Piagetian theories, this is not one of them. Teachers and parents constantly confirm the remarkable things children say at this age. The poet Sandra McPherson would tell her three-year-old daughter every time she said something extraordinary, "Let's write down what you just said.

You spoke a poem." Children are able to speak so creatively, and adults react with delight because at this stage all words do not mean to children what they mean to adults; the child's mental structures are qualitatively different.

Besides, words carry different meanings and images when the brain and cognition are young. That is why children laugh uproariously at the literal antics of Amelia Bedelia or at books that engage in language play, such as *The King Who Rained* or *Cloudy with a Chance of Meatballs*.

The point is clear—students learn what they see. Using abstractions or expecting students to understand something in the abstract is futile. Children do not understand because they cannot; they are not yet ready.

Children revel in novelty during this preoperational stage. Everything is new! Just as infants observe and then touch, children during this time continue to explore, discover, and glimpse the wealth of possibilities around them. Creating joyfully literate classrooms permits children to have fun with language and learning language. We should stock the room with many books, materials, pictures, and objects of various textures, configurations, shapes, and size. Encouraging children's natural use of figurative language sows seeds for the later study of figurative language that enriches literature and deepens writing.

> *Recently while sharing a book about pumpkins to urban second-graders, we read the phrase "envelopes of seeds." We looked into a sea of blank faces. Of course, how would these city kids know about those envelopes people buy full of seeds? As Piaget suggests, the words didn't mean the same to them as they mean to us. They probably envisioned bunches of seeds shaped like envelopes. It seems we underestimate learners on the one hand and forget where they are developmentally on the other. Next time we shared that book, we took envelopes of seeds to show the kids.*

These three cognitive limitations do not preclude learning, but being aware of them informs teachers' understandings. Writing for meaning, teaching skills, sowing seeds for revision, developing the fundamentals for multiple levels of simultaneous thinking, beginning response groups, and working in collaboration remain important activities on this preoperational level.

The Concrete Operational Stage (7–11). We come now to the basis of logical thought and its importance. Without this stage of concrete logical thought, students would not have the schemata in place to conceptualize the abstract. Without sufficient concrete experiences, students are stunted in later development. Piaget insists children must pass through one stage before entering the next, maintaining that each stage is both a culmination of the preceding one and a preparation for the one to follow. Teachers and parents gain nothing by pushing children too early into a stage for which they are not ready.

Piaget repeatedly emphasizes the need for plenty of concrete activities for children in this stage, believing they must act and interact to develop understanding. While restricted to the concrete, during this stage they are developing new mental capabilities such as mentally reversing an action, holding more variables in their minds as they think through a problem, and reconciling contradictions. They are becoming less egocentric. We want teachers to realize that at this stage responses are the result of generalized, observable attributes not manifestations of the ability to abstract. It is not unusual, for example, for students to call any *-ing* word a gerund by noting the attribute of *-ing*. That the word may be a participle confuses them because they cannot abstract the difference; they do not understand the concept of functionality. All of which seems to militate against teaching any concept out of a context and before the leaner is able cognitively to learn it.

At this stage children are generally unable to think purely in the abstract, yet according to at least one researcher, "a great number of texts written for middle schoolers are inappropriately abstract" (Cheatham 15). They are intellectually fettered to actual objects, real events, and genuine people. Obviously, the first implication for writing is that students write what they know—not fill in worksheets. Students should write daily about their world. They should be given real reasons to write such as for pen pals, in learning logs, as the basis for interactions with each other and the teacher. They should practice writing in different genres. They should see writing everywhere. It should become intrinsic to the classroom environment—on walls, from ceilings, in folders, on tables—everywhere. The classroom should literally drip with writing. Reading and books should also pervade the environment.

Building on Piaget's concrete operational stage, we should provide plenty of opportunity for peer response groups and teacher conferences. This helps students as they move from egocentrism. Modeling by the teacher helps students handle analytic aspects of writing and begin transitioning to more formal thought. For example, if teachers demonstrate how they combine sentences in their writing, students in this stage have a concrete model to follow. Of course, we recommend modeling throughout the writing process.

We believe and research supports teaching all English language arts skills concretely and within the writing process. Logical reasoning strategies connected to writing and life experiences, and made between writing and reading, help students advance from transduction into deductive and inductive reasoning—so important in organizing writing as well as in other disciplines such as science and mathematics. Students see reasons for writing and reading when both are integrated with other disciplines in the curriculum.

Thinking concretely, every effort should be made to use tables not desks since students need space to spread out in order to literally see all their writing. There should be flexibility yet structure in the classroom. There should be places designated for specific activities such as private reading areas where writing can happen undisturbed, conference areas, writing areas—no matter how young, kids love small places because they intensify sensory stimuli and allow for more social interaction. Most importantly, students should have blocks of time, large blocks of time, to engage in writing and reading.

The writing folder and writing portfolio become essential at this stage. Students (as well as teachers, parents, administrators, and other interested persons) are able to access and assess the work done, work in progress, and trace achievement.

The Formal Operational Stage (11–15). The main difference between this stage and the preceding ones is that students can think beyond present tasks and form theories. They are able to deal with proportions, probabilities, correlations, permutations, and aggregations. They can hold several abstract factors in their minds while considering others.

While Piaget suggests that at this point in their cognitive development, students are capable of abstract thinking, several studies suggest that this is not the case. Conrad F. Toepfer contends that overchallenging youngsters to meet unrealistic expectations for higher level thinking during the twelve to fourteen age plateau may cause almost irreversible problems. He calls for a reexamination of the assumptions held by middle-school and high-school teachers that a majority of learners can function at abstract thinking levels.

Toepfer cites studies by Herman Epstein, a prominent biophysicist, which raise serious questions about formal operational thinking in middle and high school. Toepfer attributes this jump too soon into abstraction as the cause of what he calls the "turned-off syndrome" (4). Students who are experiencing low achievement may be victims of too great an emphasis upon formal operations before they are ready. While the percents vary, albeit not appreciably, Epstein's work has been corroborated by other studies (Shayer and Arlin; Sayre and Ball; Martorano). These data are summarized here and suggest a reexamination of curricula. In brief, Epstein's research shows:

1. Nationally, no more than 1 percent of ten-year-olds, 5 percent of eleven-year-olds, and 12 percent of twelve-year-olds can even initiate formal operations.

2. Statistics on students who have initiated or can perform mature formal operations show that only 20 percent of thirteen-year-olds and 24 percent of fourteen-year-olds can learn with some degree of formality. Clearly, 80 percent of the thirteen-year-olds and 76 percent of fourteen-year-olds still cannot think and learn at the formal operational level.

3. Between the ages of fourteen and eighteen, the increase in percentage of learners having the capacity for formal operational thinking rises to the point where 15 percent of eighteen-year-olds display initiated formal operations capabilities and 19 percent have mature formal operation skills. Thus, only 34 percent can do some kind of formal operations processing, even at age eighteen.

4. It is estimated that 38–40 percent of American adults can think at the formal operations level. That means about 60 percent cannot.

5. Most disturbing is that in the final period of great brain growth at fourteen to sixteen years, learners did not, for the most part, reverse any prior poor achievement. (Toepfer 3–5)

In his early research Piaget thought formal operations began in early adolescence. Later writings, however, reflect a rethinking. Piaget thought later that his sample in Switzerland perhaps showed earlier development than other populations.

The overarching implication of Piaget's theories on the teaching of writing is that writing should be taught as a recursive process, with skills, collaboration, and modeling an integral part of that process.

Lev Semenovich Vygotsky

Lev Semenovich Vygotsky, the innovative Russian cognitive developmentalist whose investigations and research in the fields of developmental psychology and education were described as "quantitatively meager but brilliant" (Bruner 1971, 8), died an untimely death of tuberculosis at the age of thirty-eight. Briefly, Vygotsky's theories defend the mind as integral to the culture, society, and human contributions that interact as processes during its development. Ahead of his time, he insisted that psychological functions are brain based, and he advocated combining experimental cognitive psychology with neurology and physiology. In short, he believed in the biology of the mind. Gerald M. Edelman, a Nobel laureate, echoes Vygotsky. "Cognitive science is an interdisciplinary effort drawing on psychology, computer science and artificial intelligence, aspects of neurobiology and linguistics, and philosophy" (13).

While the theories of Vygotsky and Piaget generally correspond, Vygotsky differed from Piaget on four counts.

Piaget	*Vygotsky*

Egocentric speech

| 1. eventually subsides. | 1. evolves into inner speech, a "thinking for oneself," shorthand thinking. |

Human development

2. "centers upon the capacity to achieve sophisticated knowledge about numbers—or Number" (Gardner 1991, 29).

2. is an integral part and guiding function in forming a concept.

Thought and language

3. thought stimulates language.

3. language influences thought. "A word is a microcosm of human consciousness" (1962, 153).

Intelligence

4. moves from inside out.

4. moves from outside in.

Vygotsky's Stages of Intellectual Development and Implications for Teaching Writing

Vygotsky continually focuses on the process involved in the formation of a concept, holding that word and thought relate in a continual ebb and flow. The process of concept development that follows is both an abridgment and a synthesis of Chapter 5, "An Experimental Study of Concept Formation," from Vygotsky's *Thought and Language*. We have added the implications for writing and the teaching of writing. (One additional point: Vygotsky cautions that concept formation in the experimental setting differs from the process in real life where the phases mix.) We want to stress here that Vygotsky maintains that any one of any age coming to a new concept goes through these stages in some way. Vygotsky's stages of intellectual development form the foundation for the writing process.

Unorganized Heaps

Heaping is the first step toward concept formation. The child haphazardly piles objects. While seemingly serendipitous, this phase subsumes three distinct stages: (1) *trial and error*: the child heaps objects at random and adds other objects arbitrarily; (2) *line of vision*: the child heaps objects together that are seen together, that is in the same spatial area; (3) *rearrangement*: the child newly combines objects only to create different unorganized heaps. In the rearranging, it is not that the child sees bonds or connections, rather the rearrangement happens because of some chance impression that causes the child to simply put something in a different place. Vygotsky uses Blonski's term to describe this trait—"incoherent coherence" (1962, 60).

In the writing process, unorganized heaps parallel prewriting. In this messy creative stage, students plumb their minds to find or to focus ideas. Huge heaps of thought splay across papers, lists superimpose other lists, doodles and drawings hug the pages, fragments pile upon other fragments in an effort to hold ephemeral thought so it doesn't slip away. Writers are unconcerned about conventions—ideas rule.

Blueprinting, for example, yields an imprecise drawing of a place with labels that may or may not mean anything to anyone else—students label some rooms by function, others by association. Some rooms contain furniture or things; some hold the names or initials of people. Writing may be scrawled or abbreviated. The blueprint heaps memories—unsorted, stacked on the page—a virtual stockpile of images and glimmerings from the past—a treasure trove to draw from when writing.

Thinking in Complexes

During this phase, the child begins to make subjective connections among objects and to see real bonds among objects, so the child begins to discern differences. In the writing process, this is the beginning of organization, albeit still lacking the qualities of unity and conciseness. By noting the five basic complexes, we are able to more knowledgeably intervene and help the students in their struggle for a coherent, focused, unified writing.

Association Complexes. Association complexes are based on similarities or perceptually compelling ties among things. Associations are anything the child notices as the same among the sample objects. The child may add one object to the given sample—a yellow triangle—because it is the same color but another because of size. But some associations are made by made by contrast or even proximity—a green triangle, for example, or a red square that happens to be close at hand. Still the child is grouping in some way, not just heaping.

In writing, association complexes parallel the rudiments of organization. Students begin reading their prewriting with new eyes. They examine it for patterns of ideas—things that have popped up here and there but seem to belong together. Here we see arrows or circles connecting something to something else or colors used as codes of connectivity all over the pages. But because the process is recursive, and because students are still thinking in complexes, they make some connections on the basis of differences or because something juxtaposed with something else and read anew creates a eureka!

At this stage, students take their blueprinting, for example, to look at what ties the rooms together. Do they notice a particular person or a pet cropping up in several rooms? Why do they keep mentioning a birthday? Suddenly, though, reading about that birthday party reminds them of another birthday party they didn't write down. They add it. As they add that, they remember not being invited to a classmate's party. They vicariously experience the disappointment. They jot that down as well. The writing is still random and unfocused.

Collection Complexes. Collection complexes are associations by contrast rather than similarity. The grouping is determined by function. A child groups objects on the basis on one trait that differs yet complements others. A child may pick out an object that differs from the sample—a yellow triangle—in color (a yellow square), form (something triangular), size (a big blue triangle), or some other characteristic (something with points). A child could create a group of objects—for example, triangles, each of a different color, because each *is* a different color. Vygotsky says this happens because children learn some collections are assembled because of their function such as cup/saucer/spoon (each different but a logical group) or even the clothing they wear such as cap/gloves/shoes/socks.

When students write authentically through the process, they inevitably come to the point where they start adding depth to their original idea. As one idea triggers another, their thought deepens.

Again, using the example of writing out of the blueprint, students reread their ideas—playing hopscotch on the front sidewalk—and write not just a how-to rendition of the game, but they begin suffusing details about how the neighborhood bully messed up the game or what happened when a friend fell while hopping and broke her wrist. They do the same with other ideas. While students make progress and continue to add details to all their ideas, they have not settled yet on one.

Chain Complexes. Chain complexes are dynamic, consecutive links with meaning carried from one link to the next. For example, a child could pick out a few triangles because the sample is a yellow triangle, but become distracted by a blue block and begin selecting blue blocks of any shape. Then, the child, diverted by a round block, could switch again and begin choosing anything round. The complex may no longer be connected to the sample, but each object is connected by a single trait to the previous object. Vygotsky considers the chain complex the purest form of thinking at this point in the child's (or anyone's) formation of a concept because the concrete grouping is connected between single elements, nothing more.

Because "the chain formation strikingly demonstrates the perceptually concrete, factual nature of complex thinking" (Vygotsky 1962, 64), this stage holds particular significance in the writing process.

Just as a child working with triangles and blocks includes an object not because a single trait is abstracted and given a special role (as in a concept), but because the child sees all traits as functionally equal, students see everything they have written for blueprinting as homogeneous. They regard what they wrote about Dad's heart attack in his study comparable to Mom dropping all the dishes at Thanksgiving. This inability to establish hierarchical organization is important to recognize in writing because it leads to incoherency. Because all ideas are equal to students, they fail to make the connections on paper they make mentally. They stop at this stage, thinking they have produced their final product. Untrained teachers stop too.

Diffuse Complexes. Diffuse complexes are indefinite limitless ways of connecting things. Basically learners add objects to a group because something reminds them of something else. Keeping in mind that the sample is a yellow triangle, a child who picks out trapezoids as well as triangles because the trapezoids remind him or her of triangles with the tops cut off has formed a diffuse complex. Fluid, this complex repeatedly shows up in the nonpractical and nonperceptual, unverifiable thinking of children. When children give that "off the wall" response or comment, they are engaged in diffuse complex thinking. One example comes to mind: A group of kindergartners had just heard Kelley Smith Barger read *The Important Book.* When she finished, she pointed to the dust jacket where it said, "Words by Margaret Wise Brown." She asked the children what that meant. Satisfied that they understood the word *author,* she moved on, "Do you remember any other books written by that author?" Many children offered *Goodnight Moon;* someone remembered *The Runaway Bunny,* but one little tyke, obviously engaged in diffuse thinking on the complex level, shouted out, "The lady who drives the school bus is named Margaret." While not practical (not the answer to the teacher's question), not perceptual (neither the school bus nor the driver was in sight), and unverifiable (the teacher did not know the name of the driver or even which school bus the boy referenced), his response proved a personal connection to the name *Margaret.*

While surprising transitions and startling connections give writing texture, tone, and style, students at this stage do not control these extensions when organizing. If a student begins writing about a birthday party and mentions his friend Bo, which reminds him of the time they fought in the school yard, which sets off a memory of going to the principal's office, which triggers some sentences describing the principal—then this diffuse complex thinking will yield a rambling piece of unfocused discourse.

At this stage we show students how to hone in on one facet of their writing. We encourage crossing out, rearranging, reformulating. Students drop sentences that don't belong; they expunge whole paragraphs. "This has nothing to do with my dog," they'll say. "Why did I add this about my brother?" they'll ask. Thinking in diffuse complexes is not a bad thing—it is part of the process—but students must learn to recognize that thinking and work to refine it.

Pseudo-Concepts. Pseudo-concepts are just that—*pretend* concepts. Resembling genuine concepts, pseudo-concepts are essentially complexes on the way to becoming concepts, and as such form the bridge between complexes and concepts. It is essential to remember what distinguishes pseudo-concepts from genuine concepts are not visible properties but the thinking process behind them—pseudo-concepts remain rooted in concrete attributes; genuine concepts rise into the abstract.

Fig. 10.1. Pseudo-Concept Bridge.

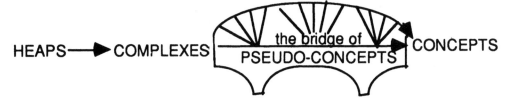

Learners produce a pseudo-concept every time they surround a sample with objects that could just as well have been assembled on the basis of an abstract concept. For instance, given the sample of a yellow triangle, the child picks out all the triangles in the experimental material. Herein lies the problem, he or she could have been guided by the abstract notion or concept of a triangle, but Vygotsky's experimental analysis shows that it is the concrete, visible likeness that guides the child. In this case, the child has not formed a genuine concept but only an associative complex limited to shape. Although the results are identical—all the triangles are identified—the process by which they are reached is not at all the same as in conceptual thinking (1962, 66).

Understanding how pseudo-concepts closely resemble genuine concepts supports teachers who use the pedagogical strategies of asking students how they arrive at an answer, probing students to explain why they think what they contend, and requiring them to supply textual evidence or data to buttress their thinking.

What makes an unawareness of pseudo-conceptual thinking dangerous in the classroom is that while pseudo-concepts carry the seed of the concept, they often fool both student and teacher. Take an example from grammar. Teacher and students worked hard on adverbs. Students filled in the blanks on worksheets, completed that section in the workbook accompanying the grammar book, and were ready for the final test.

The test, an approximation of the isolated drill from the worksheets and workbook, asked students to identify the adverb in each unrelated sentence. Later, the teacher showed us the results.

Most students missed the demonstrative adjectives; none identified *almost*; and, although all caught the adverbs ending in *-wise*, *-ly*, the concrete ending clearly signaled a pseudo-concept because the students identified *butterfly* as an adverb but missed *very*. The students who received passing grades on the test believed they understood adverbs although they were guided only by the attribute (*-wise* or *-ly*). Perhaps more disturbingly, the teacher who administered the passing grades believed the students understood adverbs. Both demonstrated pseudo-concepts—the teacher for thinking they had formed a genuine concept of adverbs and the students for thinking they had mastered adverbs.

The pseudo-conceptual stage in writing, the drafting stage, can be equally deceiving. A student, who has done the prewriting and organized the ideas, arranging them in some semblance of order, proclaims, "I'm done"—thus exhibiting pseudo-concept number one.

The paper may appear complete with multiple paragraphs, a title, neat writing or formatting, but process is far from over. That is the concrete part of the process—writing the idea and structuring it. Now, students must assume the role of reader, look at their papers more abstractly, and reenter them to make them better in a multiplicity of ways. To be truly finished, they must correct, revise, reformulate; they must proofread.

To summarize, complexes established connections. Complex thinking takes scattered impressions and organizes them. This forms the basis for developing concepts and thinking more abstractly. Vygotsky considers complex thinking a stage in the development of verbal thinking. We have applied heaps and complexes to the writing process.

Genuine Concepts

When the level of advanced genuine abstract conceptual thinking has been reached, the learner not only organizes but is able to abstract and single out elements and view those elements apart from the original concrete experience (analyze), sometimes in a new way (synthesis). Because thinking in complexes precedes synthesizing and analyzing, analysis and synthesis must be combined for genuine concept formation.

In this stage, the child groups together *maximally similar* objects such as a group of objects that are small *and* round, or red *and* flat. These "best matches" show the child paying more attention to some traits than to others—prioritizing. These "matches" have attributes that the child abstracts from the nonmatches, which the child paid less attention to or those completely ignored. Vygotsky insists, "A concept emerges only when the abstracted traits are synthesized anew and the resulting abstract synthesis becomes the main instrument of thought." The operative word here is *anew*.

Thus, in writing, if students cannot take their prewriting, writing, and post writing and work it into a final, publishable paper, if they cannot verbalize their processes, cannot paraphrase what they have written (or read), cannot apply grammar to enhance their meaning, they do not understand those concepts. Recognizing something, for example, a sentence fragment, on a worksheet but using them consistently when writing or not being able to reenter their papers to find and correct fragments, indicates the student has only a pseudo-concept of fragments. The student may be able to define the word *fragment*, but cannot synthesize it in writing, cannot reconfigure the concept *anew*. That student has not formulated the concept *fragment* on a purely abstract plane. In other words, the student doesn't understand *fragments*.

Vygotsky's theory of concept development applies to any level where students undertake new information. It applies equally to young children first learning to read and to high school students tackling algebra. It applies to learning a grammatical concept or the way a motor works. And it is a process.

General Implications for Teaching Writing

Writing as a Process

The first and overarching implication is that Vygotsky's process of concept develop parallels the writing process. Rightly so, especially if we hold—as we do—writing is thinking on paper.

High Levels of Abstraction

Second, written language requires a high level of abstraction. Vygotsky says, "In learning to write, the child must disengage himself from the sensory aspect of speech and replace words by images of words. . . . Our studies show that it is the abstract quality of written language that is the main stumbling block" (1962, 98–99). The implication is clear: Surround students with concrete examples of writing; engage them in language play, provide print-rich environments, read, read, read; and, above all else, give them many opportunities to engage in the act of writing.

Writing for Someone Absent

Third, writing to or for someone *absent* is new to a child. "Our studies show that he has little motivation to learn writing when we begin to teach it. He feels no need for it and has only a vague idea of its usefulness" (1962, 99). Therefore, having an audience—the principal, a caregiver, a friend, a classmate, the teacher—makes writing real. After being read to and reading books, writing their own books becomes both a purpose and a motivation. And this does not just pertain to young children. Middle-school and high-school students disengage themselves from writing because they see no purpose or they lack motivation.

Writing Is Analytical

Fourth, writing is analytical. When speaking, words flow, perhaps from a need for information or to convey information. People speak. They may think about what they are going to say but they rarely ponder over exact syntax. They have questions that must be asked or they have demands for answers. Requests arise naturally from situations. Whereas writing requires deliberation, analyzing the phrase, choosing the precise word. The syntax of inner speech is opposite the syntax of written speech with oral speech in the middle. In that design, writing requires, "deliberate structuring of the web of meaning" (1962, 100).

The Importance of Grammar

Fifth, the study of grammar is important in mental development, but it should be taught within writing so that that the student becomes "aware of what he is doing and learns to use his skills consciously" (1962, 101). As Vygotsky says, "Writing must be 'relevant to life' . . . writing should be meaningful for children" (1978, 118).

Vygotsky's Theory of the Zone of Proximal Development (ZPD)

Vygotsky defines the zone of proximal development as "the distance between the actual developmental level as determined by independent problem solving and the level of potential development as determined through problem solving under adult guidance or in collaboration with more capable peers" (1978, 86). Restated, it is the space between cognitive actuality and latency. Wink and Putney clarify the definition further: "After a student receives instructional support or tutelage from someone, who happens to be more capable in that particular context, the learner internalizes the new idea and will be more able to perform independently in the next similar problem-solving situation" (86).

The ZPD is most significant in the writing process. Not only does it support more capable learners assisting the less capable ones in any area of writing, but it also supports more broadly how teachers use social processes and cultural resources to help students.

To identify this zone of development, Vygotsky illuminated a niggling problem in teaching. So often we observe students who work well during and after peer consultations or teacher conferences, but seem incapable of working out a problem independently. We worry these students are not working hard enough, are becoming too dependent, or are getting off too easy. Because of these anxieties, we are tempted to derail the process by skipping any group work. But Vygotsky suggests that some functions used by students are not yet matured enough for independent work. He calls them the "buds" rather than the "fruits" of development. He offers the zone of proximal development as a tool to understand those functions that are still in the process of development.

The zone of proximal development clearly supports collaborative learning: group work, cohort groups, conferences, clusters, teams, peer tutoring, modeling with immediate application, guided practice, and collaborative activities. Using the zone of proximal development as an educational tool serves us well when teaching the writing process.

An example: Mary conferences with Miss A. During the conference, Mary lucidly describes a problem she cannot solve in her writing. Miss A. asks a series of questions, which Mary answers. This exchange helps Mary, so she leaves the conference area, returns to the writing area and sets about "getting her writing right." But this baffles Miss A. Mary is bright. She can identify problems in her paper, but she seems incapable of walking through those problems to solutions by herself. Miss A. comments, "Mary drives me crazy. She can't seem to make any decisions about her writing without checking with me first."

Explanation: Mary comes to the teacher at her actual developmental level. Her teacher works with Mary at her potential developmental level. What exists in between these two levels is Mary's zone of proximal development. When Mary hits another problem beyond her actual developmental level, the process will be repeated. Because of the changing nature of problems and levels of development, this process is dynamic; it changes with the function and the development of the student.

Fig. 10.2. Two Ways of Crossing the ZPD.

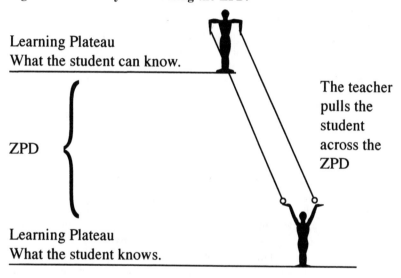

Learning Plateau
What the student can know.

ZPD

Learning Plateau
What the student knows.

The teacher pulls the student across the ZPD

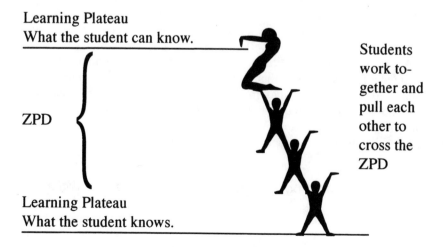

Learning Plateau
What the student can know.

ZPD

Learning Plateau
What the student knows.

Students work to-gether and pull each other to cross the ZPD

Vygotsky believes collaboration is key. His now famous line supports his belief, "What the child can do in cooperation today she can do alone tomorrow" (1962, 104; 1978, 87).

Benjamin S. Bloom

Benjamin S. Bloom, an American cognitive developmentalist, is perhaps best known for the *Taxonomy of Educational Objectives: The Classification of Educational Goals* published in 1956. Under his editorship, this taxonomy provided a new and different tool for curriculum analysis and course planning.

Earlier he, together with L. J. Border, studied the problem-solving processes of college students. They found the major difference between more able and less able problem solvers was the degree to which the students were active or passive in how they processed these problems. The students who spent extra time on a problem, developed steps for solving the problem, and looked for new ways to approach the problem did better than did those who gave up if the solution did not immediately present itself.

Coming from this perspective, Bloom differs from Piaget and Vygotsky. His taxonomy adds another dimension to cognition—the pedagogical dimension of student behavior coupled with goals. For example, by using Bloom's taxonomy, the intuitive teacher who formerly asked, "What should I teach today?" becomes teacher/researcher who systematically assesses how students respond in relation to the goals of the lesson. More specifically, a teacher intending to teach map making may have a hazy objective. With Bloom's taxonomy, that teacher begins by focusing on the knowledge level to determine what the students already know about cartography and then moves from there.

Bloom's Taxonomy of Educational Objectives: The Cognitive Domain

Bloom's Taxonomy of Educational Objectives is a hierarchical classification of the goals of an educational plan. It is arranged from the simple to the complex and implies both the behavior intended and the content or goal of that behavior. The taxonomy of cognition or thought, which in this case impacts written and oral language, deals with the development of intellectual abilities and skills. Further, it provides a way to advance students upwards from lower to higher levels of thinking.

Bloom's Taxonomy is adaptable to curriculum or lessons. For example, if one teacher states, "I want my students to really understand nouns," and another teacher says, "I want my students to internalize nouns," and a third teacher declares, "I want my students to comprehend nouns," are all three saying the same thing? More importantly, how specifically will their students demonstrate "understanding," "internalizing," and "comprehending"? Bloom's taxonomy attempts to give educators a set of standard classifications that facilitates defining such terms more precisely. Thus, if these teachers applied the taxonomy, they might rephrase their statements so that both the behavior and the goal would be explicit, "Students will be able to explain in their own words why they chose the common and proper nouns they used in the introduction of their 'How to Carve A Pumpkin' papers to illustrate their understanding of nouns."

The Six Classes of Bloom's Cognitive Taxonomy as Related to Writing

Just as biology taxonomizes plants and animals according to their natural relationships, so Bloom and his group of educators and research specialists structured levels of thinking in a way consistent with cognitive theories so that the structure would reveal relationships among the levels (17). According to Bloom's hierarchy, the objectives and behaviors in one class, such as *application,* build on the objectives and behaviors of the preceding classes of *knowledge* and *comprehension.* Bloom's taxonomy contains six classes: Knowledge, Comprehension, Application, Analysis, Synthesis, and Evaluation. Each of these classes may be applied in specific ways to writing as a process.

I. Knowledge. Knowledge involves the psychological processes of remembering. Sometimes this class is called "memory" or "the memory level." Students are expected to:

Expectation	Example
• **recall** specific information	• name the author of specific books
• **define** terminology	• "What is a noun?"
• **repeat** facts	• "Sentences begin with capital letters."
• **follow** processes	• fold an eight-page book
• **employ** conventions	• use the correct form in a documented essay
• **repeat** sequences	• employ sequence words: *first, second, then, next, last*
• **recognize** classifications	• move prewriting into a genre
• **follow** methods	• doing the pointing technique during a group activity
• **observe** rules	• not talking in the designated writing spaces
• **identify** structures	• state the elements in a story

When teaching to the knowledge level, teachers direct, tell, show, examine, read, and lecture. They expect students to memorize, recall, know the subject matter. Students demonstrate this knowledge by quoting, repeating, recording, reciting, defining, listing, naming, or stating specific bits of information. This level involves little more than retrieving information.

Students construct a timeline on cash register tape of the events in a narrative they have written. After recalling this information and setting it out visually, students move to higher levels of thought in predicting what they still need in their stories, analyzing if they have events in chronological order, and so forth.

II. Comprehension. Comprehension refers to that level of cognition where information is understood without consulting other material for further explanation or clarification. Students are expected to:

Expectation	Example
• **translate** information	• paraphrase for a peer what they heard in the writing
• **interpret**	• summarize a peer's writing in a word or sentence
• **extrapolate**	• predict what needs to be done next in their writing

When teaching for comprehension, teachers demonstrate, question, suggest comparisons or contrasts, and listen. They expect students to associate, compare, contrast, differentiate, discuss, estimate, and predict. Students demonstrate their comprehension by changing the form of the ideas without changing the meaning. Comprehension represents the lowest level of understanding.

Students illustrate their writing. Doing this enables them to interpret pictorially what their writing means while translating from one symbolic form to another.

III. Application. Application shows that whatever was learned in one situation can be used in another situation or in the same situation with new elements. Students are expected to:

Expectation   Example

• **apply**   • include metaphors in their writing

• **connect**   • find metaphors in the writing of others

• **relate**   • explain the metaphor in relation to the story

If students truly comprehended *metaphor*, they would be able to not only identify metaphor in a specific poem under study (knowledge level), tell what it means in their own words (comprehension level), but also find metaphor in other poems or write their own metaphors (application level). This transfer of learning means students have to not only know and comprehend what is being taught but be able to restructure it cognitively in order to use it elsewhere.

When teaching application, teachers show, facilitate, observe, critique, challenge and motivate, especially since one of the major reasons for lack of application is a lack of motivation. We expect students to relate, solve, apply, calculate, illustrate, use, and make connections. Students demonstrate their ability to apply when they use what they have learned. The effectiveness of any lesson depends upon students' ability to make applications.

Students write how-to books on some process learned in class. For example, the first-graders who made arachnids out of Oreo® cookies and then wrote how-to books applied the how-to process in a new situation—in a book.

IV. Analysis. Analysis involves breaking down information into constituent parts to better understand the relationship of these parts to the whole. For example, when the *Challenger* disaster occurred, everyone who watched it on television and in person saw the explosion. Later, viewing audiences saw replays of the explosion from different cameras. Still later, as experts wrestled with possible causes, audiences saw various close-ups and angles of the shuttle in its flight. Ultimately, the spurt from an O-ring, one tiny part, one almost infinitesimal part of the spacecraft, was analyzed. Experts pinpointed it as the cause of the tragedy. Thus, by analyzing the parts, they explained the entire experience. Students are expected to:

Expectation   Example

• **analyze** elements   • detect fact from opinion in a persuasive piece

• **separate** relationships   • distinguish a thesis (implicit or explicitly stated) from the information that supports that thesis

• **order** organizational   • classify the organizational structure in a piece of writing principles

When teaching for analysis, teachers probe, guide, observe, and act as a resource. They expect students to order, relate, separate, dichotomize, dissect, split up, sever, group, and classify. Students demonstrate their ability to analyze by being able to explain the various parts of what they are studying, by relating the different parts of a subject in relation to the whole, and by categorizing relationships according to facts, ideas, or other commonalties. Analysis is a more advanced level of thinking than that of comprehension and application.

Hexagonal writing invites analysis. This strategy invites students to look at a piece of literature from six perspectives. Particularly effective for literary analysis, it helps students see relationships in literature.

V. Synthesis. Synthesis calls for putting together constituent parts to form something new or to place something in a new situation. This involves working with pieces, parts, elements, sections, portions, segments, and so forth and rearranging and recombining them in a uniquely different way. This is the class of cognition that most clearly encourages creative behavior. When synthesizing, students:

Expectations	Examples
• **produce** something unique	• write a reflexive piece of writing, changing an remembered experience into a story or memoir
• **develop** a plan of work	• create a proposal for extensive piece of writing
• **design** something new	• create a language code

When teaching for synthesis, teachers reflect, extend, analyze, evaluate, and open up the process. They expect students to rearrange, recombine, construct, create, design, develop, formulate, integrate, produce, and propose. Students demonstrate their ability to synthesize by being creative, doing things in new and different ways, thinking innovatively, displaying ingenious plans, and producing original ideas. In one sense, all writing is synthesis.

Divide students into four groups. Each group comes up with a "new" idea. One group writes a biography to demonstrate their idea. Another group creates an advertisement to sell their idea. The third group conveys their idea through music. The fourth group presents their idea through art.

VI. Evaluation. When we evaluate, we make quantitative and qualitative judgments on information, materials, and ideas. These judgments must be made against an appropriate criteria or standard. Jumping from merely being able to repeat or retell something—"Shakespeare's play *Romeo and Juliet* is about star-crossed lovers"—to a judgment—"That play's stupid"—is called a snap judgment. In true evaluation, the person judging ranges through all the cognitive levels— getting to know it, expressing it indifferent words, applying it to life, taking it apart, putting it together in new and different ways—before evaluating it. To do this, students:

Expectations	Examples
• **judge** by internal standards	• decide if the writing is apt, clear, and lively
• **judge** by external standards	• ascertain the worth of their writing by comparing it to a literary model

When teachers want students to evaluate, they accept and harmonize. They expect students to appraise, assess, critique, grade, judge, measure, rank, rate, recommend, and test. Students demonstrate their ability to evaluate by making a judgment and providing supports for that judgment. Evaluation not only concludes the taxonomy of cognitive behaviors but links it to the affective domain, where values, likes, and dislikes are identified.

Students who participate with the teacher in constructing the Carroll/Wilson Analytic Scale for Classroom Use use every level of cognitive thought. The process culminates when they prioritize what was taught and learned. In creating the analytic scale, students identify the concepts that were taught, express the concepts in their own words, discuss how the concepts were used in their writing, break the concepts into parts, put them together in a new way through the class brainstorming session, and then rank them in order of importance.

Bloom's Taxonomy and Implications for Teaching Writing

To prepare students for globalization in the twenty-first century is to prepare students to think. Using Bloom's taxonomy provides educators with a helpful tool to raise the level of thinking for all students on any grade level. It also offers a base for curriculum restructuring, especially in the area of writing. Rebuilding a curriculum not of generalizations such as "Students should learn to think clearly," but one with concrete writing situations and prompts based on Bloom's classifications helps that restructuring happen in specific ways. Also, basing written examination and test questions on Bloom's ensures a movement from the recitation of simple facts to the higher levels of creating and evaluating.

We need to put Bloom in action all the time—even within our own lessons.

> *After a lesson with eleventh-grade students on perception, a lesson where we introduced the Salem Witch Trials of 1692, we asked the students what they had learned. They responded with information about Cotton Mather, the New England Puritans, and the nineteen persons who were hanged. They remembered Giles Corey, no doubt because he alone had been pressed to death. They recounted details, made assumptions, and shared connections.*
>
> *Then we asked, "What could we have done to make this lesson better?" The question struck this loquacious group of adolescents dumb. They stared at us wide-eyed. Obviously they never shared in appraising a lesson. We concluded by talking about how appraising a lesson could extend their learning and help us.*

If writing is a mode of thinking and a mode of learning as Emig suggests, then using Bloom's taxonomy assumes even greater significance for the teacher of writing. On the one hand, it offers categories that foster writing on all developmental levels; on the other hand, it presents a classification system for analyzing that writing. When a student writes a poem as a response to a piece of literature, much the way William Carlos Williams did for the Icarus and Daedalus myth, knowing Bloom's taxonomy helps the teacher identify the response as synthesis. When a student's prewriting shows arrows and asterisks connecting names and thoughts for a reflexive piece, the teacher understands those arrows and asterisks represent rudimentary analysis. Informed teachers target students who write only plot summaries in one safe genre as students stuck in comprehension. They know these students need instruction and challenge to develop patterns for higher-level thinking.

If writing is indeed thinking on paper, students should write for a variety of purposes, in many modes, and for different audiences. Through writing, students develop logical skills, clarify thought, and engage in the act of doing. Blending Bloom's taxonomy with the teaching of writing encourages students to use writing as a place to ask questions or raise concerns. A steady diet of systematic teaching helps students acquire skill in asking and answering questions.

Carmen Agra Deedy's delightful children's book *Agatha's Feather Bed* best encapsulates the power of cognitive thought. Agatha always tells her customers, especially children:

Everything comes from something,
Nothing comes from nothing.
Just like paper comes from trees,
And glass comes from sand,
An answer comes from a question.
All you have to do is ask. (9)

Jerome Bruner

Jerome Bruner has been a major influence in developmental psychology for the past five decades. Considered the founder of cognitive psychology, he moved thinking from behavoristic to cognitive. He emphasized *mentalism*, believing people make sense of the world by going beyond the information given, by manipulating mental actions. He, like Piaget and Vygotsky, developed an empirical framework to demonstrate mental processes.

Generally, the interests of this American cognitive developmentalist have centered on learning and perception. His wartime experience led him deeply into the analysis of propaganda and public opinion, which led him further into exploration into the nature of processes underlying opinion formation, such as perception, thoughts, learning, and language. Ultimately he concentrated his research on the study of development in children and the nature of the educational process.

Bruner's book *Acts of Meaning*, in addition to tracing the cognitive revolution from its beginnings to the present, brilliantly investigates what he calls "folk psychology," the narrative, and the place of meaning making as a mediator between mind and culture.

Of utmost importance to students and teachers is Bruner's contention that in constructing and listening to stories (and myths), we are able to deal with experiences and create realities. He holds that plots with beginnings, middles, and endings provide us with frameworks that allow us a context for the information we constantly process. Thus, writing of stories promotes learning as a process of constructing our ideas based on current and past knowledge.

Three of Bruner's major contributions have special relevance for the purposes of this chapter and raise implications for the teaching of writing. These are his views on the process of education, the process of knowing, and the process of discovery.

The Process of Education

In broad terms, Jerome Bruner believes that education enriches life. Learning is not simply the amassing of skills for skills' sake; rather education develops skills that are both immediately useful and develop attitudes and principles applicable to situations throughout life. Having learned how to write stories as children, for example, adults are better equipped to transfer that learning into writing letters, memos, proposals; they are better able to sort out experiences and make connections. Further, if the experience of learning to write was pleasant, encouraging, and rewarding, then people are more likely to continue self-sponsored writing into their adult lives. This writing may emerge in journals, diaries, letters to the editor, articles, or it may reappear through reading as a love of the writing of others.

More specifically, Bruner contends "any subject can be taught effectively in some intellectually honest form to any child at any stage of development" (1963, 33), a contention that lies at the very heart of teaching writing as a process. Some students learn to write, become skilled at its craft, and enjoy the process of writing, but unfortunately, some do not learn to write, remain capable of only very rudimentary marks or incoherent phrases, and avoid it at all costs. We do not serve these latter students well for the future. By embracing writing as a process, we are enabled to meet in an "intellectually honest form" the needs of any child. To do that, teachers need to understand the intellectual development in children, the act of learning, the spiral curriculum.

Intellectual Development in Children

Bruner, like Piaget, maintains there are stages of intellectual development in children and at each stage the child views the world uniquely. During the first stage, which Bruner considers a mesh of sensorimotor and preoperational (basically pre-school), children are active. They principally manipulate their world. When they move to learning symbols, they use them in generalized ways with no separation between inner self, that is, feelings or motives, and outer reality.

During the second stage, children move into operations, which means that they understand by hands-on activities, and they represent things and relations in their minds. Things become internalized. We must remember that children in this stage are only able to give structure to what is immediately present. Bruner says, "This is not to say that children operating concretely are not able to anticipate things that are not present. Rather, it is that they do not command the operations for conjuring up systematically the full range of alternative possibilities that could exist at a given time" (1963, 37).

Intellectual operations characterize the third stage. "It is at this point that the child is able to give formal or axiomatic expression to the concrete ideas that before guided his problem solving but could not be described or formally understood" (1963, 37–38).

Bruner encourages us to challenge children at every level, while cautioning us that abstract explanations before the child is ready are futile. For Bruner, a deep understanding of the mind so that its power and sensibilities may be fully developed enhances the process of education.

The Act of Learning

For Bruner, learning is an act that subsumes within it three simultaneous processes: acquisition, transformation, and evaluation. Acquisition refers to new information that sometimes demands a refinement of what was previously known. Transformation is the wielding of knowledge to fit new situations—knowing and going beyond that knowing. Evaluation checks and balances those transformations.

Think of the act of learning, for the moment, as a lesson in any typical classroom. The teacher begins the lesson usually with some artifact, challenge, or connection to prior knowledge to arouse interest or to motivate. The teacher introduces the new information or concept for the students to acquire and models this new knowledge by using it in some way. Here Bruner is adamant,

The teacher is not only a communicator but a model. Somebody who does not see anything beautiful or powerful about mathematics is not likely to ignite others with a sense of the intrinsic excitement of the subject. A teacher who will not or cannot give play to his own intuitiveness is not likely to be effective in encouraging intuition in his students. To be so insecure that he dares not be caught in a mistake does not make a teacher a likely model of daring. If the teacher will not risk a shaky hypothesis, why should the student? (1963, 90)

Next, the students manipulate the information in some way, applying it to something they have done or discussing it in relation to what they know. All this time they are working to fit it into what they know. All this time they are in the act of learning. Finally, the lesson ends with some type of check on learning such as a debriefing.

Now think of the act of learning on the continuum of life. If people are open to learning, then life provides daily opportunities, occasions for learning, nanoseconds of learning and learning that takes years, learning that is transformed, and missed moments. But when we teach writing with the objective to instill the love of learning in students, to make them lifelong writers and readers, they have the *process* of education, the *act* of learning opened for them. They, in turn, develop neurons that predispose them to continual learning, evidenced by an openmindedness, "a willingness to construe knowledge and values from multiple perspectives without loss of commitment to one's own values. Open-mindedness is the keystone of what we call a democratic culture" (1990, 30).

The Spiral Curriculum

Bruner uses the phrase *the spiral curriculum* to return to his belief that any subject can be taught to any child in some honest form. He advises respecting the ways children think and teaching to those ways. If curricula are built upon the stages of development and address the issue of continuity, they will not deteriorate into shapeless masses but spiral upward to include all subjects and all students.

The Process of Knowing

Bruner maintains that the process of knowing occurs through three modes: enactive, iconic, and symbolic. These three modes are at once representations of reality and ways to represent experience.

Enactive Knowing. With enactive or motoric knowing, students learn by doing. Here the hand predominates because things get represented through the muscles. Enactive knowing describes certain actions appropriate for achieving certain results. It also describes actions that manifest the mastery of those results. For example, if a student recombines sentences until they "feel" right, that student knows the combination works through the manipulation of the words. Bruner calls this motor amplification.

Iconic Knowing. When students learn by depicting an image, they are using iconic or ikonic knowing. Here the eye predominates. Iconic knowing uses images, pictures, and graphics to represent objects and events, and it describes images created to demonstrate that knowing. For example, a student may describe an image of the ocean from memory. Being able to re-create the image proves iconic knowing. Bruner calls this sensory amplification.

Symbolic Knowing. Through symbolic or representational knowing, students learn by a restatement in words. Here the brain predominates. Symbolic knowing includes knowledge gained through symbolic systems, such as a number system or a language system that are transformed into meaning by the mind. Using a symbolic system in a logical way, such as putting letters together to form words and words to form sentences, proves symbolic systems exist. For example, taking a totally new or creative idea from the mind and transforming it onto paper is symbolic knowing. Bruner calls this intellectual or ratiocinative amplification.

In her essay "Tolstoy, Vygotsky, and the Making of Meaning," Ann E. Berthoff echoes Bruner: "As soon as the form-finding and form-creating powers of mind are engaged, purposes are given shape; intentions are realized; meanings are created" (46). We galvanize those powers when we engage students in writing. As Janet Emig says, "If we are sighted, we make use of all three modes at once since the writing hand (motoric) produces the piece (iconic) that is a verbal symbolization (representational)" (1978, 65). Emig applies this thought to the teaching of writing by suggesting that there should be greater emphasis upon writing as the making of an icon, such as self-made books. Ann Ruggles Gere maintains that writing as a focused activity using hand, eye, brain, coupled with its linearity of word following word, "leads to more coherent and sustained thought than thinking or speaking. The physical limitations imposed on writers make writing a slow process (slow relative to thinking or talking), and this slowness seems to free some parts of the brain for the discoveries so common among writers" (4).

The Process of Discovery

Discovery in the Newtonian sense is rare, argues Bruner. For most, discovery is "in its essence a matter of rearranging or transforming evidence in such a way that one is enabled to go beyond the evidence so reassembled to new insights" (1971, 82–83). To place discovery in a perspective, Bruner defines two types of teaching: expository and hypothetical. In the former, teachers present with students as a "bench-bound listeners" (1971, 83); in the latter, teacher and students cooperate in the learning process. Therein lies the possibility for discovery. Bruner identifies four benefits for learning by discovery: intellectual potency, intrinsic and extrinsic motives, heuristics of discovery, and conservation of memory.

Intellectual Potency

Bruner's studies led him to contend that students who expect to find something in their environment or in a task show an observable increase in cognitive activity, connect information in a more organized way, and persist longer at the task than do students who did not expect to find something. This translated into an emphasis on discovery, active learning, and high expectations for both teacher and students.

Intrinsic and Extrinsic Motives

Bruner posits that extrinsic rewards tend to limit even overachievers to conform to what is expected of them or to try to please in order to get the reward. He believes that learning *about* something is less effective for cognitive development than learning *as a process* of discovery. "The degree to which the desire for competence comes to control behavior, to that degree the role of reinforcement or 'outside rewards' wanes in shaping behavior" (1971, 92). In other words, the more students discover, the greater their ability to discover, and vice versa.

Heuristics of Discovery

Bruner encourages practice for discovery: practice at trying to figure things out and practice in the heuristics of inquiry. He states, "Of only one thing am I convinced: I have never seen anybody improve in the art and technique of inquiry by any means other than engaging in inquiry" (1971, 94). So, too, with writing—one learns to write by writing.

Conservation of Memory

Basically Bruner's research shows that if students construct their own cognitive processes, what he calls "mediators" for remembering information, rather than using none at all or one given to them by someone else, they make that information more accessible for retrieval. The point is students will discover a mediator that works for them based on interest and their cognitive structures. For example, if given pairs of words to remember, according to Bruner, students who are given no mediator for remembering them will do poorly. Those given a mediator, such as "think of the two words in a story" do better at remembering them. But the students who are given the notion of a mediator or a way to remember, but who are allowed to come up with their own mediator, remember up to 95 percent of them.

APPLICATION

Vygotsky designed twenty-two wooden blocks to use for his concept formation tests. There were five different colors, six different shapes, two heights (tall and flat), and two sizes (large and small). *Lag* was written on the back of the tall large blocks; *bik* on the flat large ones; *mur* on the tall small ones; and *cev* on the flat small ones, irrespective of color.

Make a set of these blocks (bath blocks work well). Then devise a test that could be given to a group in order to check their concept formation level. (A full explanation of Vygotsky's test may be found on pages 56–57 in *Thought and Language*.) Administer the test to a group to check their concept formation level and write your conclusions.

11

EARLY LITERACY

Learning to read and write is a process of experiencing language.
There is no end product. Fluency is not some state that is finally
attained; we are all continually arriving. Writing develops continually,
sometimes inconspicuously, sometimes in dramatic spurts.
Eventually, as the various conventions are mastered,
children develop a common fund of concepts, but the
point of entry and the path of progress are different for each child.
—Judith Newman □

DEVELOPMENTAL WRITING AND CONSTRUCTED SPELLING

Pre-Alphabet

The natural writing development of children mirrors in truncation the writing development of humankind.

Consider the cave paintings of Altamira, Font-de-Gaume, Combarelles, Les Eyzies, Montignac, and other prehistoric sites. Privileged to visit the area in France between Lascaux in the north and Les Eyzies in the south, we saw the famous cave paintings. Woolly rhinoceros, mammoths, hippopotami, cave bear, horses, aurochs, bison, and other Paleolithic and Mesolithic animals painted as static *thing-pictures* exist side-by-side with more dynamic *idea-pictures* of charging bulls, a fresco of five deer swimming and running through tall grass with heads up and necks outstretched, galloping horses, a stallion pierced by seven arrows, a cavalcade of mares, ponies, and ibex. Covering the walls was a gallery of large and small animals—along the base, the top, or wedged between other images, these animals run with multiple feet and legs as if in a Duchamp painting, while Chagall-like cows seem to indeed jump over the moon. We remember a mythical dappled unicorn with an almost human face loping easily alongside a darker horse. One stunning wall depicts a hunter and a bison juxtaposed in mortal combat. Spears and rope appear in the foreground along with a bird sitting on a pole or shaft. No doubt the painter expressed several ideas on this wall— fear, valor, courage, the thrill of the hunt, even the notion of life and death.

We had two favorites: the first, an upside down horse, perhaps driven off the cliff by hunters, the details of its vertiginous fall captured in a surrealistic suspension for perpetuity; the second, the outline of a human hand, small and childlike. Standing before it, we could almost hear the author whisper across the millennia, "I am."

We could see these cave walls as our ancestors must have seen them—as huge canvasses—or as children would have seen them—as enormous sheets of butcher paper—upon which to write.

The ancients probably experienced the cave walls much like a child regards a wall at home or unlined paper in preschool or kindergarten.

These are inviting spaces to be filled; here are places to capture things and ideas. And so children fill their spaces as our ancestors filled theirs with reality, myth, color, texture, feeling, and their own idiosyncratic symbols. What children tell us as they move from just explaining what they have pictured to telling about complex relationships, sequences, and captured chronologies, we call *story*.

The Evolution of the Alphabet

- Thing pictures

- Idea pictures

- Word-sound pictures

- Syllable-sound pictures

- Letter-sound symbols known as the true alphabet

In time the pre-alphabet of cave picture writing became cumbersome, so moving forward to the Assyrians, Babylonians, and Hittites, we find cuneiform characters replacing pictures and used to represent ideas. These wedge-shaped characters, modifications of early pictures or hieroglyphics, naturally and eventually morphed into sound-symbols, considered a true alphabet, somewhere around 1700 B.C. The twenty-two-letter North Semitic alphabet is considered the earliest (Crystal 258). These sound-symbols were simple in form, easy to write and understand.

We do know, for example, that the Phoenicians had some letters such as *aleph*, which was both a letter and the word *ox*. They probably adapted it from the Babylonian character that looked like the face and horns of an ox. Just as likely, however, the Phoenician *aleph* came from the Egyptian *apis*, meaning "sacred bull," evolved into the Phoenician *aleph*, became the Greek *alpha*, and eventually, via the Romans, turned into our letter *A*. Using our imaginations, we can picture the head of a bull with two horns sticking up and two ears sticking out. We if stretch the bull's face into a *v*-shape and turn it upside down, we have the letter *A*.

Moving through time to the Greeks and Romans, we realize the word *alphabet* is composed of the first two letters of the Greek alphabet, *alpha* and *beta*. From the standard Greek alphabet the Romans took *A*, *B*, *E*, *H*, *I*, *Z*, *K*, *M*, *N*, *O*, *T*, *X*, and *Y* with little change. The letter *B*, for example, was merely a rounded form of the Greek character. Remodeling and finishing other Greek letters, the Romans produced *C* (and *G*), *L*, *S*, *P*, *R*, *D*, and *V*, *F*, and *Q* were taken from two old characters abandoned by the Greeks, making twenty-three.

Meanwhile, *Z* comes at the end of our alphabet although it was number six for the Greeks. At first the Romans dropped *Z* entirely, then discovered they needed it. When it returned, it had to go to the end of the line where it has remained ever since.

The Romans did not use *J*, *U*, and *W*. *U* and *W* grew out of the letter *V* about a thousand years ago, while *J*, our youngest letter, expanded from the letter *I* about 500 years ago (Ogg 106).

Just a cursory glance at this brief history of the development of writing illuminates the parallels between the evolution of writing in humankind and in children. Coupled with the fact that *a*, *e*, *i*, *o*, *u* were consonant symbols in the Semitic alphabet, that we wrote at first in all capital letters, and that we didn't put spaces between words until sometime in the Middle Ages, we begin to understand just how precisely matched is the comparison.

WRITING AS A NATURAL ACT

All of which brings us to the question: What if writing were a natural act? What if children come to it as they come to language? What if teachers considered writing a "natural language with signifying systems as diverse as those of myth, dress, food, cinema, kinship, politeness, painting, poetry, and cartography" (Guzzetti 177) as does semiologist Christian Metz? What if students are biologically predisposed to write? What if writing were another way to interpret or infer? What if writing were a constant constructing and reconstructing of thought, not just the adding of letters to letters or words to words? What if writing was considered implosive, that is bursting inward on the learner; as well explosive, that is exploding outward to the reader? What if writing grows out of an ability to make sense of things? If teachers thought about these questions, would writing be taught differently?

Research on Early Writing

In the past, most educators held that speaking and listening were primary activities because, in most normal circumstances, they simply happened. Reading and writing were considered secondary activities because they required systematic teaching. Seeing a child at the beach making marks in the sand or watching a child scribble did not constitute an act of writing in these educators' minds. However, the research of nativist theorists such as Eric Lenneberg and David McNeill, cognitive theorists Jean Piaget, Lev Vygotsky, and Jerome Bruner, the burgeoning brain research, the work of Gerald. M. Edelman and Carla Shatz, and articles in *Time*, *Newsweek*, *National Geographic*, *Childhood Education*, coupled with the myriad books recently published on the topic, suggest there are innate structures in humankind that enable children to process linguistic information in uniquely human ways.

If writing is a code that stands for something else, then symbolic play, for example, may be as developmentally important to writing as babbling is to speech or crawling is to walking. After all, babbling is a way of making sound just as speech is a way of making sound. Crawling is movement just as walking is movement. Just so, symbolic play constructs meaning just as writing constructs meaning. The difference lies in sophistication of degree, of extent, and of developmental significance. Each is a natural part of an incredibly complicated growth and learning process. More broadly, writing may be thought of as the manifestation of a process of comprehension that places the reality of the writer within a culture. In and through this transformation called writing, the child engages in a process of comprehension. Even so, as developmental psychologist Margaret Donaldson, reminds, "'Understanding' is a very complex notion. . . . The 'correct' interpretation of a word on one occasion is no guarantee of full understanding on another" (72–73).

Further, years of research by scholars the caliber of Durkin, Clay, Lamme, Bissex, Dyson, and others who have studied the features of writing by young children, undergird statements drafted by organizations such as the National Council of Teachers of English, the Association for Childhood Education International, the International Reading Association, and the National Association for the Education of Young Children. Each has generated position papers or published articles that support the developmentally appropriate teaching of writing. They advocate experience-centered environments; they promote activities such as scribbling, drawing, and constructing spellings; they advise teachers to "encourage risk-taking in first attempts at reading and writing, and accept what appear to be errors as part of children's natural patterns of growth and development" (Early Childhood 6).

Therefore, the artificial teaching of writing with its concomitant teaching of isolated letters and isolated skills limits learning. While the more integrated, incremental, holistic approaches to writing free children to explore and build upon a living language. Those who believe children cannot write until they have mastered the alphabet, are superceded by research that regards writing as "a particular system of symbols and signs whose mastery heralds a critical turning-point in the entire cultural development of the child" (Vygotsky 1978, 106). This research promotes a print-rich environment, one filled with words, with labels on everything. Teachers expose students to books, stacking them on tables, piling them in baskets, and covering every available shelf with them. They frequently read to and talk often with their students. They encourage students to read and talk to each other. They write and invite their students to write. And they allow plenty of time for writing. They know students can read without writing, but they cannot write without reading—the two are inextricable. They create writing and reading centers; they confer; they group. They announce the importance of writing by displaying it everywhere. Even scribbles, drawings, and awkward letters made randomly on a page, proclaim from ceilings, bulletin boards, walls, and doors the excitement of writing, the excitement of making meaning. In short, the environment becomes an eloquent social context and a joyfully literate climate, both conducive to growth.

Two Experiences

A principal called. She expressed dismay at the state-mandated writing test results of her third-graders. So she observed her primary teachers and determined they were not teaching writing. She called us to provide in-service training for them.

The school, located in one of the nicest suburbs of the city, was new, sprawling, and beautiful. The classrooms, spacious double rooms, allowed plenty of room for any activity. Entering the first-grade classroom we noticed laminated, store-bought pictures, posters, and letters displayed. A huge paper tree, obviously made by the teacher, squatted in a corner. Its branches, bereft of anything made or written by a child, curled up to the ceiling. The room was showy but without substance. We spotted one storybook on the teacher's desk—none were apparent anywhere else in the room. Then we saw cubbies and cubbies filled with worksheets, all categorized—reading, mathematics, science, and phonics.

Visiting this school immediately after working in an urban school in a poor neighborhood made this an indelible experience. That school was old with stuffy, overcrowded classrooms. In that first-grade classroom, its one window, high on the wall, provided neither ventilation nor light. These first-graders sat in oversized chairs at oversized desks, obviously leftovers from a higher grade. They literally had to kneel on their chairs to write at their desks. But the atmosphere in that room was electric. The children were eager and responsive. They shared their writing and discussed it in groups. The teacher facilitated. Writing and books were everywhere. We did not see one worksheet. We remembered Slade, whose brain tumor made learning difficult, proudly reading, "Poochie died. I got a cat. Boots is my cat."

Fig. 11.1. Slade's Writing.

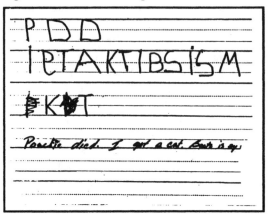

We asked him for a copy. Not to be outdone, Lindsy ran over with her writing.
Lindsy, who had been retained, wrote this note to another first-grader about the
need for proper bathroom manners. Not only humorous, it proves writing is a
survival skill.

"From Lindsy—When you go to the bathroom pretty please flush the toilet
and don't waste stuff in the bathroom. [pictures of bathroom] And please do not
potty on the side of the toilet."

Fig. 11.2. Lindsy's Writing.

Because of those memories, we asked the principal who was serving as host
at the suburban school, "Where are the children in this room?"

Misunderstanding, she nodded in the direction of fifteen well-dressed incredibly well-behaved students who were patiently sitting cross-legged on the floor.

"What we mean is, we don't see their work anywhere. The room seems sterile. There is no life" we whispered.

"That's why you're here," she whispered back.

The writing those fifteen privileged students produced that day made us heartsick. Before and after Bernard Most's *The Cow that Went Oink*, they interacted monosyllabically, with little verve, but politely. Then, when asked to write a story "about some animal you know," these children, who by all accounts should have been fluent confident writers, drew only a small box on their papers to surround an even smaller animal. A word or two accompanied the picture. Days later we discussed the terror in one child's eye as she asked us if she had spelled *kat* correctly.

Analyzing the children's writing, we realized they had reproduced worksheets—a word, a box, a drawing, a line from the box to the drawing. They modeled what they knew—worksheets. We knew why the scores were lacking in third grade—there was no writing happening in the primary grades.

The difference between these two experiences has little to do with buildings, rooms, space, or socioeconomic levels but a great deal to do with the knowledge base of the teachers. Decorating a room is decidedly different from co-creating one. When teachers and students come together in meaningful ways, the classroom becomes an extension of that meaning. The classroom becomes theirs together—not the teacher's alone. It reflects the making of meaning that has occurred there and serves to inspire the making of additional meaning.

Co-Created Classrooms

In co-created classrooms, students feel ownership. They feel comfortable. They are not disenfranchised from a context that can foster their development, nor are they simply marshaled through a series of rote activities. Just as children expand their oral language through the environs of their cultural context, so, too, they expand their written language according to the environs of their academic culture. The more that culture opens children's minds, the more it undergirds writing with sound theory and pedagogy, the more teachers understand the processes that advance the natural development of children in writing, the less it delimits that growth.

As Margaret Donaldson states, "A child's ability to learn language is indeed something at which we may wonder. But his language-learning skills are not isolated from the rest of his mental growth. . . . It now looks as though he first makes sense of situations (and perhaps especially those involving human intention) and then uses this kind of understanding to help him to make sense of what is said to him" (56).

ARENAS IN WRITING AND SPELLING DEVELOPMENT

To pull away from writing as a motor skill or mere copying and to move to writing as what Vygotsky calls "a system of signs" (1978, 106) involves knowledge of a complex of processes that are oxymora: they are chaotically structured yet complexly simple. This chapter traces these processes through seven arenas of recursive and overlapping writing and spelling development.

The Arenas of Writing Development

   I.   Rhythms

   II. Gestures

III.   Initial Visual Signs

     Random Scribbles

IV.   Symbolic Play

     Controlled Scribbles

     Named Scribbles

     Approximations and Prephonemic Spelling

     Alphabet Writing and Spelling

 V.   Symbolic Drawing

     Pictographs

     Ideographs

VI.   Transitional Writing and Spelling

     Consonant Writing and Phonemic Spelling

VII. Standard Writing and Spelling

Fig. 11.3. The Arenas of Writing.

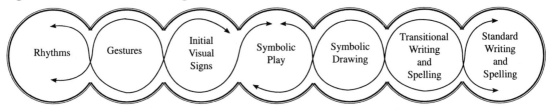

We have chosen the word *arena* to indicate a "sphere of activity." The word *stage* doesn't work because it suggests development that is linear or lock-step. The word *characteristic* doesn't work because while it denotes a distinguishing quality, it connotes that which is typical. Young children's writing is atypical since their language arenas are more closely tied to all their other learning. After years of observing and collecting children's writing, we find a child will produce an astonishing piece in one context but become almost mute in another. Kindergartners will write pages of discourse, for example, way beyond stages labeled as phonemic or letter-name spelling.

Crystal wrote: "The moon and the sun were chasing me and I felt dizzy like a tornado. Then I fell into a big, big hole. And it was soft in the hole. And I saw a shiny star on the pillow." (See Fig. 11.4.)

True, aspects of development may be typical and may be distinguished from other aspects, but the intent here is to use an inclusive, widely applicable word. Some students in middle school or even high school produce writing that looks like the writing of young children. They draw, doodle, or even use the recurring principle of repetition as they think into meaning. In other words, writing arenas overlap because the means of generating meaning overlap. (See Carroll's "Drawing into Meaning," appendix H for more on the dimensions of literacy across grade levels.)

Fig. 11.4. Crystal's Writing.

I. Rhythms

Invited to keynote at a local NAEYC conference on the topic of developmental writing, we asked to have the house lights dimmed after the introductions but before the talk. We switched on the large monitor hooked up to a VCR that held a sonogram tape. An image of a fetus dramatically appeared as if carved by some antediluvian hydrographical system in a subterranean cavern. Then it moved. Everyone saw the baby slowly, silently sway among the black and white shadows. The audience sat spellbound.

"This, ladies and gentlemen, is where writing begins."

Rhythm marks life. From the gentle swaying felt *in utero* to the diastolic expansion and systolic contraction of the heart, people are held by it. From the rising moon to the setting sun, people are reinforced by it. From sowing to spinning, people are connected by it. People work in rhythm, sing in rhythm, and pray in rhythm. Rhythm soothes and fascinates. It is the drum beat of lives, marking time. When a rhythm goes awry, people feel disconnected, fragmented, disturbed. Rhythm mesmerizes or tranquilizes; it deafens or bores; it excites or quiets, but whatever the reaction, rhythm is imprinted on the human consciousness.

Two physicians, Fernand Lamaze, author of *Painless Childbirth*, and Frederick LaBoyer, author of *Birth Without Violence* understand the significance of these imprints. Creating a metaphor that arises from the sea, LaBoyer calls birth "a tidal wave of sensation surpassing anything we can imagine" (15). To ensure positive imprints, they believe that massaging the baby throughout the birthing process continues the womb's rhythms. LaBoyer poetically explains, "the hands holding him should speak in the language of the womb" (60). They believe this action gentles the neonate's entry into the world and produces happier, untraumatized babies. As if to prove his point, LaBoyer includes pictures in his book of babies smiling not crying at birth.

Children, whether birthed by rhythm or not, begin life with some pattern of recurrence. As they mature, they continue like "dwellers by the sea [who] cannot fail to be impressed by the sight of its ceaseless ebb and flow, and are apt, on the principles of that rude philosophy of sympathy and resemblance . . . to trace a subtle relation, a secret harmony, between its tides and the life of man, of animals, and of plants" (Frazer 39). It seems likely, therefore, that those fundamental rhythms and those that run from the synaptic responses in the brain, down the arm, onto the paper, share an affinity.

Kornei Chukovsky, the most beloved author of children's books in Russia, tells how children cherish rhythm and use it to learn language. He says children think of words in pairs as if every word has a twin. Having learned one word, the child looks for another that is related—or makes one up, for example, *curly/stringly*. He claims, "Children who have just begun to talk in phrases make use of rhyme to ease the task of pronouncing two words in a row. It is easier for the very young child to say 'night-night' than 'good night,' 'bye-bye' than 'good-bye' " (63). That makes sense. Little wonder that Chukovsky calls children linguistic geniuses.

Is it such a stretch to speculate that writing and its flip side reading finds its roots in rhythm and rhyme? If children enjoy saying word twins, it is logical they would write them in their stories and poems.

Take, for example, how young children respond to Margaret Wise Brown's *Goodnight Moon*. Of course, they identify with bunny who prolongs bedtime by repeating "Goodnight" to everything in the "great green room." Of course, they expand their vocabulary through the delightful repetition. There is also the compelling rhythm created by Brown's rhyme. Children never tire of hearing it read and often chorus the lines. They take this classic and "read" it, even before preschool. Then they write it into their books. To speculate more specifically, perhaps that is what Maria Teresa Rivera did when she was a young child. Perhaps she fooled around with rhythm and rhyme; then, in fourth grade, she wrote a line that rings with alliterative rhythm, a line that contains a stunning comparison: "The moon is as black as a black apple burning" in *Wishes, Lies, and Dreams* by Kenneth Koch (94). Could this speculation, this hypothetical conjuring, lead us to poets such as Marge Piercy? What is her writing history? How did her writing metamorphose? As a child, did she imagine the moon's face? Did she mouth moon words? Might her poems "How the Full Moon Wakes You" and "The Hunger Moon" (148–149) have come from those rhythms?

Perhaps these suppositions are not too far afield. Eudora Welty tells of growing up to the whistling back and forth of her parents and the striking of clocks. She describes the dancing gyroscope and the box kite that tugged in her hands, and she remembers being read to, in a rocker, "which ticked in rhythm as we rocked, as though we had a cricket accompanying the story" (5). The point is: Language, its power and its force, is rooted in rhythm. Young children know that. So do professional authors.

While seeing friends who had recently become parents, we visited the nursery as they prepared Londi for bed. As luck would have it, she became restive and would not settle down no matter what they tried. Finally, Londi's dad picked up a stuffed lamb and began turning the key in its back. We expected a lullaby or some rendition of "Mary Had a Little Lamb." Instead we heard a soft rhythmic whooshing sound. To erase our perplexed looks, our friends explained, "This sound is like what Londi heard *in utero*. It always puts her to sleep." Almost immediately Londi drifted into a deep slumber. Our immediate comment was, "How great. We need one of those."

The coda to the story is that merchandisers have discovered the lulling rhythm of the womb, the heartbeat, and the sea. Now for a reasonable sum anyone may purchase devices that create this "white sound" to aid those with sleeping. Rhythm is that basic.

II. Gestures

Vygotsky maintains that gestures "contain the child's future writing as an acorn contains a future oak" (1978, 107). Gestures convey meaning. People recognize the meaning of a pointed finger, crossed arms, or a shaking head. They understand a nod, thumbs up, or a clenched fist. These gestures, almost archetypal, convey in signs a universal language. Transforming gestures into writing is a matter of changing modes.

Two researchers, William S. Condon and Louis W. Sander, from the Boston University School of Medicine carried out highly sophisticated research on sixteen neonates at Boston City Hospital and Boston Hospital for Women. Their purpose was to investigate the linguistic-kinetic interactive process between neonates and adults; that is, they studied the correspondence between adult speech and infant movement. Using a Bell & Howell modified 16 mm Time/Motion Analyzer, they conducted a microanalysis of the movement of every part of the babies' bodies, frame by frame or across frames. Their equipment also did a frame-by-frame analysis of speech. They could examine an arm motion "event" for x number of frames, for example, while simultaneously hearing and seeing any speech sounds through an oscilloscopic display.

Their study reveals "a complex interactional 'system' in which the organization of the neonate's motor behavior is seen to be entrained by and synchronized with the organized speech behavior of adults in his environment" (461). To rephrase, the neonates gestured to the rhythm of the adult speech they heard around them. This occurred as early as within the first twenty-four hours of life. Further, the correspondence occurred whether the adult speaking was actually present or was taped, whether the stimulus was American English or Chinese, or whether the neonates were supine or held. Interestingly, especially in terms of reading instruction, "Disconnected vowel sounds failed to show the degree of correspondence which was associated with natural rhythmic speech" (461).

This research on language acquisition has implications for the development of writing because the acquisition of language in one form illuminates the acquisition of language in another form—in this case, writing. The results of Condon and Sander's work suggests language acquisition is organismic, not atomistic. Learning language is a living integrated human event not something reduced to mastering tiny bits of information. A new generation of "'nativist' psychologists and cognitive scientists whose more sophisticated experiments led them to theorize that infants arrive already equipped with some knowledge of the physical world and even rudimentary programming for math and language" (Brunton 95). Consider: "If the infant, from the beginning, moves in precise, shared rhythm with the organization of the speech structure of his culture, then he participates developmentally through complex, sociobiological entrainment processes in millions of repetitions of linguistic forms long before he will later use them in speaking and communicating" (Condon and Sonders, 461–462). It seems logical, then, to continue that shared organization structure when teaching writing. Just as Lamaze and LaBoyer continue the rhythm of the womb during birth, the teacher of writing continues to build on this expressive bond. Evidently, the form and structure of the culture, its rhythm, syntax, paralinguistic nuances, and body-motion styles are absorbed long before children speak. This bond of gesture linked with speech reinforces the continuation of participatory interaction within shared constructs not "isolated entities sending discrete messages" (462). That translates into the need for active learning environments where listening, speaking, writing, reading, viewing are actively integrated with culture, not silent, mindless environments. Not only does this apply to students of one culture but to all students in all cultures, which includes those enrolled in ESL and bilingual classes.

To conclude, gestures, as an outgrowth of rhythm, command a rightful arena in the development of writing. As Vygotsky says, "Gestures are writing in air and written signs are simply gestures that have been fixed" (1978, 107).

III. Initial Visual Signs

Initial visual signs are extensions of gestures and extensions of self. Random graphics—lines and scribbles—are the child's first way of saying, "I am." For example, a line scribbled on a wall or a sidewalk is nothing more than the fixed extension of the index finger. Hold a pencil in the normal position as if to write to see how it extends the index finger. Vygotsky says young children at first do not draw or write in the conventional sense; rather, they indicate. They talk as they run their hands over the paper; they make what looks like random marks to indicate what they are saying.

One holiday a former student paid a visit with three children in tow. The baby slept the entire time; the six-year-old will most assuredly grow up to be an electrical engineer since he demonstrated fascination with every electrical outlet; but the three-year-old is destined to become a writer. Taking the inside of a dress box and some crayons, she spent the afternoon "indicating" the stories she talked.

**Fig. 11.5 A Preschooler's Indication
of Visit to Park.**

Unfortunately her scribbles up the sides of the box do not show, but she covered the entire area with random scribbles that represented her recent trip to the park.

Random Scribbles. At first, children are not even aware they are making marks, for example, those of two-year-old Katie. Children most often use their index fingers to mark in sand, smear circles on frosted windows, or to track paths in their food. It is not uncommon for a young child to take a crayon and run with it along a wall, look back at the mark, and giggle. Likewise, upon finding a tube of lipstick, a young child may hold it to a wall while hopping up and down. The results delight the child, although they may exasperate the caregiver. The randomness of the marks suggest that just seeing the marks appear is enough to satisfy the child.

Crockett Johnson's book *Harold and the Purple Crayon* captures this discovery. Harold holds a purple crayon after making scribbles all over the page. Then he decides to go for a walk. From that point on, Harold creates the reality he wants, the moon, a path, an apple tree and so on. The reader participates in Harold's discovery—knowing at some point that like the random scribbles of children, Harold's initial visual signs will give way to meaningful marks.

Fig. 11.6. Katie's Scribbles.

Instructional Strategies for Random Scribbles. If young children randomly mark the page, the idea is to give them some strategies for control:

- Encourage them to make more marks but in specific places.

- Ask them to repeat a random pattern by naming it. For example, "That's a wonderfully long line. Can you make it again?"

- Respond positively the child's writing, for example, "I like what you wrote."

Never say, "What's that?" "You can't write!" or "That's not writing."

IV. Symbolic Play

Symbolic play, sometimes called dramatic play, is a key arena in the development of writing and spelling. Vygotsky believes "that symbolic representation in play is essentially a particular form of speech at an earlier stage, one that leads directly to written language" (1978, 111). This is perhaps the most crucial arena for it is the time when many aspects of language meaningfully come together for children. Margaret Donaldson calls this time "the grasp of meaning" (32–33). When children begin to make sense out of things, out of what people do and say, and out of events, they often do so through symbolic play. Here children play games with objects that stand for reality. They put pieces of colored felt together to make a sandwich. They sit in tubs of colored dry rice and pretend they are swimming. Wearing a T-shirt with a tail transforms them into the wolf. Subsumed in this arena are controlled scribbles, named scribbles, approximations, and alphabet writing and spelling.

> *Once, while observing four-year-olds, we overheard the following conversation:*
> *"I'll be the Mommy. David, you will be the Daddy."*
> *At this point another little girl quipped, "But I want to be the Mommy."*
> *Without missing a beat the first child replied, "OK. I will be the first Mommy and you can be the second Mommy."*

Controlled Scribbles. Subsumed under symbolic play are controlled scribbles, marks that show some deliberation. For example, the page may be filled with lines or circles or a combination of both. As children develop, they gain more control over their motoric actions. Instead of making an apparently wild display of marks hodgepodge on a page, children begin to deliberately make shapes and lines. Bent over their work like nuclear scientists, brows furrowed in intense concentration, they make shapes endlessly or get caught up in a movement as three-year-old Bill did as he moved his crayon repeatedly up and down.

Fig. 11.7. Bill's Repetitive Marks.

Marie Clay calls this tendency "the recurring principle" (20). Later, in another arena, this principle continues as children repeat letters, drawings, even groups of words or sentences. When self-initiated, not teacher mandated, this act of repetition often helps students experience a sense of accomplishment.

Instructional Strategies for Controlled Scribbles. Children like the challenge of making the same mark in a different way or in a different place, a longer line or a bigger circle, or a line or circle on another sheet of paper. Guiding children by asking for an extension of a line or a duplication of a shape helps them refine motor skills and gain control over their writing. Asking them to move the mark helps them hold the image in their heads and reproduce from memory. We should also encourage children to experiment with many different colored markers and crayons. Always invite, "Tell me about what you have written." In this way, children learn that marks carry meaning.

Named Scribbles. When children move into this arena, they talk-write. There is intention and that intention emerges during the writing. Given a rabbit from a coloring book to color, three-year-old Kristen turned it over, dismissing the pre-made one and opting to make one of her own. She chose purple, green, and red markers. As she "wrote," she said aloud, "This is my bunny. Here are ears. He eats lotsa carrot. He can hop. Hop bunny."

Also at this stage, children begin to differentiate between manuscript and cursive writing.

Instructional Strategies for Named Scribbles. Since children are becoming aware of letters and words, label everything in the room so children see print everywhere. Create opportunities to display their names. Provide real reasons to write: books, letters, labels, marking attendance, and library cards. Since meaning still exists in the mind of the child, and since what they have "written" is not always decipherable, we recommend taking dictation. Invite, "Tell me all about your writing."

Fig. 11.8. Kristen's Written Bunny.

Approximations and Prephonemic Spelling. Sometimes the marks children make closely resemble letters, so we call them approximations. They appear all over the page without regard for the top, bottom, or if they are upside down. While at first they may occur by accident, because the marks children make look like letters or because they are reminiscent of hieroglyphs, later they become the child's deliberate attempts to form letters.

Interestingly, prephonemic spelling begins about this time. *Prephonemic* is the word used to describe letters written by children unconnected in their minds to sounds. Just as children indicate through awkward, clumsy scribbles they lack graphic discrimination, so, too, they indicate through the haphazard making of letters they lack phonemic sense.

Approximations refer to children's writing and prephonemic spelling refers their spelling. Because they are closely related, we sometimes use the terms interchangeably. To distinguish between the two, approximations happen as the child's scribbles; afterwards the child may recognize the letter—although not always. Other times approximations occur as the child attempts to form a letter or letters.

In prephonemic spelling, children often know they are making or attempting to make letters, but they do not know that there is a letter-sound correspondence. In other words, when children are prephonemic, letters, any letters, are significant. For example, Toya made letters that look like *G* or *C*, but she read, "This is a balloon."

Fig. 11.9. Toya's Approximation.

Therefore, Toya is approximating, but when children try to form letters important to them, once they see in their name or in writing displayed in their environment, their approximations become prephonemic as they are in Aaron's writing.

Apparently Aaron is still in prephonemic spelling as his letters obviously imitate a title. Therefore, for Aaron, they are meaning-bearing symbols, probably influenced by the titles he sees on television or in books, but they are not yet connected to sounds.

Fig. 11.10. Aaron's Prephonemic Writing.

The work of Toya and Aaron illustrate why it is so important for teachers of primary writing to encourage students to talk about their writing and listen closely to what they say. These indicators of growth are often subtle and can be easily overlooked, overinterpreted, or underinterpreted without the intervention of the child as writer.

Instructional Strategies for Approximations and Prephonemic Spelling. Modeling becomes paramount. Children should see not only labels around the room but also the teacher producing those labels. Teachers should habitually say aloud the thoughts that engender their own writing so children see and hear the connections between their thought and their writing. It is not simply a matter of reading aloud what was written (while that is good pedagogy), it is also speaking from the mind—sharing what prompted the writing. For example, by saying, "Yesterday I went shopping. Maybe I could write about that today. Let me write something so I don't forget—'I like to go shopping.' I'll go from there," students are exposed to many subtleties of prewriting. Continue to take dictation, but provide plenty of opportunity for children to share their writing.

Alphabet Writing and Spelling. Children form strings of letters almost as if once they start on a letter they are unable to stop. Often letters are made upside down and backwards, but generally they are still not associated with sounds. Children in this stage try to copy writing from adults or from print.

Instructional Strategies for Alphabet Writing and Spelling. Model writing and continue to talk and write. Persist at dictation since the child's writing still cannot be read. Provide many opportunities for children to write. Point out real examples of writing, cereal boxes, magazines, letters, and advertisements to help children discover letter and sound correspondences and to help them realize the importance of writing in the world.

V. Symbolic Drawing

The arena of symbolic drawing superimposes itself upon the arena of symbolic play to lend another dimension to developing literacy. As children move from making random marks on a page to making meaningful marks, they begin to understand those marks as objects (not yet understood as symbols or representations) that convey their meaning to others. An example: When five-and-a-half-year-old Cory drew a peacock feather, he named it and colored its front in bright blue and yellow hues. Then he turned the paper over, named it again and drew it again. This time he depicted the back of the feather as a plain brown oval.

Clearly Cory saw the similarity between his drawing and the feather in his mother's vase, but just as clearly he regarded his drawing as a similar object, not a representation—hence, the attention to detail on both sides. Vygotsky verifies how children relate to drawings as if they were objects with this observation from his research. "When a drawing shows a boy with his back to the observer, the child will turn the sheet over to try to see the face. Even among five-year-olds we always observed that, in response to the question, 'Where is his face and nose?' children would turn the drawing over, and only then would answer, 'It's not there, it's not drawn'" (1978, 113).

Eventually children discover "that one can draw not only things but also speech" (Vygotsky 1978, 115). For children, drawing becomes a natural way to make meaning. It is their rudimentary writing. Usually their drawings fall into two categories: pictographs and ideographs.

Pictographs. Pictographs are pictures, signs, or symbols that capture what children know, not what they see. When a child constructs a pictograph it is tantamount to a teacher teaching or a writer writing. Just as teachers cannot teach what they do not know, just as writers cannot write what they do not know, children cannot draw what they do not know.

Jenny, two years old, "wrote" a circle with two eyes and a smile. She made five lines radiating out of the circle. "Hey, Jenny, tell us about what you wrote there," we coaxed.

Jenny smiled broadly and responded, "That's my mommy."

"Wow!" we said. "Tell us about your mommy."

"Well, she smiles a lot and give me hugs. Those are her arms." (See Fig. 11.11.)

Fig. 11.11. Jenny's Writing.

Jenny wrote about the mother she knows—the loving, warm, happy woman. Jenny doesn't understand symbolism yet, but she certainly knows how to choose marks to show what she means.

During this pictograph stage, adults working with children must not commit "assumi-cide" as did the person in Chukovksy's *From Three to Five:*

> This child was drawing flowers; around them she drew several dots:
> "What are those? Flies?"
> "No! That's how the flower smells."

When we look with adult-centric eyes and make incorrect inferences, children must either worry about us or lose confidence in their own ability to share meaning. Best to nudge them into talking about their writing.

> *Maryssa's preschool teacher asked her to make a self-portrait on the cover of her schoolbook. This book contained a collection of memories, Maryssa's experiences, and work done during the year. "Maryssa's drawn herself on the cover," the enthusiastic teacher stated as she handed Maryssa's mother the book.*
>
> *All the mother saw was a crossed-out smile, made with a heavy brown mark. When the mom got home, she sat with Maryssa so they could look at her book together. "Tell me about your cover, mi hija."*
>
> *Maryssa began, "I used purple to draw me because that's my favorite color." Pointing, she said, "That's my hair, my eyes, my nose, my mouth, and those are my green earrings."*
>
> *The mother ventured, "Why did you cross out your smile?"*
>
> *Maryssa looked at her mom puzzled and stated matter-of-factly, "I didn't cross out my smile. I made me eating a chocolate candy bar." (See Fig. 11.12.)*

Fig. 11.12. Maryssa's Writing.

Two additional examples come from five-year-old Mary. Her daddy was mowing the lawn. After watching him for a time, Mary went inside and created a pictograph. When asked about all those lines coming out of his feet, Mary simply replied, "Daddy is barefoot." Mary could not see her daddy as she drew her pictograph, but she knew he had fingers and had toes. (See Fig. 11.13.)

Fig. 11.13. Mary's Writing.

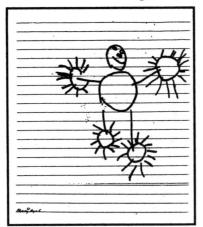

The second pictograph is of Mary's grandmother who appears happy but without a neck or body. When asked her to read her "writing," Mary was straightforward, "That's how grandma looks when I run to her. You can't see me but I'm running to hug her."

Of course, Mary's explanation makes sense. Grandma hunkers down for the hug, big smile of anticipation on her face. Mary runs to her with outstretched arms and later remembers the smile, the arms, and the legs. The body, telescoped to accommodate Mary, is nowhere to be seen on Mary's pictograph. Caught in the context of the hug, Mary didn't know neck or body—for her at that moment, it wasn't there. As Ruth Hubbard warns, "In interpreting the behaviors and motives of children, adults are liable to approach the task from their own world views and conceptions; they are often quite adultcentric" (13). We, as adults, interpret children's work from our own assumptions. Instead, we often need to invite children to "Tell me about your writing." Never ask, "What is it?"

Ideographs. Ideographs refer to written or graphic symbols that represent an idea or depict some relationship.

David's ideograph of a roller coaster illustrates the point. Five years old, he re-created the ride, its twists and turns, ascents and descents, where the ride begins and where it is. He shows the relationship of the kids in the car to the entire ride. (See Fig. 11.14.)

During a writing institute, a teacher brought us the work of her four-year-old son, Derrick. "What do you think this is?" she asked referring to his drawing.

We looked at it and suggested, "Why don't you ask him to tell you about his writing?"

The next day she returned with following explanation. "It's a map. That odd mark on the far left is where he started."

"I messed up here, so I started again," he told her. "This is where we live," he said as he ran his hand around the loosely triangular form. "Up here," he said pointing to the small circle to the left inside the triangle, "is our house. This is the road to the Gina's" (the baby-sitter), he continued

**Fig. 11.14. David's
Roller Coaster Writing.**

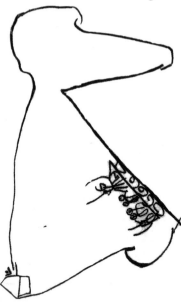

as he traced the line down under the loop and up to the second almost circle, the one in the middle. "This is Gina's."

"Did he tell you about this third larger shape?" we asked, pointing to the one on the right.

"He told me that was our church." (See Fig. 11.15.)

**Fig. 11.15. Map of
Derrick's Hometown.**

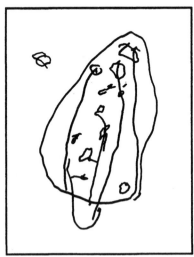

Truly this captures the entire world of that youngster. Every weekday before and after school hours, he travels to and from the baby-sitter's. On Wednesday evenings and twice on Sundays, he accompanies the family to church. Since then we have used this ideograph that so completely captures this child's world.

Often children combine both writing and drawing to create relationships. An ideograph done within writing is not regression but a swift shift to another arena. It is important to again note how very important it is to ask children about their symbolic drawing; and it is equally important to note that these arenas cut across chronological age. Sometimes a five-year-old constructs pictographs while a four-year-old attempts ideographs. These arenas are not necessarily hierarchical, but like all of writing, they are recursive.

Observing on March 28 in kindergarten, we found Garrett well on his way to becoming a writer. But when he attempted to rewrite "The Eyes of Texas," he hit a stumbling block. He couldn't spell the word *clap*. He asked Ms. Kern who told him to sound it out. He asked classmates who, busy with their own writing, just shrugged. So he made a decision, he would convey his meaning another way. (See Fig. 11.16.)

Fig. 11.16. The Eyes of Texas.

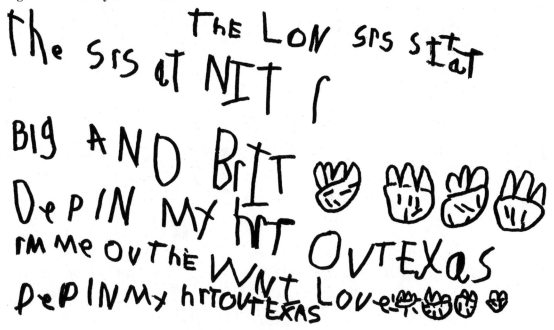

When he got to the part in the song when everyone claps, he "wrote" four pictures of hands apparently clapping. Confident he was conveying his intent, he repeated the hands a bit smaller, though, for the second verse.

Garrett's sophisticated ideograph shows the relationship not of thing to thing or person to person but writing to writing. Isn't this what illustrators do?

Three-and-a-half-year-old Amy, deeply involved in playing house with an old box, propped her doll on a chair opposite the box and placed her brother's toy boat on the floor. "Outside house," she said as she pushed the boat further away. After playing for about ten minutes, she retrieved some paper, a red marker, and pink marker. She settled down on the floor in the middle of her play area.

First she drew the box at the top of the page. "House," she said. She held the paper out in front of her as if taking inventory; then she made the marks inside the box. She picked up the pink marker and mumbled something indistinguishable about the house as she scribbled the marks to the right of the house. Next she turned the paper upside down and drew the face at the bottom of the page with the red marker. Immediately, she returned the paper to its original position. In pink, she drew the other little face. Then she talk-wrote to the top and right of the small pink face, "This is Amy's face. This is Amy's feet." (In a purely egocentric act, she named her doll after herself.) Beyond that pink writing she drew "beautiful boat" in red. Finally she made some red letters. The first few overlap the upside down face. At the risk of over-interpreting, we think one mark looks like a *D*. The *A* and *M* appear to be deliberate letters of her name and her doll's. What follows are approximations. "Done," she pronounced. (See Fig. 11.17.)

Fig. 11.17. Amy's Ideograph.

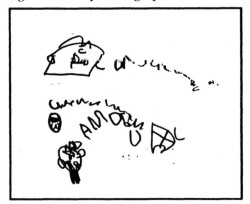

Fig. 11.18. The School Bus.

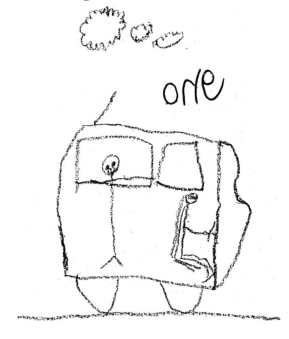

The significance of this writing event is that Amy moves fluidly from her symbolic play arena, where she clearly enacted a real event, to the arena of symbolic drawing, which was coupled with named scribbles and approximations. Her attempt to write her name may have been coincidental imitation or a degree of phonemic spelling.

One of our favorite ideographs we call "The School Bus." While visiting a kindergarten class, we found this impressive piece of "writing" on the bulletin board. During the debriefing with teachers afterwards, we asked the teacher about it. She said the child drew it and posted it. (See Fig. 11.18.)

"Did he tell you about his writing?" we probed.

"No, he just drew it and posted it on the bulletin board."

So we asked her to take it down, sit with the boy, and say, "Tell me about your writing," and transcribe what he says. She did. She told us she took one sheet of paper, fully expecting a few sentences, but he talked so much, she had to turn the paper sideways to continue transcribing.

What we find so captivating about this writing is the shift from nonfiction to fiction back to nonfiction—and the fact that the child recognizes that. "And my mom and I ran out of gas *for real.*" Most importantly, and we suspect the reason for writing and posting rises out of that astounding last sentence, "And I'm moving, too."

The whole notion that children associate school buses and cars with movement, that a kid on

Fig. 11.19. Story about the School Bus.

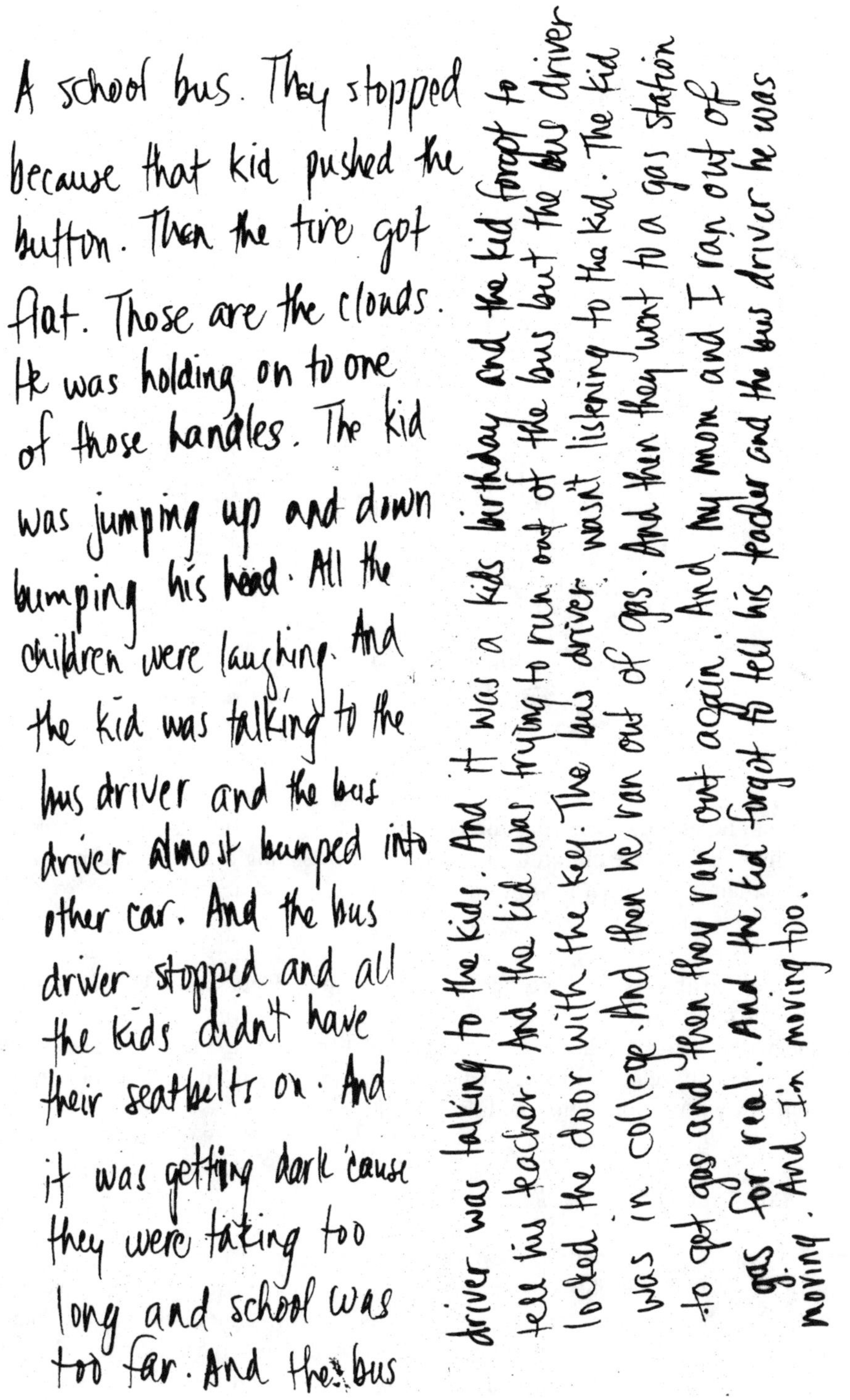

A school bus. They stopped because that kid pushed the button. Then the tire got flat. Those are the clouds. He was holding on to one of those handles. The kid was jumping up and down bumping his head. All the children were laughing. And the kid was talking to the bus driver and the bus driver almost bumped into other car. And the bus driver stopped and all the kids didn't have their seatbelts on. And it was getting dark 'cause they were taking too long and school was too far. And the bus driver was talking to the kids. And it was a kids birthday and the kid forgot to tell his teacher. And the kid was trying to run out of the bus but the bus driver locked the door with the key. The bus driver wasn't listening to the kid. The kid was in college. And then he ran out of gas. And then they went to a gas station to get gas and then they ran out again. And my mom and I ran out of gas for real. And the kid forgot to tell his teacher and the bus driver he was moving. And I'm moving too.

From *Acts of Teaching*, 2nd Edition, by Joyce Armstrong Carroll and Edward E. Wilson. Westport, CT: Teacher Ideas Press/Portsmouth, NH: Heinemann. Copyright © 2008.

the bus forgot to tell his teacher about his birthday, and the sad fact that this little writer won't get to celebrate his birthday with this class because he is moving, all come together in this ideograph that he wrote and posted for all to see. We also find it interesting that he mentions, albeit off-handedly, "Those are the clouds," but he never addresses the word *one*—one little boy shown on the bus; one little boy moving away. (See Fig. 11.19.)

Finally, some ideographs approach folk art forms. Derek, six and a half years old, produced the naive art seen in Fig. 11.17. After completing this wordless ideograph, Derek verbally identified each character by its specific name: Tyrannosaurus Rex, saber-toothed tiger, Pteranodon, Archaeopteryx, and, of course, cavemen. Obviously Derek had already learned that writing is a way to extend memory.

Fig. 11.20. Derek's Ideograph.

Instructional Strategies for Symbolic Drawing. Take dictation as children talk through their symbolic drawings. Encourage children to "write" their meaning and applaud their efforts. Establish an author's chair so children have a place to formally read and share their writing. Continue to model and provide many forums for writing.

Instructional Strategies for Pictographs, Ideographs, Consonant Writing, and Phonemic Spelling. Take dictation as children talk through heir symbolic drawings. As letters appear, and as teacher and writer can read them, stop taking dictation. Create author's chairs so the children have a place to formally read and share their writing. Continue to model, encourage, and provide many functions for writing for fiction and nonfiction.

VI. Transitional Writing and Spelling

Transitional writing and spelling are terms used to define a crucial arena of passage. When children move in dynamic, implosive, and explosive ways away from rudimentary writing to the standard writing of their culture, they no longer draw things; they draw words. Their brains are growing. The neurons expand because the dendrites, which receive messages, develop synaptic connections, become heavier, and grow new branches; the supporting glial cells increase in number; the axons, or output parts of the neurons, develop coats of myelin. "By the time the child is two years old, its [the brain's] weight will triple, and by age seven its 1,250 grams will represent 90% of adult weight" (Healy 66).

Neuroscientist Gerald M. Edelman contends that language is not independent of cognition. He presents compelling data by George Lakoff, "Individual humans construct cognitive models that reflect concepts concerned with the interactions between the body—brain and the environment" (246). It seems the brain, cognition, body, and culture blend together to make meaning and at no other time in the development of a child is meaning making more manifest than within this transitional arena.

Consonant Writing and Phonemic Spelling. Consonant writing, phonemic spelling, or, as it is sometimes called, letter-name spelling, refers to an early transitional area where every letter stands for a sound, no extra letters are used, and often only the initial consonant is used to stand for a word. Children become phonemically aware, conscious that different letters carry different sounds. They try to make the fit. Interestingly, Cory's symbolic drawing of the peacock also contained consonant writing. He wrote the letter *P* to fit *pea* and the letter *K* to fit *cock*. He read *peacock.*

The transition from simple idea transmission to a systematic, phonetic writing probably occurs as naturally as it did historically—as an aid to memory. Albertine Gaur, in her comprehensive study of the history of writing, tells how the ordinary picture-writing , *kekewin,* of North American Indians differs from their specialized picture-writing, *kekinowin,* which was known only to their priests. They memorized *kekinowin* so their spells and incantations would be exact. *Kekewin* represents an idea, concept, or event—somewhat like a child's ideograph. *Kekinowin* known to only a select few, contains pictures that represent a sentence or verse with only one possible spoken form for each picture (28). Similarly, children, who live in an ever-expanding global world of ever-expanding knowledge, seem to sense their need for a system to keep track, more exactly, of what they know.

Equally interesting as testimony to the influence of environment upon writing are "semitic scripts." Characterized by consonants, almost as an abbreviation, with vowels playing a secondary part, *B* may mean book or to read a book. Eventually, as others adopted this, it developed into an alphabet with syllabic script forms (Gaur 88). What makes semitic scripts so interesting to us is that they parallel children's writing in this transitional arena.

Children use consonants to convey their meaning, for example, "srs t nt r" in the "Eyes of Texas" song, "*stars at night are* big and bright." In time, they begin to incorporate the vowels, for example, "srs at nit r." Young children write the word *because* many different ways as they develop into standard writers. Often they write the word several different ways in one piece of discourse. Following are some variations of *because* culled over an academic year from first-grade writers: *bks, bcs, bkus, bcoz, BCos, bcos, bcus, bcuse, becus, becos, becas, becoss, becuse, becase, becose, because.* Of course, not all the first-graders used all these variations. Some developed in exactly this order. Some regressed, moved forward, regressed, only to move forward with what seemed to be more security. Many jumped quickly from consonant spelling to standard spelling. At year's end, few remained in transition with this word. The point is, the transitional arena is just that—a time for the body, the brain, and cognition to gain physiological, and neurological, and cultural balance.

Kindergarten Examples

Alison wrote her response to Martin and Archambault's *Here Are My Hands* by chronicling the things she knows. "Things about you. You have eyes. You have a nose. You have a mouth. You have fingers. You have hands. You have a stomach. You have feet. You have toes. You have ears." Then she goes on to explain these things. "These things are very useful. A mouth to talk with. Ears to hear with. A nose to smell with. A stomach for things in your body to go through.

Fig. 11.21. Alison's Transitional Writing.

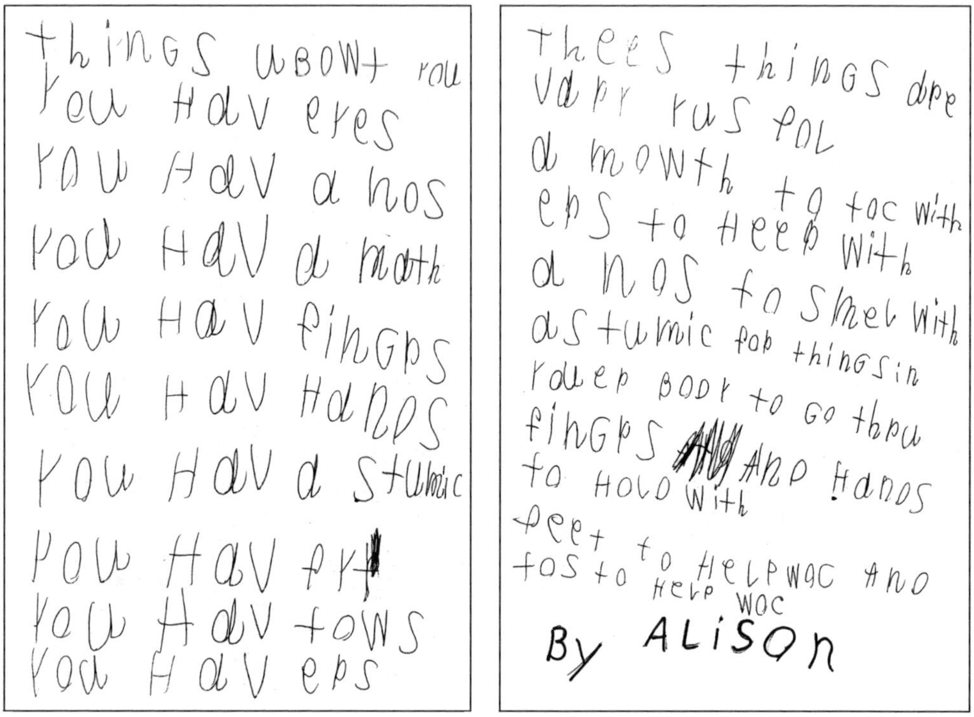

Fingers and hands to hold with. Feet to help walk and toes to help walk. By Alison." (See Fig. 11.21.)

Not only does Alison generate meaning through the repetitive pattern she uses on her first page, but she takes liberties with this pattern on her second page. Clearly Alison's writing belongs in the transitional arena. She uses standard spelling for some words such as *things, you, eyes*; she omits the final silent *e* for some words: *hav* and *nos*, common even among good spellers; she takes risks with words that are precise but obviously are not in her repertoire: *ubowt, stumic*. But where she demonstrates most that she is transitional is with the words *toes* and *feet*. On the first page she stumbles around with *fyt*, crossing out part of what might have been the letter *Y*, yet on the second page she writes the word correctly. She may have received help, remembered how it was spelled, found the word in print, or sounded it out. No matter, writing words differently in the same piece of discourse characterizes transitional writers and spellers. Similarly, she writes *tows* on page one, but *tos* on her second page. Because she is still transitioning with that word, and considering that *tow* is pronounced like *toe*, her problem may be homonymic. She omits the *E* in fingers and the *U* in mouth; reverses the *A* in ears; and inserts an *E* between the *U* and *R* in *your*. Some of her words are constructed spellings, such as *vary* for *very*, *yusfol* for *useful*, and *wac* or *woc* for walk. The most significant thing to note in analyzing Alison's writing is not her inconsistencies but that there is much more right with her writing than there is wrong.

We want to include some writing from Spanish-speaking, Spanish-writing students who are transitioning not only in their development of writing but also from Spanish to English. As early as October 3, given a Venn diagram and lots of modeling, these kindergarten children produced astonishing work.

Ms. Silva distributed to each child lined paper on which she had reproduced the Venn diagram. She asked them to compare the story she read to them and the video they watched. In the first circle, they drew what happened in the book; in the middle section, they drew something common in both; in the circle on the right, they drew something from the video. Then they wrote. One child wrote in Spanish: "The ugly ducking hid in the sugar cane. In the video the dog looked at the ugly duckling. In both it was snowing." (See Fig. 11.22.)

Fig. 11.22. The Ugly Duckling.

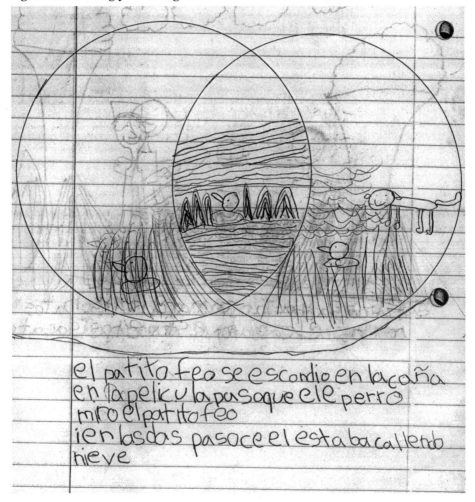

Twelve days later, Ms. Silva read *Hansel and Gretel*. This time she wanted them to tell her what they liked and didn't like about the story. One student wrote in Spanish: "I liked the part that they ate the witch's house and the witch said who's eating my house, and what I didn't like in the story was that the witch lied to the children." (See Fig. 11.23.)

Although the ideograph that accompanies that writing shows the witch and Hansel and Gretel smiling even as they are about to be thrust into the oven, the writing clearly shows a sense of moral outrage.

Our favorite of this trilogy came about two weeks later. Shorter in writing but richer in details, it fulfills the assignment: Tell your favorite part of the story "The Three Little Pigs."

Fig. 11.23. Hansel and Gretel.

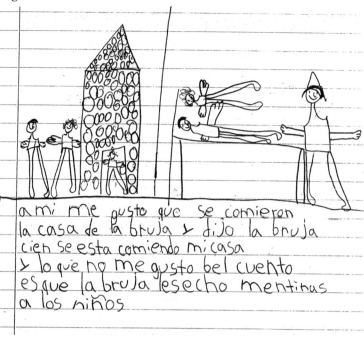

a mi me gusto que se comieron
la casa de la bruja y dijo la bruja
cien se esta comiendo mi casa
y lo que no me gusto bel cuento
es que la bruja lesecho mentiras
a los niños

Erika, not mincing any words, writes in Spanish: "The wolf destroyed the house and the little pigs ran outside." (See Fig. 11.24.)

Fig. 11.24. Erika's "The Three Little Pigs."

El lobo destrul, la Casa y los maranitos corieron
para fuera.

But look at that pigeon-toed, long-snout wolf with breath strong enough to render the house into separate sticks. Look at the smiling faces as bodies on the three pigs. Don't miss the detail of the two birds, turned away from the destruction, beaks held high as they observe another animal whose head is apparently in the clouds, perhaps oblivious to the entire event. We know this detail in drawing will emerge as detail in writing. We know Ms. Silva is not only preparing her students in writing but raising their self-esteem.

Five-year-old Jenny's parents had just purchased a bilevel home, so they laid out the perimeters to Jenny. The den was fair game. There she could munch, watch television, and visit with her friends. The living room, with its new ecru carpet, was off limits. Not too many days after they moved in, Jenny, grape juice in hand, tripped and spilled the juice on the new carpet. Dad dusted off the back of her lap and sent her upstairs to her room. Jenny cried for a while but suddenly stopped. Her mom became worried and tiptoed up the stairs to check on Jenny. Just as she reached the top step, a piece of paper slid from under Jenny's door. (See Fig. 11.25.)

Fig. 11.25. Jenny's Apology.   **Fig. 11.26. Seth's Letter.**

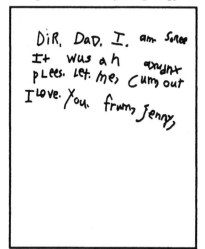   

"Dear Dad, I am sorry. It was an accident. Please let me come out. I love you. From Jenny."

Apparently Jenny, who obviously knew the conventions of letter writing, decided to apologize and to formalize that apology in a letter. Analyzing it, gives us insight into Jenny's thinking. She begins with her purpose, by extending her oral apology. In sentence two, she offers an explanation. By the third sentence, she pleads, but it is that corker of a final sentence that she hopes will be the clincher. Appealing to that soft spot in all parents, and just in case her other explanations failed, she proclaims her love. (Who said kindergartners couldn't write persuasive pieces?) Jenny closes her letter and signs it, making everything official.

There are nineteen words in Jenny's letter; thirteen are spelled correctly. The remaining six words are constructed spellings. Jenny must use words such as *soree* (sorry) and *axudnx* (accident) for accuracy even though they are not in her spelling repertoire, since no other words would adequately express her meaning.

Seth, a precocious five-year-old whose father works at NASA and whose grandfather is an inventor, also wrote a letter. This one is to his grandfather. The name and address in the top right corner has been blurred. (The place where the picture was affixed has been indicated.) (See Fig. 11.26.)

"Love Seth. Dear Granddaddy, I am interested in a laboratory. All the stuff in the catalog is for older kids. Can you design a laboratory for beginners? I already have a microscope. I cut out pictures to show you what I like. I want to be a mad scientist. I want real potions that can change real things. Tell grandmama thank you for that piano book. Love Seth."

We note that nothing is wrong with Seth's ego. He begins his letter as he ends it—with a request or a reminder or a command—to love him. Seth, like Jenny, knows letter form. Probably both see letters being written, sent, and received. In Seth's home, especially since the family live distances apart, letters from family are fussed over; they are valued, and apparently Seth realizes their value as well, but he also knows they serve a function—they are a way to request things.

Seth knows how to find information. The catalog provides him with the spelling of words such as *laboratory, catalog,* and *microscope,* although the second time he uses the word *laboratory,* he omits the *A.* Even though he demonstrates his precocity with words such as *already, love, change, stuff, cut, out, show, what, like,* and so forth, he proves he is still in the transitional arena with the constructed spelling of *intrested, oldr,* and *kides.*

Rarely do kindergartners use a hyphen, yet Seth's punctuation is remarkable. He uses it twice correctly, and the third time he almost gets it right. While he ignores commas, all his terminal punctuation is correct. There is also a sense of paragraphing.

Seth writes with purpose and knows his audience. The entire letter is geared to the request. The thank you for the piano book is placed last, an afterthought. Voice in the sentences, "I want to be a mad scientist" and "I want real potions that can change real things," shows confidence and authenticity. He knows what he wants and he knows where to get it—surely a grandfather who happens to invent things is the right audience and the right person to "design a laboratory for beginners."

We conducted a three-day workshop for primary teachers. On Monday we began with kindergarten. Among other things, we showed examples of kindergarten writing and presented strategies to help the teachers and challenged them to get their students writing. We heard the usual excuses: "They don't know the entire alphabet"; "they can't write yet"; "they will cry"; and so forth. Still, we challenged them to challenge their students. On Wednesday as we worked with second-grade teachers, Mrs. Macias sent over samples of her kindergartners' writing. She read *A House for Hermit Crab* by Eric Carle, and taking a cue from us she invited them to write what they remembered. She made her invitation casual and nonthreatening and in a manner that conveyed her high expectations. Victoria wrote: "One little crab he said I am going to move out of this house and he got big and big and one day be decided to go in another shell." (See Fig. 11.27.)

Mrs. Macias was beside herself. "They can write," she exclaimed to all who would listen. According to her, Victoria had never written *like this* in her class. We pointed out how much was correct in the writing, how she used her phonics *uv* and how she constructed the word *decided* using what she knew about words, letters, and sound *disidid.*

Unfortunately, this book is not in color for the way Victoria colored the shells as she shows the hermit crab getting bigger and bigger demonstrates her artistic sense—the shading, the way the large shell blends into the word *shell,* the way the medium shell slightly touches the largest shell.

Conducting a similar workshop in another district, we spent time on the use of word banks as one way to increase vocabulary and spelling awareness in primary students (see Carroll, *Phonics,* 1998). We modeled for the teachers. We cut a swatch of brown butcher paper in a stick-figure shape to connect "The Gingerbread Boy," the story we were about to read. Each student received a piece of brown paper to create his or her own stick figure "gingerbread boy." As spelling words, as we read, we deposited words from the story into the gingerbread word bank to be discussed, used for later reference, and for students to use when writing.

Melinda Villarreal used this idea when she taught about Christopher Columbus to her kindergartners. After she read the story, they roleplayed. The next day she gave them butcher paper and invited them to write what they remembered. Marcos remembered a lot, and because he had his word bank, he could write what he remembered. (See Fig. 11.28.)

One day there was a boy named Christopher Columbus. Christopher Columbus wanted men to go to Asia. He didn't have any men. He went to a king and queen but the king and queen said no, so Christopher Columbus went to another king and queen and they

Fig. 11.27. A House for Hermit Crab.

said yes. The king and queen send 90 men and some food and 3 boats. So they sailed for 32 weeks. So they wanted to throw Christopher Columbus out but Christopher Columbus said let's wait for 3 months. So Christopher Columbus found land. So Christopher Columbus thought he was in the Indies because they didn't have any spices. Christopher Columbus thought . . .

The ideograph, done beautifully in color truly augments his text by showing the men and the ships. Clearly the words *Christopher Columbus*, *king*, *queen*, *Indies*, and *Asia* appeared in the word bank, but Marcos was the only student who wrote that Columbus petitioned two different kings and queens, that they sailed for thirty-two weeks, and so on.

What makes this writing so remarkable is its length. Typically, just the physical exertion of writing that much text would discourage most five-year-olds. At some point Marcos tired and simply trailed off with Columbus thinking, but what a proof he offers us about kindergarten writing.

All of this self-sponsored writing by kindergartners supports the ever-increasing corpus of empirical data that indicate children are capable of more—and certainly more writing—than we ever realized. They further prove that sociocultural events affect their making of meaning.

Fig. 11.28. Marco's Writing.

First-Grade Examples

Gabriela, a recent immigrant at the time of this writing, clearly shows the ability of primary students to write about what they know. Her teacher, Ms. Jilpas, shared this example with us.

After introducing her family through a pictograph as the cover of her book "My Family," Gabriela writes a whole and coherent piece of writing about them. Her "mistakes" such as *tow* for *two*, *oun* for *one* are common at this age. *Biy* is an example of overlearning the long *i* sound, and *brouthrs* is an example of not quite understanding the *ou* phonogram or confusing it with the short *u* sound. While Gabriela places the *–er* ending on the word *sister*, she still maintains a remnant of consonant spelling when she omits the *e* in *brother*. Interestingly, she spells *brothers* correctly on page two, but spells it *brouthers* on the last page. This vacillation marks a transitional writer/speller. She vacilates, too, with the word *little*. On page one, she spells it *litte;* in the third sentence on page two, she spells it *litel;* but in the seventh sentence, she spells it correctly. (See Fig. 11.29.)

Fig. 11.29. Gabriela's Family.

> This is my family. I have a dad and a mom. I have tow twin Bruothis and oun sister. I like my family a lot. I do a lot of things with my family. I Play a lot withmy brouthrs and my litte sister. I Go with my family to the mall, we BY toys.

> Then we go and eat pizza. Then all of us go home and play mnople. Then me and my brothers and my littel sister go outside and play hide and seek. Then we play hopskach. And then we go and see move, we see Barbie and the nut chraci. Me and my little sistler like that move. Then we wach mary kate and Ashly.

> Me and my mom do lots of things. We read books, and do aert. And me and my dad do lots of stuff to. We mack woud houseis and brid houseis. My family and I love ech othr very much becase we ure a family my mom my dad, my brouthers and sister and me!

That Gabriela is a transitional speller is most evident in the word *mnople*. She constructs the spelling based on her knowledge of phonics and her reading, and we are able to read the word. With the word *hopscotch*, she chooses the hard *c/k* sound, and entirely misses the *–otch* phonogram, as she misses the *–atch* phonogram in *watch*. She consistently omits the *i* in *movie/movies*, but the *ae* in *art* could be simple phonetic confusion between the schwa or, in thinking *art* begins with *ae*, she may have created a dieresis by dividing the two adjacent vowels as two syllables rather gliding them together as a diphthong and perhaps catching her mistake.

To and *wood* are homonymic problems. *Mack* for *make* shows she needs more work on the *–ake* phonogram, but *brid* is a simple letter reversal and *houseis* is the overgeneralization children make with the endings of words. We have already discussed how children progress developmentally with the word *because*. On the whole, since there are many more correctly spelled words in Gabriela's pieces, her spelling errors show more an overlearning of her phonics than bad spelling.

What is exemplary about Gabriela's writing is its structure. She begins with a clear introduction and goes on to describe what the family does together. She becomes specific, telling her audience where they go, what they eat, and what they play. At first she tells what she does with her bothers and sister, moves to her mother, and concludes with her father. The organization flows in an orderly, clear way. Each sentence is connected. She ties everything together nicely with a restatement and a call back.

Roxanne, who spoke no English when she came to the United States from Vietnam two years prior to the writing in Fig. 11.30, grew into the English language through the rich sociocultural context created in the classroom by veteran teacher Lu Ann Kubis. Ms. Kubis integrates all the language arts, so her classroom is alive with her constant modeling and her students writing and sharing.

On the day Roxanne composed this piece, she wrote diligently during the entire writing time. Before grouping, Lu Ann conducted a mini-teach on a simplified version of Say Back. In group, Roxanne volunteered to read her piece.

Fig. 11.30. Roxanne's Writing.

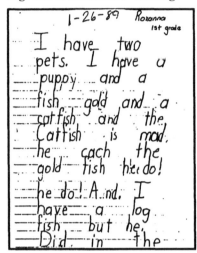
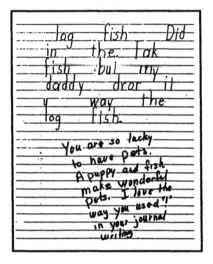

"I have two pets. I have a puppy and a fish gold, and a catfish. And the Catfish is mad. He catch the gold fish. He do! He do! And I have a long fish, but he died in the long fish died in the tank fish. But my daddy threw it away, the long fish." When she finished, she looked up ready for the "what do you like best" part of Say Back. Almost in unison, her group said, "He do! He do!"

There are several noteworthy things about Roxanne's writing. Her handwriting is impeccable. She painstakingly and deliberately forms each letter. She cares about her writing but is careful to write what she knows. Since Roxanne wrote this in her daily journal, the repetition in the next to the last sentence is most likely due to turning the page.

The words she spells inventively seem to be words with sounds that still sound foreign to her ear: the *t* in *catch* or the *th* in *threw*, which she pronounces *drew*. Interestingly, however, she spells and pronounces *the* correctly.

She still grapples with the adjective preceding the noun in English, because like Spanish, the adjectival form follows the noun form in Vietnamese. She sometimes gets the adjective placed correctly according to standard English grammar, but she sometimes places it as in the Vietnamese language. For instance, she writes *fish gold* and *tank fish*, yet she also writes *catfish* and *long fish*. The use of exclamation marks used appropriately is impressive in this writing, because unlike so many other children who first discover them, Roxanne does not overuse them.

Finally, although the "he do! he do!" is indeed delightful and reveals voice, it shows that Roxanne still follows a verb pattern from her original language. Her teacher avoids placing too much emphasis on Roxanne's verb forms in her note at the end of the writing. Rather, she affirms Roxanne's pets and emphasizes what Roxanne did well—the use of the exclamation point. Roxanne is becoming fluent; work on skills happens in this first grade when they take something from their journals to publication.

Second-Grade Examples

Justin's writing typifies the writing of second-graders once introduced to chapter books. His tale proves the power of literature influencing writing. He emulates the conventions: beginning in the classical manner of fairy tales, naming the lead character, getting him in trouble and then resolving that trouble, identifying chapters, titling them, ending each chapter with a page-turner,

Fig. 11.31. Justin's Goblen.

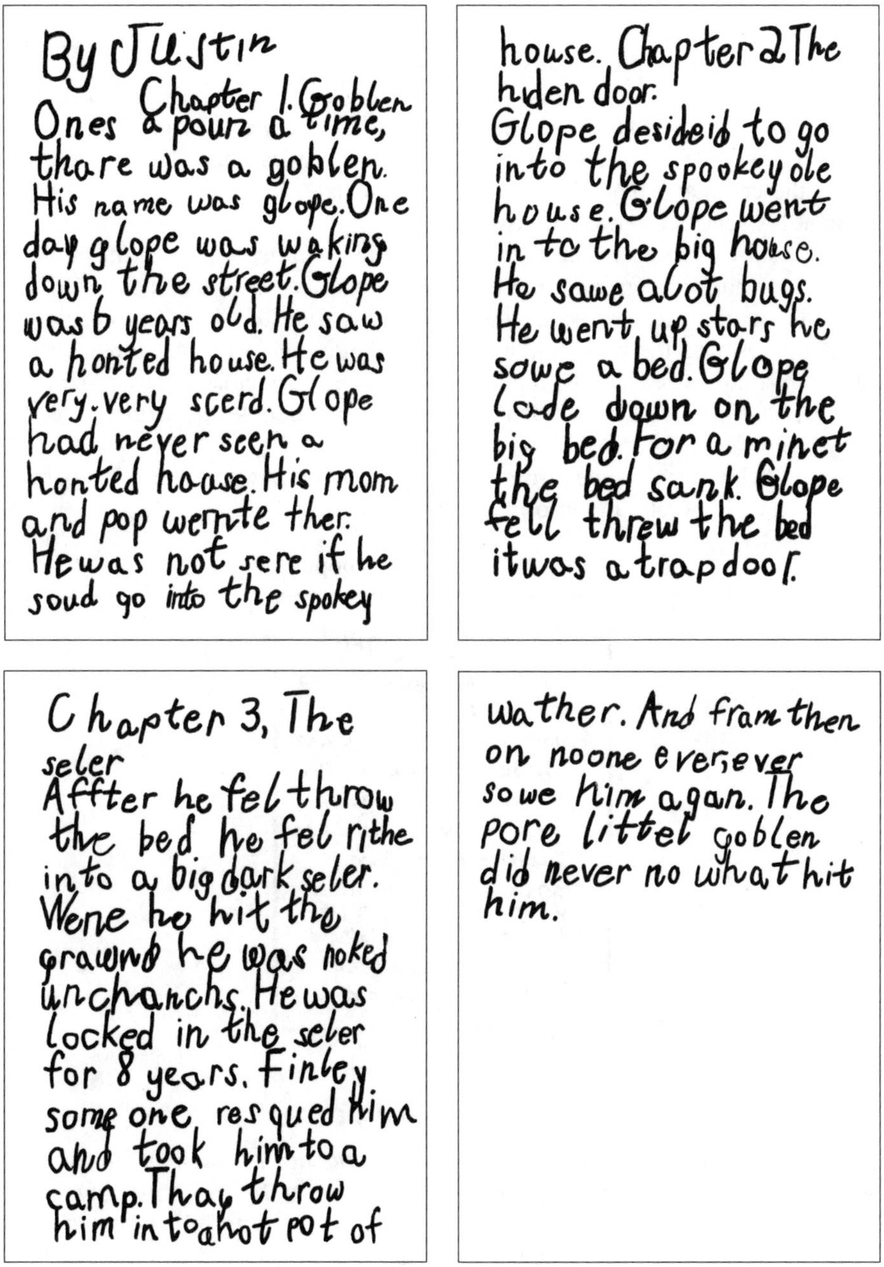

By Justin
Chapter 1. Goblen
Ones a poun a time,
thare was a goblen.
His name was glope. One
day glope was wakirg
down the street. Glope
was 6 years old. He saw
a honted house. He was
very.very scerd. Glope
had never seen a
honted house. His mom
and pop wernte ther.
He was not sere if he
soud go into the spokey

house. Chapter 2 The
hiden door.
Glope desideid to go
into the spookey ole
house. Glope went
in to the big house.
He sawe alot bugs.
He went up stars he
sowe a bed. Glope
lode down on the
big bed. For a minet
the bed sank. Glope
fell threw the bed
it was a trap door.

Chapter 3, The
seler
Affter he fel throw
the bed he fel rithe
into a big dark seler.
Wene he hit the
grawnd he was noked
unchanchs. He was
locked in the seler
for 8 years. Finley
some one resqued him
and took him to a
camp. Thay throw
him in to a hot pot of

wather. And fram then
on noone ever ever
sowe him agan. The
pore littel goblen
did never no what hit
him.

beginning the next chapter where he left off. Never does Justin stray from his point. His writing is tight, focused, and coherent. His piece conveys his voice and reveals what he knows about writing, for example, his use of punctuation.

This self-sponsored writing, while transitional in its spelling, holds the genesis of a skilled developing writer.

Justin's writing shows progression in the three chapter titles: "Goblen," "The Hiden Door," and, scariest of all, "The Cellar." Justin makes his character younger than himself, a show of power because six-year-old kids are easy to scare, but keeps him in captivity for more years than he is old—clearly a device to show what Glope feels as endless time.

Eschewing worry over spelling, Justin plunges forward to make meaning. He spells words totally by their sound: *globen*, *hanted*, *wernte*, *ther*, *hidden*, *desideid*, *ole*, *minet*, *seler*, *wene*, *noked*, *unchonshs*, *resqued.* When we present Justin's writing in our workshops, we invite the participants to read it along with us. They never miss a beat, reading *desideid* as *decided*, *noked* as *knocked*, *unchonshs* as *unconscious*, and so forth. They delight in the story and marvel that a second-grader could write such a well-developed story so early in the year—around the end of October. They note his use of the comma: After the opening phrase, between the two *verys* and the two *evers.* They are agog at his sentence sense and use of periods.

Justin's craft shows promise. The name of his goblin *Glope,* which Justin pronounces "glue pea," suggests something foreign and exotic. Justin introduces Glope and the setting in chapter one; describes the setting in more detail and adds the tension of trouble in chapter two; builds suspense, uniquely resolves the problem, and teaches the lesson in chapter three. Justin concisely crafts his story with no wasted words, rapid action, and a satisfactory ending. We as readers are left bedeviled by that corker of a last sentence. Did Justin double the negative as Shakespeare did—to emphasize?

The author of "Granpope" comes from West Texas. After a weekend in October on the ranch with his grandparents, he wrote this informative piece.

Fig. 11.32. My Granpope.

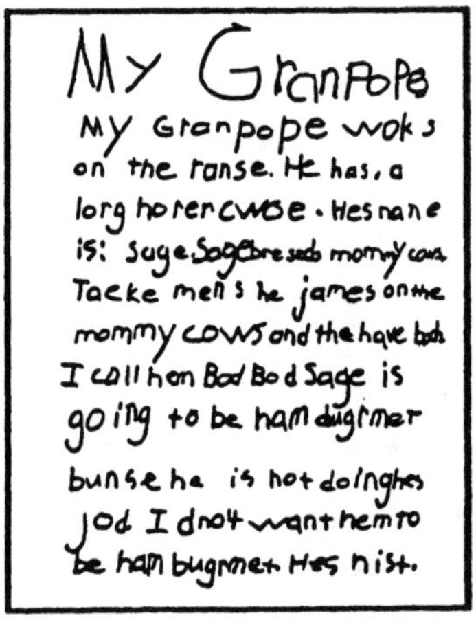
My Granpope
My Granpope woks
on the ranse. He has, a
lorg horercwse. Hes nane
is: Suge. Sage bresds mommy cows.
Tacke men's he james on the
mommy cows and the have bab
I call hen Bad Bad Sage is
going to be hamdugrmer
bunse he is not dolnghes
jod I dnot want hem to
be ham bugrmet. Hes nist.

My Granpope

My grandpop works on the ranch. He has a long horn cow. His name is Sage. Sage breeds mommy cows. That means he jumps on the mommy cows and they have babies. I call him Bad. Bad Sage is going to be hamburger meat because he is not doing his job. I don't want him to be hamburger meat. He is nice.

Perhaps better than any other piece in this chapter, this writing clearly shows the influence of culture. Discussing the ranch, bulls, cows, breeding, and its consequences are as natural in a ranching community as clients, accounts, and paying bills might be elsewhere. So this young man writes about the world he knows.

Clearly this writer is in the transitional arena. He may have overlearned the silent *e*. He tacks it onto *Granpope*; he writes it on *ranse*; and he puts it at the end of his invented spelling of *cwoe*.

He also makes some errors in word details. For example: *horen, breseds, dno't*. Marie Clay says that often these errors occur "because the child is trying to write down his speech, using what he knows of letter-sound correspondence" (58).

Sometimes he reverses the letters themselves, as he did in the obvious attempt to correct the *b* in *hamburger* and the *b* in *job*. These are the errors that signal help.

This young author displays a sense of story. He begins with a title and carries that title deftly into the defining first sentence. The piece is internally coherent, each sentence coheres to the previous sentence with the first sentence cohering to the title. His message quality is enhanced by the use of punctuation: the period, the apostrophe, and, interestingly, the colon. He uses the specificity of Sage, naming the bull and telling exactly what will happen to Sage if he does not do his job. And contrary to Piaget's theory of egocentrism, which holds that young children do not act altruistically, this author shows compassion for Sage's plight. Not incidentally, there is a growing corpus of data that demonstrate even children as young as two exhibit decentered and therefore altruistic behavior (Hubbard 1989; Black 1981; Donaldson 1978).

VII. Standard Writing and Spelling

Students in this arena write and spell using the standard conventions. Their language level indicates their knowledge of the alphabet, words, phrases, clauses, sentences, and paragraphs. Their writing is meaningful, clear, and coherent; it has voice, contains proper punctuation and correct spelling, and demonstrates craft and the elements of genre. Their spelling indicates a sense of phonics, of the rules that work, of patterns, and of vast exposure to words. While errors may occasionally occur, it is clear that the student has a firm grasp of how to write and spell.

An Elementary-Level Longitudinal Look

One way to examine writing and spelling development is by longitudinal studies. Another way is to collect one student's writing over a period of time. We have the collected writings of Jason, a kindergartner who was not formally taught writing but was given many opportunities every day to write. His teacher taught the children their names and upper- and lowercase letters. She exposed them to reading and writing and invited them daily to, "Choose something you have written today for your big books." Applying Piaget's theory of conservation to books, the children considered their big wallpaper books extremely important because of their immense size. They seemed to reason that because their writing went into this big important book, their writing must also be important, so they carefully chose from their daily writing an entry that they affixed to each page in the book. The samples were culled from a year of Jason's work. There are nine examples representing his writing in September, October, early November, later November, December, February, March (when Jason turned six), April, and May. (See Fig. 11.33.)

In September, Jason created an ideograph. He dictated to his teacher, "I went to go spend the night with my cousin." Aside from one boy levitating, the picture clearly depicts bunk beds and the relationship of the two cousins. Clearly, Jason begins his writing life in the arena of symbolic drawing.

Fig. 11.33. Jason's Writing Over the Course of a School Year.

By October, Jason learned his name and upper- and lowercase letters, which he practiced. Here he drew an interesting framed ideograph. Under it he strung, "Me and my dad were painting the house." With these words, he begins his trek through the levels of writing and spelling. For the most part Jason used uppercase letters, no punctuation, and no space between the words. *Wr* signals consonant writing and spelling, and despite growth into other arenas, Jason consistently stayed with *wr* for *were* during the entire year.

"On the walk," an ideograph chosen in early November, reveals an interesting perspective. Although Jason wrote about his class going on a walk and pictured the class, he made this ideograph unique by viewing the scene of which he is a part (he is fourth from the left) from an omniscient point of view. Jason also used an uppercase letter to begin his phrase and used parentheses to separate words. The children are smiling. Indeed, most of Jason's people smile.

Later in November Jason creates what K. Buhler, cited by Vygotsky, calls "x-ray drawings" (1978, 112). Two children play under the stairs. This is an example of a child writing what he knows, not what he sees. This page is cut off a bit on the left because the big book would not lie flat on the photocopy machine. It says, "Me and my friend were playing house." Jason began putting in hyphens to separate words.

Christmas presented a dilemma for Jason. Told their Christmas tree was as tall as Dad, Jason stretched his father to match the height of the tree. He wrote, "Me and my dad are putting up our Christmas tree." To Jason *are* and *our* sound the same, so he is consistent, albeit incorrect, in spelling both words. This example of consistent inconsistency is common in young writers. Prior to this writing, Jason asked his teacher, "Why doesn't my writing look like the writing in books?"

"Because you don't leave space between the words," she replied.

"Why didn't you tell me that?" asked Jason, arms akimbo. He strutted back to his table and began putting in spaces as he wrote.

Sentences, beginning with capital letters and ending with terminal punctuation, made their way into Jason's writing by February. Although he still relied on pictographing and ideographing, his compound sentence indicates a developing syntactical maturity. "My friend came over yesterday and we played star wars."

Cognitive development is apparent in the March entry with the extended compound sentence that Jason wrote. "Yesterday Cory came to my house and we went to the creek and we threw rocks in the water." He constructed the spelling of several words, but Jason is clearly mastering connections between what he thinks and what he writes.

Jason no longer needs symbolic drawing by April. As he gained more control over his thinking and writing, the less he needed the other symbolizing system. Interestingly, this writing shows indenting in the extreme. The sentence beginning with *And* is three-quarters of the way across the page, an example of how learners tend to exaggerate something new. Jason writes, "Last night I had a tee ball game. And it was a tie 43 to 43 and it was on until 7 o'clock." This piece of writing is informative, clear, and detailed. He capitalized *Game* because it was important to him. He capitalized *It* because it references an important game. While he does not put the apostrophe in *o'clock*, he leaves space as if he knows something might go there.

In May Jason shows a sense of paragraphs—this time block type. He used capital letters and punctuation. His cognitive ability to hold several ideas in his mind while writing those ideas in sequence is obvious. He took spelling risks. *Miniature* is not a word considered part of a kindergartner's written vocabulary, but it is the precise word. "Yesterday I saw a play. And after that me and Dad went to play miniature golf. Saturday while Mom and Uncle Ronnie were judging and Sunday while Mom and Grandma were having a drink."

A Secondary Longitudinal Look

Another longitudinal look comes from a high-school student, one of many students who participated in the original New Jersey Writing Project Study. The Educational Testing Service used the now-famous "Tomato Lady" as the prompt for students in the project and control schools midway through the year.

Fig. 11.34. Tomato Lady, Writing Topic.

```
                        WRITING TOPIC II
        Here is a picture of a woman with some tomatoes.  Look at
        the picture for awhile and decide what is going on.  When
        you have decided, write about what is happening in the
        picture and what is likely to happen next.
```

We used a different prompt at the conclusion of the year, but the "Tomato Lady" responses were used to train all of us in holistic scoring mid-way through the project. We were then re-trained with different anchor papers from the students' final test. The following piece written by a tenth-grader was so outstanding, it would have skewed any results, and so we were unable to use it as an anchor paper. Had this been given a 4 (the highest score) in the calibration of papers, no other student would have achieved a score of 4.

Fig. 11.35. Tenth Grader's Writing to the Tomato Lady.

The elderly woman in the picture has just found the tomato of her dreams. For fifty years she's been traveling to the same market in the same neighborhood looking for the ultimate tomato. A quest can make a life worth living no matter how trivial it seems to the rest of the world. The quest for the perfect tomato has kept this woman going through two world wars, three husbands, the age of rock-and-roll, measly Social Security checks, and Watergate. While all the world may seem to crumble around her, the quest lives on bright, perfect, shiny, and complete as the perfect tomato she seeks as the light at end of her tunnel. She shops at this little market everyday. Now that it is open on Sundays, she goes directly after church. It has become a holy ritual now, these Sundays of seeking: get up, dress up in one of your good "Sunday" clothes, put on the string of pearls your

*late (and latest) husband gave you on your 10th anniversary, go to church, pay
your money, light your candle, and then on . . . to the real business at hand.*

*Things have changed a lot since she first began her quest too many years ago
to remember. Back then, she had needed some purpose, some ideal, some goal,
to lift her above the drudgery and earth-shattering boredom of her new life as a
young bride. While other young wives turned to men and drink, she turned with an
equal lust, and finally, obsession to the tomato stand at the neighborhood market.*

*And as the years passed, it did become an overpowering obsession. After her
first husband died (of fewed poisoning—they said it was something in the stewed
tomatoes he had at dinner that last awful night—ah, the wizardry of those red round
bewitchers!), she kept the house through two more marriages, and one divorce.*

*Now in her later years, the boredom had returned, greater and more shocking
and complete. While others of her age went to Florida to live "the good life" in
mobile homes, or to old folks homes to be gently and slowly carried out of life, she
turned to her tomato stand as some turned to their children. Those little round-
cheeked darlings of hers distracted her, amused her, entertained her, and com-
peted for her attention—why, they really needed her!*

Then today, she had gone as usual after church-and there it was. The PER-
FECT TOMATO. Grinning and shining up at her through all that damned cellophane. What was he doing in the same package with those other inferior vegetables? But she, after making sure that no one was watching, gently squeezed him
lovingly, removed him and knew that because of the quest her life, which could end
now, had been worthwhile.

After the test, we interviewed the young lady who wrote this outstanding piece. Her parents were
Princeton professors and as a small child she made the commitment to become a writer. "I saw
this prompt," she said, "as another way to prove I am a writer."

Indeed she is.

Her essay demonstrates unusual competence. To analyze this essay, we decided to use Irmscher's criteria, which are not unlike Diederich's scales, as opposed to holistically scoring it.

Irmscher's Criteria

Content. His first criterion is *content*. Irmscher says, "The first mark of the *A*-paper is that
it invites reading" (162). Further he notes that even if the prompt is bland, "the writer finds a way
of making something of nothing, either by humor or irony or fantasy" (162).

The author of the "Tomato Lady" piece certainly fulfills that criterion. After her first sentence,
we want to read on. Faced with a picture of an old woman holding a package of tomatoes, she
creates a story filled with humor and irony. Who could miss the tongue-in-cheek of "While other
young wives turned to men and drink, she turned with equal lust, and finally, obsession to the
tomato stand at the neighborhood market"? And who could miss the irony of the first husband
dying of "fewed"—deliberately misspelled for rhetorical effect—poisoning from "something in
the stewed tomatoes he had at dinner that last awful night"?

Irmscher also notes that *A*-essay writers "draw upon both reading and experience for details
and examples . . . *A*-writing is often fertile, leading to diverse interpretations and richness of meaning. These are the marks of mature prose" (163).

This tenth-grader shows the marks of mature prose by drawing upon the "quest" theme she
has most assuredly studied, morphing it into a "holy ritual," surely born of the experience of
dressing for church on Sunday, eschewing the mundane of "Florida," "mobile homes," or "old
folks homes," probably the result of conversations with grandparents, personifying the tomatoes

as children, "little round-cheeked darlings" who "really *needed* her"—a slice of her own life—and concluding with a return to the archetypical quest ending, achieving the goal, rescuing the maiden, slaying the dragon, or in this case, finding the "PERFECT TOMATO" now transmogrified into a "he" to bring her "Tomato Lady" fantasy to a satisfying close with that gentle loving squeeze. There is no doubt this writer is a reader.

The reader is left with the possibility of many interpretations of this text—is the "Tomato Lady" daft, senile, whimsical, a romantic? Did she really poison that first husband? Why has she been married so many times? What caused the divorce? Is that "string of pearls" symbolic? Are the tomatoes symbolic—they are blood red after all—but caged in cellophane?

Form. Form is the next criterion Irmscher identifies. "A writer with a good rhythmic sense will perceive the ebb and flow of generalization and particularity in the development of thought, will know the importance of ending as well as beginning, will recognize where emphasis is needed" (163).

"Tomato Lady" is not your typical five-paragraph paper—introduction, three points, conclusion. This author tells the outcome in her opening sentence, "The elderly woman in the picture has just found the tomatoe [*sic*] of her dreams." How perfectly she sets up the tale. How perfectly she moves into a flashback extending back fifty years without losing control of her story, her character, or her logic. Her final sentence, a nice syntactically mature one, embedded with everything she wants to emphasize, is a call back to her lead. She shows remarkable control of form and craft.

Diction. In diction, the third item on Irmscher's list, this young author excels. "The most characteristic feature of the language of an *A*-paper is the individuality and aptness of the diction" (163). These writers use words they own; they avoid the trite and the pompous. They use big and small words as a matter of style.

Our author chooses her words and phrases carefully: *trivial, crumble, drudgery, earth-shattering boredom, round-cheeked*; she correctly uses the words *lust, wizardry, bewitchers*; the context of finally fulfilling her quest only to be separated by *that damned cellophane* works even though it is a fragment. She comes close to a cliché but saves it from banality with one word. She doesn't write "light at the end of the tunnel," but personalizes it as "light at the end of *her* tunnel," and that slight change makes all the difference.

Mechanics. Irmscher's fourth criterion for *A*-writing, mechanics are generally acceptable in *A*-papers with a tendency to overpunctuate and misspell some words (Irmscher notes that "students who are unusually competent in other regards may be wretched spellers" [164].)

The young author of "Tomato Lady" vacillates in her spelling of *tomato*, and typically in one place, she marks out the *e* and then replaces it, demonstrating her insecurity about the spelling of this word. She also falters with the word *passed*, first writing *past* and then reconsidering, she writes *passed* over it, which is correct. She adds an extra *l* to *traveling,* but uses only one *l* in *cellophane*. We find nothing glaring, nothing distracting in her spelling.

Her punctuation and its range illuminate her literacy. She uses hyphens appropriately in "rock-and-roll," and dashes sparing and correctly; her commas in words and phrases in a series are correct; the colon before the list of the Sunday morning ritual, and all her parentheses are perfectly placed, as is her ellipsis. She puts commas after introductory words and phrases and nonrestrictive clauses, dares to begin a paragraph with *And*, places quotation marks around the adage "the good life" and around "Sunday," shows italics by underlining *needed,* and emphasizes *the perfect tomato* with capital letters. Her terminal punctuation is correct, including the question mark after "What was he doing in the same package with those other inferior vegetables?" She uses one exclamation point after *bewitchers* and the other after "they really *needed* her!" So she does not succumb to the overuse of that mark.

Style. The final criterion is style. Perhaps more than any other element, style marks the *A*-writer. Irmscher tells us that they "have already developed an identifiable style. They are fluent. They know how to control sentences for rhetorical purposes. They use their intuitive senses to create effects that not only emphasize meaning but evoke reaction" (164–165).

"Tomato Lady" is nothing but style. Nice use of items in a series, great parallel structures, attention to detail, specificity such as "10th Anniversary," a command of simple, compound, complex, compound/complex sentences, and something worthwhile to say. What she writes both refreshes and surprises.

Although much more research, perhaps never-ending research, is needed to more closely pinpoint the relationship of writing to cognition, much can be learned by close analysis, observing students as they write, listening closely as students read their writing, and by talking frequently to students about their intended meaning.

APPLICATION

Convey your understanding of the information in this chapter by responding to the quote that opens this chapter. You may respond by sharing examples of children's writing, by writing, by drawing, through discussion, or in some other way.

12

RESEARCH

A fundamentally important aspect of inquiry is its relationship
to reading and writing.
—Barbara K. Stripling □

THE TRUTH ABOUT INQUIRY

No one has all the answers to all the questions. Most have hunches; some have indications; others have proofs. Sometimes while searching for answers more questions evolve. Often when writers need answers they go to the library, they interview, they access reliable sources on the Internet. They know to ask questions of experts. They have learned to investigate. They read. They collect from the most and least likely places. They observe. In this way, they immerse themselves in inquiry.

Why then does this inquiry process seem so foreign to the research done in most schools? To answer this question, we must first examine the way some teachers "cover" research.

Primary School

Typically in the past, primary teachers have not engaged their students in inquiry in any formal way.

Intermediate School

Generally in intermediate classrooms, teachers assign a topic to each student, usually one related to science or social studies. For example, Mrs. Blank tells Marie to write a report about Italy. Marie goes to the library. She finds the "I" volume of the *World Book Encyclopedia.* She takes it to a library desk, because reference materials may not leave the Learning Resource Room. She finds "Italy" wedged between entries on Itaipu and Ithaca. She copies down information like: "Chief manufactures include iron and steel, refined petroleum, chemicals, textiles, motor vehicles, and machinery." Marie continues her report with "North and Central Italy saw the rise of separate city-states; these, despite constant internecine warfare, built huge commercial empires, dominated European finance, and produced the great cultural flowering know as the Renaissance." Marie writes pages about Italy, including words and information she does not understand. Marie persists. She includes information about Vatican City, the Etruscans, the Roman Empire, the Lombards, the Papal States, Risorgimento, the Triple Alliance, and finishes it off with a word about the Red Brigade.

Mostly she unintentionally plagiarizes because she has no context for understanding.

Marie turns in her report. She gets a high mark as she should—fine writers and researchers spent years writing what she has turned in for a grade. Marie and her teacher feel successful. They celebrate Marie's report and those of other students by having a food day. Marie brings pizza. Her friend Joey brings Swiss cheese—the teacher assigned him Switzerland. Her other friend Tamara brings corn chips for Mexico.

And so it goes. Research becomes entrenched in the brain as something tedious, a careful copying of information, not a discovery process of what students want to know.

Middle School

In middle school the scenario goes something like, "Write a report on euthanasia." Students scurry to the library or the Internet. Some go to the encyclopedias; others go to the subject card catalog or they google book titles; they copy Internet articles. If their books have two pages of typeface, they stretch it into a six-page report. If the encyclopedia has a paragraph, they elongate it into several pages. Sometimes if the teacher is pressed for time, the assignment becomes specific, "Write a one-page report on euthanasia." Some students, panicking once they see the magnitude of the topic, search for the shortest entry. Some write that page, fulfill the assignment, and simply stop—mid-sentence, mid-paragraph, mid-point. They have written their page.

Meanwhile, the students at the subject card file scramble for the "E" drawer. If the subject catalog has a single entry for euthanasia, students head for the book on the shelf. Depending upon the library's holdings, there might be one book or there might be several. These students then look for the chapter, subhead, or section on euthanasia. They copy what is there, changing a word or two, claiming it as their own.

If the subject catalog has no entries on the topic, students often give up or go with their friends who have consulted the encyclopedia or called up the word on the Internet. Sometimes students even reject a book listed in the subject catalog if the title does not explicitly contain the word "euthanasia." These "researchers" tend to be highly literal; they do not see research as creative, interactive, satisfying, or a process of following a thread or a lead.

Occasionally, there is a student whose parent takes him or her to the local public library or even a college or university library. If a research librarian helps the youngster, they have more information than they know how to assimilate. They resort to copying again—this time bits and pieces. Sometimes parents write the report.

There are students who opt to fail. They refuse to do the assignment; they don't care about the assignment. Perhaps these are the most honest. Occasionally, there is the student who writes the highly original report about "Youth in Asia."

Teachers actually try to grade this "research." Students with the same paper receive a disciplinary notice for copying another student's work. The "copied from" student sighs, relieved the teacher did not discover the "copier's" source. Usually all students with similar reports fail. If the teacher is creatively punitive, sometimes that block of students share one grade—say a 90 divided equally among the conspirators. Most often, however, students get high marks for writing a "good report."

To circumvent plagiarism, some teachers resort to placing certain books or articles on reserve for student use. These and only these may be used. From time to time, Mrs. Blank laments, "These students don't know how to do research."

High School

By the time students reach high school, the research paper has become a highly refined neurotic exercise. Tom Romano characterizes it this way, "Such repeated, narrow engagement in composition, I believe, prevents students from developing open, flexible attitudes about writing. It inhibits their ability to use writing as a learning tool, and it promotes habits of mind and perceptions of how writing is done that may cripple their growth as writers" (2000, 131).

Typically high school research papers come in two varieties: "literary" and "current events." The literary paper, usually teacher driven, finds the teacher selecting the topics (see intermediate school) or distributing a list of topics from which students draw their topics lottery style. We have even heard of topic auctions that range from classical literary personages—Shakespeare, Yeats, Shelley, and thematic approaches—"the water imagery in Donne's metaphysical poetry," to corpus collections—"the collected works of D. H. Lawrence." Teachers who employ these methods truly believe they are preparing their students for college and see themselves as protectors of the literary canon.

The current topic research paper slightly sophisticates the "research" approach of the middle grades. Rules engulf this process. Requirements such as fifty note cards for an A, five books and ten magazine articles as sources, and exact margins are tenets the students must master.

We hear the teachers' mantra echo on all levels, "We must prepare them for next year."

This so-called research swamps the curriculum, taking up six or nine weeks of valuable class time. Three weeks spent in the library—in libraries unable to support the research being required—and three weeks writing. And what do the students do? Again some make valiant, genuine attempts. Most, though, produce bland papers that lack ownership and voice. If these classrooms were financial institutions they would go bankrupt from the "high" cost of this assignment. Classroom time and learning are too valuable to whittle away "doing" the research paper.

Saner voices must prevail amid this research mania. Rational examinations reveal when students become involved in real research for appropriate reasons, they actually cognitively enjoy it, find it exciting, and rise to its challenge. Effective teachers on all levels incorporate research and library skills into lessons in multitude of ways. This chapter examines some of those ways.

AUTHENTIC INQUIRY

Young children can and should be introduced to inquiry skills at this level. One of the best series we have found to begin beginners on the road to inquiry is Arnone's *Curious Kids Series.* This storybook approach to research skills is novel, colorful, and sound. This series integrates both literacy and skills within a context. Students locate, collect, and organize information. There is a fine *Educators' Guide,* written by Arnone and Coatney, that accompanies each book.

Primary children write reports—actually they love to write about what they have learned or about what they find interesting. Their first engagement with inquiry rises most naturally from all-about books. After hearing them and reading them, they want to write all they know about their expertise. For example, Troy, a first-grader, writes about dinosaurs.

> the is up the hill.
> the dinosar aet met.
> the dinosar is a brontusaris.
> the brontusaris kild a bad dinosar.
> he kild a trontusarirex at the kav
> he ess plans at his kav on his
> prpde and under the sun shin.

[The dinosaur is up the hill. The dinosaur eats meat. The dinosaur is a Brontosaurus. The Brontosaurus killed a bad dinosaur. He killed a Tyrannosaurus Rex at the cave. He has plants at his cave on his property and under the sunshine.]

Troy studied dinosaurs in his class. He read picture and story books about them. He does not need to copy what someone else writes because he is developing his own knowledge of the dinosaur.

Teachers should not quickly dismiss the interest of the child researcher. Jean Piaget classified all of the known mollusks in the Geneva museum by the age of twelve. Children know a great deal about those things that are important to them. They can talk for extended periods of time about *their* topics. Good teachers tap students' interests or motivate students to help them develop interests.

We remember, for instance, Mrs. Crosby, a quirkily delightfully alive person, who taught fourth grade. Shorter than any of her fourth-grade students, she outweighed them by 300 pounds. She did not walk; she waddled. One summer before school started, Mrs. Crosby visited Egypt. For the first three days of class she showed slides. There were fifty-six trays of them—one of her on a camel. The kids spent hours theorizing how she even got on that camel, but they loved those slides because they transported them to a then unknown world. Most of their parents had never traveled outside their home state. A few had fathers who had been drafted in World War II or served in Korea, but they didn't talk about those experiences. So exotic Egypt enthralled the class.

Memory fades the details of how research on Egypt started that year, but memory does not dim the effects of the research. The students built a replica of the Nile River, complete with barges and papyrus ships, down the counter of the room.

They reproduced the Valley of the Kings, temples, and the Sphinx. Their play, *Dr. Livingston, I Presume*, was a sell out. They constructed a mummy, built a sarcophagus, carved death masks, and learned to write in hieroglyphics. Egyptology filled the year. Everything they read, heard, or watched in math, science, social studies, art, music, or language arts centered around one of the world's oldest, developed civilizations. Not once did any of them copy a report from a book, instead they read books to became experts about different aspects of Egypt. Their love affair with everything foreign to their small town had begun. When the Tutankhamen exhibit opened in the National Museum in Washington, they knew and identified with Howard Carter's words when asked if he could see anything, "Yes, wonderful things."

If practices like those of Mrs. Crosby and Troy's teacher indicate how research should be taught, then what do students and teachers need to hear these saner voices? The first step is to understand the inquiry method and its attendant research processes.

The Inquiry

"Inquiry-based learning is an approach to instruction that centers on the research process" (Kuhlthau in Donham et al. 1). The key word is *process*. Writing before, during, and after inquiry ensures a systematic journey throughout the research. Still, like all writing, inquiry is recursive. We have designed a model for inquiry schemata applicable for all levels with allowances made for time, topic, and diversification.

Inquiry for Primary Students

Young students begin their inquiry, as does everyone, by tapping previous knowledge, experiences, and observations. This helps the young researcher select a topic for research. With proper guidance from the teacher, they develop some questions, make some predictions, and formulate a hypothesis, which they investigate. They, like any researcher, read, think, and eventually write their findings. The point to remember here is that developmentally the process can happen on the primary level.

Previous knowledge, most probably, is the basis for choosing a topic in the first place. For

Fig. 12.1. Carroll/Wilson Inquiry Schemata.

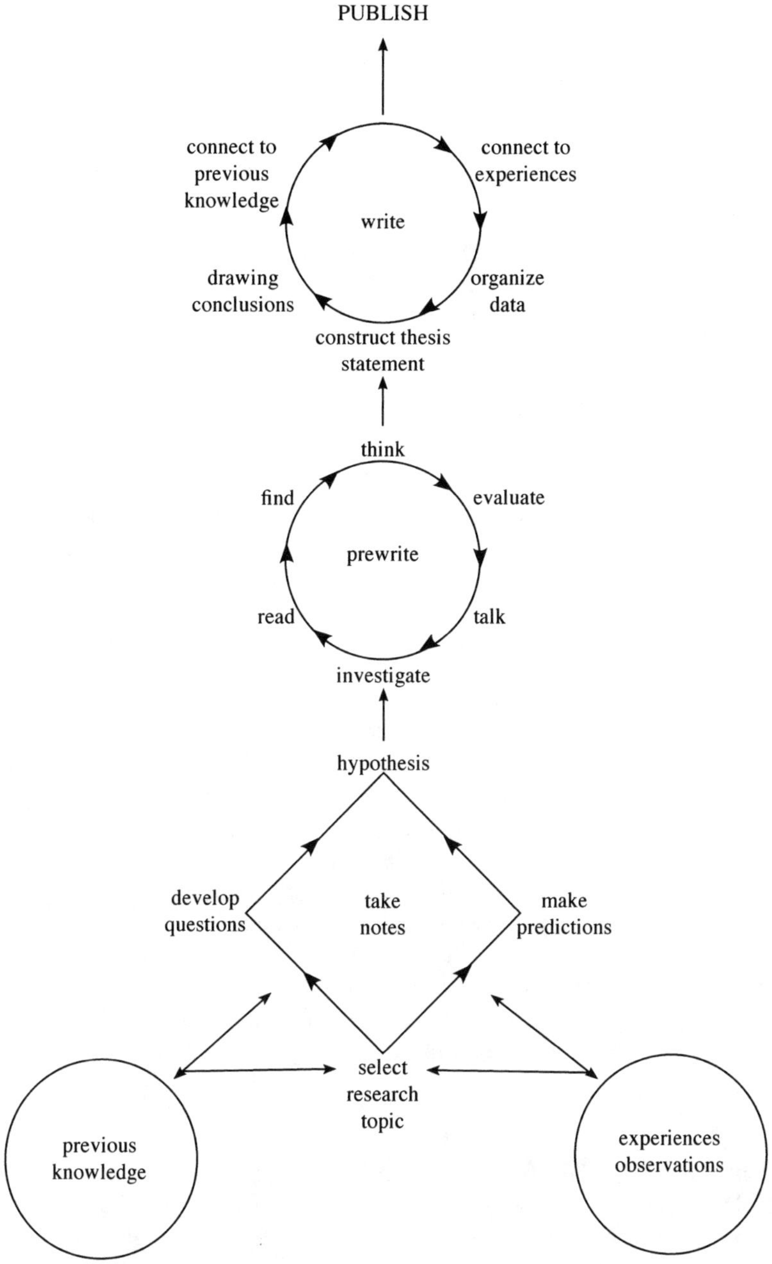

PUBLISH

connect to previous knowledge

connect to experiences

write

drawing conclusions

organize data

construct thesis statement

think

find

evaluate

prewrite

read

talk

investigate

hypothesis

develop questions

take notes

make predictions

select research topic

previous knowledge

experiences observations

example, Audrey chose to write about "The Mice" because there were mice in the classroom, so she had prior knowledge about mice. When the mice had babies, Audrey coupled her prior knowledge with her experiences and observations. She eagerly watched the mice and shared her observations in writing. For an egocentric first-grader, convinced her observations were as new to readers as they were to her, she wrote with passion. More importantly she clearly showed germinating research skills. She was excited about keeping a journal, anticipating as all good researchers anticipate, new and important revelations.

The Mice
by Audrey

Over the weekend our mice had
babys and there were twelve babys.
My teacher said that Leah and I could
have a baby mouse but Leah has first
choise. The mice are pink and thier
ears and eyes are clossed when they
are born. They sort of look like
very very small pigs. They are very
cute and they were born on Saturday.
We are going to keep a journal about
the mice and write a little every
day.

Leah, on the other hand, conveys her sense of Eureka! She provided the details that interested her: the tension of waiting two weeks, exactly when they were born, and how the daddy was moved. She speculated about their appearance and was as joyful as Audrey about keeping a journal.

The Mice

After about 2 weeks of waiting the
baby mice were born! They were born
late Friday night. I called
Mrs. Dombroski Saterday to ask it
Dewey had her babys. She said yes she
also said she moved the dady into the
other kage incase he ate any babys.
& she said I could come Sunday to see
the baby mice. Some times I wunder
how little pink harless baby mice
will become beutiful mice like thair
Mom and Dad. Thair were at least 12 or
more. We are going to keep ajrnal on them.

by Leah

Both students were not only becoming experts on baby mice but also experts on research skills. Already they knew the importance of establishing a context—the time and place of the research. They made careful observations and wrote accurate descriptions. Audrey understood her audience. She knew not all children have seen baby mice, so she used a metaphor of the more common pig to better inform her reader. Leah manifested superior insight because she projected that there would be nothing left—no more data if the daddy ate the babies.

They both expect to learn more; they both know the power and permanency of recording their observations in journals to keep track of what they discover.

Ross, age six, who planted his bean, also showed his research capabilities. Notice how he divided his paper by days and attempted to both write about the experiment and illustrate it. He clearly observed it until it "rodid" and he began helping Jessica. (See Fig. 12.2.)

Fig. 12.2. Ross's Science Paper.

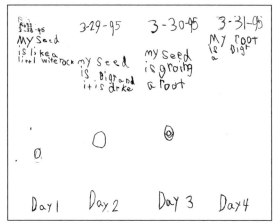
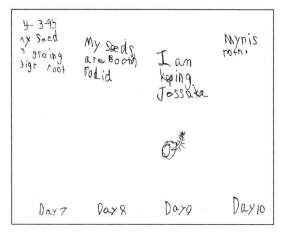

Audrey, Leah, Ross, and Troy have teachers who understand not only the young student, but also the inquiry process. With guidance from their teachers, these students selected an area to research. Key to this process was the focus and organization that the act of selection required. As they dismissed some material and prioritized other material, the direction from their teachers allowed for exploration and risk-taking.

When Troy wrote about dinosaurs, his research area, he showed that he had a working knowledge of the prehistoric beasts. When he narrowed his topic to the Brontosaurus, he demonstrated something all researchers learn—you can't study and write about everything. And although his hypothesis about Brontosaurus being a meat eater was incorrect, he knew that plants were key to their survival and that dinosaurs were territorial.

Troy's process follows the inquiry schema. He investigated, read, thought, evaluated, and discussed dinosaurs. He read several books and watched a video in an effort to analyze the information. He talked to his classmates about the Brontosaurus. His interview, while not reflected in his writing, consisted of a dialogue with an all-important third-grader he had met in the library. The third-grader shared his favorite dinosaur book with Troy.

When Troy started to write, he dismissed many of the things he could have said. His drafts showed evidence of selecting and constructing information that stuck to his topic. When he conferred with is teacher, he added the "trontusarirex" after his teacher asked him what kind of dinosaur the Brontosaurus killed.

He typed his piece on the computer and shared it with students in a read-around. His research completed for the time being, he went on to write about other dinosaurs he had learned about while researching the Brontosaurs.

Young Students as Experts

The goal for young students involved in inquiry is not to have them master some type of form or genre of writing, but to nurture their affection for and attraction to discovery. Young students epitomize true inquiry because they naturally want to know more about things; however, they do not always want to know about the things the teacher decides are important. They prefer to select what they want to discover. Their needs are interpersonal and representational—interpersonal in the sense that they co-discover as classmates discover, and representational in the sense that they want tangible proof of what they have learned. When teachers allow students to choose their own topics, both are rewarded by the natural high that true inquiry brings.

Often teachers worry needlessly over the preoccupation of children about a given topic. But the truth is children become consumed with writing, learning, experiencing, and using everything related to their area of inquiry. This is nothing more than the inchoate stage of becoming an expert on the topic.

Instead of discouraging such inquiry, the teacher should facilitate the study. Children taught at a young age to trust their own learning make better researchers. Personal knowledge translates into formal knowledge. What a child discovers today, he or she may study more deeply tomorrow.

We have a sample book begun by Josh, a second-grader who told us unequivocally that he was writing a book about gorillas "for little kids 'cause there aren't any books on gorillas for them." Fascinated with the primates since preschool, this student had already read all the books on gorillas in the districts' elementary and middle schools. He began his book in second grade and had completed ten chapters. He readily gave us copies. Reading them, we could easily see that he had internalized the information on gorillas and was gearing his language to "little kids."

Fig. 12.3. Josh's Gorillas.

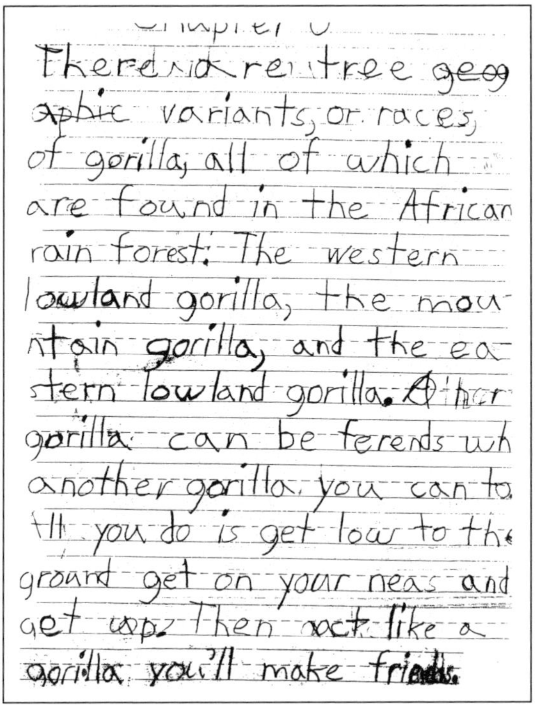

One example from his Chapter 6: "There are three geographic variants, or races of gorilla, all of which are found in the African rain forest: the western lowland gorilla, the mountain gorilla, and the eastern lowland gorilla. Another gorilla can be friends with another gorilla. You can too. All you do is get low to the ground, get on your knees, and get up. Then act like a gorilla. When he sees you you'll make friends."

Notice, he simplifies the first sentence by crossing out the adjective *geographic,* and while he knows the word *variants,* he isn't sure his young readers will, so he supplies an easier synonym.

He also addresses his audience when giving directions on becoming friends with gorillas. What a sense of audience.

Interestingly he spells *variants* correctly, but he misses *friends* and *knees.* If we hadn't watched him writing this portion of his book, we would have been tempted to explain it away by saying he copied the first part. But, indeed, he did not. All of that information came from his head.

When we touched base with his fifth-grade teacher, she told us he was still working on his gorilla book—for publication. Reconnecting again when he was in middle school, we were told he received a scholarship to work with the gorillas at the San Diego Zoo. His book helped him attain this award. We have no doubt he will emerge as a leading gorilla expert in his lifetime.

Third-grader Julie Fannin shared her original and important research, "How I Got My Name," with an impressive eye and ear for detail. She has learned the lessons of accuracy. She quoted her sources. She learned the power of showing not telling. As she took the reader through the experience, she informed and settled for all time how and why she got her name.

Fig. 12.4. Julie's Research.

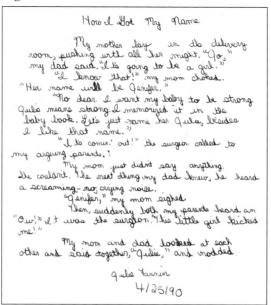

What is more important to a child—exploring her name or copying information? How much easier it will be to engage Julie in extensions after her initial research into her name. True research leads to new and often unexpected places. Julie may learn there are experts in the field of names, that the study of names is called *onomastics,* and that *etymology* is the study of the meanings of names and words; she may enjoy discovering what these experts say. Julie's curiosity may be peaked by reading books about how people got their names such as the major character in Bill Martin's *Knots on a Counting Rope* or books about how kids feel about their names such as the major character in Kevin Henkes's *Chrysanthemum.* She may watch videos about names and family histories with more understanding. Allowing Julie to become acquainted with her topic and discovering the richness of the topic may get her involved with genealogy as an extension of her original research. Julie's teacher may have endowed her with an area that becomes an avocation, which, in turn, may enhance the quality of Julie's life. The point of inquiry is not always the destination but the journey.

Nor does the child have to report the research in dry, dull prose. Bruner in *Acts of Meaning* reminds teachers of the power of the narrative.

Narrative requires . . . four crucial grammatical constituents if it is to be effectively carried out. It requires, first, a means for emphasizing human action or agentivity—action directed toward goals controlled by agents. It requires, secondly, that a sequential order be established and maintained—that events and states be linearized in a standard way. Narrative, thirdly, also requires a sensitivity to what is canonical and what violates canonicality approximating a narrator's perspective: it cannot, in the jargon of narratology, be voiceless. (77)

If teachers want to engage young students into the ownership of research, then the research should be narrative in nature and in structure and in voice.

Inquiry for Intermediate and Middle School Learners

The intermediate and middle school student, like the elementary student, has a wealth of knowledge and a diversity of interests upon which to draw. Part of the difficulty working with them, though, is they think they don't know enough. Because they are moving from an egocentric perception of their world to a more adult perception, they realize they may not be the center of the universe and therefore may not have enough of a handle on a topic to be considered an expert. While debatable and in many ways erroneous, this perception nevertheless exists.

Intermediate and middle school students find the Inquiry Schemata helps them focus and proceed in a systematic way through their processes. Focus is their Waterloo. We see it in their approach to daily living. They experiment with clothing styles, hairstyles, attitudes, and peer groups quickly and randomly. They are the instant generation, text messaging, IM-ing, iPods dangling, cell phones ringing, they jump from topic to topic like meerkats on the warpath. Getting them to focus is difficult, but not impossible. By following the schemata, they have a consistent path to follow, yet one that is not formulaic. We suggest they use the K-W approach as their launch. By writing out what they know about a topic and what they want to know, they more easily move into developing questions, making predictions, and formulating a reasonable hypothesis.

Instead of concentrating a large amount of time and effort on one big research project, these students profit by undertaking smaller projects and shorter papers. Projects more manageable and less intimidating work best.

The TV Model. "TV and Term Papers" outlines one possible approach to turn research into more creative assignments. By following the model of television news shows such as *Sixty Minutes*, students are challenged to be accurate and integrate their research into readable, friendly prose (Carroll 85). She suggests assimilating research skills into the format students absorb when watching TV news shows or the new rage of cop forensic shows. Both demonstrate research, documentation, investigation, exploration, and inquiry. Carroll's article clearly shows that by shifting the focus from the genre to the methods of research, students explore within limitations.

Documented Essays. Documented essay also work with students of all ages. (See Appendix E.) Even fifth-graders respond to them. Jodi Hughes describes, in *Encouraging the Process: Teaching Reading and Writing in the Fifth Grade Classroom,* how she moved from the "typical research report about a famous person or an animal" to a documented essay. When she did, the students embraced the documented essay with zeal.

A student writing about bike riding looked at different types of bikes, bike trails found in the area, and bicycle safety rules. One student, interested in Marine Biology because she loves dolphins and whales, researched information about Sea World trainers and ways to train animals. Once the students shared their pieces and discussed the ways to incorporate research, they felt comfortable with their topic and found appropriate places to add citations. (Forthcoming from Absey & Co.)

Multigenre Papers. Tom Romano has given us the multigenre paper. Inspired by Michael Ondaatje's *The Collected Works of Billy the Kid,* Romano tells us, "Out of his inquiry into Billy the Kid, Ondaatje created a complex, multilayered, multivoiced blend of genres, each revealing information about his topic, each self-contained, making a point of its own, unconnected to other genres by conventional transitional devices" (2000, 4). The "multi-" in "multigenre" is exactly what appeals to intermediate and middle school students.

Further supporting multigenre research, Camille Allen, inspired by Tom Romano, itemizes how this type of inquiry helps students build skills. Students

- learn to conduct research

- read often

- write

- speak in small- and large-group settings

- learn to listen

- learn to self-evaluate

- learn to use technology

- develop thinking and problem-solving skills

- learn to think creatively and imaginatively

- learn organizational skills

- learn to collaborate. (9–11)

When introducing inquiry to intermediate and middle-school students, we pull the prewriting techniques covered in previous chapters. In fact, the writing process does not change because of research. Actually, if you ask any scientist, they will tell you "all is process." The key for the middle-school student is selecting the research area, developing questions, making predictions, and settling upon a hypothesis. We ask students to read primary sources and conduct interviews. The publishing aspect of this level can also be broadened to include other ways of going public with research. Again, the idea of designing a news program format or using a multigenre approach intensifies the challenge and motivates students. For students unable to use or acquire video equipment, live performances are equally motivational.

Research Areas for the Middle School

Regardless of the socioeconomic or educational background, all students have interests. Working with a group of eighth-grade, urban students revealed their interests differed considerably from their suburban cousins. One inner-city student expressed dismay when his teacher announced they would be researching the medieval period. "What are you interested in?" we asked. "Weapons," he answered. Undaunted we responded, "Then you're going to love the weaponry of this period. Why don't you see what you can find out about cat-o'-nine-tails and the catapult?"

As the class made its way through a study of Arthurian legends and a selection of *Canterbury Tales*, the students delved into topics such as alchemy, dungeons, and dragon lore. They read Cynthia Voigt's *On Fortune's Wheel* and Christopher Paolini's *Eragon*; they studied herbology and illumination. The young man who had scoffed at medieval studies produced a series of drawings depicting ancient weapons and their uses. Not only did he search out information, but he also spoke with local collectors of weapons. The principal of the school was surprised when this student arranged for a local retired general to speak to the class about his collection.

What on the surface had the earmarking of gang activity and antisocial behavior, was productively rechanneled. We guided the student into research that directly placed the student in contact with one of the most conservative members of the community—a general. Was this student saved from the ravages of gang neighborhoods and a fascination with the bizarre? No. But neither was the student alienated from research, discovery, or inquiry. Neither was the student turned away from a learning process and a place called school. In fact, the retired general made quite an impact on the young man, especially when the general invited him to help with the display of his weapons collection at a local museum.

Following the Research

The major consideration at the intermediate and middle-school level is not so much mastering the conventions of writing research as it is mastering an understanding of the concept of research and the skills required to conduct it. Developmentally, intermediate and middle school is not the time to snare students into the mechanics of documentation, but it is the time to trap students into understanding the power of documentation. As they say on the forensic shows, students must learn "to follow the evidence" in order to formulate a hypothesis. They must learn that they don't "make the evidence" fit their hypothesis. And, most importantly, they must look at the evidence in context.

These young writers don't need to copy, copy, copy. They need to distinguish between their own idea or words and those that are borrowed. Tapping another TV show, *Numb3rs*, we offer an apt analogy between borrowing data for inquiry and borrowing in mathematics. Borrowing from the "tens" column for the "ones" column has consequences. The borrowing must be noted or something is lost. Sometimes when the borrowing is done incorrectly, or if too much is borrowed mathematically, the answer is wrong. Because students have been working with this concept since the second grade, under good teaching, they easily transfer it to research. When information is borrowed, it needs to be accounted for by giving credit. If too much is borrowed, the paper is incorrect because it is no longer theirs; they have merely copied the work or works of others. The concept is relatively simple. Simple attribution works but worrying students over correct bibliographical form at this age only repels them instead of attracting them to research.

Once they internalize the "rightness" of giving credit, intermediate and middle-school students must grapple with giving credit. We expect students to give credence to the validity of others. When students write and incorporate the ideas and words of others, then they are developing the skills that will allow them to become better researchers. Carroll in her article, "Plagiarism: The Unfun Game" recommends the "personnoting page." This page, which parallels acknowledgments, is "the place where students can acknowledge everyone who helped with their papers in any way—teachers, friends, family, librarians, authors, lyricists, lecturers, and editors (even Webster and Roget)" (93). Her kid-friendly term and practical idea cultivates the student researcher.

Cultivating Researchers

A researcher is not made in a day. Researchers are nurtured and guided through the processes of inquiry. Never should research be an isolated exercise done in one paper on one occasion during the year—as in the infamous fifteen-page research paper. Research is a state of mind. Again, saner voices must influence the curricula of middle schools. Students who only engage in research once a year for one paper hardly have the time to internalize the skills necessary to understand and use research as a lifelong skill.

Teachers intuitively and educationally know this to be true. They know that research is not something done once, in May. They, too, have been the victims of too many courses where the end product is a research paper. They remember what and how they went about doing this research. They remember when it was real research and when it was a pseudo-academic. Teachers, who record what they do in their classrooms, what they diagnose, treat, and cure, what they watch die, and what they watch come to life are the real researchers. These teachers use their research abilities not only for graduate study but for professional reasons. These teachers have learned the lessons of supporting evidence and borrowed ideas. They readily give credit to ideas they use, and they eagerly receive the recognition for what they have discovered in their inquiry of teaching and learning. Teachers who actively engage in and write research have students who do the same.

Research is not so foreign to middle school students. After all, they are constantly studying and researching what it takes to become teenagers. They are not immune or allergic to inquiry. With the right direction, these students understand the need for research and grow to respect it.

Inquiry for High School Students

Every phase of the Inquiry Schemata demands that high school students produce deeper, more sophisticated, more rigorous, more detailed, more precise papers. At this level, the scrutiny becomes formalized, the writing meticulous, the documentation standardized. But the Inquiry Schemata remains the same. At this level, students have more previous knowledge, experiences, and observations upon which to draw. Their topics range from contemporary social problems to ideological ones. No longer interested in weaponry or how a bean grows, these students gravitate to issues and ideas.

The advanced level of the inquiry process that works best with high school students starts in the reflexive mode and moves to the extensive. Starting with their journals and prewriting, students explore their interests. They reread their writing to consider extrapolating an issue or a problem. This process parallels the one where the student identifies the best genre for a piece of writing, except here we encourage students to choose topics based on the evidence. In this way, they will already have basic support for the topic.

For example, Jerry, an eleventh-grade student, wrote one of his reflexive pieces about hitting a dog while driving down the street. To move Jerry into the extensive mode, it was easy to suggest he write a letter to the editor about the necessity of leash laws and the value of dog tags. Once he completed that inquiry and writing, we helped Jerry identify clearly factual points as opposed to points based on conjecture or opinion.

At this point Jerry began his investigation in earnest. He examined what others discovered and recorded about his topic. He interviewed people working with animal control, veterinarians, breeders, and pet owners. He read statutes and opinions on the subject. During this process, we taught him research skills—everything from how to use a periodical index to how to ascertain and access reliable sources on the Internet, from how to paraphrase to how to record findings. When he shared with his group in class, Jerry was able to articulate his findings and, together with the group, evaluate them.

Jerry moved his writing from the letter genre to the essay genre; he was still intensely interested and focused upon in his topic.

Requirements of fifty note cards became superfluous for this type of inquiry; Jerry had much more: audio and videotapes, photocopies of articles, pictures of animals. For emotional appeal, he had a letter from an elderly lady who lost her dog to a drunk driver. She begged drivers to be more careful. The kids sat riveted as Jerry read the letter—most thought of their own pets.

Jerry used the tools of a good researcher—everything out there. Vygotsky would say he "heaped." When he wrote his documented essay, he constructed his data into complexes—what connected in like ways and what differed; he grouped items by function and linguistically made dynamic links that explained his position. Jerry did not suffer from the pseudo-concepts carefully copied note cards sometimes yield. He learned that research is messy work and everything does not fall neatly into preordained cognitive slots.

Then Jerry was left to draw conclusions based on the evidence and the connections. He had to use his higher-level thinking to decide how he would present his views and the views of others. He had to consider his purpose. Did he want to persuade or inform? Did he want to inject some narrative anecdotes into his essay? Did he want to set up his paper as one of argumentation? We couldn't advise him at this point until he explored more, wrote more, and thought more about the impact of his research.

After Jerry completed his essay, he reconsidered his hypothesis. He had data now, he had to use the data (evidence) and his hypothesis to write his thesis statement. If Jerry were in a traditional classroom, he would have been asked before he had done any type of inquiry "to write a thesis statement." Too often teachers bypass the hypothesis and have students jump directly to writing a thesis statement. (And teachers wonder why students do poorly on research.) In doctoral research it is common for the researcher to develop a hypothesis, write a proposal, conduct tests, do preliminary research, and finally write a thesis that proves or disproves the hypothesis. In the research loop of the traditional classroom, students and the teacher skip this process and "jump to the chase." Students not quite certain about the importance of the thesis statement, often end up with a weak one.

With all his reading and study, Jerry was ready to document his sources and present a piece of writing that convincingly and coherently dealt with his topic. Jerry moved from what he knew into what others helped him to know better, more deeply, or differently. He never had to completely leave the arena of his own knowledge. He never had to report on those things about which he knew nothing.

Jerry became a lifelong learner because he had the Carroll/Wilson Inquiry Schemata to use over and over again for everything from how to buy a car, to the effect of inflation on his net income. With that rock solid basis, he continued to research any of his inquiries.

What do students think of research? Mike Gill's essay, "The Eyes of the Beholder," gives us a glimpse. Satirical in tone, there are underlying messages in phrases like, "dreaded junior-year composition research paper," "total self-abuse and mind-wracking impossibilities," "writing failures," "possessed by the devil," and "total doom." His essay, reprinted here with its chilly ending of spending all that time, of feeling pleased with what he had accomplished, only to garner an eighty-seven, lives as a reminder to all secondary teachers about the hazards of just going through the motions of research instead of making it an inquiry process.

The Eyes of the Beholder

Michael M. Gill, Senior

Christmas break was finally over and with the fond memories of my relatives and many gifts still rumbling through my mind, I grumpily walked up to the bleak, puke green doors that led into the academic halls. I stood there for a couple of minutes contemplating suicide, for on the other side of those doors was the most feared task my feeble human brain could ever conceive—the dreaded Junior composition research paper. I shrugged my shoulders, gave a small meaningless stone a kick, and flung the doors open; sadly committing myself to eight weeks of total self abuse and mind wracking impossibilities.

I walked down the corridor, entered room twenty-three twenty-three, and quickly took my seat by the trashcan. Coincidently, I knew I'd probably be having to use the receptacle either to vomit or to discard many writing failures. I looked around the room and noticed that everyone in the class looked as boring as they had last month. You see, nobody wears their new clothes they got for Christmas until later in the week because that's the "cool" thing to do.

But then my theory was totally ruined when Gary Emptyboat walked in wearing new everything—even bright red ropers. My theory was then further demolished as Mrs. Hildabroom walked into the room flaunting her new dress from Sax Sixth Street. She had undoubtedly purchased the dress with her slightly overused American Express Platinum card. She seemed so righteous as she walked up to the table where she began to pass out little neatly stacked pieces of paper. I thought, for a second, that I heard lightning and thunder along with a hideous laugh. "No, that's impossible." So I decided to forget the whole thing.

Mrs. Hildabroom then spoke in a tone that I had never heard her speak in before. It was as if she were possessed by the devil.

"As you all know, this semester we will be working on your Junior composition research papers. I hope that you've been thinking about what you are going to research, since we start taking note cards on Wednesday."

I could hear her laugh deep in her throat as she walked down the aisle. Then, as if the world were about to end, a moan went up over the entire room. Such was the noise, Mr. Fixitcorridor and his sidekick Mr. Small would probably be down in the room in a minute having a cow in the hallway. Then I thought to myself, "Hmm, what can I do my research paper on? I'm not interested in anything but swimming and that would be boring." Then like a flash of lightning I thought, "Hey, I'm a party kinda guy and what kind of parties are the best? Fraternity parties! I'll do my paper on fraternities—yeah, that's the ticket."

Well, from that point on, I had nothing but pure hard work ahead of me and the subject seemed to beckon me like the sirens to Ulysses. It sounded great but I was headed towards total doom and a certain early grave. As my peers stood up and proudly told Hazel Hildabroom their subjects they had chosen, I gradually began to think my topic was not worthy enough to compete with the others in class. First of all, there was somebody researching brains and brain surgeons and another euthanasia. Then some dweeb actually wanted to learn about the effects of sugar substitutes on the body. Finally to top things off, Willy Snide wanted to find out if dreams and R.E.M. could ever be reality or something to that extent.

When it was my turn to speak, I felt my stomach knot up as I lifted myself from the chair.

"Fraternities," I said as I blended my words with a cough.

"What was that Michael?" She called me Michael, because she thought it was really a cute name.

I spoke again, "Fraternities and the benefits of the Greek way of life in college."

Apparently she was not impressed, but what really made me sick was when she said in a very bored voice, "Oh, that's very nice." And she went on, not bothering to ask why or anything. I knew right then and there I was in Big Time Trouble. If she didn't think my subject was worthy of her class, she would probably just laugh at it when I turned the paper in. "I'll show her," I thought to myself, "I'm going to write the best damn research appear she's ever seen!" That very night I went down to the public library and began on my quest for information on my so called "great" subject. I looked and searched and searched some more. Nothing! Not one damn thing on fraternities. Then I figured, "Hey, college libraries must have something about fraternities. Right!"

Wrong. Not one of the libraries in town had anything I could use in my paper that would prove my thesis. That's when I really started to worry about how I could find the information I needed. Well, to make a long story short, the next six weeks were spent writing letters to colleges all over America, getting bits of information here or scrounging magazines from there. I wrote to so may Inter-Fraternity Councils that I figured it would be easier to just xerox the letters or better yet, not even do the whole thing. Just then the haunting figure of Mrs. Hildabroom, dressed in her furs from Padre's came flashing into my mind.

"Oh, Michael Darling—" as if she were trying to imitate ZaZa Gabore, "if you don't receive a passing grade on this research paper, you won't ever graduate! Ha, Ha, Ha, Ha, Ha."

The laughs went right through my soul like Chinese food goes through a Wisconsin dairy farmer with a bad case of the runs. I was left standing in a cold sweat as I placed another letter into our little blue mailbox in the front yard. This was the same box, which I prayed would in a week or two bring me the massive amounts of letters, articles, or books thus saving me from another year of Junior composition. Well, to say the least, I received about three pieces of literature which I could actually use. The rest was kindling for the fire inside the mailbox. I guess I just started blaming that stupid box for its inadequacy to pick up letters of the opposite sex, or something like that, and burned the little sucker to the ground.

I guess by now, you can tell that, yes, I was getting a little crazy about the whole gosh-darn thing. But just as I was getting ready to commit hara-kiri, my brother Larry, back from college, was reading something with great intensity. As he walked by, ignoring the fact that his only brother was about to sacrifice his body to the God of English, I noticed the book said something about Fraternities! I jumped up amid the candle and incense, threathened my brother's life, and grabbed the book from his shaking hands. I looked at the cover and cried tears of joy. The cover read: "A Modern Guide to Fraternities and Sororities."

I was saved. It was a gift from the great god of English, Neddy Wilso, who in his infinite wisdom had sent a miracle to a poor distressed sixteen year old. Now I was having more success than ever. By now miracles were happening daily. I was receiving books from people I had never even written and even got a phone call from a member of the Phi Theta Delta Fraternity in Lubbock, Texas. I don't think it really counted though, it was only my brother asking us to send him some clean underwear, and babbling about a little accident that happened during hell week.

The weeks went by very fast as I was writing and recopying. By now, the week before the paper was due, I had the whole thing ready to be sent to my father's trusty secretary. Yes, I was three days ahead of schedule and very proud of myself. I think I might have even impressed Mrs. Hildabroom . . . just a little bit. Now all I had to do was take it easy. Relax. Let everyone else sweat it out. I was done with everything and those who weren't could go jump for all I cared. I actually enjoyed myself, in a sick kind of way, walking around the room telling people that they had typed their whole bibliography wrong. Or saying that we were supposed to use double space lines instead of single space.

But what really got me off was rubbing salt into the wounds of all those "brilliant" people who chose so called marvelous topics to write about. They just kept telling me things like "Oh, I'll get it done by tomorrow," or "Sure, I can type this in a couple of hours. No problem."

I just had to laugh out loud, and I'm sure those people got together after class and planned to beat me senseless on the way to school Friday morning. To my pleasure, everything, went fine and I was not killed driving to school. In fact, everything from that day on seemed to be just a little bit better than they were eight weeks ago. I walked to those same puke colored doors, as I had done all year and before I opened them, I examined them even closer. To my surprise, they didn't at all look too badly discolored. In fact, the whole world looked better to me. The grass was greener, the people still looked the same, but they seemed a bit more friendly. I opened the doors, and to my amazement, they did not creak any longer.

On the way up to Mrs. Hildabroom's desk, I looked down at the manila envelope that held my hard work and hundreds of hours of research, and was very pleased with myself. Pleased was I, because I accomplished something that just a few weeks ago, seemed to be an almost impossible task. Not only had I increased my knowledge, but I felt that I had matured a great deal in this small period of time.

I still received an eighty seven. Oh, well, such is life.

The Personal Pronoun in Research

We heard a teacher say, "Students cannot use the first person pronoun in the research paper because they are not experts on what they are researching." In fact, this teacher held to this tenet so tightly, her grading policy reflected her strong belief—automatic failure on the entire paper. Since her school had the policy that the "junior research paper" on a current topic had to be mastered before a junior could receive credit for the year's course, the principal had initiated a review board comprised of teachers and parents to arbitrate disputes about grades.

One year a student who used the first person pronoun and her mother met with this panel to complain that the teacher's dictum was unfair. The girl and parent both reluctantly agreed that the dictum had been posted in advance, but the student had elected to disregard it. When the panel questioned this absolute rule she reiterated, "Students are not experts on what they are researching."

Sensing failure and frustration, the student exploded in front of everyone. No one could have predicted her vehement and impassioned response. She turned to the teacher and asked, "Have you had an abortion? I have, and I think I earned the right to be an expert on the topic." No student should ever be thrust into this situation.

School is no place for rules that reflect the attitude that students cannot be experts. Russell Stovall, by the time he had reached high school, had already syndicated his news column, "Whiz Kid," in national papers, appeared on Johnny Carson, and knew more about computers than 98 percent of the faculty. He was an acknowledged expert.

Consider the expertise of this young writer:

Arthritis and Rheumatism: The Common Chronic Cripplers

"Twisted," "distorted," "grotesque" these are harsh words to say about some-one I love, but they create an image of his body. I can see the pain in his eyes. He has trouble doing things that seem trivial to the rest of us. He seems like another man—feeble and old.

Although the memory is vague, I still remember when he was a strong hard working farmer. He used to lift me up to the tractor seat and let me help plow. After all the chores were finished, it was time for fun. On this farm was the world's best fishin' hole. When we would go there I got to ride in the back of the pickup. I did not really like fishing, but I would do anything to be with him. Perhaps he felt the same because he did not make me put those dirty worms on the hook to take those slimy fish off; he took care of that. Then something happened, he began to lose weight and his hands and feet became useless appendages. He would sit in his chair all day wringing his crippled hands refusing any help. He had too much pride.

Once or twice after he became ill we went fishing—only this time it was different. Instead of riding in the back of the pickup, I drove. The truck had to be backed up to the porch so that he would only have to exert a minimum amount of effort. We would slowly drive to the tank, being careful not to hit any hard bumps. When there, he would slowly creep up the ramp that had been specially built. I took a great deal for me to bait his hook with worms and take the fish off, but being unable to do these things himself, it was up to me to do the dirty work.

What kind of illness could be so bad that it could totally disable my grandfa-ther? A common disease. Usually not thought of as a chronic crippler, arthritis crippled him. Arthritis stole my grandfather.

Arthritis, rheumatism, and gout are among the oldest diseases known to af-fect human being. Even before the time of Hippocrates, evidence of the occur-rence of the disease has been found in mummies and other ancient civilizations.

The writer of this research has good reason to search for answers to her questions about arthritis. She considers them in her conclusion. "Will I become a victim like my grandfather?" How absurd it would be if she were to write, "Will *one* become a victim like *one's* grandfather?" Taking the first person out of research is to distance the research from what the discoverer is discovering. Practices that promote this type of writing are bound to produce perfectly bland pa-pers, contested papers, hostility, and reluctance to or avoidance of inquiry.

The I-Search Paper

Ken Macrorie sums up the issue of the learner as researcher in two words: I search. That's the truth of any inquiry. *Re*-search implies complete detachment, absolute objectivity. Time to clear that miasma and admit that the best searchers act both subjectively and objectively and write so that professionals and the public can understand their searches and profit from them. Time to get down to the basics, which are not note cards, but curiosity, need, rigor in judging one's findings and the opinions of experts in helping others test the validity of the search.

In *Searching Writing*, Macrorie details steps for the I-search paper. An alternative to the research paper, which he feels "are bad jokes. They're funny because they pretend to be so much and actually are so little" (1980, 161). He says a search should be done when someone wants to answer a question. We recommend those interested in learning more about this alternative method of inquiry, read his book.

Narrative Inquiry

Jerome Bruner in *Acts of Meaning* reminds us of the power of the legal narrative. Mimi Guarneri in *The Heart Speaks* talks about the medical narrative. Patricia Lambert Stock, in her 2004 Presidential Address presented at the NCTE 94th Annual Convention, spoke of story in educational research. Referencing Vivian Paley's work, Stock says, "One of the things I mean when I speak of the integrity of Paley's work is that she uses story and storytelling not only as a means of teaching but also as a means of shaping, conducting, sharing, and arguing for the findings of her research" (14). The business world uses story as a differentiator. Why has story become so popular in our new paradigm? Stephen Denning, in *The Springboard: How Storytelling Ignites Action in Knowledge-Era Organizations,* sums it up best, "Storytelling doesn't replace analytical thinking. It supplants it by enabling us to imagine new perspectives and new worlds. . . . Abstract analysis is easier to understand when seen through the lens of a well-chosen story" (xvii). We believe what is true in law, medicine, corporate governance, finance, and higher education pertains equally—perhaps even more—to young students coming early to inquiry in their educational journey. The research in which students engage can be illuminated and comprehended best through a well-placed narrative—an anecdote, a slice of memory, an event that gives context to the text.

With facts so widely available, so accessible on the Internet, so easy to google, so easy to manipulate, so handy anyone can instantaneously offer a statistic or a fact to support or counter other statistics and facts, what begins to make the difference is the affective context that narrative provides. "When our lives are brimming with information and data, it's not enough to marshal an effective argument. Someone somewhere will inevitably tract down a counterpoint to rebut your point. The essence of persuasion, communication, and self-understanding has become the ability also to fashion a compelling narrative" (Pink 65–66).

We encourage teachers to consider promoting the narrative because as Hillocks reminds us, "Without question students should become proficient in many kinds of writing. But there are many reasons for including narrative throughout the curriculum. Knowing how to write narratives can become a base for other kinds of writing and for studying literature" (2007, 9).

On the Web site "We All Use Math Every Day," a consultant for *Numb3rs*, the popular TV show, illustrates through episode 318, "Democracy," aired March 9, 2007, that inductive reasoning, problem solving, pattern analysis and recognition, and probability and simulation are just some of the math concepts the show tackles through story. To reinforce the power of story in math on a personal level, while watching it we often say, "Now if we had had a teacher like that in mathematics, one who used such great stories and grand analogies, we would probably be teaching math!"

To conclude our thoughts on the narrative we offer a paraphrase of E. M. Forster's famous observation: A fact: "The queen died and the king died." A story: "The queen died and the king died of a broken heart." It isn't difficult to decide which is most compelling.

The Inquiry Box

Consider what students of all ages are capable of doing. They are capable of discovering information about a topic they already know something about, or about a topic they want to discover more about, or about a topic in which they have interest. They are capable of asking questions and following threads—regardless of their ages.

No student really *needs* to write a "research" paper; instead students *need* to engage in personal inquiry. Students and teachers *need* to drop the adherence to outdated, unjustifiable ideas such as footnotes, witch hunts for errors, specific numbers of sources, outlines, and note cards. Authentic inquiry allows students to discover, rediscover, uncover, and document. We offer a step-by-step approach to conducting inquiry that we call the "inquiry box."

Implementing the Inquiry Box

1. Invite students to bring in a box—about shoebox size—that will serve as a repository for all their research. Tell students to walk around for a couple of days with small notepads, looking at things and thinking about what they would like to know. As ideas pop into their heads, they jot them down and place them in the box.

   Suggest they keep their notepads by their bed to record ideas that present themselves before or during sleep, or upon waking up. Scientists have discovered that the relaxation of sleep fosters our most productive ideas. They add these to the box.

2. They take their boxes to class or to their group. Others respond by offering tips, names, addresses, phone numbers of experts, books, films, tapes, newspapers, articles, Web sites, and so forth. All this goes into the box.

3. To use Vygotsky's term, the students are "heaping."

4. At some point, the teacher invites each student to sort and categorize what is in his or her box. With that, students progress into ways to find the core issues of their inquiry. Teachers encourage students to explore, to follow threads.

5. Before students interview experts, conduct surveys, design questionnaires, or pursue research, the teacher provides inquiry strategies. Students keep these strategies in the box for ready reference.

6. Students continue to place all collected information in the box.

7. Tape the box shut.

8. Students prewrite about their topics, leaving the box sealed. They write everything they remember reading, their suppositions, hypotheses, their thoughts, and connections.

9. Students open the box and use the research to write more, to support what they have written, to hone, to add, and to revise.

10. Students document where necessary.

Inquiry in a box keeps students from simply copying information. They are forced after the box is sealed to paraphrase and to put what they are discovering in their own words. Students love the novelty of the "box" and the suspense of opening it after their prewriting.

DOCUMENTATION FORMS

Currently the major method of documentation is internal documentation (this text, for example, uses internal documentation). It is easily recognizable immediately after quoted or paraphrased information by the author's name and page number between the parentheses.

Internal documentation whether MLA (Modern Language Association) or APA (American Psychological Association) style eliminates much of the cumbersome mechanics of citing references. If the sole reason for having students to do research is because they will need it "next year," then no wonder students throw up their hands in frustration. As Larson points out in the article in Appendix D, different teachers and different disciplines have distinct documentation styles. Trying to second-guess what students will need next year is like throwing a handful of beans at a door hoping one will go into the key hole. While it is important that students learn other documentation styles, they will be better served if they learn one consistent, workable form of documentation. If they learn one style well, they will easily master others because they will understand the necessity of validation and credibility.

CONCLUSION

Earlier is this chapter we referenced the work of Jerome Bruner to support the narrative in writing. Macrorie agrees. In *Searching Writing* he writes, "The most fundamental mode of human communication is telling stories" (98). Ending this chapter on inquiry it seems appropriate reinforce the validity of story. As Joseph Campbell tells us in *The Hero with a Thousand Faces* there are no new stories, just the same story retold. As Willa Cather says in *O Pioneers!*, "There are only two or three human stories, and they go on repeating themselves as fiercely as if they had never happened before." Inquiry uses these stories—therein lies its truth.

APPLICATION

Write your memories of writing research papers when you were in school. Be honest. Compare your memories to others. Compare your memories with how you teach inquiry. Draw conclusions.

13

WRITING AS A MODE OF LEARNING

Writing represents a unique mode of learning—
not merely valuable, not merely special, but unique.

—Janet Emig □

WRITING IN OTHER DISCIPLINES

When Janet Emig wrote her essay "Writing as a Mode of Learning" in 1977 (see Appendix F), she referenced Lev Vygotsky, A. R. Luria, and Jerome Bruner as others who "have all pointed out that higher cognitive functions, such as analysis and synthesis, seem to develop most fully only with the support system of verbal language—particularly, it seems, of written language" (1983, 123).

When Mikhail Bakhtin, one of great thinkers of the twentieth century, wrote, "We are all authors," he was talking, among other things, about how people appropriate meaning. Further, he maintained, "the word is a two-sided act. It is determined equally by whose word it is and for whom it is meant. . . . A word is territory shared by both addresser and addressee" (Clark and Holquist 15). What he means is that when people use language to talk or write about a subject, they literally take ownership of that subject. Then when others read or hear these words, they begin their own appropriation of meaning. In this way, words belong in part to the authors and in part to the hearers or readers; words are shared meaning.

In a real sense this is what happens when students read and write in other disciplines. Words embedded in a context called "reading" or "mathematics" or "social studies" or other disciplines carry unique meaning within that discipline. Students partake of that meaning as they read. Then, when they write, they extend their understanding. As students write responses, they become authors of meaning about or because of the words that have been shared. This appropriation of meaning and shared ownership is called *writing to learn*.

The importance of writing to learn helps students develop the habit of writing, to understand writing as a representation of what they think, and to use writing to foster further, deeper thinking and to integrate knowledge. If students believe writing only belongs in English or language arts classes, they may thwart positive brain patterning that develops when they write often and for many purposes. In a sense they may be fragmenting their own learning. If writing in all contexts is a manifestation of appropriated information, why is there sometimes resistance to writing in other disciplines?

Resistance to Writing in Other Disciplines

Need for Strategies

One major reason for resistance to writing in other disciplines is a need by teachers other than ELA teachers for specific and effective writing strategies to bring about learning. This chapter, indeed this book, offers myriad strategies that counter resistance.

Faulty Perceptions

Another difficulty lies in faulty perceptions by both teachers and students. Some teachers, for example, interpret the phrase "writing in other disciplines" to mean that they should teach writing. This immediately sets off signals, and red flags go up. "That's the English teacher's job." "I can't even cover what I'm suppose to, and they want me to teach writing too." "I hate writing. That's why I didn't become an English teacher." "I don't have time to grade the writing." "I wouldn't know how to grade it." For students, the response is generally more straightforward, "This isn't English. Why do you want me to write?"

So it seems three misconceptions prevail: (1) Writing (implicit is teaching all the conventions and correcting all the grammar) would have to be taught in addition to the subject matter; (2) writing means students generate more papers and more papers mean more grading; and (3) writing should occur only in English and language arts classes. These misconceptions are ubiquitous, pervasive, and sometimes debilitating.

We need to reexamine these misconceptions. Writing, one of the most rigorous intellectual activities, one that demands the writer take ephemeral, abstract thoughts and reconstitute them on a blank page in a comprehensible way, is both a manifestation and mode of thought. With so much information bombarding students daily, they need strategies to cope with the surge of information. Hazy, lazy thinking does not serve students well. So it seems prudent that teachers in all disciplines and on all levels come to grips with a definition of writing that includes thought and learning. When we do, we will be better equipped to incorporate writing to maximize learning and enhance the intellectual rigor of students.

Leon Botstein, President of Bard College, in the foreword to *Writing to Learn Mathematics and Science*, says, "Ordinary language, particularly in its notated forms—writing—must be construed as part of everyday experience. Even at low levels of general literacy, the complex cognitive and epistemological processes imbedded in everyday speech (as opposed to tacit experience) and action constitutes a sufficient link to understanding mathematics and science. The act of writing in the process of learning these subject areas is essential to developing curiosity and comprehension in the learner" (Countryman xiv).

> *Sometimes people ask, "Not everyone will be employed in these higher-level thinking professions. What of the housekeeper or the gardener? Why do they need to learn to write?" While there are several responses to that line of thinking—one that questions whether these folks would teach to the lowest common denominator, the other that questions their touch with reality and what the future promises. But to us the most tactful response is this parable of the gardener.*
>
> *Because we travel frequently, we have hired a young man to take care of our yard. We rarely see him. He sends the bills and we pay them. Recently, we thought it would be nice to put in some bedding plants, so we wrote him a note explaining what we had in mind. He sent us a reply asking for more specifics—co-*

lor, type, exact placement, and amount. We answered with more directions. He responded with questions about fertilizers, quotes of prices, and other pertinent information. Eventually the flowers were planted.

Misconception One: Writing Would Have to Be Taught in Addition to the Subject Matter. Maintaining that writing belongs in all disciplines is not an effort to convert all teachers into English language arts teachers, although all teachers teach English because they model it daily. In all practicality, it may be necessary to rethink exactly who teaches what.

English language arts teachers could incorporate more information from other disciplines into their lessons—say, historical information—while teachers in other disciplines could integrate more written responses into their class work. Teachers need to pool their efforts by team teaching or at least, team planning. To borrow Madeline Hunter's term, lessons need to be designed with an "'educational wiggle' that will accommodate students who need different 'catch hold' points in a content area" (53). Expanding time into longer blocks for more sustained integration and grouping students by their mastery of objectives would maximize learning. If depth is the desired goal, then time must be allotted to plumb the depths. Madeline Hunter suggests that in the old paradigm *time* was the constant, but in the new paradigm *learning* is (2). This jibes with cognitive theory and brain research—as no two students learn the same way. This is also the concept good school librarians model—they meet weekly or monthly with grade-level teams or cross-discipline teams acting as the catalyst to collaborative integrated teaching and assessment across the disciplines with inquiry as the center. This level of planning works well if teachers have been trained in this type of effort.

Three Examples of Integration

Example 1: Mathematics. Laurye Webb, a math teacher, opens her students to interesting writing assignments that connect to mathematics. Her middle school students worked in small groups on designing games. Not only did the criteria of mathematical concepts have to be present in the final product, but also the directions had to be written in clear, appropriate English. Laurye checked the precision of their language as much as their mathematics as she monitored the groups, advised, probed, nudged, and facilitated.

Example 2: Science. The third-graders of Dawn Mathews McLendon became deeply engaged in all aspects of earthquake investigation following the one that hit the San Francisco area. They roleplayed television interviewers, jotted notes, and wrote news articles; they researched the sites of prior earthquakes and predicted future earthquakes; they figured the projected costs for reclamation in areas hit by earthquakes; they had maps and globes and rulers and paper and pencils everywhere. Each cluster of students fine-tuned their area of expertise because they knew they would be sharing it with others in the class who also knew a great deal about the subject. When we observed, we couldn't tell where one subject ended and another began. Students were writing their science and using science in their writing. They were reading, writing, calculating, and computing. They were listening, speaking, and thinking. They posed some problems and solved others. Because these students were totally immersed in their study, they understood the true nature of how knowledge crosses and criss-crosses itself in what Vygotsky calls a "web of meaning."

Example 3: History. The study of ballads in senior English led to a discussion of folklore and eventually to discussion of some specific local folklore—a phantom lady that supposedly appears on the local lake. In sharing their renditions of this lore, the students became intensely interested in the variations of the tale. They became so taken with the story that the history and

English teacher combined classes to give students more time for deeper study. Thus began research into Fort Phantom, the supposed site of the story, which led next to discoveries about Fort Phantom Hill, some ten miles or so from Abilene, Texas. That, in turn, ushered in history, most especially the mistaken geography of a Major General Smith who thought he was to build the fort to protect settlers on the Brazos and Trinity Rivers.

After thorough investigations of local histories, old newspapers, and interviews with elderly residents, students decided they needed empirical data, so in caravans of cars, these twelfth-graders drove out to the Fort Phantom. Later some even claimed to have seen the phantom. They wrote their own versions of the ballad, which they performed at an all-school assembly. Subsequently, these seniors were featured in the local paper and interviewed on the local television station. It is not likely that they, or their teachers, will soon forget ballads and how history envelops them. The entire experience echoed what Anne Ruggles Gere says, "Secondary education should provide students a way of thinking, not a set of facts" (3).

Admittedly, these examples indicate a longer, deeper, more intense study of mathematics, science, social studies, and literature with writing as the thread that wound the learning events together into a fabric of larger meaning. However, writing also may be used for shorter responses. Every class need not explore the entire lode in the mine; sometimes studying a nugget will do.

Nuggets

Admit and Exit Slips. Strategies such as "Admit" and "Exit" slips, suggested by authors in Gere's *Roots in the Sawdust*, and popularized in Janet Allen's neat flip book *Tools for Teaching Content Literacy*, are brief written responses that are collected as "tickets" in or out of any class.

Learning Logs. Students in any class could write in a learning log what they have learned each class period or at the end of the day. These bursts of writing provide opportunities for students to capture their learning. Instead of writing when they enter class or at the start of the day, they write as closure. These logs are then available as references to analyze their thinking processes, to see where they were, and to judge where they are going. Students often add, extend, alter, or elaborate upon what is there. What better way for teacher and student to see what was internalized?

Brainstorming. Tried and true in any discipline, brainstorming works as a class or in small groups.

Listing. Listing sets students thinking, then writing. The old adage, "If you can't write it, you don't know it" holds.

Clips of Meaning. Cris Tovani often stops during a lesson and invites students to "show me your thinking." This invitation at once tells students they always should be thinking and making meaning while enabling them to write a "clip" of their meaning. It's easy to talk out of that "clip."

Clearly, old boundaries are crumbling. The days of standing in front of a class of row-upon-row of students, assigning a paper, and expecting that paper to happen are past. Vito Perrone, director of programs in Teacher Education at the Harvard Graduate School of Education and Senior Fellow of the Carnegie Foundation for the Advancement of Teaching, urges restructuring that is "within a framework of consequential purposes. Otherwise, what passes for restructuring will be formulaic and limited in substance, leading ultimately to greater cynicism" (132). He contends, "teachers need to construct for themselves a more powerful voice" (133). Teachers cannot construct a voice without recent and continuous study in the way students learn.

Misconception Two: Writing Means Students Generate More Papers and More Papers Mean More Grading. Of course writing needs to be evaluated, but there are different purposes for evaluating just as there are different purposes for writing. Reading prewriting and drafts holistically, for example, meets the need for a general impression of where the piece is in its rough form. Sometimes students just need assurance they are on the right track. Whereas papers that have gone through the process require more deliberate assessment, perhaps through an analytic scale, but much of the writing that happens daily as reader response is either shared immediately, is filed for further consideration, or is simply judged as work in process.

Reconsider the three previous examples. The middle-school students working on their game wrote reams. They filled pages with descriptions of their designs. They wrote problem cards, challenge cards, trivia cards as part of the game. They wrote directions, mini "how-to" essays. They tested, corrected, revised, and reformulated what they had written. They wanted their game to "work." Laurye walked around, clipboard in hand, making notes, giving credit for work in process, then she assessed the final product according to the criteria everyone was given at the onset. Another point: Because her students had worked in groups, she had six or seven games to evaluate per class, not twenty-five or thirty.

The third-graders were constantly writing. There was so much writing by the end of their study that Dawn asked them to gather it together "archeologically," that is, what they did first was on the bottom; what they did last was on top. Then she led them brilliantly through some self-assessment (all the while taking notes in her grade book): What did they learn? How did they learn it? What would they do differently? What was best among their efforts? She did not read every word in every packet, but she knew exactly what each student had done. Grading for Dawn was easy.

The English teacher evaluated the high-school students' ballads according to the characteristics of a ballad and the conventions of English; the history teacher evaluated the historical research. Then the history teacher read the ballads for historical accuracy while the English teacher read the research for English conventions. Each student received a grade in each discipline; they also received a grade for process.

Reading: One Additional Example. Carolyn L. Johnson, a middle-school teacher, describes a workable classroom management strategy that enables maximum reader response without teacher burnout. After studying the response theory of Robert Probst, Carolyn initiated readers' logs and literary letters in her classes. As an ongoing process, students responded in their readers' logs to whatever they had read that day. Sometimes give them questions as nudges, "What struck you most in your reading? Why?"

At the conclusion of the week, students read through their logs and wrote a literary letter to her; to a classmate, a student in another class, or a friend; or to a caregiver, parent, or trusted adult. Carolyn's strategy works like this:

Week 1: third period writes their letters to her; fifth period writes to a classmate; seventh period writes to their parents.

Week 2: third period writes to a classmate; fifth to their parents; seventh to her.

Week 3: third period writes to their parents, fifth to her, and seventh to a classmate.

This rotation continues throughout the year with occasional scheduled breaks. In this way, Carolyn explains, there is a continuity of student writing, but she only responds to one class per week, not to every student every week.

Clearly, one implication is that students should be writing every day for many purposes, but every piece of that writing does not have to undergo traditional scrutiny. In the real world, people are judged on their best work, not on every attempt. Dancers practice for hours and make many mistakes, but audiences see only the final performance. Advertising agents create many concepts for clients, but they disregard all but their best for the final conference. Chefs experiment with sauces but serve only the most exquisite. Students should write, practice, create, experiment, but they also should be graded on their best.

Misconception Three: Writing Should Occur Only in English and Language Arts Classes. If writing occurs only in English language arts classes, students regard it as a limited tool, something associated with literature or isolated grammar. Indeed, some students (who grow up to be parents) think grammar *is* writing. In today's world, typically students are not exposed to much writing in their homes—the phone has replaced the letter, the cell phone has replaced the home phone in many households. Certainly, while programs on TV have been written, students do not see evidence of it. Even the teleprompter has become so sophisticated viewers do not even see speakers' notes or papers.

Students do not see people generating notes, memos, lab reports, logs, articles, books, or letters. Informal and formal surveys (King 1979) of teachers reveal that many do not write with their students—indeed, many do not write at all. Therefore, it seems students have few models. No wonder students wonder at the brouhaha about writing. It must seem a worthless endeavor to learn—one created, no doubt, to bedevil them.

In truth, writing is an inextricably important skill in the world. All business telephone calls are followed up with letters. Reports of all types on all levels are part of the work-a-day world. Firefighters write reports, so do police officers, inspectors, insurance people, mid-management, and CEOs. People who cannot write clearly and coherently are disadvantaged at best and, at worst, exploitable. Historically, one way used to keep people in lower social strata was to limit their ability to write and read. In addition to the pragmatic application of writing, there is its aesthetic value. As a major symbolizing system, writing and an appreciation of writing enrich life through its levels of meaning, and its nuances. As thinking on paper, writing enables people to clarify and refine thought. It also empowers. The most effective way to communicate the importance of writing is by valuing it daily in the classroom.

> *We received a call from a CEO of a large food store chain. After the usual amenities, the distinguished-sounding voice on the other end asked, "Do you do for businesses what you do for teachers? Do you offer training in writing?"*
>
> *Before answering, we inquired about the reason for his call. He replied, "We like to encourage our people to work hard. And we reward them. We have some folks working for us who began as baggers, who were promoted to stockers, and who eventually worked their way into mid-management positions. But I'm sitting here right now with three memos written by employees that make no sense to me; I can't understand them, and I'm the CEO."*

Robert J. Marzano, Deputy Director of Training and Development at the Mid-continent Regional Educational Laboratory in Aurora, Colorado, maintains that "a fundamental goal of schooling is for students to learn whatever is deemed important in a given subject—in other words, to acquire and integrate knowledge" (31). If students are to integrate knowledge, then schools should be structured and classes taught in a way that facilitates integration.

THE READING/WRITING CONNECTION
ACROSS THE CURRICULUM

New Criticism

In order to gain a historical perspective on the reading/writing connection and how it applies across the curriculum, we first look at New Criticism. This theory, primarily espoused by I. A. Richards, held that the text was central and primary to the learning experience, for it was the repository of truth and wisdom, and anything extraneous to the text was considered irrelevant. Professors and teachers, considered authorities, albeit authorities by degree, were powerful. They were charged with transmitting this truth and wisdom to students, who, as neophyte readers-as-critics of the text, could never completely ascertain its truths or understand its wisdom without help.

Clem Young of the Brisbane College of Advanced Education contends that New Criticism caught students in "a theory of deficits" (11). Once a professional postulated the "true" or "correct" response, any other response jarred the integrity of the work and was therefore considered "incorrect." So the job of the student became one of "learning the techniques of unlocking textual meanings and internalizing the canons of literary judgement and taste" (Young 11). Thus, the correctness of the response was judged according to its match with the postulations of the piece—the closer the match, the higher the grade. The final critique was all important. Therefore, New Criticism stands as a product approach to teaching and learning that affected the way teachers taught reading, literature, and other subjects since the 1920s.

Reader-Response

Reader-response, sometimes called transactional theory, grew out of Louise M. Rosenblatt's studies at the Sorbonne in the 1930s and ran alongside the writings of William James, C. S. Peirce, George Santayana, and John Dewey. Rosenblatt succinctly states, "I rejected the notion of the poem-as-object, and the neglect of both author and reader" (1978, xii).

In essence, Rosenblatt and her followers reintroduce the author and the reader into the learning experience—the author creates the text; the reader co-creates it. Wolfgang Iser, an adherent to the reader-response theory, posits that a painting or a sculpture or any text cannot be entirely taken in all at one time, so the understanding is dynamic, ever-changing, "a moving viewpoint which travels along inside that which it has to apprehended" (108–109). This makes sense. Most people admit when they read a text on any given day, they get certain meanings, but upon rereading the same text at a later date, they arrive at new, different, often deeper meanings. All that has transpired in the interim, including experiences, mood, fatigue level, time, changes the reader's perceptions. Indeed, "Scientific research shows that there are a minimum of 500,000,000,000 possible different responses to a given text, that's at least 200 different responses for everybody in the world! And they are all related" (Purves 38–39). In light of recent brain research, that figure is probably conservative.

Reader-response theory invites the reader to call upon not just five senses, but what M. C. Richards identifies as "twelve senses: touch, life, movement, balance, smell, taste, sight, warmth, hearing, word, thought, and ego. The sense of ego is the highest. It is the sense one has of another" (146). In reading the work of others, no matter what discipline or what level, the reader must sense self and others for what Rosenblatt calls "understanding, " which she defines as implying "the full impact of the sensuous, emotional, as well as intellectual force of the word" (1983, 112).

The way to help students develop this ability to participate in a text, according to Rosenblatt, "is to encourage them to engage in such imaginative writing. In this way they will themselves be involved in wrestling with the materials offered them by life or by their reaction to it; they will discover that problems of form and artistry are not separable from the problems of clarifying the particular sense of life or the particular human mood that the work of art is destined to embody" (1983, 48–49).

Taken to the latest educational forum, reader-response has become known as text-to-self, text-to-text, text-to-world, or what we call "text to the third power" responses. Students read the text and make connections. Following a student's response, a teacher would not say, "No, that is wrong. World War II should not remind you of your uncle's death." "No, that mathematical problem must be solved this way." Rather the teacher receives the individual responses, lets them reverberate with each other, then as Rosenblatt says, "the teacher will be able to lead him [the learner] to the various kinds of knowledge that will enable him to achieve the experiences offered by this particular text" (1983, 114). Because reader-response at its very core validates the equality of personal meanings, esteems the both/all answer, respects the primacy of individual responses, and the plurality of meaning, it rests comfortably in the process/globalization/conceptual paradigm.

THE PROCESSES OF READING AND WRITING

Writing has been called the flip side of reading because cognitively composing and comprehending emerge as two sides of the same process. When composing, we create meaning; when comprehending, we re-create it. When composing, students write what they mean, then they return—sometimes over and over again—to understand what they have written, to develop, extend, and reconsider it as a reader in a act of re-creation.

When reading, we also compose and comprehend. First we read what someone has written, then we compose its meaning for ourselves (what Bakhtin calls "appropriating meaning"), finally, we comprehend that meaning—what it means to us.

This process best describes what writing across the curriculum does—it elicits responses from students after they have read a given text. These responses illuminate what meaning has been appropriated and what may be built upon for further learning. To begin the trek of writing in other disciplines, teachers are best served when they recognize the fact that both writers and readers compose.

"Writing about reading is one of the best ways to get students to unravel their transactions so that we can see how they understand and, in the process, help them to elaborate, clarify, and illustrate their responses by reference to the associations and prior knowledge that inform them" (Petrosky 24). The following strategies are some ways to generate these responses from students in any discipline.

READING/WRITING STRATEGIES

Read and retell, shielding, the tri-fold, the dialectical notebook, text renderings, text tampering, sub-texting, sequence charts, building meaning, and reading/writing connections are among the reading/writing strategies that tease meaning out of literature, art and music, the performing arts, mathematics, science, social studies, physical education, computer study, ESL, and the industrial arts and onto the page. Also the prewriting strategies offered in Chapter 1 generate reader responses: the pentad, hexagonal writing, trigger words, and so forth. These strategies offer a unique way into meaning just once or many times. The pedagogy here is—repeat and vary.

Read and Retell

Explanation. This strategy developed by Hazel Brown and Brian Cambourne has been adapted from their book *Read and Retell*. Easy to prepare, suitable across the curriculum, flexible, read and retell provides practice over a range of skills that include reading, writing, listening, talking, thinking, interacting, comparing, matching, selecting, organizing, remembering, and understanding.

Implementation.

- Divide class into groups of four or five students.

- Provide the title of the text to be studied.

- On the basis of the title, students write a brief prediction of the text.

- Share predictions in group.

- Students comment on each other's predictions.

- Teacher reads the text aloud.

- Students read the text silently as many times as they need or wish to read it.

- Students, not looking at the text, quickly write out what they remember.

- Students share and compare what they have written.

- Debrief.

Remarks. Read and retell begins with a level of surprise. Its novelty usually captures students' interest. It involves intensive reading and collaboration and demands intensive listening and attending. Writing engages the learner in a gamut of language processes. Sharing and comparing invites multiple readings and rereadings, different shifts of focus, and metacognitive assessments. Brown and Cambourne claim observable growth in "knowledge of text forms; knowledge of text conventions; the conscious awareness of processes involved in text construction; the range and variety of text forms and conventions being employed in other writing tasks; control of vocabulary; reading flexibility; confidence" (11–12). When using read and retell, skilled teachers also extend learners to other levels beyond the paraphrasing level.

Shielding

Explanation. Shielding is a prewriting/reader response strategy. Most students are aware of heraldry in some form or fashion. If not, examples of family shields are readily available. The Web site www.heraldica.org is a great place to find examples of family shields. Students create their own shields to better understand the concepts of plot, theme setting, irony, and symbolism.

Implementation.

- Students create a shield; they may use paper, cardboard, wood, aluminum foil, or any safe material or combination of materials.

- They divide their shields into four equal parts and draw a circle in the center.

- Students label the top left-hand corner PLOT; the top right-hand corner SETTING; the lower left-hand corner IRONY; the lower right-hand corner THEME; and the circle SYMBOL.

- After writing a story connected to their lives, they return to their shields. They write a summary of their lives in the section labeled PLOT. They need something from the beginning, the middle, and the end. We explain to students that the end of where they are in the life in the present is the "end" of the story of their life up to that point. The same thing holds true for a piece of literature. The end of *Because of Winn-Dixie* is not the death of Opal. "End" and "death" are not synonymous.

- In the SETTING section, students list all the places they have lived. For some there will be many; for others, few.

- The THEME corner is where students write a quote that sums up who they are. It is best to have students avoid clichés, which makes a fine mini-lesson. There can also be a mini-lesson on documentation and proper attribution.

- The IRONY corner will be difficult for most students. We ask them to write about how they think people perceive as opposed to how they really are—therein lies the irony. We use the Shakespearean notion of "appearances versus reality" to help define irony. The purpose of this section is not to invade a student's privacy but to understand that everyone's life is filled with irony.

- In the center students write about or draw a symbol that best represents who they are. After students have completed their shields, they may decorate it to correspond to each section. The purpose is not the art, but to invite another level of thought. (Wilson 43–47)

Remarks. The rationale for this strategy is based on moving from self to others. If students understand the plot, theme, setting, irony, and symbolism in their lives, they better understand these devices in a piece of literature. A wonderful extension of this strategy is to have students create shields for characters in a piece of literature or for historical characters they are studying.

The shielding strategy may be used in all classes, but it works particularly well when integrated with the study of medieval history, heraldry, or when taken in conjunction with any study related to King Arthur. Another effective way to use shielding is as an introduction—a project begun the first day of class. Not only do teachers gain insights into students, but students gain insights into other students. It becomes a reflexive writing activity that can be called upon repeatedly throughout the grading period, semester, or year. For example, "We're going to study symbolism. Let's look at some of the symbols we put on our shields."

Projects

The notion of the ongoing use of the shield as a point of reference in later classes suggests the advantage of other ongoing projects. Cooperative ventures undertaken by individuals or groups of students expand the concepts taught and invite practical and immediate application of these concepts. Howard Gardner offers projects as one way to achieve performance-based education and assessment that go "beyond the bubble." He says that "Students in these [Vermont, California, Connecticut] and some other states are being asked to carry out extended projects, often cooperatively, in which they demonstrate 'in practical situations' their understandings of concepts in mathematics, science, and other disciplines" (1991, 259). He cites examples where students argue controversial issues, design fiscally sound programs, assess toxic water supplies, and determine accurate media reporting. He portrays projects as a way around what can be faked because performance-based learning "requires sufficient mastery of concepts and principles so that students are able to bring them to bear appropriately on large multifaceted problems of the sort for which learnings ought to be mobilized" (1991, 259).

Tri-Folds

Explanation. The tri-fold is a listening and thinking strategy that uses reader response as its springboard. Workable with any discipline across the curriculum, it is a quick and nonthreatening way to involve all students, because they begin with what they consider important.

Implementation.

- Students use one sheet of paper, which they fold into thirds. (In elementary classes this is a teachable moment for fractions.)

- Teacher or student reads a story, poem, section from a text, or a chapter. Students are cautioned to listen carefully.

- After the reading, students write in the center third what struck them most and why.

- They write in the top third what came before what they wrote in the center section.

- They write in the bottom third what came after what they wrote in the center.

- They divide into groups and share. They begin by reading their centers, then they share their before and after sections. After that they discuss the commonalities and differences in their responses.

- Conduct a debriefing on what was learned.

Remarks. This strategy gives students ownership over the material. They determine, in a truly reader-response way, what is important to them. Most often students will identify the main idea, but they do the identifying. Through sharing, they hear the responses of others, which extends their thinking. The strategy is also good for sequencing, with the starting point decided by the student. It is also makes class discussion more interesting since there will be differences in all sections of the tri-fold that permit the validation of diversity. Tri-folds also serve as excellent prewriting for a longer piece of discourse, which students read. Students find that the center section offers the nugget for a thesis or a proposition with little refining, perhaps combining it with something gleaned from another student or from one of the other sections of their tri-fold.

Mathematics Adaptation

Mary Ryan adapted this strategy for her pre-algebra class. She invited her students to write three positive and three negative integers in the center section. In the top section they created a word problem using the integers from the center section. They exchanged papers. The recipient of the paper solved the problem in the bottom section and explained the process used to arrive at the solution. The papers were returned and checked by the originator of the problem. The teacher had only to double-check these. Grading went quickly since Mary monitored the students during their work in process. Following is an excerpt from a Maria, an ESL student.

Fig. 13.1. Maria's Math Tri-Fold.

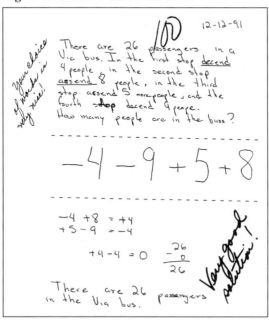

Maria clearly has difficulty with the English language, but not with positive and negative integers. There can be no doubt that by writing in math class, and in other classes across the curriculum, she is receiving practice using English as well as the opportunity to integrate it with other knowledge.

Dialectical Notebooks

Explanation. Ann E. Berthoff describes the dialectical notebook, sometimes called the double-entry notebook or the interactive notebook or journal, as a place for construing and constructing. A double-entry notebook invites the student to write notes on one side and notes about those notes on the other side. Berthoff says, "The important thing is to separate your notes from notes about notes so that you can carry on a dialogue between you-as-listener and you-as-reviewer, the One Who Listens and Looks Again" (26).

Implementation.

* Students draw a line vertically down the center of each page in a standard spiral notebook. They label the column on the left "Notes"; they label the column on the right "Notes on Notes."

- Students use the left side of these pages to take notes from whatever source, for example, pacewalking in physical education, Copernicus in science, recent newspaper reports in social studies, and so forth. They may include reading or observational notes, direct quotations, sketches, passages, fragments, lists, images (verbal and visual), and paraphrases.

- On the right side, students write commentary on the notes. These may include their own notes or observations, comments, responses, reactions, comparisons, contrasts, summaries, questions, suggestions, revisions, and aphorisms.

Remarks. Berthoff calls this activity the "audit of meaning," a continuous effort to review thought and meaning. It is metacognitive because there is continual opportunity to "see" that thinking and rethink its meaning.

Emily Flores uses the dialectical notebook with her eighth-grade students. She says it benefits them in four ways: it strengthens note taking and listening skills, provides a valuable study and review tool, serves as a writing-to-learn tool in other classes, and works as a spark for future writing topic possibilities. Emily collects dialectical notebooks five times during a six-week marking period. Each check is worth a maximum of twenty points. Students receive ten points for thoroughness and completion; five points for effort on both sides of the notebook; five points for conscientious upkeep of notes and responses, neatness, and practicality of notebook contents. Following is an excerpt from Richard's notebook. (See Fig. 13.2.)

Richard records his connection between the Greek amphitheater, which he is studying, and contemporary amphitheaters such as the Astrodrome, which is part of his experiential knowledge. That is an important association; he is linking ideas; he is making connections. The dialectical notebook has enabled him to integrate his knowledge. This subjective organization of information is key to memory. Richard also identifies with the bravery of Thespis, a typical and therefore genuine response from an adolescent. Perhaps most telling on the left side, however, is the way he organized the Greek writers, with numbers following their names. It is not apparent until the bottom of the column that Richard used them as an identification code. Does Richard know he needs space (and perhaps time) between received information so he can process it? Was Richard mimicking some model quiz he read or saw in a magazine? Was the information given this way in the source? Was Richard testing himself as he took the notes? Whatever the answers to these questions, it is clear that the dialectical notebook helped Richard appropriate meaning. It also gives Emily as clear picture of Richard's learning at this point.

Text Renderings

Explanation. Text rendering comes from the idea in music of rendition. When students "render" a text they interpret it; they create their version of it. Like the jazz greats, they improvise on a theme, repeat chords, omit what seems extraneous—but they never lose the original melody, the harmonious relationships—they just play around with them.

Implementation.

- Divide students into groups. Assign a poem, story, passage, chapter, or section to be rendered.

- Model a short text rendering.

Fig. 13.2. Richard's Dialectical Notebook.

①   Richard

Notes From Source (4 - 19)   Me and Mine

Origins of Drama

     Aristophanes ①
     Aeschylus ②
     Euripides ③
     Sophocles ④
- Religious ceremonies
to fertility God - Dionysus
amphitheater

       audience
       chorus

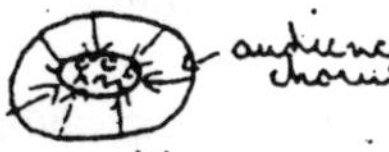

    - usually semicircular
    - seats elevated
    - like astrodom
    - 1st used for religious
ceremonies.
     Thespis - equivalent
of 1st actor. seperated from chorus
and sang and meditated by
himself.
    - other actors would single
themselves out to. Changed from
religious ceremonies to entainment.

Greek writers from top.
   ① first comedy writer
   ② comedy and tragedy
   ③ tragedy
   ④ heavy tragedy.

It's funny that all of
these Greek gods that Greeks
worshiped inspired not
great crops or good weather but
instead it inspired
Drama.
    I always thought that
the astrodome etc. were
high-tech new inventions.
It's interesting that
these ideas were sprouted
by ancient greeks and that,
thousands of years later,
these ideas are still being
used.
    I think Thespis most
of been a pretty brave guy
because I know I would
be chicken to stand out
of a group and single myself
out. He put his behind
on the line of humiliation
or historic importance.
I'm glad somebody stood
out.
    It is fascinating that
in ancient times only
peasants and "nobodys"
would go to the theater.

- Groups decide how they will render their assignment, but they must keep to the following guidelines:

  a. Convey the basic information;

  b. Repeat, interweave (as in counterpoint), rearrange, or improvise;

  c. Omit nothing important;

  d. Add nothing new—stay with the words in the text;

  e. Say parts singularly or in chorus, chant, rap, or in any combination;

  f. Words may be emphasized by drawing them out, by tone, pitch, or repetition;

  g. Groups may ask other groups to participate in all or part of their rendering.

- Groups present their renderings orally to the class.

Remarks. This strategy electrifies a class. Novel and collaborative, it allows, even encourages different learning styles, and it is fun. Additionally, and importantly, students who are aural learners benefit, as do those who are kinetic learners. Perhaps most importantly, it demands close reading, and the repetition of the information during practice in groups helps students remember the material. This works with children's books, passages from texts, and rules for teams to remember. It reinforces musical concepts, encourages a transfer to art concepts, and assists ESL students who learn language through repeating and using it. What would happen in science, if students rendered their lab reports? What would happen in mathematics, if students rendered their word problems? What would happen in social studies, if students rendered a poignant passage on the issue of slavery, or a powerful section on war, or a somewhat dull chapter on various treaties?

At first students render more as a chorus or a reader's theater, but the elegance of this strategy becomes apparent with additional implementations. Students borrow and use ideas for renderings after hearing each other. Callie Vassar used it successfully during her appraisal lesson to introduce her twelfth-graders to Chaucer. She confided that all the students became involved, and that she received high marks from her appraiser.

Text Tampering

Explanation. Building on Rosenblatt's concept of co-creating a text, Iser's concept of coming to a text from a moving viewpoint, and Jacques Derrida's theory of deconstruction, text tamperings actually invite students to take the text and manipulate it into meaning. Bill Corcoran, Senior Lecturer in English Education at James Cook University of North Queensland, Australia, claims that tampering with texts "have long been in the repertoire of inspired teachers who have played with, distorted, and cut the texts to shape their students rather than contorting their students to the shape of the text" (66). And readers have always done this. Who has not mentally rewritten the dialogue for a beloved character, created a different ending, predicted an outcome, put themselves into the text, or played "what if" while reading? This strategy simply asks students to do this tampering on paper.

Consider the implicit invitation to tamper with the text in this book. The articles have an accompanying commentary and wide margins, which bids readers to add their commentary—thereby together co-creating additional meanings.

Implementation. There are three major ways to tamper with a text. Each of these may be adapted in various ways, so that there are many possible permutations and innovations.

- Find gaps: The first is to find the gaps in a story, passage, or chapter, or even in a sentence or two. For example, take the first book in the *Chronicles of Narnia*. C. S. Lewis begins with these two sentences: "Once there were four children whose names were Peter, Susan, Edmund and Lucy. This story is about something that happened to them when they were sent away from London during the war because of the air-raids."

  Students (or teacher, but it is far better for students to do this) identify the gaps unfulfilled for them, places where they may insert their own projections. As they travel along the book, they may modify or change their projections. For instance, students may find a gap in not immediately knowing the ages of the children. They may, therefore, project what they think the ages to be. Then, before the opening paragraph is over, they will discover who is the youngest and next youngest. They may have to change their projection, or they may feel good about being correct. Students may wonder what war the author means. Filling in that gap for most would entail research and analysis of the clues in the text.

  Students working in groups may collaborate on any subject using this strategy. There are gaps in other genre besides narratives, for example, rules, directions, and experiments to name a few.

  Young children do this almost naturally when they make predictions based on the pictures in the book. They also predict as the story is being read to them, "I think they will find the princess." Teachers help this along by stopping regularly while reading aloud to ask children to predict, project, identify, comment, or consider what the authors did not tell.

- Write new parts: Another way to tamper with texts is by writing different beginnings or endings, or by extending the story with a sequel. While this is not a new notion and can become somewhat trite, there are many stories and opportunities that lend themselves to this activity. Also, it provides an effective way for students to search out the seeds in a passage or story in order to make their changes fit. It is not enough to write a new ending to a story, for example. That ending must flow from the story, which assumes comprehension, and it must bring events to a reasonable conclusion. Writing, for example, that all the children in Margaret Wild's *Let the Celebrations Begin!* lived happily ever after is to belie any knowledge of the survivors of concentration camps, their physical and mental health, their desire to locate parents, and so forth.

- Insert self: Writing self into a story, or a passage is a third way to text tamper. Students do this by becoming a new character, an observer, or the scientist or mathematician who is being studied. ESL students conduct an interview by alternating languages with a character in the story. In the industrial arts, students take some information, such as building a bookcase or roofing a house, and rewrite it for the television show *Home Improvement*. When inserting self, the students may take great liberties as they cozy into a text, but they must remain faithful to its information.

Remarks. This strategy promotes risk taking, thinking, research, close reading, remembering, rereading, checking, cross-checking, integrating information, and writing. Students enjoy finding the gaps and filling them in, writing different parts, and placing themselves in the context. They experience self-satisfaction, gain confidence, and develop some aesthetic sense. Also, this skill of projecting and inferring is an important one for a future that promises rapid change and many unknowns; it will be the basic skill called upon to cope.

Sub-Texting

Explanation. Sub-texting is an idea used in drama by Roslyn Arnold of the University of Sydney, but is applicable to other disciplines as well. Arnold defines sub-texting as a method "of articulating and bringing to the surface all the ideas and associations the reader has in response to the text" (220).

Implementation. (Adapted from Arnold 218–233.)

• Divide students into large groups (Arnold suggests ten in a group).

• Distribute copies of the text, or assign sections of the text to each group.

• Model sub-texting for students.

• Students, in turn, read several lines or sentences as originally written, then they write those lines in first person, as if they were the character, or as if they were present. Finally they read them as a free translation.

• Validate all responses no matter how trivial, silly, or confused they may be. Responses often vary, but with that diversity students begin to see what the text means when it is enacted by others.

• After sub-texting once, the text may be reworked again. (Arnold claims that in the reworking often aberrant interpretations are excised for the more conventional ones.)

Following is an example of how a group of ninth-graders sub-texted a portion of *Romeo and Juliet.*

Romeo and Juliet I i, 163–173

Enter Romeo

TEXT	SUB-TEXT
BENVOLIO: Good morrow, cousin.	Romiester! What's going down?
ROMEO: Is the day so young?	This day's a drag. Is it still only morning?
BENVOLIO: But new struck nine.	It's nine. What's your problem?
ROMEO: Ay me! sad hours seem long. Was that my father that went hence so fast?	I'm bummed—tired of waiting. Hey, was that Dad in the Porsche? Whoa!
BENVOLIO: It was. What sadness lengthens Romeo's hours?	Yeah. One more time, what's your problem?
ROMEO: Not having that which having makes them short.	Not hangin' with my girl.

BENVOLIO: In love?	Man, are you falling in love?
ROMEO: Out—	I'm out of it, I think.
BENVOLIO: Of love?	Why love? You could have your pick.
ROMEO: Out of her favor where I am in love.	She wants a jock, but I'm crazy about her.
BENVOLIO: Alas! that love, so gentle in his view, Should be so tyrannous and rough in proof!	That's a real bummer, man. She's hot, but she sure is making it rough on you.

Remarks. Perhaps more than any reader-response strategy, this one elicits engagement and ownership. In answer to those who may express concern that sub-texting is not authentic reading, Arnold states, "I reiterate the purpose of sub-texting as one of coming to terms with the author's language through a dynamic process of making it one's own. When the process has been experienced effectively, the author's language lives for the reader, in its own right, and as part of the reader's range of experienced language options" (232). Besides, recently published textbooks have so many annotations for almost every line of Shakespeare, the pages look like a dialectical notebook. With sub-texting, at least the annotations are the students' own.

Sequence Charts

Explanation. Sequence charts, while not new, are ideal ways to incorporate writing into a temporal perspective. They may be used to chronicle some historical occurrence, the course of events in a story, stages in a problem, the arrangement of procedures for making or creating something, the steps for following directions, the proceedings of a meeting, or the succession of happenings. They work for any discipline.

Implementation.

• Divide students into small groups.

• Assign text to be sequenced.

• Distribute long sheets of butcher paper or long pieces of cash register tape (about 4′ or 5′) to each group.

• Students reenter the text and sequence it on paper. They may write, draw, cut out suitable pictures, affix small symbolic objects, or use of combination of media, textures, and words.

• Groups share their sequence charts by explaining them to the class and then displaying them somewhere in the room or hall.

Remarks. This strategy, because it is collaborative, enriches the knowledge of each student. It invites reexamination of the text for a particular purpose. It lends itself to variation and specificity. For example, one variation is to keep the sequence chart daily, that is, end each class period with ten minutes or so of work on the chart for students to add what they learned that day. Also, teachers often make sequence charts specific, for example, sequence events by people or chronicle events by dates. Then when the sequence chart is complete, students may go back to add labels, other data, and further explanations. This acts as a review.

Building Meaning

Explanation. This is an ongoing strategy that invites writing in bursts; it is visual, enables review, and almost demands a final product. Building meaning works for any discipline.

Implementation.

- Distribute "bricks" in the form of 3″ × 5″ index cards (or paper cut that size) to students at the end of a week, every several days, or even daily—depending on the class.

- Students quickly write on their cards what is most significant to them. (For teachers with multiple classes, the cards may be color-coded to a class, for example, first period uses green cards; third period, blue.)

- When they have completed their cards, they affix them on the wall. (Qwik-Tac or other reusable adhesives work well because they can be used again and usually do not mar walls.) They begin at the bottom. In this way they quite literally build a writing wall of meaning.

- At the end of the marking period, divide students into groups. Students retrieve their bricks and discuss in groups what they have learned. This serves as a review.

- Students use the information on their cards to synthesize what they have learned and write into a sustained paper.

Remarks. Not only does this strategy enable writing for a purpose, but the writing becomes a visible entity in the room. Students begin writing more as the wall progresses and they see what others have written. The collaborative nature of the final sharing is a novel and interesting way for students to review what they have learned and to continue to learn from others in their group.

Reading/Writing Connections

Explanation. We typically focus students on the concept underway or about to be underway by reading a selection from children's literature, which, while brief, ensures the lesson's direction or purpose. For example, if we are working with students of American literature, we introduce Emily Dickinson through Michael Bedard's delightful book *Emily*. If we are working in social studies, we present the African American experience through an excerpt from Walter Dean Myers's nonfiction work *Now Is Your Time!* If the lesson is aerodynamics in science, Robert Burleigh's award-winning *Flight* fills the bill.

After the reading, students make or we give an artifact associated with the concept. For example, *Emily*, a copy of her poem for the little girl on parchment, a white flower or something else white, or a flower bulb works. This also serves as a prompt for writing.

Often there is the same sense of discovery in the making or receiving of an artifact as there is in writing. As M. C. Richards so eloquently says, "The exchange between the crafts, the mergers and the interpretations, are also witnesses to this centering attitude, which cuts across the lines an allows the values of color and shape and texture and innerness and architecture and use and inspiration all to blow like different currents of air into a single breath through whatever object we make" (63).

Implementation.

- No matter what the level, we gather the students around us as we read. This closeness generates an intensity of purpose and better focuses the lesson.

- Read the book, selection, or excerpt.

- Discuss, predict, raise questions.

- Create a word bank from the vocabulary in the text. (See Carroll's *Authentic Strategies*, pp. 123–129.)

- Distribute or make the artifact.

- Students write something that rises out of the text, the artifact, or both. For *Emily*, creating a poem would be natural, although writing description or conducting research would be appropriate. Another approach invites students to freewrite to the lines, "I brought you some spring," or, "No, you are poetry. This only tries to be."

- This strategy concludes with some type of sharing.

Remarks. "There is a continuum between the child's earliest retelling of the familiar picture-book story and the critical article in a learned journal" (Protherough 79). Knowing that, teachers on every grade level need to rethink the viability of using children's literature from time to time as doors to deeper more sophisticated concepts. Besides the obvious literary connections, the promised artifact always generates anticipation and surprise. Using children's literature as a springboard into any discipline and on any level enables quick access into the purpose of the lesson.

> *"I want to thank you for an idea you gave me," said Peggy Meathenia, Director of C & I.*
> *"What idea is that?" we asked.*
> *"Using children's literature to focus a presentation. Now whenever I have a staff meeting, I find a book that has the message I want to convey encapsulated in it. I use it to start the meeting. People love the books, and it sets a comfortable tone and gets our meetings off on a positive note."*

Artifacts

Explanation. Artifacts associated with concepts, learning, and lessons have been around since records have been kept. Great teachers always used them. Pythagoras used rope, knots, and tiles to clarify his theorems, and Christ used mustard seeds, loaves, and fishes to reinforce his lessons. Indeed, the very invention of written language attributed to the Greeks, is a visual artifact of thought.

The research for the use of artifacts rests upon synectics. Gordon in 1961 named this approach to creative thinking as one that depends upon a comprehension of that which is apparently different. (The prefix *syn-* means together; *ec-* means out; and the suffix *-ics* means a scientific or social system.) So synectics literally is a system that takes out meaning from disparate things. With its main tools of analogy and metaphor, synectics is not unlike Pink's R-Directed Thinking, which he identifies as "simultaneous, metaphorical, aesthetic, contextual, and synthetic" (26).

Because powerful mental connections are made with artifacts—consider the power of happening upon an old photograph of a deceased family member or a class ring or old penknife—we recommend giving careful consideration to the link between lesson and artifact.

Sometimes the artifacts are given to students at the beginning or end of lessons; sometimes they students create them as part of the lesson.

Implementation.

- Students should have some receptacle, a bag, box, or pouch to store their artifacts.

- Teachers introduce a lesson with an artifact to start the creative process, to raise awareness or curiosity, or to capitalize on the learning theory of novelty. Recently, to introduce a workshop on conflict in literature, we used a small piece of white rope tied in a knot. We asked, "Why would we start a workshop this way?" This generated much discussion and conjecture. We concluded the workshop by distributing inexpensive "friendship" bracelets, expandable because they were tied with two knots. This (friendship/knots) reinforced irony, paradox, and other figurative devices authors craft to support conflict in their writing. Every teacher wore his or her bracelet.

- Teachers construct the lesson so students fashion the artifact. For example, after reading Eve Bunting's *The Wall*, a story about a father and son who visit the Vietnam Veterans Memorial in Washington, DC, students do pencil rubbings like the one in the book. When artifacts are so integrated with the lesson they aid moving the lesson into the students' long-term memory.

- The most common use of artifacts is when teachers distribute them at the conclusion of a lesson. Then they act as a concrete metaphor or analogy of the concept taught. For example, after studying Abraham Lincoln, students receive a penny; after studying volcanoes, students receive a piece of pumice (lava rock).

- Students keep these artifacts in their receptacles. At the end of a unit of study or before a test, they extract them one by one for review.

Remarks. Artifacts are not given every day or for every lesson, but are given to introduce, solidify, create interest, reinforce lessons or to develop text-to-self, text-to-text, and text-to world connections.

After working with second-graders on a friendship unit as we modeled for teachers, we gave students long pieces of string and taught them some string games. We read Lizzie and Harold *by Elizabeth Winthrop and Martha Weston because in the book the two friends play string games. Then we upped the ante by inviting the students to write a how-to essay for a friend, explaining how to play the string game of their choice. After the students shared, we let them keep their strings.*

The following year, we returned to the same school. As the principal walked us to our destination, she stopped by a third-grade classroom. "Some of the children in here were in that class you taught last year," she explained. We three stepped inside.

"Boys and girls, do any of you remember these folks?"

"They're the people with the string," a few chorused.

"You remembered," we said. "What else do you remember from that lesson?" One girl remembered the book was about friends, another added "playing string games," another student remembered writing. One boy said the book was about a boy and a girl. In short, one year later, because of the artifact, these students were able to quite accurately reconstruct the lesson. That is powerful learning. Artifacts help that learning.

IMPLEMENTATION MODELS

Overview

In an effort to help teachers incorporate writing as a process and reader response in their disciplines, we have included seven implementation models in this chapter: Language Arts, Social Studies, Science, Mathematics, Kindergarten, plus two high-school models. These models may be adapted, adopted, and modeled to fit to any level. A high-school English teacher may take the kindergarten idea of working with a corpus of work by an author, or a science teacher may work with a genre, for example, the informative essay. Also, these models are meant as suggested time-lines. Some students may require an accelerated adaptation, while others students may demand more time be spent in certain areas. Skilled teachers may even adapt these to smaller groups with the class or even to individual learners within the class.

To design a day-by-day implementation guide, teachers decide upon a key concept or genre, choose children's books or other literature that illuminate that concept or genre, establish the skills to be covered, and progress through the days in natural reader-response ways.

Regardless of the discipline, students should keep writing folders. They should retrieve them from their storage box or file at the beginning of the class, file any writing done during that class in them, and replace them in their proper place at the conclusion of the class. Each student should write his or her name on the file and be fully responsible for keeping its contents in order. If portfolios are part of the system, these writing folders will assume an even more important role as the repository of all their written work.

Areas in the room for writing, the conference, group work, as well as places for materials should all be clearly delineated on the first day of implementation. Having clear classroom procedures up front will save valuable instructional time in the long run, set the tenor and pace for more successful implementation, and place some responsibility upon the student.

The Language Arts Model

This model is based on six weeks of study, a forty-five- to fifty-five-minute period of time. The genre is the narrative, but this model could be reworked for poetry, persuasive essays, drama, or any other genre. The reading/writing connection follows the format of reading a related book or excerpt that embodies that genre, distributing or making an artifact, writing a response that rises out of the reading and artifact, modeling that writing, sharing and debriefing.

Day 1—Generally introduce the narrative genre, perhaps referring to their language arts textbook. Read a story and discuss informally. Lead students through a "warm-up" based on that story, such as trigger words or freewriting. Distribute writing folders. Talk about their purpose. File prewriting. Discuss classroom procedures.

Day 2—Reading/Writing Connection, for example, *Aunt Isabel Tells a Good One* by Kate Duke. Discuss. Distribute miniature mice (either plastic ones available in the miniature section of craft stores or students may make them from paper or felt). Pair students so they may together write a story following the model in the book. Teacher writes too. Students will not finish, but they have a start. Take a few moments at the end of the class to share story ideas. Debrief. File.

Day 3—Reading/Writing Connection, e.g., Read *Cyclops* by Leonard Everett Fisher. Discuss. Distribute paper plates and one plastic eye (available at craft stores). Students construct quickly a Cyclops mask. Under the eye, they make a small hole. Then they take their masks, sit somewhere in the room, and write a description of what they see through their Cyclopian eye. Teacher writes too. Several students share. Debrief. File.

Day 4—Mini-teach on description as part of a good story. Build upon writing done the day before. Use textbook to augment lesson. Debrief.

Day 5—Mini-teach on setting as part of a good story. Build upon writing done day 3. Discuss how that could be a setting for a story. Debrief.

Day 6—Reading/Writing Connection. Read an excerpt from *Bearstone* by Will Hobbs. Discuss. Distribute clay. Students fashion their own "bearstones." They write about why they chose the animal or symbol they chose. Teacher writes too. Several students share. Debrief.

Day 7—Reading/Writing Connection, e.g., Demi's *The Empty Pot*. Distribute or make tiny clay pots. Discuss. Students write about a time when they did the right thing and were rewarded (or they can make up a time). Several students share. Debrief.

Day 8—Free reading/Freewriting—Student/Teacher Conferences. This day permits students to pursue independent reading, finish something that is in their folder, do other writing, or conference with the teacher about an unclear concept. This also allows the teacher to "catch up" any students who may have been absent.

Day 9—Free reading/Freewriting—Student/Teacher Conferences.

Day 10—Reading/Writing Connection. "The People Could Fly" a story in the book by the same name, written by Virginia Hamilton. Distribute feathers. Students (and teacher) write a response to the sentence stub—"If I could fly . . . " Several students share. Debrief. (Students now have at least five pieces of prewriting in their folders.)

Day 11—Introduce the elements of the narrative. Use "Little Miss Muffet." Students write out these elements on a sheet of paper. Study a literary sample of the narrative, perhaps from the textbook or another piece of children's literature such as Margaret Hodges's retelling of *Saint George and the Dragon*. Review the elements in the stories taken through the reading/writing connections thus far.

Day 12—Students review the elements (usually by reciting "Little Miss Muffet"). They turn over the sheet on which they listed them in order to make a grid. Do not make these grids for the students. Remember, as they are constructing their grids, they

Fig. 13.3. Elements of a Narrative in "Little Miss Muffett."

Elements of narrative in "Little Miss Muffet

Little Miss Muffet sat on a tuffet (introduction of protagonist,- action, and setting)

Along came a spider (introduction of antagonist)

And sat down beside her (conflict)

And frightened Miss Muffet away. (resolution)

are in the act of remembering. Their learning is being reinforced. Students then reread all their prewriting and record the elements they have from each prewriting onto the grid. For example, students may only check a protagonist and antagonist for their response to *Aunt Isabel*; or they may only have a setting for *Cyclops*, but for the *Empty Pot*, they may have a protagonist, antagonist, setting, and problem. After they have recorded their prewriting on their grids, they examine what they have already written, and make a decision. They must make a commitment to develop one prewriting into a narrative. That is their challenge. Students make their decisions. Discuss and debrief.

Day 13—Teachers model using their own prewriting for a mini-teach on moving prewriting into a narrative genre, what has to be added, deleted, elaborated upon, what elements are missing, and so forth.

Day 14—Mini-lesson on ways to begin a narrative. Students practice leads for their story. Share. Debrief.

Day 15—Mini-lesson on elaboration strategies for the narrative. Work on the laminae of meaning. Use plenty of models from literature and from teacher and student work. Students practice. Share. Debrief.

Table 13.1. Grid to Analyze Elements of Narative in Students' Prewriting.

Narrative Elements	Day 2 Prewriting	Day 3 Prewriting	Day 6 Prewriting	Day 7 Prewriting	Day 10 Prewriting
Protagonist	✔			✔	
Antagonist	✔				✔
Setting		✔		✔	
Action/Plot					
Conflict/Problem				✔	
Resolution					
Beginning					
Middle					
Ending					
Interest					

Day 16—Mini-lesson on conclusions for the narrative. Students practice. Share. Debrief. For days 14, 15, and16, it is a good idea to incorporate examples from literature in the mini-lesson.

Day 17—Skills lessons: Teach quotation marks direct and indirect dialogue, the proper way to punctuate dialogue, or other skills appropriate for the narrative, the level and needs of the learner.

Day 18—Skills lessons: Teach the paragraph and when and how to indent dialogue. An effective way to teach indention is with a quick object lesson. Hold up an empty soda pop can. When all eyes are focused on the can, squeeze it. Ask students to offer words to describe what you have just done. They will suggest words such as "squeezed," "crushed," "squashed." Eventually someone will say, "You dented it!" When they do, draw a parallel between the dent in the can and the dent made with words. Show how there can be no dent if the words do not first go inward (like the dent in) and then come outward (like the part not dented in). Explain how "indenting" is the same as "denting in." Make the concept concrete.

Day 19—Student grouping technique. Use "Say Back." Student/Teacher Conferences.

Day 20—Free reading/Freewriting—Student/Teacher Conferences.

Day 21—Ratiocination. If quotation marks and paragraphing have been taken as skills lessons, students might take red markers and "put lipstick" on their quotation marks. This helps them check that they have both opened and closed their quoted material. This also helps students double check where they have placed the terminal marks. For paragraphs, they might check indentions with red arrows or mark their paragraphs as TRIPSQA, transitions, or paragraph blocs.

Day 22—Final publication will be in the format of an eight-page book. Fold books, identify the cover, title page, and the dedication page. Number pages, and label the last page "All About the Author." Teach titles, strategies for getting a title, and how to write a title.

Day 23—Visit the library. Find the narrative section. Examine the books. Distribute library cards and envelopes. Each student makes a card and envelope to be affixed in his or her book.

Day 24—Students reenter their writing to check spelling.

Day 25—Analytic Scale.

Day 26—Writing final copy.

Day 27—Writing final copy.

Day 28—Clocking.

Day 29—Free reading/Freewriting—Student/Teacher Conferences.

Day 30—Publication Day—Celebration of the Publication—Read around.

Kindergarten Implementation Model

Day 1—General introduction/creating an environment for kinders/reading/writing. Classroom rules and management strategies. Create an author's corner, for example, on David McPhail. Consult Sharron L. McElmeel's *Bookpeople: A First Album.*

Day 2—Reading/Writing Connection. Talk about pets. Read McPhail's *Emma's Pet.* Students write (draw) a story (narrative) about a pet they had, have, or wish they had, or a friend or family member's pet. Share from Author's Chair.

Day 3—Reading/Writing Connection. Talk about something that broke and needed to be fixed. Read *Fix-It* by David McPhail. Students write (draw) a "How To" fix something. Share from Author's Chair.

Day 4—Mini-teach on the *B* sound since Emma is a bear. Find objects in the room with that letter. Work with that letter in a context.

Day 5—Mini-teach on bears. Connect to animal study and science.

Day 6—Students do dramatic play activities on bears. They walk like them, make the sounds, and reenact the stories.

Day 7—Reading/Writing Connection. Talk about the family, the members of the family. List words associated with family such as *mother, father, brother, sister, aunt,* and so forth. Read McPhail's *Sisters.* Students write about someone in their family. Share in Author's Chair.

Day 8—Reading/Writing Connection. Talk about a time when students were lost or felt lost, for example in the supermarket. Read McPhail's *Lost!.* Students write about a time when they were lost or when someone they knew was lost. Share in Author's Chair.

Day 9—Reading/Writing Connection. Talk about losing a tooth or having a toothache. Read David McPhail's *The Bear's Toothache*. Students write about a time when they lost a tooth or had a toothache. Share in Author's Chair.

Day 10—Students make "Bear-bag name places" out of grocery bags. (See Carroll's *The Best of Dr. JAC*, 4.)

1. Save enough large brown paper grocery shopping bags so you have one per child.

2. Cut the brown shopping bag down the two folds on each side, making two large bear arms.

3. Students draw or paint a head in the inside section of the front panel (this usually contains the name of the market).

4. They draw or paint a body inside the section that was the bottom of the bag, and legs on the inside of the section that was the back of the bag.

5. Students write their names across the bear's chest.

6. Girls make a red paper bow for the bear's head; boys place the bow as a tie at its neck.

7. They sit these bears in their chairs for parents' night. They fold their bear's arms around a folder that contains their work.

8. Parents find their child's bear when they visit.

Day 11—Reading/Writing Connection. Talk about a time it snowed, what kids do in the snow, what snow feels like, and so forth. Read McPhail's *Snow Lion*. Students make snowflakes and paste them on paper and display. Students do movement activities like snowflakes falling. Play "Let it Snow, Let it Snow" or something like "Jingle Bells."

Day 12—Reading/Writing Connection. Talk about something special, what makes something special, and so on. Read McPhail's *Something Special*. Students make something special (provide materials). Share in Author's Chair.

Day 13—Model/Mini-teach. Review the *B* sound. Teach the *S* sound. Create a word bank of words that begin with the letter *S*.

Day 14—Reading/Writing Connection. Talk about airplanes, flying, and travel. Read McPhail's *First Flight*. Students write an informative paper about a kind of travel they know. Share in Author's Chair.

Day 15—Reading/Writing Connection. Continue the word on locomotion and travel. Read McPhail's *The Train*. Students form groups. Each group makes a part of a train. They write something on it (words of what trains do, a name, numbers, letters). Display by groups in the room.

Day 16—Reading/Writing Connection. Continue the word on locomotion and travel. Read Emilie Warren McLeod's (illustrated by David McPhail) *The Bear's Bicycle*. Students decide if this book, illustrated but not written by McPhail, should go in the Author's Corner.

Day 17—Look at all the books by David McPhail. Walk over to the Author's Corner and review the books. Invite students to tell what they remember about the books, which one they liked best and why. Perhaps reread a favorite.

Day 18—Count the number of bears in a book; in several books. Give the bears' names. Distribute bear cookies or gummy bears.

Day 19—Rhythmic activity. Use Bill Martin Jr.'s *Brown Bear, Brown Bear, What Do You See?*

Day 20—Read a version of *Goldilocks and the Three Bears*. Students write a letter to Baby Bear.

Day 21—Bear's habitats: Locate on a map places where bears live, such as wilderness areas and national parks.

Day 22—Library skills appropriate to that concept. Take students to library to find other bear books. Teach proper behavior in the library.

Day 23—Rhythmic activity. Use Bill Martin Jr.'s *Polar Bear, Polar Bear, What Do You Hear?*

Day 24—Check out nonfiction bear books from the library, such as *The Little Polar Bear* series by Hans de Beer.

Day 25—Work with students on writing a book, how they would go about it, ideas.

Day 26—Students make an eight-page book about bears.

Day 27—Students group and read their books to peers.

Day 28—Students continue writing, edit, and conference with teacher.

Day 29—Students illustrate their books.

Day 30—Publication Day—Celebration of the Publication—Share a selected portion of the report in a read around.

Social Studies Implementation Model

Day 1—General introduction/creating an environment for a Social Studies/reading/writing classroom—Time/creating a sense of how social scientists work/establishing the key concept, for example, the Holocaust.

Day 2—Reading/Writing Connection on the Holocaust. Read *Let the Celebrations Begin!* by Margaret Wild and Julie Vivas. Students begin a "Holocaust Notebook" of the key words and words of special interest, and Holocaust facts. Keep books shared as resources in the classroom. Share several. Debrief.

Day 3—Reading/Writing Connection on that Holocaust. Read Eve Bunting's *Terrible Things: An Allegory of the Holocaust.* Students write their reaction to the allegory in their notebooks. Share. Debrief.

Day 4—Mini-teach on one aspect of the holocaust, such as the Nazi Party, Adolf Hitler, concentration camps, boycott of Jewish businesses, book burnings, the political climate in Europe, and so forth. Consult social studies book information—add to notebooks. Debrief.

Day 5—View a nonfiction video on Anne Frank, Alan Resnais's documentary *Night and Fog*, or portions of Leni Riefenstahl's *Triumph of the Will*. Add information to notebooks. Share. Debrief.

Day 6—Reading/Writing Connection on the Holocaust. Read portions of Lois Lowry's *Number the Stars*. Students take the position of Annemarie and write what they would do for a friend in those circumstances. Share. Debrief.

Day 7—Reading/Writing Connection on the Holocaust. Read selected passages from Jane Yolen's *The Devil's Arithmetic*. Students assume the persona of Chaya and write how they feel about the numbers tattooed on their arms. Share. Debrief.

Day 8—Divide students into groups. Distribute long strips of butcher paper. Students create a timeline. The begin in 1919 when Adolf Hitler joined the German Workers' Party, which a year later became the National Socialist German Workers' Party—the Nazi Party—and end with the liberation, May 8, 1945, when Germany surrendered to the Allies.

Day 9—Free reading/Freewriting—Student/Teacher Conferences.

Day 10—Reading/Writing Connection on the Holocaust—e.g., Share Inge Auerbacher's personal biography *I Am a Star: Child of the Holocaust*. Students write about innocent children as victims of the Holocaust in their notebooks. Share. Debrief.

Day 11—Introduce Art Spiegelman's *Maus*, a two-book graphic novel series on the Holocaust. Students add their reaction to the Holocaust via cartoons to notebooks. Play some Jewish folk music; play some German folk music; play a symphony by Wagner. Share. Debrief.

Day 12—Grid the Holocaust, for example, Auschwitz and other concentration camps, nonfiction accounts, fictionalized accounts, Hitler, wearing the Star of David, relocations, and so forth. Chart responses as possible foci for a paper. Make decisions—discuss.

Day 13—Model/Mini-teach an informative essay. Discuss/study/work on the format of this type of essay for final publication.

Day 14—Teach the appropriate beginnings for an essay (although informative essays are usually formal, personal anecdotes or quotations are often as effective a lead as is a startling statistic or fact).

Day 15—Teach the appropriate elaboration for this essay (include ways to support information and references).

Day 16—Teach the appropriate endings (indication that further study is needed or what was learned is often better than a dull summary).

Day 17—Teach appropriate related social studies concepts.

Day 18—Teach appropriate related social studies concepts.

Day 19—Teach appropriate related social studies concepts.

Day 20—Teach appropriate related social studies concepts.

Day 21—Teach appropriate related social studies concepts.

Day 22—Library skills appropriate to the Holocaust in general and each student's focus specifically. Take students to library to check data, find any additional support or information to add to their paper.

Day 23—Ratiocination.

Day 24—Student grouping—use "Say Back."

Day 25—Analytic Scale (work with students)

Day 26—Students write final copy.

Day 27—Free reading/Freewriting and/or make-up work—Student/Teacher Conferences.

Day 28—Clocking the final paper.

Day 29—Final six-week test.

Day 30—Publication Day—Celebration of the Publication—Share a selected portion of the report in a read around.

Mathematics Implementation Model

Day 1—General introduction/creating an environment for a mathematics/reading/writing classroom—time/creating the science area/the lab/supplies/a sense of how mathematicians work/establish the key concept, for example: problem solving. Share the following parallels with students:

Composing	Problem Solving
• prewriting	• experiencing the phenomenon
• writing	• stating the problem
• revising	• constructing a mathematical model
• editing	• manipulating algebraic statements and stating a solution
• publishing	• interpreting the solution in a mathematical context and in the real world

(Adapted from Joan Countryman's *Writing to Learn Mathematics.*)

Day 2—Reading/Writing Connection on that concept. Read Margarette Reid's *The Button Box.* Students begin a "Math Notebook" by listing in it the kind of thinking involved in the story. Relate to thinking involved in a problem. Share several lists. Discuss.

Day 3—Reading/Writing Connection on that concept. Read *Let the Celebrations Begin!* by Margaret Wild and Julie Vivas. Pose the problem: Based on the information in the book and other information students may know about concentration camps and prisons, students estimate the area of the camp. Students add to notebooks with their reasons. Share. Debrief.

Day 4—Mini-teach on one aspect of area using problem solving, teach how to figure the area of a circle. Formula states: Area = pi times radius time radius or $A = \pi r^2$. Conduct an experiment to reinforce the area of a circle—divide students into groups. Distribute circular lids. Students determine the area of the lid. Change to metric. Then tell students the second hand of the clock is 6 in. (15 cm) long. Figure the area the hand sweeps in 1 minute. In their notebooks, students explain how they worked the problems. Consult mathematics book for information. Debrief.

Day 5—Mini-teach on another aspect of area using problem solving, teach how to figure surface area. Formula states: Area = Length × Width. Conduct an experiment to teach surface area—divide students into groups. Give each group different size boxes, cereal boxes, open boxes, and so forth. Students compute the area. In their notebooks, students explain how they worked the problems. Consult mathematics book for more information. Debrief.

Day 6—Groups find an area in the school, for example, the classroom, cafeteria, outside playground, principal's office. Each group writes a problem involving area for another group to solve. Exchange problems. Solve. Share. Add to notebooks. Debrief.

Day 7—Reading/Writing Connection on the concept. Read Daniel Barbot's *A Bicycle for Rosaura.* Students working in groups determine the problem and offer possible solutions. Debrief.

Day 8—Reading/Writing Connection on problem solving on the concept of estimating. *A Million Fish . . . More or Less* by Patricia C. McKissack. In their notebooks, students write what is necessary to estimate and what makes a good estimate. Share and discuss.

Day 9—Reading/Writing Connection on problem solving on the concept of money. Read David M. Schwartz's *How Much Is a Million?* and *If You Made a Million* or *The Go-Around Dollar* by Barbara Johnston Adams. Divide students into groups. Distribute catalogs. Students list what they would buy, and compute other problems using money.

Day 10—Use Marilyn Burns's *Math for Smarty Pants* for other unique problem-solving situations.

Day 11—Use Janice Van Cleave's *Math for Every Kid* for additional activities on problem solving.

Day 12—Grid Problem Solving. Students reread their notebooks. Chart responses as possibilities for a report. Make decisions. Discuss.

Day 13—Model/Mini-teach for creating a book of problems. Discuss/study/work on the format for this type of book.

Day 14—Teach the appropriate format: introduction that explains the book's purpose; an organized way to categorize the problems such as: fractions, subtraction, ratio; or word problems, number problems; or easy, difficult, almost impossible.

Day 15—Teach clarity of expression, appropriate word choice and include ways to illustrate complex problems. Use the mathematics textbook as a resource.

Day 16—Start draft of Book of Problems.

Day 17—Teach appropriate related mathematics concepts.

Day 18—Teach appropriate related mathematics concepts.

Day 19—Teach appropriate related mathematics concepts.

Day 20—Teach appropriate related mathematics concepts.

Day 21—Teach appropriate related mathematics concepts.

Day 22—Library skills appropriate to that concept. Take students to library to check data, find any additional support or information to add to their paper/book.

Day 23—Ratiocination.

Day 24—Student grouping—Use "Say Back."

Day 25—Analytic Scale (work with students)

Day 26—Students write final copy.

Day 27—Free reading/Freewriting and/or make-up work—Student/Teacher Conferences.

Day 28—Clocking the final paper.

Day 29—Final six-week test.

Day 30—Publication Day—Celebration of the Publication—Share a selected portion of the report in a read around.

Science Implementation Model

Day 1—General introduction/creating an environment for a Science classroom—time/creating the science area/the lab/supplies/a sense of how scientists work/establishing the key concept, for example, space.

Day 2—Reading/Writing Connection on that concept. Read "Our Launchpad" from Heather Couper and Nigel Henbest's *The Space Atlas*. Students begin a "Space Facts Notebook" of the key words and words of special interest, and space facts. Keep books shared as resources in the classroom. Share several. Debrief.

Day 3—Reading/Writing Connection on that concept. Read Robin and Sally Hirst's *My Place in Space*. Students add to notebooks. Share. Debrief.

Day 4—Mini-teach on one aspect of space, spiral galaxy—conduct an experiment to reinforce the concept. 1. Fill a jar about three-quarters full of water; 2. Sprinkle with about twenty paper circles cut from a hole punch; 3. Quickly stir water in a circular motion with a straw; 4. View the motion of the water and circles from top and sides when you stop. Compare to the Milky Way Galaxy. Consult science book information—add to notebooks. Debrief.

Day 5—Visit a planetarium or museum with a space display or consult the yearly *National Geographic Educational Service's Film and Video Catalog* for excellent videos on space. (Published through the National Geographic Society, Washington, DC) Add to notebooks. Share. Debrief.

Day 6—Reading/Writing Connection on that concept. Read Ruth Young's *A Trip to Mars*. Students add to their notebooks. Share. Debrief.

Day 7—Reading/Writing Connection on that concept. Read Jeanne Willis's *Earthlets as Explained by Professor Xargl*. Students choose some things from their notebooks and using Earthlets as their model, they write them up from a different point of view. Share. Debrief.

Day 8—Free reading/Freewriting—Student/Teacher Conferences.

Day 9—Free reading/Freewriting—Student/Teacher Conferences.

Day 10—Reading/Writing Connection on that concept. Read Laurence Santrey's *Discovering the Stars*. Students add to notebooks. Share. Debrief.

Day 11—Introduce Seymour Simon's series on planets. Play portions of Gustav Holst's *The Planets*. Students add to notebooks. Share. Debrief.

Day 12—Grid space (entering space, living in space, space suits, space travel, and so forth); galaxies (spiral, Milky Way, movement, exploding, and so forth); planets (Earth, Mercury, Venus, Mars, Jupiter, Saturn, Uranus, Neptune, orbiting speed, rotations, heat shields, magnetic fields, and so forth); stars (brightness, nearest, shooting, size, twinkling, variable, and so forth). Students reread their notebooks— chart responses as possibilities for a report. Make decisions—discuss.

Day 13—Model/Mini-teach a report. Discuss/study/work on the format of a report for final publication.

Day 14—Teach the appropriate beginnings for a report (although a report is informative and usually formal, personal anecdotes or quotations are often as effective a lead as is a startling statistic or fact).

Day 15—Teach the appropriate elaboration for a report (include ways to support information and references).

Day 16—Teach the appropriate endings (indication that further study is needed or what was learned is often better than a dull summary).

Day 17—Teach appropriate related science concepts.

Day 18—Teach appropriate related science concepts.

Day 19—Teach appropriate related science concepts.

Day 20—Teach appropriate related science concepts.

Day 21—Teach appropriate related science concepts.

Day 22—Library skills appropriate to that concept. Take students to library to check data, find any additional support or information to add to their paper.

Day 23—Ratiocination.

Day 24—Student grouping—Use "Say Back."

Day 25—Analytic scale (work with students).

Day 26—Students write final copy.

Day 27—Free reading/Freewriting and/or make-up work—Student/Teacher Conferences.

Day 28—Clocking the final paper.

Day 29—Final six-week test.

Day 30—Publication Day—Celebration of the Publication—Share a selected portion of the report in a read around.

For this second edition of *Acts of Teaching*, we invited our assistant Jill Aufill to share two of her high-school implementation models from her forthcoming book (*In the Evidence*, Absey, 2008), to include here. The first is ELA; the second is Social Studies.

Twenty-One-Day ELA Implementation Model—High School

Writing Rubric

Open-ended Rubric

Day 1
Preview Vocabulary—word bank with *S*.
Brainstorm words for "shame."
Prewrite on the idea of "shame" and share responses.
Read "Shame" by Dick Gregory (memoir—expository).
Teach and model: Drawing pictures/symbols (paragraphs/chunks of paragraphs).

Day 2
Return to "Shame."
Teach:
  • Topics, Themes, and Prompts (Carroll's *Authentic Strategies*)
Write to one of the prompts for ten to fifteen minutes.
Share drafts or parts of drafts as time allows.

Day 3
Return to the draft.
Teach:
  • Developing a working title (focus and coherence)
  • Prove Its! (depth and development of ideas) (Carroll's *Guide to Writing* 2–3)
  • Thought Bubbles (depth of ideas) (Carroll's *Guide to Writing* 7–9)
Share examples of each strategy as time allows.
Peer Conferences—Point out what you like about this piece.

Day 4
Teach:
  • Alternate leads—"Post-It notes possibility" (organization) (Carroll's *Guide to Writing* 28)
  • write three new leads for the composition
  • add one or two to the composition for depth of ideas
  • Conclusions (organization) (Carroll's *Conclusions*)
  • write three new conclusions for the composition
  • add one or two to the composition for depth of ideas
Share examples of each strategy as time allows.
Continue working on draft.

Day 5
Finish draft.
Ratiocinate for "be" verbs, first words, and sentence variety.
Make revisions.

Day 6
Clocking.
Make final corrections.
Collect drafts and final copies.
Use writing rubric to assess.

Day 7

Discuss the open-ended rubric.

Teach purpose for reading.

Return to "Shame."

Model the two-column graphic organizer to gather textual evidence (Aufill's *In the Evidence*).

Choose one:

How does poverty affect the narrator's behavior?

Why is the author embarrassed in "Shame?"

What does the author learn about shame?

How is self-esteem important in "Shame?"

How does the author's attitude toward his poverty change in "Shame?"

Note: Support you answer with evidence from the text.

Day 8

Return to "Shame."

Students write open-ended responses.

Share answers in peer groups of three.

Teach "evolving" open-ended responses (Aufill's *In the Evidence*).

Day 9

Return to "evolving" open-ended responses.

Use samples from Day 8 as models.

Use the open-ended rubric to collaboratively "evolve" sample responses through the score points.

Model embedding textual evidence.

Collect "evolved" responses to check that students have successfully completed the task.

Day 10

Read "The Moustache" by Robert Cormier (fiction—literary).

Draw pictures/symbols (paragraphs/chunks of paragraphs).

Day 11

Return to "The Moustache."

Discuss main idea and summary.

Write a summary of "The Moustache" using the "hand" method (Carroll's *Authentic Strategies*).

Day 12

Return to "The Moustache" by Robert Cormier.

Review purpose for reading and the open-ended rubric.

Use the two-column graphic organizer to gather textual evidence (Aufill's *In the Evidence*).

Choose one:

- In "The Moustache," what does the reader learn about Mike?
- In "The Moustache," what does the reader learn about old age?
- What does Mike learn about maturity in "The Moustache?"
- Note: Support your answer with evidence from the selection.

Students write open-ended responses.

Share answers in peer groups of three using the open-ended rubric.

Day 13
Select several responses from Day 12.
Model and work whole class to " evolve" several sample responses.
Students should revise their own responses.
Collect "evolved" responses.
Use the open-ended rubric to assess.

Day 14
Read excerpt from *Crossing the Wire* by Will Hobbs.
Vocabulary—word bank with a drawing of the Mexican-American border (or any other
    border).
Reader response to excerpt from *Crossing the Wire* by Will Hobbs.

Day 15
Brainstorm:
   • Topics, Themes, and Prompts (Carroll's *Authentic Strategies*)
Write to the prompt for twenty to thirty minutes.
Share examples of each strategy as time allows.

Day 16
Return to the draft.
Review and ask students to include evidence of these in their drafts:
   • Working Title
   • Prove Its! (Carroll's *Guide to Writing* 2–3)
   • Snapshots (Lane's *After THE END* 32–35)
   • Thought Bubbles (Carroll's *Guide to Writing* 7–9)
   • Leads (Carroll's *Guide to Writing* 28–31)
   • Conclusions (Carroll's *Conclusions*)
Teach:
   • Dialogue (Carroll's *Guide to Writing* 41–42)
   • Thesis/Antithesis (Carroll's *Guide to Writing* 34–35)
Share examples of each strategy as time allows.
Collect and scan.

Day 17
Return to the draft.
Peer/teacher conferences.
Revise compositions to add comments from peer/teacher conferences.

Day 18
Finish draft.
Ratiocinate for "be" verbs and sentence variety.
Finish revisions.

Day 19
Clocking.
Make final corrections.
Collect drafts and final copies.
Use writing rubric to assess.

Day 20
Read "Autopsies done on 5 bodies found in the Rio Grande."
Create a visual thematically linking *Crossing the Wire* excerpt and "Autopsies."
Discuss the "Welcome to America" visual (Watkins, 2006).
Discuss the expectations of the crossover question.
Work on crossover questions for excerpt from *Crossing the Wire* and "Autopsies."

What do immigrants risk (or have to overcome) in the excerpt from *Crossing the Wire* and "Autopsies?"
Support your answer with evidence from *both* selections.

Or
What is one common characteristic the author of "Shame" and Mike in "The Moustache" share? Support your answer with evidence from *both* selections.

Write an open-ended answer.
Collect and assess using the rubric.

Day 21
Review and debrief strategies. Review test-taking strategies.

Fifteen-Day Writing Implementation Model for Social Studies

We do not write in order to be understood; we write in order to understand.
—C. Day Lewis

Writing is thinking on paper.
—Dr. Joyce Armstrong Carroll

Academic Journal. These journals serve a variety of writing and thinking purposes, the most important of which is to provide a context and a record of new learning. For students, their individual academic journal creates a record of interaction with social studies texts, becomes a place to keep class notes, record class discussions, write drafts of essays, and collect primary and secondary source documentation for research papers. A place to ask and answer questions, explore new concepts, discuss issues, and extend thinking from the concrete to the abstract are only some of journal possibilities.

Day 1
Preview of content: begin with quotes that reflect the content/concept. For example:

"I hate war as only a soldier who has lived it can, only as one who has seen its brutality, its futility, and its *stupidity*."
—Dwight D. Eisenhower

"The first casualty, when war comes, is truth."
—Hiram Johnson, Governor, Senator, and the 1912 Vice-Presidential
candidate on the ticket with Theodore Roosevelt

"Wars are inevitable so long as society is divided into classes, so long as the exploitation of man by man exists."

—Lenin

"There was never a good war or a bad peace."

—Benjamin Franklin

"I am a firm believer in the people. If given the truth, they can be depended upon to meet any national crisis. The great point is to bring them the real facts."

—Abraham Lincoln

> Students choose a quote and write a short response in their academic journal.
> Share written responses as time allows.
> Discuss the purposes and patterns of war.

Instructional Goal. Through the writing and reading of responses as an anticipatory activity, the teacher solicits opinions from students. This approach creates student ownership—students are engaged through offering their personal perspectives.

Day 2

Ask students to imagine fighting in a battle. Ask them to write their thoughts in their academic journals using sensory images: How would the fighting look? What might they smell during the battle? What might they hear? Might there be a sense of taste (blood, fear, danger, adrenaline)? How might it feel to be fighting?

Introduce content: The Battle of Gettysburg and its impact on the Civil War. Read a short excerpt from *The Red Badge of Courage* by Stephen Crane (fiction) and/or *Soldier's Heart* by Gary Paulsen (nonfiction). *A Soldier's Heart*, based on the life of real fifteen-year-old Charley Goddard, sharply contrasts the glory of war with its horror. Also read the textbook account.

Discuss and compare student responses to those in *The Red Badge of Courage, Soldier's Heart,* and the textbook.

Instructional Goal. Teacher provides content information on Gettysburg and students take notes in their academic journals.

Day 3

Preview five to seven words from *The Gettysburg Address.* The students record these words on either a gray or blue piece of fabric or colored paper that they can later staple into their academic journals.

Vocabulary suggestions: *fourscore (and seven years ago), conceived, proposition, consecrate, hallow, nobly* (and any other words students may not know in this context.)

Students keep a record of these words in their academic journals.
Read aloud *The Gettysburg Address.* Stop as the previewed vocabulary appears in context.

The Gettysburg Address

November 19, 1863

Fourscore and seven years ago our fathers brought forth upon this continent a new nation, conceived in liberty and dedicated to the proposition that all men are created equal.

Now we are engaged in a great civil war, testing whether that nation or any nation so conceived and so dedicated can long endure. We are met on a great battlefield of that war. We have come to dedicate a portion of that field as a final resting-place for those who here gave their lives that that nation might live. It is altogether fitting and proper that we should do this.

But in a larger sense, we cannot dedicate, we cannot consecrate, we cannot hallow this ground. The brave men, living and dead who struggled here have consecrated it far above our poor power to add or detract. The world will little note nor long remember what we say here, but it can never forget what they did here. It is for us the living rather to be dedicated here to the unfinished work that they who fought here have thus far so nobly advanced. It is rather for us to be here dedicated to the great task remaining before us—that from these honored dead we take increased devotion to that cause for which they gave the last full measure of devotion—that we here highly resolve that these dead shall not have died in vain, that this nation under God shall have a new birth of freedom, and that government of the people, by the people, for the people shall not perish from the earth.

Instructional Goal. Introducing and leading students through a discussion of content specific vocabulary scaffolds reading comprehension. Teach *The Gettysburg Address*.

Day 4

Students draft a response to Lincoln's speech in their academic journals. Offer students choice: They can write their response in any genre (letter, newspaper report, poem, editorial, etc.), and they can write as either a Southerner or a Northerner. Be sure each class has some students writing as Southerners and some students writing as Northerners.

Instructional Goal. Perspective influences content.

Day 5

Return to *The Gettysburg Address*.
Teach:
- Topics, Themes, and Prompts using a tri-fold.

See *Authentic Strategies for High-Stakes Tests* by Joyce Armstrong Carroll (pp. 17–21).

Topics. What topics are addressed in *The Gettysburg Address*? These topics or subjects should just be a word or two. Typical examples are: "war," "death," "heroes." The speech elicits many possibilities.

Themes. What was Lincoln trying to convey to the audience gathered at the battle site? What are possible themes? Remind students that the Civil War was not yet over. Generally, themes are written as phrases or sentences. They are not just a word or two. Examples: "War means death." "There are no winners in a civil war." "Soldiers should not die in vain." "We should honor those who serve our country."

Instructional Goal. Point out themes are universal and in this case would apply to Gettysburg as well as to other battles of other wars. This reinforces the idea of historical patterns.

Prompts. Turn each theme into a prompt (statement or question). For example: The topic "war" becomes a springboard to the theme "War means death," which can then generate several prompts:

- Write an essay about the price of war.

- Who are the victims of war?

- How does the death of a soldier impact his/her family?

- How is the death of a civilian different from the death of a soldier?

Brainstorm a list of words to describe aspects of war. Remind students of war words or ideas they used while writing in their academic journals.

Day 6

Discuss how aspects of war are portrayed in film.

Show short clips of several films. Students should take notes in their academic journals.

Film suggestions: *The Patriot* (Revolutionary War); *Glory, Red Badge of Courage, Gone with the Wind* (Civil War); *All Quiet on the Western Front, Flyboys, Gallipoli,* or *Sergeant York* (WW I); *Pearl Harbor* (the bombing), *Saving Private Ryan, Patton, Casablanca, Schindler's List, Battle of the Bulge, A Bridge Too Far, Sands of Iwo Jima, The Longest Day, Tora! Tora! Tora!* (WW II); *Pork Chop Hill, The Bridges at Toko-Ri,* clips from *M*A*S*H*—the TV series (Korea); *Apocalypse Now, Good Morning, Vietnam, We Were Soldiers, Forrest Gump, Rumor of War* (Vietnam); *Renaissance Man, Black Hawk Down, A Few Good Men* (peace time).

Instructional Goal

Students return to the prompts of Day 5 and choose one.
Prewrite for ten to fifteen minutes in their academic journals.
Students should incorporate pertinent information from the film clips.
The students will eventually produce a persuasive documented essay.
Share drafts or parts of drafts as time allows. Students should begin to identify historical patterns.

Day 7
Return to the draft.
Take students to the library and/or internet to research their prompts.
- Students locate both primary and secondary sources
- Students keep a bibliography of sources in their academic journals

Review:
- Primary and secondary sources
- Developing a working title for focus and coherence
- Prove Its! for depth and development of ideas

See *Dr. JAC's Guide to Writing with Depth* by Joyce Armstrong Carroll (pp. 2–3).
Share examples of each strategy as time allows.
Allow time for students to continue to work on their essay.

Instructional Goal. Students work through the process of writing a documented essay.

Day 8
Teach:
- Developing a working title for focus and coherence
- Prove Its! for depth and development of ideas

See *Dr. JAC's Guide to Writing with Depth* by Joyce Armstrong Carroll (pp. 2–3).

Instructional Goal. Students read their drafts in a small group with two other peers who point out what they *like* about the essay.

Day 9
Teach:
- Bruffee's organizational patterns

Use short persuasive articles or editorials. Ask students to identify the organization pattern the author uses to convey his message. Was the author persuasive?

Instructional Goal. *Meaning dictates form.* Bruffee's patterns are useful once students have done some drafting of their persuasive essays—students need something written to work with before they can decide which organizational pattern best fits their intended meaning.

Day 10
Students return to their persuasive documented drafts. Teach integration of sources using student examples.

Instructional Goal. Students decide which organizational pattern best accommodates their meaning and revise their drafts accordingly.

Day 11
Finish essays.
Ratiocinate for "be" verbs and sentence beginnings.
Finish revisions.
Collect drafts and final copies.
Use rubric to assess.

Instructional Goal. Final revision of content.

Day 12
Review reading strategies:
- Draw pictures/symbols (paragraphs/chunks of paragraphs)
- Annotation

Teach:
- Purpose for reading
- Open-ended question concept and expectations
- Model writing open-ended answers

Use a two-column graphic organizer to gather textual evidence.

Possible open-ended questions:
- What is the lesson of *The Gettysburg Address*?
- What is one message Lincoln conveys in *The Gettysburg Address*?
- How does *The Gettysburg Address* support, challenge, or qualify the political circumstances of 1863?
- What does the reader learn about Lincoln's perspective from *The Gettysburg Address*?

Note: Support your answer with evidence from the text.

See *In the Evidence* by Jill Elizabeth Aufill (forthcoming, Absey & Co.).

Instructional Goal. Ideas should be generated and supported by textual evidence.

Day 13

Return to *The Gettysburg Address*.

Students write individual open-ended responses.

Students should read their answers aloud in peer groups of four.

Teacher shares one answer from each group with the whole class (as many as time allows).

Instructional Goal. Open-ended question allows for a variety of correct answers and thinking as long as the answer is supported by relevant text.

Day 14

Teach additional Civil War content using text rendering.

Instructional Goal. Text rendering demands close reading.

Day 15

Teach additional Civil War content using text rendering.

Instructional Goal. Text rendering demands close reading.

CONCLUSION

We would like to share a final thought about writing to learn. Writing in the various disciplines ranges from the technical to the memo, from directions to reports, from plans to explanations. To only teach these specific modes limits students; we need to plumb the depths of many genres. The point is to teach writing in such a way that students learn how to write, so they may carry it with them and call upon it when necessary. If skilled teachers begin by teaching writing reflexively *and* move to extensive writing, students will enter the world armed with viable strategies

A West Point cadet was interviewed on a local news program. In the course of the interview the cadet discussed his training. "When I was a plebe," he said, "we learned about combat. Now I am about to graduate and we are learning about

humanitarian efforts. The world's changed, and so we changed. What I know is that when I am on any assignment, I will have both to call upon. But I am sure of what I know." The analogy seems clear: We learn different material in different disciplines, but above all, we need students to go out into whatever job or profession secure in what they know. With the world undergoing rapid and unprecedented change, students will need the knowledge that will enable them to change and to cope with the change. Writing makes learning visual, establishes a process by which to learn, and preserves that learning.

The point is, and it is a point not made without care, colleagues in other disciplines cannot afford not to use writing in their instruction. If all of the scientific research is true, if all of the theory is true, if all the best practices are true, then writing must occur in every lesson covered in all disciplines.

We are reminded of one young teacher who taught four classes of English language arts and two periods of girls' volleyball. After implementing writing in her ELA classes and seeing the profound learning that writing enabled, she required her varsity girls to keep a "Winner's Journal." After every game, before showering, before traveling home, before anything, she had her players write what it felt like to be a winner. When they lost, she had them to write what they learned in the game. Before the next game, she had them read what it felt like to be a winner and what they learned. She and her team consistently went to the state finals.

Imagine if a coach used writing to win games, how much the students of math, science, or social studies would benefit from writing in a variety of ways. One such teacher is Gary Dergerstorm. He embraces writing as a foundation for everything he teaches in photography. He is passionate about the difference it has made. His students write what they learn and how they learn it. He produces hundreds of photographers every year. Writing is indeed a mode of learning.

APPLICATION

Text tampering also includes underlining, highlighting, labeling, annotating, commentary, and questions. Reenter a text or book you have studied or read. Examine it with the intention of tampering with the text. Do some tampering, and then evaluate how the tampering helped the purpose of your study or your reading. Be prepared to share your conclusions.

BIBLIOGRAPHY

Abrams, M. H. *A Glossary of Literary Terms.* New York: Holt, Rinehart and Winston, 1991.

Ackerman, Sandra. *Discovering the Brain.* Washington, DC: National Academy Press, 1992.

Ada, Alma Flor. *Alma Flor Ada and YOU.* Westport, CT: Libraries Unlimited, 2005.

Adams, Barbara Johnston. *The Go-Around Dollar.* New York: Macmillan, 1992.

Adams, Richard. *Watership Down.* New York: Avon, 1976.

Allen, Camille A. *The Multigenre Research Paper: Voice, Passion, and Discovery in Grades 4–6.* Portsmouth, NH: Heinemann, 2001.

Allen, Janet. *Tools for Teaching Content Literacy.* Portland, ME: Stenhouse, 2004.

Altenbernd, Lynn and Leslie L. Lewis. *A Handbook for the Study of Fiction.* New York: Macmillan, 1966.

Anderson, Carl. *How's it Going?* Portsmouth, NH: Heinemann, 2000.

Anderson, Jeff. *Mechanically Inclined.* Portland, ME: Stenhouse Publishers, 2005.

Arbuthnot, May Hill and Zena Sutherland. *Children and Books.* Glenview, IL: Scott, Foresman and Company, 1972.

Aristotle. *Aristotle Poetics.* Translated by Gerald R. Else. Ann Arbor, MI: University of Michigan Press, 1978.

Armstrong, Thomas. *Awakening Genius In The Classroom.* Alexandria, VA: Association for Supervision and Curriculum Development, 1998.

Arnold, Roslyn. "The Hidden Life of a Drama Text." *Readers, Texts, Teachers,* edited by Bill Corcoran and Emrys Evans. Upper Montclair, NJ: Boynton/Cook Publishers, 1987.

Arnone, Marilyn P. *Digging for Answers.* Westport, CT: Libraries Unlimited, 2006.

———. *Squiggly Question.* Westport, CT: Libraries Unlimited, 2005.

———. *Squiggly Question: Educators' Guide.* Westport, CT: Libraries Unlimited, 2005.

Asia Society. *Math and Science Education in a Global Age: What the U.S. Can Learn from China.* New York: Asia Society, 2006.

Atkins, Andrea. "Big Business and Education: Will Corporate Cash Aid Schools?" *Better Homes and Gardens* (March 1991): 32–34.

Atwell, Nancie. *In The Middle: Writing, Reading, and Learning with Adolescents.* Portsmouth, NH: Boynton/Cook Publishers, 1987.

Auerbacher, Inge. *I Am A Star: Child of the Holocaust.* New York: Prentice Hall Books, 1986.

Aufill, Jill Elizabeth. *In the Evidence.* Spring, TX: Absey & Co., 2008.

"Autopsies Done on 5 Bodies Found in Rio Grande." www.newschannel5.tv, October 24, 2006.

Barbot, Daniel. *A Bicycle for Rosaura.* New York: Kane Miller, 1991.

Barnstone, Aliki and Willis Barnstone. *A Book of Women Poets from Antiquity to Now.* New York: Schocken Books, 1980.

Barrett, Judi. *Cloudy With a Chance of Meatballs*. New York: Aladdin Paperbacks, 1978.

Barth, John. "Writing: Can It Be Taught." *Late City Final Edition*. Section 7; Page 1, Column 1; Book Review Desk, June 16, 1985.

Beach, Richard. *Writing About Ourselves and Others*. ERIC, 1977.

Bedard, Michael. *Emily*. New York: Delacorte Press, 1992.

Begley, Sharon, et al. "Mapping the Brain." *Newsweek* (20 April 1992): 66–72.

Berger, Eric. "Lab Decoding Decision-Making." *Houston Chronicle* (October 24, 2006): Sec. B, p. 2.

Berthoff, Ann E. "Tolstoy, Vygotsky, and the Making of Meaning." In *Composition and Its Teaching*, edited by Richard C. Gebhardt. Findlay, OH: Ohio Council of Teachers of English Language Arts, 1979.

Black, Janet K. "Are Young Children Really Egocentric?" *Young Children* (September 1981): 51–55.

Bloom, Benjamin S., Max D. Engelhart, Edward J. Furst, Walker H. Hill, and David R. Krathwohl, eds. *Taxonomy of Educational Objectives: The Classification of Educational Goals*. New York: David McKay Company, 1956.

Blythe, Ronald, ed. *The Pleasures of Diaries: Four Centuries of Private Writing*. New York: Pantheon Books, 1989.

Booth, Wayne. "Rhetoric, Mere Rhetoric, and Reality: Or, My Basics Are More Basic Than Your Basics." In *The English Curriculum Under Fire: What Are the Real Basics?* Urbana, IL: NCTE, 1982.

Braddock, Richard, Richard Lloyd-Jones, and Lowell Schoer. *Research in Written Composition*. Urbana, IL: NCTE, 1963.

Brancato, Claudia. *Borrowings*. Spring, TX: Absey & Co., 2002.

Britton, James, et al. *The Development of Writing Abilities (11–18)*. London: Macmillan, 1975.

Brizendine, Louann, M.D. *The Female Brain*. New York: Morgan Road Books, 2006.

Brock, Paula. *Nudges*. Spring, TX: Absey & Co., 2002.

Brown, Hazel and Brian Cambourne. *Read and Retell*. Portsmouth, NH: Heinemann, 1987.

Brown, Margaret Wise. *Goodnight Moon*. New York: Harper & Row, 1947, renewed 1975.

———. *The Important Book*. New York: Harper & Row, 1949.

———. *The Runaway Bunny*. New York: Harper & Row, 1942.

Browne, Malcolm W. "How Brain Waves Can Fly a Plane." *New York Times* (March 7, 1995).

Brownlee, Shannon. "Inside the Teen Brain." *U.S. News & World Report* (August 9, 1999): 46–54.

Bruffee, Kenneth A. *A Short Course in Writing*. Cambridge, MA: Winthrop, 1980.

Bruner, Jerome S. *Acts of Meaning*. Cambridge, MA: Harvard University Press, 1990.

———. *On Knowing: Essays for the Left Hand*. New York: Atheneum, 1971.

———. *The Process of Education*. New York: Vintage Books, 1963.

Brunton, Michael. "What Do Babies Know?" *Time* (January 29, 2007).

Brunvand, Jan Harold. *The Choking Doberman and Other "New" Urban Legends*. New York: W.W. Norton and Company, 1984.

———. *The Vanishing Hitchhiker: American Urban Legends and Their Meaning*. New York: W.W. Norton and Company, 1986.

Bullock, Sir. A., F.B.A. *A Language for Life*. London: Her Majesty's Stationery Office, 1975.

Bunting, Eve. *Terrible Things: An Allegory of the Holocaust*. New York: The Jewish Publication Society, 1989.

———. *The Wall*. New York: Clarion Books, 1990.

Burke, Kenneth. *A Grammar of Motives*. Berkeley: University of California Press, 1969.

———. "Introduction: The Five Key Terms of Dramatism." In *Contemporary Rhetoric: A Conceptual Background with Readings,* edited by W. Ross Winterowd. New York: Harcourt Brace Jovanovich, 1975.

Burleigh, Robert. *Flight*. New York: Philomel Books, 1991.

Burns, Marilyn. *Math for Smarty Pants*. Boston, MA: Little, Brown and Company, 1982.

Burns, Olive Ann. *Cold Sassy Tree*. New York: Laurel Trade Paperback, 1984.

Burstyn, Ellen. *Lessons in Becoming Myself*. Riverhead Hardcover, 2006.

Caine, Renate Nummela and Geoffrey Caine. *Making Connections: Teaching and the Human Brain*. Alexandria, VA: Association for Supervision and Curriculum Development, 1991.

Calkins, Lucy McCormick. *The Art of Teaching Writing*. Portsmouth, NH: Heinemann, 1986.

———. *Lessons From a Child: On the Teaching and Learning of Writing*. Portsmouth, NH: Heinemann, 1983.

Campbell, Joseph. *Creative Mythology*. New York: Penguin Publishing, 1968.

———. *The Hero with a Thousand Faces*. Princeton, NJ: Princeton University Press,1972.

Canadian Council of Teachers of English. "Evaluation Policy." *Classmate* 16(2), (1985): 27–30.

Capote, Truman. *A Christmas Memory*. New York: Random House, 1956.

Carle, Eric. *A House for Hermit Crab*. Saxonville, MA: Picture Book Studio, 1987.

———. *The Very Hungry Caterpillar*. New York: Philomel Books, 1969.

Carroll, Joyce Armstrong. *Authentic Strategies For High Stakes Tests*. Spring, TX: Absey & Co., 2007.

———. *The Best of Dr. JAC*. Spring, TX: Absey & Co., 1998.

———. *Conclusions*. Spring, TX: Absey & Co., 2004.

———. "Drawing into Meaning: A Powerful Writing Tool." *English Journal,* 80, no. 6 (October 1991): 34–38.

———. *Dr. JAC's Guide To Writing With Depth*. Spring, TX: Absey & Co., 2002.

———. "Grappling with Grammar: A Matter of Timing." *Florida English Journal*, 23 (Spring 1987): 51–56.

——— "Journal Making." *Media & Methods* (November 1972): 61–63.

———. *Phonics Friendly Books*. Spring, TX: Absey & Co., 1998.

———. "Plagiarism: The Unfun Game." *English Journal* (September 1982): 92–95.

———. "Process into Product: Awareness of the Composing Process Affects the Written Product." Ed.D. diss., Rutgers University, New Brunswick, NJ, 1979.

———. "Process into Product: Teacher Awareness of the Writing Process Affects Students' Written Products." *New Directions in Composition Research*, edited by Richard Beach and Lillian S. Bridwell. New York: The Guilford Press, 1984.

———. "Publishing: The Writer's Touchdown." *English Journal* (April 1983): 93–94.

———. "Ratiocination and Revision, or Clues in the Written Draft." *English Journal* (November 1982): 90–92.

——. "Talking Through the Writing Process." *English Journal* (November 1981): 100–102.

——. "TV and Term Papers." *English Journal* (October 1985): 85–86.

——. "Visualizing the Composing Process." *English in Texas* (Spring 1982): 11–14.

Carroll, Joyce Armstrong and Edward E. Wilson. *Acts of Teaching: How to Teach Writing.* Englewood, CO: Teacher Ideas Press, 1993.

——. *Poetry After Lunch.* Spring, TX: Absye & Co., 1997.

Carver, Raymond. *A New Path to the Waterfall.* Introduction by Tess Gallagher. New York: The Atlantic Monthly Press, 1989.

Cather, Willa. *O Pioneers!* New York: Viking Penguin, 1989.

Cheatham, Judy. "Piaget, Writing Instruction and the Middle School." *Middle School Journal* (March 1989): 14–17.

Chukovsky, Kornei. *From Two to Five.* Translated by Miriam Morton. Berkeley: University of California Press, 1963.

Ciardi, John. "Everyone Wants to Be Published, But . . . " In *The Writer's Handbook*, edited by Sylvia Burack. Boston, MA: The Writer, 1989.

Clark, Barbara. *Growing Up Gifted: Developing the Potential of Children at Home and at School.* (Fourth Edition). New York: Macmillan, 1992.

Clark, Katerina and Michael Holquist. *Mikhail Bakhtin.* Cambridge, MA: Harvard University Press, 1984.

Clay, Marie M. *What Did I Write?* Portsmouth, NH: Heinemann, 1975.

Coatney, Sharon and Marilyn P. Arnone. *Digging for Answers: Educators' Guide.* Westport, CT: Libraries Unlimited, 2006.

Coatsworth, John H. "Globalization, Growth, and Welfare in History." In *Globalization: Culture and Education in the New Millennium*, edited by Marcelo M. Suarez-Orozco and Desiree Baolian Qin-Hillard. Berkeley: University of California Press, 2004.

Cohen, A. S. *Tests: Marked for Life.* Toronto, Canada: Scholastic, 1988.

Condon, William S. and Louis W. Sander. "Synchrony Demonstrated between Movements of the Neonate and Adult Speech." *Child Development* (1974): 456–462.

Cooper, Charles R. and Lee Odell. *Evaluating Writing: Describing, Measuring, Judging.* Urbana, IL: NCTE, 1977.

Corballis, Michael C. "The Origins and Evolution of Human Laterality." In *Neuropsychology and Cognition*, Vol. 1, edited by R. N. Malateska and L. C. Hartlage. The Hague, Netherlands: Martinus Nijhoff Publishers, 1982.

Corcoran, Bill. "Teachers Creating Readers." In *Readers, Texts, Teachers*, edited by Bill Corcoran and Emrys Evans. Upper Montclair, NJ: Boynton/Cook Publishers, 1987.

Corder, Jim W. "Asking for a Text and Trying to Learn It." In *Encountering Student Texts*, edited by Bruce Lawson, Susan Sterr Ryan and W. Ross Winterowd. Urbana IL.: NCTE, 1989.

Corder, Jim W. and John J. Ruszkiewicz. *Handbook of Current English.* Glenview, IL: Scott, Foresman and Company, 1985.

Cormier, Robert. *The Chocolate War.* New York: Dell Publishing, 1976.

——. *I Am the Cheese.* New York: Pantheon Books, 1977.

——. "The Moustache." In *Eight Plus One.* New York: Bantam Doubleday Dell Books for Young Readers, 1991.

Countryman, Joan. *Writing to Learn Mathematics.* Portsmouth, NH: Heinemann, 1992.

Couper, Heather and Nigel Henbest. *The Space Atlas.* New York: Harcourt Brace Jovanovich, 1992.

Cowan, Gregory and Elizabeth Cowan. *Writing.* New York: John Wiley & Sons, 1980.

Cowley, Malcolm, ed. *Writers at Work.* New York: Penguin Books, 1958.

Crane, Stephen. *The Red Badge of Courage.* New York: Bantam Books, 1981.

Crouch, Luis. "South Africa: Overcoming Past Injustice." In *Balancing Change and Tradition in Global Education Reform,* edited by Iris Rotberg. New York: Rowman & Littlefield, 2004.

Crystal, David. *The Cambridge Encyclopedia Of The English Language.* New York: Cambridge University Press, 1995.

Damasio, Antonio R. and Hanna Damasio. "Brain and Language." *Scientific American* (Special Issue, September 1992): 89–95.

de Beer, Hans. *The Little Polar Bear.* New York: North-South Publishers, 1993.

Decker, Randall E. *Patterns of Exposition.* Boston, MA: Little, Brown and Company, 1980.

Deedy, Carmen Agra. *Agatha's Feather Bed: Not Just Another Wild Goose Story.* Atlanta, GA: Peachtree, 1991.

Demi. *The Empty Pot.* New York: Henry Holt, 1990.

Denning, Stephen. *The Springboard: How Storytelling Ignites Action in Knowledge-Era Organizations.* Burlington, MA: Butterworth Heinemann, 2001.

Diamond, Marian. *Enriching Heredity: The Impact of the Environment on the Anatomy of the Brain.* New York: The Free Press, 1988.

DiCamillo, Kate. *Because of Winn-Dixie.* Cambridge, MA: Candlewick Press, 2000.

Diederich, Paul B. *Measuring Growth in English.* Urbana, IL: NCTE, 1974.

Dilena, Mike and Jane Leaker. "Literary Assessment: Assessing Achievements in Real Reading and Writing." In *The Literacy Agenda: Issues for the Nineties,* edited by Elaine Furniss and Pamela Green. Portsmouth, NH: Heinemann, 1991.

Dillard, Annie. *The Writing Life.* New York: Harper & Row, 1989.

Donaldson, Margaret. *Children's Minds.* New York: W. W. Norton and Company, 1978.

Donham, Jean, Kay Bishop, et al. *Inquiry-Based Learning: Lessons from Library Power.* Worthington, OH: Linworth Publishing, 2001.

Dorris, Michael. *A Yellow Raft in Blue Water.* New York: Warner Books, 1988.

Drake, Barbara. *Writing Poetry.* New York: Harcourt Brace Jovanovich, 1983.

Duke, Kate. *Aunt Isabel Tells a Good One.* New York: Dutton Children's Books, 1992.

Eads, Vivian Athens. Through Baylor University in 1989 replicates the data of the NJWP original study.

Early Childhood and Literacy Development Committee. *Literacy Development and Prefirst Grade.* Newark, DE: International Reading Association, 1988.

Edwards, Betty. *Drawing on the Artist Within.* New York: Simon & Schuster, 1986.

———. *Drawing on the Right Side of the Brain.* Los Angeles, CA: J. P. Tarcher, 1979.

Edelman, Gerald M. *Bright Air, Brilliant Fire: On the Matter of the Mind.* New York: Basic Books, 1992.

Elbow, Peter. *Embracing Contraries.* New York: Oxford University Press, 1986.

———. *Writing Without Teachers.* New York: Oxford University Press, 1973.

———. *Writing with Power.* New York: Oxford University Press, 1981.

Elbow, Peter and Pat Belanoff. *A Community of Writers.* New York: McGraw-Hill, 1999.

Emig, Janet. *The Composing Processes of Twelfth Graders.* Urbana, IL: NCTE, 1971.

———. "Hand, Eye, Brain: Some 'Basics' in the Writing Process." In *Research on Composing: Points of Departure*, edited by Charles R. Cooper and Lee Odell. Urbana, IL: NCTE, 1978.

———. *The Web of Meaning.* Upper Montclair, NJ: Boynton/Cook Publishers, 1983.

Estes, Clarissa Pinkola. *Women Who Run with the Wolves.* New York: Ballentine Books, 1996.

Fant, Joseph L. and Robert Ashley. *Faulkner at West Point.* New York: Vintage Books, 1969.

Faulkner, William. *As I Lay Dying.* New York: Vintage Books, 1957.

Fischbach, Gerald D. "Mind and Brain." *Scientific American* (Special Issue, September 1992), 48–57.

Fisher, Leonard Everett. *Cyclops.* New York: Holiday House, 1991.

Fowler, H. Ramsey. *The Little, Brown Handbook.* Boston, MA: Little, Brown and Company, 1980.

Frazer, James George. *The Golden Bough.* Abridged ed. Vol. 2. New York: Macmillan, 1972.

Freedman, Glenn and Elizabeth G. Reynolds. "Enriching Basal Reader Lessons with Semantic Webbing." *The Reading Teacher* (March 1980): 677–684.

Fritz, Jean. *Homesick.* New York: Putnam Juvenile, 1982.

Frost, Robert. "Out, Out-." In *Poetry After Lunch*, edited by Joyce Armstrong Carroll and Edward E. Wilson. Spring, TX: Absey & Co., 1997.

Fry, Edward Bernard, Jacqueline E. Kress, and Dona Lee Fountoukidis. *The Reading Teacher's Book of Lists*, 3rd edition. New York: The Center for Applied Research in Education, 1993.

Fulwiler, Toby. *The Journal Book.* Portsmouth, NH: Heinemann, 1987.

Gardner, Howard. *Frames of Mind: The Theory of Multiple Intelligences.* New York: Basic Books, 1983.

———. *Intelligence Reframed: Multiple Intelligences for the 21st Century.* New York: Basic Books, 1999.

———. *The Unschooled Mind: How Children Think and How Schools Should Teach.* New York: Basic Books, 1991.

Gaur, Albertine. *A History of Writing.* New York: Cross River Press, 1992.

Gentry, J. Richard. *SPEL . . . Is a Four-Letter Word.* Portsmouth, NH: Heinemann, 1987.

Gere, Anne Ruggles, ed. *Roots in the Sawdust: Writing to Learn Across Disciplines.* Urbana, IL: NCTE, 1985.

Giblin, James Cross, ed. *The Century That Was; Reflections on the Last One Hundred Years.* New York: Atheneum Books, 2000.

Giddens, Anthony. *Runaway World.* New York: Routledge, 1999.

Gill, Michael. "The Eyes of the Beholder." In *Commentarius*, edited by Megan Hawkins and Scott O'Hara. Abilene, TX: O.H. Cooper High School, 1987, 62–64.

Ginsburg, Herbert and Sylvia Opper. *Piaget's Theory of Intellectual Development: An Introduction.* Englewood Cliffs, NJ: Prentice Hall, 1969.

Glasser, William. *The Quality School.* New York: Perennial Library, Harper & Row, 1990.

Goldberg, Bonni. *Room to Write.* New York: Putnam, 1996.

Goldberg, Natalie. *Writing Down the Bones*. Boston, MA: Shambhala, 1986.

Golding, William. *Lord of the Flies*. New York: Harcourt Brace Jovanovich, 1969.

Goldman-Rakic, Patricia S. "Working Memory and the Mind." *Scientific American* (Special Issue, September 1992): 111–117.

Gordon, W. J. J. *Synectics*. New York: Harper & Row, 1961.

Gould, June. *The Writer in All of Us*. New York: E. P. Dutton, 1989.

Gould, Stephen Jay. *Bully for Brontosaurus: Reflections in Natural History*. New York: W. W. Norton and Company, 1991.

Govenar, Alan. *Extraordinary Ordinary People*. Cambridge, MA: Candlewick Press, 2006.

Graham, Steve and Dolores Perin. *Writing Next: A Report to Carnegie Corporation of New York*. New York: Carnegie Corporation, 2007.

Graves, Donald H. *Balance the Basics: Let Them Write*. New York: Ford Foundation, 1978.

Graves, Donald H. and Bonnie S. Sunstein, eds. *Portfolio Portraits*. Portsmouth, NH: Heinemann, 1992.

Gregory, Dick. "Shame." In *Nigger: An Autobiography*. New York: E. P. Dutton, 1964.

Guarneri, Mimi, M.D., FACC. *The Heart Speaks*. New York: Simon & Schuster, 2006.

Guralnik, David B. (Editor of Webster's New World Dictionary). *Webster's New World Misspeller's Dictionary*. New York: Simon & Schuster, 1983.

Guzzetti, Alfred. "Christian Metz and the Semiology of the Cinema." In *Film Theory and Criticism*, edited by Gerald Mast and Marshall Cohen. New York: Oxford University Press, 1985.

Gwynne, Fred. *The King Who Rained*. New York: Simon & Schuster, 1988.

Hamilton, Virginia. *Anthony Burns: The Defeat and Triumph of a Fugitive Slave*. New York: Alfred A. Knopf, 1988.

———. *The People Could Fly*. New York: Alfred A. Knopf, 1985.

Harris, Peggy. "Writing Boosts Learning in Science, Math, and Social Studies." *The Council Chronicle* 16 (September 2006).

Hart, Leslie A. *How the Brain Works*. New York: Basic Books, 1975.

Hartwell, Patrick. "Grammar, Grammars, and the Teaching of Grammar." *College English* (February 1985).

Hawking, Stephen W. *A Brief History of Time*. New York: Bantam Books, 1988.

Healy, Jane M. *Endangered Minds: Why Our Children Don't Think*. New York: Simon & Schuster, 1990.

Henkes, Kevin. *Chrysanthemum*. New York: Greenwillow Books, 1991.

Hermann, Ned. "Theories of Brain Organisation." In *The Creative Brain*. Lake Lure, NC: Brain Books, 1988.

Hillocks, George, Jr. *Narrative Writing*. Portsmouth, NH: Heinemann, 2007.

———. "Synthesis on Research Writing." *Educational Leadership* 44 (May 1987): 71–76, 78, 80–82.

Hirst, Sally and Robin Hirst. *My Place in Space*. New York: Orchard Books, 1988.

Hobbs, Will. *Bearstone*. New York: Atheneum, 1989.

———. *Crossing the Wire*. New York: HarperCollins, 2006.

Hodges, Margaret. *Saint George and the Dragon*. Boston, MA: Little, Brown and Company, 1984.

Holst, Gustav. *The SOLTI Collection: The Planets.* London: The Decca Record Company Limited, 1979.

Hoopfer, L. and M. Hunsberger. "An Ethnomethodological Perspective on Reading Assessment." Forum in *Reading and Language Education,* 1(1), 1986.

Hubbard, Ruth. *Authors of Pictures, Draughtsmen of Words.* Portsmouth, NH: Heinemann, 1989.

Hunt, Kellogg W. "Early Blooming and Late Blooming Syntactic Structures." In *Evaluating Writing,* edited by Charles R. Cooper and Lee Odell. Urbana, IL: NCTE, 1977, 91–106.

Hunter, Madeline C. *How to Change to a Nongraded School.* Alexandria, VA: ASCD, 1992.

Irmscher, William F. *Teaching Expository Writing.* New York: Holt, Rinehart and Winston, 1979.

Iser, Wolfgang. *The Act of Reading.* Baltimore, MD: Johns Hopkins Press, 1978.

Iyer, Pico. "In Praise of the Humble Comma." *Time* (13 June 1988): 80.

Jacques, Brian. *Mossflower.* New York: Putnam, 1988.

————. *Redwall.* New York: Putnam, 1987.

Janeczko, Paul. *The Music of What Happens: Poems That Tell Stories.* New York: Orchard Press, 1988.

Jean, Georges. *Writing: The Story of Alphabets and Scripts.* New York: Harry N. Abrams, 1992.

Jensen, Eric. *Teaching with the Brain in Mind.* Alexandria, VA: ASCD, 1998.

Johmann, Carol. "Sex and the Split Brain." *Omni* (August 1983) 5, (26 & 113).

Johnson, Crockett. *Harold and the Purple Crayon.* New York: Scholastic, 1955.

Johnson, Robin D. "A Study of the Effects of a Three-week Teacher Training in Writing on Teacher Attitude, Student Attitude, and Student Achievement." Ed.D. diss. Texas A & M University, Commerce, forthcoming.

Joyce, Bruce and Beverly Showers. "Improving Inservice Training: The Messages of Research." *Educational Leadership* (February 1980): 379–385.

Judine, Sister M. IHM, ed. *A Guide for Evaluating Student Composition.* Urbana, IL: NCTE, 1965.

Kennedy, X. J. *Literature: An Introduction to Fiction, Poetry and Drama.* New York: Scott, Foresman and Company, 1987.

Kerr, M. E. *Me, Me, Me, Me, Me: Not a Novel.* New York: New American Library, 1983.

Kimura, Doreen. "Sex Differences in the Brain." *Scientific American* (Special Issue, September 1992), 119–125.

King, Barbara. "Two Modes of Analyzing Teacher and Student Attitudes Toward Writing: The Emig Attitude Scale and the King Construct Scale." Ed. D. diss., Rutgers University, 1979.

King, Stephen. *On Writing: A Memoir of the Craft.* New York: Pocket Books, 2000.

Kingston, Maxine Hong. Letter to Joyce Armstrong Carroll, October 16, 1980.

Klivington, Kenneth. *The Science of Mind.* Cambridge, MA: MIT Press, 1989.

Knott, William C. *The Craft of Fiction.* Reston, VA: Reston Publishing, 1973.

Koch, Kenneth. *Wishes, Lies, and Dreams.* New York: Vintage Books, 1970.

Kraus, Robert. *Leo the Late Bloomer.* New York: Simon & Schuster, 1971.

Krevisky, Joseph and Jordan L. Linfield. *The Bad Speller's Dictionary.* New York: Random House, 1963.

Kuhn, Thomas. *The Structure of Scientific Revolutions.* Chicago: University of Chicago Press, 1970.

Kurtz, Jane. *Jane Kurtz and YOU*. Westport, CT: Libraries Unlimited, 2007.

LaBoyer, Frederick. *Birth Without Violence*. New York: Knopf, 1974.

Lamaze, Fernand. *Painless Childbirth*. New York: Contemporary Books, 1987.

Lambert, Dorothy. "Keeping a Journal." *The English Journal*. 56(2) (Feb. 1967): 286–288.

Lane, Barry. *After THE END*. Portsmouth, NH: Heinemann, 1993.

Langer, Susanne. *Philosophy in a New Key*. Cambridge: Harvard University Press, 1957.

Larson, Richard L. "Discovery Through Questioning: A Plan for Teaching Rhetorical Invention." In *Contemporary Rhetoric: A Conceptual Background with Readings,* edited by W. Ross Winterowd. New York: Harcourt Brace Jovanovich, 1975, 144–154.

Lasky, Kathryn. *The Librarian Who Measured the Earth*. New York: Little Brown and Company, 1994.

Lassek, A. M. *The Human Brain from Primitive to Modern*. Springfield, IL: Charles C. Thomas, 1957.

Le Doux, Joseph. *The Emotional Brain: The Mysterious Underpinnings of Emotional Life*. New York: Simon & Schuster, 1996.

———. *Synaptic Self: How Our Brains Become Who We Are*. New York: Penguin Books, 2002.

L'Engle, Madeline, "Don't Think: Write!" *The Writer's Handbook,* edited by Sylvia K. Burrack. Boston, MA: The Writer, 1989.

Levitt, Peggy. *The Transnational Villagers*. Berkeley: University of California Press, 2001.

Lewis, C. S. *The Lion, the Witch and the Wardrobe*. New York: Collier Books, 1950.

Lilly, John. *The Mind of the Dolphin*. New York: Avon Books, 1969.

Lincoln, Abraham. "The Gettysburg Address." Delivered at Gettysburg, PA: November 19, 1863.

Lloyd-Jones, Richard. "Primary Trait Scoring." In *Evaluating Writing*, edited by Charles R. Cooper and Lee Odell. Urbana, IL: NCTE, 1977.

Loomis, Roger Sherman and Laura Hibbard Loomis, eds. *Medieval Romances*. New York: Modern Library, 1957.

Lowry, Lois. *Number the Stars*. Boston, MA: Houghton Mifflin, 1989.

Lucas, Joni. "Teaching Writing." ASCD Curriculum Update. Alexandria, VA: ASCD, January 1993.

MacCann, Richard Dyer. *Film: A Montage of Theories*. New York: E. P. Dutton, 1966.

MacLean, Paul D. "A Mind of Three Minds: Educating the Triune Brain." In *Education and the Brain: The Seventy-seventh Yearbook of the National Society for the Study of Education*, edited by Jeanne S. Chall and Allan F. Mirsky. Chicago: University of Chicago Press, 1978.

Macrorie, Ken. *Searching Writing*. New York: Hayden Book Company, 1980.

———. *Telling Writing*. New York: Hayden Book Company, 1970.

Markham, Beryl. *West with the Night*. Albany, CA: North Point Press, 1983.

Marrou, H. I. *A History of Education in Antiquity*. New York: Mentor, 1964.

Martin, Bill, Jr. *Brown Bear, Brown Bear, What Do You See?* New York: Henry Holt, 1983.

———. *Polar Bear, Polar Bear, What Do You Hear?* New York: Henry Holt, 1991.

Martin, Bill, Jr. and John Archambault. *Here Are My Hands*. New York: Henry Holt, 1985.

———. *Knots on a Counting Rope*. New York: Henry Holt, 1987.

Martorano, S. "A Development Analysis of Performance on Piaget's Formal Operations Tasks." *Developmental Psychology* 13 (1977): 666–672.

Marzano, Robert J. *A Different Kind of Classroom: Teaching with Dimensions of Learning.* Alexandria, VA: The Association for Supervision and Curriculum Development, 1992.

McAuliffe, Suzanne. "Researchers Compare Notes on Mapping the Brain." *San Antonio Light*, 1 December 1992, B-1.

McConkey, Max. Letter to Kaye Dunn, 3 April 1993, published in *NJWPT for the Improvement of Teaching.*

McCrum, Robert, William Cran, and Robert MacNeil. *The Story of English.* New York: Viking, 1986.

McElemeel, Sharon L. *Bookpeople: A First Album.* Englewood, CO: Libraries Unlimited, 1990.

McEwen, B. S. and R. M. Sapolsky. *Current Opinion Neurobiology* 5 (1995): 205–216.

McKinnley, Robin. *The Blue Sword.* New York: Greenwillow Books, 1982.

———. *The Hero and the Crown.* New York: Greenwillow Books, 1985.

McKissack, Patricia C. *A Million Fish More or Less.* New York: Alfred A. Knopf, 1992.

McLeod, Emilie Warren. *The Bear's Bicycle.* Boston, MA: Little, Brown and Company, 1975.

McPhail, David. *The Bear's Toothache.* Boston, MA: Joy Street Books, 1988.

———. *Emma's Pet.* New York: Dutton, 1985.

———. *First Flight.* Boston, MA: Little, Brown and Company, 1987.

———. *Fix-It.* New York: Dutton, 1984.

———. *Lost!* Boston, MA: Little, Brown and Company, 1990.

———. *Sisters.* New York: Harcourt Brace Jovanovich, 1984.

———. *Snow Lion.* Boston, MA: Parents Magazine Press, 1982.

———. *Something Special.* Boston, MA: Little, Brown and Company, 1988.

———. *The Train.* Boston, MA: Little, Brown and Company, 1977.

McPherson, Elisabeth. "Spelling, Revisited." *Slate Starter Sheet.* Urbana, IL: NCTE, January, 1984.

Metz, Virginia Ellen. "Training Teachers to Teach Writing: Impact on Teacher Attitudes and Student Products." Ph.D. diss. Texas A & M University, 1993.

Mezey, Stephen and Robert Berg, eds. *Naked Poetry: Recent American Poetry in Open Form.* Saddle River, NJ: Prentice Hall, 1969.

Miller, Casey and Kate Swift. *The Handbook of Nonsexist Writing.* New York: Harper & Row, 1980, 1988.

Moffett, James. *Teaching the Universe of Discourse.* Boston, MA: Houghton Mifflin, 1968.

Monroe, Walter S., ed. *Encyclopedia of Educational Research.* New York: Macmillan, 1950.

Most, Bernard. *The Cow That Went Oink.* New York: Harcourt Brace Jovanovich, 1990.

Murray, Donald M. *A Writer Teaches Writing: A Practical Method of Teaching Composition.* New York: Houghton Mifflin, 1968.

Myers, Walter Dean. *Now Is Your Time! The African-American Struggle for Freedom.* New York: HarperCollins, 1991.

Nash, J. Madeleine. "The Frontier Within." *Time* (Special Issue, Fall 1992): 81–82.

———. "The Gift of Mimicry." *Time* (January 19, 2007): 108–113.

Newman, Judith. *Children's Writing.* Spring, TX: Absey & Co., 2001.

Nims, John Frederick. *Western Wind.* New York: Random House. 1983.

Noguchi, Rei R. *Grammar and the Teaching of Writing*. Urbana, IL: NCTE, 1991.

Nolan, Christopher. *Under the Eye of the Clock*. Preface by John Carey. New York: St. Martins Press, 1987.

Noyce, Pendred. "Professional Development: How Do We Know If It Works?" *Education Week* (September 13, 2006).

Noyes, Alfred. "The Highwayman." In *Collected Poems*. New York: Frederick A. Stokes, 1913.

Numeroff, Laura Joffe. *If You Give A Mouse A Cookie*. New York: Harper & Row, 1985.

Odell, Lee. "Measuring Changes in Intellectual Processes as One Dimension of Growth in Writing." In *Evaluating Writing*, edited by Charles R. Cooper and Lee Odell. Urbana, IL: NCTE, 1977.

Ogg, Oscar. *The 26 Letters*. New York: Thomas Y. Crowell Company, 1961.

Olney, James. *Metaphor of Self: The Meaning of Autobiography*. Princeton, NJ: Princeton University Press, 1972.

O'Neil, John. "Preparing for the Changing Workplace." *Educational Leadership* 49 (March 1992): 6–9.

Ornstein, Robert E., ed. *The Nature of Human Consciousness: A Book of Readings*. San Francisco, CA: Freeman & Co., 1973.

Ornstein, Robert and Richard F. Thompson. *The Amazing Brain*. Boston, MA: Houghton Mifflin, 1984.

Paolini, Christopher. *Eragon*. New York: Alfred A. Knopf, 2003.

Parish, Peggy. *Amelia Bedelia*. New York: Harper & Row, 1963.

Patron, Susan. *The Higher Power of Lucky*. New York: Atheneum, 2006.

Paulsen, Gary. *Soldier's Heart*. New York: Random House, 1998.

Payan, Irene. "Peer Proofreading." *How to Handle the Paper Load*, edited by Gene Stanford. Urbana, IL: NCTE, 1979–1980, 124–125.

Pearson, David P. and Dale D. Johnson. *Teaching Reading Comprehension*. New York: Holt, Rhinehart & Winston, 1978.

Perrone, Vito. *A Letter to Teachers: Reflections on Schooling and the Art of Teaching*. San Francisco, CA: Jossey-Bass, 1991.

Petrosky, Anthony R. "From Story to Essay: Reading and Writing." *College Composition and Communication* 33 (1982): 24–25.

Piaget, Jean. *Judgment and Reasoning in the Child*. Totowa, NJ: Littlefield, Adams & Co., 1976.

———. *The Language and Thought of the Child*. New York: The World Publishing Co., 1969.

Piercy, Marge. *Mars and Her Children*. New York: Alfred A. Knopf, 1992.

Pink, Daniel H. *A Whole New Mind*. New York: Riverhead Books, 2005.

Pinkers, Lyndsay. *Who's Counted? Who's Counting? Understanding High School Graduation Rates*. Washington, DC: Alliance for Excellent Education, 2006.

PIRLS Report. timss.be.edu/pirls2001i/PIRLS2001_new.htm.

Polanyi, Michael. *Personal Knowledge: Toward a Post-Critical Philosophy*. Chicago: University of Chicago Press, 1958.

Protherough, Robert. "The Stories That Readers Tell." In *Readers, Texts, Teachers*, edited by Bill Corcoran and Emrys Evans. Upper Montclair, NJ: Boynton/Cook Publishers, 1987.

Purves, Alan C., ed. *How Porcupines Make Love: Notes on a Response-Centered Curriculum.* Lexington, MA: Xerox College Publishing, 1972.

Raiten-D'Antonio, Toni. *The Velveteen Principles.* Deerfield Beach, FL: Health Communications, 2004.

Reaske, Christopher R. and Robert F. Willson Jr. *Student Voices/One.* New York: Random House, 1971.

Reich, Robert B. *Education and the Next Economy.* Washington DC: National Education Association, 1988.

Reid, Margarette S. *The Button Box.* New York: E. P. Dutton, 1990.

Resnais, Alan. *Night and Fog.* Skokie, IL: Films Inc. (also available in video stores).

Restak, Richard M. *The Brain.* New York: Bantam Books, 1984.

————. *The New Brain.* New York: Rodale, 2003.

Richards, I. A. *Practical Criticism.* New York: Harcourt, Brace & World, 1929.

————. *The Principles of Literary Criticism.* New York: Harcourt, Brace and Co., 1948.

Richards, M. C. *Centering in Pottery, Poetry, and the Person.* 5th printing. Middletown, CT: Wesleyan University Press, 1972.

Richardson, Samuel. *Pamela; or Virtue Rewarded.* London: G. Woodfall, 1801.

Rico, Gabriele Lusser. *Creating Re-creations.* Spring, TX: Absey & Co., 2000.

Rief, Linda. *Seeking Diversity.* Portsmouth, NH: Heinemann, 1992.

Riefenstal, Leni. *Triumph of the Will.* Skokie, IL: Films Inc. (also available in video stores).

Rodriguez, Richard. *Hunger of Memory: the Education of Richard Rodriguez.* New York: Bantam Books, 1982.

Romano, Tom. *Blending Genre, Altering Style: Writing Multigenre Papers.* Portsmouth, NH: Heinemann, 2000.

————. *Clearing the Way.* Portsmouth, NH: Heinemann, 1987.

Rotberg, Iris C., ed. *Balancing Change and Tradition in Global Education Reform.* Lanham, MD: Rowman & Littlefield, 2004.

Rothman, Robert. "RAND Study Finds Serious Problems in VT. Portfolio Program." *Education Week.* Volume XII, Number 15 (December 16, 1992).

Rosaldo, Renato. *Culture and Truth: The Remaking of Social Analysis.* Boston, MA: Beacon Press, 1989.

Rosenblatt, Louise M. *The Reader, the Text, the Poem.* Carbondale: Southern Illinois University Press, 1978.

Russell, Peter. *The Brain Book.* New York: E. P. Dutton, 1979.

Sagan, Carl. *Dragons of Eden: Speculations on the Evolution of Human Intelligence.* New York: Ballantine Books, 1977.

Sanborn, Jean. "Grammar: Good Wine before Its Time." *English Journal* (March 1986): 72–79.

Sanders, Judith. "Teaching the Metaphoric Lesson." Paper presented at the annual convention of TJCTE, Houston, TX, February 1985.

Santrey, Laurence. *Discovering the Stars.* Mahwah, NJ: Troll, 1982.

Sapolsky, R. M. "Why Stress Is Bad for Your Brain." *Science* 273 (1996): 749–750.

————. *Why Zebras Don't Get Ulcers.* New York: Freeman, 1998.

Sayre, S., and D. W. Ball. "Piagetian Cognitive Development and Achievement in Science." *Journal of Research in Science Teaching* 12 (1975): 165–174.

Schacter, Daniel L. *Searching for Memory.* New York: Basic Books, 1996.

Schotter, Roni. *Nothing Ever Happens on 90th Street.* New York: Orchard Books, 1997.

Schwartz, David M. *How Much Is a Million?* NY: Lothrop, Lee & Shepard Books, 1989.

———. *If You Made a Million.* New York: Lothrop, Lee & Shepard Books, 1989.

Sedlacek, Gary C. "Voices." *English Journal* (March 1987): 48–51.

Shakespeare, William. *Romeo and Juliet.* In *The Yale Shakespeare*, edited by Richard Hosley. New Haven, CT: Yale University Press, 1965.

———. *The Tragedy of Macbeth*, edited by Eugene M. Waith. New Haven, CT: Yale University Press, 1966.

Shapard, Robert and James Thomas, eds. *Sudden Fiction.* Salt Lake City, UT: Gibbs M. Smith, 1986.

Shatz, Carla J. "The Developing Brain." *Scientific American* (Special Issue, September 1992): 61–67.

Shayer, M. and P. Arlin. "The Transescent Mind: Teachers Can Begin to Make a Difference." *Transescence* 10 (1982): 27–34.

Shaywitz, Sally. *Overcoming Dyslexia.* New York: Alfred A. Knopf, 2003.

Shweder, Richard, Martha Minow, et al., eds. *Engaging Cultural Differences: The Multicultural Challenge in Liberal Democracies.* New York: Russell Sage, 2002.

Silverstein, Shel. "Sarah Cynthia Sylvia Stout Would Not Take the Garbage Out." In *Where the Sidewalk Ends.* New York: Harper & Row, 1974.

Simon, Seymour. *Jupiter.* New York: William Morrow and Co., 1985.

———. *Mars.* New York: Mulberry Books, 1987.

———. *Neptune.* New York: Morrow Junior Books, 1991.

Smith, Frank. *Writing and the Writer.* New York: Holt, Rinehart and Winston, 1982.

Smith, Kelly R. *Phonics Friendly Families.* Spring, TX: Absey & Co., 1999.

Snowdon, David, PhD. *Aging with Grace.* New York: Bantam Books, 2001.

Sohn, David A. Film*: The Creative Eye.* Dayton, OH: Geo. A. Pflaum, 1970.

Soler, Eloise Ida Scott. "Brain Hemisphere Characteristics and Leadership Style of Selected School Superintendents in Texas." Ph. D. diss., Texas A&M University.

Soyinka, Wole. *Ake: The Years of Childhood.* New York: Vintage, 1989.

Sparks, Dennis. "13 Tips for Managing Change." *Education Week* (June 10, 1992): 22.

Spiegelman, Art. *Maus: The Survivor Tale.* New York: Panetheon Books, 1986 (1) and 1991 (2).

Springer, Sally P. and George Deutsch. *Left Brain, Right Brain.* New York: W. H. Freeman and Company, 1989.

Stafford, William. *The Animal That Drank Up Sound.* New York: Harcourt Brace Jovanovich, 1992.

Steinbeck, John. *The Grapes of Wrath.* New York: Bantam Books, 1969.

———. *Of Mice and Men.* New York: Bantam Books, 1977.

Stern, Arthur A. "When is a Paragraph." *College Composition and Communication* (October 1976). In *ACTS of Teaching: How to Teach Writing*, edited by Joyce Armstrong Carroll and Edward E. Wilson. Englewood, CO: Teacher Ideas Press, 1993.

Sternberg, Robert. *The Triarchic Mind.* New York: Viking Penguin, 1988.

Stewart, Mary. *The Last Enchantment.* New York: William Morrow, 1979.

Strindberg, August. *Miss Julie.* Mineola, NY: Dover Publications, 1992.

Stillman, Peter. *Families Writing.* New York: Boynton/Cook Publishers, 1998.

Strickland, Bill, ed. *On Being a Writer.* Cincinnati, OH: Writer's Digest Books, 1989.

Stock, Patricia Lambert. "Practicing the Scholarship of Teaching What We Do with the Knowledge We Make." *The Council Chronicle* 15(September 2005): 13–16.

Strong, William. *Creative Approaches to Sentence Combining.* Urbana, IL: ERIC, 1986.

———. *Sentence Combining.* New York: Random House, 1983.

Stull, William L. *Combining & Creating.* New York: Holt, Rinehart and Winston, 1983.

Suarez-Orozco, Marcelo. "Rethinking Education In the Global Era." *Phi Delta Kappan* (November 2005): 209–212.

Suarez-Orozco, Marcelo and Desiree Baolian Qin-Hillard, eds. *Globalization Culture and Education in the New Millennium.* Berkeley: University of California Press, 2004.

Sylwester, Robert. *The Adolescent Brain: Reaching for Autonomy.* Thousand Oaks, CA: Corwin Press, 2007.

Tan, Amy. *The Kitchen God's Wife.* New York: G. P. Putnam's Sons, 1991.

Thoreau, Henry David. *Walden.* New York: Doubleday, 1960.

Thurber, James. *Many Moons.* New York: Harcourt Brace Jovanovich, 1973.

Tierney, Robert J., Mark A. Carter, and Laura E. Desai. *Portfolio Assessment in the Reading-Writing Classroom.* Norwood, MA: Christopher-Gordon Publishers, 1991.

Tierney, Robert, John E. Readence, and Ernest K. Dishner. *Reading Strategies and Practices; A Compendium.* Boston, MA: Allen and Bacon, 1995.

Toepfer, Conrad F., Jr. "Brain Growth Periodization: Implications for Middle Grades Education." *Schools in the Middle* (April 1981): 1–6.

Toffler, Alvin. "Other Forms of Literacy." www.edu-cyberpg.com/Literacy/otherforms.asp.

Tovani, Cris. *I Read It, But I Don't Get It.* Portland, ME: Stenhouse, 2000.

Trimble, John R. *Writing with Style.* Englewood Cliffs, NJ: Prentice Hall, Inc. 1975.

Truffault, François. *Hitchcock.* New York: Simon & Schuster, 1983.

Truss, Lynne. *Eats, Shoots & Leaves.* New York: Gotham Books, 2003.

UNESCO Institute for Statistics. www.UIS.unesco.org.

Van Cleave, Janice. *Janice VanCleave's Math for Every Kid: Easy Activities that Make Learning Math Fun.* New York: Jossey-Bass, 1991.

Voigt, Cynthia. *Dicey's Song.* New York: Fawcett Juniper, 1982.

———. *On Fortune's Wheel.* New York: Simon Pulse, 1999.

Vygotsky, L. S. *Thought and Language.* Translated by Eugenia Hanfmann and Gertrude Vakar. Cambridge, MA: MIT Press, 1962.

———. *Mind in Society.* Edited by Michael Cole, Vera John-Steiner, Sylvia Scribner, and Ellen Souberman. Cambridge, MA: Harvard University Press, 1978.

Wakoski, Diane. "Good Water." In *Poetry After Lunch*, edited by Joyce Armstrong Carroll and Edward E. Wilson. Spring, TX: Absey & Co., 1997.

Waller, Robert James. *The Bridges of Madison County.* New York: Warner Books, 1992.

Walsh, Mark. "Whittle Unveils Team To Design New Schools." *Education Week* 4 (March 1992), 1, 13.

Watkins, Dale. "Welcome to America." www.sentimentalrefugee.com/maze_final_SR.jpg, April 8, 2006.

Watson, James D. "Foreword." In *Discovering the Brain*, by Sandra Ackerman. Washington, DC: National Academy Press, 1992.

Weaver, Constance. *Grammar for Teachers: Perspectives and Definitions*. Urbana, IL: NCTE, 1979.

Weintraub, Stanley, ed. *The Portable Bernard Shaw*. New York: Penguin Books, 1983.

Welty, Eudora. *One Writer's Beginnings*. Cambridge, MA: Harvard University Press, 1984.

Whitehead, Alfred North. *The Aims of Education and Other Essays*. New York: Free Press, 1968.

Wild, Margaret and Julie Vivas. *Let the Celebrations Begin!* New York: Orchard Books, 1991.

Wilde, Sandra. *You Kan Red This! Spelling and Punctuation for Whole Language Classrooms, K–6*. Portsmouth, NH: Heinemann, 1992.

Wileman, Bud and Robin Wileman, eds. *Webster's Bad Spellers' Dictionary*. New York: Barnes & Noble, 1985.

Willis, Jeanne and Tony Ross. *Earthlets: As Explained by Professor Xargle*. New York: Puffin, 1994.

Willis, Judy. *Brain-Friendly Strategies for the Inclusion Classroom*. Alexandria, VA: Association for Supervision and Curriculum Development, 2007.

Wittrock, M. C. "Education and the Cognitive Processes of the Brain." In *Education and the Brain: The Seventy-seventh Yearbook of the National Society for the Study of Education*, edited by Jeanne S. Chall and Allan F. Mirsky. Chicago: University of Chicago Press, 1978.

White, Edward M. *Teaching and Assessing Writing*. San Francisco, CA: Jossey-Bass, 1985.

Whitehead, Alfred North. *The Aims of Education and Other Essays*. New York: Free Press, 1968.

Wilson, Edward E. "Shielding the Basic Student." *English in Texas* (Vol. 14): 43–47.

Wink, Joan and LeAnn Putney. *A Vision of Vygotsky*. Boston, MA: Allyn and Bacon, 2002.

Witkin, R. W. *The Intelligence of Feeling*. London: Heinemann, 1974.

Wolfe, Sidney. *Worst Pills Best Pills*. New York: Pocket Books, 2005.

Wolff, Geoffrey, ed. *The Best American Essays 1989*. New York: Ticknor & Fields, 1989.

Yagawa, Sumiko and Katherine Paterson. *The Crane Wife*. New York: William Morrow, 2001.

Yolen, Jane. *The Devil's Arithmetic*. New York: Viking Kestrel, 1988.

———. *Wings*. New York: Harcourt Brace Jovanovich, 1991.

Young, Clem. "Readers, Texts, Teachers." In *Readers, Texts, Teachers*, edited by Bill Corcoran and Emrys Evans. Upper Montclair, NJ: Boynton/Cook Publishers, 1987.

Young, Ed. *Seven Blind Mice*. New York: Philomel Books, 1992.

Young, Richard E., Alton L. Becker, and Kenneth L. Pike. *Rhetoric: Discovery and Change*. New York: Harcourt, Brace & World, 1970.

Young, Ruth. *A Trip to Mars*. New York: Orchard Books, 1990.

Zinsser, William. *On Writing Well*. New York: Harper & Row, 1988.

PART

III

APPENDICES

A

GENRES

Adapted from Camille A. Allen, *The Multigenre Research Paper: Voice, Passion, and Discovery in Grades 4–6* (Portsmouth, NH: Heinemann, 2001). Copyright © 2001 Heinemann.

ads
allegories
announcements
autobiographies
awards
baseball cards
bedtime stories
billboards
biographies
book jackets
book reviews
brochures
bulletins
bumper stickers
calendars
campaign speeches
captions
cartoons
certificates
character sketches
children's books
comic strips
contracts
conversations
critiques
crossword puzzles
course syllabi
dedications

definitions
diaries
diplomas
directions
directories
double voice poems
editorials
epitaphs
encyclopedia entries
essays
fables
fairy tales
family trees
flash fiction
flip books
game rules
graffiti
good news/bad news
grocery lists
headlines
how-to speeches
impromptu speeches
interviews
job applications
journals
laboratory notes
letters
lists

lyrics
magazines
maps
memos
memoirs
menus
mission statements
mysteries
myths
newscasts
newsletters
newspapers
novellas
novels
novels (graphic)
obituaries
observational notes
pamphlets
parodies
plays & skits
poems
posters & banners
postcards
prayers
propaganda sheets
product descriptions
puppet shows
puzzles

questionnaires
questions
quizzes
quotations
real estate notices
recipes
remedies
requests
requisitions
research pieces
resumes
reviews
riddles
sales pitches
schedules
slogans
speeches
stamps & stickers
stories
tables of content
telegrams
tickets
time lines
tombstones
tributes
TV commercials
Web pages
wills
word searches

GRAMMAR, GRAMMARS, AND THE TEACHING OF GRAMMAR

PATRICK HARTWELL
From *College English*, February 1985. Copyright 1985 by the
National Council of Teachers of English. Reprinted with permission.

For me the grammar issue was settled at least twenty years ago with the conclusion offered by Richard Braddock, Richard Lloyd-Jones, and Lowell Schoer in 1963.

In view of the widespread agreement of research studies base upon many types of students and teachers, the conclusion may be stated in strong and unqualified terms: the teaching of formal grammar has a negligible or, because it usually displaces some instruction and practice in composition, even a harmful effect on improvement in writing.[1]

Indeed, I would agree with Janet Emig that the grammar issue is a prime example the "magical thinking": the assumption that students will learn only what we teach and only because we teach.[2]

But the grammar issue, as we will see, is a complicated one. And, perhaps surprisingly, it remains controversial, with the regular appearance of papers defending the teaching of formal grammar or attacking it.[3] Thus Janice Neuleib, writing on "The Relation of Formal Grammar to Composition" in *College Composition and Communication* (23 [1977], 247–150), is tempted "to sputter on paper" at reading the quotation above (p. 248), and Martha Kolln, writing in the same journal three years later ("Closing the Books on Alchemy," *CCC*, 32 [1981], 139–151), labels people like me "alchemists" for our perverse beliefs. Neuleib reviews five experimental studies, most of them concluding that formal grammar instruction has no effect on the quality of students' writing nor on their ability to avoid error. Yet she renders in effect a Scots verdict of "Not proven" and calls for more research on the issue. Similarly, Kolln reviews six experimental studies that arrive at similar conclusions, only one of them overlapping with the studies cited by Neuleib. She calls for more careful definition of the word *grammar*—her definition being "the internalized system that native speakers of a language share" (p. 140)—and she concludes with a stirring call to place grammar instruction at the center of the composition curriculum: "our goal should be to help students understand the system they know unconsciously as native speakers, to teach them the necessary categories and labels that will enable them to think about and talk about their language" (p. 150). Certainly our textbooks and our pedagogies—though they vary widely in what they see as "necessary categories and labels"—continue to emphasize mastery of formal grammar, and popular discussions of a presumed literacy crisis are almost unanimous in their call for a renewed emphasis on the teaching of formal grammar, seen as basic for success in writing.[4]

An Instructive Example

It is worth noting at the outset that both sides in this dispute—the grammarians and the anti-grammarians—articulate the issue in the same positivistic terms: what does experimental research tell us about the value of teaching formal grammar? But seventy-five years of experimental research has for all practical purposes told us nothing. The two sides are unable to agree on how to interpret such research. Studies are interpreted in terms of one's prior assumption about the value of teaching grammar: their results seem not to change those assumptions. Thus the basis of the discussion, a basis shared by Kolln and Neuleib and by Braddock and his colleagues—what does educational research tell us?"—seems designed to perpetuate, not to resolve, the issue. A single example will be instructive. In 1976, and then at greater length in 1979, W.B. Elley, I.H. Barham, H. Lamb, and M. Wyllie reported on a three-year experiment in New Zealand, comparing the relative effectiveness at the high school level of instruction in transformational grammar, instruction in traditional grammar, and no grammar instruction.[5] They concluded that the formal study of grammar, whether transformational or traditional, improved neither writing quality nor control over surface correctness.

> After two years, no differences were detected in writing performance or language competence; after three years small differences appeared in some minor conventions favoring the TG [transformational grammar] group, but these were more than offset by the less positive attitudes they showed towards their English studies. (p. 18)

Anthony Petroskey, in a review of research ("Grammar Instruction: What We Know," *English Journal*, 66, No. 9 [1977], 86–88), agreed with this conclusion, finding the study to be carefully designed, "representative of the best kind of educational research" (p. 86), its validity "unquestionable" (p. 88). Yet Janice Neuleib in her essay found the same conclusions to be "startling" and questioned whether the finding could be generalized beyond the target population, New Zealand high school students. Martha Kolln, when her attention is drawn to the study ("Reply to Ron Shook," *CCC*, 32 [1981], 139–151), thinks the whole experiment "suspicious." And John Mellon has been willing to use the study to defend the teaching of grammar; the study of Elley and his colleagues, he has argued, shows that teaching grammar does no harm.[6]

It would seem unlikely, therefore, that further experimental research, in and of itself, will resolve the grammar issue. Any experimental design can be nit-picked, any experimental population can be criticized, and any experimental conclusion can be questioned or, more often, ignored. In fact, it may well be that the grammar question is not open to resolution by experimental research, that, as Noam Chomsky has argued in *Reflections on Language* (New York: Pantheon, 1975), criticizing the trivialization of human learning by behavioral psychologists, the issue is simply misdefined.

> There will be "good experiments" only in domains that lie outside the organism's cognitive capacity. For example, there will be no "good experiments" in the study of human learning.

> This discipline . . . will, of necessity, avoid those domains in which an organism is specifically designed to acquire rich cognitive structures that enter into its life in an intimate fashion. The discipline will be of virtually no intellectual interest, it seems to me, since it is restricting itself in principle to those questions that are guaranteed to tell us little about the nature of organisms. (p. 36)

Asking the Right Questions

As a result, though I will look briefly at the tradition of experimental research, my primary goal in this essay is to articulate the grammar issue in different and, I would hope, more productive terms. Specifically, I want to ask four questions:

1. Why is the grammar issue so important? Why has it been the dominant focus of composition research for the last seventy-five years?

2. What definitions of the word *grammar* are needed to articulate the grammar issue intelligibly?

3. What do findings in cognate disciplines

suggest about the value of formal grammar instruction?

4. What is our theory of language, and what does it predict about the value of formal grammar instruction? (This question—"what does our theory of language predict?"—seems a much more powerful question than "what does educational research tell us?")

In exploring these questions I will attempt to be fully explicit about issues, terms, and assumptions. I hope that both proponents and opponents of formal grammar instruction would agree that these are useful as shared points of reference: care in definition, full examination of the evidence, reference to relevant work in cognate disciplines, and explicit analysis of the theoretical bases of the issue.

But even with that gesture of harmony it will be difficult to articulate the issue in a balanced way, one that will be acceptable to both sides. After all, we are dealing with a professional dispute in which one side accuses the other of "magical thinking," and in turn that side responds by charging the other as "alchemists." Thus we might suspect that the grammar issue is itself embedded in larger models of the transmission of literacy, part of quite different assumptions about the teaching of composition.

Those of us who dismiss the teaching of formal grammar have a model of composition instruction that makes the grammar issue "uninteresting" in a scientific sense. Our model predicts a rich and complex interaction of learner and environment in mastering literacy, an interaction that has little to do with sequences of skills instruction as such. Those who defend the teaching of grammar tend to have a model of composition instruction that is rigidly skills-centered and rigidly sequential: the formal teaching of grammar, as the first step in that sequence, is the cornerstone or linchpin. Grammar teaching is thus supremely interesting, naturally a dominant focus for educational research. The controversy over the value of grammar instruction, then, is inseparable from two other issues: the issues of sequence in the teaching of composition and the role of the composition teacher. Consider, for example, the force of these two issues in Janice Neuleib's conclusion: after calling for yet more experimental research on the value of teaching grammar, she ends with an absolute (and unsupported) claim about sequences and teacher roles in composition.

> We do know, however, that some things must be taught at different levels. Insistence on adherence to usage norms by composition teachers does improve usage. Students can learn to organize their papers if teachers do not accept papers that are disorganized. Perhaps composition teachers can teach those two abilities before they begin the more difficult tasks of developing syntactic sophistication and a winning style. ("The Relation of Formal Grammar to Composition," p. 250)

(One might want to ask, in passing, whether "usage norms" exist in the monolithic fashion the phrase suggests and whether refusing to accept disorganized papers is our best available pedagogy for teaching arrangement.)[7]

But I want to focus on the notion of sequence that makes the grammar issue so important: first grammar, then usage, then some absolute model of organization, all controlled by the teacher at the center of the learning process, with other matters, those of rhetorical weight—"syntactic sophistication and a winning style"—pushed off to the future. It is not surprising that we call each other names: those of us who question the value of teaching grammar are in fact shaking the whole elaborate edifice of traditional composition instruction.

The Five Meanings of "Grammar"

Given its centrality to a well-established way of teaching composition, I need to go about the business of defining grammar rather carefully, particularly in view of Kolln's criticism of the lack of care in earlier discussions. Therefore I will build upon a seminal discussion of the word *grammar* offered a generation ago, in 1954, by W. Nelson Francis, often excerpted as "The Three Meanings of Grammar."[8] It is worth reprinting at length, if only to re-establish it as a reference point for future discussions.

The first thing we mean by "grammar" is "the set of formal patterns in which words of a language are arranged in order to convey larger meanings." It is not necessary that we be able to discuss these patterns self-consciously in order to be able to use them. In fact, all speakers of a language above the age of five or six know how to use its complex forms of organization with considerable skill; in this sense of the word—call it "Grammar 1"—they are thoroughly familiar with its grammar.

The second meaning of "grammar"—call it "Grammar 2"—is the branch of linguistic science which is concerned with the description, analysis, and formulization of formal language patterns." Just as gravity was in full operation before Newton's apple fell, so grammar in the first sense was in full operation before anyone formulated the first rule that began the history of grammar as a study.

The third sense in which people use the word "grammar" is "linguistic etiquette." This we may call "Grammar 3." The word in this sense is often coupled with a derogatory adjective: we say that the expression "he ain't here" is "bad grammar." . . .

As has already been suggested, much confusion arises from missing these meanings. One hears a good deal of criticism of teachers of English couched in such terms as "they don't teach grammar any more." Criticism of this sort is based on the wholly unproven assumption that teaching Grammar 2 will improve the student's proficiency in Grammar 1 or improve his manners in Grammar 3. Actually, the form of Grammar 2 which is usually taught is a very inaccurate and misleading analysis of the facts of Grammar 1; and it therefore is of highly questionable value in improving a person's ability to handle the structural patterns of his language. (pp. 300–301)

Francis' Grammar 3 is, of course, not grammar at all, but usage. One would like to assume that Joseph Williams' recent discussion of usage ("The Phenomenology of Error," *CCC*, 32 [1981], 152–168), along with his references, has placed those shibboleths in a proper prospective. But I doubt it, and I suspect that popular discussions of the grammar issue will be flawed by the intrusion of usage issues as past discussions have been. At any rate I will make only passing references to Grammar 3—usage—naively assuming that this issue has been discussed elsewhere and that my readers are familiar with those discussions.

We need also to make further discriminations about Francis' Grammar 2, given that the purpose of his 1954 article was to substitute for one form of Grammar 2, that "inaccurate and misleading" form "which is usually taught," another form, that of American structuralist grammar. Here we can make use of a still earlier discussion, one going back to the days when *PMLA* was willing to publish articles on rhetoric and linguistics, to a 1927 article by Charles Carpenter Fries, "The Rules of the Common School Grammars" (42 [1927], 221–237). Fries there distinguished between the scientific tradition of language study (to which we will now delimit Francis' Grammar 2, scientific grammar) and the separate tradition of "the common school grammars," developed unscientifically, largely based on two inadequate principles—appeals to "logical principles" like "two negatives make a positive," and analogy to Latin grammar; thus, Charlton Laird's characterization, "the grammar of Latin, ingeniously warped to suggest English" (*Language in America* [New York: World, 1970], p. 294). There is, of course, a direct link between the "common school grammars" that Fries criticized in 1927 and the grammar-based texts of today, and thus it seems wise, as Karl W. Dykema suggests ("Where Our Grammar Came From," *CE*, 22 [1961], 455–465), to separate Grammar 2, "scientific grammar," from Grammar 4, "school grammar," the latter meaning, quite literally, "the grammar used in the schools."

Further, since Martha Kolln points to the adaptation of Christensen's sentence rhetoric in a recent sentence-combining text as an example of the proper emphasis on "grammar" ("Closing the Books on Alchemy," p. 140), it is worth separating out, as still another meaning of *grammar*, Grammar 5, "stylistic grammar," defined as "grammatical terms used in the interest of teaching prose style." And, since stylistic grammars abound, with widely variant terms and emphases, we might appropriately speak parenthetically of specific forms of Grammar 5— Grammar 5 (Lanham); Grammar 5 (Strunk and White); Grammar 5 (Williams, *Style*); even Grammar 5 (Christensen, as adapted by Daiker, Kerek, and Morenberg).[9]

The Grammar in Our Heads

With these definitions in mind, let us return to Francis' Grammar 1, admirably defined by Kolln as the "internalized system of rules that speakers of a language share" ("Closing the Books on Alchemy," p. 140), or, to put it more simply, the grammar in our heads. Three features of Grammar 1 need to be stressed: first, its special status as an internalized system of rules," as tacit and unconscious knowledge; second, the abstract, even counterintuitive, nature of these rules, insofar as we are able to approximate them indirectly as Grammar 2 statements; and third, the way in which the form of one's Grammar 1 seems profoundly affected by the acquisition of literacy. This sort of review is designed to firm up our theory of language, so that we can ask what it predicts about the value of teaching formal grammar.

A simple thought experiment will isolate the special status of Grammar 1 knowledge. I have asked members of a number of different groups—from sixth graders to college freshmen to high-school teachers—to give me the rule for ordering adjectives of nationality, age, and number in English. The response is always the same: "We don't know the rule." Yet when I asked these groups to perform an active language task, they show productive control over the rule they have denied knowing. I ask them to arrange the following words in a natural order:

French   the   young   girls   four

I have never seen a native speaker of English who did not immediately produce the nature or-

der, "the four young French girls." The rule is that in English order of adjectives is first, number, second, age, and third, nationality. Native speakers can create analogous phrases using the rule—"the seventy-three aged Scandinavian lechers"; and the drive for meaning is so great that they will create contexts to make sense out of violations of the rule, as in foregrounding for emphasis: "I want to talk to the French four young girls." (I immediately envision a large room, perhaps a banquet hall, filled with tables at which are seated groups of four young girls, each group of a different nationality.) So Grammar 1 is eminently usable knowledge—the way we make our life through language—but it is not accessible knowledge; in a profound sense, we do not know that we have it. Thus neurolinguist Z.N. Pylyshyn speaks of Grammar 1 as "autonomous," separate from common-sense reasoning, and as "cognitively impenetrable," not available for direct examination.[10] In philosophy and linguistics, the distinction is made between formal, conscious, "knowing about" knowledge (like Grammar 2 knowledge) and tacit, unconscious, "knowing how" knowledge (like Grammar 1 knowledge). The importance of this distinction for the teaching of composition—it provides a powerful theoretical justification for mistrusting the ability of Grammar 2 (or Grammar 4) knowledge to affect Grammar 1 performance—was pointed out in this journal by Martin Steinmann, Jr., in 1966 ("Rhetorical Research," *CE*, 27 [1966], 278–285).

Further, the more we learn about Grammar 1—and most linguists would agree that we know surprisingly little about it—the more abstract and implicit it seems. This abstractness can be illustrated with an experiment, devised by Lise Menn and reported by Morris Halle,[11] about our rule for forming plurals in speech. It is obvious that we do indeed have a "rule" for forming plurals, for we do not memorize the plural of each noun separately. You will demonstrate productive control over that rule by forming the spoken plurals of the nonsense words below:

thole   flitch   plast

Halle offers two ways of formalizing a Grammar 2 equivalent of this Grammar 1 ability. One form of the rule is the following, stated in terms of speech sounds:

a. If the noun ends in /s z ŝ ẑ ĉ ĵ/, add /Iz/'

b. otherwise, if the noun ends in / p t k f Ø/, add /s/;

c. otherwise, add /z/.

This rule comes close to what we literate adults consider to be an adequate rule for plurals in writing, like the rules, for example, taken from a recent "common school grammar," Eric Gould's *Reading into Writing: A Rhetoric, Reader, and Handbook* (Boston: Houghton Mifflin, 1983):

Plurals can be tricky. If you are unsure of a plural, then check it in the dictionary.

The general rules are

Add *s* to the singular: *girls, tables*

Add *es* to nouns ending in ch, sh, x or s: *churches, boxes, wishes*

Add *es* to nouns ending in *y* and preceded by a vowel once you have changed *y* to *i*: *monies, companies.* (p. 666)

(But note the persistent inadequacy of such Grammar 4 rules: here, as I read it, the rule is inadequate to explain the plurals of *ray* and *tray*, even to explain the collective noun *monies*, not a plural at all, formed from the mass noun *money* and offered as an example.) A second form of the rule would make use of much more abstract entities, sound features:

a. If the noun ends with a sound that is [coronal, strident], add /Iz/;

b. otherwise, if the noun ends with a sound that is [non-voiced], add /s/;

c. otherwise, add /z/.

(The notion of "sound features" is itself rather abstract, perhaps new to readers not trained in linguistics. But such readers should be able to recognize that the spoken plurals of *lip* and *duck*, the sound [s], differ from the spoken plurals of *sea* and *gnu*, the sound [z], only in that

the sounds of the latter are "voiced"—one's vocal cords vibrate—while the sounds of the former are "non-voiced.")

To test the psychologically operative rule, the Grammar 1 rule, native speakers of English were asked to form the plural of the last name of the composer Johann Sebastian *Bach*, a sound [x], unique in American (though not in Scottish) English. If speakers follow the first rule above, using word endings, they would a reject a) and b), then apply c), producing the plural as /baxz/, with word-final /z/. (If writers were to follow the rule of the common school grammar, they would produce the written plural *Baches*, apparently, given the form of the rule, on analogy with *churches*.) If speakers follow the second rule, they would have to analyze the sound [x] as [non-labial, non-coronal, dorsal, non-voiced, and non-strident], producing the plural as /baxs/, with word-final /s/. Native speakers of American English overwhelmingly produce the plural as /baxs/. They use knowledge that Halle characterizes as "unlearned and untaught" (p. 140).

Now such a conclusion is counterintuitive—certainly it departs maximally from Grammar 4 rules for forming plurals. It seems that native speakers of English behave as if they have productive control, as Grammar 1 knowledge, of abstract sound features (= coronal, = strident, and so on) which are available as conscious, Grammar 2 knowledge only to trained linguists—and, indeed, formally available only within the last hundred years or so. ("Behave as if," in that last sentence, is a necessary hedge, to underscore the difficulty of "knowing about" Grammar 1.)

Moreover, as the example of plural rules suggests, the form of the Grammar 1 in the heads of literate adults seems profoundly affected by the acquisition of literacy. Obviously, literate adults have access to different morphological codes: the abstract print –s underlying the predictable /s/ and /z/ plurals, the abstract print –ed underlying the spoken past tense markers /t/, as in "walked," /əd/, as in "surrounded," /d/, as in "sacred," and the symbol /Ø/ for no surface realization of "I walked to the store." Literate adults also have access to distinctions preserved only in the code of print (for example, the distinction between "a good sailer" and "a good sailor" that Mark Aranoff points out in "An English Spelling Convention," *Linguistic Inquiry*, 9 [1978], 299–303). More significantly, Irene Moscowitz speculates that the ability of third graders to form abstract nouns on analogy with pairs like *divine::divinity* and *serene::serenity*, where the spoken vowel changes but the spelling preserves the meaning, is a factor of knowing how to read. Carol Chomsky finds a three-stage developmental sequence in the grammatical performance of seven-year-olds, related to measures of kind and variety of reading; and Rita S. Brause finds a nine-stage developmental sequence in the ability to understand semantic ambiguity, extending from fourth graders to graduate students.[12] John Mills and Gordon Hemsley find that level of education, and presumably level of literacy, influence judgments of grammaticality, concluding that literacy changes the deep structure of one's internal grammar; Jean Whyte finds that oral language functions develop differently in readers and nonreaders; José Morais, Jésus Alegria, and Paul Bertelson find that illiterate adults are unable to add or delete sounds at the beginning of nonsense words, suggesting that awareness of speech as a series of phones is provided by learning to read an alphabetic code. Two experiments—one conducted by Charles A. Ferguson, the other by Mary E. Hamilton and David Barton—find that adults' ability to recognize segmentation in speech is related to degree of literacy, not to amount of schooling or general ability.[13]

It is worth noting that none of these investigators would suggest that the developmental sequences they have uncovered be isolated and taught as discrete skills. They are natural concomitants of literacy, and then seem best characterized not as isolated rules but as developing schemata, broad strategies for approaching written language.

Grammar 2

We can, of course, attempt to approximate the rules of schemata of Grammar 1 by writing fully explicit descriptions that model the competence of a native speaker. Such rules, like the rules for pluralizing nouns or ordering adjectives discussed above, are the goal of the science of linguistics, that is, Grammar 2. There are a number of scientific grammars—an older structuralist model and several versions within a generative-transformational paradigm, not to mention isolated schools like tagmemic grammar, Montague grammar, and the like. In fact, we cannot think of Grammar 2 as a stable entity, for its form changes with each new issue of each linguistics journal, as new "rules of grammar" are proposed and debated. Thus Grammar 2, though of great theoretical interest to the composition teacher, is of little practical use in the classroom, as Constance Weaver has pointed out (*Grammar for Teachers* [Urbana, Ill.: NCTE, 1979], pp. 3–6). Indeed Grammar 2 is a scientific model of Grammar 1, not a description of it, so that questions of psychological reality, while important, are less important than other, more theoretical factors, such as the elegance of formulation or the global power of rules. We might, for example, wish to replace the rule for ordering adjectives of age, number, and nationality cited above with a more general rule—what linguists call a "fuzzy" rule—that adjectives in English are ordered by their abstract quality of "nouniness": adjectives that are very much like nouns, like *French* or *Scandinavian*, come physically closer to nouns than do adjectives that are less "nouny," like *four* or *aged*. But our motivation for accepting the broader rule would be its global power, not its psychological reality.[14]

I try to consider a hostile reader, one committed to the teaching of grammar, and I try to think of ways to hammer in the central point of this distinction, that the rules of Grammar 2 are simply unconnected to productive control over Grammar 1. I can argue from authority: Noam Chomsky has touched on this point whenever he has concerned himself with the implications of linguistics for language teaching, and years ago transformationalist Mark Lester stated unequivocally, "there simply appears to be no correlation between a writer's study of language and his ability to write."[15] I can cite analogies offered by others: Francis Christensen's analogy in an essay originally published in 1962 that formal grammar study would be "to invite a centipede to attend to the sequence of his legs in motion,"[16] or James Britton's analogy, offered informally after a conference presentation, that grammar study would be like forcing starving people to master the use of a knife and fork before allowing them to eat. I can offer analogies of my own, contemplating the wisdom of asking pool player to master the physics of momentum before taking up the cue or of making a prospective driver get a degree in automotive engineering before engaging the clutch. I consider a hypothetical argument that if Grammar 2 knowledge affected Grammar 1 performance, then linguists would be our best writers. (I can certify that they are, on the whole, not.) Such a position, after all, is only in accord with other domains of science: the formula for catching a fly ball in baseball ("Playing It by Ear," *Scientific American*, 248, No. 4 [1983], 76) is of such complexity that it is beyond my understanding—and, I would suspect, that of many workaday centerfielders. But perhaps I can best hammer in this claim—that Grammar 2 knowledge has no effect on Grammar 1 performance—by offering a demonstration.

The diagram on the next page is an attempt by Thomas N. Huckin and Leslie A. Olsen (*English for Science and Technology* [New York: McGraw-Hill, 1983]) to offer, for students of English as a second language, a fully explicit formulation of what is, for native speakers, a trivial rule of the language—the choice of definite article, indefinite article, or no definite article. There are obvious limits to such a formulation, for article choice in English is less a matter of rule than of idiom ("I went to college" versus "I went to a university" versus British "I went to university"), real-world knowledge (using in-definite "I went into a house" instantiates definite "I look at the ceiling" and indefinite "I visited a university" instantiates definite "I talked with the professors"), and stylistic choice (the last sentence above might alternatively end with "the choice of the definite article, the indefinite article, or no article"). Huckin and Olsen invite non-native speakers to use the rule consciously to justify article choice in technical prose, such as the passage below from P.F. Brandwein (*Matter: An Earth Science* [New York: Harcourt Brace Jovanovich, 1975]). I invite you to spend a couple of minutes doing the same thing, with the understanding that this exercise is a test case: you are using a very explicit rule to justify a fairly straightforward issue of grammatical choice.

Imagine a cannon on top of ____ highest mountain on earth. It is firing ____ cannonballs horizontally. ____ first cannonball fired follows its path. As ____ cannonball moves, ____ gravity pulls it down, and it soon hits ____ ground. Now ____ velocity with which each succeeding cannonball is fired is increased. Thus, ____ cannonball goes farther each time. Cannonball 2 goes farther than ____ cannonball 1 although each is begin pulled by ____ gravity toward the earth all ____ time. ____ last cannonball is fired with such tremendous velocity that it goes completely around ____ earth. It returns to ____ mountaintop and continues around the earth again and again. ____ cannonball's inertia causes it to continue in motion indefinitely in ____ orbit around earth. In such a situation, we could consider ____ cannonball to be ____ artificial satellite, just like ____ weather satellites launched by ____ U.S. Weather Service. (p. 209)

Most native speakers of English who have attempted this exercise report a great deal of frustration, a curious sense of working against, rather than with the rule. The rule, however valuable it may be for non-native speakers, is, for the most part, simply unusable for native speakers of the language.

Fig. B.1. Choice of Definite Article.

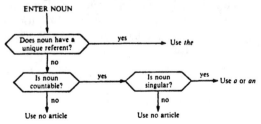

Cognate Areas of Research

We can corroborate this demonstration by turning to research in two cognate areas, studies of the induction of rules of artificial languages and studies of the role of formal rules in second language acquisition. Psychologists have studied the ability of subjects to learn artificial languages, usually constructed of nonsense syllables or letter strings. Such languages can be described by phrase structure rules:

$$S \Rightarrow VX$$
$$X \Rightarrow MX$$

More clearly, they can be presented as flow diagrams, as below:

Fig. B.2. Flow Diagram.

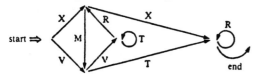

This diagram produces "sentences" like the following:

VVTRXRR.   XMVTTRX.   XXRR.
XMVRMT.   VVTTRMT.   XMTRRR.

The following "sentences" would be "ungrammatical" in this language:

*VMXTT.   *RTXVVT.   *TRVXXVVM.

Arthur S. Reber, in a classic 1967 experiment, demonstrated that mere exposure to grammatical sentences produced tacit learning: subjects who copied several grammatical sentences performed far above chance in judging the grammaticality of other letter strings. Further experiments have shown that providing subjects with formal rules—giving them the flow diagram above, for example—remarkably degrades performance; subjects given the "rules of the language" do much less well in acquiring the rules than do subjects not given the rules. Indeed, even telling subjects that they are to induce the rules of an artificial language degrades

performance. Such laboratory experiments are admittedly contrived, but they confirm predictions that our theory of language would make about the value of formal rules in language learning.[17]

The thrust of recent research in second language learning similarly works to constrain the value of formal grammar rules. The most explicit statement of the value of formal rules is that of Stephen D. Krashen's monitor model.[18] Krashen divided second language mastery into *acquisition*—tacit, informal mastery, akin to first language, acquisition—and formal learning—conscious application of Grammar 2 rules, which he calls "monitoring" output. In another essay Krashen uses his model to predict a highly individual use of the monitor and a highly constrained role for formal rules:

> Some adults (and very few children) are able to use conscious rules to increase the grammatical accuracy of their output, and even for these people, very strict conditions need to be met before the conscious grammar can be applied.[19]

In *Principles and Practice in Second Language Acquisition* (New York: Pergamon, 1982) Krashen outlines these conditions by means of a series of concentric circles, beginning with a large circle denoting the rules of English and a smaller circle denoting the subset of those rules described by formal linguists (adding that most linguists would protest that the size of this circle is much too large):

Fig. B.3. Krashen's Conditions Outline.

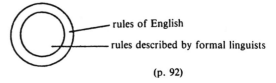

(p. 92)

Krashen then adds smaller circles, as shown below—a subset of the rules described by formal linguists that would be know to applied linguists, a subset of those rules that would be available to the best teachers, and then a subset of those rules that teachers might choose to present to second language learners:

Fig. B.4. Krashen's Continued Outline.

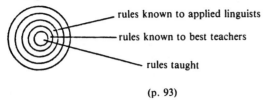

— rules known to applied linguists

— rules known to best teachers

— rules taught

(p. 93)

Of course, as Krashen notes, not all the rules taught will be learned, and not all those learned will be available, as what he calls "mental baggage" (p. 94), for conscious use.

An experiment by Ellen Bialystock, asking English speakers learning French to judge the grammaticality of taped sentences, complicates this issue, for reaction time data suggest that learners make an intuitive judgment of grammaticality, using implicit or Grammar 1 knowledge, and only then search for formal explanations, using explicit or Grammar 2 knowledge.[20] This distinction would suggest that Grammar 2 knowledge is of use to second language learners only after the principle has already been mastered as tacit Grammar 1 knowledge. In the terms of Krashen's model, learning never becomes acquisition (*Principles*, p. 86).

An ingenious experiment by Herbert W. Seliger complicates the issue yet further ("On the Nature and Function of Language Rules in Language Learning," *TESOL Quarterly*, 13 [1979], 359–369). Seliger asked native and non-native speakers of English to orally identify pictures of objects (e.g., "an apple," "a pear," "a book," "an umbrella"), noting whether they used the correct form of the indefinite articles *a* and *an*. He found no correlation between the ability to state the rule and the ability to apply it correctly, either with native or non-native speakers. Indeed, three or four adult non-native speakers in his sample produced a correct form of the rule, but they did not apply it in speaking. A strong conclusion from this experiment would be that formal rules of grammar seem to have no value whatsoever. Seliger, however, suggests a more paradoxical interpretation. Rules are of no use, he agrees, but some people think they are, and for these people, assuming that they have internalized the rules, even inadequate rules are of

heuristic value, for they allow them to access the internal rules they actually use.

The Incantations of the "Common School Grammars"

Such a paradox may explain the fascination we have as teachers with "rules of grammar" of the Grammar 4 variety, the "rules" of the "common school grammars." Again and again such rules are inadequate to the facts of written language; you will recall that we have known this since Francis' 1927 study. R. Scott Baldwin and James M. Coady, studying how readers respond to punctuation signals ("Psycholinguistic Approaches to a Theory of Punctuation," *Journal of Reading Behavior*, 10 [1978], 363–383), conclude that conventional rules of punctuation are "a complete sham" (p. 375). My own favorite is the Grammar 4 rule for showing possession, always expressed in terms of adding –'s or –s' to nouns, while our internal grammar, if you think about it, adds possession to noun phrases, albeit under severe stylistic constraints: "the horses of the Queen of England" are "the feathers of the duck over there" are "the duck over there's feathers." Suzette Haden Elgin refers to the "rules" of Grammar 4 as "incantations" (*Never Mind the Trees*, p. 9; see footnote 3).

It may simply be that as hyperliterate adults we are conscious of "using rules" when we are in fact doing something else, something far more complex, accessing tacit heuristics honed by print literacy itself. We can clarify this notion by reaching for an acronym coined by technical writers to explain the readability of complex prose—COIK: "clear only if known." The rules of Grammar 4—no, we can a this point be more honest—the incantations of Grammar 4 are in the code of print, then the advice to add –'s to nouns makes perfect sense, just as the collective noun *monies* is a fine example of changing –*y* to –*i* and adding –*es* to form the plural. But if you have not grasped, tacitly, the abstract representation of possession in print, such incantations can only be opaque.

Worse yet, the advice given in "the common school grammars" is unconnected with anything remotely resembling literate adult behavior. Consider, as an example, the rule for not writing a sentence fragment as the rule is described in the best-selling college grammar text, John C. Hodges and Mary S. Whitten's *Harbrace College Handbook*, 9th ed. (New York: Harcourt Brace Jovanovich, 1982). In order to get to the advice, "as a rule, do not write a sentence fragment" (p. 25), the student must master the following learning tasks:

Recognizing verbs.
Recognizing subjects and verbs.
Recognizing all parts of speech. (*Harbrace* lists eight.)
Recognizing phrases and subordinate clauses. (Harbrace lists six types of phrases, and it offers incomplete lists of eight relative pronouns and eighteen subordinate conjunctions.)
Recognizing main clauses and types of sentences.

These learning tasks completed, the student is given the rule above, offered a page of exceptions, and then given the following advice (or is it an incantation?):

Before handing in a composition . . . proofread each word group written as a sentence. Test each one for completeness. First, be sure that it has at least one subject and one predicate. Next, be sure that the word group is not a dependent clause beginning with a subordinating conjunction or a relative clause. (p. 27)

The school grammar approach defines a sentence fragment as a conceptual error—as not having conscious knowledge of the school grammar definition of *sentence*. It demands heavy emphasis on rote memory, and it asks students to behave in ways patently removed from the behaviors of mature writers. (I have never in my life tested a sentence for completeness, and I am a better writer—and probably a better person—as a consequence.) It may be of course, that some developing writers, at some

points in their development, may benefits from such advice—or, more to the point, may think that they benefit—but, as Thomas Friedman points out in "Teaching Error, Nurturing Confusion" (*CE*, 45 [1983], 390–399), our theory of language tells us that such advice is, at best, COIK. As the Maine joke has it, about a tourist asking directions from a farmer, "you can't get there from here."

Redefining Error

In the specific case of sentence fragments, Mina P. Shaughnessy (*Errors and Expectations* [New York: Oxford University Press, 1977]) argues that such errors are not conceptual failures at all, but performance errors—mistakes in punctuation. Muriel Harris' error counts support this view ("Mending the Fragmented Free Modifier," *CCC*, 32 [1981], 175–182). Case studies show example after example of errors that occur *because of* instruction—one thinks, for example, of David Bartholmae's student explaining that he added an *–s* to *children* "because it's a plural" (The Study of Error," *CCC*, 31 [1980], 262). Surveys, such as that by Muriel Harris ("Contradictory Perceptions of the Rules of Writing," *CCC*, 30 [1979], 218–220), and our own observations suggest that students consistently misunderstand such Grammar 4 explanations (COIK, you will recall). For example, from Patrick Hartwell and Robert H. Bentley and from Mike Rose, we have two separate anecdotal accounts of students, cited for punctuating a *because*-clause as a sentence, who have decided to avoid using *because*. More generally, Collette A. Daiute's analysis of errors made by college students show that errors tend to appear at clause boundaries, suggesting short-term memory load and not conceptual deficiency as a cause of error.[21]

Thus, if we think seriously about error and its relationship to the worship of formal grammar study, we need to attempt some massive dislocation of our traditional thinking, to shuck off our hyperliterate perception of the value of formal rules, and to regain the confidence in the tacit power of unconscious knowledge that our theory of language gives us. Most students, reading their writing aloud, will correct in essence all errors of spelling, grammar, and, by intonation, punctuation, but usually without noticing that what they read departs from what they wrote.[22] And Richard H. Haswell ("Minimal Marking," *CE*, 45 [1983], 600–604) notes that his students correct 61.1% of their errors when they are identified with a simple mark in the margin rather than by error type. Such findings suggest that we need to redefine error, to see it not as a cognitive or linguistic problem, a problem of not knowing a "rule of grammar" (whatever that may mean), but rather, following the insight of Robert J. Bracewell ("Writing as a Cognitive Activity," *Visible Language*, 14 [1980], 400–422), as a problem of metacognition and metalinguistic awareness, a matter of accessing knowledges that, to be of any use, learners must have already internalized by means of exposure to the code. (Usage issues—Grammar 3—probably represents a different order of problem. Both Joseph Emonds and Jeffrey Jochnowitz establish that the usage issues we worry most about are linguistically unnatural, departures from the grammar in our heads.)[23]

The notion of metalinguistic awareness seems crucial. The sentence below, created by Douglas R. Hofstadter ("Metamagical Themas," *Scientific American*, 235, No. 1 [1981], 22–32), is offered to clarify that notion; you are invited to examine it for a moment or two before continuing.

Their is four errors in this sentence. Can you find them?

Three errors announce themselves plainly enough, the misspellings of *there* and *sentence* and the use of *is* instead of *are*. (And, just to illustrate the perils of hyperliteracy, let it be noted that through three years of drafts, I referred to the choice of *is* and *are* as a matter of "subject-verb agreement.") The fourth error resists detection, until one assesses the truth value of the sentence itself—the fourth error is that there are not four errors, only three. Such a sentence (Hofsadter calls it a "self-referencing sentence") asks you to look at it in two ways, simultaneously as statement and as linguistic artifact—in other words, to exercise metalinguistic awareness.

A broad range of cross-cultural studies suggest that metalinguistic awareness is a defining feature of print literacy. Thus Sylvia Scribner and Michael Cole, working with the triliterate Vai of Liberia (variously literate in English, through schooling; in Arabic, for religious purposes; and in an indigenous Vai script, used for personal affairs), find that metalinguistic awareness, broadly conceived, is the only cognitive skill underlying each of the three literacies. The one statistically significant skill shared by literate Vai was the recognition of word boundaries. Moreover, literate Vai tended to answer "yes" when asked (in Vai), "Can you call the sun the moon and the moon the sun?" while illiterate Vai tended to have grave doubts about such metalinguistic play. And in the United States Henry and Lila R. Gleitman report quite different response by clerical workers and Ph.D. candidates asked to interpret nonsense compounds like "house-bird glass"; clerical workers focused on meaning and plausibility (for example, "a house-bird made of glass"), while Ph.D. candidates focused on syntax (for example, "a very small drinking cup for canaries" or "a glass that protects house-birds").[24] More general research findings suggest a clear relationship between measures of metalinguistic awareness and measures of literacy level.[25] Willaim Labov, speculating on literacy acquisition in inner-city ghettoes, contrasts "stimulus-bound" and "language-bound" individuals, suggesting that the latter seem to master literacy more easily.[26] The analysis here suggests that the causal relationship works the other way, that it is the mastery of written language that increases one's awareness of language as language.

This analysis has two implications. First, it makes the question of socially nonstandard dialects, always implicit in discussions of teaching formal grammar into a non-issue.[27] Native speakers of English, regardless of dialect, show tacit mastery of the conventions of Standard English, and that mastery seems to transfer into abstract orthographic knowledge through interaction with print.[28] Developing writers show the same patterning of errors, regardless of dialect.[29]

Studies of reading and of writing are simply irrelevant to mastering print literacy.[30] Print is a complex cultural code—or better yet, a system of codes—and my bet is that, regardless of instruction, one masters those codes from the top down, from pragmatic questions of voice, tone, audience, register, and rhetorical strategy, not from the bottom up, from grammar to usage to fixed forms of organization.

Second, this analysis forces us to posit multiple literacies, used for multiple purposes, rather than a single static literacy, engraved in "rules of grammar." These multiple literacies are evident in cross-cultural studies.[31] They are equally evident when we inquire into the uses of literacy in American communities.[32] Further, given that students, at all levels, show widely variant interactions with print literacy, there would seem to be little to do with grammar—with Grammar 2 or with Grammar 4—that would isolate as a basis for formal instruction.[33]

Grammar 5: Stylistic Grammar

Similarly, when we turn to Grammar 5, "grammatical terms used in the interest of teaching prose style," so central to Martha Kolln's argument for teaching formal grammar, we find that the grammar issue is simply beside the point. There are two fully-articulated positions about "stylistic grammar," which I will label "romantic" and "classic," following Richard Lloyd-Jones and Richard E. Young.[34] The romantic position is that stylistic grammars, though perhaps useful for teachers, have little place in the teaching of composition, for students must struggle with and through language toward meaning. This position rests on a theory of language ultimately philosophical rather than linguistic (witness, for example, the contempt for linguists in Ann Berthoff's *The Making of Meaning: Metaphors, Models, and Maxims for Writing Teachers* [Montclair, N.J.: Boynton/ Cook, 1981]); it is articulated as a theory of style by Donald A. Murray and, on somewhat different grounds (that stylistic grammars encourage overuse of the monitor), by Ian Pringle. The classic position, on the other hand, is that

we can help find ways to offer developing writers helpful suggestions about prose style, suggestions such as Francis Christensen's emphasis on the cumulative sentence, developed by observing the practice of skilled writers, and Joseph Williams' advice about predication, developed by psycholinguistic studies of comprehension.[35] James A. Berlin's recent survey of composition theory (*CE*, 45 [1982], 765–777) probably understates the gulf between these two positions and the radically different conceptions of language that underlie them, but it does establish that they share and overriding assumption in common: that one learns to control the language of print by manipulating language in meaningful contexts, not by learning about language in isolation, as by the study of formal grammar. Thus even classic theorists, who choose to present a vocabulary of style to students, do so only as a vehicle for encouraging productive control of communicative structures.

We might put the matter in the following terms. Writers need to develop skills at two levels. One, broadly rhetorical, involves communication in meaningful contexts (the strategies, registers, and procedures of discourse across a range of modes, audiences, contexts, and purposes). The other, broadly metalinguistic rather than linguistic, involves active manipulation of language with conscious attention to surface form. This second level may be developed tacitly, as a natural adjunct to developing rhetorical competencies—I take this to be developed formally, by manipulating language for stylistic effect, and such manipulation may involve, for pedagogical continuity, a vocabulary of style. But it is primarily developed by any kind of language activity that enhances the awareness of language as language.[36] David T. Hakes, summarizing the research on metalinguistic awareness, notes how far we are from understanding the process:

the optimal conditions for becoming metalinguistically competent involve growing up in a literate environment with adult models who are themselves metalinguistically competent and who foster the growth of that competence in a variety of ways as yet little understood. ("The Development of Metalinguisitc Abilities," p. 205, see footnote 25)

Such a model places language, at all levels, at the center of the curriculum, but not as "necessary categories and labels" (Kolln, "Closing the Books of Alchemy," p. 150), but as literal stuff, verbal clay, to be molded and probed, shaped and reshaped, and, above all, enjoyed.

The Tradition of Experimental Research

Thus, when we turn back to experimental research on the value of formal grammar instruction, we do so with firm predictions given us by our theory of language. Our theory would predict the formal grammar instruction, whether instruction in scientific grammar or instruction in "the common school grammar," would have little to do with control over surface correctness nor with quality of writing. It would predict that any form of active involvement with language would be preferable to instruction in rules or definitions (or incantations). In essence, this is what the research tells us. In 1893, the Committee of Ten (*Report of the Committee of Ten on Secondary School Studies* [Washington, D.C.: U.S. Government Printing Office, 1893]) put grammar at the center of the English curriculum, and its report established the rigidly sequential mode of instruction common for the last century. But the committee explicitly noted that grammar instruction did not aid correctness, arguing instead that it improved the ability to think logically (an argument developed from the role of the "grammarian" in the classical rhetorical tradition, essentially a teacher of literature—see, for example, the etymology of *grammar* in the *Oxford English Dictionary*).

But Franklin S. Hoyt, in a 1906 experiment, found no relationship between the study of grammar and the ability to think logically; his research led him to conclude what I am constrained to argue more than seventy-five years later, that there is no "relationship between a knowledge of technical grammar and the ability

to use English and to interpret language" ("The Place of Grammar in the Elementary Curriculum," *Teachers College Record*, 7 [1906], 483–484). Later studies, through the 1920s, focused on the relationship of knowledge of grammar and ability to recognize error; experiments reported by James Boraas in 1917 and by William Asker in 1923 are typical of those that reported no correlation. In the 1930s, with the development of the functional grammar movement, it was common to compare the study of formal grammar with one form or another of active manipulation of language; experiments by I.O. Ash in 1935 and Ellen Frogner in 1939 are typical of studies showing the superiority of active involvement with language.[37] In a 1959 article, "Grammar in Language Teaching" (*Elementary English*, 36 [1959] 412–421), John J. DeBoer noted the consistency of these findings.

> The impressive fact is . . . that in all these studies, carried out in places and at all time far removed from each other, often by highly experienced and disinterested investigators, the results have been consistently negative so far as the value of grammar in the improvement of language expression is concerned. (p. 417)

In 1960 Ingrid M. Strom, reviewing more than fifty experimental studies, came to a similarly strong and unqualified conclusion:

> direct methods of instruction, focusing on writing activities and the structuring of ideas, are more efficient in teaching sentence structure, usage, punctuation, and other related factors than are such methods as nomenclature drill, diagramming, and rote memorization of grammatical rules.[38]

In 1963 two research reviews appeared, one by Braddock, Lloyd-Jones, and Schorer, cited at the beginning of this paper, and one by Henry C. Meckel, whose conclusions, though more guarded, are in essential agreement.[39] In 1969 J. Stephens Sherwin devoted one-fourth of his *Four Problems in Teaching English: A Critique of Research* (Scranton, Penn.: International Textbook, 1969) to the grammar issue, concluding that "instruction in formal grammar is an ineffective way to help students achieve proficiency in writing" (p. 135). Some early experiments in sentence combining, such as those by Donald R. Bateman and Frank J. Zidonnis and by John C. Mellon, showed improvement in measures of syntactic complexity with instruction in transformational grammar keyed to sentence combining practice. But a later study by Frank O'Hare achieved the same gains with no grammar instruction, suggesting to Sandra L. Stotsky and to Richard Van de Veghe that active manipulation of language, not the grammar unit, explained the earlier results.[40] More recent summaries of research—by Elizabeth I. Haynes, Hillary Taylor Holbrook, and Marcia Farr Whiteman—support similar conclusions. Indirect evidence for this position is provided by surveys reported by Betty Bamberg in 1978 and 1981, showing that time spent in grammar instruction in high school is the least important factor, of eight factors examined, in separating regular from remedial writers at the college level.[41]

More generally, Patrick Scott and Bruce Castner, in "Reference Sources for Composition Research: A Practical Survey" (*CE*, 45 [1983], 756–768), note that much current research is not informed by an awareness of the past. Put simply, we are constrained to reinvent the wheel. My concern here has been with a far more serious problem: that too often the wheel we reinvent is square.

It is, after all, a question of power. Janet Emig, developing a consensus from composition research, and Aaron S. Carton and Lawrence V. Castiglione, developing the implications of language theory for education, come to the same conclusion: that the thrust of current research and theory is to take power from the teacher and to give that power to the learner.[42] At no point in the English curriculum is the question of power more blatantly posed than in the issue of formal grammar instruction. It is time that we, as teachers, formulate theories of language and literacy and let those theories guide our teaching, and it is time that we, as researchers, move on to more interesting areas of inquiry.

Notes

1. *Research in Written Composition* (Urbana, Ill.: National Council of Teachers of English, 1963), pp. 37–38.

2. "Non-magical Thinking: Presenting Writing Developmentally in Schools," in *Writing Process, Development and Communication*, Vol. II of *Writing: The Nature, Development and Teaching of Written Communication*, ed. Charles H. Fredericksen and Joseph F. Dominic (Hillsdale, N.J.: Lawrence Erlbaum, 1980), pp. 21–30.

3. For arguments in favor of formal grammar teaching, see Patrick F. Basset, "Grammar—Can We Afford Not to Teach It?" *NASSP Bulletin*, 64, No. 10 (1980), 55–63; Mary Epes, et al., "The COMP-LAB Project: Assessing the Effectiveness of a Laboratory-Centered Basic Writing Course on the College Level" (Jamaica, N.Y.: York College, CUNY, 1979) ERIC 194 908; June B. Evans, "The Analogous Ounce: The Analgesic for Relief," *English Journal*, 70, No. 2 (1981), 38–39; Sydney Greenbaum, "What Is Grammar and Why Teach It?" (a paper presented at the meeting of the National Council of Teachers of English, Boston, Nov. 1982) ERIC 222 917; Marjorie Smelstor, *A Guide to the Role of Grammar in Teaching Writing* (Madison: University of Wisconsin School of Education, 1978) ERIC 176 323; and A.M. Tibbetts, *Working Papers: A Teacher's Observations on Composition* (Glenview, Ill.: Scott, Foresman, 1982).

For attacks on formal grammar teaching, see Harvey A. Daniels, *Famous Last Words: The American Language Crisis Reconsidered* (Carbondale: Southern Illinois University Press, 1983); Suzette Haden Elgin, *Never Mind the Trees: What the English Teacher Really Needs to Know about Linguistics* (Berkeley: University of California College of Education, Bay Area Writing Project Occasional Paper No. 2, 1980) ERIC 198 536; Mike Rose, "Remedial Writing Courses: A Critique and a Proposal," *College English*, 45 (1983), 109–128; and Ron Shook, "Response to Martha Kolln," *College Composition and Communication*, 34 (1983), 491–495.

4. See, for example, Clifton Fadiman and James Howard, *Empty Pages: A Search for Writing Competence in School and Society* (Belmont, Cal.: Fearon Pitman, 1979); Edwin Newman, *A Civil Tongue* (Indianapolis, Ind.: Bobbs-Merrill, 1976); and *Strictly Speaking* (New York: Warner Books, 1974); John Simons, *Paradigm: Lost* (New York: Clarkson N. Potter, 1980); A.M. Tibbets and Charlene Tibbets, *What's Happening to American English?* (New York: Scribner's, 1978); and "Why Johnny Can't Write," *Newsweek*, 3 Dec. 1975, pp. 58–63.

5. The Role of Grammar in a Secondary School English Curriculum," *Research in the Teaching of English*, 10 (1976), 5–21; *The Role of Grammar in a Secondary School Curriculum* (Wellington: New Zealand Council of Teachers of English, 1979).

6. "A Taxonomy of Compositional Competencies," in *Perspectives on Literacy*, ed. Richard Beach and P. David Pearson (Minneapolis: University of Minnesota College of Education, 1979), pp. 247–272.

7. On usage norms, see Edward Finegan, *Attitudes toward English Usage: The History of a War of Words* (New York: Teachers College Press, 1980), and Jim Quinn, *American Tongue in Cheek*: *A Populist Guide to Language* (New York: Pantheon, 1980); on arrangement, see Patrick Hartwell, "Teaching Arrangement: A Pedagogy," *CE*, 40 (1979), 348–554.

8. "Revolution in Grammar," *Quarterly Journal of Speech*, 40 (1954), 299–312.

9. Richard A. Lanham, *Revising Prose* (New York: Scribner's, 1979); William Strunk and E.B. White, *The Elements of Style*, 3rd ed. (New York: Macmillan, 1979); Joseph Williams, *Style: Ten Lessons in Clarity and Grace* (Glenview, Ill.: Scott, Foresman, 1981); Christensen, "A Generative Rhetoric of the Sentence," *CCC*, 14 (1963), 155–161; Donald A. Daiker, Andrew Kerek, and Max Morenberg, *The Writer's Options: Combining to Composing*, 2nd ed. (New York: Harper & Row, 1982).

10. "A Psychological Approach," in *Psychobiology of Language*, ed. M. Studdert-Kennedy (Cambridge, Mass.: MIT Press, 1983), pp. 16–19. See also Noam Chomsky, "Language and Unconscious Knowledge," in *Psychoanalysis and Language Psychiatry and the Humanities*, Vol. III, ed. Joseph H. Smith (New Haven, Conn.: Yale University Press, 1978), pp. 3–44.

11. Morris Halle, "Knowledge Unlearned and Untaught: What Speakers Know about the Sounds of their Language," in *Linguistic Theory and Psychological Reality*, ed. Halle, Joan Bresnan, and George A. Miller (Cambridge, Mass.: MIT Press, 1978), pp. 135–140.

12. Moscowitz, "On the Status of Vowel Shift in English," in *Cognitive Development and the Acquisition of Language*, ed. T.E. Moore (New York: Academic Press, 1973), pp. 223–260; Chomsky, "Stages in Language Development and Reading Exposure," *Harvard Educational Review*, 42 (1972), 1–33; and Brause, "Developmental Aspects of the Ability to Understand Semantic Ambiguity, with Implications for Teachers," *RTE*, 11 (1977), 39–48.

13. Mills and Hemsley, "The Effects of Levels of Education on Judgments of Grammatical Acceptability," *Language and Speech*, 19 (1976), 324–342; Whyte, "Levels of Language Competence and Reading Ability: An Exploratory Investigation," *Journal of Research in Reading*, 5 (1982). 123–132; Morais, et al., "Does Awareness of Speech as a Series of Phones Arise Spontaneously?" Cognition, 7 (1979), 323–331; Ferguson, Cognitive *Effects of Literacy: Linguistic Awareness in Adult Literacy: Linguistic Awareness in Adult Nonreaders* (Washington, D.C.: National Institute of Education Final Report, 1981) ERIC 222 857; Hamilton and Barton, "A Word Is a Word: Metalinguistic Skills in Adults of Varying Literacy Levels" (Stanford, Cal.: Stanford University Department of Linguistics, 1980) ERIC 222 859.

14. On the question of the psychological reality of Grammar 2 descriptions, see Maria Black and Shulamith Chiat, "Psycholinguistics without 'Psychological Reality'," *Linguistics*, 19 (1981), 37–61; Joan Bresnan, ed., *The Mental Representation of Grammatical Relations* (Cambridge, Mass.: MIT Press, 1982); and Michael H. Long, "Inside the 'Black Box': Methodological Issues in Classroom Research on Language Learning," *Language Learning*, 30 (1980), 1–42.

15. Chomsky, "The Current Scene in Linguistics," *College English*, 27 (1966), 587–595;

and "Linguistic Theory," in *Language Teaching: Broader Contexts*, ed. Robert C. Meade, Jr. (New York: Modern Language Association, 1966), pp. 43–49; Mark Lester, "The Value of Transformational Grammar in Teaching Composition," *CCC*, 16 (1967), 228.

16. Christensen, "Between Two Worlds," in *Notes toward a New Rhetoric: Nine Essays for Teachers*, rev. ed., ed. Bonniejean Christensen (New York: Harper & Row, 1978), pp. 1–22.

17. Reber, "Implicit Learning of Artificial Grammars," *Journal of Verbal Learning and Verbal Behavior*, 6 (1967), 855–863; "Implicit Learning of Synthetic Languages: The Role of Instructional Set," *Journal of Experimental Psychology: Human Learning and Memory*, 2 (1976), 889–894; and Reber, Saul M. Kassin, Selma Lewis, and Gary Cantor, "On the Relationship Between Implicit and Explicit Modes in the Learning of a Complex Rule Structure," *Journal of Experimental Psychology: Human Learning and Memory*, 6 (1980), 492–502.

18. "Individual Variation in the Use of the Monitor," in *Principles of Second Language Learning*, ed. W. Richie (New York: Academic Press, 1978), pp. 175–185.

19. "Applications of Psycholinguistic Research to the Classroom," in *Practical Applications of Research in Foreign Language Teaching*, ed. D.J. James (Lincolnwood, Ill.: National Textbook, 1983), p. 61.

20. "Some Evidence for the Integrity and Interaction of Two Knowledge Sources," in *New Dimensions in Second Language Acquisition Research*, ed. Roger W. Anderson (Rowley, Mass.: Newbury House, 1981), pp. 62–74.

21. Hartwell and Bentley, *Some Suggestions for Using Open to Language* (New York: Oxford University Press, 1982), p. 73; Rose, *Writer's Block: The Cognitive Dimension* (Carbondale: Southern Illinois University Press, 1983), p. 99; Daiute, "Psycholinguistic Foundations of the Writing Process," *RTE*, 15 (1981), 5–22.

22. See Bartholmae, "The Study of Error"; Patrick Hartwell, "The Writing Center and the Paradoxes of Written-Down Speech," in *Writing Centers: Theory and Administration*, ed. Gary Olson (Urbana, Ill.: NCTE, 1984), pp. 48–61;

and Sondra Perl, "A Look at Basic Writers in the Process of Composing," in *Basic Writing: A Collection of Essays for Teachers, Researchers, and Administrators* (Urbana, Ill.: NCTE, 1980), pp. 13–32.

23. Emonds, *Adjacency in Grammar: The Theory of Language-Particular Rules* (New York: Academic, 1983); and Jochnowitz, "Everybody Likes Pizza, Doesn't He or She?" *American Speech*, 57 (1982), 198–203.

24. Scribner and Cole, *Psychology of Literacy* (Cambridge, Mass.: Harvard University Press, 1981); Gleitman and Gleitman, "Language Use and Language Judgment," in *Individual Differences in Language Ability and Language Behavior*, ed. Charles J. Fillmore, Daniel Kempner, and William S.-Y. Wang (New York: Academic Press, 1979), pp. 103–126.

25. There are several recent reviews of this developing body of research in psychology and child development: Irene Athey, "Language Development: Factors Related to Reading Development," *Journal of Educational Research*, 76, 1983), 197–203; James Flood and Paula Menyuk, "Metalinguistic Development and Reading/Writing Achievement," *Claremont Reading Conference Yearbook*, 46 (1982), 122–132; and the following four essays: David T. Hakes, "The Development of Metalinguistic Abilities:What Develops?," pp. 162–210; Stan A. Kuczaj, II, and Brooke Harbaugh, "What Children Think about the Speaking Capabilities of Other Persons and Things," pp. 211–227; Karen Saywitz and Louise Cherry Wilkinson, "Age-Related Differences in Metalinguistic Awareness," pp. 229–250; and Harriet Salatas Waters and Virginia S. Tinsley, "The Development of Verbal Self-Regulation: Relationships between Language, Cognition, and Behavior," pp. 251–277; all in *Language, Thought, and Culture*, Vol. II of *Language Development*, ed. Stan Kuczaj, Jr. (Hillsdae, N.J.: Lawrence Erlbaum, 1982). See also Joanne R. Nurss, "Research in Review: Linguistic Awareness and Learning to Read," *Young Children*, 35, No. 3 (1980), 57–66.

26. "Competing Value Systems in Inner City Schools," in *Children In and Out of School: Ethnography and Education*, ed. Perry Gilmore and Allan A. Glatthorn (Washington D.C.: Cen-

ter for Applied Linguistics, 1982), pp. 148–171; and "Locating the Frontier between Social and Psychological Factors in Linguistic Structure," in *Individual Differences in Language Ability and Language Behavior*, ed. Fillmore, Kemper, and Wang, pp. 327–340.

27. See, for example, Thomas Farrell, "IQ and Standard English," *CCC*, 34 (1983), 470–484; and the responses by Karen L. Greenberg and Patrick Hartwell, *CCC*, in press.

28. Jane W. Torrey, "Teaching Standard English to Speakers of Other Dialects," in *Applications of Linguistics: Selected Papers of the Second International Conference of Applied Linguistics*, ed. G.E. Perren and J.L.M. Trim (Cambridge, Mass.: Cambridge University Press, 1971), pp. 423–428; James W. Beers and Edmund H. Henderson, "A Study of the Developing Orthographic Concepts among First Graders," *RTE*, 11 (1977), 133–148.

29. See the error counts of Samuel A. Kirschner and G. Howard Poteet, "Non-Standard English Usage in the Writing of Black, White, and Hispanic Remedial English Students in an Urban Community College," *RTE*, 7 (1973), 351–355; and Marilyn Sternglass, "Close Similarities in Dialect Features of Black and White College Students in Remedial Composition Classes," *TESOL Quarterly*, 8 (1974), 271–283.

30. For reading, see the massive study by Kenneth S. Goodman and Yetta M. Goodman, *Reading of American Children Whose Language Is a Stable Rural Dialect of English or a Language Other Than English* (Washington, D.C.: National Institute of Education Final Report, 1978) ERIC 175 754; and the overview by Rudine Sims, "Dialect and Reading: Toward Redefining the Issues," in *Reader Meets Author/ Bridging the Gap: A Psycholinguistic and Sociolinguistic Approach*, ed. Judith A. Langer and M. Tricia Smith-Burke (Newark, Del.: International Reading Association, 1982), pp. 222–232. For writing, see Patrick Hartwell, "Dialect Interference in Writing: A Critical View," RTE, 14 (1980), 101–118; and the anthology edited by Barry M. Kroll and Roberta J. Vann, *Exploring Speaking-Writing Relationships: Connections and Contrasts* (Urbana, Ill.: NCTE, 1981).

31. See, for example, Eric A. Havelock, *The Literary Revolution in Greece and Its Cultural Consequences* (Princeton, N.J.: Princeton University Press, 1982); Lesley Milroy on literacy in Dublin, *Language and Social Networks* (Oxford: Basil Blackwell, 1980); Ron Scollon and Suzanne B.K. Scollon on literacy in central Alaska, *Inter-ethnic Communication: An Athabascan Case* (Austin, Tex.: Southwest Educational Development Laboratory Working Papers in Sociolinguistics, No. 59, 1979) ERIC 175 276; and Scribner and Cole on literacy in Liberia, *Psychology of Literacy* (see footnote 24).

32. See, for example, the anthology edited by Deborah Tannen, *Spoken and Written Language: Exploring Orality and Literacy* (Norwood, N.J.: Albex, 1982); and Shirley Brice Heath's continuing work: "Protean Shapes in Literacy Events: Ever-Shifting Oral and Literate Traditions," in *Spoken and Written Language*, pp. 91–117; *Ways with Words: Language, Life and Work in Communities and Classrooms* (New York: Cambridge University Press, 1983); and "What No Bedtime Story Means," *Language in Society*, 11 (1982), 49–76.

33. For studies at the elementary level, see Dell H. Hymes, et al., eds., *Ethnographic Monitoring of Children's Acquisition of Reading/ Language Arts Skills In and Out of the Classroom* (Washington, D.C.: National Institute of Education Final Report, 1981) ERIC 208 096. For studies at the secondary level, see James L. Collins and Michael M. Williamson, "Spoken Language and Semantic Abbreviation in Writing," *RTE*, 15 (1981), 23–36. And for studies at the college level, see Patrick Hartwell and Gene LoPresti, "Sentence Combining as Kid-Watching," in *Sentence Combining: Toward a Rhetorical Perpective*, ed. Donald A. Daiker, Andrew Kerek, and Max Morenberg (Carbondale: Southern Illinois University Press, in press).

34. Lloyd-Jones, "Romantic Revels—I Am Not You," CCC, 23 (1972), 251–271; and Young, "Concepts of Art and the Teaching of Writing," in *The Rhetorical Tradition and Modern Writing*, ed. James J. Murphy (New York: Modern Language Association, 1982), pp. 130–141.

35. For the romantic position, see Ann E. Berthoff, "Tolstoy, Vygotsky, and the Making

of Meaning," *CCC*, 29 (1978), 249–255; Kenneth Dowst, "The Epistemic Approach," in *Eight Approaches to Teaching Composition*, ed. Timothy Donovan and Ben G. McClellan (Urbana, Ill.: NCTE, 1980), pp. 65–85; Peter Elbow, "The Challenge for Sentence Combining,"; and Donald Murray, "Following Language toward Meaning," both in *Sentence Combining: Toward a Rhetorical Perspective* (in press; see footnote 33); and Ian Pringle, "Why Teach Style? A Review-Essay," *CCC*, 34 (1983), 91–98.

For the classic position, see Christensen's "A Generative Rhetoric of the Sentence"; and Joseph Williams' "Defining Complexity," CE, 41 (1979), 59–609; and his *Style: Ten Lessons in Clarity and Grace* (see footnote 9).

36. Courtney B. Cazden and David K. Dickinson, "Language and Education: Standardization versus Cultural Pluralism," in *Language in the USA*, ed. Charles A. Ferguson and Shirley Brice Heath (New York: Cambridge University Press, 1931), pp. 446–468; and Carol Chomsky, "Developing Facility with Language Structure," in *Discovering Language with Children*, ed. Gay Su Pinnell (Urbana, Ill.: NCTE, 1980), pp. 56–59.

37. Boraas, "Format English Grammar and the Practical Mastery of English," Diss. University of Illinois, 1917; Asker, "Does Knowledge of Grammar Function?" *School and Society*, 17 (27 January 1923), 109–111; Ash, "An Experimental Evaluation of the Stylistic approach in Teaching Composition in the Junior High School," *Journal of Experimental Education*, 4 (1935), 54–62; and Frogner, "A Study of the Relative Efficacy of a Grammatical and a Thought Approach to the Improvement of Sentence Structure in Grades Nine and Eleven," *School Review*, 47 (1939), 663–675.

38. "Research on Grammar and Usage and Its Implications for Teaching Writing," *Bulletin of the School Education*, Indiana University, 36 (1960), pp. 13–14.

39. Meckel, "Research on Teaching Composition and Literature," in *Handbook of Research on Teaching*, ed. N.L. Gage (Chicago: Rand McNally, 1963), pp. 966–1006.

40. Bateman and Zidonis, *The Effect of a Study of Transformational Grammar on the Writing of Ninth and Tenth Graders* (Urbana, Ill.: NCTE, 1966); Mellon, *Transformational Sentence Combining: A Method for Enhancing the Development of Fluency in English Composition* (Urbana, Ill.: NCTE, 1969); O'Hare, *Sentence-Combining: Improving Student Writing without Formal Grammar Instruction* (Urbana, Ill.: NCTE, 1971); Stotsky, "Sentence-Combining as a Curricular Activity: Its Effect on Written Language Development," *RTE*, 9 (1975), 30–72; and Van de Veghe, "Research in Written Composition: Fifteen Years of Investigation," ERIC 157 095.

41. Haynes, "Using Research in Preparing to Teach Writing," *English Journal*, 69, No. 1 (1978), 82–88; Holbrook, "ERIC/RCS Report: Whither (Wither) Grammar," *Language Arts*, 60 (1983), 259–263; Whiteman, "What we Can Learn from Writing Research," *Theory into Practice*, 19 (1980), 150–156; Bamberg, "Composition in the Secondary English Curriculum: Some Current Trands and Directions for the Eighties," *RTE*, 15 (1981), 257–266; and "Composition Instruction Does Make a Difference: A Comparison of the High School Preparation of College Freshmen in Regular and Remedial English Classes," *RTE*, 12 (1978), 47–59.

42. Emig, "Inquiry Paradigms and Writing," *CCC*, 33 (1982), 64–75; Carton and Castiglione, "Educational Linguistics: Defining the Domain," in *Psycholinguistic Research: Implications and Applications*, ed. Doris Aaronson and Robert W. Rieber (Hillsdale, N.J.: Lawrence Erlbaum, 1979), pp. 497–520.

Patrick Hartwell, Professor of English at Indiana University of Pennsylvania, is the co-author, with Robert H. Bentley, of *Open to Language: A New College Rhetoric* (Oxford University Press, 1982).

Professor Hartwell wishes to thank Wayne Edkin, Camden (New York) Public Schools; Michael Marier, Brigham Young University-Hawaii; and Ron Shook, Utah State University, for discussing these issues with him, and particularly to thank his colleague Dan J. Tannacito for references and discussion.

RATIOCINATION AND REVISION OR CLUES IN THE WRITTEN DRAFT

JOYCE ARMSTRONG CARROLL
(From English Journal, November 1982. Copyright 1982 by the
National Council of Teachers of English. Reprinted with permission.)

My fascination with clues began with a Captain Marvel decoder ring. After drinking jars of Ovaltine, I collected enough labels to send for that prize. When it arrived, the clues read by the radio announcer at program's end no longer formed incomprehensible cryptograms. Eagerly I copied them; anxiously I turned the ring's painted silvery dial to decode them. Figuring every word became an adventure—every message a solved mystery.

Progressing from radio to reading, I collected Carolyn Keene's books like those Ovaltine labels. Nancy Drew, her chum Helen Corning, and I were amateur detectives. No clue escaped us. Soon, my literary tastes refining, Sherlock Holmes and Dr. Watson replaced Nancy and Helen, then Agatha Christie's Hercule Poirot became my hero—I had been well prepared for secret packets and revolutionary coups d'état. But my fascination flowered while following C. August Dupine, Edgar Allan Poe's smart (and I knew handsome) sleuth, especially when I discovered the sophisticated word for this process of logically reasoning out clues—*ratiocination.*

Although no Holmes, Poirot, or Dupin, in one *eureka!* moment I realized how I apply this ratiocinative process, how like a detective I become while revising. Relentlessly I go back through my writing searching for clues in the language, decoding them in order to make the writing better. For example, in an early draft, my opening sentence read: My fascination with clues may have started with a . . . When I reentered the writing, *may* and *have* provided clues for decoding. *May* expresses contingency; *have* indicates the perfect tense. Since I wanted certainty in the

Commentary:

Carroll chronicles a childhood where words and wonder were a natural part of her growing up. Unfortunately, today's society seems to militate against childhoods where imagination and rich reading experiences abound. Day care, Little League, T-ball, computer camp, latch-key, TV, poverty, pull at children's lives. Helen at the Red Balloon Bookstore in San Antonio says that 10 percent of the American public purchase 90 percent of the books. In an informal survey of the parents of 150 seniors at Cooper High School in Abilene, Texas, 47 of the seniors reported not having a single book in their homes. Thirty-two of the homes had one book—a dictionary. It is highly unlikely that these students had childhoods that were rich with literary experiences.

Knowing how to revise requires years and years of experiencing writing. Emergent writers do not readily revise. Neophyte writers struggle with revision. And the experienced writer can still find it difficult.

The teacher who approaches teaching revision by pronouncement, has the same effect on a student's writing as a politician at a national convention. Proclaiming a candidate as a "man or woman of the people" doesn't make it so. Telling isn't teaching. The uninformed, untrained teacher announces, "today you will revise your paper." Then the teacher wonders why the students did not revise. Revision must be taught in order for it to be incorporated into writing.

One good way to teach this technique makes use of a chart that shows the relationship of the code to the clue and the decoding tips. On the chalkboard the teacher can write:

past, both proved inaccurate—the sentence had to be revised.

Students, however, do not share this relentlessness; they cower during revision as if terrorized, failing to realize that a piece of writing, like a story, is essentially over at the beginning, the crime already committed when the author introduces the clues. Usually the structure of the story revolves around the detective figuring out those clues to discover the culprit and bring the story to a satisfactory close. So, too, with a written draft in need of revision. It's an unsolved mystery. Most everything is essentially there, but the writer must reenter the writing as a detective, checking the significance of linguistic clues to bring the piece to a satisfactory close.

Students, most neophyte writers, most unskilled detectives of language, are unable to reenter their writing without clues, are unable to do revision as Frank Smith describes it in *Writing and the Writer:* " . . . review the draft of the text from their own point of view to discover what the text contains" (p. 127). Therefore students avoid revision: they abhor it and, if pressed, usually do a shoddy job of it. Directions, fine as they may be for the practiced writer, (*lower the noun/verb ratio"* or *transform passive constructions into active ones* in Linda Flower's *Problem-Solving Strategies for Writing* [New York: Harcourt, 1981, pp. 177–179]), strike students as vague or meaningless since they give no clues pointing where to begin.

If clues hold the secret to revision, then teachers must show student how to code the clues which will enable them to reenter their papers the way practiced writers do. Further, by following those coded clues and by using the process of logical reasoning to decode them, students figure out words and meanings to solve the mystery of their written drafts and bring their papers to a satisfactory close.

The Procedure

Instruct students to bring colored markers, pens, pencils, or crayons—colored coders—or keep a box of these in class. After students have shaped their prewritings (clearly labeled at the top) into trial rough drafts (also clearly labeled), introduce "Clue Day."

Present the clues (see "Coding the Clues" below) that you want students to code for this paper. For example, if you want students to work on the first clue, you might list all the "to be" verbs on the board, telling students, "Each time you come across one of these verbs, circle it clearly with one color." For the next clue, they would use another color. Depending upon the length of the papers, and the number of clues, this coding process could easily take the rest of the period. What emerges are drafts clearly filled with visually coded clues.

Next, explain how decoding their clues involves logical thinking (ratiocination—although you may not wish to introduce the term at this time) as well as decision making since there are many options and alternatives available when working with language (see "The Decoding" below). After this explanation, students reenter their trial rough drafts decoding their clues, making decisions, and rewriting onto what will become their rough drafts. As students engage in decoding, the teacher may move about the room offering individual help.

When students polish their rough drafts into their final papers, they hand in all their drafts fastened together in descending order with the final paper on top. This order makes assessment easier, while the coding and the decoding make it more thorough, more specific, and quicker. Grading should be keyed directly to the concepts covered in the clues and to the quality of writing after decoding those clues.

For the first paper, I'd recommend presenting the first two clues; for the second paper, review them; then add one or two more depending upon the level and writing abilities of the students. For slow students, one clue per paper is sufficient. I have sequenced these clues in a workable order so that by the end of the semester, through this process of accumulation, all ten clues will become part of the student's repertoire. A word of caution: do not rush this giving of clues because the ratiocination which each clue generates is highly complex and intricate transformational process.

Code	Clue	Decoding
◯ (circle)	"to be" verbs is am are was were be being been	• do not change • change to a livelier verb • indicates passive voice • indicates a knotted, weak sentence • do not change if the "to be" verb is in a quote • consider leaving it in dialogue—characters speak this way

A word about using the chalkboard versus using the overhead. The chalkboard invites interaction and simultaneous discover. Presentation on the chalkboard keeps the pacing of the presentation at a comfortable rate for students.

Ratiocination guarantees that students will use:

- *higher-order thinking skills,*
- *revision skills in a context, and*
- *concrete signals to reenter their own writing.*

With ratiocination, teachers find they use some codes, clues, and decodes with every piece of discourse. In time, student writers internalize some clues.

As with most good techniques, however, ratiocination can be abused. One well-meaning teacher may insist that her students use all ten codes, clues, and decodes on each paper they write, and the result: cognitive overload and illegible drafts. This overteaching can be detrimental and discouraging.

Coding the Clues

1. Circle all "to be" verbs.
2. Make a wavy line under repeated words.
3. Underline each sentence.
4. Bracket each sentence beginning.
5. Draw an arrow from subject to predicate in each sentence.
6. Place a box around clichés.
7. Mark words that might be imprecise with a check.
8. X out the word *very*.
9. Draw two vertical lines next to anything underdeveloped.
10. Put *it* in a triangle.

The Decoding

One teacher told us that "to be" verbs is the only code she uses with her students. Through it she is able to teach everything from word choice and grammatical concepts to syntax and style.

1. When decoding a circle, students determine if the "to be" verb should be untouched because changing it would diminish the composition or if it should be replaced because changing it to a livelier verb would enhance the composition. Sometimes a "to be" verb signals a passive construction which might entail either revising its order to subject-verb-complement or leaving it to focus on the complement. Other times a "to be" verb suggests a weak sentence which should be omitted or drastically revised.

2. When approaching a wavy line, students consider if the repetition is necessary and should remain to make the meaning emphatic, to show continuity between sentences or paragraphs, to retain parallel form, or to make the sentence function as is the case with words such as *a, an, the*. If the repetition is unnecessary, it should be eliminated or changed because it reveals careless word choice or confuses by using homonymic words.

We have learned from other teachers that this works best when the students underline the sentences in alternating colors.

3. Underlining invites students to study their sentences. For example, if they are

about the same length, shortening or lengthening a few adds variety and provides visual relief. If choppy (each sentence contains a minimal number of words or a simple idea divided into two or more sentences), combining sentences produces a smoother effect. If stringy (ideas are strung together with coordinating conjunctions as if all elements are equal), cutting down on conjunctions and subordinating ideas solves the problem.

4. Bracketing heightens awareness of the tendency to start each sentence with a noun or pronoun subject, thereby lowering the overall impact of the writing. Students decode by experimenting with a variety of beginnings—modifiers, phrases, clauses.

See Chapter 5.

5. While most arrows will point to subject/predicate agreement, some will uncover dialect problems*: I do, you do, he do, she do, it do*. Using a current handbook *and* the student's writing, individualize instruction on this problem. Students should compare examples in handbooks with what they have written since many rules and exceptions govern these situations.

6. Students might miss boxing in all their trite expressions. Because they are so common, students use them without thinking. When they do catch a cliché, they decode the clue by asking how they could more freshly express the hackneyed.

This is a good time to work collaboratively.

7. Word precision problems arise when students fail to distinguish nuances of meaning. Decoding a check demands cross reference work with both thesaurus and dictionary.

8. *Very* in my class is considered a four-letter word and as such gets X-ed. But students should understand the rationale behind the X so they may intelligently

Teachers have extended this to include a lot (as one word), really, good, and other overused words.

One way to help students develop is by using charts and the SEE strategy (see Table 6.1 and Chapter 6).

This may be extended to all personal pronouns.

Primary teachers may adapt ratiocination to their students' appropriate developmental level. For example: Code: Red dot. Clue: Stop! Every place you stop when you read . . . Decode: Put a period (.), an asking mark (?), or an excitement mark (!).

decode it. As an adverb, *very* acts as an intensifier for the word it precedes. There's nothing wrong with that, although students often grab *very* instead of mentally wrestling with precise word choice. To avoid this corroding of precision, students determine if they have used *very* as an adjective or if they have used it as an adverb. If adjectival, it remains; if adverbial, it tips off imprecision. Students untangle this clue by omitting *very* and choosing an exact word for its modificand.

9. By the time students reach this clue, they should have had ample work on development by detail, narration, example, illustration, and fact. Coding with two vertical lines encourages close reading to be sure all points have been developed; decoding reminds that more writing is needed.

10. *It,* clearly a pronoun meant to refer to an idea previously expressed, is often used by students to refer to an idea still in their heads. (How many times have we received compositions beginning with *it*?) The triangle warns students to examine the referent. If the referent is clear, it remains; if unclear or nonexistent, it must be replaced with something specific, or the sentence must be reworked.

The Objectives

These clues and decodings

1. enable teachers to integrate lexical, syntactical, rhetorical, and grammatical concepts with composition instruction *during* the writing process;

2. encourage students to test these concepts immediately in a context that matters to them;

3. provide students with visual ways for re-entry into their writing in order to make it better;

4. help students take the responsibility for their own writing;

5. permit students to revise *during* their process thereby improving their papers *before* they are handing in for a grade;

6. aid teachers' work evaluating those papers and lightening their paper load.

After all this detective work, our class may close as a Carolyn Keene mystery closes. Students discussing this venture will wonder if they'll ever have another so thrilling. Assure them they will, perhaps calling the next paper "Secrets of Sentence Beginnings" or "Hidden Word Meanings." And be sure to explain that this, their first paper in a series, should serve as a pleasant reminder of their first solved mystery. Just fiction? Maybe. But maybe not.

Ratiocination is one technique, one strategy, one concrete way teachers have to integrate the teaching of grammar with the teaching of writing during revision. Too many writing projects, too many classrooms, too many writing courses spend too much time on prewriting and not enough time on revision. Ratiocination is the single most effective way 475 teachers surveyed have found to teach revision.

D

THE "RESEARCH PAPER" IN THE WRITING COURSE: A NON-FORM OF WRITING

RICHARD L. LARSON

From *College English*, December 1982. Copyright 1982 by the National Council of Teachers of English. Reprinted with permission.

Commentary:

Teaching research does not happen only in the traditional sense of a research paper. Research should be an ongoing activity rather that an event undertaken once a year usually during one entire marking period.

Remember, this is a college course description, and while the change in course description is significant, it is also developmentally appropriate for that level. Inclusion here does not mean to suggest it is equally appropriate for middle school or high school, although documentation in authentic ways may be adapted to various levels. Informed curricula writers adjust their scope and sequence to lay foundations rather that to engage students in watered-down versions of college courses.

Let me begin by assuring you that I do not oppose the assumption that student writers in academic and professional settings, whether they be freshman or sophomores or students in secondary school or intend to be journalists or lawyers or scholars or whatever, should engage in research. I think they should engage in research and that appropriately informed people should help them learn to engage in research in whatever field these writers happen to be studying. Nor do I deny the axiom that writing should incorporate the citation of the writer's sources of information when those sources are not common knowledge. I think that writers must incorporate into their writing the citation of their sources—and they must also incorporate the thoughtful, perceptive evaluation of those sources and of the contribution that those sources might have made to the writer's thinking. Nor do I oppose the assumption that a writer should make the use of appropriate sources a regular activity in the process of composing. I share the assumption that writers should identify, explore, evaluate, and draw upon appropriate sources as an integral step in what today we think of as the composing process.

In fact, let me begin with some positive values. On my campus, the Department of English has just decided to request a change in the description of its second-semester freshman course. The old description read as follows:

This course emphasizes the writing of formal analytic essays and the basic methods of research common to various academic disciplines. Students will write frequently in and out of class. By the close of the semester, students will demonstrate mastery of the formal expository essay and the research paper. Individual conferences.

The department is asking our curriculum committee to have the description read:

This course emphasizes writing of analytical essays and the methods of inquiry common to various academic disciplines. Students will write frequently in and out of class. By the close of the semester, students will demonstrate their ability to write essays incorporating references to suitable sources of information and to use appropriate methods of documentation. Individual conferences.

I applauded the department for requesting that change, and I wrote to the college curriculum committee to say so.

While thinking about this paper—to take another positive example—I received from the University of Michigan press a copy of the proofs of a forthcoming book titled *Researching American Culture: A Guide for Student Anthropologists*, sent to me because members of the English Composition Board of the University of Michigan had decided that the book might be of use as a supplementary text at Michigan in writing courses that emphasize writing in the academic disciplines. Along with essays by professional anthropologists presenting or discussing research in anthropology, the book includes several essays by students. In these essays the students, who had been instructed and guided by faculty in anthropology, report the results of research they have performed on aspects of American culture, from peer groups in high school to connections between consumption of alcohol and tipping in a restaurant, to mortuary customs, to sports in America. If anyone was in doubt about the point, the collection demonstrates that undergraduate students can conduct and report sensible, orderly, clear, and informative research in the disciple of anthropology. I am here to endorse, indeed to applaud, such work, not to

We have here a clear example of Vygotsky's zone of proximal development.

Again, learning research must take place within a context. Doing research because the curriculum guide says so is not helping students see the connections between research and what they are learning.

A challenge for English language arts teachers may be to brainstorm what would constitute research for the level they teach.

Preoccupation with card catalogs and guides to periodic literature is both antiquated and shortsighted. Teachers like Larson want to broaden the definition of research.

question the wisdom of such collections as that from Michigan or to voice reservations about the capacity of undergraduates for research.

Why, then, an essay whose title makes clear a deep skepticism about "research papers"? First, because I believe that the generic "research paper" as a concept, and as a form of writing taught in a department of English, is not defensible. Second, because I believe that by saying that we teach the "research paper"—that is, by acting as if there is a generic concept defensible entitled the "research paper"—we mislead students about the activities of both research and writing. I take up these propositions in order.

We would all agree to begin with, I think, that "research" is an activity in which one engages. Probably almost everyone reading this paper has engaged, at one time or another, in research. Most graduate seminars require research; most dissertations rely upon research, though of course many dissertations in English may also include analytical interpretation of texts written by one or more authors. Research can take many forms: systematically observing events, finding out what happens when one performs certain procedures in the laboratory, conducting interviews, tape-recording speakers' comments, asking human beings to utter aloud their thoughts while composing in writing or in another medium and noting what emerges, photographing phenomena (such as the light received in a telescope from planets and stars), watching the activities of people in groups, reading a person's letters and notes; all these are research. So, of course, is looking up information in a library or in newspaper files, or reading documents to which one has gained access under the Freedom of Information Act—though reading filed and catalogued documents is in many fields not the most important (it may be least important) activity in which a "researcher" engages. We could probably define "research" generally as the seeking out of information new to the seeker, for the purpose, and we could probably agree that the researcher usually has to interpret, evaluate, and organize that information before it acquires value. And we would probably agree that the researcher has to present the fruits of his or her research, appropriately ordered and interpreted, in symbols that are intelligible to others, before that research can be evaluated and can have an effect. Most often, outside of mathematics and the sciences (and outside of those branches of philosophy that work with nonverbal symbolic notation), maybe also outside of music, that research is presented to others, orally or in writing, in a verbal language.

But research still is an activity; it furnishes the substance of much discourse and can furnish substance to almost any discourse except, possibly, one's personal reflections on one's own experience. But it is itself the subject—the substance—of no distinctively identifiable kind of writing. Research can inform virtually any writing or speaking if the author wishes it to do so; there is nothing of substance or content that differentiates one paper that draws on data from outside the author's own self from another paper—nothing that can enable one to say that this paper is a "research paper" and that paper is not. (Indeed even as ordered, interpreted reporting of altogether personal experiences and responses can, if presented purposively, be a reporting of research.) I would assert therefore that the so-called "research paper," as a generic, cross-disciplinary term, has no conceptual or substantive identity. If almost any paper is potentially a paper incorporating the fruits of research, the term "research paper" has virtually no value as an identification of a kind of substance in a paper. Conceptually, the generic term "research paper" is for practical purposes meaningless. We cannot usefully distinguish between "research papers" and non-research papers; we can distinguish only between papers that should have incorporated the fruits of research but did not, and those that did incorporate such results, or between those that reflect poor or inadequate research and those that reflect good or sufficient research. I would argue that most undergraduate papers reflect poor or inadequate research, and that our responsibility . . . should be to assure that each student reflect in each paper the appropriate research, wisely conducted, for his or her subject.

I have already suggested that "research" can take a wide variety of forms, down to and in-

Consider the work of Donald Graves, Lucy McCormick Calkins, Tom Romano, and Nancie Atwell as examples of substantive research based primarily on personal observation taken systematically and organized in literate and interesting ways.

Consider, too, the difference between a research paper and research skills.

At best, this is merely copying; at worse, it is plagiarism. Additionally, most elementary, middle, and high school libraries are inadequate. Sending students to university libraries results in either frustration on the students' part, or aggravation on the librarian's part, or both. Case in point: A high school student from an honors class was told to research every article in the Washington Post *related to the first thirty days of the Clinton presidency. The student sat at the microfilm reader in tears when she realized the enormity of the task. The college reference librarian finally walked off in disgust saying, "I don't know what your teacher wants."*

In this sentence Larson opens up research, which, unfortunately, has been too often viewed as a closed activity.

Richard L. Larson is without peer as a scholar of integrity. He is equally respected by members of the Modern Language Association and the National Council of Teachers of English. That a professor of this caliber holds that the "research paper" has no formal substantive or procedural identity should give all teachers of English pause.

cluding the ordered presentation of one's personal reflections and the interpretations of one's most direct experiences unmediated by interaction with others or by reference to identifiably external sources. (The form of research on composing known as "protocol analysis" or even the keeping of what some teachers of writing designate as a "process journal," if conducted by the giver of the protocol or by the writer while writing, might be such research.) If research can refer to almost any process by which data outside the immediate and purely personal experiences of the writer are gathered, then I suggest that just as the so-called "research paper" has no conceptual or substantive identity, neither does it have a procedural identity; the term does not necessarily designate any particular kind of data nor any preferred procedure for gathering data. I would argue that the so-called "research paper," as ordinarily taught by the kinds of texts I have reviewed, implicitly equates "research" with looking up books in the library and taking down information from those books. Even if there [are goings on] in some departments of English instruction that [get] beyond those narrow boundaries, the customary practices that I have observed for guiding the "research paper" assume a procedural identity for the paper that is, I think, nonexistent.

As the activity of research can take a wide variety of forms, so the presentation and use of research within discourse can take a wide variety of forms. Indeed I cannot imagine any identifiable design that any scholar in rhetoric has identifies as a recurrent plan from arranging discourse which cannot incorporate the fruits of research, broadly construed. I am not aware of any kind or form of discourse or any aim, identified by any student of rhetoric or any theorist of language or any investigator of discourse theory, that is distinguished primarily—or to any extent—by the presence of the fruits of "research" in its typical examples. One currently popular theoretical classification of discourse, that by James Kinneavy (*A Theory of Discourse* [Englewood Cliffs, N.J.; Prentice-Hall, 1971]), identifies some "aims" of discourse that might seem to furnish a home for papers based on research: "referential" and "exploratory" discourse.

But, as I understand these aims, a piece of discourse does not require the presence of results, of ordered "research" in order to fit into either of these classes, even though discourse incorporating the results of ordered research might fit there—as indeed it might under almost any of Kinneavy's categories, including the category of "expressive" discourse. (All discourse is to a degree "expressive" anyway.) The other currently dominant categorization of examples of discourse—dominate even over Kinneavy's extensively discussed theory—is really categorization based upon plans that organize discourse: narration (of completed events, of ongoing processes, of possible scenarios), casual analysis, comparison, analogy, and so on. None of these plans is differentiated from other plans by the presence within it of fruits from research; research can be presented, so far as I can see, according to any of these plans. And if one consults Frank J. D'Angelo's *A Conceptual Theory of Rhetoric* (Cambridge, Mass.: Winthrop, 1975) one will not find, if my memory serves me reliably, any category of rhetorical plan or any fundamental human cognitive process—D'Angelo connects all rhetorical plans with human cognitive processes—that is defined by the presence of the fruits of research. If there is a particular rhetorical form that is defined by the presence of results of research, then, I have not seen an effort to define that form and to argue that the results of research are what identify it as a form. I conclude that the "research paper," as now taught, has no formal identity, as it has no substantive identify and no procedural identity.

For me, then, very little is gained by speaking about and teaching, as a generic concept, the so-called "research paper." If anything at all is gained, it is only the reminder that responsible writing normally depends on well-planned investigation of data. But much is lost by teaching the research paper as a separately designated activity. For by teaching the generic "research paper" as a separate activity, instructors in writing signal to their students that there is a kind of writing that incorporates the results of research, and there are (by implication) many kinds of writing that do not and need not do so. "Research," students are allowed to infer, is a spe-

Once again, integration, not fragmentation, is the key.

First, it is interesting to note that Larson comfortably uses personal pronouns, and these personal pronouns in no way distract from the import of his meaning. Second, I visited a high school class in La Joya, Texas. The students in Linda Garcia Perez's class had undertaken exciting research. They had interviewed the joyas *(jewels), that is, the older members of the community, about their experiences. They were encouraged to note facial expressions and capture direct dialogue. Most students worked with tape recorders. The results were bound together in an anthology entitled* Our Town, Nuestro Pueblo, *which won second place in the national Arts and Entertainment 1990 Teacher Grant Competition, May 14, 1990, in Washington, D.C. As I read through Monica A. Gonzalez's account of her great aunt's memories of picking cotton, Miguel Ramos's interview with his grandfather who was paid seventy-five cents a day pruning orange trees, or Noralisa Leo's essay, "The Medicis of La Joya," I was struck with the individual style of each writer as he or she documented the data of their interviewee. The results were poignant, sometimes sad, often humorous, but always interesting. I couldn't put the anthology down. I even requested a copy to share with other teachers. Besides this rich book of heritage sat the students' other research. These papers were on such topics as John Donne's metaphysical poetry and the use of symbolism in the collected*

cialized activity that one engages in during a special course, or late in a regular semester or year, or but that one does not ordinarily need to be concerned about and can indeed, for the most part, forget about. Designating the "research paper" as a separate project therefore seems to me to work against the purposes for which we allegedly teach the research paper: to help students familiarize themselves with ways of gathering, interpreting, drawing upon, and acknowledging data from outside themselves in their writing. By talking of the "research paper," that is, we undermine some of the very goals of our teaching.

We also meet two other, related difficulties. First, when we tend to present the "research paper" as in effect paper based upon the use of the library, we misrepresent "research." Granted that a good deal of research in the field of literature is conducted in the library among books, much research that is still entitled to be called humanistic takes place outside the library. It can take place, as I mentioned earlier, wherever "protocol" research or writers' analyses of their composing processes take place: it can take place in the living room or study of an author who is being interviewed about his or her habits of working. It can take place in the home of an old farmer or rancher or weaver or potter who is telling a student about the legends or songs of his or her people, or about the historical process by which the speaker came from roots at home or abroad. Much research relies upon books, but books do not constitute the corpus of research data except possibly in one or two fields of study. If we teach the so-called "research paper" is such a way as to imply that all or almost all research is done in books and in libraries, we show our provincialism and degrade the research of many disciplines.

Second, though we pretend to prepare students to engage in the research appropriate to their chosen disciplines, we do not and cannot do so. Faculty in other fields may wish that we could relieve them of the responsibility of teaching their students to write about the research students do in those other fields, but I don't think that as teachers of English we can relieve them of that responsibility. Looking at the work of the students who contributed to the University of Michigan press volume of *Researching American Culture*, I can't conceive myself giving useful direction to those students. I can't conceive myself showing them how to do the research they did, how to avoid pitfalls, assure representativeness of data, draw permissible inferences, and reach defensible conclusions. And, frankly, I can't conceive many teachers of English showing these students what they needed to know either. I can't conceive myself, or very many colleagues (other than trained teachers of technical writing) guiding a student toward a report of a scientific laboratory experiment that a teacher of science would find exemplary. I can't conceive myself or many colleagues guiding a student toward a well-designed experiment in psychology, with appropriate safeguards and controls and wise interpretations of quantitative and nonquantitative information. In each of these fields (indeed probably in each academic field) the term "research paper" may have some meaning—quite probably a meaning different from its meaning in other fields. Students in different fields do write papers reporting research. We in English have no business claiming to teach "research" when research in different academic disciplines works from distinctive assumptions and follows distinctive patterns of inquiry. Such distinctions in fact are what differentiate the disciplines. Most of us are trained in one discipline only and should be modest enough to admit it.

But let me repeat what I said when I started: that I don't come before you to urge that students of writing need not engage in "research." I think that they should engage in research. I think they should understand that in order to function as educated, informed men and women they have to engage in research, from the beginning of and throughout their work as writers. I think that they should know what research can embrace, and I think they should be encouraged to view research as broadly, and conduct it as imaginatively, as they can. I think they should be held accountable for their opinions and should be required to say, from evidence, why they believe what they assert. I think that they should be let to recognize that data from "research" will affect their entire lives, and that they should

works of D. H. Lawrence. I randomly selected a few to read. Style, voice, and verve were gone. Lifeless prose, obviously copied from much too advanced scholarly works, rose up to greet me. At the end of the day, I stood with the anthology in one hand and the "research papers" in the other. "Do you see any difference?" I asked Linda. Of course she had. And it is doubtful that Linda as teacher-researcher will ever put her students through the generic research paper again.

If Julie as a third-grader (Chapter 12) was able to research her name, and Audrey and Leah as kindergartners (Chapter 12) were able to research mice, most certainly students on all levels are capable of research and should, in Larson's words, "be required to say, from evidence, why they believe what they assert."

know how to evaluate such data as well as to gather them. And I think they should know their responsibilities for telling their listeners and readers where their data came from.

What I argue is that the profession of the teaching of English should abandon the concept of the generic "research paper"—that form of what a colleague of mine has called "messenger service" in which a student is told that for this one assignment, this one project, he or she has to go somewhere (usually the library), get out some materials, make some notes, and present them to the customer neatly wrapped in footnotes and bibliography tied together according to someone's notation of style sheet. I argue that

We have often said that this cogent article by Larson should be photocopied (with permission, of course) and dropped by crop dusters over schools across the nation.

the generic "research paper," so far as I am familiar with it, is a concept without an identity, and that to teach it is not only to misrepresent research but also quite often to pander to the wishes of faculty in other disciplines that we spare them a responsibility that they must accept. Teaching the generic "research paper" often represents a misguided notion of service to other departments. The best service we can render to those departments and to the students themselves, I would argue, is to insist that students recognize their continuing responsibility for looking attentively at their experiences; for seeking out, wherever it can be found, the information they need for the development of their ideas; and for putting such data at the service of

This kind of service best serves democracy.

every piece they write. That is one kind of service we can do to advance students' humanistic and liberal education.

THE DOCUMENTED ESSAY

JOYCE ARMSTRONG CARROLL

Change is everywhere; it's in the air—corporations no longer require business suits, restaurants have gone casual, even church services have relaxed. While my alma mater grapples with decisions revolving around graduate classes and how to preserve the pristine estate of George Jay Gould at Georgian Court University, Burka asks about Texas A&M, "Can the forces of change overcome the forces of resistance?" ("Corps Values," *Texas Monthly*, May 2004).

Ah! A noble question. A question worthy of some high school teachers and college professors who remain wedded to the fifteen-page research paper, requiring note cards—fifty for an A (do they really not know about photocopy machines?)—endnotes (or even footnotes) on quaint topics easily accessible (plagiarized?) from the Internet. Their resistance, often offered in the name of scholarship, is not only outdated but also downright antediluvian.

The much-quoted Marcus Aurelius Antoninus (121–180) cautioned in his *Meditations III,* "Everything is in a state of metamorphosis. Thou thyself art in everlasting change" (translated by Gregory Hayes, Oxford University Press, 1998). But some hold onto that research paper!

So I got to thinking. Perhaps they are unfamiliar with the documented essay, research writing that includes a limited number of research sources, providing full documentation parenthetically within the text. This form works well and invites students not to put all their eggs in one research basket, but to illuminate what they know about subjects in shorter pieces with more teeth.

How grand to invite one documented essay that includes a survey or an interview; another with research out of journals, newspapers, and magazines; a third with sources from the Internet; a fourth with books as the documentation; a fifth with a touch of TV, other media, or a combination of sources. How quickly the teacher could assess, refine, correct, and hone the research capabilities of students—immediately, not at the end of a semester when the students, with great heaves and sighs, turn in the dreaded paper knowing they will pass or fail but in either case move on.

All of which reminds me that in October 1985, I wrote an article titled "TV and Term Papers," published in *English Journal.* Way before state-mandated tests contained open-ended items that invited connections, I began with a quote from Wilfred Trotter, "Knowledge comes from noticing resemblances and recurrences in the events that happen around us." I invited teachers to consider the times and programs such as *20/20, The Today Show, Good Morning America,* or *60 Minutes* which tick through topics as diverse as SIDS, "The Minister of Cocaine," and a profile on Red Smith. I asked them to eschew "term paper time," and I assimilated "into the teaching of the term paper what students assimilate when watching TV shows that research, document, investigate, explore, and inquire" (85).

I used as support Janet Emig's "Hand, Eye, Brain: Some 'Basics' in the Writing Process," where she states, "the eye is probably the major sense modality for presenting experience to the brain" (Cooper and Odell, *Research on Composing,* NCTE, 1978), information most re-

Reprint by permission from: *R&E Journal.* "From the Director's: The Documented Essay." Spring/Summer 2004, Spring, TX: New Jersey Writing Project in Texas, vol. xii, no. 1, pp. 10–11.

cently reinforced in Richard Restak's *The New Brain* (Rodale Books, 2003). I also tapped the work of my students—one who told about how she was accepted by Ford Modeling, another who explained how her family dealt with her brain-damaged brother. These students were doing research in every sense of the word, true research, research that captured their interest, research they owned about topics they truly wanted to know more about. Isn't that at the basis of all good writing?

Now over twenty years later, I again make a plea for the documented essay. Though it may make use of personal observations and examples, it is not a personal essay. While a documented essay may be biographical, historical, scientific, or general informational, it

- documents research and gives supporting references;

- provides information on a specific topic;

- contains references to source material *within* the text of essay;

- is shorter than a term paper (which suggests by its very name prolonged work over six or nine weeks);

- contains fewer sources;

- is clearly and effectively organized. (For a Self-Assessment Rubric for the documented essay, see *Prentice Hall Writing and Grammar: Communication in Action, Diamond Level*, p. 266.)

Students are able to efficiently write a documented essay about something that interests them, something about which they are expert. Over the years, students have written three- to five-page documented essays on high school, college, hobbies, the beauty of a foreign country, football, math class, pets, cheerleading, painting, and books. All valid essays. All documented. All pithy and interesting.

I urge teachers to validate the documented essay in class; I urge teachers to write one or more and submit to appropriate publications. I urge us all to incorporate the documented essay into many, indeed all, assignments—replacing the one "biggy" with bantam but better papers. My experience has led me to realize that when students write many essays with spurts of documentation, they actually do more research, better research, and authentic research. The by-product is that teachers then have the opportunity to catch flaws along the way—all along the way. It's a win/win situation.

(Just for the record, please note that you have just read a documented essay.)

WRITING AS A MODE OF LEARNING

JANET EMIG

From *College Composition and Communication,* May 1977. Copyright 1977 by the National Council of Teachers of English. Reprinted with permission.

Writing represents a unique mode of learning—not merely valuable, not merely special, but unique. That will be my contention on this paper. The thesis is straightforward. Writing serves learning uniquely because writing as a process-and-product possesses a cluster of attributes that correspond uniquely to certain powerful learning strategies.

Although the notion is clearly debatable, it is scarcely a private belief. Some of the most distinguished contemporary psychologists have at least implied such a role for writing as heuristic. Lev Vygotsky, A. R. Luria, and Jerome Bruner, for example, have all pointed out that higher cognitive functions, such as analysis and synthesis, seem to develop most fully only with the support system of verbal language—particularly, it seems, of written language.[1] Some of their arguments and evidence will be incorporated here.

Here I have a prior purpose: to describe as tellingly as possible *how* writing uniquely corresponds to certain powerful learning strategies. Making such a case for the uniqueness of writing should logically and theoretically involve establishing many contrasts, distinctions between (1) writing and all other verbal languaging processes—listening, reading, and especially talking; (2) writing and all other forms of composing a painting, a symphony, a dance, a film, a building; and (3) composing in words and composing in the two other major graphic symbol systems of mathematical equations and scientific formulae. For the purposes of this paper, the task is simpler, since most students are not permitted by most curricula to discover the values of composing, say, in dance, or even in film; and most students are not sophisticated enough

Commentary:

Teachers of other content areas will need to understand the effect of Emig's straightforward thesis. No longer can they ignore the importance of writing. Writing in the content areas can serve these teachers well. Not only will their students benefit from the writing experience, but they will have evidence of the students' learning.

Since Emig wrote her article in 1977, too little change has occurred in the teaching of English. Too many classrooms are still exclusively reading and listening—lecturing is still the method of instruction in most high schools. During one week of spring 1992, we examined a large high school. One hundred ten out of 123 English classes per day were devoted to lecture four out of five days per week. The social studies department did not fare any better—ninety classes per day out of ninety-one were devoted to lecture five of the five days. The only time the lecture method was not in use was during testing. The schedule in 98 out of 105 math classes was divided equally between lecture and seat work (working problems every day) except when tests were given. The one teacher in the math department who used collaborative learning and group presentation was labeled a rebel.

Nor did we find a medium-sized college English department a paragon of change. Out of the thirty-six sections of Freshman Writing, thirty were taught by the lecture method with writing assigned, not taught. Of the ninety-two classes devoted to literature study, all but the three classes on film were taught by the lecture method. The one course devoted to teacher education was process oriented and student centered.

Sometimes distinctions are made that are neat and tidy but, upon closer inspection, became blurred.

Consider children who mark up walls and "write" in their food.

Actually, watching television comes closer to passivity than does reading.

It proves interesting to graph these four processes according to one's own experiences. Then share and compare them to the experiences of others.

to create, to originate formulations, using the highly abstruse symbol system of equations and formulae. Verbal language represents the most *available* medium for composing; in fact, the significance of sheer availability in its selection as a mode for learning can probably not be overstressed. But the uniqueness of writing among the verbal languaging processes does need to be established and supported if only because so many curricula and courses in English still consist almost exclusively of reading and listening.

Writing as a Unique Languaging Process

Traditionally, the four languaging processes of listening, talking, reading, and writing are paired in either of two ways. The more informative seems to be the division many linguists make between first-order and second-order processes, with talking and listening characterized as first-order processes; reading and writing, as second-order. First-order processes are acquired without formal or systematic instruction; the second-order processes of reading and writing tend to be learned initially only with the aid of formal and systematic instruction.

The less useful distinction is that between listening and reading as receptive functions and talking and writing as productive functions. Critics of these terms like Louise Rosenblatt rightfully point out that the connotation of passivity too often accompanies the notion of receptivity when reading, like listening, is a vital, construing act.

An additional distinction, so simple it may have been previously overlooked, resides in two criteria: the matters of origination and of graphic recording. Writing is originating and creating a unique verbal construct that is graphically recorded. Reading is creating or re-creating *but not* originating a verbal construct that is graphically recorded. Listening is creating or re-creating but not originating a verbal construct that is *not* graphically recorded. Talking is creating *and* originating a verbal construct that is *not* graphically recorded (except for the circuitous routing of a transcribed tape). Note that a distinction is being made between creating and originating, separable processes.

For talking, the nearest languaging process, additional distinctions should probably be made. (What follows is not a denigration of talk as a valuable mode of learning.) A silent classroom or one filled only with the teacher's voice is anathema to learning. For evidence of the cognitive value of talk, one can look to some of the persuasive monographs coming from the London Schools Council project on writing: *From Information to Understanding* by Nancy Martin or *From Talking to Writing* by Peter Medway.[2] We also know that for some of us, talking is a valuable, even necessary, form of pre-writing. In his curriculum, James Moffett makes the value of such talk quite explicit.

But to say that talking is a valuable form of pre-writing is not to say that writing is talk recorded, an inaccuracy appearing far too many composition texts. Rather, a number of contemporary trans-disciplinary sources suggest that talking and writing may emanate from different organic sources and represent quite different, possibly distinct, language functions. In *Thought and Language*, Vygotsky notes that "written speech is a separate linguistic function, differing from oral speech in both structure and mode of functioning."[3] The sociolinguist Dell Hymes, in a valuable issue of *Daedalus*, "Language as a Human Problem," makes a comparable point: "That speech and writing are not simply interchangeable, and have developed historically in ways at least partly autonomous, is obvious."[4] At the first session of the Buffalo Conference on Researching Composition (4–5 October 1975), the first point of unanimity among the participant-speakers with interests in developmental psychology, media, dreams and aphasia was that talking and writing were markedly different functions.[5] Some of us who work rather steadily with writing research agree. We also believe that there are hazards, conceptually and pedagogically, in creating too complete an analogy between talking and writing, in blurring the very real differences between the two.

This very issue—that writing is not written talk—coupled with the desire to model, causes the dilemma in preschool, pre-kindergarten, kindergarten, and even first grade concerning the value of taking dictation, that is, writing the talk of children. More research may be needed in this area.

In "Non-Magical Thinking: Presenting Writing Developmentally in Schools" Emig hypothesizes on a revision of her statements here. She writes, "But what if, as evidence from many disciplines now suggests, writing is developmentally a natural process? What if it is just as natural . . . to write books and to read them as it is natural to die or be born?" Natural for this content must be quickly defined: As humans we seem to have a genetic predisposition to write as well as to speak; and, if we meet an enabling environment, one that possesses certain characteristics and presents us with certain opportunities, we will learn" (Janet Emig, The Web of Meaning, *ed. Dixie Goswami and Maureen Butler (Upper Montclair, N.J.: Boynton/Cook, 1983), p. 136).*

Vygotsky in "A Prehistory of Written Language" writes, "The gesture is the initial visual sign that contains the child's future writing as an acorn contains a future oak. Gestures, it has been correctly said, are writing in air, and written signs frequently are simply gestures that have been fixed" (L. S. Vygotsky, Mind in Society, *ed. Michael Cole, Vera John-Steiner, Sylvia Scribner, and Ellen Souberman (Cambridge, Mass.: Harvard University Press, 1978), p. 107).*

Writing allows us to see the mind at work. No other symbolizing system is so complete. If students cannot write clearly, then they have not thought clearly. If their writing is unorganized, then their thinking is random and nonsequential. They have not harnessed their own thoughts, and writing shows this.

What are These Differences?

(1) Writing is learned behavior; talking is natural, even irrepressible, behavior.

(2) Writing then is an artificial process; talking is not.

(3) Writing is a technological device—not the wheel, but early enough to qualify as primary technology; talking is organic, natural, earlier.

(4) Most writing is slower than most talking.

(5) Writing is stark, barren, even naked as a medium; talking is rich, luxuriant, inherently redundant.

(6) Talk leans on the environment; writing must provide its own context.

(7) With writing, the audience is usually absent; with talking, the listener is usually present.

(8) Writing usually results in a visible graphic product; talking usually does not.

(9) Perhaps because there is a product involved, writing tends to be a more responsible and committed act than talking.

(10) It can even be said that throughout history, an aura, an ambience, a mystique has usually encircled the written word; the spoken word has for the most part proved ephemeral and treated mundanely (ignore, please, our recent national history).

(11) Because writing is often our representation of the world made visible, embodying both process and product, writing is more readily a form and source of learning than talking.

Unique Correspondences between Learning and Writing

What then are some *unique* correspondences between learning and writing? To begin with some definitions: Learning can be defined in many ways, according to one's predilections and training, with all statements about learning of course hypothetical. Definitions range from the chemo-physiological ("Learning is changed patterns of protein synthesis in relevant portions of the cortex")[6] to transactive views drawn from both philosophy and psychology (John Dewey, Jean Piaget) that learning is the re-organization or confirmation of a cognitive scheme in light of an experience.[7] What the speculations seem to share is consensus about certain features and strategies that characterize successful learning. These include the importance of the classic attributes of re-inforcement and feedback. In most hypotheses, successful learning is also connective and selective. Additionally, it makes use of propositions, hypotheses, and other elegant summarizers. Finally, it is active, engaged, personal—more specifically, self-rythmed—in nature.

It may be helpful to write out two definitions, one for writing and one for learning. Doing this may be revealing.

Jerome Bruner, like Jean Piaget, through a comparable set of categories, posits three major ways in which we represent and deal with actuality: (1) enactive—we learn "by doing"; (2) iconic—we learn "by depiction in an image"; and (3) representational or symbolic—we learn "by restatement in words."[8] To overstate the matter, in enactive learning, the hand predominates; in iconic, the eye; and in symbolic, the brain.

NJWPT trainers read from a suggested reading list and synthesize their reading into summaries. They always remark how this part of their training benefits them. For most, it becomes exactly what Emig describes as involving "the fullest possible functioning of the brain."

What is striking about writing as a process is that, by its very nature, all three ways of dealing with actuality are simultaneously or almost simultaneously deployed. That is, the symbolic transformation of experience through the specific symbol system of verbal language is shaped into an icon (the graphic product) by the enactive hand. If the most efficacious learning occurs when learning is re-inforced, then writing through its inherent re-inforcing cycle involving hand, eye, and brain marks a uniquely powerful multi-representational mode for learning.

Writing is also integrative in perhaps the most basic possible sense: the organic, the functional. Writing involves the fullest possible functioning of the brain, which entails the active participation in the process of both the left and the right hemispheres. Writing is markedly bispheral, although in some popular accounts, writing is inaccurately presented as a chiefly left-hemisphere activity, perhaps because the linear written product is somehow regarded as analogue for the process that created it; and the left hemisphere seems to process material linearly.

The right hemisphere, however, seems to make at least three, perhaps four, major contributions to the writing process—probably, to the creative process generically. First, several researchers, such as Geschwind and Snyder of Harvard and Zaidal of Cal Tech, through markedly different experiments, have very tentatively suggested that the right hemisphere is the sphere, even the seat, of emotions.[9] Second—or perhaps as an illustration of the first—Howard Gardner, in his important study of the brain-damaged, notes that our sense of emotional appropriateness in discourse may reside in the right sphere:

> Emotional appropriateness, in sum—being related not only to *what* is said, but to how it is said and to what is *not* said, as well—is crucially dependent on right hemisphere intactness.[10]

After working with the concepts and strategies that make up this book, after reading and rereading the theories of the scholars and the pedagogies of the teachers presented here, we agree that the process of writing this book became a unique and penetrating learning experience.

Third, the right hemisphere seems to be the source of intuition, of sudden gestalts, of flashes of images, of abstractions occurring as visual or spatial wholes, as the initiating metaphors in the creative process. A familiar example: William Faulkner noted in his *Paris Review* interview that *The Sound and the Fury* began as the image of a little girl's muddy drawers as she sat in a tree watching her grandmother's funeral.[11]

Also, a unique form of feedback, as well as reinforcement, exists with writing, because information from the *process* is immediately and visibly available as that portion of the *product* already written. The importance for learning of a product in a familiar and available medium for immediate, literal (that is, visual) re-scanning and review cannot perhaps be overstated. In his remarkable study of purportedly blind sculptors, Géza Révész found that without sight, persons cannot move beyond a literal transcription of elements into any manner of symbolic transformation—by definition, the central requirement for reformulation and re-interpretation, i.e., revision, that most aptly named process.[12]

As noted in the second paragraph, Vygotsky and Luria, like Bruner, have written importantly about the connections between learning and writing. In his essay "The Psychobiology of Psychology," Bruner lists as one of six axioms regarding learning: "We are connective."[13] Another correspondence then between learning and writing: in *Thought and Language*, Vygotsky notes that writing makes a unique demand in that the writer must engage in "deliberate semantics"—in Vygotsky's elegant phrase, "deliberate structuring of the web of meaning."[14] Such structuring is required because, of Vygotsky, writing centrally represents an expansion of inner speech, that mode whereby we talk of ourselves, which is "maximally compact" and "almost entirely predicative"; written speech is a mode which is "maximally detailed" and which requires explicitly supplied subjects and topics. The medium then of written verbal language requires the establishment of systematic connections and relationships. Clear writing by definition is that writing which signals without ambiguity the nature of conceptual relationships, whether they be coordinate, subordinate, causal, or something other.

Successful learning is also engaged, committed, personal learning. Indeed, impersonal learning may be an anomalous concept, like the very notion of objectivism itself. As Michael Polanyi states simply at the beginning of *Personal Knowledge*: "the ideal of strict objectivism is absurd." (How many courses and curricula in English, science, and all else does that one sentence reduce to rubble?) Indeed, the theme of *Personal Knowledge* is that

We are reminded of Jasper Neel's words that when students engage in the traditional classes of expository writing "they can avoid writing altogether by providing shells with no interior: spelling, punctuation, sentences, paragraphs, structure, and coherence that are nothing but spelling, punctuation, sentences, paragraphs, structure and coherence" (Jasper Neel, Plato Derrida, Writing [Carbondale: Southern Illinois Press, 1988], p. 165). What they produce is not writing, but antiwriting. This type of writing does not show the mind at work, it shows writing conventions at work.

into every act of knowing there enters a passionate contribution of the person knowing what is being known, . . . this coefficient is no mere imperfection but a vital component of his knowledge.[15]

In *Zen and the Art of the Motorcycle Maintenance*, Robert Pirsig states a comparable theme:

The Quality which creates the world emerges as a *relationship* between man and his experience. He is a *participant* in the creation of all things.[16]

Finally, the psychologist George Kelly has as the central notion in his subtle and compelling theory of personal constructs man as a scientist steadily and actively engaged in making and re-making his hypotheses about the nature of the universe.[17]

We are acquiring as well some empirical confirmation about the importance of engagement in, as well as self-selection of, a subject for the student learning to write and writing to learn. The recent Sanders and Littlefield study, reported in *Research in the Teaching of English*, is persuasive evidence on this point, as well as being a model for a certain type of research.[18]

As Luria implies in the quotation above, writing is self-rythmed. One writes best as one learns best, at one's own pace. Or to connect the two processes, writing can sponsor learning because it can match its pace. Support for the importance of self-pacing to learning can be found in Benjamin Bloom's important study "Time and Learning."[19] Evidence for the significance of self-pacing to writing can be found in the reason Jean-Paul Sartre gave last summer for not using the tape-recorder when he announced that blindness in his second eye had forced him to give up writing:

I think there is an enormous difference between speaking and writing. One re-reads what one rewrites. But one can read slowly or quickly: in other words, you do not know how long you will have to take deliberating, over a sentence . . . If I listen to a tape recorder, the listening speed is determined by the speed at which the tape turns and not by my own needs. Therefore I will

Perhaps each of us should create a huge banner that reads ONE WRITES BEST AS ONE LEARNS BEST, AT ONE'S OWN PACE. This banner might be hung in classrooms everywhere.

always be either lagging behind or running ahead of the machine.[20]

Writing is connective as a process in a more subtle and perhaps more significant way, as Luria points out in what may be the most powerful paragraph of rationale ever supplied for writing as heuristic:

> Written speech is bound up with the inhibition of immediate synpractical connections. It assumes a much slower, repeated mediating process of analysis and synthesis, which makes it possible not only to develop the required thought, but even to revert to its earlier stages, thus transforming the sequential chain of connections in a simultaneous, self-reviewing structure. Written speech thus represents a new and powerful instrument of thought.[21]

But first to explicate: writing inhibits "immediate synpractical connections." Luria defines *synpraxis* as "concrete-active" situations in which language does not exist independently but as a "fragment" of an ongoing action "outside of which it is incomprehensible."[22] In *Language and Learning*, James Britton defines it succinctly as "speech-cum-action."[23] Writing, unlike talking, restrains dependence upon the actual situation. Writing as a mode is inherently more self-reliant than speaking. Moreover, as Bruner states in explicating Vygotsky, "Writing virtually forces a remoteness of reference on the language user."[24]

Luria notes what has already been noted above: that writing, typically, is a "much slower" process than talking. But then he points out the relation of this slower pace to learning: this slower pace allows for—indeed, encourages—the shuttling among past, present, and future. Writing, in other words, connects the three major tenses of our experience to make meaning. And the two major modes by which these three aspects are united are the processes of analysis and synthesis: analysis, the breaking of entities into their constituent parts; and synthesis, combining or fusing these, often into fresh arrangements or amalgams.

If there is any truth to the theory that there is intelligence in every molecule of the body, Luria's "fragment" theory assumes vast implications.

Again we find Emig further defining her stance. In "Non-Magical Thinking: Presenting Writing Developmentally in Schools" she writes,

What are the possible implications of these research finding for the presentation of writing in schools?

1. Although writing is natural, it is activated by enabling environments.
2. These environments have the follow-

**Fig. F.1. Unique Cluster of Correspondences between Certain
Learning Strategies and Certain Attributes of Writing**

Selected Characteristics of Successful Learning Strategies	Selected Attributes of Writing, Process and Product
(1) Profits from multi-representational and integrative re-inforcement	(1) Represents process uniquely multi-representational and integrative
(2) Seeks self-provided feedback:	(2) Represents powerful instance of self-provided feedback:
(a) immediate	(a) provides product uniquely available for *immediate* feedback (review and re-evaluation)
(b) long-term	(b) provides record of evolution of thought since writing is epigenetic as process-and-product
(3) Is connective:	(3) Provides connections:
(a) makes generative conceptual groupings, synthetic and analytic	(a) establishes explicit and systematic conceptual groupings through lexical, syntactic, and rhetorical devices
(b) proceeds from propositions, hypotheses, and other elegant summarizers	(b) represents most available means (verbal language) for economic recording of abstract formulations
(4) Is active, engaged, personal—notably, self-rhythmed	(4) Is active, engaged, personal—notably, self-rhythmed

*ing characteristics: they are safe,
structured, private, unobtrusive, and
literate.*

3. *Adults in these environments have
   two especial roles: they are fellow
   practitioners, and they are providers
   of possible content, experiences and
   feedback.*
4. *Children need frequent opportunities
   to practice writing, many of these
   playful.*

*None of these conditions is met in
our current schools; indeed, to honor
them would require nothing less than
paradigm shift in the ways we present
not only writing but also other major
cognitive processes as well (Emig
139).*

Finally, writing is epigenetic, with the complex evolutionary development of thought steadily and graphically visible and available throughout as a record of the journey, from jottings and notes to full discursive formulations.

For a summary of the correspondences stressed here between certain learning strategies and certain attributes of writing see Figure 1.

This essay represents a first effort to make a certain kind of case for writing—specifically, to show its unique value for learning. It is at once over-elaborate and under specific. Too much of the formulation is in the off-putting jargon of the learning theorist, when my own predilection would have been to emulate George Kelly and to avoid terms like re-inforcement and feedback since their use implies that I live inside a certain paradigm about learning I don't truly inhabit. Yet I hope that the essay will start a crucial line of inquiry; for unless the losses to learners of not writing are compellingly described and substantiated by experimental and speculative research, writing itself as a central academic process may not long endure.

Notes

1. Lev S. Vygotsky, *Thought and Language*, trans. Eugenia Hanfmann and Gertrude Vakar (Cambridge: The M.I.T. Press, 1962); A.R. Luria and F. Ia. Yudovich, Speech *and the Development of Mental Processes in the Child*, ed. Joan Simon (Baltimore: Penguin, 1971); Jerome S. Bruner, *The Relevance of Education* (New York: W.W. Norton and Co., 1971).

2. Nancy Martin, *From Information to Understanding* (London: Schools Council Project Writing Across the Curriculum, 11–13, 1973); Peter Medway, *From Talking to Writing* (London: Schools Council Project Writing Across the Curriculum, 11–13, 1973).

3. Vygotsky, p. 98.

4. Dell Hymes, "On the Origins and Foundations of Inequality Among Speakers," *Daedalus*, 102 (Summer, 1973), 69.

5. Participant-speakers were Loren Barrett, University of Michigan; Gerald O'Grady, SUNY/Buffalo; Hollis Frampton, SUNY/Buffalo; and Janet Emig, Rutgers.

6. George Steiner, *After Babel: Aspects of Language and Translation* (New York: Oxford University Press, 1975) p. 287.

7. John Dewey, *Experience and Education* (New York: Macmillan, 1938); Jean Piaget, *Biology and Knowledge: An Essay on the Relations between Organic Regulations and Cognitive Processes* (Chicago: University of Chicago Press, 1971).

8. Bruner, pp. 7–8.

9. Boyce Rensberger, "Language Ability Found in Right Side of Brain," *New York Times*, 1 August 1975, p. 14.

10. Howard Gardner, *The Shattered Mind: The Person After Brain Damage* (New York: Alfred A. Knopf, 1975) p. 372.

11. William Faulkner, *Writers at Work: The Paris Review Interviews*, ed. Malcolm Cowley (New York: The Viking Press, 1959), p. 130.

12. Géza Révész, *Psychology and Art of the*

What are teachers and schools waiting for before they change? What research do these teachers and schools have to support their adherence to the aging paradigm?

Blind, trans. H.A. Wolff (London: Longmans-Green, 1950).

13. Bruner, p. 126.

14. Bygotsky, p. 100.

15. Michael Polanyi, *Personal Knowledge: Toward a Post-Critical Philosophy* Chicago: University of Chicago Press, 1958), p. viii.

16. Robert Pirsig, *Zen and the Art of Motorcycle Maintenance* (New York: William Morrow and Co., Inc., 1974), p. 212.

17. George Kelly, A Theory of Personality: *The Psychology of Personal Constructs* (New York: W.W. Norton and Co., 1963).

18. Sara E. Sanders and John H. Littlefield, "Perhaps Test Essays Can Reflect Significant Improvement in Freshman Composition: Report on a Successful Attempt," *RTE*, 9 (Fall 1975), 145–153.

19. Benjamin Bloom, "Time and Learning," *American Psychologist*, 29 (September 1974), 682–688.

20. Jean-Paul Sartre, "Sartre at Seventy: An Interview," with Michel Contat, *New York Review of Books*, 7 August 1975.

21. Luria, p. 118.

22. Luria, p. 50.

23. James Britton, *Language and Learning* (Baltimore: Penguin, 1971), pp. 10–11.

24. Bruner, p. 47.

WRITE BEFORE WRITING

DONALD M. MURRAY
From College Composition and Communication, NCTE December 1978. Copyright 1978 by the National Council of Teachers of English. Reprinted with permission.

We command our students to write and grow frustrated when our "bad" students hesitate, stare out the window, dawdle over blank paper, give up and say, "I can't write," while the "good" students smugly pass their papers in before the end of the period.

When publishing writers visit such classrooms, however, they are astonished at students who can write on command, ejaculating correct little essays without thought, for writers have to write before writing.

The writers were the students who dawdled, stared out windows, and, more often than we like to admit, didn't do well in English—or in school.

One reason may be that few teachers have ever allowed adequate time for prewriting, that essential stage in the writing process which precedes a completed first draft. And even the curricula plans and textbooks which attempt to deal with prewriting usually pass over it rather quickly, referring only to the techniques of outlining, note-taking, or journal-making, not revealing the complicated process writers work through to get to the first draft.

Writing teachers, however, should give careful attention to what happens between the moment the writer receives an idea or an assignment and the moment the first completed draft is begun. We need to understand, as well as we can, the complicated and intertwining processes of perception and conception through language.

In actual practice, of course, these stages overlap and interact with one another, but to understand what goes on we must separate them and look at them artificially, the way we break down any skill to study it.

Commentary:

If published writers and students were given the opportunity to impact curricula and testing situations, how would they change them? Query: What would the impact be if these writers and students were members of curriculum meetings and testing committees? Who would be threatened by their membership? Why can't these writers and students have more to say in the way writing is practiced in classrooms and tests?

There is still the misconception that knowing the words that denote the writing process is to know the writing process. Most teachers would recognize the word angiography, *but surely none would be comfortable performing an angiography. Knowing the words alone does not ensure correct praxis.*

This understanding does not come from reading about theses processes alone, it also comes from experiencing them.

This also applies to professors who teach and train future teachers. Periodically, and for extended time, they need to go into classrooms on all levels and teach.

In Tom's classroom, which is in a large urban school, a student appeared to be unengaged and disinterested with the writing being pursued. Suddenly, with apparently no prompting, he began. The results showed a deep interest. Uninformed teachers and misdirected classroom evaluators can inadvertently short-circuit the resistance to writing and allow for no writing to be produced because of their compulsion for all students to be engaged at all times. How sad it is that they do not understand the writing process enough to know this negative force is a positive, vital aspect to writing.

While we were writing this book, the Weather Channel became the diversion. When a section became troublesome, or tiring, the forecasts for cities became stopovers in the process of finding the words.

First of all, we must get out of the stands where we observe the process of writing from a distance—and after the fact—and get on the field where we can understand the pressures under which the writer operates. On the field, we all discover there is one principal negative force which keeps the writer from writing and four positive forces which help the writer move forward to a completed draft.

Resistance to Writing

The negative force is *resistance* to writing, one of the real natural forces of nature. It may be called the Law of Delay; that writing which can be delayed, will be. Teachers and writers too often consider resistance to writing evil. When, in fact, it is necessary.

When I get an idea for a poem or an article or a talk or a short story, I feel myself consciously draw away from it. I seek procrastination and delay. There must be time for the seed of the idea to be nurtured in the mind. Far better writers than I have felt the same way. Over his writing desk Franz Kafka had one word, "Wait." William Wordsworth talked of the writer's "wise passiveness." Naturalist Annie Dillard recently said, "I'm waiting. I usually get my idea in November, and I start writing in January. I'm waiting." Denise Levertov says, "If . . . somewhere in the vicinity there is a poem then, no I don't do anything about it, I wait."

Even the most productive writers are expert dawdlers, doers of unnecessary errands, seekers of interruptions—trials to their wives or husbands, friends, associates, and themselves. They sharpen well-pointed pencils and go out to buy more blank paper, rearrange offices, wander through libraries and bookstores, chop wood, walk, drive, make unnecessary calls, nap, daydream, and try not "consciously" to think about what they are going to write so they can think subconsciously about it.

Writers fear this delay, for they can name colleagues who have made a career of delay, whose great unwritten books will never be written, but, somehow, those writers who write must have the faith to sustain themselves through the necessity of delay.

Forces of Writing

In addition to that faith, writers feel four pressures that move them forward towards the first draft.

The first is *increasing information* about the subject. Once a writer decides on a subject or accepts an assignment, information about the subject seems to attach itself to the writer. The writer's perception apparatus finds significance in what the writer observes or overhears or reads or thinks or remembers. The writer becomes a magnet for specific details, insights, anecdotes, statistics, connecting thoughts, references. The subject itself seems to take hold of the writer's experience, turning everything that happens to the writer into material, and this inventory of information creates pressure that moves the writer forward towards the first draft.

Classrooms and teachers became the magnets for this endeavor. They acted as the source on occasion. They served as confirmation at other times. But they could never be too far away.

Usually the writer feels an *increasing concern* for the subject. The more a writer knows about the subject the more the writer begins to feel about the subject. The writer cares that the subject be ordered and shared. The concern, which at first is a vague interest in the writer's mind, often becomes an obsession until it is communicated. Winston Churchill said, "Writing a book was an adventure. To begin with, it was a toy, and amusement; then it became a mistress, and then a master. And then a tyrant."

This becomes a type of ownership for the student. Any parent who has had a child involved in soccer, drama, or the self-sponsored activities in which children involve themselves can attest to the devotion and ownership that the child displays. When students feel the same concern for their writing, teaching writing ceases to be the onerous task in a curriculum and becomes the confirmation of thinking and learning.

The writer becomes aware of a *waiting audience*, potential readers who want or need to know what the writer had to say. Writing is an act of arrogance and communication. The writer rarely writes just for himself or herself, but for others who may be informed, entertained, or persuaded by what the writer has to say.

Bob Rath, interestingly, upset the canon of the waiting audience in his research that reveals the writer only writes for him- or herself. Self is the ultimate audience.

And perhaps most important of all is the *approaching deadline*, which moves closer day by day at a terrifying and accelerating rate. Few writers publish without deadlines, which are imposed by others or by themselves. The deadline is real, absolute, stern, and commanding.

If the deadline is unrealistic and imposing, the brain will perceive it as a threat, and this can result in downshifting.

Rehearsal for Writing

There is a significance to Murray's term rehearsal. *The writer must "rehear" what he or she has chosen to say.*

What the writer does under the pressure not to write and the four countervailing pressures to write is best described by the word, *rehearsal*, which I first heard used by Dr. Donald Graves of the University of New Hampshire to describe what he saw young children doing as they began to write. He watched them draw what they would write and heard them, as we all have, speaking aloud what they might say on the page before they wrote. If you walk through editorial offices of a newspaper city-room you will see lips moving and hear expert professionals muttering and whispering to themselves as they write. Rehearsal is a normal part of the writing process, but it took a trained observer, such as Dr. Graves, to identify its significance.

Rehearsal covers much more than the muttering of struggling writers, As Dr. Graves points out, productive writers are "in a state of rehearsal all the time." Rehearsal usually begins with an unwritten dialogue within the writer's mind. "All of a sudden I discover that I have been thinking about a plot," says Edward Albee. "This is usually between six months and a year before I actually sit down and begin typing it out." The writer thinks about characters or arguments, about plot or structure, about words and lines. The writer usually hears something which is similar to what Wallace Stevens must have heard as he walked through his insurance office working out poems in his head.

What the writer hears in his or her head usually evolves into note-taking. This may be simple brainstorming, the jotting down of random bits of information which may connect themselves into a pattern later on, of it may be journal-writing, a written dialogue between the writer and the subject. It may even become research recorded in a formal structure of note-taking.

A teacher cannot underestimate the power of this collaboration. It gives the writer balance. It keeps the writer on track. For too long writing classrooms have been classrooms where the only voice heard was the teacher's. If students are to become writers, then they must hear their own voices.

Sometimes the writer not only talks to himself or herself, but to others—collaborators, editors, teachers, friends—working out the piece of writing in oral language with someone else who can enter into the process of discovery with the writer.

For most writers, the informal notes turn into lists, outlines, titles, leads, ordered fragments, all sketches of what later may be writing, devices to catch a possible order that exists in the chaos of the subject.

In the final state of rehearsal, the writer produces test drafts, written or unwritten. Sometimes they are called discovery drafts or trial runs or false starts that he writer doesn't think will be false. All writing is experimental, and the writer must come to the point where drafts are attempted in the writer's head and on paper.

Some writers seem to work more in their head, and others more on paper. Susan Sowars, a researcher at the university of New Hampshire, examining the writing processes of a group of graduate students found

Students will not experiment in classrooms where risk taking is not valued and rewarded. The cost is too high. Jimmie Kanning, a teacher San Antonio, is an excellent example of the teacher valuing and rewarding risk taking. Working with seniors who have been disenfranchised by a system, she placed magical safety nets to catch any student who falls from academic grace. They risk under her guidance. They learn failure is just another way of signaling learning.

a division ... between those who make most discoveries during prewriting and those who make most discoveries during writing and revision. The discoveries include the whole range from insights into personal issues to task-related organizational and content insight. The earlier the stage at which the insights occur, the greater the drudgery associated with the writing-rewriting tasks. It may be that we resemble the young reflective and reactive writing. The less developmentally mature reactive writers enjoy writing more than reflective writers. They may use writing as a rehearsal for thinking just as young reactive writers draw to rehearse writing. The younger and older reflective writers do not need to rehearse by drawing to write or by writing to think clearly or to discover new relationships and significant content.

Teela McKee uses students' natural interest in self to engage her students in writing. They collect old photos, stuffed animals, blankets, and other childhood memorabilia. From these, they share explorations in writing persuasively.

This concept deserves more investigation. We need to know about both the reflective and reactive prewriting mode. We need to see if there are developmental changes in students, it they move from one mode to another as they mature, and we need to see it one mode is more important in certain writing tasks that others. We must, in every way possible, explore the significant writing stage of rehearsal which has rarely been described in the literature on the writing process.

The Signals Which Say "Write"

During the rehearsal process, the experienced writer sees signals which tell the writer how to control the subject and produce a working first draft. The writer Rebecca Rule points out that in some cases when the subject is found, the way to deal with it is inherent in the subject. The subject itself is the signal. Most writers have experienced this quick passing though of the prewriting process. The line is given and the poem is clear; a character gets up and walks the writer through the story; the newspaperman attends a press conference, hears a quote, sees the lead and the entire structure of the article instantly. But many times the process is far less clear. The writer is assigned a subject or chooses one and then is lost.

To recognize these signals, the teacher of writing must become a diagnostician. The teacher must learn to not only recognize but also assist the writer in knowing what to do in the writing. This is no easy task.

E.B. White testifies, "I never knew in the morning how the day was going to develop. I was like a hunter, hoping to catch sight of a rabbit." Denise Levertov says, "You can smell the poem before you see it." Most writers know these feelings, but students who have never seen a rabbit dart across their writing desks or smelled a poem need to know the signals which tell them that a piece of writing is near.

What does the writer recognize which gives a sense of closure, a way of handling a diffuse and overwhelming subject? There seem to eight principal signals to which writers respond.

One signal is *genre*. Most writers view the world as a fiction writer, a reporter, a poet, or an historian. The writer sees experience as a plot or a lyric poem or a news story or a chronicle. The writer uses such literary traditions to see and understand life.

Lesson planning becomes a developmental process rather that a checklist of accomplishments. Although on the one hand it is important for the teacher to plan what he or she is going to do with the students who are engaged in the writing process, it is equally important to leave this planning open-ended and dynamic. Principals who want to see six-week lesson plans, semester lesson plans, or even weekly lesson plans do not want to see writers who are learners, or learners who are actively discovering what they know and need to know. This type of learning does not occur because the lesson plan says it will happen on day fourteen of the six weeks. Learning and writing happen best when facilitated. Facilitation requires planning, replanning, chance, and good teaching.

"Ideas come to a writer because he has trained his mind to seek them out," says Brian Garfield. "Thus when he observes or reads or is exposed to a character or event, his mind sees the story possibilities in it and he begins to compose a dramatic structure in his mind. This process is incessant. Now and then it leads to something that will become a novel. But it's mainly an attitude; a way of looking at things; a habit of examining everything one perceives as potential material for a story."

Genre is a powerful but dangerous lens. It both clarifies and limits. The writer and the student must be careful not to see life merely in the stereotype form with which he or she is most familiar but look at life with all of the possibilities of the genre in mind and to attempt to look at life through different genre.

Another signal the writer looks for is *point of view*. This can be an opinion towards the subject or a position from which the writer—and the reader—studies the subject.

A tenement fire could inspire the writer to speak out against tenements, dangerous space-heating systems, a fire-department budget cut. The fire might also be seen from the point of view of the people who are the victims or who escaped or who came home to find their home gone. It may be told from the point of view of a fireman, an arsonist, an insurance investigator, a fire-safety engineer, a real-estate planner, a housing inspector, a landlord, a spectator, as well as the victim. The list could go on.

Still another way the writer sees the subject is through *voice*. As the writer rehearses, in the writer's head and on paper, the writer listens to the sound of the language as a clue to the meaning in the subject and the writer's attitude toward that meaning. Voice is often the force which drives a piece of writing forward, which illuminates the subject for the writer and the reader.

A writer may, for example, start to write a test draft with detached unconcern and find that the language appearing on the page reveals anger or passionate concern. The writer who starts to write a solemn report of a meeting may hear a smile and then a laugh in his own words and go on to produce a humorous column.

News is an important signal for many writers who ask what the reader needs to know or would like to know. Those prolific authors of nature books, Lorus and Margery Milne, organize their books and each chapter in the books around what is new in the field. Between assignment and draft they are constantly looking for the latest news they can pass along to their

In a writing institute, one member looked somewhat surprised when another group member responded with, "I think you have the makings of a poem there." She responded, "But I didn't start out to write a poem." It is much like Einstein's "apple" quote in the film Why Man Creates.

Katherine Paterson says in The Spying Heart, *"An idea is something that makes a sound in the heart (the heart in Japanese . . . being the seat of intelligence as much as the seat of feeling)" (28). The point is that writers should listen to the sound of their hearts.*

In the poem "August Pickings," by Joyce Armstrong Carroll (English Journal, 1990), she starts with, "I hear the swamp berries are ready, Dad announced with a grin." She tells how when working with a group of teachers on prewriting techniques, she wrote the words "berry picking." She fully intended to move on from those words, but instead she felt the pull of the words compelling her to write about the times her father took her berry picking. Had she not been open to the resonance of the line, she would have missed the poem.

Many times the first line that leads the way into a writing never finds its way into the final piece. Mundo, a student in Beverly McKinley's high school class, discovered this. His prewriting began, "Back in the 40's and 50's my father hunted as a young boy with his father." Subsequently, he scratched this line out and wrote beside it, "cheesy story." This line, however, galvanized a poignant story titled "On the Hunt." It begins, "Long ago my father introduced hunting to his three oldest sons." The story chronicles his passage from a punk kid armed with a slingshot aimed at lizards to a responsible hunter of bigger game. Nowhere in Mundo's rather lengthy story does that original line appear. And the story is anything but "cheesy."

readers. When they find what is new, then they know how to organize their writing.

Writers constantly wait for the *line* which is given. For most writers, there is an enormous difference between a thesis or an idea or a concept and an actual line, for the line itself has resonance. A single line can imply a voice, a tone, a pace, a whole way of treating a subject. Joseph Heller tells about the signal which produced his novel *Something Happened:*

I begin with a first sentence that is independent of any conscious preparation. Most often nothing comes out of it: a sentence will come to mind that doesn't lead to a second sentence. Sometimes it will lead to thirty sentences which then come to a dead end. I was alone on the deck. As I sat there worrying and considering what to do, one of those first lines suddenly came to mind: "In the office in which I work, there are four people of whom I am afraid. Each of these four people is afraid of five people." Immediately, the lines presented a whole explosion of possibilities and choices—characters (working in a corporation), a tone, a mode of anxiety, or of insecurity. In that first hour (before someone came along and asked me to go to the beach) I knew the beginning, the ending, most of the middle, the whole scene of that particular "something" that was going to happen; I knew about the brain-damaged child, and especially, of course, about Bob Slocum, my protagonist, and what frightened him, that he wanted to be liked, that his immediate hope was to be allowed to make a three-minute speech at the company convention. Many of the actual lines throughout the book came to me—the entire "something happened" scene with those solar plexus lines (beginning with the doctor's statement and the ending with "Don't tell my wife" and the rest of them) all coming to me in that first hour on that Fire Island deck. Eventually I found a different opening chapter with a different first line ("I get the willies when I see closed doors") but kept the original, which had spurred everything, to start off the second section.

Newspapermen are able to write quickly and effectively under pressure because they become skillful at identifying a lead, that first line—or two or three—which will inform and entice the reader and which, of course, also gives the writer control over the subject. As an editorial writer, I found that finding the title first gave me control over the subject. Each title became, in effect, a pre-draft, so that in listing potential titles I would come to one which would be a signal as to how the whole editorial could be written.

Poets and fiction writers often receive their signals in terms of an *image*. Some times this image is static; other times it is a moving picture in the writer's mind. When Gabriel García Márquez was asked what the starting point of his novels was, he answered, "a completely visual image . . . the starting point of *Leaf Storm* is an old man taking his grandson to a funeral, in *No One Writes the Colonel*, it's an old man waiting, and in *One Hundred Years*, an old man taking his grandson to the fair to find out what ice is." William Faulkner was quoted as saying, "It begins with character, usually, and once he stands up on his feet and begins to move, all I do is trot along behind him with a paper and pencil trying to keep up long enough to put down what he says and does." It's a comment which seems facetious—if you're not a fiction writer. Joyce Carol Oates adds, "I visualize the characters completely; I have heard their dialogue, I know how they speak, what they want, who they are, nearly everything about them."

Although image has been testified to mostly by imaginative writers, where it is obviously most appropriate, I think research would show that nonfiction writers often see an image as the signal. The person, for example, writing a memo about a manufacturing procedure may see the assembly line in his or her mind. The politician arguing for a pension law may see a person robbed of a pension, and by seeing that person know how to organize a speech or the draft of a new law.

Many writers know they are ready to write

These examples of Murray's attest to the need for a variety of prewriting experiences. Not all writing for all students will come from one prewriting activity. A variety allows for student writers to find their topics and their genre and to feel success.

Although published writers see this gestalt, it is not so clear to the student writer. With practice, much practice, the student writer develops this "sight." When and how this occurs is worthy of more study and research. Marsha White spends time in her classroom allowing students to verbalize the "how" of their gestalt. She listens to her students and offers possibilities to guide them in their discoveries.

For the new paradigm, the skill of asking questions, the right questions, will become even more valuable. With the information explosion, knowing the answers is an impossibility, so society needs people who can ask the right questions.

when they see a *pattern* in a subject. This pattern is usually quite different from what we think of as an outline, which is linear and goes from beginning to end. Usually the writer sees something which might be called a gestalt, which is, in the word of the dictionary, "a unified physical, psychological, or symbolic configuration having properties that cannot be derived from its parts." The writer usually in a moment sees the entire piece of writing as a shape, a form, something that is more that all of its parts, something that is entire and is represented in his or her mind, and probably on paper, by a shape.

Marge Piercy says, "I think that the beginning of fiction, of the story, has to do with the perception of patter in event." Leonard Gardner, in talking of his fine novel *Fat City*, said, "I had a definite design in mind. I had a sense of circle . . . of closing the circle at the end." John Updike says, "I really begin with some kind of solid, coherent image, some notion of the shape of the book and even of its texture. *The Poorhouse Fair* was meant to have a sort of wide shape. *Rabbit, Run* was kind of zigzag. *The Centaur* was sort of a sandwich."

We have interviews with imaginative writers about the writing process but rarely interviews with sciences writers, business writers, political writers, journalists, ghost writers, legal writers, medical writers—examples of effective writers who use language to inform and persuade. I am convinced that such research would reveal that they also see patterns or gestalts which carry them from idea to draft.

"It's not the answer that enlightens but the question," says Ionesco. This insight into what the writer is looking for is one of the most significant considerations in trying to understand the freewriting process. A most significant book based on more than ten years of study of art students, *The Creative Vision, A Longitudinal Study of Problem-Finding in Art,* by Jacob W. Getzels and Mihaly Csikszentmihalyi, has documented how the most creative students are those who come up with the problem to be solved rather than a quick answer. The signal to the creative person may well be the problem, which will be solved through the writing.

We need to take all the concepts of invention from classical rhetoric and combine them with what we know from modern psychology, from studies of creativity, from writers' testimony about the prewriting process. Most of all we need to observe successful students and writers during the prewriting process, and to debrief them to find out what they do when they move effectively from assignment or idea to completed first draft. Most of all, we need to move from failure-centered research to research which defines what happens when the writing goes well, just what is the process followed by effective student and professional writers. We know far too little about the writing process.

Implications for Teaching Writing

Our speculations make it clear that there are significant implications for the teaching of writing in a close examination of what happens between receiving an assignment or finding a subject and beginning a completed first draft. We may need, for example, to reconsider our attitude towards those who delay writing. We may, in fact, need to force many of our glib, hair-trigger student writers to slow down, to daydream, to waste time, but not to avoid a reasonable deadline.

We certainly should allow time within the curriculum for prewriting, and we should work with our students to help them understand the process of rehearsal, to allow them the experience of rehearsing what they will write in their minds, on the paper, and with collaborators. We should also make our students familiar with the signals they may see during the rehearsal process which will tell them that they are ready to write, that they have a way of dealing with their subject.

The prewriting process is largely invisible; it takes place within the writer's head or on scraps of paper that are rarely published. But we must understand that such a process takes place, that it is significant, and that it can be made clear to our students. Students who are not writing, or not writing well may have a second chance if they are able to experience the writer's counsel to write before writing.

See Chapter 1 for classical invention and classical invention for the contemporary student.

Murray advocates student responsibility. It is time for students to be the ones responsible for what goes on the classrooms. Teachers are not the only decision makers present in classrooms.

Murray's article invites mini-teaches on the four forces of writing: increasing information, increasing concern for subject, a waiting audience, and the approaching deadline. Also, it begs for mini-teaches on rehearsal and "the signals which say 'write.'": genre (see Chapter 2), point of view, voice, news, line, image, and patterns.

DRAWING INTO MEANING: A POWERFUL WRITING TOOL

JOYCE ARMSTRONG CARROLL
From *English Journal* 80, no. 6 [October 1991]. Copyright 1991 by the National Council of Teachers of English. Reprinted with permission.

" . . . and [he] told her she could keep it forever and ever."

"Now we're going to write," said Ms. Smith. Promptly, twenty-one kindergartners, some with crayons, some with fat or skinny pencils, began talking and turning their oversized unlined papers this way and that. Soon the chatter generated by Joan de Hamel's *Hemi's Pet* (1985) slowed as drawings of real and make-believe animals flew, trotted, crawled, and ran across the students' papers.

Background

When we watch children in primary or elementary grades, we delight in all this drawing; we accept it as a way of meaning; we accept it as writing. "Read what you have written," we invite. So automatically playing the "believing game" (Elbow 1973, 148), they read their circles with lines radiating out as "a bright sunny day"; they read their row of stick figures as "I love my family." Yet somewhere up the ladder of academe, we educate out of students this powerful writing tool we let middle- and high-school students know in subtle and sometimes not-so-subtle ways that drawing belongs to little kids.

I find this curious since I draw when I write. I usually line up boxes along my top margin like square soldiers. Then, apparently depending upon the nature of the writing, I fill them in with lines and shading—the more complex the piece of writing, the more intricate the details in the boxes. I don't do this consciously, perhaps because they are "fugitives of my unconscious" (Torrey 1989, 65), yet boxes always appear on my papers.

So curious (or obsessive) did I become about connections between drawing and writing, I began a quiet and admittedly unscholarly research project—no control groups, no statistics—just random glancing at people engaged in the act of writing. I saw much drawing going on surreptitiously—clouds, smoke, flowers, houses, hands, cowboys, and cats sat side by side scribbles and squiggles on page after page. Some people even drew beautiful, suitable-for-framing designs like the elaborate mandalas a friend of mine creates before he ever writes a word.

Theory

As is usually the case when something strikes the mind, I noticed articles on this "frittering" everywhere. Obviously my curiosity was shared by readers ranging from *American Baby* (Lamme 1985) to *Omni* (Torrey), from *Psychology Today* (Winner 1986) to *College English* (Fulwiler and Petersen 1981). I wondered: if drawing, scribbling, and doodling fascinate us all, if all these loops and lines hold tacit meaning, why don't we use drawing in middle and high schools as the powerful writing tool it is?

In a jointly written article, Toby Fulwiler and Bruce Petersen validate this notion of drawing as a writing tool by not only identifying three types of doodles and suggesting doodling as analogous "to journal writing, free writing, and rough drafting" but also by explaining that doodles help "develop concrete records of otherwise incompletely synthesized intellection" (626). In other words, they believe that doodles help make visible that which might remain ethereal.

Ruth Hubbard (1989b), borrowing the terms *disigno interno* (inner languages) and *disigno esterno* (visual modes) from the Italian painter Frederico Zuccari, echoes Fulwiler and Petersen: "These final products—on the canvas or printed page—are only a representation, of perhaps interpretation, of what goes on in our minds" (134). Further, she quotes Walter Grey's study of the modes in which people communicate; "15% of the population thinks exclusively in the visual modes, another 15% thinks only in verbal terms, and the remaining 70% uses a mixture of approaches" (133–134). When I read those statistics, I began to realize why so many people naturally turn to drawing while writing.

Then I heard about Judy Skupa's dissertation (1985). In it, she analyzes the writings of three groups of elementary students: those permitted to draw and look at their drawings before writing, those permitted to draw but not look at their drawing before writing (blind drawers), and those who were not permitted to draw at all before writing. Her data show that those permitted to draw and look at their drawings wrote best.

Skupa's research supports that of psychologists James Gibson and Patricia Yonas. They recorded the delight two-year-olds took in making marks across a page, but they noted that if they replaced the child's marker with one that left no trace, the children would stop writing (Winner 25).

I am reminded here of Janet Emig's observation about Sartre's blindness and his frustration at not being able to read his own work: "The eye . . . permits individual rhythms of review to be established and followed" (1978, 66). It seems obvious that the graphic symbol, born from the self for the self, different yet similar to the written one, contains its own intrinsic power, power arising from its unique ability to display a visual knowing and from its unique ability to enable a focused concentration.

Beginning to understand why drawing emerges as so powerful a writing tool, I hypothesized that meaning embodied in a graphic symbol

leads to what Susanne Langer calls "symbolic expression" (Cassirer 1946, ix). Put another way, drawing provides "a cognitive economy in its metaphoric transformations, which make it possible for a seemingly limited symbol to spread its power over a range of experience" (Bruner 1971, 14).

Perhaps Betty Edwards (1986) most clearly explains it. Making a case that perceptual skills (those used when drawing) enhance *thinking* skills. She proposes that

learning to see and draw is a very efficient way to train the visual system, just as learning to read and write can efficiently train the verbal system. . . . And when trained as equal partners, one mode of thinking enhances the other, and together the two modes can release human creativity. (8)

That's power.

To withhold that power from middle- and high-school students—no matter how well-intentioned—to permit only elementary students access to that symbolizing system ignores the importance of drawing as powerful preliminary of writing. Along with brainstorming, mapping, classical invention, the pentad, and other prewriting strategies, students should be encouraged to draw into meaning, whether as prewriting for their reflexive or extensive pieces or as initial responses to literature. In order to help that happen, we need to

1. Enable students to reenter texts in visual, non-threatening ways

2. Encourage drawing as a prewriting technique

3. Appropriate drawing as a springboard for further writing

4. Consider drawing an initial graphic probe, a strategy for tapping deeper or other awarenesses.

Application

In an effort to capitalization the power in drawing (as well as to test my hypothesis), I visited many middle and high schools, and through interactive inservice (teaching classes, being observed by teachers, then meeting with those teachers afterwards), I was able to invite drawing as response to literature, then to see where that response might lead.

First, I talked to the students about symbolic drawing. I explained that such drawing is a symbolizing system just as writing is a symbolizing system: the former is one of images, the latter is one of words; the former is visual, the latter is verbal. Together we talked about the cave drawings found to date back as far as 16,000 BC, to the Old Stone Age. I showed pictures of symbolic drawings taken from the caves at Altamira, Combarelles, Les Eyzies, and Font de Gaume in France. The students were hooked.

I followed with examples from the archaeological finds at Novgorod. These birchbark manuscripts show actual school exercises done by Onfim, a six- or seven-year-old boy, in the first half of the thirteenth century. Some are letters; some are syllables; some are remarkably contemporary looking "drawings of himself, battle scenes and pictures of his teacher" (Yanin 1990, 89). Onfim used letters and drawing to give form to his meaning.

Next, I showed a *pictograph* and defined pictographs as capturing the essence of what the reader knows. The one I chose was a simple stick figure of a man with twenty or so lines emanating out of each foot because five-year-old Mary told me as she pointed to her picture, "My father's barefoot."

"She drew what she knew," I explained.

Next I showed four-year-old Derrick's map as another example of symbolic drawing, the *ideograph*, a more sophisticated visual that the pictograph since it conveys relationships. Here I pointed out the way Derrick outlined the trip from his house to the babysitter's house as well as from his house to church. As Hubbard (1989a) says,

> As each of us attempts our search for meaning, we need a medium through which our ideas can take shape. But there is not just one medium; productive thought uses many ways to find meaning. (3)

Through discussion, it was made clear that drawing as a powerful tool of writing was not the same as drawing as an art form. The students realized that such drawing gives form to thought for self then communicates that meaning to others. This got them past the reluctance to participate, even to try because of the "I-can't-draw" syndrome, meaning "I'm not an artist."

Making connections between the history of writing and the symbol system children create, the students grew more curious. They wondered whether they could still tap drawing as a medium of meaning. The students were anxious to try the "new" symbol system; they were ready to put it to use, so I placed Richard Brautigan's poem "In a Café" on the overhead.

> I watched a man in a café fold a slice of
>   bread
> As if he were folding a birth certificate or
>   looking
> At the photograph of dead lover
>   (Brautigan 1979, 46)

After reading it aloud as students followed along, I said, "Let's tackle this poem by fooling the usual and perhaps dominant hemispheres of our brain. Take your pen or pencil in the hand opposite the hand with which you usually write and draw what you know." Heads down they worked. I did, too.

In about five or seven minutes, I intervened. "Switch to your comfortable hand and write what you discover in your drawing." Again heads bowed down as they worked. Mine did too.

"Let's see what happened. Who would like to share?" I invited. Many hands shot up.

Stephanie shared her drawing of an eye in the upper left corner and a tear in the upper right corner, She read,

> My Scottish grandfather wore khakis. He was a railroad man—

his box house was next to the station. They were both painted

railway yellow with coal black trim. I only saw him twice.

"Talk to us about any connections you see between the poem and what you drew and wrote," I invited.

"The poem made me feel sad. All of a sudden I thought about my grandfather who I only saw twice. I think I thought about him because I feel bad I only saw him twice before he died. Maybe he sat at a table alone. Maybe he thought about me."

"What did your drawing and writing tell you about the poem?" I press.

Stephanie thought a long while as she studied her work and Brautigan's. Finally she said, "My grandfather was a loner. When you read the poem, I felt lonely. That made me think of Papa Mac. When I thought of him, I thought of what he did and where he lived. That's what first popped into my mind. The colors came later.

"Now I think I'd add that the poet wanted to tell us not just about being lonely but also about being lonely even when you are around people, like in a café or by a railroad where you'd see lots of people."

"The more I think about this, it's like my mind keeps changing because now I'm thinking more of isolation than loneliness. Maybe the man in the café, like Papa Mac, wanted to be alone, wanted to be isolated. That piece of bread wasn't bread at all, not when he really looked at it. It became the birth certificate or the photograph. The poet could be telling us something about wanting to see something so badly you do see it. Maybe the whole poem is about out perceptions."

Stephanie's writing and subsequent telling seem to validate Lev Vygotsky's contention that drawing is not representational but rather it yields "predispositions to judgments that are invested with speech or capable of being so invested" (1978, 112). It's unlikely that if Stephanie had been given the poem in the traditional setting any mention of Papa Mac would have occurred. It's even less likely that the sequence of conjectures following that telling would have

occurred. Later, when Stephanie drafted her essay about the poem, there was a quality, a depth to her writing which, according to her teacher, hitherto did not exist.

Continuing the sharing, another student held up a shaky sketch of a seated man. She read, "withered and solitary the man sits and waits. Auschwitz thin in striped pajamas, quietly letting go."

T: How did your drawing cause that writing, Cathy?

C: Unexpectedly I thought about *The Diary of Anne Frank*, I think because we just finished reading it. When you read the poem I thought how that man in the poem could be a Jew who had been in a concentration camp. Then after the war he came to France. I thought of France because of the word "café." He could have trouble eating because every time he goes to eat he thinks of the concentration camp.

T: Do those thoughts help you understand the poem?

C: Well, it's awfully short—like Anne Frank's life. I think the poet wanted to condense everything like Anne had to condense everything in that tiny room.

I know poems are always condensed, but in this one it's like it shows what it means. You can get a lot of meaning into a little space if you choose carefully. I want to choose carefully. I want to my life to be full even if I'm only thirteen years old.

These thoughts shared aloud echo Hubbard's own exploration of the relationship between her words and images. Here Cathy conveys the complexity of that relationship. First, Brautigan's poem caused an association with a book Cathy had just finished, which came out through the shaky drawing and the thin man. That, in turn, caused an allusion to a concentration camp to surface in the writing. When sharing, Cathy made application to her own life, her own desire to live life to the fullest.

As with Stephanie, the tendency is to use

drawing as the basic response, then to move in hierarchical, heuristical ways from the known (their graphic representation) to discoveries, to transformations, and to higher levels of knowing.

Another example comes from a twelfth grader named Raul who drew a large trash can. Bits of paper spilled over and cluttered the area around it. He wrote simply, "The man is a discard. No one cares about him." Raul didn't elaborate orally. At first blush it seemed nothing further had been triggered. However, when I revisited Raul's class several weeks later, he thrust a neatly written two-page paper at me. "Read this," he murmured, "I wrote it after your drawing class." The title "A Disenfranchised Man" promised and the prose delivered a profound look at a person living in America, homeless, without privilege, without identity.

Raul and others had used drawing as a visual probe, a method of inquiry which helped them transform the raw data of the poem into something they and others could understand.

Conclusion

In *Authors of Pictures, Draughtsmen of Words*, in which Hubbard investigates how children use drawings and words to make meaning, she also cites adult authors (not just picture-book authors) who found drawing helpful in their works (see chapter 6) Writers like E.B. White, e.e. cummings, D.H. Lawrence, John Dos Passos, William Faulkner, S. J. Perelman, Gabriel García Márquez, Flannery O'Connor, and John Updike rise up to remind us not to relegate only to little kids the joy of making meaning through drawing.

Finally, referencing several teachers at the middle-school and high-school levels who are giving their students the freedom "to use visual as well as verbal solutions to their problems" (152), Hubbard concludes,

Drawing is not just for children who can't yet write fluently, and creating pictures is not just part of rehearsal for real writing. Images *at any age* are part of the serious business of making meaning—partners with

words for communicating our inner designs. (157)

My experience again and again with drawing into meaning permits me to redouble her words. We must try to facilitate an environment where middle-and and high-school students discover this powerful writing tool, for as Gabriele Rico reminds us, "Before there are words, there are images" (1983, 157).

Works Cited

Brautigan, Richard. 1979. "In a Café." *Postcard Poems: A Collection of Poetry for Sharing.* Ed. Paul B. Janeczko. New York: Bradbury, 46.

Bruner, Jerome S. 1971. *On Knowing:Essays for the Left Hand.* New York: Atheneum.

Cassirer, Ernest. 1946. *Language and Myth.* Trans and preface by Susanne K. Langer. New York: Dover.

de Hamel, Joan. 1985. *Hemi's Pet.* Boston: Houghton.

Edwards, Betty. 1986. *Drawing on the Artist Within.* New York: Simon.

Elbow, Peter. 1973 *Writing Without Teachers.* New York: Oxford UP.

Emig, Janet. 1978. "Hand, Eye, Brain: Some 'Basics' in the Writing Process." *Research on Composing: Points of Departure.* Eds. Charles R. Cooper and Lee Odell. Urbana, IL: NCTE. 59–71.

Fulwiler, Toby, and Bruce Petersen. 1981. "Toward Irrational Heuristics: Freeing the Tacit Mode." *College English* 43.6 (Oct.): 621–629.

Hubbard, Ruth. 1989a. *Authors of Pictures, Draughtsmen of Words.* Portsmouth, NH: Heinemann.

———. 1989b. "Inner Designs." *Language Arts* 66.2 (Feb.): 119–136.

Lamme, Linda. 1985. "From Scribbling to Writing." *American Baby* 47.8 (Aug.): 47–48, 50.

Rico, Gabriele Lusser. 1983. *Writing the Natural Way*. Los Angeles: Tarcher.

Skupa, Judith Ann. 1985. "An Analysis of the Relationship Between Drawing and Idea Production in Writing for Second Grade Children across Three Aims of Discourse." Diss. U. of Texas at Austin.

Torrey, Joanna. 1989. "Breaking the Code of Doodles." *Omni* 11.7 (Apr): 65–69, 120–125.

Vygotsky, Lev S. 1978. *Mind in Society: The Development of Higher Psychological Processes*. Ed. Michael Cole et al. Cambridge: Harvard UP.

Winner, Ellen. 1986. "Where Pelicans Kiss Seals." *Psychology Today* 20.8 (Aug.): 24.26, 30–35.

Yanin, Valentin L. 1990. " The Archaeology of Novgorod." *Scientific American* 262.2 (Feb.): 84–91.

I

WHEN IS A PARAGRAPH?

ARTHUR A. STERN

From *College Composition and Communication,* October 1976. Copyright 1976 by the National Council of Teachers of English. Reprinted with permission.

Commentary:

This experiment is worth conducting not only with teachers, but also with students. A favorite section we like to use is affectionately referred to as "Queen Victoria." It can be found in Teaching Expository Writing *by William F. Irmscher (New York: Holt, Rinehart & Winston, 1979) or* The Sentence and the Paragraph *by Alton Beckner (Champaign, IL: National Council of Teachers of English, n.d., p. 35). The piece, written by Lytton Strachey, is about the English Constitution. Strachey wrote the piece as one paragraph.*

The English Constitution—that indescribable entity—is a living thing, growing with the growth of men, and assuming ever-varying forms in accordance with the subtle and complex laws of human character. It is the child of wisdom and chance. The wise men of 1688 molded it into the shape we know, but the chance that George I could not speak English gave it one of its essential peculiarities—the system of a Cabinet independent of the Crown and subordinate to the Prime Minister. The wisdom of Lord Grey saved it from petrification and set it upon the path of democracy. Then chance intervened once more. A female sovereign happened to marry an able and pertinacious man, and it seemed likely that an element which had been quiescent within it for years—the element of irresponsible administrative power—was about to become its predominant characteristic and change com-

For the past few years, for reasons that will soon become apparent, I have asked students in one of my courses to take part in a small, informal experiment. Each student receives a duplicated copy of the same 500-word expository passage. The passage, I explain, has been transcribed verbatim from Cleanth Brooks and Robert Penn Warren's *Fundamentals of Good Writing* (New York: Harcourt, Brace & Co., 1950), pp. 290–291, departing from the original in only one respect: the original passage was divided into two or more paragraphs; the copy contains no paragraph indentations. Their task is simply to decide into how many paragraphs they think it should be divided and to note the precise point (or points) at which they would make their divisions.

The exercise usually takes fifteen minutes or so, and we spend another ten or fifteen analyzing the results, which are invariably intriguing. We discover that some students have divided the passage into two paragraphs, others into three, still others into four or five. What is more, nearly all of these possible divisions seem justifiable—they "feel right." Most surprising of all is the fact that only five students out of the more than 100 who have tried the experiment have paragraphed the passage precisely as Brooks and Warren originally did.

These results are hardly earthshaking, I realize. They prove, if they prove anything, only that different students have different intuitions about paragraphing and that many of these intuitions turn out to be equally acceptable, equally "correct." But perhaps a few facts I have so far neglected to mention will make this discovery less trivial that it may at first appear.

First of all, the students who took part in the

exercise were not college freshmen; they were teachers of English. Secondly, most of them were committed to the theory, promulgated by many handbooks, that the paragraph is a purely "logical" unit of discourse. They believed, that is to say, that a paragraph is a group of sentences developing one central idea. They believed that good paragraphs always (or usually) contain identifiable topic sentences which always (or usually) occur toward the beginning of the paragraphs. They believed that a well-developed paragraph is "a composition in miniature." They believed accordingly, that good English teachers should concentrate on teaching their students to write good paragraphs, because good paragraphs are really good essays writ small.

My purpose in having them try my little experiment was to induce them to question the adequacy of the theory they had accepted. If, as the handbooks declare, a paragraph represents a "distinct unit of thought," why is it that we can't recognize a unit of thought when we see one? If every paragraph contains an identifiable topic sentence, then why don't all of us identify the same topic sentence? If good paragraphs are really compositions in miniature, why do some of us, given a passage not marked off into paragraphs, find in it two mini-compositions, while others find three or four or five? Aren't compositions—even miniature ones—supposed to have clear beginnings, middles, and conclusions?

Too many of us, I suspect, have based our teaching of the paragraph on a theory whose origins we do not know and whose validity we have not tested. Like the poet's neighbor in Frost's "Mending Wall," we go on repeating our fathers' sayings without ever going behind them.

Behind the logical (or "organic") theory of the paragraph lies a history replete with facts that cast doubt upon it authenticity. That history, as Paul C. Rodgers, Jr. has told us, begins a little more than a hundred years ago with Alexander Bain, a Scottish logician.[1] The fact that Bain was a logician, not a teacher of rhetoric, is itself of first importance; for he conceived the paragraph as a deductive system, a collection of sentences animated by unity of purpose, a pur-

pletely the direction of its growth. But what chance gave, chance took away. The Consort perished in his prime, and the English Constitution, dropping the dead limb with hardly a tremor, continued its mysterious life as if he had never been.

Watching teachers and students mark where they would paragraph the selection gives the same types of results that Stern chronicles. So often teachers and students paragraph and have little metacognitive reasons behind this paragraphing. Most paragraph intuitively.

When writing a paragraph, teachers in Stern's classes and other writing institutes do not follow the rule that they teach their students. Their response is, "But students must first learn how to do it by the rules before they can break them." Rather than reexamining the rule, their approach is to promulgate the rule.

There exists the possibility that answers to questions such as Stern's could vary between cultures and experiences. A unit of thought in a culture that values brevity will be radically different from the thought in a culture that values indirect and implied meaning. A case in point: Growing up in the Panhandle of Texas, language experience in our family was different from the language experience in a family from the Northeast. A typical childhood exchange would have included certain avoidance of the real issue. In fact, so often, we talked around the problem, without ever directly assaulting the situation.

In contrast to the language of my paternal family was the language of my maternal grandfather. Born and raised in Scotland, he was a man of few words. He, like Bain, dismissed anything not logical. Both grandparents raised animals for food consumption and as a child, I thought feeding the animals was a treat. Often I would adopt and anthropomorphize a chick or a bunny. When it was time for grandmother to wring the neck of the pullet, she would say something like, "I have to get dinner" or "You like my fried chicken, don't you?" On the other hand, my grandfather would say, "Don't get attached. I will have to kill the rabbit for food."

The point is that life and language affect the way we perceive structure and function. When communicating with my grandmother, I could be more lyrical. With my grandfather, I made my point and accepted his reply knowing there would be no lengthy discussions.

Soon, Rodger's observation will read, "for placing twenty-first century paragraph rhetoric . . . "

See Chapter 6.

pose announced in an opening topic statement and developed through a logically ordered sequence of statements that "iterate or illustrate the same idea."[2]

What is more, Bain appears to have constructed his deductive model by a purely deductive procedure. Making no empirical analysis of actual paragraphs, he simply transferred to his collection of sentences the classical rules governing the individual sentence—rules, now discredited, which defined the sentence as a group of words containing a subject and predicate and expressing a "complete and independent thought." Bains paragraph, notes Rodgers, "is simply a sentence writ large,"[3] that is, an extension by analogy of logic-based grammar.

Others—John Genung, Barrett Wendell, and George R. Carpenter among them—subsequently refined Bain's theory without questioning its assumptions, reducing Bain's original six principles of paragraph construction to the now familiar triad of Unity, Coherence, and Emphasis, and tacking on the added notion that the paragraph is the discourse in miniature. Bain's influence is thus responsible, Rodgers observes, "for placing twentieth-century paragraph rhetoric in a deductive cage, from which it had yet to extricate itself."[4]

The work of extrication has been quietly going forward, however. The most recent empirical testing of Bain's theory, and the most damaging to it, was undertaken by Richard Braddock in 1974.[5] Braddock's study, completed shortly before his untimely death, took specific aim at two of Bain's assertions: that all expository paragraphs have topic sentences and that topic sentences usually occur at the beginnings of paragraphs. Braddock's method of research and his findings call into question not only Bain's century-old paragraph theory but also, as I shall try to show, the procedures and generalizations of such "new" rhetoricians as Francis Christensen and Alto L. Becker.

Braddock began by making a random selection of essays published in *The Atlantic, Harper's, The Reporter, The New Yorker,* and *The Saturday Review.* Almost immediately, he ran into trouble, finding it extremely difficult to define the very item he was looking for—the topic sentence. "After several frustrating attempts to underline the appropriate T-unit where it occurred," Braddock reported, "I realized that the notion of what a topic sentences is, is not at all clear."[6] In an effort to define this central term, he developed an entire catalogue of "types" of topic sentence: the *simple* topic (the kind handbooks say all paragraphs should contain); the *delayed-completion* (a topic stated in two T-units, not necessarily adjacent); the *assembled* (not actually a sentence at all, but a composite, gummed together from fragments of several sentences running through the paragraph); and the *inferred* (a "topic sentence" nowhere explicitly stated by the writer, but construed by the reader).

Teaching paragraph "types" would extend students' awareness of the complexity of topical paragraphs.

But even after thus extending—one might say stretching—the definition of "topic sentence," Braddock found that a considerable proportion of the paragraphs in his sample contained no topic sentence of any type. In some instances, a single topic sentence governed a sequence running to several paragraphs; in others, the indentions seem "quite arbitrary." All told, fewer that half the paragraphs contained a simple topic sentence even when topic sentences of the delayed completion type were included, the total came to little more that half (55%). How many paragraphs *began* with topic sentences? Fewer than one out of seven (13%) in all the paragraphs Braddock analyzed.

This is what Irmscher calls the paragraph bloc.

These findings, Braddock noted with quiet understatement, "did not support the claims of textbook writers about the frequency and location of topic sentences in professional writing."[7] Although scientific and technical writing might present a different case, with respect to contemporary professional exposition the textbooks' claims were "just not true."[8]

This seems to be a chicken-or-egg syndrome. Textbooks propagate a notion of the topic sentence "because teachers demand it." Teachers teach it "because that's the way it is in the textbooks." And so it goes.

Braddock's study thus effectively disposes of the hand-me-down Bainalities of the textbooks. But it does more that: as I have already suggested, Braddock's empirical method and his findings cast some doubt upon certain conclusions reached by Francis Christensen and A.L. Becker, and upon the evidence those conclusions are based on.

Banality—*ordinary and uninteresting.*
Bainality—*overgeneralized or incorrect.*

In his "Generative Rhetoric of the Paragraph," Professor Christensen proposes, as did

Sometimes teachers assign writing in ways that assume collective, universal knowledge of such terms as topic sentence. This often breeds misunderstanding.

If considered from the perspective of the old paradigm A = 1, 2, 3, TRIPSQA suggests a cause and effect that is logical, linear, rigid, and absolute.

If considered from the perspective of the new paradigm that subsumes the particle, wave, and field theory of quantum physics, TRIPSQA suggests something quite different. According to Gary Zukav in The Dancing Wu Li Masters *(1984), quantum theory does not state that something can be wavelike and particlelike simultaneously, rather it depends upon the field (200–201).*

Applying particle, wave, and field quantum theory to TRIPSQA implies that paragraphing can be static and dynamic, depending upon its context.

Alexander Bain, "that the paragraph has, or may have, a structure as definable and traceable as that of the sentence and that it can be analyzed in the same way."[9] From this premise he moves rather swiftly to conclusions hardly distinguishable from Bain's:

1. The paragraph may be defined as a sequence of structurally related sentences.

2. The top sentence of the sequence is the topic sentence.

3. The topic sentence is nearly always the first sentence of the sequence.[10]

Although he subsequently allows for exceptions (some paragraphs have no topic sentence; some paragraphing is "illogical"), there is no mistaking that Christensen's second and third "rules" are essentially those which Braddock found to be false. Unlike Braddock, Christensen seems to believe that the term *topic sentence* is self-explanatory, requiring no precise definition. In support of his claims, Christensen cites the "many scores of paragraphs I have analyzed for this study."[11] He does not tell us how these paragraphs were selected or from what sources; he tells us only that in the paragraphs he analyzed "the topic sentence occurs almost invariably at the beginning."[12] Had he detailed his procedures as he did in his study of sentence openers,[13] we would have reason to be more confident of his conclusions. But he doesn't. The evidence underlying his statements about the paragraph is soft and rather vague.

A.L. Becker's "Tagmemic Approach to Paragraph Analysis," viewed in the light of Braddock's study, seems similarly flawed. Like Christensen, Becker applies to the paragraph the instruments of sentence-analysis, with the purpose of "extending grammatical theories now used in analyzing and describing sentence structure . . . to the description of paragraphs."[14] He cautions at the outset that he intends to examine the paragraph from only one of three possible perspectives—the "particle" perspective—and that his description will necessarily be somewhat distorted because it suppresses the "wave" and "field" aspects of paragraph structure. But this disclaimer hardly prepares us for his subsequent assertion that there are "two major patterns of paragraphing in expository writing,"[15] and only two: the TRI (Topic-Restriction-Illustration) pattern and the PS (Problem-Solution) pattern. Becker continues:

> Although there are more kinds of expository paragraphs than these two, I would say that the majority of them fall into one of these two major types. Many expository paragraphs which at first appear to be neither TRI or [*sic*] PS can be interpreted as variations of these patterns. . . . There are also minor paragraph forms (usually transitional paragraphs or simple lists)—and, finally, there are "bad" paragraphs, like poorly constructed, confusing sentences.[16]

Use TRIPSQA to ratiocinate a paragraph (see "Application," at the conclusion of Chapter 6), rather than as a way to write up to a paragraph.

Again, one is left in doubt as to the evidence on which these generalizations rest. Surely, in preparing his study, Professor Becker cannot have read *all* expository paragraphs; how, then, can he justify a claim concerning a "majority" of them? What were his sampling procedures? Were "bad" paragraphs included in his total count, or were they summarily rejected as unworthy of consideration? To these and other questions he provides no answers. We know only that his findings conflict sharply with Braddock's, and that, in Becker's case as in Christensen's we find somewhat disguised by modern terminology, the century-old claim that a "good" paragraph begins with a topic sentence and develops the idea stated by the topic sentence.

William Irmscher had his students replicate Braddock's research. They found much the same. Braddock is so well respected as a researcher that the National Council of Teachers of English awards outstanding research in his name each year. The Braddock Award is coveted and worthy of his legacy.

If we are ever to rid ourselves of Bain's lingering legacy we must, it seems clear, abandon his exclusively sentence-based, "particle" approach to paragraph description, an approach that treats the paragraph as if it were an isolated, self-contained unit, and imposes upon it a rigid set of logical and quasi-grammatical rules. We must adopt an approach that describes not only the internal structure of a paragraph but also its external connections with adjoining paragraphs and its function in the discourse as a whole. What we need, Paul Rodgers proposes, is "a flexible, open-ended *discourse centered* rhetoric of the paragraph":

It has been thirty-one years since Stern called for an adoption of an approach to paragraphing that describes the internal and external functions of a paragraph, and still texts have not changed.

Rhetorical choice, of course, fosters higher-level thinking skills.

All we can usefully say of *all* paragraphs at present [Rodgers explains] is that their authors have marked them off for special consideration as *stadia of discourse*, in preference to other stadia, other patterns, in the same material. Paragraph structure is part and parcel of the discourse as a whole; a given stadium becomes a paragraph not by virtue of its structure but because the writer elects to indent, his indentation functioning, as does all punctuation, as a gloss upon the overall literary process under way at that point.[17]

Paragraphing, Rodgers here suggests, is governed by rhetorical choice rather than by logical or grammatical rule. Like the structure of a sentence or that of a fully developed essay, the structure of a paragraph arises out of an *ethos* and a *pathos* as well as out of a *logos*—out of the writer's personality and his perception of his reader as well as out of his perception of the structure of his subject matter. The logic and "grammar" of a given paragraph are conditioned—sometimes powerfully—by what may be termed the psychologic and socio-logic of a particular rhetorical occasion.

"Someday it will be possible to teach paragraphing by rule and formula, though, I frankly doubt it." Powerful words from Stern. The rules are not there to support the continuation of teaching paragraphing as if there were such rules. No wonder students feel cheated when they find out they were taught and graded on something that was not even true.

As every experienced writer knows, paragraphing helps establish a tone or "voice." (Editors know this, too. That is why they frequently re-paragraph a writer's prose to bring it into conformity with their publication's image.) Short paragraphs appear to move more softly than long ones; short paragraphs lighten up the appearance of a page, whereas long ones, containing the identical information, give the page a heavier, more scholarly look. Just as he adjusts his sentences and his diction, the writer may adjust his paragraphs, deliberately or intuitively, to achieve a variety of rhetorical effects—formality of informality, abruptness or suavity, emphasis or sub-junction.

One powerful activity to use with students is a comparison of paragraphs from a work of Charles Dickens to those of most contemporary writers.

Paragraphing practices are also governed by changes in fashion and social convention. Today's paragraphs are considerably shorter than those of fifty or a hundred years ago. "In books of the last century," Paul Roberts reminds us, "a paragraph often ran through several pages, but the modern reader wants to come up for air oftener. He is alarmed by a solid mass of writing and comforted when it is broken up into chunks."[18] In consequence of this change in literary fashion, nineteenth century rules of "logical" paragraphing dubious in their own day, are outmoded now. What might once have appeared as a single paragraph is today routinely broken up into smaller units which, taken together, comprise what William Irmscher has labeled a "paragraph bloc."[19] Indeed, when Richard Braddock observed that one topic sentence frequently governed the entire sequence of paragraphs, he was suggesting that contemporary professional writers use blocs rather than single paragraphs as logical units much of the time.

In sum, today's paragraph is not a logical unit and we should stop telling our students it is. It does not necessarily begin with a topic sentence; it does not necessarily "handle and exhaust a distinct topic," as the textbooks say it must do. It is not a composition-in-miniature, either—it is not an independent, self-contained whole, but a functioning part of discourse; its boundaries are not sealed but open to the surround text; it links as often as it divides. Shaped by the writer's individual style and by the reader's expectations as well as by the logic of the subject-matter, the paragraph is a flexible, expressive rhetorical instrument.

Perhaps some day it will be possible to teach paragraphing by rule and formula, though I frankly doubt it. In any case, the rules and formulas that govern the paragraphing practices of professional writers have yet to be discovered. Let us, therefore, focus our students' attention on what they have to say—on the arguments they want to present, the points they want to make—and not on the number of indentations they should use in saying it. Let us make them think about the topics they plan to discuss rather than about he "correct" location of their topic sentences. Let us, in other words, make our teaching discourse-centered. If the whole does in indeed determine the parts, their paragraphs should improve as their essays mold them into form.

We must also stop telling students to begin a paragraph with such statements as, "I'm going to tell you a story about . . ." or "This is about . . . "

Stern, and many scholars like him, keep saying the same thing over and over—we must teach, in context, all that is to be learned. Students will learn how to paragraph if paragraphing is taught within the writing process.

464 APPENDIX I

Notes

1. Paul C. Rodgers, Jr., "Alexander Bain and the Rise of the Organic Paragraph," *Quarterly Journal of Speech,* 51 (December, 1965), 399–408.

2. Alexander Bain, *English Composition and Rhetoric* (London: Longmans, Green, 1866), cited by Rodgers, p. 404.

3. Rodgers, "Alexander Bain," p. 406.

4. Ibid., p. 408.

5. Richard Braddock, "The Frequency and Placement of Topic Sentences in Expository Prose," *Research in the Teaching of English*, 8 (Winter, 1974), 287–302.

6. Ibid., p. 291.

7. Ibid., p. 307.

8. Ibid., p. 298.

9. *Notes Toward a New Thetoric* (New York: Harper & Row, 1967), p. 54.

10. Ibid., pp. 57–58.

11. Ibid., p. 58.

12. Ibid.

13. Ibid., pp. 39–51.

14. A. L. Becker, "A Tagmemic Approach to Paragraph Analysis," in Francis Christensen et al., *The Sentence and the Paragraph* (Champaign, Il.: National Council of Teachers of English, 1966), p. 33.

15. Ibid., p. 34.

16. Ibid., p. 36.

17. Paul C. Rodgers, Jr., "A Discourse-Centered Rhetoric of the Paragraph," in Francis Christensen et al., *The Sentence and the Paragraph* (Champaign, Il.: National Council of Teachers of English, 1966), p. 42.

18. Paul Roberts, *Understanding English* (New York: Harper & Row, 1958), p. 423.

19. William F. Irmscher, *The Holt Guide to English* (New York: Holt, Rinehart and Winston, Inc., 1972), p. 86.

"THE COMPOSING PROCESS: MODE OF ANALYSIS" AND "IMPLICATIONS FOR TEACHING"

JANET EMIG
From The Composing Processes of Twelfth Graders, NCTE 1971. Copyright 1971 by National Council of Teachers of English. Reprinted with permission.

Chapter 3
The Composing Process: Mode of Analysis

The purpose of this chapter is to delineate dimensions of the composing process among secondary school students, against which case studies of twelfth-grade writers can be analyzed. As with some of the accounts of the creative process in chapter 1, the premise of this chapter is that there are elements, moments, and stages within the composing process which can be distinguished and characterized in some detail.

This delineation is presented in two forms: as an outline and as a narrative. The use of an outline, which is of course linear and single layered, to describe a process, which is laminated and recursive, may seem a paradoxical procedure; but its purpose is to give a category system against which the eight case studies can be examined. The narrative portion, in contrast, is an attempt to convey the actual density and "blendedness" of the process.

Although this category system is set forth before the analysis of the data, it was derived from an extensive analysis of the eight case studies. The procedure for analyzing the data was inductive; the presentation is deductive.

Commentary:

Students of all ages have been shown to have elements, moments, and stages within the composing process. The idiosyncratic characteristics are developmental to each grade level.

Consider the visual of placing all of these models in a three-dimensional fractal, capable of being dynamic and static at the same time. Possibly, it is akin to the quantum dot—capable of existing as a particle and wave simultaneously or separately at any given time. The quantum dot is to the silicon chip, what the microwave oven is to the campfire—highly complex.

Dimension of the Composing Process among Twelfth-Grade Writers: An Outline

1. **Context of Composing**
   Community, Family, School

2. **Nature of Stimulus**
   Registers:
   Field of Discourse—encounter with natural environment; encounter with induced environment or artifacts; human relationships; self.
   Mode of Discourse—expressive-reflexive; expressive-extensive.
   Tenor of Discourse
   Self-Encountered Stimulus
   Other-Initiated Stimulus:
   Assignment by Teacher—external features (student's relation to teacher; relation to peers in classroom; relation to general curriculum and to syllabus in English; relation to other work in composition); internal features or specification of assignment (registers, linguistic formulation, length, purpose, audience, deadline, amenities, treatment of written outcome, other).
   Reception of Assignment by Student—nature of task, comprehension of task, ability to enact task, motivation to enact task.

3. **Prewriting**
   Self-Sponsored Writing:
   Length of Period
   Nature of Musing and Elements Contemplated—field of discourse; mode of written discourse; tenor or formulating of discourse.
   Interveners and Interventions—self, adults (parents, teachers, other), peers (sibling, classmate, friend); type of intervention (verbal, nonverbal), time of intervention, reason for intervention (inferred), effect of intervention on writing, if any.
   Teacher-Initiated (or School-Sponsored) Writing:
   (Same categories as above)

These modes of discourse strike teachers as much more workable than those of other rhetoricians, such as James L. Kinneavy in Theory of Discourse. Could it be what strikes these teachers is the fact that Emig's classifications come inductively from student work, whereas Kinneavy's has been deductively imposed onto students' work?

Current state competency testing seems to ignore all or most of these elements. They place students, writing, and curricula in jeopardy with hidden agendas. Students spend hours trying to guess, "What do they want?" and "How do they want it?" Little attention is being paid to what students have to say.

It is important note that even in self-sponsored writing, peers and others still play a role in the contemplation of writing.

4. **Planning**

Self-Sponsored Writing:

Initial Planning—length of planning; mode of planning (oral; written: jotting, informal list of words/phrases, topic outline, sentence outline); scope; interveners and interventions.

Later Planning—length of planning; mode; scope; time of occurrence; reason; interveners and intervention.

Teacher-Initiated Writing:

(Same categories as above)

Here Emig refers to types of planning. Clearly, the implications for the classroom point to the use of more prewriting opportunities and the use of heuristics.

5. **Starting**

Self-sponsored Writing:

Seeming Ease or Difficulty of Decision

Element Treated First Discursively—seeming reason for initial selection of that element; eventual placement in completed piece.

Context and Conditions under Which Writing Began

Interveners and Interventions

Teacher-Initiated Writing:

(Same categories as above)

Although the starting of self-sponsored and school sponsored types of writing are the same, the results are radically different. The ownership is different. Students care far more about their own writing than they do for the writing forced upon them in schools. They keep and maintain their own writing; they seem to tolerate the school sponsored attempts.

6. **Composing Aloud: A Characterization**

Selecting and Ordering Components:

Anticipation/Abeyance—what components projected; when first noted orally; when used in written piece.

Kinds of Transformational Operations—addition (right-branching, left-branching); deletions; reordering or substitution; embedding

Style—preferred transformations, if any; "program" of style behind preferred transformations (source: self, teacher, parent, established writer, peer); (effect on handling of other components—lexical, rhetorical, imagaic).

Other Observed Behaviors:

Silence—physical writing; silent reading; "unfilled" pauses.

Vocalized Hesitation Phenomena—filler sounds (selected phonemes; morphemes of semantically-low content; phrases and clauses of semantically-low content); critical comments (lexis, syntax; rhetoric); expressions of feelings

Many of these phenomena are what inept evaluators of writing classroom characterize as poor learning environments or lack of teacher direction. As teachers move to understanding the composing processes of their students, administrators will need to move toward understanding the teaching processes of teaching writing. Mindless activity in place of real thinking cannot be allowed to flourish in classrooms.

and attitudes (statements, expressions of emotion—pleasure/pain) toward self as writer to reader; digressions (ego-enhancing; discourse-related).

Tempo of Composing:
Combinations of Composing and Hesitational Behaviors
Relevance of Certain Theoretical Statements concerning Spontaneous Speech

7. **Reformulation**
   Type of Task:
   Correcting; Revising; Rewriting
   Transforming Operations:
   Addition—kind of element; stated or inferred reason for addition.
   Deletion—kind of element; stated or inferred reason for deletion.
   Reordering or Substitution—kind of element; stated or inferred reason.
   Embedding—kind of element; stated or inferred reason.

8. **Stopping**
   Formulation:
   Seeming Ease or Difficulty of Decision
   Element Treated Last—seeming reason for treating last; placement of that element in piece.
   Context and Conditions under Which Writing Stopped
   Interveners and Interventions
   Seeming Effect of Parameters and Variables—established by others; set by self.
   Reformulation:
   (Same categories as above)

9. **Contemplation of Product**
   Length of Contemplation
   Unit Contemplated
   Effect of Product upon Self
   Anticipated Effect upon Reader

10. **Seeming Teacher Influence on Piece**
    Elements of Product Affected:
    Register—field of discourse; mode of written discourse; tenor of discourse.
    Formulation of Title or Topic; Length;

Again, the capriciousness of competency tests comes to mind. Requiring students to complete a draft of writing that shows evidence of elaboration that normally doesn't occur immediately in the writing process strikes many as unfair and as poor test construction. Performance testing appears to be the only way that an accurate assessment could be made of an impromptu situation. Portfolios show a more accurate picture of students' processes.

In many classrooms the reason for stopping a piece of writing is because of the due date. In writing/reading classrooms, teachers and students are moving away from the "due date" to a "due window." Like a space shot, there are only certain days available for launching. Certain days are given for the assignment to be turned in for evaluation. The rigid "it is due today, before the end of the period" strikes teachers and students who are involved in their own processes as antiquated.

Purpose; Audience; Deadline; Amenities; Treatment of Written Outcomes;Other.

Dimensions of the Composing Process Among Twelfth-Grade Writers: A Narrative

The first dimension of the composing process to note is the *nature of the stimulus* that activates the process or keeps it going. For students, as for any other writers, stimuli are either self encountered or other initiated. Either the student writes from stimuli with which he has privately interacted or from stimuli presented by others— the most common species of the second being, of course, the assignment given by the teacher. Both kinds of stimuli can be nonverbal or verbal, although it is an extremely rare and sophisticated teacher who can give a nonverbal writing assignment.

All areas of experience, or fields of discourse, can provide the stimuli for writing. It is useful to pause here to present the schema of registers devised by the British linguists Halliday, McIntosh, and Strevens because of the applicability of their category-system to this inquiry.

Registers these linguists define as the varieties of language from which the user of that language makes his oral and written choices.[1] Registers are divided into the following three categories: (1) the field of discourse, or the area of experience dealt with; (2) the mode of discourse, whether the discourse is oral or written; and (3) the tenor of discourse, the degree of formality of treatment.

Although, to the investigator's knowledge, the three linguists do not attempt to specify the various fields of discourse, it seems a refinement helpful for a closer analysis of the composing process. In his essay on poetic creativity, the psychologist R.N. Wilson divides experiences tapped by writers into four categories: (1) encounters with the natural (nonhuman) environment; (2) human interrelations; (3) symbol systems; and (4) self.[2] For the analysis of student writing in this inquiry, "symbol systems" becomes "encounters with induced environments or artifacts."

Linda Waitkus revealed in her study ("The Effect of Poetic Writing on Transactional Writing: A Case Study Investigating the Writing of Three High School Seniors." Ed.D. diss. [New Brunswick, NJ: Rutgers University, 1982]) that students who learned skills, mechanics, and grammar while engaged in writing reflexively retained this knowledge, while the information conveyed during extensive writings were not retained. Often she found students regressed in their manipulations of such skills.

Here we are reminded of Halliday's uses of language ("The Uses of Language," Language Arts 54, no. 6 [September 1977]: 638–644):

1. *instrumental—I want—language used for getting things done, for satisfying material needs*
2. *regulatory—Do as I tell you—language used for controlling the behavior, feelings, attitude of others*
3. *interactional—Me and you; me against you—language used for getting along with others, for establishing status*
4. *personal—Here I come—language used to express individuality or awareness of self*
5. *heuristic—Tell me why—language used to seek and test knowledge*
6. *imaginative—Let's pretend—language used to create new worlds*
7. *representational—I've got something to tell you—language used to communicate*

Frank Smith adds three of his own:

8. *divertive—Enjoy this—language used to have fun*

9. *contractual—How it must be—language used to regulate*
10. *perpetuating—How it was—language used to preserve*

To which Yetta Goodman ("Relating Reading and Writng," speech given at the 32nd annual meeting of the Conference on College Composition and Communication, 26–28 March 1981, Dallas) has added:

11. *ritualistic—How are you; Fine— (phatic) language used for getting along with others*
12. *extending memory—I can remember this now—language used to retain data*
13. *instructional—Here is what I know— language used by authority to test knowledge.*

The case of language being dynamic and mutative is evidenced here. American English and British English are changing dennotatively and connotatively. Britton et al.'s terms do not work for us.

Another useful refinement of the system of registers is to divide the category "the written mode of discourse: into species. In their speculations on modes of student writing, Britton, Rosen, and Martin of the University of London have devised the following schema:

Fig. J.1. Modes of Student Writing.

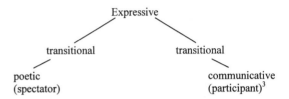

They regard all writing as primarily expressive—that is, expressing the thoughts and feelings of the writer in relation to some field of discourse. But beyond sheer expressiveness, writing evolves toward, or becomes, one of two major modes; *poetic*, in which the student observes some field of discourse, behaving as a spectator; or *communicative*, in which the student somehow participates through his writing in the business of the world. The many exemplars of writing Britton, Rosen, and Martin regard as mid-mode they have called *transitional* writings. (One longs to give the two kinds of transitional writing exponents, as with Hayakawa's cow[1] and cow[2].)

To this investigator, the notion that all student writings emanate from an expressive impulse and that they then bifurcate into two major modes is useful and accurate. Less satisfactory are the terms assigned to these modes and the implications of these terms about the relation to the writing self to the field of discourse. The terms are at once too familiar and too ultimate. Both *poetic* and *communicative* are freighted with connotations that intrude. *Poetic*, for example, sets up in most minds a contrast with prose, or prosaic, although in this schema the poetic mode includes certain kinds of prose, such as the personal fictional narrative. Second, they are too absolute: rather than describing two general kinds of relations between the writer and his world, they specify absolute states—either passivity or participation.

The following schema seems at once looser and more accurate:

Fig. J.2. Modes of Student Writing.

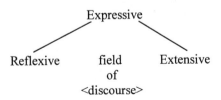

Modes of Student Writing

The terms *reflexive* and *extensive* have the virtue of relative unfamiliarity in discussions of modes of discourse. Second, they suggest two general kinds of relations between the writing self and the field of discourse—the *reflexive*, a basically contemplative role: "What does this experience mean?"; the *extensive*, a basically active role: "How, because of this experience, do I interact with my environment?" Note that neither mode suggests ultimate states of passivity or participation. Note too that the mid-modes or transitional writings have been eliminated from this schema as a needless complexity—at this time.

Subcategories can be established as well for the register, "tenor of discourse," which concerns the distance observed between the writing self and field of discourse, expressed by the degree of formality observed in the writing itself. Formality or decorum in written discourse can be established by one or more of the following means: lexical choices, syntactic choices, rhetorical choices. Obviously, the most formal discourse would employ all three means. The next question, of course, is what constitutes decorum for these three means.

Most past and current composition guides have been predicated upon the belief that there are established and widely accepted indices of written decorum and that student writers of all ages can learn and employ them. Levels of diction really refer to corpora of lexical items that are consigned some place on a formality continuum. Syntactically, certain orderings of words are regarded as more formal than others: the

It is this loose and accurate terminology that makes reflexive and extensive so applicable to the classroom. In contrast, Kinneavey uses narrative, descriptive, and classificatory as his modes of writing. To these he added purposes: expressive, persuasive, and informative. Finding real writing that adheres to a strict definition for the modes and purposes is difficult, if not impossible. Real writers overlap, weave in and out of Kinneavey's divisions. Worse yet is trying to produce a piece of writing that sticks to a single mode. Emig's terms are more fluid. They come from the real writing of real students, so to find examples is easy—to produce is natural. Kinneavy's discourse is old paradigm—either/or. It arises from Aristotelian rhetoric. Emig's discourse is new paradigm—both/all. It reflects newer philosophies of Bakhtin, Richards, Langer, Derrida, and Pierce. It is a kind of abduction; it allows for the mind to range over all possibilities.

Because of the fractuality (fractual is motion) of these lexical items, their changes are varied and sometimes hurried. Teaching these to student writers can become frustrating. Because texts are often three years old before adoption; because they stay in adoption for up to ten years, the

changes can come and go before some even have the opportunity to dismiss them as "new." So the need for teachers to maintain their own reading and writing becomes a most important task of teaching.

"balanced" sentence, for example, as against the "loose" sentence. Rhetorically, certain arrangements of sentences and the kinds of signals that precede and connect them are also regarded as more formal than others; for example, the use of explicit "lead sentence" and explicit transitional devices such as *nevertheless* and *however.*"

The teacher-initiated assignment as stimulus has specifiable dimensions. It occurs within a context that may affect it in certain ways. Included in this context are relationships the student writer may have with his peers or, more importantly—given the teacher-centered nature of very many American classrooms—with his teacher; the general curriculum in English being enacted, and the specific activities in composition of which the assignment is a part; and the other stimuli that have immediately accompanied the assignment, with the sequence and mode of these probably very important. As an example of the last: if a teacher shows a film as stimulus for writing, do her words precede the film, or follow it, or both? Here, as with the other dimensions specified, no research of any consequence has been undertaken.

Internal aspects of the assignment that may bear upon the student's writing process, and product, include the following specifications: (1) registers—the field of discourse, the written mode, and the tenor; (2) the linguistic formulation of the assignment; (3) the length; (4) the purpose; (5) the audience; (6) the deadline; (7) the amenities, such as punctuation and spelling; and (8) the treatment of written outcome—that is, if the teacher plans to evaluate the product, how—by grade? comment? conference? peer response? or by some combination of these?

The reception of the assignment by the student is affected by the following: (1) the general nature of the task, particularly the registers specified; (2) the linguistic formulation of the assignment; (3) the student's comprehension of the task; (4) his ability to enact the task; and (5) his motivation to enact the task. There is now some empirical evidence that not all students can write with equal ease and skill in all modes.[4] For the less able student some species of mode present almost insuperable difficulties—for example, the impersonal argument in which the

Joyce Carroll Oates's words seem poignant here: "[We] can't pretend to not know what is known" ("Excerpts from a Journal," Georgia Review *44, nos. 1 and 2: 121–134).*

writer is to present "dispassionately" more than one side, or aspect, of a case. Consequently, if a teacher gives an assignment requiring writing in this sub-mode, certain students may be unable to complete adequately, or even to begin, such an assignment. Along with being intellectively unable to perform the assignment, the student may also be unmotivated or psychically unable to perform the assignment. Such "block" may emanate from strikingly different sources: the student may find the task too boring, or he may find the task too threatening. He may not want to write, again, about his summer vacation or the function of Banquo's ghost; or about family life, if his father has just lost his job or if his mother has just threatened divorce.

Next, there are two possible preludes to the act of writing: *prewriting* and *planning*. *Prewriting* is that part of the composing process that extends from the time a writer begins to perceive selectively certain features of his inner and/or outer environment with a view to writing about them—usually at the instigation of a stimulus—to the time when he first puts words or phrases on paper elucidating that perception.

Planning refers to any oral and written establishment of elements and parameters before or during a discursive formulation. Prewriting occurs but once in a writing process; planning can occur many times.

Whether or not a piece of writing is self- or other-initiated affects both prewriting and planning. If the piece is teacher-initiated and if the assignment is highly specific, particularly as to a fairly immediate deadline, it is likely that the prewriting period will be brief—or that the paper will be late. Planning is intricately affected by the nature of the assignment as well. One way of regarding an assignment is as the part the teacher takes in the planning of a piece of writing. If the teacher's part is extensive—as in specifying registers, length, purpose, audience —it is obvious that the part a student plays in his own planning is diminished. There seems to be some evidence that a delicate balance, if not a paradox, exists in the giving of assignments. If the teacher sets too many of the variables for a piece of writing (we need to know far more about how many are too many, and which vari-

Faulkner's career illuminates this dichotomy between what the writer wants to write and what the writer is told to write. While Faulkner's novels propel readers headlong into intellectual discovery, his films sent the viewer out for popcorn. He could not write under a Hollywood system, though he could write what he wanted to write.

At first glance, the response to "Prewriting occurs but once," might be "I don't think so." But upon reflection, a new prewriting starts a new process. Prewriting signals another start.

Schools are still full of teachers who say, "I give my students choices." Which is translated into, "Select one of the following topics for your paper." Sure the student has a choice—he/she gets to pick from one of the teacher's topics. And teachers wonder why students have malaise about writing.

Secondary teachers are finding that honors, gifted, and Advanced Placement students resist with fervor ambiguity or freedom. These students have learned to play a certain academic game and balk when they feel the rules have changed. Examining their writing reveals they have mastered the formula. They know what gets the A. They are not too eager to take risks in their writing for fear of a lower GPA. Curricula cannot be governed by the pressures these students and their parents can place upon them. Thinking and discovery should govern the curriculum, not the ranking of a student average.

ables are more significant than others), some students feel too confined, too constricted by the limitations to write "well." If the teacher does not specify enough variables (again, how many are enough, and for what student?), the task may daunt at least some students by its ambiguity or by its degrees of freedom. If there are individual differences here, which students learn from highly specified assignments and which from loose assignments? And if future empirical studies suggest giving more than a single assignment to accommodate these differences in responses, how can the teacher be certain there is some equality in the tasks he assigns? Again, far more research needs to be undertaken in this area of the teaching of composition.

For the phases of prewriting and planning, as in almost every other phase that follows, a category in the outline is "Interveners and Interventions." It is an extremely rare situation for writers, particularly student writers, to proceed from initial stimulus to final draft, or revision, without interruption. Rather, events and people—teachers, notably—intervene; and in major enough ways to affect the process of writing, and the product.

Interveners, for the purposes of this study, will be defined as persons who enter into the composing process of another. For student writers, interveners are most often two sorts of adults, teachers and parents; and one sort on contemporary, a friend, in self-sponsored.

Starting is a specifiable moment in the process of writing—and the one perhaps most resistant to logical characterization and analysis. Certain psychoanalytic or certain learning theories provide explanations as to why a writer starts to write. If one accepts the major Freudian metaphor of the tri-partite self, starting can be regarded as the moment when the id, or the unconscious, is, in R.N. Wilson's terms, "the least amenable to ego mastery," and breaks through the controls usually exerted by the ego and super-ego.[5]

Because of the clearly profound, and opaque, nature of this moment, the kinds of elements that can be accurately specified, that exhibit themselves in behavior, are contextual—and, usually, trivial. Examples here are where, physically, the writer is when he begins and what habits or rituals he observes. Perhaps the most significant feature of starting that can be readily observed is what element the writer first places on paper, and where in the finished piece that element occurs, if at all.

For the purposes of this inquiry, eight twelfth graders attempt to compose aloud. The assumption here is that *composing aloud*, a writer's effort to externalize his process of composing, somehow reflects, if not parallels, his actual inner process.

At least three interesting questions can be asked about this particular, and peculiar, form of verbal behavior. First, are there recurring characteristics as one or more persons compose aloud? Second, if so, can a category-system be devised by which these behaviors can be usefully classified? Three, can provocative hypotheses be generated to account for these behaviors?

Composing aloud can be characterized as the alternation of composing behaviors that directly pertain to the selection and ordering of components for a piece of written discourse, and those which do not.

Anticipating is different from planning in the following three ways: Planning involves the projection of a total piece of discourse; anticipating, the projection of a portion of discourse. Planning does not occur in the language of the piece; anticipating often employs the exact lexicon and syntax that will appear in the finished piece of discourse.

Finally, anticipating, as Jerome Bruner notes, shuttles between the present and the future; planning does not:

The speaker or writer rides ahead of rather than behind the edge of his utterance. He is organizing ahead, marshaling thoughts and words and transforming them into utterances, anticipating what requires saying. If the listener is trafficking back and forth between the present and the immediate past, the speaker is principally shuttling between the present and the future . . . The tonic effect of speaking is that one thrusts the edge of the present toward the future. In one

Composing aloud is uniquely different from speech. Early childhood educators can attest to children "languaging" differently when they are "reading" from scribbles, than when they are talking. In writing institutes we have noted a few participants who due to their writing anorexia would compose aloud in grouping or sharing sessions. These compositions always resemble writing more than talk.

Nancy Willard describes it this way:

The game was simple. It required two people: the teller and the listener. The teller's task was to describe a place as vividly as possible. The object of the game was to convince the listener she was there. The teller had to carry on the description until the listener said, "Stop, I'm there." . . . At the height of my telling, something unforeseen happened. My sister burst into tears.

"Stop!" she cried. "I'm there!"

I looked at her in astonishment . . .

But to cry at a place pieced together out of our common experience and our common language, a place that would vanish the minute I stopped talking! That passed beyond the bound of the game altogether . . .

The joy of being the teller stayed with me, however, and when people asked me, "What do you want to be when you grow up?" I answered, "I want to tell stories" (153–154).

(Nancy Willard, "The Well-tempered False-hood: The Art of Storytelling," A Nancy Willard Reader: Selected Poetry and Prose *[Hanover: Middlebury College Press, 1991], pp. 153–154.)*

The kind of self-censoring due to lack of knowledge or interest should be acceptable, valid reasons to eliminate options, but when self-censoring occurs due to environment, prejudices, or teacher bias, then students have an obligation to resist this type of censorship.

Another excellent way to see this breakdown is in William L. Stull's Combining and Creating: Sentence Combining and Generative Rhetoric. *Two hundred and thirty-seven professional writers such as Steinbeck, Hemingway, and Faulkner, as well as essayists such as Joan Didion, Lewis Thomas, and Walter Lippmann make up 90 percent of the sentence combining exercises. Examination of their style becomes a natural extension to the sentence combining.*

case anticipation is forced into abeyance. In the other it dominates the activity.[6]

Student writers frequently demonstrate the phenomenon of anticipation in their writing as they compose aloud. They anticipate the use of a theme or of an element, then return to the present portion of discourse, to fill out the intervening matter. There are clear signs of efficiently divided attention, as they focus upon the here-and-now while at the same time considering where the future element will eventually, and best, appear.

There are other strategies a writer follows in dealing with the elements or components of discourse: he can accept, and immediately employ, an element; he can accept, then immediately abandon or delete his choice (if too much time intervenes, the action becomes reformulation or revision); or he can combine the element in some way with other elements in the discourse. (*Author's note:* The kind of self-censoring that eliminates an option before it is uttered is outside the purview of this inquiry.)

When dealing with syntactic components—and one must note at once that there are also lexical, rhetorical, and imagaic components—these actions córrespond to the basic transforming operations—addition; deletion; reordering or substitution; and combination, especially embedding.[7]

In his article, "Generative Grammars and the Concept of Literary Style," Richard Ohmann gives the following definition of style: "Style is in part a characteristic way of deploying the transformational apparatus of a language."[8] As illustrations, he breaks down passages from Faulkner ("The Bear"), Hemingway ("Soldier's Home"), James ("The Bench of Desolation"), and Lawrence (*Studies in Classic American Literature*) into kernel sentences and notes that, for each, a different cluster of optional transformations is favored. The special "style" of Faulkner, for example, seems partially dependent upon his favoring three transformations: the relative, or *wh,* [who, where, etc.], transformation, the conjunctive transformation, and the comparative transformation.[9]

There is no reason to believe that nonprofessional writers do not also have their characteristic ways "of deploying the transformational apparatus of a language," although these ways may be less striking, with less reliance on "a very small amount of grammatical apparatus."[10] (Query: when teachers or critics say that a writer has "no style," is what they mean that the writer in question has no strongly favored ways of transforming?)

The next question, of course, becomes why one favors a given cluster of transforms. One explanation seems to be that a writer is following some sort of "program" of style, a series of principles, implied or explicit, of what constitutes "good" writing. For example, he might break the concept "coherence" into a set of behavioral objectives, such as "Be clear about referents" and "Repeat necessary lexical elements."

Composing aloud does not occur in a solid series of composing behaviors. Rather, many kinds of hesitation behaviors intervene.[11] The most common of these are making filler sounds; making critical comments; expressing feelings and attitudes, toward the self as writer, to the reader; engaging in digressions, either ego-enhancing or discourse-related; and repeating elements. Even the student writer's silence can be categorized: the silence can be filled with physical writing (sheer scribal activity); with reading; or the silence can be seemingly "unfilled"— "seemingly" because the writer may at these times be engaged in very important nonexternalized thinking and composing.

While not the same type of silence, Tillie Olsen's Silences *(1989) is a poetic and powerful account about the silences in the lives of writers who are women.*

The alternation of composing behaviors and of hesitation phenomena gives composing aloud a certain rhythm or tempo. It is interesting to speculate that a writer may have a characteristic tempo of composing, just as he may use a characteristic cluster of transforms.

Composing aloud captures the behaviors of planning and of writing. Partly because of the very definition of reformulation, and partly because of the attitudes of the twelfth graders toward this portion of the composing process, it does not capture reformulating.

Writing and reformulating differ in significant ways. One is in the role memory is asked

*John Frederick Nims (*Western Wind *[New York: Random House, 1974]) writes, "According to Robert Frost, there 'are virtually but two [rhythms], strict iambic and loose iambic'." Nims continues, "Walking, too, with our legs and arms swinging in pendulum time, has developed our feeling for rhythms. Goethe composed many of his poems while walking. So, in our own day, did Voznesensky: 'I may be walking down a street or in the woods . . . and a rhythm starts inside, maybe connected with my breathing. . . . ' The kind of work that man and woman did for countless centuries— sowing, mowing, woodchopping, spinning,* *rocking the cradle—encouraged rhythmical expressions. Robert Graves believes that our most vigorous rhythms originated in the ringing of hammers on the anvil and the pulling of oars through the sea."*

to play. Another is in the nature and number of interferences in the two portions of the composing process. In writing, the memory is seldom asked to recall more than the words and the structures in the given unit of discourse upon which the writer is working and, possibly, in the unit immediately preceding. In reformulating, the memory is asked to recall larger units of discourse for longer periods of time, again the "noise" of all intervening experiences. (In writing itself, the major form of "noise" seems to be the physical act of writing, the scribal activity.)

A third way they differ is in the relative roles of encoding and decoding in the two portions of the process. In writing, encoding—the production of discourse—is clearly dominant. Decoding during the act of writing for the most part consists of rereading one's own recently formulated, and remembered, words in short, retrospective scannings. In reformulation, decoding plays a larger role because of the intervention of a longer period of time and the consequent forgetting that has occurred. One becomes more truly the reader, rather than the writer, of a given piece of discourse—that is, he views his writing from the point of view of a reader who needs all possible grammatical and rhetorical aids for his own comprehension.

Writing takes on important implications to reading instruction. When the student writes, the student is engaged in the act of reading and rereading. Writing demands both writing and reading. Reading alone does not demand as rigorous a commitment to the mind as writing.

Reformulation can be of three sorts: correcting, revising, and rewriting. The size of the task involved differs among the three: correcting is a small, and usually trivial, affair that consists of eliminating discrete "mechanical errors" and stylistic infelicities. Another-imposed task, correcting is synonymous with composing in the minds of many secondary and elementary school teachers of composition. Revising is a larger task involving the reformulation of larger segments of discourse and in more major and organic ways—a shift of point of view toward the material in a piece; major reorganizations and restructurings. While others may recommend correcting, the writer himself must accede to the value of the task of revising. Rewriting is the largest of the three, often involving total reformulation of a piece in all its aspects; or the scrapping of a given piece, and the writing of a fresh one.

Many teachers mistake grading for the act of correcting. Grading means to determine the quality of, or evaluate. These same teachers spend eons of their time correcting papers. They spend very little time grading. And detrimental to students, they bestow grades based on the correcting.

Stopping represents a specifiable moment—

rather, moments—in the writing process because, of course, a writer stops more than once
although the final stopping, like the first starting—the first placement of words on a page—
has special, or exaggerated, characteristics. One
stops at the ends of drafts or versions of a piece
of writing; he stops when he thinks the piece is
finished—when he feels he has worked through
or worked out the possibilities, contentive and
formal, that interest him in the piece; he also
stops for the purpose of presenting a piece in a
given state for the reading—and, usually, evaluation—of one or more others.

Maybe writing is never finished; maybe it is just abandoned.

These moments and motives for stopping do
not necessarily coincide. Again, whether or not
a piece of writing is assigned affects stopping as
it affects almost every other phase in the writing
process. If an imposed deadline forces the writer
to submit a piece of writing for reading and
evaluation before he is content with his formulation, before he experiences closure, states of
tension develop that make the act of stopping
painful, if not impossible. Hypothesis: Stopping
occurs most "easily" when one's personal sense
of closure occurs at the same time as a deadline
imposed by oneself or by others.

How can teachers structure classrooms where the closure and the deadline are "easy" for the writer?

The next moment to be noted is the *contemplation of product*—the moment in the process
when one feels most godlike. One looks upon
part, or all, of his creative and finds it—good?
uneven? poor? If he has not steadily, or even
erratically, kept his reader in mind during the
process, the writer may think of him now and
wonder about the reception the piece will experience in the world.

The final category concerns the *seeming influence* by a teacher or by a group of teachers
upon the piece of student writing. There are five
sources of information about this elusive matter
of influences: student statement; student practice; teachers' written evaluations of former
pieces, if available; student descriptions of composition teaching experienced; and, the most
difficult information to obtain, what those composition teachers actually do in the classroom as
they "teach" composition.

Portfolio assessment will allow for teach-ers and students to analyze and hypothe-size about these influences of writing.

This chapter represents a theoretical sketch of
one of the most complex processes man engages
in. Although it is roughly taxonomic, it does not

of course purport to be exhaustive. Nonetheless, almost every sentence contains or implies hypotheses upon which one could spend a lifetime in empirical research. Perhaps investigators other than the writer will find here materials for provocative questions and generative hypotheses about the composing process, particularly of students.

Chapter 7
Implications for Teaching
(excerpt)

This inquiry strongly suggests that, for a number of reasons, school-sponsored writing experienced by older American secondary students is a limited, and limiting, experience. The teaching of composition at this level is essentially unimodal, with only extensive writing given sanction in many schools. Almost by definition, this mode is other-directed—in fact it is other-centered. The concern is with sending a message, a communication out into the world for the edification, the enlightenment, and ultimately the evaluation of another. Too often, the other is a teacher, interested chiefly in a product he can criticize rather than is a process he can help initiate through imagination and sustain through empathy and support.

A species of extensive writing that recurs so frequently in student accounts that it deserves special mention is the *five-paragraph theme*, consisting of one paragraph of introduction ("tell what you are going to say"), three of expansion and example ("say it"), and one of conclusion ("tell what you have said"). This mode is so indigenously American that it might be called the Fifty-Star Theme. In fact, the reader might imagine behind this and the next three paragraphs Kate Smith singing "God Bless America" or the piccolo obligato from "The Stars and Stripes Forever."

Why is the Fifty-Star Theme so tightly lodged in the American composition curriculum? The reason teachers often give is that this essentially redundant form, devoid, or duplication, of content in a least two of its five parts,

Forty years later, school-sponsored writing is still the major experience by most secondary students. The real tragedy is not just the fact that so little change has occurred, but that the "push down" effect on middle school and elementary school curricula have younger writers experiencing more and more extensive writing. A balance is still to be found. Might the fact that 49 percent of high school students drop out of school be attributed to the type of curriculum? Students involved in the process of learning stay in school. Students tested daily on the products of learning lose interest.

Critics of writing as a process clamor over the loss of this formula. Because the only thing they understand about composition is this formula, they cannot imagine teaching anything else.

As recently as the April/May, 2007 issue of Reading Today, *to our horror, a headline blared: "The Five-Paragraph Essay Goes Digital." We immediately wrote to IRA and received this reply: "Thank you for your letter of concern about the Essay Map. The rationale for developing that resource was that, for better or worse, many teachers use that essay format as a way to prepare students for the types of writing they face on standardized tests, and the highlighted lessons on ReadWriteThink.org* exists outside their classrooms, and in very high places—notable, freshman English classes; "business"; and in the "best practices" of the "best writer"—that, in other words, this theme somehow fulfills requirements somewhere in the real world.

This fantasy is easy to disprove. If one takes a constellation of writers who current critical judgment would agree are among the best American writers of the sixties—Norman Mailer, Truman Capote, Philip Roth, Saul Bellow; and their juniors, Gloria Steinem and Tom Wolfe— where, even in their earliest extensive writings, can one find a single example of any variation of the Fifty-Star Theme?

As to freshman English classes, the assumption is that freshman English is a monolith, rather than a hydra-headed monster with perhaps as many curricula and syllabi as there are harassed section men and graduate assistants. In "business," where can one write the Fifty-Star Theme except as a letter to an unheeding computer or as a Pentagon memorandum?

The absence of match between what is being taught secondary—and, undoubtedly, elementary—students and the practices of the best current writers is partially attributable to teacher illiteracy: how many of the teachers described in this inquiry, would one guess, have read one or more of the writers mentioned above? Yet without such reading of wholly contemporary writers, teachers have no viable sources of criteria for teaching writing in the seventies, even in the single mode they purport to teach. No wonder that many of the students who are better- and newer-read reject models that are as old as exemplars in the secretary guides of the late eighteenth century and as divorced from the best literature of their time. (This is not to say that the only models should be works of the late twentieth century; great works from all centuries are contemporary, as the writings of Donne, Swift, Coleridge, and Carroll will attest.)

More crucial, many teachers of composition, at least below the college level, themselves do not write. The have no recent, direct experience of a process they purport to present to others. One reason may be that there are in the United

help teachers and students use the format in a more interesting, interactive way."

Also, the online tool is simply a graphic organizer to help students map out (or organize) their information/thoughts before writing. As such, it could be used as an optional resource to support various forms of writing for those teachers who feel it will benefits (sic) the needs of their students (Bridget Hilferty, Project Manager, ReadWriteThink.org, International Reading Association).

"For better or worse"? In light of Emig's research, this so called "tool" is neither useful nor does it promote reading, writing or thinking. It is formula pure and simple and cannot be guised otherwise.

Gabriele Lusser Rico, in October 1988 issue of English Journal, *wrote, "Against Formulaic Writing." In that article, she states, "Indeed, the five-paragraph essay rewards formulaic writing, and formulaic writing is more often that not dull and lifeless . . . The human mind is not a straight thinker. It makes associative leaps, responds to the rhythms and patterns of language, and takes deep pleasure in shaping wholes meaningful to the writing self; for writing is first and foremost an act of self-definition, and the shape it takes is part of that self-defining process. If we superimpose a formula on this indeterminate process, we will hobble this innate mental capability and block diversity of expression" (57).*

We were working with a group of English teachers in one of the largest cities in the United States, in one of the most progressive school districts in the city. They were given the opportunity to reveal what they knew about the last twenty years of Pulitzer Prize–winning poets. Out of 150 teachers, middle school and high school, only 7 knew of or recognized more than seven of the twenty poets. Over 90 percent of the teachers admitted to never reading any of these poets. They all recognized every eighteenth-century poet and poem given. One implication might be their knowledge of poetry is three centuries behind. By now, hopefully they are not four centuries out of touch.

Many teachers believe that knowing the terms of the writing process are the same as experiencing them. As long as they have the belief system, they will continue to underconceptualize and oversimplify.

Many secondary teachers still see themselves as "American Lit" teachers, or "British Lit" teachers. They do not see their roles as writing teachers. They will not be what they are not—writers.

Teachers often assign revision as a homework assignment. Consider this as precursor to failure. If a student is asked to revise without teacher intervention and assistance, how and what will the student revise?

States very few teacher-training institutions which have intensive and frequent composing as an organic part of the curriculum for young and for experienced teachers of English. In England, such programs seem more common, as do experiences in allied arts through creative arts workshops.[1] When, if ever, have our secondary school teachers painted, sung, or sculpted under any academic auspices?

Partially because they have no direct experience of composing, English err in important ways. They underconceptualize and oversimplify the process of composing. Planning degenerates into outlining; reformulating becomes the correction of minor infelicities.

They truncate the process of composing. From the accounts of the twelfth-grade writers in this sample one can see that in self-sponsored writing, students engage in prewriting activities that last as long as two years. In most American high schools, there are no sponsored pre-writing activities: there is no time provided, and no place where a student can ever be alone, although all accounts of writers tell us a condition of solitude is requisite for certain kinds of encounters with words and concepts. (If teachers assume that the student will find elsewhere the solitude the school does not provide, let them visit the houses and apartments in which their students live.)

At the other end of the process, revision is lost, not only because it is too narrowly defined but because, again, no time is provided for any major reformulation or reconceptualization. Despite the introduction of modular scheduling in a few schools, a Carnegie-unit set toward writing, and the other arts, still prevails.

Much of the teaching of composition in American high schools is probably too abstract for the average and below-average students. This inquiry has shown that some able students can translate an abstract directive such as "Be concise" into a set of behaviors involving the selection of lexical, syntactic, and rhetorical options. But there is no indication they were taught how to make such a translation in schools. There is also no indication that less able students can do such translating on their own—at least, without constant and specific guidance by their teachers.

Much of the teaching of composition in American high schools is essentially a neurotic activity. There is little evidence, for example, that the persistent pointing out of specific errors in student themes leads to the elimination of these errors, yet teachers expend much of their energy in this futile and unrewarding exercise. Another index of neurosis is the systematic confusion of accidents and essences (one wonders, at times, if this confusion does not characterize American high schools in general). Even the student who, because of the health of his private writing life, stays somewhat whole is enervated by worries over peripherals—spelling, punctuation, length. In *The Secret Places*, as elsewhere in his writing, David Holbrook describes these emphases:

> Children become terrified of putting down a word misspelt, particularly an unfamiliar word, that they don't put down any words. I have seen it happen to a child of 8, who wrote long marvelous stories. After a year with a teacher who wrote 'Please be more tidy,' 'Your spelling is awful,' 'Sloppy'— and never a good word, she stopped altogether. She wrote little lies, a sentence at a time, in a 'diary.' 'Coming to school today I saw an elephant.' It wasn't true. But that was all she was damn-well going to write— neat, complete, grammatical, well-spelt, short, and essentially illiterate lies. For her the word had been divorced from experience. The deeper effect is to make the learning process one separated from sympathy, and a creative collaborative interest in exploring the wonder of being.[4]

What is needed for the reversal of the current situation? Assuredly, frequent, inescapable opportunities for composing for all teachers of writing especially in reflexive writing, such as diaries and journals.

For teachers at all levels, given the mysterious nature of learning and teaching, surely some value will adhere to having their own experi-

One teacher told us that spelling tests were a part of the culture of the school and community, and the culture could not be changed.

One teacher evaluator came into the room while the teacher and students were involved in the act of writing, he said, "I'll come back when you are teaching."

Change is happening. Once a teacher understands and teaches according to learning, reading, and writing processes, they cannot go back to the skill and drill approach.

ences shaped into words for pondering, perhaps into meaning and illumination.

Perhaps their students will gain benefits as well, as the result of such teacher training. Perhaps teachers will abandon the unimodal approach to writing and show far greater generosity in the width of writing invitations they extend to all students. One wonders at times if the shying away from reflexive writing is not an unconscious effort to keep the "average" and "less able" students from the kind of writing he can do best and, often, far better than the "able," since there is so marvelous a democracy in the distribution of feeling and of imagination.

Finally, a shift may consequently come in who evaluates whom, and to what end. In this inquiry we have seen that the most significant others in the private, and often the school-sponsored, writing of twelfth graders are peers, despite the overwhelming opportunity for domination teachers hold through their governance of all formal evaluation. American high schools and college must seriously and immediately consider that the teacher-centered presentation of composition, like the teacher-centered presentation of almost every other segment of a curriculum, is pedagogically, developmentally, and politically an anachronism.

There is too much at stake for teachers not to make this change. Failure to do so threatens the very fabric of our society. The change reflects a geo-political shift as well as the educational one. Threatened paradigms that refuses to change are ultimately destroyed within. Already evidence of a newer paradigm can be seen. Adherence to a dying paradigm is not productive. Emig's words speak truth—the world has little tolerance for anachronistic practices.

Notes

Chapter 3

1. M.A.K. Halliday, Angus McIntosh, and Peter Strevens, *The Linguistic Sciences and Language Teaching,* p. 77.

2. Wilson, "Poetic Creativity," p. 167.

3. Harold Rosen, Lecture, NDEA Institute in English Composition, University of Chicago, July 1968.

4. Research of James Britton, Nancy Martin, and Harold Rosen, Institute of Education, University of London.

5. Wilson, "Poetic Creativity," p. 168.

6. Jerome Bruner, "Teaching a Native Language," *Toward a Theory of Instruction,* p. 103. Copyright 1966 by Belknap Press of Harvard University Press. Used by permission.

7. For an interesting discussion of the ordering of elements, see Francis Christensen's "A Generative Rhetoric of the Sentence," *Notes Toward a New Rhetoric,* pp. 1–22.

8. Richard Ohmann, "Generative Grammars and the Concept of Literary Style," *Word* (1964), p. 431.

9. Ibid., p. 433.

10. Ibid.

11. The terminology employed in this section is, for the most part, borrowed from the studies of hesitation phenomena, particularly from "Hesitation Phenomena in Spontaneous English Speech" by Howard Maclay and Charles E. Osgood, *Readings in the Psychology of Language,* pp. 305–24.

Chapter 7 (excerpt)

1. See the accounts, for example, in Sybil Marshall, *An Experiment in Education;* and David Holbrook, *The Secret Places: Essays on Imaginative Work in English Teaching and on the Culture of the Child.*

2. From *The Secret Places* by David Holbrook, p. 69. Copyright © by David Holbrook. Used by permission of the University of Alabama Press.

INDEX

ABOUT THE AUTHORS

JOYCE ARMSTRONG CARROLL (Ed.D., H.L.D.) has taught most grade levels, was professor of English and Writing at McMurry University, and is co-director of Abydos Learning International, formerly the New Jersey Writing Project in Texas (NJWPT), with her husband Edward E. Wilson. Carroll has served as President of the Texas Council of Teachers of English Language Arts, served on the National Council of Teachers of English's Commission on Composition, and was Chair of NCTEs Standing Committee Against Censorship. She has written numerous books for teachers such as *Dr. JAC's Guide to Writing with Depth, Authentic Strategies for High-stakes Tests, Phonics Friendly Books* plus hundreds of journal articles. Carroll co-authored with her husband Prentice Hall's *Writing and Grammar* series 6-12.

EDWARD E. WILSON is co-director of Abydos Learning International, formerly the New Jersey Writing Project in Texas (NJWPT), with his wife, Joyce Armstrong Carroll. Wilson has taught on the elementary, secondary, and junior college levels and is a member of NCTE, TCTELA, and ASCD. A poet, he co-edited *Poetry After Lunch* with Carroll and co-authored with her Prentice Hall's *Writing and Grammar* series 6-12. Wilson is also the owner of Absey & Co., and is a publisher committed to educational excellence and creative works of literary merit.